# VINTAGE WINE BOOK:
# A PRACTICAL GUIDE
# TO THE HISTORY OF WINE,
# WINEMAKING, CLASSIFICATION,
# AND SELECTION
# SECOND EDITION

Sommelier Executive Council

## SOME ADVANCE REVIEWS

"Concise, precise, accurate, especially for the complicated Italian wines. A must for any beginner or enthusiast."

**Bruno Ceretto**
Piedmont, Italy

"Clarity and coherency are two most elusive qualities in much modern documentation. [This] book, however, achieves great heights on both counts and will constitute, I am sure, a veritable 'bible' for sommeliers and restauranteurs alike . . . . A fascinating and practical aid to the world of wine."

**Louis Latour**
Beaune, Cote d'Or, France

"One of the best books for training sales people and restauranteurs. . . . . Not intimidating for a beginner."

**Cesar Baeza**
Executive Vice President/Winemaker
Brotherhood Winery
Washingtonville, New York

# Vintage
# Wine Book

## *A Practical Guide to the History of Wine, Winemaking, Classification, and Selection*
### *Second Edition*

## FOOD PRODUCTS PRESS

An Imprint of The Haworth Press, Inc.
Robert E. Gough, PhD, Senior Editor

# Vintage Wine Book

## A Practical Guide to the History of Wine, Winemaking, Classification, and Selection

### Second Edition

Sommelier Executive Council
Norman Sickels, President
Anthony Verdoni, Vice President
Joseph Wolkomir, Vice President
Richard Stolarz, Secretary

Food Products Press
An Imprint of The Haworth Press, Inc.
New York • London • Norwood (Australia)

Published by

Food Products Press, an imprint of The Haworth Press, Inc., 10 Alice Street, Binghamton, NY 13904-1580.

Index by Deborah Oksutcik Johnston.

**Library of Congress Cataloging-in-Publication Data**

Vintage wine book / Sommelier Executive Council.
    p.  cm.
   Includes index.
   ISBN 1-56022-008-2 (alk. paper) — ISBN 1-56022-009-0 (pbk. : alk. paper)
   1. Wine and wine making. I. Sommelier Executive Council.
TP548.V488   1991
641.2′2 — dc20
                                             91-8360
                                             CIP

*"Bacchus" art: From the Collection of the Museo del Vino Torgiano, Italy.*

# DEDICATION

He was known by many names. His symbol, the tiger, indicates that viticulture probably originated in Asia. The Classical Greeks and Romans deified him. Judaism and Christianity both embraced the vine and incorporated wine into their religious services. When colonists settled the Americas and Australia, they carried vines with them. Today, tens of millions celebrate the spring's rebirth of the vine and its autumnal harvest.

The ancient Greek tragic poet, Euripides, tells us that there are two great spirits in the world, Demeter who gives us food, and Dionysus who gives us wine.

"He found the liquid shower hid in the grape. He rests man's spirit dim from grieving, when the vine exalteth him. He giveth sleep to sink the fretful day in cool forgetting."[1]

We call him by his Roman name, *Bacchus,* and dedicate our book to him.

[1]Euripides, *BACCHAE*, trans. Gilbert Murray.

# CONTENTS

Foreword....................................................ix

Acknowledgements .........................................x

Introduction................................................1
    Some Historical Notes ........................1
    What Is Wine? ....................................1
    Components of Wine ...........................9
    Bottle Shapes ....................................13
    Wine and Age....................................14
    Health and Wine ................................14
    Serving Wine ....................................15
    The Art of Tasting ..............................24
    Odds and Ends ..................................27
    Reading Wine Labels ..........................28
    A Parting Shot...................................33

FORTIFIED WINES ......................................35

Sherry: The World's Dominant Fortified Wine .........36
    Origin .............................................36
    Types of Sherry..................................36
    Factors in Producing Sherry ..................37

Porto: The British Are Coming! .....................42
    Origin .............................................42
    Types of Porto....................................42

Marsala: From the "Swamp of God" ...............45

Madeira: Thank You, Napoleon! ...................45

Other Fortified Wines ...............................47

AROMATIZED WINES ................................51

Vermouth.................................................52

Other Aperitifs ........................................54

SPARKLING WINES ...................................59

"True" Champagne......................................60
    The Champagnes of France ....................60
    Factors of Champagne Production ............61

Variations in the Champagne Method ................73
    Classic Method ..................................73
    Charmat—Bulk Process ......................73
    Transfer Method ...............................73
    Rustic Method...................................74
    Carbonation.......................................74

Other Sparkling Wines.................................76
    France ............................................76
    Germany ..........................................77
    Austria............................................79
    Spain .............................................79
    Italy...............................................80
    The United States ..............................82
    Other Countries .................................84

TABLE WINES..........................................87

The Wines of the United States......................88
    The Archaic Period (1619-1920) ..............89
    The Dark Ages (1920-1933).....................89
    The Renaissance (1933-1968) ..................90
    The Golden Age (1968-Present)................91
    Where Do We Go From Here?..................94
    Classifying U.S. Wines ........................94
    The California Fraternity ......................95
    Viticultural Areas ..............................96

The Wines of France...................................115
    Introduction....................................115
    The Wine Regions of France ..................118

Bordeaux . . . . . . . . . . . . . . . . . . . . . .118
Northern Burgundy . . . . . . . . . . . . . . . . . .133
Southern Burgundy . . . . . . . . . . . . . . . . . .151
Côtes-Du-Rhône . . . . . . . . . . . . . . . . . . .159
Alsace . . . . . . . . . . . . . . . . . . . . . . . .165
The Loire . . . . . . . . . . . . . . . . . . . . . .167
Other Wine Regions of France . . . . . . . . . . . .171
Glossary of French Terms . . . . . . . . . . . . . .175

**The Wines of Italy** . . . . . . . . . . . . . . . . . .**177**
Introduction . . . . . . . . . . . . . . . . . . . . .177
The Wine Regions of Italy . . . . . . . . . . . . . .187
Northern Italy . . . . . . . . . . . . . . . . . . . .187
Northeastern Italy . . . . . . . . . . . . . . . . . .197
Central Italy . . . . . . . . . . . . . . . . . . . . .205
Southern Italy . . . . . . . . . . . . . . . . . . . .221
Glossary of Italian Terms . . . . . . . . . . . . . .231

**The Wines of Germany** . . . . . . . . . . . . . . . .**233**
Introduction . . . . . . . . . . . . . . . . . . . . .233
The Wine Regions of Germany . . . . . . . . . . . .240
Popular German Wines . . . . . . . . . . . . . . . .244
Glossary of German Terms . . . . . . . . . . . . . .248

**The Wines of Iberia** . . . . . . . . . . . . . . . . .**249**
Wines of Portugal . . . . . . . . . . . . . . . . . .250
Wines of Spain . . . . . . . . . . . . . . . . . . . .252

**The Wines of Other Countries** . . . . . . . . . . . .**259**
Other European Countries . . . . . . . . . . . . . .259
Eastern Europe . . . . . . . . . . . . . . . . . . . .260
North Africa . . . . . . . . . . . . . . . . . . . . .265
The Middle East . . . . . . . . . . . . . . . . . . .265
Asia . . . . . . . . . . . . . . . . . . . . . . . . .267
South America . . . . . . . . . . . . . . . . . . . .270
Mexico . . . . . . . . . . . . . . . . . . . . . . . .273
Canada . . . . . . . . . . . . . . . . . . . . . . . .273
Australia . . . . . . . . . . . . . . . . . . . . . . .275
New Zealand . . . . . . . . . . . . . . . . . . . . .280
South Africa . . . . . . . . . . . . . . . . . . . . .280

**Alcoholic Beverages Reference Guide** . . . . . . . . .**283**
Part One: Distilled Spirits . . . . . . . . . . . . . .283
Part Two: Malt Beverages . . . . . . . . . . . . . .312

**Epilogue** . . . . . . . . . . . . . . . . . . . . . . . .**319**

**Indexes** . . . . . . . . . . . . . . . . . . . . . . . .**323**
Subject Index . . . . . . . . . . . . . . . . . . . .325
Name Index . . . . . . . . . . . . . . . . . . . . .365

# FOREWORD

## *"Just what we needed! Another wine book!"*

Well, this one is different. And we think that once you look it over, you will see that it fills gaps left by the others. In fact, this text will enable you to enjoy other wine books even more, because it is a basic primer aimed at the initiate. We have pressed into it lots of information with ample color and good extract.

We will update it with each vintage and make these supplements available to you, our readers. This will enable you to keep track of trend changes and new factors in the world of wine. That is why we call it the **"Vintage" Wine Book.**

It is possible for you to earn a wine diploma by following the simple instructions at the end of the book. You will also be put on our mailing list so that you can receive update notices, supplements, and advanced chapters at nominal costs.

We have tried to make the text as crisp and clear as a fresh Muscadet, serious but not pretentious, like a supple Napa Valley Chardonnay. Updates will enable this text to serve you for as long a time as would a case of Brunello di Montalcino. We hope that you use it, enjoy it and learn from it, as you use, enjoy and learn from wine.

Remember, if you do not learn anything, then we have not taught you anything!

# ACKNOWLEDGEMENTS

We, the members of the Sommelier Executive Council, have been a part of the wine fraternity for many years. Collectively, we have written thousands of wine lists, conducted hundreds of formal symposiums, seminars, and courses. We have participated in the sales and marketing of well over 1,000,000 cases of wine. With a total industry experience of over a century, we have come to know a lot of wine people. We would like to thank a few who have helped us, taught us, guided and encouraged us through the years.

They include: Guido Truffini, Robert Gourdin, Peter Sichel, and Smitty Kogan, as well as the late Gordon Bass, Frank Packard, Frank Schoonmaker, and Gloria Call.

We have included labels throughout our text. We wholeheartedly recommend each product whose label appears in this book. Most of them are vintage dated. Very often the vintage appears on a neckband, not on the label itself. In some cases the vintage on the sample label may not be the one in current distribution. We have chosen to make objective, educational comments on these products and do not wish to be viewed as showing partiality to one wine or another. Actually, we salute all the winemakers, distillers, and brewers who have brought us these fine products. We thank them and their marketing and sales representatives who submitted the labels to us. If you see several Chardonnays, Gavis, Cabernet Sauvignons, and Pinot Grigios, it is indicative of a trend in today's market.

We would like to thank the many importers, distributors, and producers who have aided and supported our project.

Special thanks, too, to the Mohawk Liqueur Corporation for permitting us to edit and reprint their "Spirits and Beer A to Z Supplement."

# A WORD OR TWO ABOUT THE SECOND EDITION

So much has happened between editions! Wine consumption in America has dropped for three consecutive years. A closer look, however, indicates that although wine coolers are down, interest in better wines is strongly up. Domestic wines, especially those from California, are taking more and more business from the traditional imports. You can find better American wines today in England, Japan, Italy, Germany, or France, as well as in the great hotels of Singapore and Bangkok. American wines have truly become cosmopolitan.

Those of us who believe in wine and perceive it as an ancient and noble drink, an outpouring of Western thought and culture, are more often than not being forced to defend its use and place in the civilized world. We point out its value at the table, as a part of the good life. Moderation is a word you hear from us quite often.

Opponents point to the dangers of drunk driving, health problems for pregnant women, and other items on their well-planned agenda. Eventually obvious tax increases will drive wine prices further upward. Arguments will become even more emotional than rational. It is ironic that as the U.S.A. takes its place among the superstatus wine nations of the world, we are subjected to such a degree of social pressures.

One thing is certain: Through this complicated maze of events, better wines are selling better. In our many lectures, we have never seen a greater interest in quality wines — a grander thirst for a basic understanding of the world of wines. We are quite sure that wine will not only survive, but will prevail. Remember that word "moderation" again. Remember also that for 3,000 years now, friends have been lifting their glasses and saying things like "À Votre Santé" or "Salute"; that is, "To Your Health"! Three thousand years is a long time.

*"WINE is light, held together by water."*

Galileo (1564-1642)

*"The sun, with all those planets revolving around it and dependent on it, can still ripen a bunch of grapes as if it had nothing else in the universe to do."*

Galileo (1564-1642)

*"God makes WINE. Only the ungrateful or the purblind can fail to see that sugar in the grape and yeast on the skins is a divine idea, not a human one."*

Father Robert Capon, *The Supper of the Lamb*

*"I feast on WINE and BREAD, and feasts they are!"*

Michelangelo (1475-1564)

*"Nothing more excellent nor more valuable than WINE was ever granted to mankind by God."*

Plato (427-347 B.C.)

*"Drink no longer water, but use a little WINE for thy stomach's sake."*

I Timothy S:23, S. Paul the Apostle 5:23

*"WINE was given by God, not that we might be drunken, but that we might be sober. It is the best medicine when it has moderation to direct it. WINE was given to restore the body's weakness, not to overturn the soul's strength."*

St. Chrysostom (347-407)

*"No Nation is drunk where wine is cheap."*

Thomas Jefferson

# INTRODUCTION

## SOME HISTORICAL NOTES

Today, one human being in a hundred in the Western world is a winegrower, a winemaker or a wine merchant. The world's wine harvest is enough to supply every one of the inhabitants of the globe with six bottles a year. There are 20 million acres of vineyard sites.

Wine is older than history. The vine was evident in 6000 B.C. in Egypt, 3000 B.C. in Phoenicia, and 2000 B.C. in Greece. We do not know when man first tasted wine. Some early Cromagnon cave frescos show use of libation cups some millions of years ago.

Noah became a winegrower for the last three and a half centuries of his life. He is supposed to have found water insupportable as a beverage after the flood—it tasted of sinners—"because all things corrupt therein, both man and beast were drowned for sin." At the time of the Exodus, the Jews regretted and worried over leaving behind the wines of Egypt. They need not have feared, for the Land of the Philistines and the Plain of Sharon were green with vines, and Palestine came to be rich in vineyards.

The Syrians and Phoenicians sent their wine by the old caravan routes to Arabia and Egypt, on to India, and as far as China, and their famous Chalybon went to the courts of Persian kings.

Ancient Greek wine was not much—having been cooked with resin to a concentrated honey-like consistency. The Greeks spread viticulture to Italy, southern France, Spain, and northwest Africa. Their wine was potent and had to be diluted with water. Usually the formula was one part water to one part wine. The wine that Odysseus gave the Cyclops was so powerful that 20 parts of water were necessary. The milk-drinking Cyclops mistakenly drank it straight. You know what happened next!

Roman wine, after being pressed, was carried about in the fiacre bottle with a string on it for a handle. Olive oil was poured down the long neck to prevent the wine from turning—the cork had not yet been developed. Roman wines were fortified by spices and resin. The retsina wines of the Romans, and to some degree the Greeks, were usually made from what we call black currants.

Some wines lived to be a century old. It was a practice to put aside a wine from the year of one's birth to be consumed years later at a special occasion. Roman wines were made from the aristocratic family of vines, *Vitis vinifera*. Roman soldiers planted these vines throughout what we know today as France, Switzerland, Germany, and Romania. These grapes are responsible for all the modern wines of Europe, South Africa, Asia, and California.

Winemaking was preserved by Christian monks. Certain varietals were brought back by the Crusaders from Mideastern shores. Missionaries spread the vine to California and South America. European settlers brought vineshoots with them to South Africa and Australia.

Wherever Western thought has gone, the vine has accompanied it. As the exclusive beverage of the Christian and Jewish faiths, wine has become an indelible part of Western civilization. In most European countries, wine is indispensable at mealtime.

## WHAT IS WINE?

Wine is simply the fermented juice of grapes. Or more romantically, it is the rain that falls to the earth recaptured through the vine—the juice of grapes.

All that is needed to turn grape juice into wine is the simple, entirely natural process of fermentation. Fermentation is the chemical change of sugar into alcohol (and carbon dioxide gas) brought about by yeasts that live on the skin. They need only to have the grape skin broken to start working on the sugar.

## FORMULA FOR FERMENTATION
GRAPE SUGAR + YEAST =
ALCOHOL + CARBON DIOXIDE + HEAT
$$C_6H_{12}O_6 + YEAST = 2C_2H_6O + 2CO_2$$

Under normal conditions, the yeast will go on working until all the sugar in the grape is converted into alcohol, or until the alcohol level in the wine reaches 15%. Left to nature, almost all wines would be dry. However, it is possible to stop fermentation before all the sugar is used up, either by adding alcohol to raise the level up to 15% or by adding sulphur—both of these anesthetize the yeast. The charts on the opposite page will help you to more fully understand the basic method of winemaking, a process which has not fundamentally changed in 3,000 years.

The quality of a wine is determined by five factors:

1. The Vine
2. The Soil
3. The Climate
4. Geographic Location
5. Humans

Great wines are made when perfect harmony is achieved, each supporting and complementing the other.

## The Vine

All in all, there are 10 genera in the botanical family of grapes *(Ampelidaceae),* but for winemaking only one of these, the genus *Vitis*, is significant. *Vitis* vines are cultivated in temperate zones. One species, *Vitis vinifera*, is responsible for most of the world's finest wines. Types include the reds: Cabernet Sauvignon, Pinot Noir, Zinfandel, Merlot, Nebbiolo, Sangiovese, and Aglianico; and the whites: Chardonnay, Sauvignon Blanc, Chenin Blanc, Muscat, Riesling, and Trebbiano. There are literally thousands of these types (Italy has well over 1,000), but we can safely say that

the world's most famous wines are derived from a couple of dozen.

When Leif Ericson sailed to what is now New England, he called it "Vineland." The wild grapes cultivated there were not vinifera, but rather of the species *Labrusca* (not Lambrusco). These hardy vines can withstand harsh winters. Examples of this type are Concord and Catawba. Settlers in America combined these original American vines with European through a process called hybridizing. Hybrids include Baco Noir, Chancellor Noir, Foch, Seyval Blanc, and Seibel.

The *Vitis vinifera* of Europe were all but wiped out in the late nineteenth century by a vine louse called *Phylloxera vastatrix*. This pest spread from France to Spain to Italy and Germany, attacking the roots of the vines. Eventually root stock from the hardy American vines were grafted onto the vinifera varietals. Thus they were saved.

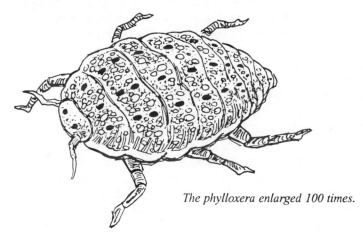

*The phylloxera enlarged 100 times.*

**The Flight of the Phylloxera**

*This dreaded louse, the* Phylloxera vastatrix *(the "ravaging leaf drier"), brought vinifera vines almost to extinction. It arrived in Bordeaux in the 1870s, in Spain and Portugal by 1890, Italy by 1880 and Eastern Europe by 1875. In Argentina the phylloxera got into the irrigation system and spread like wildfire. It hit California in 1876 and struck South Africa and Australia by 1885. Almost every vine in the world has been grafted to a resistant Native American root stock. Only Chile and a few small areas in both Portugal and Australia have been spared this pest. Believe it or not, the phylloxera is starting to rear its ugly head once again today.*

2

# HOW WINE IS MADE

## RED WINES

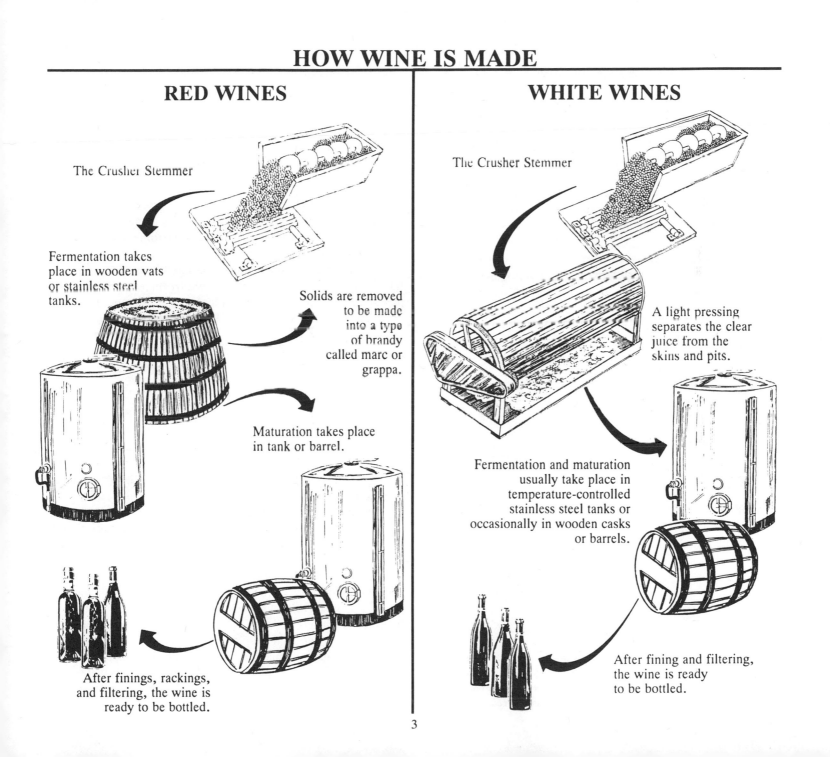

The Crusher Stemmer

Fermentation takes place in wooden vats or stainless steel tanks.

Solids are removed to be made into a type of brandy called marc or grappa.

Maturation takes place in tank or barrel.

After finings, rackings, and filtering, the wine is ready to be bottled.

## WHITE WINES

The Crusher Stemmer

A light pressing separates the clear juice from the skins and pits.

Fermentation and maturation usually take place in temperature-controlled stainless steel tanks or occasionally in wooden casks or barrels.

After fining and filtering, the wine is ready to be bottled.

To review, there are three major categories of grapes:

1. *Vitis vinifera:* Europe, California, South America, Australia, Middle East, North Africa
2. *Vitis labrusca:* Northeastern U.S.A., Canada
3. Hybrids: America, Europe

Vines are pruned and trained according to many systems to allow for optimum exposure to sunlight and, in general, for healthier grapes. Major methods include:

1. *Cordon:* Vines grow along supportive wires, which run parallel to the ground. One famous variation is called Guyot.
2. *Gobelet:* Several arms grow unsupported in the approximate shape of a vase.
3. *Espalier:* Also called the Trellis Method, supported by a wire or trellis.

*The Gobelet Method*

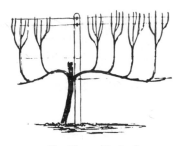

*The Guyot Method*

**PRUNING**

*The less abundant the fruit, the higher its quality. Cutting back vines, sometimes training them along trellises, enhances the fruit. Methods and techniques of pruning and head training vary from area to area. Scientific pruning dates back at least as far as the ancient Greeks.*

Most vines can withstand temperatures just below freezing (25° F) to above 100° F. Any additional excess will have a negative effect. Hail and wind can do harm as well. Excessive moisture and drought are to be avoided. Soil deficiencies, toxic fertilizers, and insecticides all do damage. Moths, beetles, mites, and various rots take their toll. And when the hardy vine overcomes all of these obstacles, the grower must watch out for birds, who savor the delicious fruit.

Vines do not produce grapes in their first two or three years. As they get older, vines yield fewer but better grapes. Eventually, after two generations or more, vines must be torn up and replaced due to a lack of productivity.

Different grape varieties are responsible for the differences in flavor and quality. The care that the vines receive—their training, pruning, and fertilizing—controls the amount of grapes they will bear and the degree of ripeness they will reach. The fewer the grapes, the better the fruit. Or more technically, the lower the yield per acre, the better the wine.

## The Soil

The geographical location of the vineyard, the direction it faces, the makeup of the soil, and the climate it enjoys all have a bearing on the variety of grape that may be grown and the degree of ripeness it will reach. The natural selection of the variety that does best and gives the best quality, combined with reasonable quantity and reasonable resistance to disease, has taken place gradually over the centuries. The soil must satisfy certain requirements. If it does not, there is no hope of making a great wine. In general, poor soil with a complex structure is needed to make a fine wine. Wine has its origin as water in the soil. A poor soil with layers of gravel and sand are plus factors for quality as they let the rain run through and encourage the vine to root deeply, thus allowing it to discover valuable resources in the elements that reside far from the surface. It is from the soil that a wine gets its character.

### FAMOUS SOILS

*"If our soil was not so poor, we would not be so rich!"* The words of the Burgundian vigneron ring true. Wine grapes like poor soil with good drainage and minerals. Soil imparts a special character to the grapes.

Famous soils and subsoils include:

> The gravel of Graves,
> The rocks of Chateauneuf-du-Pape,
> The chalk of Champagne,
> The "dust" of Rutherford in Napa Valley,
> The slate of the Mosel,
> The iron-rich clay of Serralunga near Barolo, and
> The "ponca" marl of Friuli.

## The Climate

Heat and rainfall are direct influences on vines. Moderately cold, rainy winters and fairly long, hot summers, with some, but not too much rain, are the most desirable.

The first cold of the late autumn or early winter encourages the vine to become dormant and allows the wood to toughen and mature. Severe cold, however, will kill it. Sufficient summer heat is necessary to mature the fruit. Sunshine is essential for the vines and their grapes to develop. Rain is equally vital. However, too much rain will increase the yield, swelling the grapes with water and producing wines inferior in quality, diluted and thin. Every drop of rain, every hour of sunshine and degree of heat has its eventual effect on the quality and character of the wine. Being blessed with the right soil, ideal climate, and the correct vines, however, is not enough to produce a great wine.

# ISOTHERMIC WORLD MAP

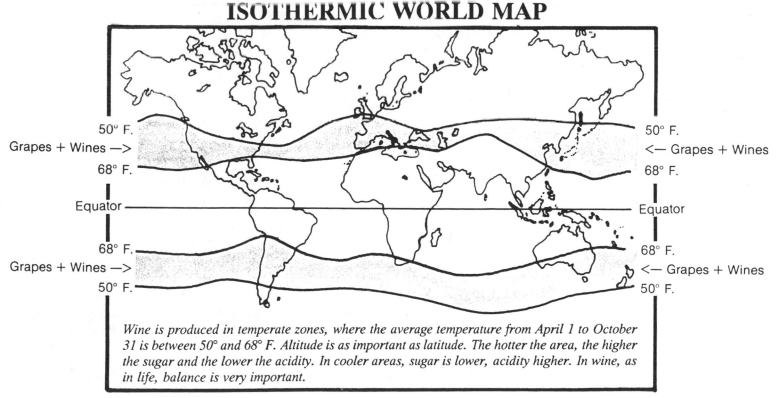

*Wine is produced in temperate zones, where the average temperature from April 1 to October 31 is between 50° and 68° F. Altitude is as important as latitude. The hotter the area, the higher the sugar and the lower the acidity. In cooler areas, sugar is lower, acidity higher. In wine, as in life, balance is very important.*

# GRAPE VARIETIES

## VINIFERA

| RED | WHITE |
|---|---|
| Aglianico | Airen |
| Aleatico | Albana |
| Alicante | Aligote |
| Barbera | Alvarinho |
| Bobal | Arinto |
| Bonarda | Arneis |
| Brunello (Sangiovese) | Azal Branco |
| Cabernet Franc | Burger |
| Cabernet Sauvignon | Catarratto |
| Canaiolo | Chardonnay |
| Cannonau | Chasselas (Gutedel) |
| Carignan | Chenin Blanc (Steen, |
| Charbono | Pineau de la Loire) |
| Cinsault (Hermitage) | Cortese |
| Corvina | Fiano |
| Criolla | Folle Blanche |
| Dolcetto | Furmint |
| Freisa | Garganega |
| Gaglioppo | Gewürztraminer |
| Gamay | Green Hungarian |
| Gamay Beaujolais | Greco |
| Grenache (Garnacha) | Grillo |
| Grignolino | Grüner Veltliner |
| Harriague | Inzolia |
| Kadarka | Macabeo |
| Lagrein | Malvasia |
| Lambrusco | Moscato |
| Malbec | Nuragus |
| Mavron (Mavrud) | Palomino |
| Merlot | Pedro Ximenes |
| Mission | Picolit |
| Monastrell | Pinot Blanc (Weissburgunder) |
| Montepulciano D'Abruzzo | Prokupac |
| Napa Gamay | Prosecco |
| Nebbiolo | Riesling (Johannisberger, White) |
| Negroamaro | Rkatsiteli |
| Nerello | Sauvignon Blanc (Fume) |
| Nero D'Avola | Sauvignon Vert |
| Pais | Savagnin |

## VINIFERA

| RED | WHITE |
|---|---|
| Perricone | Semillon |
| Petite Sirah | Sereksia |
| Petite Verdot | Sultana |
| Piedirosso | Sylvaner (Silvaner) |
| Pinot Gris (Pinot Grigio, | Thompson Seedless |
| Tokay D'Alsace, Ruländer)· | Tocai Friulano |
| Pinot Meunier | Trebbiano (Ugni Blanc) |
| Pinot Noir | Verdeca |
| Pinot St. George | Verdicchio |
| Portugieser | Verduzzo |
| Ramisco | Vernaccia |
| Refosco | Viura |
| Rossese | Xarel-Lo |
| Sangiovese (Brunello, Prugnolo) | Xynisteri |
| Schiava (Vernatsch) | |
| Souzao | |
| Syrah | |
| Tempranillo | |
| Tinta Madeira | |
| Tourigo | |
| Vespolina | |
| Zinfandel | |

**THE GRAPE**

*Grapes have petioles, internodes, rachises, and pedicels. If you like that sort of stuff, try ampelography, the study of grapes. For this book, it is enough to know that the grape is the perfect fruit for fermentation—for wine. The color, almost always, is derived from the skins and pits. Although there are thousands of grape varieties, most of the world's finest wines come from about two dozen or so.*

# GRAPE VARIETIES

## FRENCH-AMERICAN HYBRIDS

| RED | WHITE |
|-----|-------|
| Baco Noir | Aurora |
| Cascade | Cayuga |
| Chambourcin | Isabella |
| Chancellor | Okanagan Riesling |
| Chelois | Seyval Blanc |
| DeChaunac | Vidal |
| Foch | Vignoles (Ravat 51) |
| Landot | Villard |
| Millot | |
| Rosette (Seibel 1000) | |

## NATIVE AMERICAN

| RED | WHITE |
|-----|-------|
| Catawba | Delaware |
| Clinton | Diamond |
| Concord | Dutchess |
| Cynthiana (Norton) | Niagara |
| Steuben | |

## MUSCADINE

| RED | WHITE |
|-----|-------|
| Bountiful | Dearing |
| Chief | Dixie |
| Cowart | Higgins |
| Noble | |

BRONZE:
Carlos
Magnolia
Scuppernong

## VINIFERA "CROSSES"

### RED

Carnelian
*(Grenache + Carignan + Cabernet)*

Ruby Cabernet
*(Cabernet + Carignan)*

Pinotage
*(Pinot Noir + Hermitage)*

### WHITE

Bacchus
*(Silvaner + Riesling)*

Emerald Riesling
*(Riesling + Muscadelle)*

Faber
*(Müller-Thürgau + Weissburgunder)*

Flora
*(Gewürztraminer + Semillon)*

Kerner
*(Trollinger + Riesling)*

Morio-Muskat
*(Silvaner + Riesling)*

Müller-Thürgau
*(2 clones of Riesling)*

Scheurebe
*(Silvaner + Riesling)*

## YEASTS

Yeasts are natural to the skins of grapes. Often a winemaker adds a special yeast to assure a successful fermentation. Below are three examples with their University of California at Davis (UCD) designations:

Montrachet . . . . . . . . . . . . . . . UCD 522
Pasteur Champagne . . . . . . . . UCD 595
Flor Sherry . . . . . . . . . . . . . . . UCD 519

## Geographic Location

The Romans used to say, "Bacchus loves the open hills." Vines thrive on slopes that allow for ample sunlight and proper drainage. Altitude is a factor as well since the cool nights, coupled with sunny days, help the grapes achieve good sugar acid balance. Many great vineyard areas, most notably Bordeaux in France and the Rheingau and Mosel in Germany, get temperature stabilization and additional light units from proximity with rivers and other bodies of water. In New York State, it is the glacial Finger Lakes that allow vines to grow in an area that would otherwise be unsuitable for viticulture.

## Humans — The Vinification Process

In any human endeavor error must always be considered. Transferring the full quality of the grapes to the wine takes all of a grower's experience, attention, and skill. Without this the harvest will hardly be worth the effort. The skills required in making and maturing the wine have a tremendous effect on its eventual quality. In the fields, when to harvest and how to prune and train are just two of the many decisions that will have tremendous impact on a wine's quality. At the winery, the way in which the pressing is carried out and the time and temperature of fermentation, the racking and maturing of the wine, and the methods used in bottling all have an influence on the finished product. Winemakers today are skilled agronomists who have probably studied at a great university, such as Bordeaux (France), Geisenheim (Germany), Conegliano (Italy), or the University of California at Davis. Remember: To make wine is a science; to make *great* wine is an art.

## The Effect of the Vintage

There is another quality factor: vintage. We list it only as an afterthought because too much is made of it. Consumers seek out great years, not great winemakers, and this is a gross error. Off vintages are very often lighter, faster-maturing and *far less costly* wines. Talented, competitive vintners accept the challenge to produce fine wines when the fickle seasons have not blessed them.

Should you buy a Chateau Mouton-Rothschild in an off year or a lesser wine in an outstanding year, both being offered at the same price? Our advice is to steer toward the Mouton. You have the same soil, the same grape varieties, the same slopes, and the same winemaker as you would have in a great year. You may not want to cellar it, but what a treat for current drinking.

---

### A YEAR AT THE WINERY

#### AUTUMN

*This is the time of the harvest that may last for two weeks or more. It is the most hectic and critical period. Grapes must be brought in quickly. Usually migrant workers, students, and the like help the vigneron. After this exhausting period, a final plowing aerates the soil and covers the base of the vines to protect them for the oncoming winter.*

#### WINTER

*In the fields, repair work is done to supportive wires and posts. Pruning of the sleeping vines takes place. At the winery, fermented wine is racked and set aside for barrel aging. Fresh, young, white wines are bottled in late winter, as are lighter reds.*

#### SPRING

*More plowing and weeding. At the time of budding, excess buds are removed to keep the quality high and the yield low. New vines are planted now. Vineshoots are attached to supportive wires.*

*Bottling and aging processes continue at the winery.*

#### SUMMER

*More trimming, weeding, and plowing. Checking vines for mites, rots, and other maladies occupies the vintner's time. If the vintner can rest at all, it is in late summer, while nature ripens the grapes. (Rest is needed — the exhausting fall harvest is just ahead.)*

Be cautious, however! Check the bottle top for leakage or evaporation. Try a bottle before buying a case. And remember: Buy the wine that you believe in. *You* have to drink it and serve it to your guests. Do not buy what we like. Please yourself.

Although vintage champagne and vintage porto are indeed special wines you may prefer a non-vintage table wine (one from several years or harvests) to a vintage one. Do not become a slave to the Vintage Chart, the most requested and dangerous piece of wine literature to be placed in the hands of consumers.

# COMPONENTS OF WINE

Wine is a composite of thousands of constituents, esters, compounds, and congeners. Some come from the grape, others from the fermentation or aging processes. Since wine, the most fascinating of beverages, lends itself to detailed analysis, it is important, even for the beginner, to understand the major components. Thus we can tell why a wine smells, looks, and tastes the way it does. Good wine always has a pleasant balance of these components.

**Water.** Much of the grape is water, like life itself. The less watery a finished wine is, the greater the richness, body, and extract. Water dilutes the taste of wine. Water, that is, rainfall at harvest time, will bloat up the grape berries, causing a thinner, less concentrated wine. This is one reason for a light or lesser vintage.

**Alcohol.** Wine contains many alcohols, the most common being ethyl alcohol. Alcohol adds weight and body to the wine, plus a little hotness, even sweetness. You may feel a burning sensation, especially on the tongue, if the alcohol is not in balance. Alcohol is a natural result of the fermentation process.

**Tannin.** This is a flavoring and preserving element, derived mostly from the skins and pits of the grapes. Tannin makes a wine firm and very hard, and in time becomes solid sediment. As a tannic wine ages, it will soften. Tannin makes us pucker; you get tannin from over-brewed tea. A bit of tannin comes from wood in the aging process.

**Glycerin.** This is a colorless, odorless, sweetish liquid with a

## VINTAGE CHART 1978-1988

| | 1978 | 1979 | 1980 | 1981 | 1982 | 1983 | 1984 | 1985 | 1986 | 1987 | 1988(E) |
|---|---|---|---|---|---|---|---|---|---|---|---|
| BORDEAUX-MEDOC | 18L | 17E | 12C | 17L | 19L | 17L | 14E | 17E | 18L | 15E | 17L |
| BORDEAUX-ST. EMILION | 17E | 18E | 12C | 17E | 19L | 17L | 14E | 17E | 19L | 14E | 18L |
| BORDEAUX-SAUTERNES | 16E | 17E | 16E | 17L | 15E | 18L | 14E | 17E | 19L | 14E | 19L |
| BEAUJOLAIS-CRU | - | - | - | 16C | 12C | 18C | 12C | 18E | 16E | 17E | 17E |
| BURGUNDY-NUITS | 18L | 15E | 16E | 14L | 15E | 17L | 14E | 19E | 16E | 17E | 17 |
| BURGUNDY-BEAUNE | 18L | 15E | 15E | 14E | 16E | 17L | 13E | 18E | 15E | 16E | 17 |
| BURGUNDY-WHITE | 18L | 17E | 15E | 17E | 18L | 17L | 16E | 17E | 17E | 15E | 16 |
| ALSACE | - | - | - | - | - | 18L | 10C | 17E | 16L | 16E | 17 |
| LOIRE | 17C | 17C | 14C | 17C | 17C | 17C | 14C | 18E | 18E | 16E | 18E |
| RHONE | 18L | 16E | 15E | 17E | 17L | 19L | 16E | 19E | 18L | 17E | 18L |
| PIEDMONTE | 19L | 17E | 14E | 16L | 18L | 17L | 13E | 18L | 15E | 17E | 18L |
| TUSCANY | 17E | 15E | 14C | 16E | 17E | 16E | 12E | 18E | 16E | 15E | 18L |
| VERONA | 16E | 18E | 16E | 15E | 15E | 18L | 13E | 17L | 16L | 15L | 18L |
| GERMANY | 14C | 17E | 13C | 16E | 15E | 18L | 14E | 17E | 16E | 15E | 16E |
| CALIFORNIA-CABERNET | 17E | 15E | 16E | 16E | 16E | 17L | 18E | 19L | 18E | 17L | 16E |
| CALIFORNIA-CHARDONNAY | 17C | 17C | 16C | 17C | 17C | 17C | 18E | 19E | 18E | 18E | 17E |

KEYS: NUMBERS 10=POOR  20=BEST,  LETTERS E=EARLY MATURING  L=LATE MATURING  C=CAUTION

viscous, almost oily texture. It adds richness and texture to the wine and is a natural by-product of ripe grapes. It is most common in big reds and dessert wines, especially those affected by *Botrytis cinera* (a beneficial mold that dehydrates the grapes, resulting in a high concentration of sugar).

**Acids.** Acid is the skeleton of a wine. It may seem like a dirty word, but it adds life and vitality, just as a lemon makes a grilled swordfish even more delicious. Without acidity a wine would be fat and flabby. Acids, like sugar, come primarily from the grape. There are many acids, most of them "fixed," that is, not volatile or able to be smelled. Some of the main fixed acids are:

Malic Acid: Found in young wines. Gives freshness, crispness, sometimes assertive hardness to a wine.

Lactic Acid: A softer acid found in older wines. Many wines, especially reds, undergo a malo-lactic, secondary fermentation, which takes place in the spring. This softens the wine.

Tartaric Acid: This is a sour acid. In cold weather it crystallizes, sometimes on the cork; at other times into the wine itself. It is harmless cream of tartar. If found in German late-picked wines, tartar is a sign of high quality.

An acid with volatile acidity (V.A.) is acetic acid, which is common in vinegar. The pungent fragrance and prickly taste are clear signs that the wine has been exposed to oxygen, either in the fermentation or aging process or due to defective corking.

**Sugar.** Natural to the grape, sugar converts to alcohol in the fermentation process. Sometimes sugar is added to fermenting musts. This does not add to a wine's sweetness but rather affords an easier fermentation. Some sweet wines will have residual sugar, that is, sugar left over after fermentation. This sweetness must be balanced by good acidity. Remember, an imperfect wine can be sweetened to disguise its defects. Usually the label for this caliber of wine will say, "Serve very cold." Remember, too, that a completely dry wine with no sugar at all will still have fruitiness. There is a difference between fruit and sugar.

**Methyl Anthranilate.** This is the constituent that adds the "foxy" character to native American Labrusca varietals, like Concord. Europeans, especially the French, felt that Labrusca smelled like a dead fox. Proponents of Concord, Catawba, etc.,

feel that the aroma shows a pleasant fruitiness. It is interesting to taste a native American wine, a hybrid, and a vinifera side by side to make your own judgment. Remember that in California, European vinifera grapes are most frequently used. In the cold northeast, the movement has been away from the native American to hybrids and vinifera. These Labrusca are also used in jellies, jams, and juices and in the production of kosher wines.

**Sulfur Dioxide.** This gas, also called $SO_2$, is the only agent that the winemaker needs to add to otherwise completely natural wine. It is a sulfite and is usually added in the form of a tablet. $SO_2$ aids yeasts during fermentation by inhibiting harmful bacteria. It also prevents oxidation, especially necessary for young whites and sweet whites. Maximum levels are prescribed by government agencies. Those who are allergic to sulfites are cautioned to avoid wine consumption. The smell of a burnt match is associated with $SO_2$. Exposure to air will dissipate this smell.

Tasting is the best way to increase your analytical skills. You may want to set up a vertical tasting — a tasting in which you show several vintages of the same wine. This will give you a good idea as to the effects of aging and vintage variation. You may prefer a horizontal tasting, in which you show many examples of one type of wine from the same vintage. This will show you the varietal traits, distinctions in the philosophy of wineries, plus the character of the vintage. These tastings are best done with small groups of interested friends in conjunction with a meal. Remember, food makes wine taste better, and wine makes food taste better.

Two terms which are associated with "bad" wine are oxidation and maderization.

**Oxidation.** If a wine is exposed to air, its freshness and color fade and it will spoil. A defective cork, allowing oxygen to come into contact with the wine, is usually the culprit. Beware of brown wines.

**Maderization.** Wine exposed to excessive heat will take on a spoiled, baked taste. The experience is much like oxidation but with the added element of a burnt character. Remember: Controlled oxidation (Marsala and sherry) and controlled maderization (Madeira) produce distinctive and wonderful wines.

# Colors of Wines

Wine comes in two colors: red (colored) and white (uncolored).

Red wines possess many hues. Pink or rose is in the red family. Young red wines are usually purple. As they age, they take on brownish tinges. Young whites are of a pale greenish hue. They become yellow, gold, and finally brown as they age. In addition to hue, one should look for brilliance and density or depth of color in a wine.

## COLOR CHART

### REDS

Purple —> Ruby —> Red —> Mahogany —> Tawny —> Brown
( — YOUNG — )   ( —MATURE — )   ( — OK, IF PORT — )   ( —DEAD — )

### WHITES

Pale Green —> Pale Straw —> Yellow —> Gold —> Amber —> Brown
(—YOUNG—) (—RICH, SWEET or DRY—) (—GOOD IF SWEET—) (—OK for SHERRY—) (COULD BE DEAD)

### ROSE

| Pinkish Gray | Blush | Onion Skin | Partridge Eye | Orange |
|---|---|---|---|---|
| Rose D'Anjou | From U.S.A. or Weissherbst from Germany | Tawny Roses from Provence | Topaz, Salmon hue from Italy, France or U.S.A. | Full-bodied Tavel |

## You Can Learn This F.A.S.T.

There are many ways of classifying wines. We prefer to place them into four groups:

**FORTIFIED:** Wines to which some form of alcohol, usually brandy, is added. This raises the alcohol content to between 16%–20%. Examples include port, sherry, Marsala, and Madeira. They may be dry or sweet.

**AROMATIZED:** Wines to which herbs, spices, and botanicals are added to impart a special flavor. These wines, for the most part, have also been fortified for stability. The famous example is vermouth, which is available in sweet (red), dry (white), and bianco (sweet white).

**SPARKLING:** Wines to which bubbles have been added. These festive and popular wines are usually between 8% and 12% alcohol. Examples are Champagne, Asti Spumante, and Sekt. They may be white or various shades of red, including pink.

**TABLE:** Wines to which nothing has been added. Usually between 8% and 14% alcohol.

There are other wine types that do not fit comfortably into the four groups. These include pop wines, fruit wines, wine coolers, and flavored wines.

# SELF-EVALUATION

BEFORE READING ON, see if you have mastered the data set forth in the last few pages. Check the answer section at the back of the book for the correct answers. If you have not answered at least 70% of the questions below correctly, please reread the previous section.

## INTRODUCTION—PART I

| TRUE | FALSE | |
|------|-------|---|
| _____ | _____ | 1. Wine is simply unfermented grape juice. |
| _____ | _____ | 2. The climate is one factor in determining the quality of wine. |
| _____ | _____ | 3. There are three major families of wine grapes. |
| _____ | _____ | 4. Cordon, Gobelet, and Espalier are three methods of pruning vines. |
| _____ | _____ | 5. Fermentation is the chemical change of sugar into alcohol and carbon dioxide gas brought about by yeasts within the skins of the grapes. |
| _____ | _____ | 6. Cabernet Sauvignon is an example of a red *Vitis vinifera* grape. |
| _____ | _____ | 7. Thee are four ways in which to classify wines: Fortified, Aromatized, Table, and Other. |
| _____ | _____ | 8. Wine comes in three colors: Red, White, and Pink. |
| _____ | _____ | 9. If a red wine is brown, this is generally an indication that it is a fine, mature wine at its peak. |
| _____ | _____ | 10. If a white wine is pale green, it may well be young and light. |

# BOTTLE SHAPES

Although there are numerous variations, there are three basic bottle shapes:

1. **BORDEAUX:** Perfect for long aging. Used also in California and Tuscany. A variation exists for vintage porto and for sherry.
2. **BURGUNDY:** Used also in Piedmont, California. The champagne bottle is an offshoot.
3. **FLUTE:** In Germany, brown for Rhein, green for Mosel. Also used, mostly for whites and pinks, in Italy, California, and Alsace.

One interesting shape is that of the *bocksbeutel*. This squat bottle, used for certain Portuguese roses and German whites, is named for an unmentionable part of a goat's anatomy.

### BOTTLE SIZES

| Metric Size | Fluid Ounces | Name |
| --- | --- | --- |
| 187 ML | 6.3 oz. | Split |
| 375 ML | 12.7 oz. | Half-bottle |
| 750 ML | 25.4 oz. | Bottle |
| 1 L | 33.8 oz. | Liter |
| 1.5 L | 50.7 oz. | Magnum |
| 3 L | 101.4 oz. | Double Magnum (Jeroboam) |
| 4 L | 135.2 oz. | Jug |
| 4.5 L | 152.2 oz. | Rehoboam |
| 6 L | 202.9 oz. | Methuselah |
| 9 L | 304.3 oz. | Salmanazar |
| 12 L | 405.8 oz. | Balthazar |
| 15 L | 507.2 oz. | Nebuchadnezzar |

Splits usually have screw-off caps and are meant for immediate consumption. Half-bottles are a good size for dessert wines, since we would drink fewer ounces of these honeyed nectars. Half-bottles as a rule do not age well. Jugs are available in 1.5, 3, and 4 liter sizes, as well as in 5 liter and 18 liter cardboard "bag in the box" dispensers. Some wineries even offer 30 and 60 liter (approximately) kegs, similar to beer barrels, for easy, efficient han-

**The Bordeaux (Claret) Bottle**

*Also used for sherry, vintage port, Chianti, and other Tuscan reds.*

**The Burgundy Bottle**

*Also used for champagne, wines from the Loire and Rhone, and many Barolos.*

*The claret shape bottle is easiest to stack. It is ideal for aging wine because there is room for a larger cork and it has a deep punt and neck to catch sediment.*

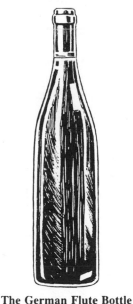

**The German Flute Bottle**

*Also used for Alsatian wines and many Italian whites.*

**The Franconian Bocksbeutel**

*Also used for Portuguese reds.*

13

dling in large restaurants and hotels. Oversized bottles are recommended for prolonged cellar aging.

# WINE AND AGE

The vast majority of wines do not (DO NOT) improve with age. Almost all whites and roses, sparkling wines, lighter reds, and great reds from lesser vintages fit into this category. Factors that assist the longevity of a wine include:

1. alcohol level
2. residual sugar
3. tannins and acids
4. grape varieties used
5. color and extract
6. method of vinification

If you want to put some wines aside for future use, we cautiously recommend: vintage porto; Cabernet Sauvignon-based wines from California, Bordeaux, Italy, and Australia; sweetish Sauternes and Barsacs from France; German Auslese, Beerenauslese, Trockenbeerenauslese and Eiswein; Hungarian Tokaji Essencia; Italy's Brunello di Montalcino and Barolo; and great Burgundies from the Cote D'Or in France. Two factors are important: proper storage conditions, and patience—remember these are great wines and you probably will not want to wait to drink them.

## Wine Storage

You may store most wines safely for six months or more in your home or apartment. Remember that wine is a living (or rather dying) thing and has some formidable enemies. They include:

1. air
2. direct sunlight;
3. vibration
4. temperature variation

For long-term storage, the perfect place to keep wines and spirits is cool and dark, is free from drafts and vibrations, and has a

constant temperature of about 55° F. Lying thus undisturbed, wines age slowly but surely, which explains why they are often found in the cellars of great chateaux and British country houses, still in their prime after very many years.

Wine bottles should be stored on their sides so that their corks are kept moist. If corks dry out they shrink, admitting air to the detriment of the wine.

### What To Do With the Opened Bottle

An unfinished bottle of fine wine should never be discarded. Ideally you should do something to eliminate the air space in the bottle, reseal it, and put it in a refrigerator to slow down the wine's metabolism. There are nitrogen systems, vacuum pumps, and other high-tech devices which help to keep the oxygen away from the wine. However, you need only transfer the unfinished wine into a smaller bottle to limit the air space. Here is an old trick: Keep putting marbles into the bottle until the wine level rises to the top of the bottle, then recork it.

You may find that a big rich wine will taste even better the next day. A pressurized champagne stopper can keep the sparkle in your bubbly for a few days. If you forget about an unfinished bottle of wine and later discover that it tastes a bit oxidized, you can still use it for cooking. Very often such wines add complexity to a dish.

# HEALTH AND WINE

Wine is an agricultural product that has been made and consumed for over 6,000 years. It has been closely associated with Jewish and Christian religious services. Louis Pasteur called it "the most hygienic and healthiest of drinks." It is as integral a part of the Mediterranean diet as is fresh fruit, bread, or good olive oil. Wine is a complex symphony of natural chemicals, minerals, and vitamins.

The only additive needed by the winemaker is sulphur dioxide. This helps control wild yeast and bacteria during the fermentation process. These sulfites have been used by vintners for centuries. In a well-made wine, there may be as little as 100–150 parts per million. However, asthmatics and others may be allergic to these sulphur compounds. Most countries forbid a quantity of 350 PPM or more. The U.S. Bureau of Alcohol, Tobacco, and Firearms (BATF) requires that any wine containing 10 PPM or more state "Contains Sulfites" on the front or back label. This includes virtually every commercial wine.

According to law and custom, wine should never be taken by anyone in excess and is never served to the young. (Plato said it best: "The fire of wine should not be added to the fire of youth!") Of course, one should never, never drive if one has drunk too much. There are strict punishments (and more severe consequences) for offenders. The wine industry is policed nationally by the BATF, statewide by a licensing and enforcing agency (in New York, the SLA; in New Jersey, the ABC), and locally by a municipal group. There are legal guidelines for wine tastings, wine courses, and the like.

Wine contains over a dozen acids and alcohols. A glass of dry wine contains about 100 calories. Wine is rich in iron, potassium, and phosphorus. It is low in sodium. Wines have traces of calcium, magnesium, manganese, zinc, chlorine, boron, silicon, fluoride, copper, vanadium, iodine, cobalt, and molybdenum. Wine contains useful amounts of vitamin B (riboflavin and niacin) and vitamin P. We have not seen any research that indicates that moderate consumption of well-made wine is harmful to the public. To the contrary, the research has been favorable.

### Mandatory Government Warnings

*Any wine bottled after November 18, 1989, must have the following warning printed clearly somewhere on its bottle if it is to be sold in the United States. It is usually found on the back label.*

## Louis Latour

For two centuries, Louis Latour has been involved in the production, selection, ageing and bottling of the finest wines of Burgundy.

Small yields and traditional methods are of utmost importance if the highest possible quality is to be maintained every year.

## SERVING WINE

### When Serving More Than One Wine

If you are staging a formal, multicourse dinner, or just tasting two or more wines, remember these guidelines:

LEAST before BEST
WHITE before RED
DRY before SWEET
LIGHT before FULL
YOUNG before OLD

If you are at a tasting that offers many wines, do not just wander from table to table, drinking capriciously. Decide which wines you wish to try and put them into logical order according to these guidelines. *SPIT*, do not swallow each and every wine. If there is a rare or very special wine at the tasting, we must admit that we break all the rules and run to taste it first. We are afraid that there may be none left by the time we get around to taste it. And with really special stuff, we swallow and never spit.

# GUIDELINES
## for the
# ORDER OF SERVING WINES

*Allow for overlapping due to style and vintage variations.*

## I. Aperitif and Dry Sparkling Wines

Champagne
Dry Vermouth
Dry Madeira

Fino Sherry
Manzanilla

Marsala Vergine
White Porto

## II. Light-Bodied Dry Whites

Chenin Blanc
Entre-Deux-Mers
Frascati

Mosel Wine
Muscadet

Orvieto
Pinot Grigio

## III. Medium-Bodied Dry Whites

Albana di Romagna
Alsatian Riesling
California Sauvignon Blanc
Chablis
Corvo

Gavi
Graves Blanc
Macon Blanc
Pouilly-Fuisse
Pouilly-Fume

Rhine Wines
Soave
Verdicchio
Vernaccia di San Gimignano
Vouvray

## IV. Full-Bodied Dry Whites

Blanc de Noirs types
California Chardonnay
Corton-Charlemagne

Greco di Tufo
Fiano di Avellino
Hermitage Blanc

Meursault
Puligny-Montrachet

### V. Dry Roses

| | | |
|---|---|---|
| Chiaretto del Garda | Tavel Rose | Varietal Roses |
| Provencal Rose | | from California |
| (Blush Wines and Rose D'Anjou may be a bit sweet) | | |

### VI. Light-Bodied Dry Reds

| | | |
|---|---|---|
| Bardolino | Chinon | Napa Gamay |
| Beaujolais | Dolcetto | Valpolicella |
| Bourgueil | | |

### VII. Medium-Bodied Dry Reds

| | | |
|---|---|---|
| Bordeaux | Cotes du Rhone | Dole de Sion |
| Chianti | Cru Beaujolais | Nebbiolo D'Alba |
| Corvo | (Fleurie, Chiroubles, etc.) | Rioja |
| Cotes de Beaune | Dao | Spanna |

### VIII. Full-Bodied Dry Reds

| | | |
|---|---|---|
| Amarone | Chateauneuf-du-Pape | Hermitage |
| Barbaresco | Chianti Riserva | Pommard |
| Barolo | Cote Rotic | Rioja Reserva |
| Brunello di Montalcino | Egri Bikaver | Taurasi |
| California Cabernet Sauvignon | Gattinara | Vino Nobile di Montepulciano |
| California Pinot Noir | Gevrey-Chambertin | Volnay |

### IX. Dessert Wines (Including Sparkling)

| | | |
|---|---|---|
| Asti Spumante | Madeira — Bual, Malmsey | Sauternes, Barsac |
| (and Moscato D'Asti) | Marsala — Sweet | Tokaji (3-5 Puttonyos or |
| Champagne Demi-Sec | Oloroso Sherries | Essencia) |
| German Auslese, BA, TBA, | Porto | |
| Eiswein | | |

## Wine Glasses

You may want to gather a complete collection of copitas for sherry, tulips for champagne, green-stemmed hock glasses, a balloon for burgundies, etc., etc. We prefer to keep things simple. Avoid small "shot glass" size bowls; avoid saucers or birdbaths for champagnes. Invest in a set of professional tasting glasses endorsed by the I.S.O. (International Standardization Organization). This glass with a capacity of about 10 oz. comfortably holds about 3–4 oz. of wine. It is a pleasure to use whether your pleasure is red or white, sparkling, port, sherry, or any combination thereof.

*The copita is traditionally used for sherries.*

*A tall, slender flute will keep the bubbles of fine champagne streaming.*

*The standard I.S.O. glass is suitable for all wines, especially dry whites.*

*Big balloons give reds a chance to breathe.*

*Whatever the shape, do not overpour. Wine, like mankind, needs lots of room to bring out the best. For fortified or table wines, pour only until one-third full. You can be more generous with sparkling wines.*

*Legend has it that saucer glasses were created in the shape of the breasts of Marie Antoinette and Helen of Troy. However, the saucer is suitable for chocolate mousse—not the mousse of fine champagne.*

## Wine and Food

In most cases, food makes wine taste better and wine makes food taste better. But there are certain dishes which are enemies of wine. Here is a partial list.

### Enemies of Wine

- broths and soups
- chocolate
- coffee
- hot spices (chili, curry, mustard, tabasco sauce)
- vinegar (pickled items)
- tomatoes
- certain fruits (citrus, bananas, pineapples)
- highly sweetened foods (including molasses)
- onions and garlic
- ice cream
- certain vegetables (artichokes and asparagus)

With sweeter items, you may opt for a liqueur or just plain water. With piquant Szechuan, Mexican, or Cajun dishes, or a pungent Indian curry, you may prefer a beer or ale.

### Perfect Marriages

Over time, many classic food/wine affinities have become quite famous:

- Burgundy and roast beef
- Champagne and caviar
- Beaujolais and chicken
- Chablis and oysters
- White Burgundies and poached fish with butter sauce
- Porto and Stilton cheese
- French Sauternes and peaches or blue veined cheeses
- Big Italian Reds (Barolo, Brunello) and Parmigiano Reggiano cheese

Remember: The fun of wine and food is to substitute and experiment.

## Tips on Which Wines to Serve

Wine should not be selected solely on its affinity to a particular food dish. You should take the following into consideration:

1. Your Guests: Are they avid wine drinkers? Beginners? People you are trying to impress?
2. The Occasion: Is it a formal dinner with an elaborate list of wines? A barbeque?
3. The Weather: You might not want a Barolo with your grilled steak when it is 95° outside. You may prefer a Soave.

You may want to highlight a great wine. This is done best by offering simply prepared food. Always have a bottle or two in reserve, just in case a faulty cork conspires to undermine your party. Offer a light aperitif, sparkling wine, or the like to your guests when they arrive. You may want to have a dessert wine as the finishing touch. Many "wine nuts" (ourselves included) select the wines first and then marry them to the proper dish, instead of the other way around.

## Wine Service

When presenting a bottle of wine in a restaurant, the waiter should show the bottle, label foremost, for the customer's approval before opening it in the customer's presence. When the wine is to be served from the bottle and not decanted, the waiter should cut the capsule round the top with a knife for neatness, then draw the cork and wipe the lip of the bottle with a clean napkin. The waiter should then present the cork to the host and pour a little into the host's glass for the host to taste and approve before the guests are served. If, in the process, any pieces of cork are seen in the wine, the waiter should exchange the host's glass for a clean one. The women should be served first, then the men, and finally the host.

# COMPLEMENTARY FOODS & WINES

### CHEESES

I. Aperitif and Dry Sparkling Wines

Brillat-Savarin
Mozzarella

II. Light-bodied Dry Whites

Havarti
Muenster
Doux de Montagne

III. Medium-bodied Dry Whites

Jarlsberg
Bel Paese
Emmenthal
Gruyere

IV. Full-bodied Dry Whites

Fontina
Taleggio
Swiss
Monterrey Jack

V. Dry Roses

VI. Light-bodied Dry Reds

Chevre
Camembert
Brie
Asiago

VII. Medium-bodied Dry Reds

Caciocavalla
Grana Padano
Parmigiano Reggiano
Provolone

VIII. Full-bodied Dry Reds

Cheddar
Gouda
Edam

IX. Dessert Wines

Gorgonzola
Blue Cheese
Roquefort

### FOODS

Antipasti
Hors d'oeuvres

Some Soups
Quiche

Prosciutto
Cold Cuts

Pasta — Fish Sauces

Most Risottos
Pasta — Cream & Butter Sauces
Seafood Paella

Seafood Stews

Burgers
Liver
Meat Paella

Pasta — Red Sauces and Meat Sauces

Stews
Casseroles

Cakes
Fruits
Foie Gras
Puddings

Fish

Shellfish

Light Poultry

Rabbit
Salmon
Poultry

Ham
Veal
Pork
Sausages

Turkey

Duck
Lamb
Beef
Game

LIGHT, MILD FOODS

STRONG, PUNGENT FOODS

20

Should the customer be dissatisfied, the waiter should then taste the wine. If it seems out of condition, the waiter should express regret and offer another bottle immediately. Even if it seems all right, it is best to offer another bottle and to keep one's own counsel.

Follow the same principles when you open a bottle or two at home. Do not pour out too much. Fill the glasses up to the halfway point only, so that the fragrance of the wine can be better appreciated.

## Champagne Service

Many initiates are a bit cautious about extracting champagne corks. Once they have 10 or 15 behind them, it not only becomes a snap, but it is actually fun. Remember that the wine is under great pressure and if left unprotected, the cork could well fly out on its own. Such corks can damage ceilings, people, whatever they are aimed at. Also, wine and bubbles can be lost.

Here are a few tips:

- Place a napkin over the cork and hold it with your thumb at all times to prevent unwanted departures.
- When you unwind the wire hood (whether you remove it or not), realize that the cork is now unprotected. Now the napkin or thumb becomes more important.
- As you remove the cork, twist the bottle away from the cork. Twisting the cork can snap it in half. If the cork snaps, insert a corkscrew *through* the napkin and into the cork. It should come out quite easily. Remember—pressure is helping you. It is pushing the cork out.
- Never *POP* the cork. Ease it out. The French say that the sound should never be louder (please excuse the chauvinism) than a woman's sigh!
- Have glasses ready for foam as it streams out. Tilting the bottle 45° will minimize such spillage.
- Serve as you would any other wine, but pour more carefully to prevent bubbles (mousse) from overflowing, and more generously (1/2 to 2/3 full).
- ENJOY!

## Decanting

There are two basic reasons for decanting:

1. To separate clear wine from sediment (which develops naturally over a period of time); and
2. To allow young, hard wine to aerate; that is, "breathe" a bit, so as to soften it.

A period of oxidation in a decanter usually does good things for a great red wine, whether young or old. The greater the sediment that a wine lays down with age, the more necessary decanting becomes. A wine served muddy or even a little bit "veiled" will never appear to the taster to be at the top of its form.

Then there is the ritual, almost religious side of decanting. When you think of the enormous effort, skill, and care that have gone into the making of a great bottle, the symbolic task of decanting it seems a fitting participation which prepares the taster for the art that is about to be exercised and the pleasure that will be enjoyed.

Once decanted, very old clarets and burgundies can die within an hour or so; the time to decant them is a few minutes before they are to be drunk. Young red wines, on the other hand, improve from "breathing" in a decanter for as much as 24 hours. Big wines, like Barolo and Chateauneuf-du-Pape, benefit greatly from being allowed to "breathe" for a few hours. Beyond this, timing is a matter of experience, but two hours beforehand is about right for five- to ten-year-old clarets.

For some wines, like vintage porto, it is easier to use cheesecloth to capture the "crust" that has developed. Elaborate wine funnels with finely meshed screens serve the same purpose. With vintage porto and older red wines, the corks may be brittle, soaked through, or very difficult to extract. Sometimes the cork will crumble or fall into the bottle. In such a case, simply pour the wine through cheesecloth into a decanter.

## Note on Temperatures

Most American homes and apartments are much warmer than they were a generation ago. For this reason, the practice of *cham-*

# DECANTING

## STEP ONE

1. Bring up the bottle about 45 minutes before drinking it. Keep it horizontal and put it on the edge of a table without jarring it. Cushion it from each side so it does not roll.
2. If the bottle is very dusty, clean its neck and shoulders with a damp cloth.
3. Completely remove the metal capsule, cutting it with the point of a corkscrew.
4. Be careful that the bottle remains in the position in which you originally put it, even if the label is not on top.

## STEP TWO

1. Light a candle and put it on the very edge of the table, beside the bottle.
2. Rinse a decanter with a tiny amount of barely tepid water and make sure that it is absolutely free of odor (certain detergents, incompletely rinsed away, can ruin a wine's bouquet).
3. After draining it, put the decanter on the other side of the bottle.
4. With the help of a double corkscrew, sink the screw-wire into the cork without shifting the position of the bottle.

A hint: Do not store your decanters closed with their own stoppers, but instead stuff the necks gently with a bit of tissue paper.

## STEP THREE

1. Once the screw-wire has completely penetrated into the cork, begin to turn the withdrawal screw, very gently.
2. When you feel the cork is about to come free of the neck, lean the bottle very slightly upwards, keeping the bottom in contact with the table. Lift it just enough so the wine does not spill when the cork comes out. Easy does it.
3. If the inside of the bottle neck is dirty, clean it delicately with a dish towel.
4. Put down the corkscrew and hold the bottle by its mid-section in your right hand and the decanter by its neck in your left hand.

## STEP FOUR

1. Pour very slowly, making the wine trickle against the interior wall of the decanter. To do this, depending on its shape, incline it more or less.
2. The candle light will enable you to see the wine pass through the neck of the bottle. You should keep an eye on the point of the bottle where the neck merges with the shoulder.
3. When the first "cloud" of sediment reaches the neck, lift the bottle quickly in order to keep it back from the rest of the wine.
4. Stopper the decanter, and if you are serving several red wines, make sure you have some way of identifying each one.

It is quite simple to learn to decant by watching someone demonstrate it and then practicing on a bottle or two.

*brer*-ing wine, bringing it to room temperature, has lost much of its original meaning. Room temperature usually means about 60°–65°F, the temperature of typical rooms a century ago.

It is better to have a wine a little too cool than a wine that is too warm. Your hand beneath the bowl of a glass can warm up a wine quite quickly and well.

Big red wines are normally served at about 65°–70° F, but some of the lighter red wines that are drunk young can be slightly chilled (Beaujolais, for example).

Rose wines, sparkling wines, and finer dry white wines must not be made so cold that the delicacy of bouquet and flavor is lost.

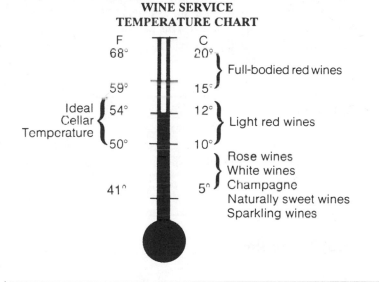

**WINE SERVICE TEMPERATURE CHART**

## Chilling Wines

Do not overchill! Most dry wines and sparklers should be 40° to 50° F. An ice bucket should be deep enough for water and ice to cover the shoulder of the bottle. If the upper part of the bottle is not chilled, leave the bottle upside down for a few minutes to permit cold wine to sink to the neck.

Use enough water with ice cubes so that bottle can be reinserted without too much effort. *NEVER USE ICE ALONE.* Ice plus water chills much faster than ice alone. Fifteen minutes in a bucket will properly chill any rose or dry white wine. In a refrigerator, one and a half to two hours is sufficient for dry wines.

Full-bodied, sweet whites should be colder (40°–45° F) than delicate, light wines (45°–50° F). Champagne takes longer to chill because of the thickness of the glass.

Reds should never be served tepid. The temperature should not be higher than 70°. Big reds are best at 65°–70° F, light reds at 55°–65° F, and roses and nouveau-type wines at 50°–55° F.

## Scoring Wines

Whenever you taste, take notes. The mind forgets, but the pen does not. You should have a method that makes it easy for you to recall which vintage was best, which wine was the best value, etc. You should also constantly sample wines in your own collection to see how they are developing. We suggest the following S.E.C. scoring card.

| Product Name: _____ Vintage: _____ | | 0 | 1 | 2 | 3 | 4 |
|---|---|---|---|---|---|---|
| Country of Origin: _____ Region: _____ | Appearance | | | | | |
| Brief Description: _____ | Nose | | | | | |
| _____ | Taste | | | | | |
| _____ | Finish | | | | | |
| Comments: _____ | General | | | | | |
| _____ | Total Score: _____ | | | | | |

# THE ART OF TASTING

Part of the fun of wine is developing your ability to taste wines comparatively so that you can make the best possible selections. You must decide how deeply you wish to delve into the art of tasting. You may be content with just finding good, solid, tasty wines or you might want to be very analytical. Whichever path you choose, remember to:

1. Conduct tastings in a smokeless room.
2. Use a white background to judge the color of a wine.
3. Keep written notes on your impressions. Unfortunately, unlike a fine Bordeaux or Brunello, most of us do not improve with age, so we tend to forget.
4. Use good glasses.
5. Remember your S's.

## Seeing a Wine

Look for color, clarity, brilliance, and viscosity. Some terms you may use to describe a wine's appearance are: clear, bright or dull, hazy or cloudy; thick/oily or thin/watery; pale or dark; weak or intense. Check out a wine's "legs." In sparkling wines, look for a steady stream of fine, abundant bubbles.

## Smelling a Wine

Really get your nose into the glass and take deep inhalations, after having swirled. Go back and sniff the wine several times to see if there is any change in your initial olfactory impression. Check for signs of "opening up" or conversely, oxidation. Remember, you will be encountering many fragrances: floral, fruity, vegetal, mineral, spicy, balsamic, chemical. Aroma is technically the fragrance of the grape; bouquet is the fragrance imparted by the winemaking and aging processes. Descriptive words include perfumed, woody, young, baked, complex, short, closed, acrid, corky, moldy, skunky, minty, vegetal, grassy. You will detect fruit smells: apples, currants, pears, peaches, strawberries; wood/ plant smells: eucalyptus, lilacs, jasmine, roses, violets; spice/nut smells: clove, cinnamon, almond, vanilla, caramel.

## Savoring a Wine

In tasting a wine, determine if the sweetness and the acidity are in balance. Take note of its body, taste, and flavor. A great wine will usually taste the way it smells and looks. Tasting, for the most part, is a confirmation of what your eyes and nose have already told you. Plus, of course, it is a lot of fun. Tasting terms include syrupy, cloying, hot, biting, raw, harsh,mild, fat, tannic, alcoholic, nervous, round, big, firm, clumsy, flabby, velvety, soft, generous, complex, chewy. You will taste the fruits, nuts, spices, etc., that you have just smelled.

## Swallowing a Wine

Note the finish on a wine, its persistence or length in your mouth. Light, crisp wines will finish clean; great, complex wines will have a lingering finish.

## Overall Impression

After having gone through this ritual, we can now say that the wine is well-bred, luxurious, voluptuous, refined, exquisite, delicate, honest, classy, weighty, noble, faded, unattractive, or just plain dead. We are fairly certain that we do not use such a rich corpus of terms to recall our taste impressions of Coca-Cola. Wine is truly civilization's most interesting beverage.

The finest book that we have seen on the subject of developing tasting appreciation skills is Steven Spurrier and Michel Dovaz's *Academie du Vin Complete Wine Course.* We think they would agree that the best, and only way, to become a better, more analytical taster is to taste, taste, and taste some more. Of course, you should spit. Fine wine, immoderately excellent, should always be drunk in moderation.

# THE U.C. DAVIS WHEEL

*Analysis begins in the center of the circle. Broad impressions become more particular as you reach the outside circle.*

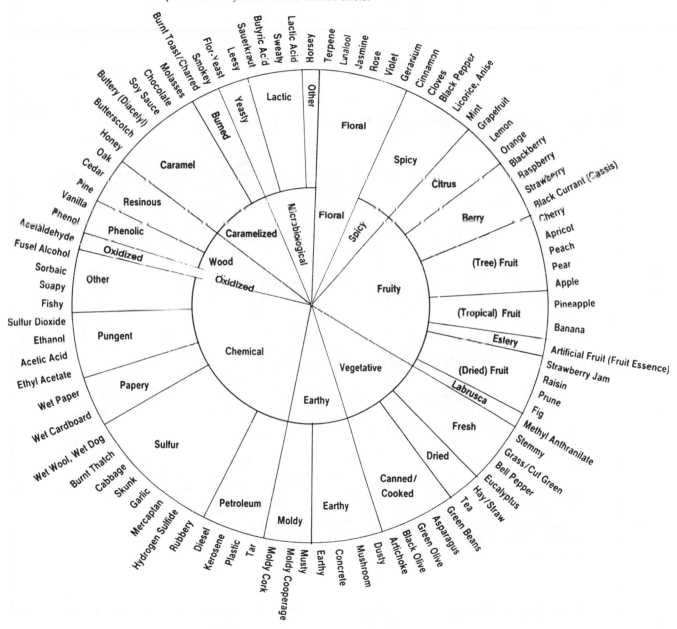

25

# HOW TO TASTE WINE

## Remember Your "S's"

No special science is required to appreciate a good thing. Tasting wines is always an enjoyable experiment.

The first step is to *look at the wine* in the glass. See how bright it looks; compare the different shades of the reds, which go from a brilliant ruby to a purple hue. The color is part of the typical characteristics of the wines of each place name. **SEE**

The next step is to *swirl the wine* in the glass. This is not done just to show off as an expert, but in order for the wine to "breathe" and come in contact with the air to develop its wonderful aroma and bouquet. It is for this reason that very little wine is poured into a large glass—so that there is plenty of room for the "perfume" of the wine to expand and develop in the glass. **SWIRL**

Now that the swirling has brought out the aroma and bouquet of the wine, *sniff it*. Smelling the wine in the glass is one of the greatest pleasures of wine tasting because the bouquet of the wine gives a foretaste of the wine itself. **SNIFF**

Next, *sip the wine*. Do not swallow it yet. It is with our mouth that we taste, and therefore, swallowing the wine immediately cuts short all the sensations that may be derived from the tasting. Let the wine roll in your mouth. **SIP (Savor)**

After you have *swallowed* the wine, there is still one step in the art of wine tasting. Concentrate on the aroma that lingers in the mouth. A good wine leaves a lasting fragrance after being swallowed, and the greater the wine, the longer this fragrance lasts. So do not shorten your pleasure by rushing to a new wine right after having tasted the previous one. If you are tasting many wines, you may prefer to spit out your wine into an appropriate ice bucket or pitcher. This will keep your mind and wits clear. **SWALLOW or SPIT**

# ODDS AND ENDS

## Corkscrews

Neophytes will find the butterfly lever type easier to use, but most professional wine waiters prefer the lever type, which fits in their pockets. There is also the "Ah-So", popular in California, which does not penetrate the cork but wedges itself around it. The best corkscrew has a hollow spiral worm with the point in continuation of the spiral. The outside of the spiral should have a groove to give a stronger grip to the cork. The spiral should be long enough to penetrate the bottom of a two-inch cork. If all else fails, the teflon coated screwpull is almost foolproof. But remember, practice makes perfect.

**Ah-So**

*Wine isn't good until you get the cork out. Practice makes perfect. Look for a corkscrew with a spiral worm, not an auger.*

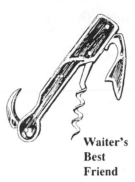

**Waiter's Best Friend**

**Auger**
*"Bad Worm"*

**Spiral**
*"Good Worm"*

**Screwpull**

**Double-Action**

**Butterfly**

## Baskets

Wicker baskets are primarily used to carry mature red wines gently from the cellar to the table. Some restaurants serve all red wines in a basket; others simply stand a young red on the table.

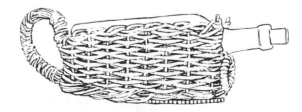

**The Wine Basket**

*This basket is a help in your attempt to separate clear wine from sediment. Its original use was to transport wine from the cellar to the table.*

27

## Sediment in Wine

Do not discard wine that contains sediment. All wines may throw sediment in normal and natural development. White wine sediment is usually colorless and does not affect taste or quality. (This may be from pectins or tartars and usually disappears in a warm room.) Otherwise, stand the bottle up to allow sediment to drop to the bottom.

Cloudy wine is usually unfit to drink. Sediment in red wines is unpleasant and bitter and should never be poured into the glass. Sediment is a natural sign of the maturation process. It is derived from tannins or color pigments. Wines with sediment should be stood up for several hours and carefully decanted.

IMPORTERS:
DEINHARD & PARTNERS, INC.
TENAFLY, N.J.

**Wine Diamonds**

You will notice that there are some crystals at the bottom of this bottle. The reason for this is that certain fine wines with a high extract tend to a crystallization of tartaric acid after being bottled. It is a perfectly natural development, and in no way harms the taste of the wine. On the contrary, connoisseurs and experts often name these crystals »Wine Diamonds«

**Sediment**

*Sediment is natural in wine. Actually, it is quite special and to be expected in older reds. Crystals are sometimes found in very special German wines, as this back label shows.*

## Legal Standards for Wine

Most countries have established legal standards for their wines. Realize that these laws regulate a wine's color, the grapes to be used, methods of pruning, the ages of vines, geographic zones, yield per acre, and many other factors. They contribute to a wine's quality, but the final determination of a wine's excellence is dependent on the quality factors, not on legal mandate.

**How Some Countries Regulate Quality:**
**Commonly Seen Abbreviations**

**France**
    Vin de Table (Vin Ordinaire)
    V.D.Q.S. (Vins Delimites de Qualité Superieure)
    A.C. or A.O.C. (Appellation d'Origine Contrôlée; the tightest standards and controls)

**West Germany**
    DTW (Deutscher Tafelwein—German table wine)
    QbA (quality wine)
    QmP (quality wine with distinction)

**Italy**
    Vino da Tavola (table wine)
    D.O.C. (like the French A.O.C.)
    D.O.C.G. (extremely rigid quality controls)

**Spain**
    D.O. (like the French A.O.C.)
    D.E. (control for Spanish sparkling wines)

# READING WINE LABELS

The wine label contains a wealth of information for you. Each company has an agency appointed to supervise and regulate its wine business. Usually it is a division in the agriculture or commerce areas. Read through the commonly seen technical terms and then peruse the labels. Do not be ashamed to ask your waiter or wine merchant questions. Also feel free to contact the shipper or importer. You will understand label designations better after reading further in the text.

## Commonly Seen Labeling Terms

Below are some technical terms that you may find on labels. We call it "California wine language:"

**Alcohol by Volume.** This must be stated on the label. There is an allowance for 1.5% variation. Table wines do not exceed 14%.

**Barrel Fermented.** Wine may be fermented in wooden barrels instead of large glass-lined or stainless steel tanks. This provides for subtlety, balance, and richness, but there is a greater risk of oxidation.

**Bottled by.** If a wine label states "Produced and Bottled by," it indicates that the winery was involved in at least 75% of the crushing, fermenting, aging, and bottling process. "Made and Bottled by" is quite another story. Here the winery is involved in only a minimum of 10% of the production. "Cellared by" and "Vinted by" are impressive sounding but legally meaningless terms.

**Brix (or Balling).** This usually indicates the ripeness or the sweetness level of the grapes at harvest. One-half of the brix gives an approximation of how much alcohol will be in the wine, if it is fermented completely dry (for example, 20° brix will be a bit more than 10% alcohol; 25° brix will be a bit more than 12.5% alcohol).

**Carbonic Maceration.** A process where the weight of the grapes alone causes fermentation; there is no crushing or pressing. Used for Beaujolais or Nouveau-styled reds, it adds fruitiness to the finished product.

**Cask #, Lot #:** These are designations of individual wineries for some of their best wines. Sometimes unscrupulous wineries will throw a curveball here.

**Cold Stabilization.** This is a clarification method that clears wines without filtering out too much of the flavor.

**Estate Bottled.** This does not have the legal clout that you might think. Find out what you can about the estate and its owner.

**Late Harvest.** The longer a grape remains on the vine, the riper it gets. Riper grapes mean more sugar, maybe even residual sugar. This term usually refers to a dessert-style wine.

**PH (or _p_H).** A way of measuring grape ripeness. On a PH scale from 0-14, a lemon is 2.0. Most table wines are 3.0–3.5; dessert wines may be as high as 3.9. Acid is a low number; alkaline is high.

**Total Acidity.** Some back labels may show this. Most dry wines are 0.6% to 0.75% total acidity. Dessert wines would be higher.

1. Bottle Size: 750 ML (25.4 oz)
2. Alcohol Content: 12%—Table
3. Vintage: 1989
4. Origin: Italy; the Adige Valley in the northeast
5. Color: White
6. Brand: La Colombaia
7. Type of Wine: Pinot Grigio
8. Government Designation: D.O.C. for Pinot Grigio wine from Valdadige
9. Importer: American BD Co., Hawthorne, NJ
10. Special Attributes: Estate bottled.

**1985**

# Badia a Coltibuono

## Chianti Classico
*Denominazione di origine controllata e garantita*

### —Riserva—

Net Cont. 750 ml
CONTAINS SULFITES

Alc. 13.5% by vol.
PRODUCT OF ITALY

*Estate bottled by*
*Tenuta di Coltibuono s.r.l. - Gaiole in Chianti - Italy*

Imported by William Grant & Sons. Inc. New York, N.Y.

1. Bottle Size: 750 ML (25.4 oz)
2. Alcohol Content: 13.5%
3. Vintage: 1985
4. Origin: Italy; a small, excellent subzone (Classico) in the Chianti area of Tuscany.
5. Color: Red (Chianti must be red)
6. Brand: Badia a Coltibuono
7. Type of Wine: Chianti Classico
8. Government Designation: D.O.C.; from the 1984 vintage on, Chianti will be D.O.C.G.
9. Importer: William Grant & Sons, Inc., New York, NY
10. Special Attributes: Riserva (aged at least 3 years). The fine print shows that it is estate bottled. Chianti is a blend of several grapes, mostly Sangiovese.

GRAND VIN DE BORDEAUX

PRODUCE OF FRANCE

# Château Taillefer
## POMEROL
APPELLATION POMEROL CONTROLÉE
**1978**

e
75cl

Héritiers MARCEL MOUEIX
PROPRIÉTAIRES A POMEROL (GIRONDE)

MIS EN BOUTEILLE AU CHATEAU

1. Bottle Size: 75 cl = 750 ML (25.4 oz)
2. Alcohol Content: Would be shown on a strip label— 12.5%—Table
3. Vintage: 1978
4. Origin: France; Pomerol, a small commune in Bordeaux
5. Color: Red (Pomerol must be red)
6. Brand: Château Taillefer
7. Type of Wine: Pomerol
8. Government Designation: A.O.C.
9. Importer: Would be shown on strip label—Favin Importers, Bayonne, NJ
10. Special Attributes: Pomerol is made basically from Merlot grapes. This one is chateau (estate) bottled.

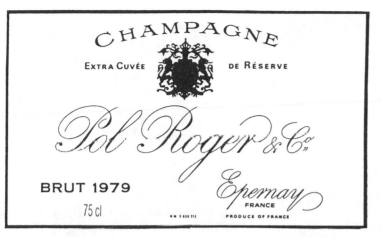

**CHAMPAGNE**

EXTRA CUVÉE    DE RÉSERVE

*Pol Roger & C⁰*

**BRUT 1979**

75 cl

*Epernay*
FRANCE
PRODUCE OF FRANCE

1. Bottle Size: 750 cl (25.4 oz)
2. Alcohol Content: Not shown (about 12%) — Sparkling
3. Vintage: 1979
4. Origin: France; the Champagne region
5. Color: White (but made from red and white grapes)
6. Brand: Pol Roger & Co.
7. Type of Wine: Champagne Brut
8. Government Designation: A.O.C. (does not have to be spelled out for French Champagne)
9. Importer: Not shown
10. Special Attributes: Must be very dry. Made by the costly Champagne method.

RED BURGUNDY WINE    ALCOHOL 11.5% BY VOLUME

MAISON FONDÉE EN 1819

*Cruse*

**Beaujolais Villages**

APPELLATION BEAUJOLAIS CONTROLÉE

MIS EN BOUTEILLE PAR *Cruse & Fils Frères* PRODUCT OF FRANCE
NÉGOCIANTS A NUITS·SAINT·GEORGES · CÔTE·D'OR

SOLE DISTRIBUTORS FOR THE UNITED STATES
LEONARD KREUSCH, INC, MOONACHIE, N.J.    750 ML

1. Bottle Size: 750 ML (25.4 oz)
2. Alcohol Content: 11.5% — Table
3. Vintage: Would be shown on neck label
4. Origin: France; a small group of about 39 choice villages in the Beaujolais zone in Southern Burgundy
5. Color: Red
6. Brand: Cruse
7. Type of Wine: Beaujolais Villages
8. Government Designation: A.O.C.
9. Importer: Leonard Kreusch, Inc., Moonachie, NJ
10. Special Attributes: Beaujolais Villages is made from Gamay grapes. A negociant is a shipper who buys grapes or wine and ages, blends, and bottles them.

*Leonard Kreusch* GmbH & Co

750 ml

LK

MOSELLE WINE - MOSEL-SAAR-RUWER

QUALITÄTSWEIN
A P Nr 3 907 229 21 86

*Zeller Schwarze Katz*

SOLE AGENT FOR USA: LEONARD KREUSCH INC., MOONACHIE, N.J.
Net Contents 750 ml - 25,4 Fl. Oz – Alcohol 9½ % by Volume

1. Bottle Size: 750 ML (25.4 oz)
2. Alcohol Content 9.5% — Table
3. Vintage: Would be shown on neck label
4. Origin: Germany; Schwarze Katz, a delimited vineyard area around the town of Zell on the Mosel River
5. Color: White
6. Brand: Leonard Kreusch
7. Type of Wine: Zeller Schwarze Katz
8. Government Designation: Qualitätswein (QbA)
9. Importer: Leonard Kreusch, Inc., Moonachie, NJ
10. Special Attributes: Most likely from the Noble Riesling vine

1. Bottle Size: 750 ML (25.4 oz)
2. Alcohol Content: 18% — Fortified
3. Vintage: Non-Vintage
4. Origin: Italy; Marsala, a small zone in western Sicily
5. Color: Amber
6. Brand: Florio
7. Type of Wine: Marsala Fine; Dry
8. Government Designation: D.O.C. for Marsala Fine
9. Importer: Julius Wile Sons, New York, NY
10. Special Attributes: By law, it must be made from Grillo, Inzolia, or Catarratto vines.

1. Bottle Size: 750 ML (25.4 oz) (would be superimposed on this sample label)
2. Alcohol Content: 12.8% — Table
3. Vintage: 1985
4. Origin: California; Napa Valley
5. Color: Red
6. Brand: J. Wile & Sons
7. Type of Wine: Cabernet Sauvignon
8. Government Designation: BATF standards for a varietal from the Napa Valley
9. Importer: Domestic
10. Special Attributes: Must be at least 75% Cabernet Sauvignon by law.

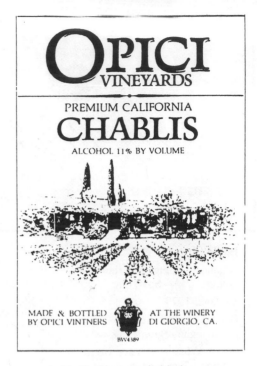

1. Bottle Size: Available in several sizes from 375 ML (12.7 oz) to 4 L (135.2 oz)
2. Alcohol Content: 11% — Table
3. Vintage: Non-Vintage
4. Origin: Grapes must come from California
5. Color: White
6. Brand: Opici
7. Type of Wine: Chablis
8. Government Designation: BATF standards for a wine from California
9. Importer: Domestic
10. Special Attributes: This is a generic wine, a blend of several grapes. It is a good, sound wine at an affordable price.

1. Bottle Size: 750 ML (25.4 oz)
2. Alcohol Content: 19.5% — Fortified
3. Vintage: Non-Vintage
4. Origin: Spain; Jerez (sherry)
5. Color: Amber
6. Brand: Williams & Humbert
7. Type of Wine: Pando
8. Government Designation: Complies with Spanish government's regulations for very dry Fino Sherry
9. Importer: (Not Shown) Julius Wile Sons, New York, NY
10. Special Attributes: As a Fino Sherry, it will be fine and dry due to rare, special flor. Palomino grapes are used.

## A PARTING SHOT

Now we will set sail to the great ports of the world to sample wines country by country. No single country has a monopoly on great vineyards, fine grape varieties, and gifted, dedicated vintners. Who makes the best wine? We can safely answer: France makes the best French wine; Italy makes the best Italian wine; America makes the best American wine; and so on and so forth. What is the best wine? Not the one with all the write-ups, or the most expensive one. The best wine is the one *YOU* like most.

To paraphrase the Greek philosopher, Heracleitus: "You cannot taste the same fine wine twice." Not only do wines change slightly from vintage to vintage, but we change, too. We are constantly looking for better, more complex wines. Wine is a unique beverage. We do not seek a greater quantity of it, but a higher quality. Each year we have thousands to evaluate and pick from. That is what makes it so interesting.

# SELF-EVALUATION

BEFORE READING ON, see if you have mastered the data set forth in the last few pages. Check the answer section at the back of the book for the correct answers. If you have not answered at least 70% of the questions below correctly, please reread the previous section.

## INTRODUCTION – PART II

TRUE    FALSE

_____    _____ 1. There are three basic shapes of bottles: Burgundy, Bordeaux, and Chianti Fiasco (straw).

_____    _____ 2. As a rule of thumb, wine, in general, may be stored safely for up to nine months.

_____    _____ 3. A copita is the most widely used wine glass by professionals.

_____    _____ 4. There are two basic reasons for decanting: (1) to separate clear wine from sediment; and (2) to aerate a wine.

_____    _____ 5. In tasting wine there are five S's: See, Swirl, Sniff, Savor, Spit (or Swallow).

_____    _____ 6. When one has a bottle of wine with sediment in it, it should be discarded.

_____    _____ 7. Red wines should never be served tepid.

_____    _____ 8. Air, temperature, movement, and sunlight enhance the characteristics of wine.

_____    _____ 9. A standard glass for all wines should be at least 10 ounces.

_____    _____ 10. The best wine is the one you like the most.

# FORTIFIED WINES

Fortified wines are enriched with brandy or some other spirit. They are usually between 16%–20% alcohol and are used as appetizer or dessert wines. They may be produced anywhere in the world, but the most significant fortified wines are the following:

SHERRY . . . . . . . . . . . . . . . . . . . . . . . . . . . . . . . . . . . . . . . . . . . . . . . .from Spain
PORTO . . . . . . . . . . . . . . . . . . . . . . . . . . . . . . . . . . . . . . . . . . . .from Portugal
MARSALA . . . . . . . . . . . . . . . . . . . . . . . . . . . . . .from the Italian island Sicily
MADEIRA . . . . . . . . . . . . . . . . . . . . . . . . . . . .from the Portuguese island Madeira

The trend in this category as well as in aromatized wines is down slightly.

*Maybe it is the salty Mediterranean air, but whatever the reason, most of the world's famous fortified wines come from the Mediterranean basin. Many were created by Arabs, who were forbidden to drink. These wines were used as elixirs, medicinal tonics, and secret potions.*

# SHERRY
## *The World's Dominant Fortified Wine*

## ORIGIN

According to a Common Market agreement, true sherry comes only from a very strictly defined area in the province of Andalusia near the city of Cadiz in the southwest corner of Spain. Although other so-called sherries are produced in other parts of the world, Europeans refer to them as sherry-type wines. In England, the world's largest market for sherry, the law states that the term sherry used on its own applies only to wine produced in the clearly defined area centered around Jerez-de-la-Frontera in Spain. Sherry-style wines from other countries must be described as American sherry, South African sherry, or Australian sherry, according to British law.

Since the United States does not comply with this agreement, we do see on American labels Gallo Sherry, Taylor Sherry, etc. Americans argue that sherry is a generic term for an amber fortified wine. A similar conflict exists with port, Chablis, burgundy, Chianti, and the like.

The production area in Spain consists of approximately fifty thousand acres. It forms a rather crude triangle with the towns of Jerez (pronounced Hay-reth: the word "sherry" is a corruption of the name of the town), Sanlucar de Barrameda, and Puerto de Santa Maria at the corners.

There are records that wine has been produced in this part of Spain for more than 2,500 years, although its distinctive style has evolved only in the past few centuries. There was a cruder style of sherry, shipped 400 years ago in the time of Shakespeare, who called it "sherry" and "sack".

Sherry is a still, amber-fortified wine. "Still" means that it is not sparkling; the "amber" color comes from white grapes (it could broadly be called a white wine); and "fortified" means that it is strengthened by adding distilled grape brandy.

## TYPES OF SHERRY

There are two basic types of sherry — **Fino** and **Oloroso** — but variations result in a range of wines of infinite scope, from the very dry, almost astringent Manzanilla, produced in the area around Sanlucar, to the rich, sweet Oloroso and brown sherries. The main variations are:

### DRY FINO

**Manzanilla:** A fino-type wine, grown and produced near the coast at Sanlucar and described as having a hint of saltiness (from the sea air) in its flavor. Very pale and very dry.

**Fino:** Again, a pale and dry wine. This is the favorite style of the Spaniards.

### MEDIUM TO SWEET OLOROSO

**Amontillado:** Originally a fino, this wine has not developed *flor* (explained in the section on sherry production) and has remained a long time in wood, gaining body, color, and a nutty character. Usually medium dry.

**Oloroso:** This is a popular category in both England and the U.S. Traditionally blended to be rich, golden, and sweet, some of these genuine old wines are expensive.

**Cream Sherry:** This is blended to be very dark and sweet. Most popular in the U.S.A.

Montilla wines, grown and produced near Cordoba, should not be referred to as sherries. Montilla wines have an identity all their own, even though some may be reminiscent of the wines of Jerez.

# FACTORS IN PRODUCING SHERRY

## Grape Varieties and Soil

Although in the past a number of grape varieties were used, sherry is now produced almost exclusively from the Palomino grape with a small quantity of the sweeter Pedro Ximenez (known as the P.X.) blended into the sweet wines.

The best vineyards are located on the very fine, chalky soil known as *albariza*. *Barros* soil, which is a mixture of clay and limestone, produces much wine, although the quality is not considered as good. *Arenas*, a sandy type of soil, produces some good wines, but it is not regarded as highly as albariza in general.

## The Harvest

Vintage time is in September, and bunches of grapes are gathered individually, as they ripen. A vineyard may be combed four or even five times before all the grapes are gathered. The grapes are placed on circular *esparto* grass mats in the sun, where they remain to dry for about 24 hours, being covered at night to protect them from dew.

After this drying period, in the traditional method of making sherry, the grapes are taken indoors to *lagars,* or pressing troughs, which can be either wood or concrete and are approximately 12 feet square. Some 1,500 pounds of grapes are put into the lagar and a team of treaders crush the grapes with *zapatos*, boots of calves leather with angled rows of nails in the soles. This allows grapes to be crushed without crushing the pits and stalks, which contain tannins and oils.

The unfermented grape juice, or *mosto,* is run off into casks. The mash that is left is heaped into a pile around a central wooden screw set in the lagar and bound into a "pie" with strips of esparto grass matting. A wooden plate is then screwed down onto the pie, extracting much of the remainder of the juice, which joins that from the first (foot) pressing. Third and fourth mechanical pressings follow. These yield juice of inferior quality to be used either for local consumption, for conditioning casks, for distillation into brandy, or for making vinegar.

# HOW A FINE FINO SHERRY IS MADE

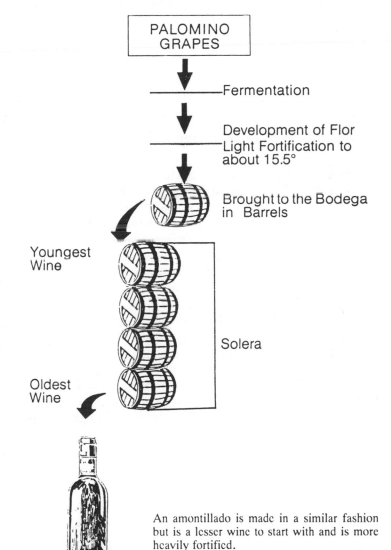

PALOMINO GRAPES

Fermentation

Development of Flor
Light Fortification to about 15.5°

Brought to the Bodega in Barrels

Youngest Wine

Solera

Oldest Wine

An amontillado is made in a similar fashion but is a lesser wine to start with and is more heavily fortified.

An oloroso contains sweet Pedro Ximenez wine or a color wine and is made similarly, but from wines that develop no flor at all.

The roughest wine is cooked for color wine or distilled to make brandy.

Due to increasing costs, many of the larger establishments are replacing foot crushing with gentle mechanical presses. It is claimed that such pressings produce mosto of a higher quality.

Once the pressing has taken place, the juice is transported in casks or by road tanker to a *bodega,* a large storage and treatment warehouse, where the wine will spend many, many years before its final bottling.

## Fermentation and Maturing

Wine is simply grape juice that has been allowed to ferment — a natural process where the natural sugar in the grape juice is transformed into alcohol. This chemical reaction is brought about by yeasts that are present in the "bloom" on the grapes and which start to work upon the grape juice the moment the two come into contact.

For sherry, fermentation is a two-stage process. The first phase lasts from 7 to 10 days, where the wine moves with a violent, "boiling" motion. The second stage is a much more gentle affair, which continues for several weeks throughout the winter and into early spring.

Since fermentation continues uninterrupted, all the sugar in the grape is turned into alcohol. Once fermentation is complete, the resulting wine is completely dry. It will remain so until final shipping, when it will be blended with sweetening wines according to taste. After fermentation, the young wines are very lightly fortified with brandy.

## Classification for Type

Classification of the wine is made by experts. Wines are constantly tasted, retasted, and reclassified.

A fascinating feature of sherry is that no one can predict with certainty how any particular cask of mosto will develop. Two casks of mosto from the same vineyard, even from the same pressing, may develop into wines that are quite different. It can be said, however, that certain vineyards tend to produce wines of similar style over the years provided that weather conditions,

treatment of the vines, and the subsequent vinification are all similar. It is also a fair generalization to say that particularly hot and dry years produce more wines of the oloroso rather than the fino type.

Certain casks of wine develop a white film on the surface known as *flor.* This entirely natural phenomenon is very necessary for fino types, since flor imparts a special character to the wine. Such special lots of fino wines are once again fortified, this time to about 15$1/2$% alcohol by volume, which is the maximum at which flor will live.

Other casks will either show no tendency to grow flor or will display a marked reluctance to do so. These cannot become true finos but are destined to develop into olorosos or at least heavier wines. Consequently, these particular casks are fortified to about 17$1/2$% or 18% alcohol by volume, since the growth of flor is no longer a factor in their development.

Within a year of the vintage, the wine will have shown its characteristics and will have been fortified to its appropriate level. It now must be very closely watched so that any signs of waywardness can be quickly checked and treated.

Although precise methods of handling wines vary from shipper to shipper, most keep their young wines in a mosto bodega for one year before passing them on to a *criadera* or nursery bodega. The criadera is the point at which a wine starts its "education," before going on to join a *solera* many years later.

## The Solera System

Sherry is essentially a blended wine, and there is no such thing as a vintage sherry.

The basis of the sherry solera system is that young wine, if blended in the right proportion with older wines of a similar style, will identify itself precisely with the older one, making for a better wine. If the blending is done carefully and intelligently, continuity of a particular type or style of wine can be guaranteed. It is essential that sufficient stocks of older wines in various styles be built up to support any given solera.

In a nutshell, the solera is a system of progressive, fractional blending of wines of one style. As a result, young wine is slowly educated, by virtue of judicious blending, to acquire the precise characteristics of the older wine to which it is married. This is carried out over a great many years and is achieved through a great many scales or stages.

Bodegas will often be organized with the very young wines on one side, the criadera wines in the middle, and the solera wines, (that is, the final scale) on the other side of the bodega. Shippers strive to have wines of only one particular type in a bodega. Since a limited amount is drawn out of the lowest scale of a solera, there is a gradual movement of younger wines to support and replace what has been taken. Thus the oldest wine is replaced, the next oldest, and so forth, until the *anada* wines (that is, the wines of one particular year, before they arc blended) are introduced into the criadera to begin their long and slow education.

This system is a tribute to the master blenders who organize special *cuvees* of wines and skillfully combine them just at the correct time. It is interesting to see their "wine thieves," which are used to draw samples from barrels. These master blenders have a sign language all their own, putting colorful code symbols called *rayas* on the sides of casks. These rayas enable them to keep track of each cask's development.

The average age of the wines in a bodega is difficult to gauge, but it is not unusual for wines of great quality to average over half a century. Certain soleras are well over one century old. The investment in stocks of old wine, coupled with the infinite care and treatment they are given over the years, makes finer wines expensive. This is why most sherry shippers are large in size and offer a wide assortment of styles.

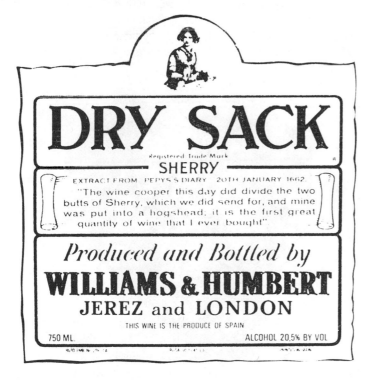

*Shakespeare called sherry "sack." Dry Sack is an excellent all-purpose sherry. It is not completely dry.*

*This oloroso is produced by Williams and Humbert, the makers of Dry Sack. The marking for aging (illustrated below Dos Cortados) is traditionally used on barrels of wine that show good potential.*

## Coloring and Sweetening

Since all sherry is allowed to ferment until completely dry, sweetening and deep coloring come at a later stage. There are three main methods:

1. **P.X.:** Wine made from the Pedro Ximenez grapes. These grapes are picked in the same way as the Palomino, but instead of being allowed to dry in the sun for 24 hours, they are left out for up to three weeks. By then they are hardly more than half-dried raisins with very little juice but an immensely high sugar content. The yield is small but syrupy and concentrated. At a certain level of alcohol, fermentation stops and the wine is left with a great deal of its original sweetness. The P.X. wines are then matured in special bodegas.
2. **MISTELAS:** This is a much lighter sweetening wine, usually made from Palomino grapes. Fermentation is arrested by the addition of alcohol before the wine is completely dry. Thus it retains some of the grape's natural sugar.
3. **COLOR WINE:** This, as its name implies, is a coloring wine made by cooking or simmering fresh mosto (to which brandy has been added to stop fermentation) for approximately 24 hours. A dark brown syrup results. This may be lightened with another sherry. Just before shipping, it can be added to a sherry to achieve the desired degree of color. *Arrope* is the most concentrated form of color wine. *Sancorcho* is less so, with a slightly lower alcoholic content.

Sweetening and coloring take place only when the wine is being prepared for shipment. Afterwards the sherry is allowed to rest for some time in order to ensure a perfect union of the wines involved. It is then "fined" to obtain brilliance and clarity. Fining is usually done by using a mixture of whites of eggs and "Spanish earth" (a highly absorbent clay), which is thoroughly mixed with the wine. Over a period of days, this mixture slowly sinks to the bottom, taking all matter in suspension with it. Do not be shocked or concerned if you see sediment in a sherry. It is natural for wine to throw such a deposit after a few years.

Just before the wine is shipped, it is raked into another cask and a final fortification is made, bringing the total alcohol content as high as 20% by volume, especially if the wine is intended to travel to the British or U.S. markets.

## Serving of Sherry

In England, the serving of sherry has long been one of the most gracious ways of entertaining. It has ousted the cocktail as a pre-prandial drink. It is quite normal in British society for nothing but sherry to be served at a reception or drinking party. In Spain, dry finos are savored with *tapas,* small dishes of finger foods. Manzanilla and fino wines are usually served only as aperitif wines. Amontillado can be served at any time, as indeed can some of the finer olorosos. In the U.S., oloroso has become very much an after-dinner drink, an alternative to brandies or cordials. Dry sherries are usually served chilled in a small glass called a copita. Sweeter types may be enjoyed neat at room temperature or over shaved ice.

There are a wide variety of sherries with differing degrees of dryness or sweetness. Whatever the palate, there should be a sherry to match it. Always look for a reliable shipper. They include boutique shippers such as Lustau and Macenista, and the larger, consistently excellent Williams and Humbert, Harveys, Duff Gordon, and Osborne.

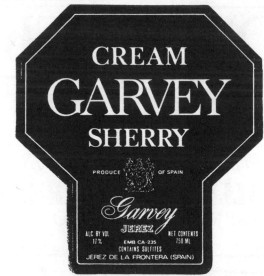

*Garvey S. A., one of the most prestigious sherry producers in Spain, states, "Garvey Cream Sherry, as a result of its aging process through the solera system, is truly an outstanding product." It has a delicious raisin palate with outstanding length and structure.*

# SELF-EVALUATION

BEFORE READING ON, see if you have mastered the data set forth in the last few pages. Check the answer section at the back of the book for the correct answers. If you have not answered at least 70% of the questions below correctly, please reread the previous section.

## SHERRY

TRUE     FALSE.

_____     _____   1. True sherry, according to the Common Market, comes only from a very strictly defined area in the province of Cadiz in the southwestern corner of Spain.

_____     _____   2. There are two basic types of sherry: Fino and Oloroso.

_____     _____   3. Manzanilla, a fino-type wine, is traditionally blended to be rich, golden, and sweet.

_____     _____   4. Sherry is made exclusively from Pedro Ximenez grapes.

_____     _____   5. The best vineyards are located on very fine, chalky soil known as albariza.

_____     _____   6. For sherry, fermentation is a two-stage process.

_____     _____   7. Flor is an entirely natural phenomenon which imparts a special character to fino-type wines.

_____     _____   8. Sherry is essentially a blended wine, and there is no such thing as vintage sherry.

_____     _____   9. The solera is a system of blending younger wines with older ones.

_____     _____   10. Fining is usually done by using a mixture of whites of eggs and Spanish earth, to obtain brilliance and clarity.

# PORTO

## *The British Are Coming!*

## ORIGIN

Porto, the fortified wine of Portugal, is as closely connected to England as it is to the land of its birth. The names of the producers are a tip-off: Taylor-Fladgate, Calem, Croft, Dow, Cockburn (pronounced KOH-burn) Smithes, Graham, Sandeman, and Smith Woodhouse, just to mention a few. To balance things there are Ferreira, Fonseca, Guimaraens, and Quinta do Noval on the Portuguese side. Perhaps it is the climate of England, but porto is the wine of the British club and boardroom. Porto was first fortified to enable it to be shipped easily to Great Britain.

Porto originates in a delimited zone in northern Portugal, stretching from the town of Oporto along the Douro River, and eastward to Pinhao, close to the Spanish border. It is made from many grapes grown on hillsides and in valleys, then blended usually in lodges or warehouses of Vila Nova de Gaia. The best soil for these grapes consists of a rocky substance, called *schist*.

White porto is made from white grapes, the Verdelho, Malvasia, and Rabigato among others. Touriga, Bastardo, Mourisca, Sousao, Tinta Cao, and Tinta Francisca form the reds. Porto is fortified to about 20% alcohol by the addition of brandy. This fortification takes place during fermentation when the alcohol is 4%–6% and the residual sugar is up to 8%. This makes most portos sweet and ideal for dessert. The white is ordinarily dry and is best used as an aperitif.

The wines are made up-river at large agricultural estates called *quintas,* a term that also applies to individual vineyard sites. Although most of these farms have mechanical harvesters, a few still cling to the old custom whereby the clusters are picked by hand. The harvesters then place the grapes in wicker baskets, which they balance on their backs by means of a forehead band. These grapes are brought to the winery by foot and put into granite troughs called *lagares.* In a chain line, a team of treaders crush the grapes with their bare feet, chanting and dancing in four-hour shifts until the crush is completed. It was believed that this method was not only good for the wine, but that contact with the grapes would also insure the health of the crushers.

After the fortification, the young wine rests. Then it is transferred to *pipes*, wooden casks of over 500 liters, or about 138 gallons. In the spring, these pipes are placed into a railcar or a truck or onto a colorful sailboat called a *rabelo.* Thus the wine casks are brought to the *armazens*, the blending and aging lodges in Vila Nova de Gaia. Many of these lodges were originally codfish warehouses. Across the Douro River are the export firms of Oporto, from which according to law all porto must be shipped.

Good porto requires skillful blending. About 85% of porto production is exported. Quite surprisingly, England is not the leading market; France is.

## TYPES OF PORTO

### Porto Blanco

White port is made differently from other portos, almost like a sherry. It is fortified toward the end of fermentation, when most of the sugar is gone. The finished product is less sweet, to be enjoyed as an aperitif. It is still grapey and fruity, topaz in hue. It is made from white grapes only.

### Bottled Portos

**Vintage Porto:** In exceptional years shippers "declare" a vintage. Each shipper acts independently in this regard, setting aside a small lot of the best wine to be bottled in its second or third year. The maturation of vintage porto takes place in the bottle. Vintage porto throws a large sediment and must be decanted; pouring it through cheesecloth is recommended. Most vintage portos require at least 10–15 years of aging to approach their zenith. There is a trend toward single-vineyard or quinta vintage portos. Some exceptional vintages include 1983, 1980, 1977, 1970, 1963, 1958, 1955, 1948, 1935, and the legendary 1927. All are necessarily expensive.

**Crusted Porto:** This is a multi-vintage blend that is bottled early. It is lighter than vintage porto. Crusted Porto must be decanted, may be enjoyed young, and is quite rare.

## Wood Portos

**Ruby:** This is a sweet, richly colored, young, multi-vintage wood-aged blend. It may be hard and fiery, but it has a youthful zest and fruitiness. It is aged in barrels usually for an average of five years or less.

**Tawny:** The winemasters say that these wines are "bred" or "financed," not blended. They are charming, tawny in color from prolonged contact with wood, and very smooth and elegant. Rubies and tawnies are consistent from vintage to vintage. Each house has its own style. Tawny porto usually spends 7–10 years in the barrel. Some tawnies specify an age of 10 to 20 years in wood. You can make cheap tawny by blending ruby and white porto. Tawny porto usually represents the best value among all porto wine.

**Special Blends:** Many shippers develop their own special cuvees, which might be blends of ruby and tawny. Some examples are Sandeman's Partners Port, Dow's Boardroom Port, and Cockburn's Special Reserve.

**Vintage Porto Look-Alikes:** You may find a porto with a vintage date on it which is not a true, bottle-matured vintage porto. Late Bottled Vintage (LBV) is kept longer in wood, sometimes for more than five years. You may see the word *colheita* on the label, which indicates LBV. Some people refer to these as "vintage tawnies".

All wood portos are clear when bottled and ready to drink. They may throw a deposit with time. Once opened, porto will hold up better than table wine, due to the extra alcohol. We have found that after a week or so, the personality and character start to fade. Enjoy white porto chilled, the others at cool room temperature. Some people squeeze a lemon into ruby porto. Store wood-aged porto upright; store vintage porto on its side.

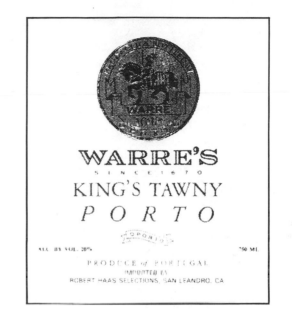

*This is an elegant wood-aged tawny, fit for a king. But you will not need a king's treasure chest. Tawny porto is almost always a good value.*

*This is a true vintage porto from a single vineyard, a quinta. Expect some natural sediment. We recommend decanting through cheesecloth.*

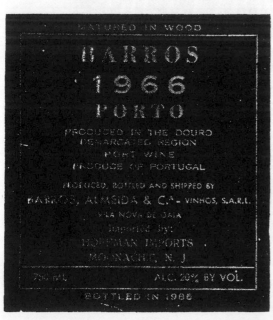

*A true vintage porto, full, rich and capable of great aging. Warre is one of the top two or three producers. Notice it was bottled only two years after the wine was made.*

*This is a sweet fine Marsala from the leading premium producer, Florio. This wine is also used to make the custard dessert, zabaglione.*

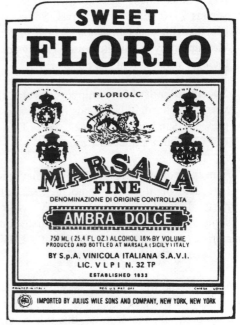

*This is a fine, wood-aged tawny, bottled 20 years after the vintage. It is not a true vintage porto, but rather an LBV (Late Bottled Vintage).*

# MARSALA

## *From the "Swamp of God"*

In 1773 John Woodhouse created Marsala wine as a substitute for porto and sherry for the English market. Made in and around the town of Marsala on the western coast of Sicily, this wine is known worldwide today not only for sipping but also as a cooking ingredient. Marsala in Arabic means "The Port or Swamp of God." Marsala wine was traditionally made from white Grillo, Catarratto, or Inzolia grapes, or a combination of them, grown within the provinces of Trapani, Palermo, or Agrigento. New wine legislation, referred to as Law 851, enacted in 1984, has both broadened the scope of Marsala and, hopefully, raised its standards. The D.O.C. zone has been restricted to include only a specific section of the province of Trapani. Approved varietals are the reds: Perricone, Calabrese, and Nerello Mascalese; and the whites: Grillo, Catarratto, Damaschino, and Inzolia, now officially called the Ansonica.

Each firm has its own formula or production method, but Marsala is almost always natural white wine blended with a sweet wine and grape alcohol mix called *sifone* and a cooked down must called *cotto*. Under the Italian government's D.O.C. laws, there are four types of Marsala:

1. **Marsala Fine:** These are 17% alcohol and can be called oro (gold) or ambra (amber). They must be aged for one year. The traditional name, IP (Italia Particolare), may be applied only to Fine.

2. **Marsala Rubino Fine:** This new "ruby" red is 17% alcohol and, like all Marsala Fine and Marsala Superiore, may be made dry (secco), demi-sec or sweet (dolce). The dry version is superb as an aperitif or with sharp cheeses, especially pecorino. The sweeter versions are excellent sipping and dessert wines.

3. **Marsala Superiore:** This category is 18% alcohol and is aged for two years. With four years of age, it can be called Riserva. The following traditional names may be applied

only to Superiore: SOM (Superior Old Marsala), GD (Garibaldi Dolce), LP (London Particular), and Vecchio (old). The dry is subtle with the nuttiness of a fino sherry, but with a distinctively woody, spicy, and citrus-like complexity, as well as a pleasant burnt character. The demi-sec is similar to an all-purpose oloroso. The sweet is like a cream sherry, but with a "baked" quality, similar to a Malmsey Madeira. Please note that cotto and sifone may be added only to ambra, never to oro or rubino.

4. **Marsala Vergine:** This is one of the world's greatest aperitif wines, made without cotto or sifone. It is a multi-vintage blend. Some wineries use a solera, as in sherry. The drier version is pale in color, fragrant, nutty, and only lightly fortified. It is wonderful with sharp, strong, pungent cheeses, such as cacciocavallo or pecorino siciliano. Only the very finest fino sherry and Chateau-Chalon from France's Jura Mountains can rival Vergine as an aperitif. Sweeter versions are excellent sipping wines. With 10 years of aging, Vergine may be called Stravecchio or Riserva. Needless to say, such rare gems are deservedly costly.

These new laws should upgrade the production of Marsala. Bottling of Marsala must take place within the province of Trapani only. Special flavored concoctions, with the addition of eggs, coffee, almonds, and the like may no longer call themselves Marsala.

Quality Marsala producers include Florio, Rallo, Mineo, Fici, Pellegrino, Woodhouse, and Mirabella. The firm of DeBartoli produces not only exquisite D.O.C. Marsala, but also the superb aperitifs Vecchio Samperi and Inzolia di Samperi.

# MADEIRA

## *Thank you, Napoleon!*

The island of Madeira was "discovered" by the Portuguese Henry the Navigator in 1419, although it had been known to the

Phoenicians over two millennia earlier. It is a volcanic chain about 500 miles southwest of Portugal in the Atlantic Ocean. Madeira wine was a favorite in colonial America.

The soil is a contributing factor to what is described as the "burnt" taste and character of Madeira wine. Legend has it that a captain named Zarco found it so difficult to advance through the thick forests of the island that he set them ablaze. The fire raged for seven years. When the trees were gone, the humus, volcanic soil became rich and fertile and imparted a burnt or baked flavor to what was planted in it.

Madeira wine was not a fortified wine until the mid-eighteenth century. During the Napoleonic era, porto, sherry, and Marsala were hard to come by due to the warring fleets. Madeira business boomed. Today Madeira is sold not only in the U.S. and England, but in virtually all of Europe and Canada. The island is, by culture and government, Portuguese. Other businesses of Madeira include wicker and tourism.

Madeira is a wine that is supposed to be blessed by the ravages of nature; cold winters and hot summers "weather" the wines. The old ocean voyages supposedly improved Madeira's flavor. In the early nineteenth century, a system of *estufagem* was developed to weather the wines. An *estufa* is a storage area into which casks of wine are placed, usually from 90 days to 6 months, and where the temperature is brought up to about 110° F. This environment closely simulates the conditions of a year-or-so duration sea voyage in the tropics. Sweeter Madeiras are fortified before estufagem; dry versions are not.

After estufagem, the wine rests for a year and is fortified, not with brandy but with 99.6% alcohol. Finished Madeira is usually about 18% alcohol and held for five years in Funchal, the island's capital, before being shipped. Some solera-dated or vintage-dated Madeira may be found, but these are rare and costly. Maybe it is the soil, the estufa, or the fortifying agent, but certain Madeiras can age for a century or more.

Madeira is usually named for grape varieties:

1. **Sercial:** The driest, pale in color, best as an aperitif. Memorable fragrance. Serve chilled.
2. **Verdelho:** Golden-hued, medium bodied. Serve chilled or at room temperature. Try it with soup. An excellent cooking ingredient. Usually soft, but with a dry finish.
3. **Bual (Boal):** Darker, fuller, sweeter, more fragrant. Serve at cool room temperature as a dessert wine. Ages well.

4. **Malmsey (Malvasia):** The richest, most luscious. Possesses great body and bouquet. Serve at cool room temperature for after dinner drinking. Ages best of all.

Extremely rare are wines made from the Terrantez or Bastardo vines. One grape, called Negra Mole, produces a wine called Tinta or Tent. There are also blends of different grapes and styles. They include Rainwater, which is pale, light, and of medium body, and Southside, which is sweeter. Quality producers found in the U.S. include Blandy, Leacock, Cossart Gordon, and Henriques and Henriques.

*This fortified wine from southern Portugal is one of the finest expressions of the Muscat grape. Another Setúbal, with less time in oak, is also offered by Da Fonseca.*

# OTHER FORTIFIED WINES

Some top-flight fortified wines originate in the United States and Australia. In these countries, amber wines are generically called port. Examples of superb American fortified wines include Ficklin Ports, J.W. Morris Ports, Quady Ports (including their orange Muscat called Essencia, and black Muscat called Elysium), and Woodbury Vintage Port. Many larger producers include excellent fortified wines in their assortments. Some recommended examples are Gallo Livingston Cream Sherry, Christian Brothers Zinfandel Port, Beringer Malvasia Bianca, Almaden Flor Fino Sherry, Paul Masson Rare Souzao Port, Novitiate Black Muscat, Papagni Dry Sherry, Taylor Cream Sherry, and Widmer Solera Sherries.

Officially, American fortified wines are called appetizer and dessert wines. As a result of legislation in 1954, the word fortified may not appear on the label. Australian brands of interest are Morris, and Baily and Chambers. A look at the map on page 35 indicates that most other prestigious fortified wines come from the Mediterranean basin. Perhaps this is due to the hot, dry climate or to the sweet grape varieties (particularly Malvasia and Muscat) that thrive there. Below is a list of some of the best known.

Some of these wines are not fortified by adding brandy. A higher concentration of alcohol might be due to evaporation caused by weathering, by a later grape harvest, or, by drying the grapes before pressing them.

Fortified wines provide the wine lover with an excellent alternative to the cocktail before a meal or to the cordial at the meal's end. Remember that, by definition, fortified wines are more potent than table and sparkling wines and should be enjoyed in moderation. Port wine is traditionally served with Stilton cheese or with nuts. Some dip their cigars into port (or cognac), but we are not in their number.

## OTHER FORTIFIED WINES

| Type | Area of Origin | Basic Grapes |
|---|---|---|
| Montilla | Spain | Pedro Ximenez |
| Malaga | Spain (Andalusia) | Pedro Ximenez, Lairen |
| Setubal | Southern Portugal | Muscat |
| Banyuls | Midi (Southern France) | Grenache |
| Maury | Midi (Southern France) | Grenache |
| Muscat de Frontignan | Midi (Southern France) | Muscat |
| Chateau-Chalon | Jura (France) | Savagnin |
| Muscat de Beaumes-de-Venise | Rhone (France) | Muscat |
| Commanderie of St. John | Cyprus | Mavron, Xynisteri |
| Muscat of Samos | Samos (Greece) | Muscat |
| Mavrodaphne | Greece | Mavron |
| Vin Santo | Italy | Usually Trebbiano or Malvasia |
| Malvasia delle Lipari | Sicily (Italy) | Malvasia |
| Moscato di Pantelleria | Sicily (Italy) | Muscat |

# FORTIFIED WINES IN REVIEW

- These wines are higher in alcohol content, usually due to the addition of brandy. They should be drunk very sparingly.

- The most renowned fortified wines are sherry from Spain, porto and Madeira from Portugal, and Marsala from Italy.

- Dry varieties of fortified wines are used as aperitifs; sweet ones as dessert wines.

- Fino and Oloroso are the two types of sherry.

- Good sherries are made by the solera system.

- Porto may be classified as white porto, bottled porto, and wood porto.

- Vintage porto is the finest of the bottled portos.

- Long-lived Madeiras can be dry (Sercial, Verdelho) or sweet (Bual, Malmsey).

- Marsala from Sicily may be Fine, Rubino Fine, Superiore, or Vergine.

- Fortified wines are made worldwide, but the most famous originate in the Mediterranean Basin.

*This is a dessert wine similar to a cream sherry in style and use. It is made from Moscatellone (Zibibbo) grapes that have been dried (passito) to almost raisiny sweetness on the island of Pantelleria. Named for the Phoenician goddess of wine, Tanit.*

# SELF-EVALUATION

BEFORE READING ON, see if you have mastered the data set forth in the last few pages. Check the answer section at the back of the book for the correct answers. If you have not answered at least 70% of the questions below correctly, please reread the previous section.

## OTHER FORTIFIED WINES

| TRUE | FALSE | |
|------|-------|---|
| ———— | ———— | 1. Quinta is a term that applies to an individual vineyard site. |
| ———— | ———— | 2. Porto wines come from southern Portugal. |
| ———— | ———— | 3. Verdelho, Malvasia, and Rabigato are three essential red grapes for making porto. |
| ———— | ———— | 4. Porto requires skillful blending. |
| ———— | ———— | 5. England is the leading importer of porto wines. |
| ———— | ———— | 6. All Marsala comes from around the town of Marsala in Sicily. |
| ———— | ———— | 7. Crusted porto and tawny portos are wood portos. |
| ———— | ———— | 8. Marsala Superiore is made without *cotto* or *sifone*. |
| ———— | ———— | 9. An *estufa* is a hot aging area in which casks of Madeira wines are placed. |
| ———— | ———— | 10. Sercial is a type of Madeira wine. |

# NOTES

# AROMATIZED WINES

## Vermouths and Aperitifs

*Wines to which herbs, roots,*
*botanicals, and the like have been added.*

The term aperitif *(aperitivo or apertif)* comes from the Latin verb *aperire,* which means "to open," As aperitif wine "opens" the meal as an appetizer and prepares the palate and stomach for the food to follow. Quite simply aperitifs are wines to which herbs, peels, flowers, bark, etc., have been added to achieve a special flavor.

This category of wine usually has a low alcohol content. By displaying nuances of bitterness and sweetness, they excite our *gustatory papillae* (taste buds) and initiate the secretion of juices responsible for better disposing us toward our meals. They accentuate subtleties of foods placed at our dinner table.

Sipping an aperitif, not only before meals but at most any time of the day, is a common and much appreciated practice in the cafes of the world. It is said that the aperitif prepares the stomach for food and the tongue for conversation. They are the beverages of hospitality and are as old as civilization itself. When herbs and botanicals were first added to wine, to mask oxidation or to serve as a stimulant or tonic, this category was born.

## How Do We Taste?

This is a good time to note how our senses react to various tastes. Of course, appearance (color, brilliance) and fragrance (aroma, bouquet) are connected to any taste experience. Taste buds line most of the surface of the tongue and palate (including the inner cheeks and lips). Their sensory nerve endings are responsible for communicating various stimuli to the brain. These taste buds are concentrated most heavily on the tongue. In fact, the four basic taste sensations strike different areas of the tongue.

1. **Sweet:** Taste buds located at the tip and forward sides of the tongue, make us aware of sweetness, the most obvious flavor. These buds, like all others, wear out in time, and are not always regenerated. When people are heard to say that their tastes have changed, it may well be due to the lack of replacement of worn out buds. The forward position may also explain why the young accept sweetness with such willingness.
2. **Salt:** Just behind the sweet on both sides of the tongue are the taste buds which distinguish the taste of salt. These taste buds are sprinkled throughout the whole area of the tongue but are mostly concentrated behind the sweet.
3. **Sour:** Taste buds responsible for giving us the sensation of sour are located behind the sweet and salty.
4. **Bitter:** Toward the back of the tongue is a V-shaped area that senses if a substance is bitter or metallic.

Certain foods and drinks excite only one of these sensitive areas. Others offer more complex flavors (sweet-sour sauces or bitter-sweet chocolate). Aperitif wines provide an organoleptic explosion by stimulating all of our taste buds. In fact, aperitifs create a fascinating tension among the four basic tastes.

Recall that taste reinforces our visual and olfactory experiences. Cloudy beverages, like cloudy skies, do not usually put us in a good mood. Without smell everything appears bland (you might say tasteless). Whenever you have a cold and the mucous membranes of your nose become gorged (obstructing your nasal passage), you may have remarked that you cannot taste. Tasting, then, is a multi-sensual experience.

## The History of Aperitifs

Aperitifs appear in the literature of Homer (in Greece in the second millennium before Christ). Specially seasoned raisin wine was considered the proper beverage to serve before dinner for special occasions. We know that Greek physicians around 500 B.C. mixed herbs and wines together in a drink called Hippocras. This elixir was a relaxant and a tonic.

In the time of the Roman Empire, the Latin poet Horace described how to make an exceptional aperitif by mixing a fine wine, the then well-regarded Falernian, with honey: the resultant mixture was called "mulsum." Plants, fruits, and herbs were also added to wine, as healing agents.

By the formulas of diligent monks in the Dark Ages, the art of flavoring wines became more widespread. With the advancing knowledge and technical know-how of the Industrial Revolution, this art became more scientific and commercial. In general, these wines and even some spirits, flavored with plants, herbs, and aromatic spices, have acquired the designation of appetizers or aperitifs. Surely the golden age of aperitifs was the late nineteenth early twentieth centuries in Paris. Artists painted larger-than-life posters for Dubonnet and other companies. The cafe scene was at its peak with people, famous or insignificant, flocking to sip absinthe, vermouth, or the like as they discussed politics, art, and life.

This golden age has surely faded. Aperitif beverages, still popular in Europe and South America, are slowly yielding to soft drinks and cocktails. In the U.S., by contrast, even more sophisticated people, opposed to the cocktail which deadens the palate, are turning to aperitifs, especially Campari.

The most popular aperitifs today, however, are white table wine or a glass of the bubbly.

# VERMOUTH

Vermouth comes from the German *wermut* or wormwood with which the Germans at one time infused their Rhine wine. This wood and its flowers are addictive and hallucinogenic and are no longer used.

The first commercial vermouth came in 1776, developed by Antonio Benedetto Carpano of Torino, Italy, both the father and the founder of the vermouth industry. A generation later, Louis Noilly of Lyons, France, developed a somewhat drier vermouth. Thus the sweet red type has come to be known as Italian and the dry white type as French. There is also a sweet white called Bianco. Some houses, notably the U.S. firm of Tribuno, have marketed a mixture of sweet red and dry white called Half & Half. The Italians also produce a great deal of dry vermouth (Italy is by far the largest producer and exporter of vermouth) and the French likewise are accountable for a goodly portion of the sweet. Each company has its own secret formula, which it guards with the same tenacity as does Coca-Cola. Originally produced only in Italy and France, vermouths of both basic types are made today in other vermouth-consuming countries. The United States produces well over 50% of its annually consumed volume, which is almost 10 million gallons. The Argentineans make more than 15 million gallons annually, which they consume in its entirety.

*Jägermeister is Germany's most famous spirit. It is world-renowned as an aperitif or a digestive aid.*

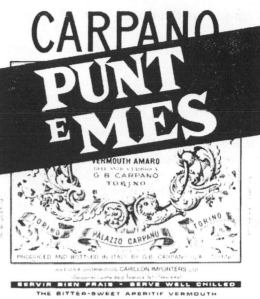

It sparkles. It has cognac in it and natural flavors as well. You may enjoy *Petite Liqueur* at either end of a meal. It is the only sparkling aperitif or cordial that we are aware of.

A superlative bitter vermouth from the founder of the vermouth industry, Carpano. Punt e Mes (Point and a Half) is a stockbroker's term. Legend has it that an attentive waiter, hearing a broker shout "Punt e Mes" in an animated table discussion, brought one part vermouth and one half bitters. The broker liked it; so did the others. And so we have it, thanks to a nameless waiter.

This, the most famous of Italian bitters, can also be drunk after meals as a "digestivo" to aid digestion. Try it neat, with mineral water or in coffee. This spirits-based tonic, derived from a secret formula of herbs, can be found in almost every Italian household.

"Bianco" is a designation for a sweet white vermouth. Cinzano has been a renowned producer of vermouth for over 230 years. You may be familiar with their ashtrays, umbrellas, and bicycling team (from the film "Breaking Away"), or their Asti Spumante.

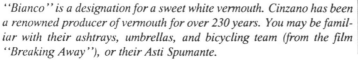

## How Vermouth is Produced

Several ingredients are required to make vermouth: wine; a mixture of unfermented grape juice and brandy called *mistelle*; alcohol; and a variety or combination of herbs, spices, peels, flowers, aromatics, and botanicals. The production of vermouth also requires equipment for pasteurizing, refrigeration, filtering, and measuring. However, the most important factor in producing vermouth is the formula.

Since the wine undergoes so many treatments, its original quality does not seem to be too important. The Italians used to employ Moscato D'Asti, but now bulk wine from southern Italy and the islands find their way to the great vermouth houses of Turin. The French sometimes weather their wine; that is, they bake it in the summer sun and force it to endure winter's cold to induce a "maderized" result. This adds flavor and concentration, promoting an evaporation of about 10% over the course of two years. This costly process has gradually yielded to a quicker cooking and cooling of the wine base.

The delicate, dry A.O.C. white wine of Chambery from the mountain vineyards of Savoy is all but gone. Most of the wine for French vermouth now comes from the Midi, in the south of France. The simple truth is that inexpensive, good, strong wine, red or white, is preferred. Masking by the addition of alcohol, mistelle, and botanicals, and filtering and refrigerating all make the nature of the original wine rather meaningless. The formula, not the freshness or quality of the wine, is the significant factor. This may explain why Martini and Rossi and Cinzano have established additional vermouth wineries closer to their strongest markets, notably in Central and South America.

The botanicals used may be fresh, liquid concentrates, distillates of the flavors, or any combination of the three. They are added to alcohol to extract flavor by maceration—that is, placed in a vat and left in contact with the alcohol (like a tea bag)—or by infusion, a process similar to coffee percolation. Eventually the flavored alcohol will be added to the wine and mistelle. The skill of the blender determines when this should be done.

Altogether up to 50 different herbs, spices, aromatics, and botanicals may be used. They include hyssop, marjoram, linden tea, elder, gentian, coriander, wormwood flower, juniper, cloves, camomille, orange peel, rose petals, ginger, allspice, forget-me-not, thistle, angelica, sage, thyme and invariably, quinine.

After the mixture is blended, it is clarified, sometimes by the addition of gelatin. Pasteurization then ensues, followed by refrigeration as low as 14° F for about two weeks or so. A vigorous filtration removes any sediment or tartrate particles, after which the vermouth is allowed to rest for a few months before final bottling and shipping.

Technology has reduced the time needed to produce quality vermouth from four years to a few months. This same technology may be vermouth's worst enemy, however, since light, dry white wine can no longer be viewed as fickle, inconsistent, short-lived, or unavailable in distant markets. An unopened bottle of vermouth can survive the vagaries of Arctic winters or summers in the Sahara. Once opened, it will oxidize over a period of time. Vermouth, especially the dry version, is an excellent substitute for table wine for cooking (the herbs and spices are already *in* the vermouth). What a shame for it to have degenerated into being a flavoring agent for the Martini, Rob Roy, or Manhattan. One must search very far and wide to find a beverage that better stimulates the palate or promotes moderation for social consumption.

# OTHER APERITIFS

There are a number of aperitifs produced around the world. The charts on the following two pages will help you to identify and understand the components of some of the major ones.

## AROMATIZED WINES IN REVIEW

- These are wines to which herbs and spices have been added.
- Vermouth is the most famous aromatized wine.
- There are three types of vermouth: sweet, dry, and bianco.
- Italy dominates the import market; France is a distant second.
- Although enjoyed as an aperitif, vermouth is more famous as a cocktail ingredient in the U. S.

# WINE-BASED APERITIFS

| APERITIF NAME | ORIGIN | INGREDIENTS or CHARACTERISTICS |
|---|---|---|
| AmerPicon | France | Orange Peel, Bitters |
| Byrrh | France | Quinine, Brandy Orange and Bitters |
| St. Raphael | France | Bitter-sweet, red wine, quinine, reminiscent of currants and peaches, #1 in France |
| Dubonnet | U.S.A., formerly France | Sweet wine, bark, quinine, both red and white are available. |
| Lillet | France | Semi-dry, white and red wine, similar to Vermouth; orange peel |
| Ratafia | France, U.S.A. | Specially sweetened wine, e.g., Panache, Angelique |
| Banyuls | Southern France | Sweet wine, like a Port |
| Maury | France | Onion-skin color, sweet wine |
| Muscat de Frontignan | France | Sweet wine |
| Muscat Beaumes-de-Venise | France | Sweet wine |
| Pineau des Charentes | France | Wine, cognac |
| Fino | Spain | Dry sherry |
| Manzanilla | Spain | Dry Sherry, a salty character |
| Montilla | Spain | Similar to dry Sherry |
| Jerez-Quina | Spain | Sherry wine, quinine |
| Marsala-Vergine | Italy | Similar to a dry Sherry or Madeira |
| Punt-E-Mes | Italy | Red Vermouth with quinine |
| Rosso Antico | Italy | Red wine, peels and bitters |
| Barolo Chinato | Italy | Barolo wine, quinine |
| Porto Branco | Portugal | White, dry Porto wine |
| Sercial | Madeira (Portugal) | Dry, fortified wine, like a Fino |
| Verdelho | Madeira (Portugal) | A bit less dry than Sercial |

# SPIRIT-BASED APERITIFS

| APERITIF NAME | ORIGIN | INGREDIENTS or CHARACTERISTICS |
| --- | --- | --- |
| Pernod | France | Anis seed, herbs |
| Ricard | France | Licorice, herbs, anis |
| Pastis | France | Licorice, herbs, from Marseilles, anis |
| Anis | France, Spain | Anis seed |
| Calisay | Spain | Brandy, quinine |
| Campari | Italy | Reddish bitters, herbs, orange peel |
| Fernet-Branca | Italy | Bitters, herbs, a mint variety is also available |
| Cynar | Italy | Brownish-red bitters, artichokes |
| Bianco Sarti | Italy | Pale yellow bitters, similar to Campari |
| Averna | Italy | Brown bitters, Sicilian, highly regarded |
| Unicum | Italy | Strong brown bitters, over 40 herbs and roots used. |
| Escarchado | Portugal | Anis-based, with solid sugar inside |
| Akvavit | Scandinavia (esp. Denmark) | Distillate of carroway seeds |
| Jagermeister | Germany | Bitters, herbs |
| Underberg | Germany | Bitters, like Fernet |
| Boonekamp | Germany | Bitters, like Fernet |
| Ouzo | Greece | Anis seed |
| Club Raki | Turkey | Anis seed |
| Montenegro | Italy | Mild bitters; as with most of these Aperitifs, it may be used as a *digestivo,* or digestive, after-dinner drink. |

# SELF-EVALUATION

BEFORE READING ON, see if you have mastered the data set forth in the last few pages. Check the answer section at the back of the book for the correct answers. If you have not answered at least 70% of the questions below correctly, please reread the previous section.

## AROMATIZED WINES

TRUE     FALSE

\_\_\_\_\_     \_\_\_\_\_    1. The term *aperitif* comes from the Latin verb *aperire,* which means "to open."

\_\_\_\_\_     \_\_\_\_\_    2. This category of wine usually has a high alcohol content.

\_\_\_\_\_     \_\_\_\_\_    3. The four basic taste sensations that strike the tongue are sweet, salt, sour, and bitter.

\_\_\_\_\_     \_\_\_\_\_    4. Italy is the largest producer and exporter of vermouth.

\_\_\_\_\_     \_\_\_\_\_    5. The United States produces well over 50 percent of its annually consumed volume of vermouth.

\_\_\_\_\_     \_\_\_\_\_    6. The most important factor in producing vermouth is the formula.

\_\_\_\_\_     \_\_\_\_\_    7. Bianco is dry white vermouth.

\_\_\_\_\_     \_\_\_\_\_    8. Vermouth takes four years to produce.

\_\_\_\_\_     \_\_\_\_\_    9. No more than 10 different herbs, spices, aromatics, and botanicals may be used in a vermouth formula.

\_\_\_\_\_     \_\_\_\_\_    10. Botanicals are equipment used in the processing of vermouth.

# NOTES

# SPARKLING WINES

Wines with bubbles in them have been popular ever since wine-makers tried to capture some of the carbon dioxide that is so natural to the process of wine fermentation. Sparkling wine may be sweet or dry; red, white, or pink; reasonably priced or expensive. It may be produced almost anywhere in the world. It is always festive.

The French tell us that "true" champagne must come from a delimited zone in northern France. It must be made according to a strictly regulated process. Only three grape varieties are permitted in "true" champagne production.

The Italians call their sparklers *spumanti*. One out of every two bottles of imported sparkling wine drunk in the U.S. is Italian in origin. Dry bubblies from Italy are downright spectacular, but it is the sweetish Asti Spumante that is best known in the U.S.A.

The Germans produce excellent sparkling wine called Sekt. And the Germans love their Sekt! It is hard to find better value than what is offered by the Spanish in their CAVA wines. The United States has made contributions on all levels of sparkling wines, from the inexpensive to the sublime.

With consumption of sparkling wines increasing each year with no peak in sight, growth in the U.S.A. seems assured.

# "TRUE" CHAMPAGNE

## THE CHAMPAGNES OF FRANCE

### Prestigious Sparklers — "Drinking Stars"

The very word champagne conveys pleasure and festivity. It conjures up an aura of sparkling elegance, of gracious charm, and of luxury in the minds of hosts as well as their guests. The delicious sparkling wine of the Champagne region is known the world over as the "King of Wines . . . the Wine of Kings." No wine merchant, restaurant, club, or hotel who is serious about wine can afford not to carry it.

Now, what is so special about this sparkling wine of France? Why does it enjoy a well-deserved reputation for completeness, perfection, and grandeur? What is there about it that creates a mood of anticipation, and instant zest and exhilaration? What makes it unique — and the most imitated of all wines?

### Crafted by Hand

Authentic champagne is the most carefully made wine in the world. It is the result of the *Methode Champenoise,* the complicated, time-consuming, costly process that is unique to the champagne region of France. Noted champagne historian Patrick Forbes says that the wine in a bottle of champagne has been attended to by some 300 pairs of hands before it is ready to drink. The number and intricacy of these hand operations is one of the things that gives champagne its special grace and style that is often imitated, but never equalled.

The "secret" of champagne lies in a combination of factors:

1. The unique soil and subsoil of the Champagne district, which is not to be found anywhere else.
2. The micro-climate of Champagne, which is the northernmost wine field in France.
3. The method of cultivation, which is strictly regulated to yield quality rather than volume.

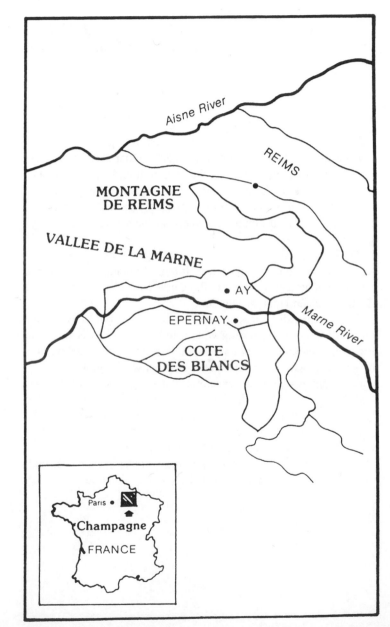

4. The types of grapes used in making champagne.
5. The rapid pressing of the grapes, which is done in the villages where the grapes are grown.
6. The blending, bottling, and aging of the finished product according to the *Methode Champenoise*.

## Definition

In simplified terms, champagne is a mixture of French white wines, usually pressed from both red and white grapes, that is made sparkling by causing the blended wine to ferment a second time in a stoppered bottle.

According to a French law dated July 1927, the only sparkling wine that can legitimately be called champagne must be produced in a small, carefully defined region located about 90 miles east of Paris. Sparkling wines made in other places may come in equally handsome bottles and be dressed and packaged to look like champagne, but none of them are genuine champagne.

The champagne-growing area consists of some 44,000 acres of vineyards in 250 different villages, most of them clustered around the cities of Rheims and Epernay.

## The Village Rating System

Each of these villages has a percentage rating, from 80–100%, which determines the price that will be paid for grapes of that area. The price is set for the villages rated at 100%, and the others are compensated in proportion to their rating.

About 40 villages are rated between 90% and 100%, and these are usually found in the three noble grape-growing areas: the Mountain of Rheims, the Valley of the Marne, and the Cote des Blancs ("white slope") around Epernay. Mountain and Marne Valley villages grow black grapes, the Pinot Noir and Pinot Meunier. On the "white slope," Chardonnay grapes are grown.

In a classical champagne blend, approximately 70% of the wine is pressed from red grapes. Typically the grapes come from more than one village, and a single bottle may therefore be a blend of 20 or 30 different wines. A number of firms also blend a *blanc de blancs* champagne made from white grapes only. The average village rating of *Grandes Marques* champagnes—that is, the well-known brands imported into the United States—is between 92% and 97%.

## Authentic French Champagnes and Other Sparklers

To be sure you are serving true French champagne, look for the words "Product of France" on the label. If the word "champagne" is modified by the name of another country or state on the main label or neck label, it indicates that the sparkling wine is not made according to the tenets and restrictions set forth in the previous paragraphs. You will not find the word "champagne" on any other Common Market country's sparkler. The Italians call theirs spumanti; the Germans and Austrians, Sekt; the Spanish, espumantes. In fact, sparkling wines from other zones within France are forbidden to use the word "champagne." Countries outside of the European Economic Community (EEC), however, who do not abide by its rules, commonly put "champagne" on their labels. Thus you will find American champagne, Australian champagne, and the like.

Recent joint ventures in California between United States and true French champagne houses, such as Moët and Chandon, and Piper-Heidsieck, have proven interesting. The word champagne is not used for these high-quality sparkling wines. Instead they are called Domaine Chandon Napa Brut and Piper-Sonoma Brut.

# FACTORS OF CHAMPAGNE PRODUCTION

## Climate and Soil

During the 35-year life of the vines, the climate and soil of Champagne work their magic. At an average annual temperature of 50° F, and under the peculiar growing conditions found in the region, the vines fight for survival. Paradoxically, these borderline conditions are what give a vigor and nobility to the grapes but at the expense of low yield and vintage variation.

The soil and subsoil of Champagne complement the effects of the climate. A chalky, porous subsoil extends for hundreds of feet below a 30-inch fertile top layer of earth to assure perfect drainage. The chalk base allows excess water to seep away, yet preserves just the right amount of humidity for proper growth and cultivation. In addition, the chalk stores and reflects the warmth of the sun, automatically regulating the elements essential to the ripening of the grapes on the vines.

The chalky subsoil of Champagne also provides ideal cellars for making the wine. The galleries, some of which date from Greco-Roman times, provide constant temperature and constant humidity that are needed for making champagne. Today this system of galleries extends between 200 and 300 miles under the towns of Rheims, Epernay, and Ay.

## The Vines and Vineyards

The three grapes from which champagne is made — Pinot Noir, Pinot Meunier, and Chardonnay yield a very special kind of wine when grown in the delimited region. (In other winefields, such as Burgundy, the same grapes produce an entirely different wine.)

The three vineyard areas of the Champagne region are:

1. **Mountain of Rheims:** These vineyards are planted mainly in Pinot Noir vines bearing red grapes. These must be pressed rapidly so that none of the color of the skins will be imparted to the wine. These grapes are characterized by fullness of flavor and body, which contribute to the bouquet of champagne and add to its liveliness.
2. **Valley of the Marne:** These vineyards also produce the red Pinot Noir and Pinot Meunier grape varieties. These yield the roundest, softest, and ripest wines with lots of bouquet.
3. **The Cote des Blancs:** This area is planted in white Chardonnay, which give freshness, lightness, and elegance to the final blend.

## Cultivation

The peculiarities of the Champagne soil and climate require that fastidious attention be given to the vines if they are to produce high-quality grapes every year. Vines are planted in rows, about three feet apart, and trained to grow along two or three strands of wire. They demand careful valeting: precise and thorough pruning, regular plowing, dressing, weeding, composting, paring, stripping of leaves, spraying, and protection with an earth cover. Pruning is controlled by law. Only four pruning methods are permissible in the Champagne vineyards, and prizes are awarded each year to winners of pruning competitions in the villages.

For the most part, Champagne vineyards are family holdings averaging about two and a half acres. They are carefully watched over by the vinegrowers, who cultivate them with much the same devotion they would give to a family garden. In a single year, the earth is plowed three times and fertilized to aerate, clean, and enrich the soil. Vines are sprayed five or six times to preserve the shoots and ensure healthy grapes.

Work in the vineyards goes on all year long, and the vinegrower stays busy from harvest to harvest. Flowering of the vines occurs in late May or early June and lasts four or five days. Rain, fog, or an unseasonal cold spell during this short period can destroy an entire year's work. Good conditions, on the other hand, influence the fruitfulness of the grapes and, hence, the abundance of the harvest which will take place about 100 days later.

## Harvesting and Pressing

Harvesting starts toward the end of September or early October. The exact time picking begins is determined by the Comite Interprofessional du Vin de Champagne (C.I.V.C.), the semi-official organization in Epernay that governs all champagne activity. After laboratory tests of grape sugar content and acidity have been made, two dates are set: one for red grapes and a somewhat later one for the whites. The date chosen is the one which most nearly coincides with the full ripening of the grapes.

During the harvest, grapes destined for champagne receive special attention. Grapes that are not quite ripe will lack the sugar content needed to produce the right amount of alcohol and their acid content will be too high. Grapes that are overripe will have too low an acid content and, if they are red, will contain juice tainted with color from the skins. Also, grapes picked at their peak of ripeness contain more juice than underripe or overripe ones.

## A Communal Effort

Speed is essential at harvest time in the Champagne district. Men, women, and children of the region, aided by busloads of part-time harvesters brought from other parts of France, all go into the vineyards to pick the grapes. Within 10 to 12 days an army of 70,000 workers cut the bunches from their stems, sort out those which are spoiled or squashed, and rush them to nearby presses where they quickly are crushed into grape juice called *must*. Like all of the critical operations affecting the quality of champagne, harvesting and pressing is subject to close regulation and control not found anywhere else in the world.

A special order from the C.I.V.C. specifies: the minimum alcoholic strength the must will have to attain in order to qualify for the appellation; the maximum weight of grapes that may be gathered from each acre; and the quantity of juice that can be pressed from each 150 kilograms of grapes. In most years these controls limit production to a stingy 500 gallons of juice per acre.

*A non-vintage brut from the firm of the Widow Clicquot, who is said to have invented remuage, the process of hand riddling. The house style is medium-bodied, ripe, almost sensuous.*

*Non-vintage brut is the barometer of Grand Marque houses. This is a good example of Piper-Heidsieck's house style—elegant and in perfect balance.*

## The Epluchage

First, the grapes are picked and sorted. The cut bunches carried from the fields by porters are spread out on wicker tables where unsound and unripe grapes are discarded. This preliminary sorting, called *epluchage,* ensures that only perfect grapes will find their way into champagne.

The surviving bunches are loaded tenderly into large baskets and carefully transported to presshouses located not far from the vineyards, where they are weighed and identified. The presshouse may belong to a champagne firm, to a village, to a cooperative of vineyard owners, or to brokers or middlemen. Normally the annual work cycle of the grower ends with the delivery of his grapes to the press.

## Start the Presses

The grape purchase is considered binding when the buyer places the grapes into the press. The making of grape juice, a critical operation demanding great care, thus becomes the responsibility of the buyer of the grapes—usually one of the champagne firms.

To avoid coloration of the grape juice, a champagne press is made wide and shallow so the skins will not long remain in contact with the juice. Moreover, the quantity of juice that may be squeezed from a given weight of grapes, as well as the quality of that juice, is regulated by law.

The surface of the press is loaded with exactly four tons of grapes, called a *marc*. In a number of successive pressings this load will produce as much as 3,000 litres of juice, depending on the type and plumpness of the grapes. However, the law decrees that only the first 2,666 litres (704 gallons) can be used to make champagne. Usually 2,000 litres are quickly obtained in three rapid pressings that take one and a half to two hours; the marc is broken up between each pressing with wooden shovels.

Grandes Marques champagnes use only the liquid from the first pressing for champagne. The remaining 666 litres pressed, called the *vin de taille*, is sold off to firms specializing in private label champagnes. The small amount of additional liquid that can be drawn off at this stage is not used for champagne at all. It goes into the manufacture of regional still wines or strong alcohols.

The grape juice is transferred into purifying vats where it stays for 10–12 hours. During this cleansing process the grape seeds, skins, and other extraneous particles settle out and the must is then ready for the first fermentation, which will convert it into still wine. Accordingly, it is transported to the champagne firms located in the nearby towns and placed in appropriate containers—either vats or casks.

## The First Fermentation

In the central buildings of the champagne firms the tumultuous first fermentation, also called "boiling up," takes place in open vessels. Some champagne houses prefer the traditional oak barrels; others use tanks made of cement lined with glass, enameled steel, or stainless steel. But all of them maintain the tightest possible control over this initial fermentation.

The key to this control is temperature. For two or three weeks the fermenting liquid is kept at a constant temperature of 69° to 72° F. Many of the champagne houses have installed air-conditioning for this purpose. This causes the fermentation to take place slowly, at a regular rate, and also ensures the complete conversion of the wine's sugar into alcohol.

As soon as possible after fermentation has been completed and

analysis shows that all of the juice has been turned into wine, the new wine undergoes several rackings (a process like decanting) that eliminate solids (called *lees*) left behind by the dead yeasts. At this stage the wine is bright and clear and still. It is ready for the next step in the *Methode Champenoise*: blending.

## Blending

Perhaps the most demanding task in the long, painstaking process of making champagne is the blending or preparation of the *cuvee*—deciding which of the wines, from what vineyards, and in what proportions, should be married to produce champagne of the desired quality, aroma, delicacy, elegance, and durability. There is no prescribed formula for blending; it is a highly subjective art involving predicting how raw, new wines will complement older, more mature wines.

*A vintage-dated champagne from the very best-rated villages. Piper-Heidsieck Rare is a "tete de cuvee," a first-pressed wine of exceptional quality and distinction.*

## "TO VINTAGE OR NOT TO VINTAGE"

The expert's nose and palate evaluate samples of the new wines for smell and taste. It is first decided whether they are worthy of being turned into vintage champagne. If so, two cuvees, a vintage and a non-vintage, will be prepared. It will also be decided how much of the vintage wine should be held in reserve. Vintage champagne occurs quite rarely, perhaps four or five times in a decade. It has been called "an accident of nature." If it is to be a non-vintage year, some proportion of older wines—both red and white and of different pressings and vineyard ratings—are selected for the cuvee.

## THE STYLE OF THE HOUSE

After making, testing, tasting, comparing, and discarding innumerable sample blendings over a period of several weeks, the cellar master finally decides on a blend that has the characteristics for which the firm is known. The selected wines are then mixed in large vats according to the blend worked out by the cellar master. The cuvee is completed by the beginning of March, and by early April after a final purification, it is ready for bottling.

*A non-vintage brut from the House of Madame Bollinger. The style is full, flavorful, assertive, dry, and memorable. This firm also produces the most costly champagne, called Vieilles Vignes Fruncaises, made from vines never affected by the phylloxera.*

## Bottling and Adding the Dosage de Tirage

Until now, the champagne has been a still wine. In the spring the blended wine goes to a vat in the bottling plant to be made sparkling. During this step it will receive a dose of pure natural yeasts which will act as fermenting agents, plus a measured amount of sugar. The quantity of sugar added will depend on two things: the degree of effervescence desired in the finished wine, and the amount of natural sugar already present in the blend.

From experience, champagne producers have learned that to achieve a good sparkle, there should be a pressure of 90 pounds per square inch in the bottle, or six times that of atmospheric pressure at sea level (called six atmospheres). This much pressure, captured in wine made from excellent grapes, will give a light, lively, and long-lived foam. The bubbles will be tiny, and they will rise continuously and tirelessly from the bottom of the glass.

*A non-vintage brut from Champagne's most popular house, Moët and Chandon. The house style is fresh, vibrant, fruity, and in perfect harmony.*

The flagship of the House of Krug is Krug Grande Cuvée, a harmonious blend of over 40 to 50 wines from 6 to 10 vintages, creating a champagne with a truly unique character and taste.

Krug Rosé, first introduced in 1985, is produced in tiny quantities. Well-balanced and extremely dry, it is considered to be one of the finest rosés available in the champagne region.

Legally, champagnes must age for one to three years, but Krug champagnes are aged for six years, a practice which is unparalleled in the champagne industry. Indeed Krug is one of the only champagnes to truly age well.

Krug Clos du Mesnil is "the extraordinary exception in champagne." Produced exclusively from a unique vineyard nestled in the village of Les Mesnil-sur-Oger, it is a brut blanc du blancs made from 100% Chardonnay.

During April, May, and June, the wine is bottled. Automatic machinery fills the bottles to the required level and adds the correct proportion of yeasts and sugar, called the *dosage de tirage.* This dosage is usually less than a teaspoonful per bottle. Then the bottles are sealed temporarily with crown corks, which resemble clamps. The champagne is now ready to be transformed from a still wine into a sparkling one by fermenting the second time in the bottle.

## Transformation, or the Second Fermentation

Quality champagnes undergo this transformation in the deepest, coldest part of the cellars where the low temperature causes the second fermentation to take place slowly. Thousands upon thousands of bottles are stacked on their sides, a procedure known as *tirage,* so the wine will be in constant contact with the cork. They are checked continuously, as much to eliminate any that might leak or explode as to make certain the wine is becoming opaque. The formation of a sediment in the bottle is a sure sign of proper fermentation.

Normally, second fermentation in the bottle takes place spontaneously, with no help or interference from the champagne maker. But if necessary, the progress of fermentation can be encouraged by repositioning the bottle piles in other parts of the cellar. After three or four months, fermentation is complete. The sugar has been converted to alcohol and carbonic gas. A deposit of sediment (from the dead yeasts) has accumulated along the lowest portion of each bottle.

When the wine has become sparkling, the bottles are restacked for aging—a stage considered essential to the production of fine French champagne. By unstacking and restacking the bottles at the beginning of the long aging period, and at least once a year thereafter, sediment and wine are brought into intimate contact. This yeast contact helps develop the bouquet and makes for a mature, well-balanced champagne.

After several years of storage—usually three to five—the wine is clear and limpid. The time has come to remove the sediment from the bottles. This is accomplished in two distinct operations: *remuage* (riddling) and *degorgement* (disgorgement).

## The Work of the Riddler

In the process of *remuage,* the sediment in the bottle is slowly caused to settle in the neck, against the cork. To accomplish this, the bottles are first placed at a slight angle, neck tilted downward, in special racks called *pupitres* (pulpits). Each day a highly expert *remuer* or riddler oscillates the bottles gently, gives them a slight turn of 45°, and progressively increases the angle of the tilt. During a period of from six weeks to three months of daily shaking, the sediment slowly slides down to rest against the cork. A skillful specialist can shake about 30,000 bottles a day, and when this work is completed, they are upside down and vertical *(sur pointe).*

After remuage is completed, champagne makers customarily stack these bottles of riddled wine in great piles *(en masse),* neck down, for the remainder of the aging period. The piles are left undisturbed in this position until they are removed from the cellars for disgorgement and final dressing.

## The Disgorging

Disgorgement is the operation that removes the collected sediment from the neck of the bottle without losing any of the sparkling froth. First, the neck is dipped into a solution of frozen brine to form a small block of ice around the sediment. The operator, who ordinarily wears a fencer's mask for face protection, then removes the cork with a type of pliers. This allows internal gas pressure to expel the ice-plug containing the frozen deposit. An experienced person can disgorge about 1,500 bottles in an eight-hour day. The work must be done quickly to prevent air from coming into contact with the wine.

The small quantity of wine lost in disgorgement is replaced by topping-up with some wine of the identical cuvee plus a dosage of older champagne, sometimes blended with grape brandy. It is at this point that the degree of dryness of the champagne is determined. (Sugar, even if only a small amount, is added to almost all champagnes because during the second fermentation all of the sugar originally in the bottle has been burned up, and the wine is now extremely dry.)

R.D. means "recently disgorged" (separated from the yeasts). It possesses the rich taste of a vintage wine aged on the yeasts for many years plus the crispness of one freshly bottled.

## The Dosage de L'Expedition

With a slight touch of a sweet dosage, the champagne becomes *brut* (bone dry). Progressively increasing amounts of sugar produce champagnes called extra dry, dry *(sec),* semi-dry *(demi-sec),* and sweet *(doux).* While the degree of sweetness desired in champagne is a matter of personal taste, a brut champagne is usually preferred because a small dose of sugar cannot mask the distinctive taste of the wine.

You should note that label designations of dryness are not precise terms. Since they are the judgments of individual producers, the brut of one house may be sweeter than that of another. If dryness is a quality you value in champagne, experimentation is necessary to find the house whose style of wine will satisfy your palate.

## Final Corking

The long, labor-intensive *Methode Champenoise* is almost finished, but even at this final stage an important operation remains—the final corking. The role of the champagne cork is criti-

cal: it must hermetically seal the bottle; it must be new so that it will not impart any taste to the wine; it must be immune to extremes of heat and cold; and it must be tough to withstand years of storage without leaking. A close inspection of a champagne cork reveals that it is really three separate smaller corks bonded together.

After the new cork has been inserted and rammed into place under great pressure, it is kept firmly in position by a wire muzzle. But the champagne is not yet ready to sell or drink. It remains at rest in the cellar for a few months before the bottles are ready to be washed, polished, and dressed. It has been on a long journey, and no one can begrudge it a short vacation before it must travel once again, to wine shops and restaurants and ultimately into our glasses.

**The Champagne Cork**

*The champagne cork is actually three corks pressed tightly together. It is inserted into the bottle under great pressure, then wired securely.*

## The Champagne Firms

There are about 150 champagne houses in France making the traditional blended wine, each with its own brand name or names. These firms, called shippers or *negociant-manipulants,* purchase grapes from more than 15,000 small vineyard owners and press them, using only prime juices from the first three pressings to make champagne. Although some of the shippers have their own vineyards, very few of them have enough acreage to provide all the grapes that are needed.

The blending of still wines from various Champagne vineyards with some reserve stocks laid away in previous years is called the cuvee, and every shipper strives for a house blend that will have the same distinctive taste and style year after year. Some houses are known for producing a full-bodied, well-balanced champagne. Others prefer to blend a lighter, more delicate wine. Some are blended to emphasize elegance, others for fruitiness or fragrance. Choosing among them becomes a matter of personal taste because all are of equally high quality and differ only in style.

For several reasons the responsibility for producing fine champagne belongs to the shipper. One is that the manufacture of champagne by the *Methode Champenoise* is a complicated, time-consuming, and costly process. Very few vineyard owners could undertake a project of such magnitude.

To produce a special house style of champagne requires large reserves of still wine. These must be maintained for blending. Vast stocks of bottled wine are kept aging in cellars until they are ready for drinking. Shippers collectively strive to keep a four-year reserve supply of bottled champagne in their vast subterranean cellars. Storing and maintaining these reserves calls for a heavy long term financial commitment that only large firms can afford.

The larger champagne firms who ship their wines into the United States are known as the *Grandes Marques* (great labels). Virtually all of them are over a century old, and most are still owned and operated by descendants, or descendants by marriage, of their founders. Grandes Marques found in the U.S. include:

| | |
|---|---|
| Ayala | Mumm |
| Bollinger | Perrier-Jouët |
| Charles Heidsieck | Piper-Heidsieck |
| Clicquot-Ponsardin | Pol Roger |
| Gosset | Pommery-Greno |
| Krug | Roederer |
| Lanson | Ruinart |
| Laurent Perrier | Taittinger |
| Möet et Chandon | |

In purchasing a *Grandes Marques* champagne, consumers can be certain that they are dealing with a firm that has a great reputation to maintain, as well as the experience and resources to blend and market wines of consistently high quality. Remember that the style of each of the Grandes Marques is distinctive and different. No two will taste exactly the same but all will be very well made.

## Non-Vintage, Vintage, and Special Cuvees

Most of the Grandes Marques champagne bottles do not bear vintage dates on their labels because they are blended from wines of varying ages, selected to maintain the individual house style. The art of marrying new wine with older wines reserved in inventory for this purpose opens up vast possibilities for nuances of taste and aroma.

In a very real sense, non-vintage champagne from one of the great houses represents the character and personality of the firm that produced it. The choices—the quantities of black and white grapes, from which vineyards and from what village, how much of one year's reserve wine and how much of another—all reflect and express the ideas and beliefs of the people to whom making champagne is both an art and a science. For the shipper, non-vintage champagne means a wine with intriguing complexity, uniform balance, and continuity of a particular style. For the consumer, it means dependability and a champagne that is ready to drink when purchased.

Vintage champagne is also, of course, a blended wine—made of black and white grapes from different vineyards. Since it is made only from the grapes of one year's harvest, however, that year must have produced grapes of fine quality, all fully ripe at the time of harvesting, with rich flavor in the fruit. A shipper usually designates a vintage year when it is determined that the wine is not only uniform and exceptional but also is capable of reflecting the personality of the house. When this happens, the year the grapes were picked is indicated on the label.

While most of the fine houses will bottle some vintage wine in a vintage year, they are quite willing to be judged on the basis of their non-vintage champagne. Only one bottle in seven carries a vintage date on the label because much of the wine produced in those years is placed in reserve to be used for subsequent blending. Owing to its scarcity, and because it uses up wines that would otherwise be kept in inventory for future use, a bottle of vintage champagne must be more expensive than a non-vintage one. The purchaser can expect to spend 15%–20% more for a vintage Grandes Marques champagne than for a non-vintage bottle from the same shipper.

Some houses specialize in blanc de blanc or champagnes made exclusively from white Chardonnay grapes. These are very often light and delicate. They may be either vintage or non-vintage.

| Styles of the Grandes Marques | | |
|---|---|---|
| **Light-Bodied** | **Medium-Bodied** | **Full-Bodied** |
| Jacquesson | Ayala | Bollinger |
| Lanson | Deutz | Krug |
| Laurent-Perrier | Charles Heidsieck | Louis Roederer |
| ·Moët and Chandon | Heidsieck Monopole | Gosset |
| Perrier-Jouët | Mumm | |
| Piper-Heidsieck | Pol Roger | |
| Pommerly and Greno | Veuve-Clicquot-Ponsardin | |
| Ruinart | | |
| Taittinger | | |

Most of the major champagne houses bottle a special cuvee, sometimes called a *tête de cuvee,* which represents the highest achievement of the winemaker's art. These super deluxe wines are invariably made from only the first pressing of grapes grown in the highest rated vineyards and are almost always vintage dated and aged in the cellars longer. They are beautifully and proudly packaged, often in replicas of eighteenth century champagne bottles. These extremely limited, "special cuvee" champagnes outshine and outcost vintage ones; they may cost more than twice the price of a non-vintage champagne.

## When to Drink Champagne

In America champagne has always been identified with celebrations. It is, therefore, served on occasions such as weddings, birthdays, anniversaries, and christenings, at Christmas and on New Year's Eve, and at fancy dress balls. But champagne offers a much wider spectrum of usage; it is the most accommodating of wines. There is no menu, no gathering, no occasion, no hour of the day or night when this versatile wine cannot properly be served.

Only recently have Americans begun to realize that champagne may be served anytime and with virtually everything in addition to or instead of ordinary table wine. Champagne is an ideal predinner cocktail. It sharpens the appetite, cleanses the palate, and enhances the food and wine that will follow. Champagne cocktails, such as Mimosa (with orange juice), Kir Royale (with Cassis) or Bellini (with peach nectar), have become popular brunch items.

Champagne is also an excellent accompaniment to a meal, marrying well to fish, fowl, or meat. Several champagnes may be enjoyed with a meal, a blanc de blancs with the fish course, a red Bouzy with meat or cheese, and a demi-sec with dessert.

An elegant, anytime beverage, there is only one rule for venerable champagne: *No swizzle sticks.* It took too long to put those tiny bubbles in. Remember also that there is a great deal of pressure in each bottle. Exercise prudence and caution when opening a bottle. An errant cork can damage objects or even injure a guest or yourself.

---

## Champagne's Fine Print

| | |
|---|---|
| **R.M.** | Recoltant-Manipulant (grower-producer) |
| **C.M.** | Cooperative-Manipulant (cooperative-producer) |
| **N.M.** | Negociant-Manipulant (shipper-producer; the major champagne houses are N.M.'s) |
| **M.A.** | Marque D'Acheteur (buyer's own brand) |

## Champagne Glassware

Look for a glass with an elongated, rather than saucer-shaped, bowl to allow for a steady stream of bubbles. A regular wine glass is preferable to the infamous saucer; tulip or trumpet shapes are even better. Some are even dishwasher safe. Expensive, luxuriant crystal is certainly available, and such a treat to drink from. Crystal is so delicate, however, that more often than not, you do not get much mileage out of it. For those cursed with champagne taste and not the comparable wealth, we suggest a good supply of ordinary, mundane glassware. This philosophy affords you the capital needed to buy better champagne and more of it, and will not cause you to lament the loss of an occasional glass or two when a guest becomes too careless or excited or when the fireplace is merely too close. But, please, no plastic! Remember it *is* champagne.

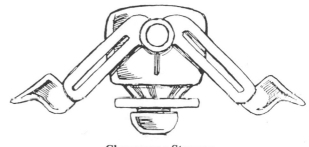

**Champagne Stopper**

*A good stopper will keep the bubbles in the wine for a few days. Quite frankly, around our houses we have no need for this invention. We finish what we start but always in moderation and under control.*

## Cooking with Champagne

You may cook with champagne just as you would with ordinary table wine. In fact, it is a great way to use up leftover champagne (if there is any leftover). Champagne is ideal for deglazing. Remember: When adding champagne to a skillet, it will fizz up. Simply remove the pan from the heat for a few seconds, then return it to the heat.

**Trumpet or Flute Champagne Glass**

*A tall, narrow glass, sometimes called a "trumpet" or a "flute," is the ideal instrument for keeping the steady stream of starry beads flowing. You should be more generous in pouring champagne than you are with table wine. Keep the glass two-thirds to three-fourths filled.*

*A delicate, supple blanc de blancs, a white wine made from white grapes (in this case, 100% Chardonnay from the best villages of the Cote des Blancs), this is a smooth, elegant, "classic" champagne by Pol Roger.*

# SELF-EVALUATION

BEFORE READING ON, see if you have mastered the data set forth in the last few pages. Check the answer section at the back of the book for the correct answers. If you have not answered at least 70% of the questions below correctly, please reread the previous section.

## CHAMPAGNE

| TRUE | FALSE | |
|------|-------|---|
| _____ | _____ | 1. Authentic champagne, made by the traditional *Methode Champenoise*, has been called the most carefully made wine in the world. |
| _____ | _____ | 2. The "secret" of champagne lies in a combination of factors, one of which is the method of cultivation, which is strictly regulated to yield quality rather than volume. |
| _____ | _____ | 3. French law mandates that sparkling wine that can be called champagne must be produced in a small defined area located 90 miles east of Paris. |
| _____ | _____ | 4. There are only three grapes from which champagne may be made. |
| _____ | _____ | 5. Chardonnay provides the softest and ripest wines with lots of bouquet. |
| _____ | _____ | 6. Epluchage is a preliminary sorting to ensure that only the perfect grapes will make champagne. |
| _____ | _____ | 7. Champagne producers are permitted to press as much juice as possible to make champagne. |
| _____ | _____ | 8. Champagne, which is white, is made from only white grapes. |

# VARIATIONS IN THE CHAMPAGNE METHOD

## *"All That Sparkles Is Not Champagne"*

## CLASSIC METHOD

The terms Classic Method and Champagne Method have come to stand broadly for sparkling wine that spends all of its time from secondary fermentation on in one specific bottle. This method is responsible for many superior bubblies worldwide, most notably in Spain, the United States, Italy, and sections of France other than the Champagne region itself. However, we have not generally found these other areas to possess the same level of tradition, dedication, and almost fanatic determination evident in true champagne.

Some particular differences include:

1. Few areas outside of Champagne utilize an epluchage, or select cluster picking, which eliminates bad grapes.
2. Few wineries reserve stocks of older, special wines to be masterfully blended into current stock.
3. Most other wines do not sit on the yeast as long as true champagnes do.
4. Many other sparklers do not reach the 5½ atmospheres of pressure mandated by the champagne process.
5. Mechanized devices, called gyropalettes, are almost always utilized outside Champagne, in place of hand riddling (we must confess that these devices are slowly replacing the riddlers in Champagne as well).
6. Most other sparkling wines are not aged as long as true champagne.

We are not saying that no one but Champagne houses can produce exceptional sparkling wine. In all honesty the best sparkling wine is the one that you enjoy the most. For us, however, champagne is the pinnacle. After extensive tasting we have found that as a rule, average brut non-vintage champagne is superior to the best produced in other regions. Even if other areas were to duplicate the true champagne method, they could never duplicate the soil, climate, village ratings, and many other factors that contribute to Champagne's excellence.

Later we will point out some exquisite examples of classic method sparkling wines, country by country.

## CHARMAT — BULK PROCESS

In the nineteenth century, Maumene Charmat and his son Eugene Charmat developed a system in which the secondary fermentation takes place in a tank rather than a bottle. In general this method, called Charmat, Bulk, Cuve Close, or Autoclave Process, allows sparkling wine to be produced en masse in a shorter period of time from less costly grapes and with a lower production cost. The result is a greater availability at a more moderate price to the consumer.

The special pressurized tanks can be as large as 25,000 gallons and are built to withstand a pressure of over 2000 pounds per square inch. Usually the wine undergoes a secondary tank fermentation for only a month or two. Mechanical agitators inside the tanks constantly circulate yeast throughout the wine. Afterwards the wine is allowed to settle, then it is filtered, and finally bottled under pressure.

Please note that there are many proponents who claim that for delicacy and charm, Charmat is superior to the classic method. Recall, too, that a decent Charmat can be one third or less the price of a Champagne Method sparkler. In the United States, where we love sparkling wines, the Charmat process types account for over 90% of all sparkling wine sales. Asti Spumante is almost exclusively made by a variation of Charmat.

## TRANSFER METHOD

A system somewhere between the classic and Charmat processes was developed in Germany in the 1930s. Called the Transfer Method, this process allows the secondary fermentation to take place in the bottle. Upon completion of this stage, the wine is chilled down to 24° F, and under pressure and in the absence of oxygen, with inert nitrogen being used, the wine is pumped from the bottle into a large tank. The wine is kept in these stainless steel pressurized vats at a low temperature until the yeasty sediment falls to the bottom and the wine clears. After the clear wine is drawn off into clean bottles, a *liqueur d'expedition* is added. All phases take place under pressure at low temperatures.

This method is quite common today in New York State and to a lesser extent in California.

# RUSTIC METHOD

There is an age-old process called the Rural or Rustic Method that is a variation of the champagne process. Or rather, the champagne process is an outgrowth of this rustic method. Developed in the Middle Ages, it is still used today to produce sparkling wines in the following regions of France: Limoux, Gaillac, Savoie, and the Clairette de Die of the Rhone area.

After the wine has undergone part of its fermentation, it is racked, filtered, and bottled. No *liqueur de tirage* is added at bottling time. The unfermented sugar creates carbon dioxide in the bottle as the fermentation process slowly continues. Called a *spontaneous fermentation,* it is not a secondary fermentation but simply a continuation of the first.

There are variations of this system. It is supposed to preserve the fresh, fruity fragrance of the grape. Critics find this method imprecise and the chief cause of occasionally cloudy, unclear sparkling wine. It is allowed by A.O.C. regulations, as, of course, is the Champagne Method. French law does not allow Charmat or Transfer Method sparklers to qualify for an Appellation Controlee. Carlo Gancia at one time used a variation of this method in Italy, but his firm has long since abandoned it.

# CARBONATION

The cheapest (not the least expensive) way to marry bubbles to wine is to inject carbon dioxide directly into it. This is usually performed at low temperatures. Of course, the wine utilized is not very good, most often sweetish and in some cases completely unsavory. There was a New York City winemaker who could produce sparkling wine in less than a day in his subterranean Manhattan cellar. He claimed that the vibrations of the passing subways assisted and ameliorated his bubbly. To say that his finished product was not quite Dom Perignon is an understatement indeed.

The U.S. government's luxury tax on carbonated wine is about 50 cents per bottle. On sparkling wine, which undergoes a secondary fermentation (such as Champagne Method, Charmat, Transfer, or Rustic), this tax is about 70 cents per bottle. The term "naturally fermented" is your guarantee that the wine has not been made by the carbonation or "soda pop" method. It usually means that the Charmat Method was used. "Fermented in the Bottle" indicates that the Transfer Method was utilized. "Fermented in This Bottle" indicates the Classic Champagne method.

*Caves de Bailly is the premier sparkling Burgundy house. Their wines, made from Chardonnay and Pinot Noir by the Champagne Method, are delicate, fresh, and less costly than Champagne. Comte de Bailly cannot be called Champagne because it lies outside of the delimited Champagne district.*

# SELF-EVALUATION

BEFORE READING ON, see if you have mastered the data set forth in the last few pages. Check the answer section at the back of the book for the correct answers. If you have not answered at least 70% of the questions below correctly, please reread the previous section.

## VARIATIONS IN THE CHAMPAGNE METHOD

TRUE      FALSE

_____      _____    1. French champagne may come from any region of Northern France.

_____      _____    2. Champagne utilizes an *epluchage* or select cluster picking, which eliminates bad grapes.

_____      _____    3. Gyropalettes are sometimes used in place of hand riddling.

_____      _____    4. Charmat process is a system in which the secondary fermentation takes place in a tank rather than a bottle.

_____      _____    5. According to the Champagne Method, the wine must spend all of the time of the secondary fermentation in one specific bottle.

_____      _____    6. Transfer Method and Champagne Method are actually the same.

_____      _____    7. In the Rural or Rustic Method, a *Liqueur de Tirage* is added at bottling time.

_____      _____    8. For the Carbonation Method, only a very high quality of grapes is used.

_____      _____    9. The U.S. government adds a "luxury tax" to sparkling wines.

_____      _____   10. "Fermented in *the* Bottle" indicates the Charmat Process.

# OTHER SPARKLING WINES

## FRANCE

Many areas outside of the Champagne region of France produce excellent bubbly. These are never called champagne, but simply *vin mousseux* (sparkling wine). They are made by various methods. The A.O.C. distinguishes several levels of atmospheric pressure in these wines. (Remember, true champagne usually is 6 atmospheres.)

The levels are designated as follows:

Perlant — 1½ to 2½ atmospheres
Petillant — 2 to 2½ atmospheres
Cremant — usually 3 to 4 atmospheres

The chart below will help you sort out some of the A.O.C. sparklers:

| AREA | TYPES | GRAPES | BRANDS |
|---|---|---|---|
| Alsace | Cremant D'Alsace | Many, including Riesling, Chardonnay, Pinot Blanc, Pinot Noir, Pinot Gris | Dopff-au-Moulin, Dopff and Irion, Sparr, Hussherr, Laugel, Willm |
| Burgundy | Bourgogne Mousseux and Cremant de Bourgogne | Various, including Pinot Noir, Pinot Blanc, Gamay Noir, Pinot Beurot | Delorme, Bouchard Pere et Fils, Bouchard Aine, Caves de Bailly |
| Jura and Savoie | Most famous are: Arbois and Seyssel | For Arbois — primarily Savagnin, Chardonnay, Pinot Noir, Pinot Gris. For Seyssel — Roussette, Molette, Chasselas | For Arbois — Domaine de las Pinte. For Seyssel — Varichon and Clerc |
| Loire | Most famous are: Saumur, Touraine, and Vouvray | Mostly Chenin Blanc, called here Pineau de la Loire; also red Cabernets Sauvignon and Franc, and Groslot | DeNeuville, Sablant, Gratien and Meyer, Amiot, Bouvet, Ackerman-Laurance, Monmousseau, Blanc Foussy, Marc Bredif |
| Rhone | Clairette de Die | Clairette and Muscat | Cave Cooperative Clairette de Die |
| Limoux | Blanquette de Limoux | Mauzac mostly plus Chardonnay and Chenin Blanc | Societe de Producteurs Blanquette de Limoux who produce the brand Saint-Hilaire |

Some of these wines are steeped in tradition. Thomas Jefferson loved Blanquette de Limoux, which is viewed as France's first sparkling wine. It originated in 1531 with the monks of Saint-Hilaire. Marc Bredif is recognized as the best producer of Sparkling Vouvray (his still wines are superb as well). Seyssel may be the best that France offers other than Champagne itself. The Cremants of the Loire, Alsace, and Burgundy represent a new, exciting category. Generally speaking, vin mousseux represents good dollar value. Many are made by the *Methode Champenoise*.

There are numerous brands of non-A.O.C. sparklers. Some which are in distribution in the U.S.A. are Champs D'Ore, Chauvenet Red Cap, Duval, Grandin, Kriter, and Remy-Pannier Brut.

French vin mousseux, A.O.C. or not, vary from bone dry to sweet and are available in red, pink, or white.


# GERMANY

**"Everything you wanted to know about Sekt, but were afraid to ask!"**

Germany is a country in love with sparkling wines. Much of it is made from grapes or wines that originate in Italy, Spain, France, or Eastern Europe. Today Germany is second only to France in production; per capita consumption of sparkling wine is over four gallons. They call their sparkling wines Schaumwein (foamy wine); the best of them they call *Sekt*.

Sekt gets its name, according to tradition, from a German actor, Ludwig Devrient, who played Falstaff in Shakespeare's Henry IV. In place of sherry (sack) on stage, he preferred a cup of the bubbly whenever he called for his "cup of sack" (Sekt). Soon others cried out "Sekt!" when they desired sparkling wine. The name stuck.

Some of the world's most famous sparkling wine names are Germanic: Heidsieck, Deutz, Geldermann, Krug, Roederer and Taittinger, and the Americans, Hanns Kornell and Adolf Heck of Cook's and later Korbel.

We are blessed in the U. S. with some of Germany's significant *Sekts*.

1. **Fürst von Metternich:** There are two dry Rieslings from the Rheingau that bear this name. They are made by the Metternich family of political and Schloss Johannisberg fame. One is a vintage-dated Methode Champenoise; the other is a non-vintage transfer method. Both are excellent. Production of this brand dates back to 1864.

2. **Deinhard:** This prestigious house founded in 1650 sold their first commercial Sekt in 1843. In 1910 they introduced Lila Imperial, which they continue to market today. It is a light, fruity cuvee made from 100% Riesling grapes grown in the Mittelrhein. Lila is a top of the line example of Charmat, having been aged for two and a half years in the tank before being released for sale.

   Deinhard also produced the now famous Bernkasteler Doktor Sekt 1978, which fetched the highest price ever for any German bubbly ($40.00 per bottle). This wine spent some time in oak as well as in Charmat tanks and was released in the fall of 1982. It is delicate, fresh with good acidity to balance out its light touch of fruity sweetness. Class!

3. **Henkell:** This firm from Wiesbaden, founded in 1832, is Germany's largest. Its 70 million bottle annual production makes it either a close second to the United States' Gallo or even first in production worldwide. Henkell Trocken can be found in widespread distribution in the U.S.A. They produce sound, reliable, clean Charmat Sekt made from Riesling, Sylvaner, and other German varietals. Henkell accounts for more than one-half of all German Schaumwein exports.

You may find Sekts from Langenbach and Sohnlein in the U.S.A. There is also Sparkling Blue Nun and a sparkling wine with strawberry fruit flavor under the label of Kroneck.

Before leaving Sekt, we must relate to you what Dr. Konstantin Frank, of German descent and the pioneer of vinifera in New York State, said: "They make Sekt when the grapes are not good enough for table wine." You may decide for yourself, after tasting several Sekts. True, late-picked Riesling table wines are the aristocrats of German wines, but we have enjoyed quite a few Schaumweins as well. Obviously, so have the German people.

Henkell is the largest exporter of Schaumwein. The Trocken (dry) is a blend of several vinifera kept on the yeasts in Charmat for over a year. It is a reliable, agreeable Sekt from the world's largest sparkling wine producer.

A light, fruity Sekt, Deinhard's Lila Imperial is made from 100% Riesling. It is aged in Charmat tanks for two and a half years before being released. It was first made by the firm of Deinhard in 1910.

## CATEGORIES OF GERMAN SPARKLING WINES

| TYPE | CHARACTERISTICS |
|------|-----------------|
| PERLWEIN | Made by carbonation method. 2½ atmospheres. Usually low alcohol, made from imported wine and consumed locally. Not exported. |
| SCHAUMWEIN | 3½ atmospheres. Usually Charmat and made from foreign wine. *Inlandischen Schaumwein* – the sparkle, not necessarily the wine, must take place inside Germany. No specified grape origin, no required aging period, usually non-vintage. The lowest category of fully sparkling stuff. Not exported. |
| SEKT (Qualitätsschaumwein) | At least 10° alcohol. Wines must be from an EEC approved area. 3½ atmospheres. Minimum of 60 days on yeast or 21 days if a stirring apparatus is used. Must be held for 9 months at the winery before being sold. Exported. |
| QbA SEKT | At least 75% of grapes must be from Germany. If a grape variety is listed (e.g., Riesling Sekt), it must be at least 75% of the mentioned varietal. If a region, village or vineyard is listed, it must be at least 75% from the mentioned zone. Vintage-dated QbA Sekt must be at least 75% from the specific vintage. Must be on the yeasts for at least 6 months. Exported. Best quality. Some *Methode Champenoise*. |

# AUSTRIA

Austria is usually just a footnote to the study of German wines. So it is with Sekt, except for the exquisite house of Schlumberger in Vienna. Since 1842 this family has been producing classic method, hand-riddled sekt from Veltliner, Welschriesling, and Voeslauer vines. Their cellars stretch for over a mile under the city of Vienna. The vintage brut is just one notch below true champagne.

# SPAIN

The *espumosos* of Spain have been one of the brightest spots on the American wine scene of late. And for a good reason! They have filled the need for delicious sparkling wine at a reasonable price. The center for Spanish "Sham-pagnes," as jealous competitors call them, is a Catalonian town near Barcelona, San Sadurni de Noya. The soil in this region, called the Penedes, is rich in chalk, similar to that of Champagne. The grapes, although not household terms like Pinot Noir and Chardonnay, are excellent. They are the white Macabeo, Parellada and Xarel-Lo and the red Monastrell.

Over 90% of Spain's sparkling wines are made from grapes that originate in the Penedes. Those made by the Champagne method have the word CAVA (short for Criado en Cava or "made in the cellar") somewhere on the label; GRAN-VAS indicates Charmat; and GASIFICADO (gaseous) signifies carbonation.

CAVA wines must be aged for at least nine months. Mechanical riddling is widespread. A device called a *girasol* ("sunflower") holds about 500 bottles. Two men can riddle about 300,000 a day by utilizing a girasol; a skilled riddler can do about 30,000 by hand.

Most of the great houses emphasize white grape varieties, especially the Macabeo. They also produce a variety of styles ranging from the driest Bruto to Seco to Semiseco to Semidulce to the sweetest Dulce. The two most popular wineries, Codorniu and Freixenet, account for 70% of all CAVA wines.

One of Spain's most famous espumosos, Castillo de Perelada, hails from Costa Brava along the Mediterranean coast. The reason for the fame (or rather the infamy) is that British courts ruled that Castillo de Perelada could not be marketed under the name of champagne in England.

## EXAMPLES OF CAVA WINES

| WINERY | TYPE | CHARACTERISTICS |
|---|---|---|
| Codorniu | Gran Codorniu | Left on the yeasts for 5 years. Made from the first 10% of the juice pressed. Dry, smooth, elegant. |
| Codorniu | Brut Natural | Aged for four years. Dry, rich. |
| Codorniu | Blanc de Blancs | Three years of aging. Delicate, dry, light. Codorniu's top seller. |
| Freixenet | Cordon Negro | Dry, well-balanced. In a distinctive black, frosted bottle. Most popular in U.S.A. |
| Freixenet | Barroco Brut | Rich, yeasty, vintage-dated. Aged for up to 7 years. Freixenet's best. |
| Castellblanch | Brut Zero | Hand riddled, not completely dry as the name implies. |
| Paul Cheneau | Blanc de Blancs Brut | Classy, dry, light. Becoming very popular in the U.S.A. |
| Segura Viudas | Brut Reserva | Dry, crisp. Must be fresh to be at its delicate best. |

CAVA
*Xènius*
BRUT
MÉTHODE TRADITIONAL CHAMPENOISE
SPARKLING WINE
NATURALLY FERMENTED IN THIS BOTTLE

RSI-30.499/B
RE-4293 B-1

Produce of Spain

Estate bottled by Covides G
750 ml.     Sant Sadurni d'Anoia     Alcohol 11'8% by vol.
IMPORTED BY WINHAM, INC., SALT LAKE CITY, UTAH

*Xènius Brut Cava (n.v.) is a remarkable product offering both quality and affordability. Xènius is produced in the Cava region of Spain by Covides, S.A., the largest cooperative of the Penedes area. In 1990, two new varieties of Xènius Cava will be introduced in the U.S.: Xènius Brut Extra and Xènius Brut Reserva.*

*Paul Cheneau* ®
BLANC DE BLANCS
*Methode Champenoise*
*Sparkling Wine*

CAVA          Produced and bottled by Can Esbert          750 ML.
PRODUCE OF SPAIN   SANT SADURNI D'ANOIA, SPAIN          ALC. 12% BY VOL.
IMPORTED BY "21" Brands NEW YORK, NY
FINE WINE SELECTIONS

*CAVA indicates the Champagne Method for this Spanish sparkler. Blanc de Blancs indicates that only white grapes are used. It is fruity, dry, and very affordable.*

## ITALY

The sparkling wines of Italy vary, as do their table wines, from cabbages to kings. They provide a variety of sparklers second to none, but also produce great quantities of mediocre *spumante,* much of it sweetish. They accounted five years ago for over half of the imported bubbly consumed in the United States. Now they comprise about $^1/_3$ of the imported sparkling wine market. What is not generally known is that at the top end, Italy's dry sparklers rival the very best the world outside of Champagne can offer. Several brands vie at least the average wines of Rheims and Epernay. The problem is that since they are so well made, they are as costly as true champagnes. Given the choice of equally priced Ca del Bosco or Moët Brut N/V, the consumer naturally sways toward the time-tested, reliable, well-known brand.

Americans may think that the word spumante connotes sweetness; it simply means foamy or frothy. The reason for the connection with sweetness is the success in the U.S. of a spumante based on the fruity Moscato (muscat) grape produced in and around the town of Asti. This wine, called Asti Spumante, is delicate, fragrant, generally has about 8% unfermented residual sugar and is only about 7.5% to 8.5% alcohol. Gancia and Contratto are families who pioneered production of this type. Both, until fairly recently, used the *Methode Champenoise.* Today Charmat is used. They say it is more precise and preserves the fresh, fruity character of the Moscato grape. It is also true that traditionally 30% to 50% of the bottles en tirage were lost due to explosions. Tank fermentation is precise, indeed, and cost effective.

Martini and Rossi is the brand leader for Asti Spumante in the U.S.A. Other popular brands include Cinzano, Villa Banfi, Cella, and Gancia. Lower priced marques, such as Zonin, Tosti, and Nando do very well. Contratto is highly regarded. Santo Stefano, controlled by the famous Ceretto brothers, is vintage-dated and estate bottled. With nuances of grapefruit, pineapple, and ever-present peaches and apricots, it may be the most charming. Traditionally, Asti Spumante is drunk with panettone, a holiday bread cake. We have found it to be a good match to cheesecake or pumpkin pie, which is a little closer to home in the American holiday kitchen. The native Piedmontese themselves prefer the lighter, fruitier, crackling Moscato D'Asti to Asti Spumante. Giacomo Bologna's limited production is very charming, as are Vietti and Santo Stefano. Moscato D'Asti has not yet caught on in

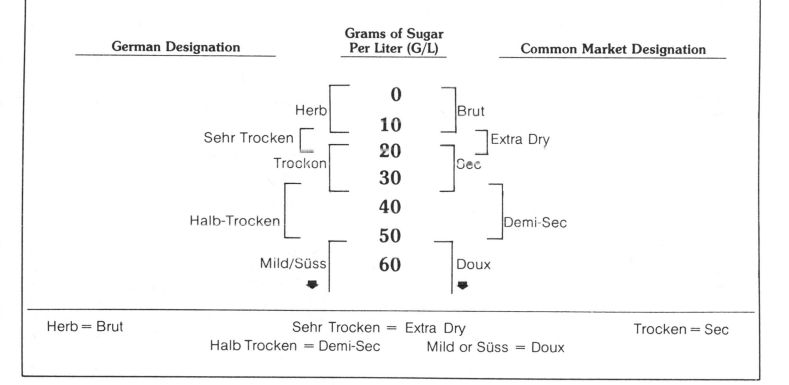

## LEVELS OF DRYNESS OF SPARKLING WINES

| German Designation | Grams of Sugar Per Liter (G/L) | Common Market Designation |
|---|---|---|
| Herb | 0 | Brut |
| Sehr Trocken | 10 | Extra Dry |
| Trockon | 20 | Sec |
| | 30 | |
| Halb-Trocken | 40 | Demi-Sec |
| | 50 | |
| Mild/Süss | 60 | Doux |

Herb = Brut          Sehr Trocken = Extra Dry          Trocken = Sec
Halb Trocken = Demi-Sec          Mild or Süss = Doux

the U.S.A. Mass-produced, lesser Moscato-based fare, such as Bosca Canei and Riunite D'Oro, sell very well.

Virtually any table wine producer may choose to dabble in spumante. The Italian government's D.O.C. laws provide for sparkling versions of popular table wine. Examples include Soave, Frascati, Verdicchio, Greco di Tufo, Lugana, Marino, and literally dozens of others. These are rarely exported. Many brands, like Bolla, Corvo, and Riunite, produce non-D.O.C. sparklers, almost always by Charmat.

One type of bubbly that is becoming chic today is Prosecco di Conegliano-Valdobbiadene, perhaps due to the Bellini or Lampone cocktails. The best of these wines, based largely on the Prosecco vine, are called *cartizze*. Prosecco as a wine is always white, but it can be made still, crackling, or fully sparkling. It varies from dry to semi-dry to sweet. Make certain you are getting the style you want. Good examples of sparkling Prosecco are Nino Franco, De Faveri, Carpene-Malvolti, Valdo, Zardetto, Venegazzu, Santa Margherita, Torresella, and Domenico de Bertiol.

## The Italian Champagne Method Institute

In 1975 a group was formed to set standards for producing *Methode Champenoise* sparklers. The following principles were established:

1. Only Chardonnay, Pinot Blanc, Pinot Grigio, and Pinot Noir may be used.
2. The grapes must come from only four zones:
   - Trentino-Alto Adige
   - Serralunga D'Alba (in Piedmont)
   - Franciacorta (in Lombardy)
   - Oltrepo Pavese (in Lombardy)
3. Secondary fermentation must take place in the bottle.
4. Age on the yeast must be at least two years.
5. Wine must be at least 3 years old.

The group started with six members and it has grown to thirteen. Members must have an annual production of over 50,000 bottles and at least five years of *Methode Champenoise* experience. You will see a special emblem depicting a riddling rack *(pupitre)* on the bottles of members. Their standards are very high. Members include Ferrari, Martini & Rossi, Riccadonna, Carpene-Malvolti, Cinzano, Antinori, Contratto, Gancia, Fontanafredda, Equipe 5, Barone Pizzini, and Berlucchi.

One of the founding members, The House of Ferrari, makes four different wines by the champagne method. For their brut, the traditional champagne varietals Chardonnay, Pinot Noir, and Pinot Meunier are used. Their vintage brut rose consists of Pinot Noir and Chardonnay. For these two varieties, the Lunelli family, which owns and runs Ferrari, buys grapes. The grapes for their 100% Chardonnay Brut de Brut Perle, and the Riserva Giulio Ferrari come from their own vineyard area. Ferrari exemplifies the high standards of the Italian Champagne Method Institute.

Some of Italy's best wineries are not members. Ca del Bosco is widely regarded as the very finest. Andre du Bois, former champagne maker for Moët and Chandon, makes several bubblies for proprietor Maurizio Zanella. Their Dosage Zero is bone dry, yeasty and firm, made from 80% white grapes (40% Chardonnay, 40% Pinot Blanc) and 20% Pinot Noir. You will find small quantities of Ca del Bosco in the U.S.A.

You may see a bit more of Berlucchi in the U.S.A. Berlucchi is the leading producer of *Methode Champenoise* in Italy. Contratto deserves special mention. In addition to producing excellent wine, Contratto puts the disgorging date on the label. Lucky consumers can tell how fresh the bubbly is. We think that others, even the French, should follow his lead.

Villa Banfi makes an exquisite Champenoise consisting of 30% Chardonnay, 20% Pinot Blanc, and 50% Pinot Noir. We would place Italy's best, together with certain U.S. brands like Schramsberg, Domaine Chandon, and Piper-Sonoma as the only serious rivals to true champagne.

# THE UNITED STATES

The earliest sparkling wines made in the U.S.A. date back to 1842, when Nicholas Longworth of Ohio offered a Sparkling Catawba for a then-pricey $3.00 per bottle. A decade later Benjamin Wilson and later the Sansevain Brothers produced bubblies, probably from the Mission vine, that fetched a substantial price of $2.00 per bottle.

By the mid-1860s on both Atlantic and Pacific Coasts, the American champagne business was in stride. U.S. wineries brought in French champagne makers and soon world medals were being earned. A California brand called Eclipse and the Pleasant Valley Wine Company of New York, now known as Great Western, were the most highly acclaimed. Important wineries of the early era included Cook's Imperial of St. Louis, and Korbel and Mirassou of California.

In California, then as now, vinifera grapes were used. Today some excellent examples of Charmat, Transfer, and Classic Method sparklers can be found in the U.S.

## Charmat Method Producers

Gallo is the titan here. Their Gallo, Andre, and Ballatore labels account for almost 6 million cases, or almost half of all the sparkling wine, imported and domestic combined, consumed in America. Other reasonably priced brands are Jacques Bonet, Cook's, the Le Domaine label of Almaden, and Canandaigua's J. Roget (note the French-sounding names). The outstanding U.S. producer of Charmat is Angelo Papagni of California.

## Transfer Method Producers

Almaden and Paul Masson apply this method on the West Coast, but New York State is where it proliferates. Gold Seal, Great Western, and Taylor are the benchmarks. Batavia Wine Cellars produces many private labels by transfer. Usually French-American hybrids, such as Aurora, Ravat, Vidal, and Seyval are used, as well as native Labruscas Catawba and Delaware. Two specific wines of great interest are Gold Seal's Charles Fournier Blanc de Blancs, created by Fournier, the former champagne maker of Veuve-Clicquot, and Taylor's Bi-Centennial Cuvee, released in 1976 at the patriotic price of $76.00 per bottle (we felt $19.76 would have been fairer, and just as patriotic).

## Classic Method Producers

Korbel dominates sales here. Since they first released Grand Pacific in 1882, they have been in the forefront of the sparkling wine industry. Their Natural, dominated by Chardonnay, with some Pinot Blanc and Pinot Noir, is their best and top-flight. They also make a Brut (their biggest seller), Extra Dry, Sec Rose, Rouge, Blanc de Noirs, and Blanc de Blancs. Their wines are clean, fruity, fresh, and in good balance.

Surely the most exciting phenomenon in California has been the joint ventures of Europeans and Americans, or simply Europeans investing in U.S. agriculture. In still wines we have Opus One (Mondavi-Rothschild), in brandy RMS (Remy Martin-Schramsberg), and in sparkling wines the following:

Piper-Sonoma (Piper-Heidsieck and Sonoma Vineyards)
Domaine Chandon (Moët Chandon in Napa Valley)
Freixenet Sonoma (Gloria Ferrer Brut)
Laurent-Perrier (with Almaden)
Maison Deutz (Deutz and Geldermann in California)
Mumm (produced at Sterling Vineyards)
Roederer (in Mendocino)
Codorniu (in San Luis Obispo County)

All produce very commendable *Methode Champenoise* sparklers.
Other noteworthy producers include Schramsberg, which is often served at White House affairs of state, Hanns Kornell, Mirassou, Chateau St. Jean, Sonoma Vineyards, and Sebastiani. Some

of the newer boutique sparklers of quality are Iron Horse, Scharffenberger, Robert Hunter, Shadow Creek, Van der Kamp, and Tijsseling. Chateau Ste. Michelle (Washington State) and Ste. Chapelle (Idaho) are doing great things in the northwest.

A careful selection of these wineries would surely uncover products that vie with the very best of the world. There is a great stylistic variation, but many are of a dry, fruity ilk and do not possess the yeasty, "chalky" character that many French champagnes strive for. Most of the progressive wineries do not label their bubbly as champagne.

Rather we see Napa Brut, Midnight Cuvee, or the like. We think this seems right. These wines will sink or swim on their particular merits, and they have characteristics all their own. America's best table wines are no longer called Burgundy and Chablis. Why should it be different for bubbly?

*Domaine Chandon, established in Napa, California in 1973, produces some of the best bubbly in the U.S. They would never call their products champagne although they are owned by the French champagne firm of Moët and Chandon. Sparklers with names like Napa Brut, Blanc de Noir, or Reserve are made under the direction of Edmond Maudiere, who also happens to make Dom Perignon.*

# OTHER COUNTRIES

**Argentina:** You may find some good quality *Methode Champenoise* wine from Toso. It is off-dry and 100% Chardonnay.

**Australia:** We will see more of these bubblies from down under. Thomas Hardy, Mildara, Seppelt, and Taltarni are names to look for.

**Chile:** Look for sparklers from the excellent table wine producers: Concha y Toro, Santa Carolina, and Undurraga.

**Hungary:** There is a decent classic method sparkler called Hungaria.

**Israel:** There are some Charmats, and one very good classic method called Carmel Sambatyon.

**Luxembourg:** You may find some Bernard-Massard in distribution in the U.S.

**Portugal:** The Portuguese have been making bubbly for a century. Their sparklers, as do their other wines, represent excellent value. Look for Caves Alianca, Caves Sao Joao, and Caves do Barrocao. These wineries specialize in the *Metodo Champanhes.*

Sparkling wines are produced in many other countries including Romania, Bulgaria, the U.S.S.R., South Africa, New Zealand, Mexico, Canada, and Brazil. Freshness is a key in finding good bubbly. Remember that the quality factors that apply to table wines also apply to sparkling wines. Try a bottle before you buy a case.

# SPARKLING WINES IN REVIEW

- Due to a combination of quality factors, true French champagne is, generally speaking, the very finest in the world.
- Bubbles get into the wine due to a secondary fermentation. This fermentation may take place in the bottle or in a tank.
- Methods of sparkling wine production include:

  1. Champagne (or Classic) Method
  2. Transfer Method
  3. Charmat Method
  4. Rustic (or Rural) Method
  5. Carbonation

- Italy makes a variety of sparklers from dry to sweet. They refer to their bubblies as spumanti.
- Germany calls it best Schaumwein (sparkling wine) Sekt. The Germans are avid consumers and boast the largest producer (Henkell) in the world.
- Spain is the most important producer of economical Champagne method wine which they refer to as CAVA.
- America is an outstanding producer and consumer of sparkling wines.
- Sparkling wines may be produced anywhere in the world.

# SELF-EVALUATION

BEFORE READING ON, see if you have mastered the data set forth in the last few pages. Check the answer section at the back of the book for the correct answers. If you have not answered at least 70% of the questions below correctly, please reread the previous section.

# OTHER SPARKLING WINES

TRUE      FALSE

_____   _____   1. Three significant brands of Sekt are Deinhard, Fürst von Metternich, and Henkell.

_____   _____   2. Four categories of German sparkling wines are Perlwein, Schaumwein, QbA Sekt, and Sehr-Trocken.

_____   _____   3. Macabeo, Parelleda, and Xarel-Lo are three basic grapes used in Spanish sparkling wines.

_____   _____   4. Spanish law specifies that CAVA wines must be aged for at least two years.

_____   _____   5. Spumante means "foaming" or "frothy" in Italian.

_____   _____   6. Moscato is the grape in Asti Spumante.

_____   _____   7. Italian *Methode Champenoise* sparkling wines are sometimes aged for up to three years.

_____   _____   8. California uses vinifera grapes in their sparkling wines.

_____   _____   9. Most of the sparkling wine sold in America is made by the classic Champagne method.

_____   _____   10. Korbel is the most popular American classic method sparkling wine brand in the United States.

# NOTES

# TABLE WINES

Those wines to which NO bubbles, herbs, brandy, flavors, or the like have been added are called table wines. Such wines are produced in temperate zones worldwide.

To explain these wines we have set up our discussions geographically. Geography, however, is only one of the quality factors that effects the making of great wine. Superb wine very often comes from the least likely area, from virtually unknown grapes, but always in combination with a talented winemaker.

There is much to discover in the table wine category. We drink these wines with our meals. They make our food taste better, and our food makes the wine taste better. The more we learn about wines, the more we will add to the enjoyment of our meals.

# THE WINES OF THE UNITED STATES

What country has been drinking wine since the early seventeenth century, been a wine producer since the eighteenth century and is considered by many to be the twentieth century "School of Wine Science and Art"? We will give you another hint: Over 80% of the states in this nation currently produce wine. Or how about: This country is sixth in the world in total production.

That's right! This wine-producing giant is our own United States of America, whose interesting, checkered history began with Captain John Smith's first sip of sherry in Jamestown, Virginia in 1609. In fact, some five hundred years earlier, Leif Ericson called America "Vineland." We know, too, that French Huguenot settlers made wine from native Scuppernong vines in 1562 just outside of what is now Jacksonville, Florida.

## AMERICA'S GRAPES

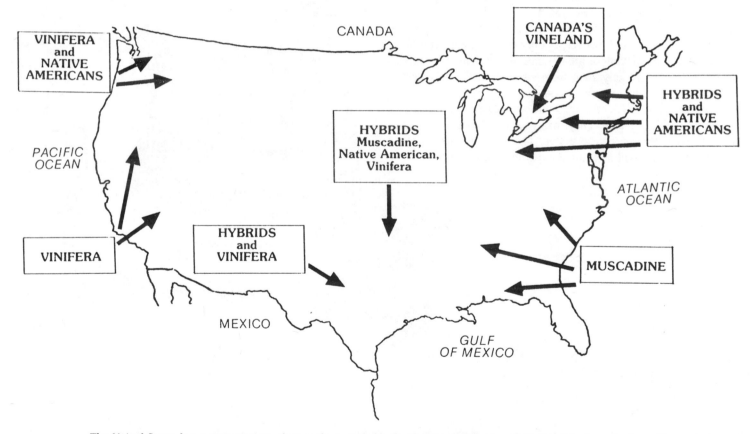

*The United States has a great variety of wines from each family of grapes: Hybrids and Native Americans in the cold Northeast; Muscadine in the deep South; and European Vinifera in California.*

## THE ARCHAIC PERIOD (1619–1920): The Battle of the Wets and the Drys

**1619–1773:** Vineplantings and winemaking actively promoted by Lord Delaware, Virginia Assembly, William Penn, John Winthrop, Lord Baltimore, and Thomas Jefferson.

**1769:** Padre Junipero Serra plants the first vinifera vines in Mission San Diego, California.

**1793:** America's first commercial winery, close to Philadelphia, is formed. The Pennsylvania Vine Company uses the Alexander grape, a hybrid of a native Labrusca and a European vinifera, to produce wine. By 1870 wine is being made from Catawba, Isabella, Concord, Elvira, and Scuppernong.

**1843:** Jean Louis Vignes brings European vinifera cuttings to his El Aliso Vineyard in Los Angeles. El Aliso becomes California's first noteworthy commercial winery.

**1849:** The Gold Rush and the Vine Rush, as the California government offers tax exemptions to promote viticulture.

**1851-1862:** Agoston Haraszthy, called both "Count" and "Colonel" although he was neither, introduces new European vinifera to California. He is also called "The Father of American Wines," which he is.

**1873:** The phylloxera strikes Sonoma, California.

**1880:** University of California establishes a Department for Viticultural Research and Instruction.

**1880–1890:** Kansas goes dry. Georgia, Oklahoma, Mississippi, North Carolina, Tennessee, West Virginia, and Virginia follow. By 1914, thirty-three states are dry.

**1880–1890:** References to alcohol are removed from school texts. Medicinal wines are dropped from the United States pharmacopeia.

**1880–1900:** Waves of European immigrants enter the U.S., bringing with them a thirst for freedom, success, and wine, and the skill and determination to slake their thirsts.

**1900:** At the Paris Exhibition, American wines win thirty-six medals. Names include Beringer, Guasti, Gundlach-Bundshu, Italian Swiss Colony, Paul Masson from California; Brotherhood Winery and Pleasant Valley Wine Co. (Great Western) from New York.

**1906:** Fifteen wineries are destroyed in the San Francisco earthquake and fire.

**1916:** Eight Canadian provinces adopt Prohibition legislation. Most are repealed by 1927.

**1920:** The 18th Amendment and the Volstead Act place the United States in Prohibition. Only about 100 wineries continue to produce sacramental, medicinal wines.

## THE DARK AGES (1920–1933): Prohibition

A few facts are interesting with reference to Prohibition's attempt to make American society safe and perfect:

- It did not work. We were worse off in 1932 than in 1919: Utopia had not been forged. Worse yet, it spread corruption, caused the collapse of our economy, and lead to the development of a criminal network that distributed illegal and lethal beverages.

- The interruption in our viticultural progress delayed our path to preeminence in quality table wine production. Only about 100 wineries in four states survived Prohibition.

- We can number ourselves among those fanatic Islamic and Communist governments that have stripped their citizenry of the freedom of moderate consumption, a policy that our friends in Western Europe have never understood.

- Prohibition did not stop people from drinking. There was "bathtub gin," the speakeasy, and the wine brick. A wine brick was a pressed concentrate of grapes, which anyone could purchase to make legal grape juice. With it came a yeast tablet and a warning that if the yeast and a gallon of water were added to the brick, fermentation would begin, thus making wine, which would be illegal.

- With repeal on December 5, 1933, Americans who had been conditioned to moonshine were not accustomed to "sour" tasting table wines. So the fortified port and sherry types became popular. American vintners did not know how to market their products. Generic names such as Burgundy, Chablis, Rhine, Chianti, Sauterne (with no "s" at the end), and Champagne came into prominence.

- The "Dry's" did not pack up and shut up with Repeal. As of 1970, local laws still forbade the sale of wine in almost 600 of our 3,000 counties, an area representing 10% of the U.S. geographically and 6% of our population. It is surmised by some that recent efforts toward higher taxes, sulfite labeling, import quotas, and the equation of the wine and spirits industry with drug dealers is the work of a dry coalition of religious teetotalers, industrialists, and therapeutic groups.

Gene Ford tells us in his magnificent *Ford's Illustrated Guide to Wines* that between 1920 and 1933, over 500,000 people were arrested, 1.5 million stills were seized, 45,000 autos and 1,300 boats were confiscated. The farming industry lost one million jobs and over $20 million in the first five years. Corn syrup sales increased six-fold; over 150,000 pounds of hops were sold as kitchen spice. Fifteen thousand Americans suffered serious injuries or death from illegal liquor. Our government lost an estimated $500 million in taxes.

# THE RENAISSANCE (1933–1968):
## Out of the Ashes . . .

From Repeal to 1968, the very year when Americans consumed as much table wine as fortified wine, the nation's wine industry expanded. The early years were dominated by giants, who set the stage for the Golden Age:

**Captain Paul Garrett:** He created a nationwide empire with his Virginia Dare label. With wine made from the native *Vitis muscadine* Scuppernong vine, Garrett established several wineries to produce a light, sweetish red and white table wine. He had called such light wines "the anti-toxin of alcoholism."

**Frank Schoonmaker:** This monumental importer and journalist encouraged U.S. firms to name their wines after the dominant grape variety. Soon new varietal names, such as Chardonnay, Pinot Noir, Niagara, etc., appeared next to already familiar Cabernet, Riesling, Catawba, and Zinfandel. Eventually Barbera, Chenin Blanc, and Petite Sirah came on the scene. European wineries even marketed their wares in America under varietal designations. Schoonmacher also advocated competitive "blind" tastings.

**Philip Wagner:** This Maryland journalist pioneered the use of French-American hybrid grapes in the northeast. Soon "foxy" Concords and Catawbas gave way to superior white Seyval Blanc and Aurora and red Baco Noir and Chelois.

**Charles Fournier:** This Frenchman from Rheims raised the American sparkling wine business to new heights at Gold Seal in the Finger Lakes region of New York. He also sponsored and supported Dr. Konstantin Frank.

**Dr. Konstantin Frank:** This German national, born and raised in the Ukraine, came to our shores in 1951. In a rags-to-riches story possible only in America, the late Dr. Frank, born on the 4th of July 1899, worked his way from dishwasher at an automat in New York City to Fournier's office at Gold Seal. Dr. Frank became the first to cultivate vinifera vines in the northeastern United States. Riesling and Chardonnay were followed by Gewurztraminer, Cabernet Sauvignon, and Pinot Noir. Dr. Frank's son, Willibald, continues his work at his Vinifera Winery. Dr. Frank's grandson is field master and winemaker for Villa Banfi, which has plantings of Chardonnay in Long Island.

**Leo Star:** There is a story told that Leo Star of the Monarch Wine Company in New York City became tired of taking back unsold kosher wines after Passover. In 1935, he put his foot down. Surprisingly, non-Jewish customers liked the sweet Concord taste. Within ten years "Man Oh Manischewitz" was on the lips of many Americans.

## Meanwhile in California . . .

At the same time, certain California wineries were establishing themselves as business giants or elite producers of world-class wines.

The giant of giants was the family-owned Gallo operation in Modesto. The largest winery in the world, it had dominated in every category under many labels, including Andre, Carlo Rossi, Bartles and Jaymes, Ballatore, and Boone's Farm. Other titanic names were Colony, Petri, Guild, Franzia, and Cribari.

Premium wineries (not that the giants did not offer premium wines) included Almaden, Paul Masson, Charles Krug (C. K. Mondavi), Christian Brothers, and Sebastiani. It was not uncommon for such firms to offer 30 wines or more ranging from port and sherry types, several sparkling wines, and vermouth to a complete line of generic, proprietary, and varietal table wines.

Super-premium wineries came into prominence. Their varietals garnered medals at prestigious international competitions and helped to put California and the U.S. on the wine map. Many were located in Napa and Sonoma, considered to be the finest viticultural sites in the United States. These proud names included Beaulieu Vineyard, David Bruce, Concannon, Ficklin, Hanzell, Heitz, Inglenook, Louis Martini, Mayacamas, Mirassou, Parducci, Martin Ray, and Wente.

Improvements in quality and production, coupled with increased consumption, set the stage for the next era.

# THE GOLDEN AGE (1968–PRESENT)

The Golden Age has witnessed California's clear emergence as the preeminent epicenter of U.S. viticulture. It also saw Americans swing away from fortified wines solidly in the direction of lighter, food-associated table wines. The rise in both quality and production led to a subsequent increase in per capita consumption. The hope of an exploding wine market caused a period of optimistic development in California. This development encompassed the following:

1. New "Boutique" Wineries
2. Traditional Wineries
3. Joint Ventures ("Eurowines")
4. Giants Changing Directions

## New Boutique Wineries

Entrepreneurs, hobbyists, and the like bought up land primarily in Napa and Sonoma to produce small quantities of wine from usually one or two grape varieties. Each of these *petite chateaux* ordinarily account for less than 25,000 cases annually, much of it very special and sought after by afficionados worldwide. Napa wineries soared from 15 to more than 150 in a decade.

Proprietors of boutique wineries include celebrities such as Pat Paulsen, the Smothers Brothers, and Francis Ford-Coppola; businessmen such as Brooks Firestone, Joseph Phelps, Ely Callaway, and Eugen Trefethen; and scientists such as Tom Jordan. Tom Burgess and Joe Heitz were Air Force pilots.

## Traditional Wineries

Traditional wineries were refurbished or bought out by corporate giants. Grape-growing families like Giumarra and Papagni built wineries. Pedrizetti and Pedroncelli remodelled in the mid-1970s. The headline, however, was the involvement of "big business" in California wine. Some of the key players included:

Nestlé — *Beringer, Napa Ridge, Meridian, Chateau Souverain*
Grand Met of England — *BV, Inglenook (formerly Heublein), Christian Brothers, Almaden (formerly National Distillers)*
Seagrams — *Sterling*
Moët-Hennessy — *Domaine Chandon, Simi*
Suntory — *Chateau St. Jean*
Tattinger — *Domaine Caraleros*
Racke USA — *Buena Vista*

## Joint Ventures — "Eurowines"

The interest of Baron Philippe de Rothschild in Napa Valley is a tribute to Robert Mondavi's vision and hard work as both a winery founder and a spokesman for California. Their superlative Opus One project becomes even more meaningful when one recalls that the Baron had supposedly said in earlier days, "California wines are like Coca-Cola — they all taste the same." Other Europeans in California are DuBoeuf, Torres, Remy Martin, and Moueix from Chateau Petrus.

# A SAMPLING OF THE MOST SUCCESSFUL "BOUTIQUE WINERIES"

| WINERY NAME | AREA & DATE OF FOUNDING | EXEMPLARY WINES |
|---|---|---|
| Acacia | Napa, 1979 | Pinot Noir, Chardonnay |
| Alexander Valley Vineyards | Sonoma, 1963 | Chardonnay, Riesling |
| Arrowood | Sonoma, 1987 | Chardonnay, Cabernet Sauvignon |
| Bonny Doon | Santa Cruz, 1983 | Vin Gris, Cigar Volant |
| Byron Cellars | Central Coast, 1984 | Chardonnay |
| Burgess | Napa, 1972 | Cabernet Sauvignon |
| Cain Cellars | Napa, 1981 | Sauvignon Blanc |
| Cakebread | Napa, 1973 | Cabernet Sauvignon |
| Calera | Hollister, 1975 | Chardonnay, Pinot Noir |
| Callaway | Riverside, 1974 | Chardonnay "Calla-Lees" Chenin Blanc |
| Carneros Creek | Napa, 1972 | Chardonnay, Pinot Noir |
| Caymus | Napa, 1972 | Cabernet Sauvignon |
| Chalone | Monterey, 1960 | Chardonnay, Pinot Noir |
| Chappellet | Napa, 1969 | Cabernet, Chardonnay |
| Chateau Montelena | Napa, 1972 | Cabernet, Chardonnay |
| Chateau St. Jean | Sonoma, 1973 | Chardonnay, Sauvignon Blanc |
| Clos du Bois | Sonoma, 1976 | Riesling, Gewürztraminer |
| Clos Pegase | Sonoma, 1980 | Chardonnay, Cabernet Sauvignon |
| Clos du Val | Napa, 1973 | Cabernet, Chardonnay |
| Conn Creek | Napa, 1974 | Cabernet |
| Concannon | Livermore, 1883 | Assemblage, Petite Sirah |
| Diamond Creek | Napa, 1972 | Cabernet |
| Dry Creek | Sonoma, 1972 | Sauvignon Blanc |
| Duckhorn | Napa, 1976 | Merlot, Cabernet, Chardonnay |
| Dunn Vineyards | Napa, 1982 | Cabernet |
| Far Niente | Napa, 1885 | Chardonnay |
| Ferrari-Carano | Sonoma, 1981 | Chardonnay, Merlot |
| Folie A Deux | Napa, 1981 | Dry Chenin Blanc |
| Firestone | Santa Barbara, 1974 | Chardonnay, Riesling, Pinot Noir |
| Freemark Abbey | Napa, 1967 | Riesling, Chardonnay |
| Grgich Hills | Napa, 1977 | Chardonnay, Johannisberg Riesling |
| Gundlach-Bundschu | Sonoma (reopened) 1973 | Cabernet |
| William Hill | Napa, 1976 | Cabernet, Chardonnay |

| WINERY NAME | AREA & DATE OF FOUNDING | EXEMPLARY WINES |
|---|---|---|
| Johnson Turnbull | Napa, 1977 | Cabernet Sauvignon |
| Jordan | Sonoma, 1976 | Cabernet, Chardonnay |
| Kalin Cellars | Novato, 1977 | Pinot Noir, Chardonnay |
| Karly | Amador, 1979 | Zinfandel, Fume Blanc |
| Robert Keenan | Napa, 1977 | Merlot, Chardonnay |
| Kenwood Vineyards | Sonoma, 1970 | Zinfandel, Chardonnay |
| LaCrema | Sonoma, 1979 | Sauvignon Blanc, Pinot Noir |
| Mantanzas Creek | Sonoma, 1978 | Merlot, Pinot Noir |
| Meridan | Santa Barbara, 1988 | Chardonnay |
| J. W. Morris | Alameda, 1975 | Ports |
| Mount Veeder | Napa, 1972 | Cabernet, Chenin Blanc |
| Newlan | Napa, 1981 | Johannisberg Riesling |
| Newton | Napa, 1978 | Merlot, Chardonnay |
| Niebaum-Coppola | Napa, 1978 | "Rubicon" |
| Robert Pepi | Napa, 1981 | Sauvignon Blanc |
| Phelps | Napa, 1973 | Cabernet, Chardonnay, "Insignia" |
| Quady | Madera, 1977 | Ports, "Essencia", "Elysium" |
| Ridge | Santa Clara, 1962 | Zinfandel, Cabernet "Montebello" |
| St. Clement | Napa, 1975 | Chardonnay, Cabernet |
| Silver Oak | Napa, 1972 | Cabernet |
| Sonoma-Cutrer | Sonoma, 1981 | Chardonnay |
| Stag's Leap Vineyard | Napa, 1972 | Petite Sirah, Cabernet |
| Stag's Leap Wine Cellars | Napa, 1972 | Cabernet, Chardonnay |
| Steltzner Vineyards | Napa, 1983 | Cabernet Sauvignon, Chardonnay |
| Robert Stemmler | Sonoma, 1977 | Pinot Noir |
| Stonegate | Napa, 1973 | Sauvignon Blanc, Merlot |
| Trefethen | Napa, 1973 | Cabernet, "Eshcol" |
| Vichon | Napa, 1980 | Cabernet Sauvignon, Chevrignon |
| Woodbury | Marin, 1979 | Ports |
| ZD Wines | Napa, 1969 | Chardonnay, Pinot Noir |

## Giants Changing Directions

With Gallo in the lead, the movement has been toward finer, lighter table wines that embellish good foods. There has been a general upgrading toward varietal wines. High tech data, such as PH, brix, total acidity, time in wood, and fermentation temperature, is often given on informative back labels. This California approach or mentality has caused a greater awareness worldwide to the basic components of wine. Technical information has become a big part of fine wine marketing. "New American Cooking," as exemplified in the restaurants of Larry Forgione, Jeremiah Tower, and Wolfgang Puck among others, has propelled U.S. food and wine into the very forefront of international cuisine.

# WHERE DO WE GO FROM HERE?

Surely the stage is set for a bright future. Perhaps a "platinum" age is at hand. But there is the shadow of neo-prohibitionists who, under pseudo-therapeutic and utopian society flags, lead the charge against wine and spirits in general. Their successful "sulfight" has put wind in their sails; along with the placement of back labels on all alcohol-bearing products indicating a danger to the health of pregnant women and their fetuses.

We advocate moderate consumption of wine and strict punishments for those who do not exercise control. A logical approach to alcohol as a food item will enable Americans to understand more fully the pleasures and limitations of wine. We believe and hope that wine will become a normal part of our diet, as it has been for over 6,000 years throughout the history of humankind.

# CLASSIFYING U.S. WINES

**Generic Names.** These are usually average quality blends of several commercial grape varieties named for famous European wine areas. Generic names are something like Finnish or Austrian Swiss cheese, broad terms depicting something pedestrian and unauthentic. We recognize the historical, post-Prohibition impor-

tance of these names, but applaud those wineries that use terms like Table Red or Napa White rather than Burgundy or Chablis. We are not trying to denigrate generic wines. In fact, certain ones, like Beaulieu Vineyard Burgundy, Chablis, and Special Burgundy, are downright superlative. We feel however, that these names are outdated and that California wines can stand on their own today without European crutches.

| RED | WHITE |
|---|---|
| Burgundy | Chablis |
| Chianti | Sauterne (no final"s") |
| Claret | Rhine |

| SPARKLING | FORTIFIED |
|---|---|
| Champagne | Ports |
| Sparkling Burgundy | Sherries |

**Varietal Names.** If 75% or more of one particular variety is used, the wine may then be labeled under the dominant grape's name. Most of the best U.S. wines are varietally named. A few examples are:

| RED | WHITE |
|---|---|
| Pinot Noir | Chardonnay |
| Merlot | Chenin Blanc |
| Barbera | Sauvignon (Fume) Blanc |
| Zinfandel | Seyval Blanc |
| Baco Noir | |
| Cabernet Sauvignon | ROSE |

| SPARKLING | ROSE |
|---|---|
| | Grenache Rose |
| | Gamay Rose |
| Champagne de Chardonnay | |

Often a vineyard designation or a special quality term is added to the varietal wines, such as Heitz Martha's Vineyard Cabernet Sauvignon, Inglenook "Cask" Cabernet Sauvignon, or Beaulieu Vineyard Private Reserve Cabernet Sauvignon.

**Proprietary Names.** These are trademark names associated with a single winery.

**RED**

Phelps Insignia
Opus One
C.K. Mondavi Fortissimo
Carlo Rossi Paisano
Dominus
Taylor Lake Country Red

**WHITE**

Colony Rhineskeller
Callaway "Sweet Nancy"
Freemark Abbey Edelwein
C.K. Mondavi Bravissimo
Ben-Marl Springwine

**ROSE (or BLUSH)**

Vose Zinblanca
Sebastiani Eye of the Swan

**SPARKLING**

Van der Kamp Midnight
Cuvee

## "POP" WINES

Alongside the traditional, easy-to-classify sparkling, fortified, aromatized, and table California wines, there has always been a stream of fun potables, which may well have been our own port of embarkation into the more serious sea of wine. The Bali Hai, Boone's Farm, and Annie Green Springs of a generation ago have given way to the wine coolers of today. These light, fruit-flavored, punch-style wines attract the same audiences as do the Italian Lambrusco and Spanish Sangria. Perhaps these attractive, festive wine products will motivate people to try basic Beaujolais, Soave, and the like, which may lead them, in turn, to more serious growths.

Potent, pint-sized, fortified, inexpensive "pocket" wines, such as Night Train, Wild Irish Rose, and Thunderbird, should be approached with extreme caution. Rather than embark on a complete tirade, let us simply say that if such wines were to disappear completely, we would never miss them.

## "Make Me Blush"

A fairly recent phenomenon is the success of blush wines. They have been around for quite some time, known as White Zinfandel or Blanc de Noirs. They are salmon- to topaz-colored wines made from red grapes, more often than not with a touch of residual sugar. Sutter Home was the popularizer of this genre. We find delicate, floral, tasty blushes from Beringer, Robert Mondavi, and Bel Arbes, produced by the Fetzer Winery.

The irony is that there have always been wonderful varietal roses from California, like Robert Mondavi's Gamay Rose, Heitz's Grignolino Rose, or Washington's Chateau Ste. Michelle Grenache Rose. The category did not attain popularity until the term blush was coined. It seems no one wants to order rose; it's what everyone's grandmother used to drink. But the fine Tavel and Provencal roses of France and Italian rose from Apulia, Sicily, and Campania are well worth searching for. They combine the complexity and size of a red with the finesse, delicacy, and chillability of a white.

Most blushes are made from Zinfandel. You will find some that are based on Barbera, Pinot Noir, or Cabernet Sauvignon. The future of this category seems secure now that titanic Gallo has issued a limited release called Blush Chablis. Gallo avoided the plunge into "light wines" a few years ago; they do not usually make mistakes. Their direction recently has been toward coolers and varietals, and now the blush.

### A Movement Toward Varietals

One happy theme in the California story is the trend toward varietal wines. Americans are drinking better and replacing Burgundy and Chablis with moderately priced Cabernets, Chardonnays, and Sauvignon Blancs. A few of the wineries that have either caused or capitalized on this wave are Gallo, Glen Ellen, Fetzer, Rutherford Estate, and Domaine St. George. One outstanding newcomer is J. Wile and Sons from Napa.

## THE CALIFORNIA FRATERNITY

Although California wineries are fiercely competitive, we have found that great admiration and interdependence exist. Winemakers have become celebrated advocates more interested in convincing us that there is a lot of good wine coming from their area than in peddling their own particular wares. History has shown that they have borrowed money from each other and bought grapes from each other. Their children have studied together (many at Christian Brothers Schools and at UC Davis). They are a tightly knit group of creative individuals, whose products have gained their own respect before attaining critical acclaim and popularity.

A good number of today's successful wineries were originally founded by European immigrants, plying the skills learned in the old world. Gustafe Niebaum from Finland (Inglenook) and the Beringer brothers from Germany are just two examples. Frenchman Paul Masson married the daughter of countryman Charles Le Franc (Almaden). Pierre Mirassou and George de Latour (BV) set up premium wineries in Monterey and Napa.

No group has made greater impact on the American wine business than Italo-Americans. Countless farmers and winemakers moved to California to help provide their compatriots in the cities of the northeast with their mandatory glass of wine. Many of these wineries were financed through Giannini's Bank of America. A special category of generous red wines, called Barberone (Big Barbera), came into prominence, reminiscent of the mellow, hearty, homemade-style wines to which Italians were accustomed.

From the jug to Opus One, the honor roll must include Gallo, the Italian-Swiss group, Perelli-Minetti, Barengo, Giumarra, Papagni, Franzia, Cribari, Foppiano, Robert Mondavi, Louis Martini, Simi, Peter Mondavi (Charles Krug), Nichelini, Parducci, Pedrizetti, Pedroncelli, Sebastiani, Scotto (Villa Armando), Cattani, and Opici, among others.

The fraternity is a sorority as well. California winemakers include an impressive group of women. Perhaps foremost is Zelma Long of Simi Winery fame.

# VITICULTURAL AREAS

The Bureau of Alcohol, Tobacco and Firearms (BATF) has approved, or is in the process of approving, almost 100 delimited wine zones in the United States. Over half of these are in California. Some are large geographic units encompassing two to five states. A wine may not be labeled as "estate bottled" unless it is from a BATF-approved area. This appellation-type ruling went into effect on January 1, 1983. The wine business is so dynamic and little niches of viticultural microclimates are so common that the number is sure to grow. Today some 41 states have wineries. It is estimated that by the year 2000, wine will be produced in every state but Alaska.

## The Northeast

The cold winters of the Northeast have made it difficult to grow vinifera successfully on a wide scale. Hybrids dominate. Of interest in New England are Rhode Island's Sakonnet Winery, and Chicama Vineyards located on the island of Martha's Vineyard in Massachusetts.

New York State is the champion of the East, with vineyards on the north fork of Long Island, the Hudson Valley, Niagara County, Chautauqua (along Lake Erie), and the Finger Lakes. Look for Hargrave Vineyard from Long Island and Ben-Marl from the Hudson Valley. Chautauqua is more noted for its Concord grape juice, jam, and jelly (remember Dr. Welch) than for its wine. These durable native American grapes are the basis for many kosher wines as well as being the hub of the table-grape industry. The Concord is considered too "foxy" to be a successful, quality wine grape.

The Finger Lakes Region, especially around Hammondsport on Lake Keuka, has a rich tradition in viticulture. The area was once the center of the U.S. champagne business. Taylor and Great Western together were third in the world in bottle-fermented champagne production. Only Henkell of Germany and France's Moët et Chandon were grander. Add Gold Seal and you have a formidable trio of quality sparkling wine producers. The transfer method is primarily used here.

It was in the Finger Lakes that Dr. Konstantin Frank initiated wide-scale planting of vinifera vines. It was here that Widmer's outdoor-aged sherries came into prominence. Though the chic wine business has moved farther west, one can still find excellent table wine from Walter Taylor's Bully Hill, Willy Frank's Vinifera Vineyards, Glenora, and Heron Hill. You will find interesting Riesling and Chardonnay and discover superior Seyval Blanc, Chelois, and Baco Noir.

New Jersey, the Garden State, has more than a dozen wineries, among them Tewksbury, Kings Road, Three Sisters, Alba, Tamuzza, Gross, and Renault. Emphasis is on hybrids, but there are vinifera at Tewksbury. Alba's flavorful Raspberry Red is delicious. Tamuzza's Vidal Blanc is crisp and fresh, along with Kings Road's exceptional Riesling.

## The Southeast

By and large, this is Scuppernong, *Vitis muscadine*, territory. Muscadine is the only grape that grows in bunches like cherries rather than in clusters. Their berries are large, about an inch in diameter, and have been growing in the Southeast and Gulf states for centuries. One winery that has impressed us with their hybrids and vinifera is Meredyth. A chateau winery, Meredyth produces exceptional Seyval Blanc as well as a commendable Chardonnay.

## Middle America — Midwest and Southwest

The Ohio River was once called the "American Rhine," due to the great number of vineyard sites. Prohibition took its toll in this area. Only two monasteries were left to produce altar wine in the Midwest. Some eighteen states between the Rockies and the Appalachians do make wine today, but collectively this vast area accounts for less than three percent of American wine production. Leon Adams, in his *Wines of America*, tells that the Midwest is the world leader in wild-growing, vine species. The area has much potential.

Some wineries of importance are Meiers Wine Cellars of Cincinnati, whose Cream Sherry #44 is one of America's best. Tabor Hill Vineyard in Michigan grows Riesling and Chardonnay. President Ford used to serve Tabor Hill Michigan Baco Noir and Trebbiano at the White House. Illinois is third in the U.S.A. in wine production. The figure is deceiving. The kosher wines of Chi-

New Jersey Blush
Produced and Bottled by
Alba Vineyard
Finesville, New Jersey

This dry table wine is produced from premium grape varieties and reflects the style and quality Alba Vineyard is known for. The scene on this label, created by internationally renowned artist Dan Campanelli, depicts one of the many historic buildings in the rural villages surrounding the vineyards from which this wine is produced. We invite you to visit us and experience, first hand, the art of winemaking. Reproductions of this artwork are available through New York Graphics Society, Greenwich, Conn.

WHITE TABLE WINE          ALC. 11.5% BY VOL.          CONTAINS SULFITES

*Vinifera can grow in the Northeast, as exhibited by this New Jersey Blush from Alba Vineyard.*

cago-based Mogen David account for the lion's share of Illinois' statistics. We should point out that Count Agoston Haraszthy of Sonoma fame had a winery in Sauk City, Wisconsin before the gold fever of 1848 drove him west.

There is a renaissance in Missouri, the state which outproduced California in the nineteenth century. Arkansas and its Ozarks are home to Wiederkehr Wine Cellars, whose annual output of well over one million gallons makes it the largest winery in the Southwest. From South Texas to the High Plains, from the Hill Country to West Texas, the Lone Star State boasts of vinifera, muscadine, hybrid and native American vines. Val Verde Winery in Del Rio, founded by the Qualia family in 1883, still garners prizes today. Messina Hof Vineyards in Bryan produces respectable wines from Chenin Blanc and Villard, as well as deep reds and ports from the Lenoir vine under the direction of proprietor Paul Bonarrigo. Fall Creek Carnelian from the Hill Country is top flight. The class viticultural area of the state is Lubbock in the High Plains. Llano Estacado Winery established there in 1976, is already being touted as a world-class winery. Its Cabernets are the pride of Texas.

## The Pacific Northwest

The only serious rivals to Californian dominance are her neighbors to the north, Oregon, Washington, and Idaho. Microclimates in the Yakima and Willamette Valleys may provide a rosier future for the Pinot Noir, White Riesling (the authentic Johannisberg Riesling), even Chardonnay, which all like it a bit cooler than Napa and Sonoma.

### IDAHO

Winter temperatures of −20°F have not stopped the Potato State from catching grape fever. Ste. Chapelle Vineyards, founded in 1976 about 25 miles northwest of Boise, dedicates about half of its production to Johannisberg Riesling, which has turned heads since first winning a bronze medal in 1977 at the Enological Society of the Pacific Northwest competition. It is surprisingly good and constantly sells out at lofty prices.

### OREGON

The Umpqua Valley is home to Hillcrest Vineyard Winery, which produces excellent White Riesling and noteworthy Chardonnay, Gewürztraminer, Semillon, Fume Blanc, as well as red Zinfandel and Pinot Noir. Most of the major wineries of the Umpqua and Willamette regions are less than a generation old, and more likely than not the founders were emigres from California. This is true of Richard Sommer of Hillcrest, Charles Coury of Charles Coury Vineyards, Richard Erath of Knudsen-Erath, just to name a few. In many cases, the emigration was preceded by a wine studies program at U.C. Davis.

Willamette Valley boasts Elk Cove Vineyards (Chardonnay), Eyrie Vineyard (Pinot Noir and Pinot Gris), Knudsen-Erath (Chardonnay, Pinot Noir), Sokol Blosser Vineyards (Sauvignon Blanc), Tualatin (White Riesling), and Adelsheim (Pinot Noir, Chardonnay). Through a network of brokers and distributors, these northern boutiques have found their way onto the shelves of fine wineshops nationwide. Salem, the capitol of Oregon, houses Honeywood Winery, the state's largest, which makes wine from Concord and White Riesling, as well as from local berries and currants.

### WASHINGTON

Washington has two BATF zones, the Columbia Basin, and the Yakima Valley where Preston Wine Cellars, Associated Vintners, and Hinzerling Vineyards are located. It may be difficult to find their wines at your favorite wineshop, but they do a superb job

The thin-skinned Chardonnay of French Burgundy acclaim grows well in the Pacific Northwest. This Chardonnay from Columbia Crest is not only excellent, but offers a great value for the consumer.

98

with Gewürztraminer, Chardonnay, Fume Blanc, and White Riesling.

You will probably be able to find the wines of Chateau Ste. Michelle, which ranks as highly as Robert Mondavi and Beringer in premium varietal sales. Grapes are trucked in from Yakima some 200 miles away to an ultra-modern facility in Woodinville, 15 miles east of Seattle. At Chateau Ste. Michelle, a complete line of table wines is produced. Most highly regarded are Johannisberger Riesling, Grenache Rose, Semillon, Fume Blanc, and Cabernet Sauvignon. A *Methode Champenoise* Blanc de Noir is exquisite indeed.

An exceptional "ice wine" was released a few years ago. That particular winter was extremely harsh, causing a loss of thousands of vines. Subsequent replanting should enable Chateau Ste. Michelle to surpass one million cases in total sales in the near future.

The main problems facing the Yakima and Columbia Basin vigneron have been faced and defeated. Irrigation has helped in this semi-arid area, which has an annual rainfall of only six to

**Chateau Ste. Michelle**

WASHINGTON

JOHANNISBERG RIESLING

1987

*Washington's most important winery, Chateau Ste. Michelle, is quite versatile. In addition to this state-of-the-art "J.R.," Chateau Ste. Michelle makes dry reds, other dry whites, a delicious Grenache Rose and a Champagne method sparkler.*

seven and a half inches. Cold winters are balanced by ample sunshine, which provides for a long, bright, frost-free growing period. Washington already ranks third in grape production, behind New York and California. If a significant part of the estimated 300,000 acres of potential vineyard area is planted, it is conceivable for Washington to surpass New York. The futures of Washington and New York are in the hands of market conditions and consumer preference.

GROWN, PRODUCED & BOTTLED BY ADELSHEIM VINEYARD NEWBERG, OREGON, USA, BW-OR-71, ALCOHOL 12½% BY VOL.

*Riesling and Pinot Noir have done well in Oregon. The thin-skinned Chardonnay likes the hills of Yamhill County. Adelsheim Chardonnay is grown, produced, and estate-bottled at the winery.*

## California:
## A Paradise for Vines

Within the borders of California are areas that provide growing conditions similar to those found in every other growing region in the world. Sections of Napa, Sonoma, and Mendocino have climates comparable to the Rhine, Bordeaux, Piedmont, or Burgundy. The Central and San Joaquin Valleys are reminiscent of France's Midi, Southern Italy, Jerez, and North Africa. And in each area, generally speaking, the vine flourishes and requires less of an effort than their European cousins. California is indeed a paradise for vines.

While the European vineyard owner usually produces two or three different wines, it is not uncommon for the California vigneron to market an assortment of twenty or more, from sparkling to table to dessert varieties. Professors Winkler and Amerine developed a method of measuring the climate of a geographic area. The heat summation chart displays the variety of climates available to California winemakers.

# HEAT SUMMATION CHART

| | NUMBER OF DEGREE DAYS | CALIFORNIA | OTHER AREAS |
|---|---|---|---|
| (COLD) | REGION I - Less than 2,500 Degree Days | Lake County, Carneros | Rhein, Mosel, Champagne, Pacific Northwest |
| | REGION II - 2,501 to 3,000 Degree Days | Much of Napa and Sonoma | Burgundy, Bordeaux, Piedmont |
| | REGION III - 3,001 to 3,500 Degree Days | Livermore, Calistoga | Rhone, Tuscany |
| | REGION IV - 3,501 to 4,000 Degree Days | Lodi, Modesto | Southern Italy, Midi |
| (HOT) | REGION V - 4,001 Degree Days or More | Southern San Joaquin Valley, Madera, Bakersfield, Fresno | North Africa, Jerez |

A Degree Day is 1 degree above 50° F in average daily temperature during the growing season. For example, if the average temperature of a day is 65° F, you have 15 Degree Days. An average daily temperature of 42° F gives you −8 degree Days.

Each region has its own recommended grape varieties. For example:

| | |
|---|---|
| Region I: | Riesling, Pinot Noir, Chardonnay |
| Region II: | Those of Region I plus Cabernet Sauvignon, Zinfandel, Fume Blanc, Nebbiolo |
| Region III: | Barbera, Semillon, Muscat, Zinfandel |
| Region IV: | French Colombard, Ruby Cabernet, Emerald Riesling, Zinfandel |
| Region V: | Port and sherry types, Alicante, Zinfandel |

100

## CALIFORNIA'S VINES

One of the accomplishments of the California wine movement has been to make drinkers more conscious of the grape varieties that form wines. Some wineries specialize in one or two varietals; others offer a veritable panoply of products. Below is a listing of some of California's important vines and a few of their most renowned exponents.

**Cabernet Sauvignon.** The noble red grape of Bordeaux thrives statewide, but especially in Napa. Over 200 wineries in the U.S. produce Cabernet Sauvignon.

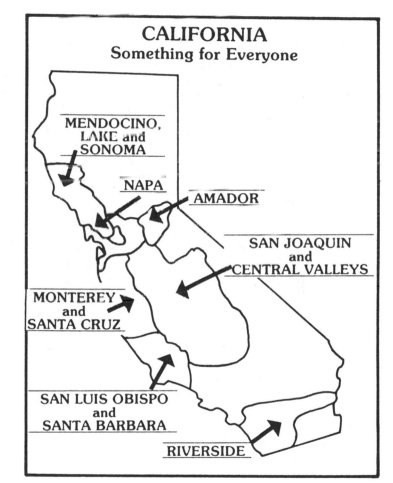

*Of California's 58 counties, 24 are principal wine-producing counties.*

| | |
|---|---|
| Ridge | Glen Ellen |
| Silver Oaks | Christian Brothers |
| Robert Mondavi | Burgess |
| Beaulieu Vineyard | Cakebread |
| Stag's Leap Wine Cellars | Caymus |
| Beringer | Freemark Abbey |
| Louis Martini | Gallo |
| Sterling | Mount Eden |
| Clos du Val | Inglenook Estate |
| Jordan | Mayacamas |
| Heitz | Phelps |
| Raymond | Simi |
| Sonoma | Villa Mt. Eden |
| Chateau Montelena | Chappellet |
| Kalin Cellars | Chateau St. Jean |
| Newton | Buena Vista |
| Clos Pegase | Arrowood |
| Flora Springs | Johnson Turnbull |
| Groth | Kendall-Jackson |

Some wineries make two or three different Cabernets; for example, Beaulieu Vineyard produces Rutherford and Beautour (moderately priced) as well as Private Reserve Georges de Latour (limited, top of the line, expensive).

**Chardonnay.** This white from Burgundy's Cote d'Or usually yields full, rich, buttery, aristocratic wines. It loves the cool hills of Sonoma and Carneros, as well as Oregon and New York State. About 200 wineries in the United States offer a Chardonnay. It is

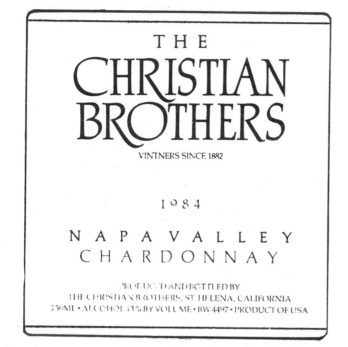

One of Napa's most important wineries, The Christian Brothers, has been producing fine wines and brandies for over a century. Their Napa Valley Chardonnay does not carry the hefty price tag of other well-made Chardonnays. Exceptional value.

Beringer is one of the largest landholders in the Napa Valley. "Produced and bottled by" indicates that Beringer is involved in at least 75% of the grape growing, crushing, and aging of the wine.

Make no mistake about it! Rodney Strong, of Sonoma Vineyard fame, grows the grapes at the Chalk Hill Vineyard, produces, ages, and bottles the wine. We approve this clear labeling. We also approve of the magnificent wine.

Bill Bonetti's Sonoma-Cutrer Chardonnays are red hot—and for good reason! He takes extraordinary steps to keep his grapes and wines fresh, with no hint of oxidation. This wine is from the Les Pierres Vineyard.

**1985**
# RUTHERFORD
E S T A T E

*Chardonnay*

N A P A   V A L L E Y

*The Rutherford Estate Chardonnay is a reflection of the new camp-style of Chardonnay. Fresh, crisp, well-balanced, dry, with good varietal character, and easy on the pocketbook.*

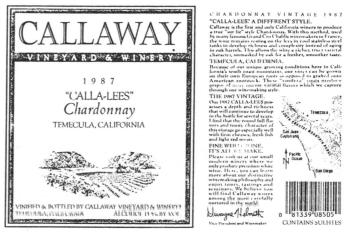

# CALLAWAY
V I N E Y A R D   &   W I N E R Y

1987
"CALLA-LEES"
*Chardonnay*
TEMECULA, CALIFORNIA

VINIFIED & BOTTLED BY CALLAWAY VINEYARD & WINERY
TEMECULA, CALIFORNIA     ALCOHOL 13 % BY VOL

CHARDONNAY VINTAGE 1987
"CALLA-LEES" A DIFFERENT STYLE.
Callaway is the first and only California winery to produce a true "sur lie" style Chardonnay. With this method, used by many famous Grand Cru Chablis winemakers in France, the wine remains resting on the lees in cool stainless steel tanks to develop richness and complexity instead of aging in oak barrels. This allows the wine a richer, truer varietal character, unmasked by oak for a fresher, smoother taste.
TEMECULA, CALIFORNIA.
Because of our unique growing conditions here in California's south coast mountains, our vines can be grown on their own European roots as opposed to grafted onto American rootstock. These "vinifera" roots produce grapes of more intense varietal flavors which we capture through our winemaking style.
THE 1987 VINTAGE.
Our 1987 CALLA-LEES possesses a depth and richness that will continue to develop in the bottle for several years. I find that the round full flavors and toasty character of this vintage go especially well with firm cheeses, fresh fish and light red meats.
FINE WINE, IT'S ALL WE MAKE.
Please visit us at our small modern winery where we only produce premium white wine. Here, you can learn more about our distinctive winemaking philosophy and enjoy tours, tastings and seminars. We believe you will find Callaway wines among the most carefully nurtured in the world.
Dwayne Helmuth
Vice President and Winemaker

CONTAINS SULFITES

0  81339 08505

*Callaway is the first and only California winery to produce a true "sur lie" style Chardonnay. With this method, used by many famous Grand Cru winemakers in France, the wine remains resting on the lees in cool stainless steel tanks to develop richness and complexity instead of aging in oak barrels. This allows the wine a richer truer varietal character, unmasked by oak, for a fresher, smoother taste.*

VINEYARDS ESTABLISHED CIRCA 1868
# GLEN·ELLEN

1985
CALIFORNIA
CHARDONNAY
PROPRIETOR'S RESERVE

VINTED & BOTTLED BY GLEN ELLEN WINERY &
VINEYARDS, GLEN ELLEN, SONOMA VALLEY, CA
B.W. 4911 ALCOHOL 12.3% BY VOLUME

*This reasonably priced Chardonnay is very popular. The grapes come entirely from California. With vineyards established over 100 years ago in cool Sonoma County, Glen Ellen has experienced a renaissance under the direction of Bruno Benzinger.*

*Buena Vista*
PRIVATE RESERVE

HARASZTHY

CARNEROS

Cabernet Sauvignon

ESTATE GROWN AND BOTTLED BY
BUENA VISTA WINERY, CARNEROS, SONOMA, CALIFORNIA, USA
Alcohol 13.0% by Volume

*This "Private Reserve" Estate bottled Cabernet is produced in the Carneros Region of Sonoma. This is an excellent wine from the Buena Vista Winery founded in the 1850s by Agoston Haraszthy, the father of California viticulture.*

*Simi produces an elegant Chardonnay. They inform us that most of the grapes (57%) are from Mendocino, the balance (43%) from Sonoma. This formerly family-owned winery has been beautifully resurrected and redirected by the Moët-Hennessy Corporation.*

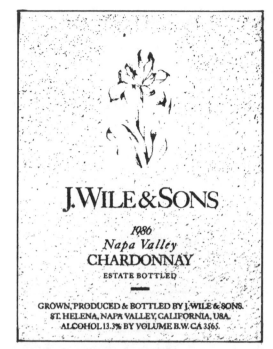

*This new estate-bottled Chardonnay is sure to enjoy success. It is full, dry, delicious, and entirely grown, produced, and bottled under the direction of the Wile family, one of America's most important wine and spirits families, and champions of wine education.*

such a popular grape that we would even presume that a Chardonnay from Mars would gain some degree of popularity.

| | |
|---|---|
| Callaway | Simi |
| Glen Ellen | Rodney Strong |
| Christian Brothers | Acacia |
| Beringer | Far Niente |
| Chateau Montelena | Firestone |
| Lambert Bridge | Hanzell |
| Freemark Abbey | Keenan |
| Inglenook Estate | Mayacamas |
| Long Vineyards | Phelps |
| Robert Mondavi | Raymond |
| Martin Ray | Sonoma Vineyards |
| St. Clement | Stony Hill |
| Sterling | Chateau St. Jean |

| | |
|---|---|
| David Bruce | Sonoma-Cutrer |
| Burgess | Chalone |
| Cakebread | Kalin Cellars |
| Arrowood | Clos Pegase |
| Newton | Buena Vista |
| Meridian | Grgich Hills |
| Flora Springs | Gaver Estate |
| Villa Zapu | |

**Pinot Noir.** Although this Burgundian red varietal has been labeled a disappointment in California, there are many wonderful examples available. The disappointment springs from the fact that California Pinot Noir does not taste like Le Chambertin, Musigny, or Romanee-Conti. But what does? Pinot Noir loves Oregon, Carneros, Napa, and Sonoma.

*The Sauvignon Blanc produces subtle wines with herbaceous, grassy nuances. This reserve wine from Gallo keeps all of the grapes' divergent overtones under control. You get true varietal character with a pleasant balance.*

| | |
|---|---|
| Chalone | Beaulieu Vineyard |
| Hanzell | David Bruce |
| Acacia | Carneros Creek |
| Firestone | Mt. Eden Vineyards |
| Robert Mondavi | Santa Cruz Mountain Vineyard |
| Robert Stemmler | La Crema |
| Kalin Cellars | Buena Vista |
| Calera | |

About 150 U.S. wineries produce a Pinot Noir.

**Sauvignon (Fume) Blanc.** This transplant from the Loire and Bordeaux produces floral, grassy, herbaceous, complex dry whites. A generation ago, it was used as a blending grape for sweeter wines. Robert Mondavi's use of the term Fume Blanc was of great influence in popularizing this vine. About 75 U.S. wineries, most of them in California, offer Sauvignon Blanc. It especially thrives in Napa.

| | |
|---|---|
| Beringer | Robert Mondavi |
| Beaulieu Vineyard | Dry Creek |
| Phelps | Cakebread |
| Chateau St. Jean | Parducci |
| Gallo | Newton |
| Robert Pepi | Preston |
| Buena Vista | McDowell |
| La Crema | |

**Johannisberg (White) Riesling.** This white from Alsace, the Mosel, and the Rhine yields dry, floral wines in California.

| | |
|---|---|
| Chappellet | Clos du Bois |
| Chateau St. Jean | Felton-Empire |
| Firestone | Freemark Abbey (Edelwein) |
| Grgich Hills | Jekel |
| Charles Krug | Robert Mondavi |
| Monterey Vineyard | Rutherford Hill |
| Stony Hill | Veedercrest |
| Wente Bros. | |

**Petite Sirah.** Deeply colored and primarily a blending grape (it is the French Duriff, not the famous Rhone Syrah), it is grown mostly in the hotter areas. About 75 wineries produce a Petite Sirah, some of which are remarkable.

| | |
|---|---|
| Concannon | Ridge |
| Fetzer | Freemark Abbey |
| Parducci | Pedrizetti |
| Stag's Leap Vineyard | Phelps |

*Firestone is responsible for one of the finest expressions of the authentic Johannisberg Riesling in the U.S. Fragrant, supple, and luxuriant, this award-winning wine is one that we are sure you will not "tire" of (forgive us). You should write the Firestone Winery for their beautifully written pamphlet, "The Praises of Wine."*

*Some people say that Sauvignon Blanc wines gained respect, credibility, and popularity in California when Robert Mondavi named his version Fume Blanc. This the grape responsible for White Bordeaux, Sancerre, and Pouilly-Fume in France.*

**Chenin Blanc.** This fruity white of Vouvray, Loire fame is popular in the U.S.A. About 100 wineries offer the grape or blend it into their generic whites. Much of it is planted in the Central Valley.

| | |
|---|---|
| Almaden | Callaway |
| Burgess | Chappellet |
| Christian Bros. | Gallo |
| Dry Creek | Kenwood |
| Grand Cru | Charles Krug |
| Mirassou | Parducci |

**Barbera.** Dry, hearty reds are made from this Piedmontese transplant. The name "Barberone," or "Big Barbera," was coined to describe the generous, homemade-style reds sought by Italo-Americans. Today over 30 wineries produce Barbera, much of it in the Central Valley. In the hands of a fine winemaker, Barbera can be a long-lived, elegant wine.

| | |
|---|---|
| Sebastiani | Louis Martini |

**Gewürztraminer.** This floral white from the Italian Tyrol village of Tramino is renowned in Alsace and Germany. Almost 100 wineries, including some east of the Rockies and in the Pacific Northwest, offer this spicy white. It may be dry, off-dry, or late harvest, even pink. It has a memorable, incomparable fragrance.

| | |
|---|---|
| Almaden | Fetzer |
| Clos du Bois | Firestone |
| Gallo | Grand Cru |
| Hacienda | Louis Martini |
| Sebastiani | Simi |
| Chateau St. John | Phelps |

**Merlot.** The star from Pomerol has achieved high marks in the U.S. About 50 wineries make a Merlot; 80% hail from California.

| | |
|---|---|
| Inglenook Estate | Clos du Val |
| Sterling | Winery Lake |
| Veedercrest | Duckhorn |
| Newton | Chateau Souverein |
| Buena Vista | Robert Keenan |

**Zinfandel.** This versatile, ubiquitous "All-American" orphan varietal is linked to the Southern Italian Primitivo di Gioia vine. It can be made in a rainbow of styles. This "mystery grape" is the most widely planted in California among red vinifera. From sparkling to blush, Nouveau to Late Harvest, Zinfandel boasts almost 200 producers. Some wineries specialize in it. We are listing only those who we feel have elevated the "Zin" to an art form.

Ridge
Carneros Creek
Burgess
Cuvaison
Dry Creek
Lytton Springs
Sausal
Sutter Home (Amador)
Amador Foothills
Storybook

Fetzer
Monterey Peninsula
Clos du Val
Delinger
Kenwood
Montevina
Sebastiani
Simi
Nalle
Santino

There are well over 100 popular grape varieties in California. It is impossible to do justice to them all. But we would like to mention just a few of the specialties that are exquisite and memorable.

Inglenook Estate Charbono
Chalone Pinot Blanc
Angelo Papagni Alicante-Bouschet
Heitz Grignolino
Paul Masson Emerald Dry (Emerald Riesling)
Seghesio Chianti Station (Sangiovese)
Bonny Doon
Robert Mondavi Moscato D'Oro
Robert Pepi Sangiovese

1989
CHARDONNAY

CALIFORNIA

ALC. 12.0% BY VOL.    1.5 LITERS

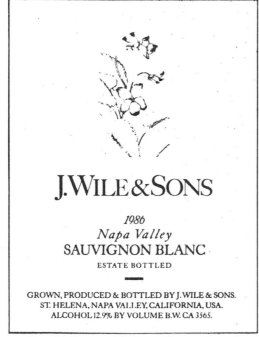

1986
*Napa Valley*
SAUVIGNON BLANC
ESTATE BOTTLED

GROWN, PRODUCED & BOTTLED BY J. WILE & SONS.
ST. HELENA, NAPA VALLEY, CALIFORNIA, USA.
ALCOHOL 12.9% BY VOLUME B.W. CA 3565.

*When you see Napa Valley on a label, it indicates that at least 75% of the grapes are from that area. This estate-bottled wine is made of grapes entirely from Napa. Sauvignon Blanc may be enjoyed young or aged for a year or two.*

*The Blossom Hill Collection of fine wines is a new label on the scene of reasonably priced California varietals. This Chardonnay exhibits all the natural flavor and characteristics one looks for in the category of white wine.*

## THE CALIFORNIA APPROACH

The California approach to wine goes beyond "try it with meat" or "smells great and tastes even better." It has awakened in the oenophile a desire to know more about the components of wine—how wine is made and a detailed analysis of a wine's characteristics.

A wine's components should be in harmony and balance. Recall that making fine wine is an art form. It starts with good grape varieties that grow well because of the location of the vineyard, the soil, and climate. The winemaker is there to guide every step of the way. California has popularized the mechanical, component approach to wine tasting, which was developed in Europe and has been followed for centuries by professionals there and elsewhere. One organization that has worked very hard to educate the trade and the oenophile to this approach is the Robert Mondavi Winery. We tip our glasses to them.

Here we see an estate-grown Cabernet Sauvignon from the popular Sonoma Winery, Glen Ellen. California Cabernets are often more intense than their Bordeaux counterparts.

*Gallo is the largest winery in the world. The family still find the time and has the interest to produce limited releases of exquisite wines at reasonable prices. The grapes for this Cabernet Sauvignon hail from Sonoma County.*

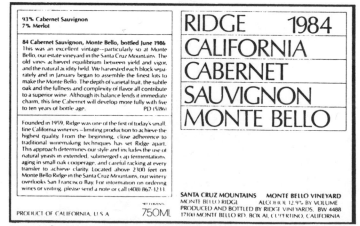

*Ridge was one of the first wineries to feature the informative wraparound label. Ridge specialized in single-vineyard wines, such as York Creek Petite Sirah or this Cabernet Sauvignon from the Monte Bello Vineyard area. Ridge is best known for its Zinfandels.*

*Many of California's fine winemakers have not only made a reputation, but are also heading up their own wineries. Mr. Arrowood, of Chateau St. Jean fame, is now producing high quality wines under his own Arrowood Estate label.*

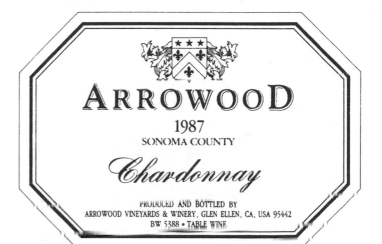

## ARROWOOD
1987
SONOMA COUNTY

*Chardonnay*

PRODUCED AND BOTTLED BY
ARROWOOD VINEYARDS & WINERY, GLEN ELLEN, CA, USA 95442
BW 5388 • TABLE WINE

# PAT PAULSEN
V I N E Y A R D S

*1986*

*Refrigerator White*

S O N O M A   C O U N T Y

(Dry White Table Wine)

PRODUCED AND BOTTLED BY PAT PAULSEN VINEYARDS
B.W.4966 CLOVERDALE, CA   ALCOHOL 13.0% BY VOLUME

*This is a sophisticated, modern, classic jug wine. It would be a fine gift to give a friend, even a friend who likes opera. A man can give this wine to another man. He cannot give lingerie to a man. A woman can give lingerie to a woman friend but a man cannot do this. He cannot even give underwear to a pal. It looks funny. Sure there is no law against it and I suppose if a man wanted to give underwear to another man he could do it. He COULD JUST GO RIGHT AHEAD AND DO THAT. I would not do that. I do not want to look weird. I own a winery and am a Big Shot. I would give him Refrigerator White.*

*Pat Paulsen*

*After all, how could a "big shot" call a wine "Chablis"?*

## Inglenook.
NAPA · VALLEY

ESTATE BOTTLED
RESERVE CASK

1983
*Cabernet Sauvignon*
NAPA VALLEY

PRODUCED AND BOTTLED BY INGLENOOK NAPA VALLEY
RUTHERFORD CALIFORNIA USA BW

*In exceptional years the Inglenook Winery sets aside special lots of Cabernet Sauvignon, which they designate as Reserve Cask. These are among the most aristocratic and longest-lived in the U.S. The 1974 is legendary.*

Beaulieu Vineyard's (B.V.) winemaker Tomy Selfridge produces four different Cabernets. This one, B.V. Rutherford Cabernet Sauvignon, is elegant and rich. A moderately priced magnum, dubbed claret, and a reasonable fifth size called Beautour are less expensive. The prestigious Georges de Latour Private Reserve is more costly. All are estate bottled.

The future of good (not great) wine may be in cardboard casks, not in bottles. Wine actually stays fresher in these packages.

The vast experience of The Christian Brothers is reflected in this estate-bottled dry red wine. The premium landholder in Napa, CB's Cabernet Sauvignon is controlled completely from the vine to the barrel to the bottle by The Christian Brothers winemaker. The year 1984 was an exceptional vintage in the Napa Valley.

The most important "Euro-American" wine venture. Robert Mondavi and Baron Phillippe de Rothschild joined forces and resources to produce Opus One. We like the understated elegance of "A Napa Valley Red Table Wine."

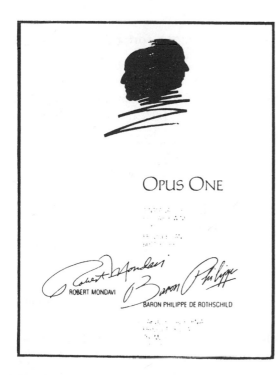

A mellow, generous blend created for the hearty tastes of Italo-Americans. The Opici family went to California to service the Italian community in New Jersey. The Mondavi's settled in Napa to make wine for their friends and customers in Minnesota.

*Oak Ridge Vineyards' "White Zinfandel" is one of the fine examples of the new "blush" category of wines. Pink in color, festive, full of fruit, and refreshing, this wine has just a hint of natural sweetness.*

# THE UNITED STATES IN REVIEW

- Despite its checkered wine history, the U.S.A. is one of the world's leading producers as well as a vital market for imported wines.

- Although wine is made in 41 states, California is the most important viticultural area in the U.S.

- U.S. wines can be divided into three groupings:

  1. Generic (named for a European Geographic Area, e.g., Burgundy)
  2. Varietal (named for a dominant grape, e.g., Chardonnay)
  3. Proprietary (a trademark, e.g., Phelps Insignia)

- The U.S. produces fortified, aromatized, sparkling and table wines.

- In the Northeastern states, Labrusca and hybrids grow well but vinifera does not due to the harsh winters.

- In California, European vinifera thrive.

- There is vintage variation for California's premium varietals.

- The U.S. produces ordinary jug wines and elegant, world-class wines. There is great variation from winery to winery.

- Premium viticultural zones in California are the Napa and Sonoma Valleys.

112

# SELF-EVALUATION

BEFORE READING ON, see if you have mastered the data set forth in the last few pages. Check the answer section at the back of the book for the correct answers. If you have not answered at least 70% of the questions below correctly, please reread the previous section.

## WINES OF THE UNITED STATES

| TRUE | FALSE | |
|------|-------|---|
| ———— | ———— | 1. In 1793 America's first commercial winery was formed. |
| ———— | ———— | 2. During Prohibition, only 50 wineries in two states survived. |
| ———— | ———— | 3. Philip Wagner pioneered the use of French-American hybrids in northeastern U.S.A. |
| ———— | ———— | 4. Dr. Konstantin Frank was the first man to cultivate vinifera grapes successfully and commercially in New York State. |
| ———— | ———— | 5. An example of *Vitis muscadine* is the Muscat grape that produces the French Muscadet. |
| ———— | ———— | 6. A "boutique" winery will usually produce more than 100,000 cases annually. |
| ———— | ———— | 7. Generic wines are named for famous European wine areas. |
| ———— | ———— | 8. In order to be labeled as a varietal, a wine must contain at least 65% of the dominant grape. |
| ———— | ———— | 9. Carlo Rossi Paisano is considered a generic wine. |
| ———— | ———— | 10. Joint ventures with European winemakers have taken place recently in California. |

# NOTES

# THE WINES OF FRANCE

## INTRODUCTION

France is truly one of the great nations of wine — its wines are constantly sought after by connoisseurs the world over. Simple proof of its greatness is the number of those who would attempt to duplicate what it seems that the poorest of soils and anything but favorable weather conditions accomplishes in its splendid wine regions. No other country seems to have the remarkable ability to produce such superb wines in the abundance and variety that it does.

France produces hundreds of individual wines — not one is an imitation of another. Its soils, variable as they are, are uniquely suited for great wines, for great wines are a result of great soils. Two wines made from the same grape variety in neighboring vineyards or villages will each have an individuality of its own, possessing what is a distinguishable quality that the riches and resources of that specific piece of soil impart to the wine.

Italy, Germany, California, Spain, and many other nations have excellent wine regions that produce great wines — but not French wines. For there is only one Corton-Charlemagne, Montrachet, Chambertin, or Romanee-Conti from Burgundy, or Chateau Lafite-Rothschild, Chateau Beychevelle, or Chateau Petrus from Bordeaux. For wine is soil — and soil is wine.

## History

Evidence of vines in French soil seem to go back to prehistory, with vineyards in the Rhone Valley and Burgundy probably fostered by the ancient Gauls, long before the Greeks arrived. But it was not until the arrival of the Roman Legions in the first century B.C. that the art of cultivating the vine and the knowledge of winemaking spread throughout Gaul. Wherever the Romans went, vineyards appeared to such an extent that they began to rival the vineyards of Italy.

The Gauls quickly became very able vinegrowers, so successful in fact that at the end of the first century the Emperor of Rome decreed that no more land was to be planted with vines and ordered scores of vineyards uprooted to protect the Roman viticulture. It was not until two centuries later that the right to plant and cultivate vines was returned.

By the fourth century, vines had been planted in the Rhone Valley, Burgundy, Bordeaux, and Champagne. Shortly thereafter the Roman Empire collapsed, and Christianity was soon embraced. As wine was always an integral part of the Mass, wherever the Church went it was necessary to have wine available. So the Church retained the vineyards, and the monks, particularly the Benedictine monks, studied and improved on the viticultural methods of the past and became the founders and producers of many of what are today France's most illustrious vineyards. By the Middle Ages wine had extended to all of the regions of France. With the ease of water transportation through the great river valleys, the wine trade began to flourish.

By the twelfth century, French wine was being exported to England, Flanders, and the Germanic countries. Shipped in casks, the wine was consumed quite young. It was not until the eighteenth century that the use of the bottle and cork were introduced to give wine the ability to age.

In the late 1800s the scourge of phylloxera devasted the vineyards, but was eventually brought under control by grafting French vines onto American roots that were immune to this pest. As a result, almost all of the vineyards of France had to be replanted, with many of the regions abandoning viticulture altogether.

## Regulation of Production

The shortages of wine that ensued soon encouraged artificial and fraudulent winemaking procedures, many using inferior varieties of grapes, opting for higher yields. The adulteration of wines became more and more widespread and the reputation of French wines began to suffer. To control this, the law of August 14th, 1889 enforced a legal definition of wine: "The result of a full or partial fermentation of fresh grapes or the juice of fresh grapes." Soon after, the *Service de la Repression des Fraudes* was instituted.

But the viticultural situation remained in turmoil, for previous laws did not make a clear enough distinction between ordinary wines and those exceptional wines from vineyards with traditions of quality that had been confirmed down through the centuries.

However, a former minister named Capus had been trying for years to promote the importance of the link between the quality and origin of a wine — or its originality. As a result of his efforts, on July 30th, 1935, the *Appellation d' Origine Controlee* (A.O.C.) laws were passed, which not only guarantee the place of origin of a wine, but also regulate the quality standards required throughout the process of producing the wine. At the same time the *Comite National des Appellations d' Origine des Vins et Eaux-de-Vie* was created to control and protect those laws, later becoming the *Institut National des Appellations d'Origine des Vins et Eaux-de-Vie* (I.N.A.O.).

## Guidelines of Control

The development of the Appellation Controlee system was a complex task. In addition to governing various aspects of viticulture, the system also had to protect and respect each region's centuries-old traditions and pride in the distinct flavors, bouquets, and characteristics of its wines.

For these reasons, the I.N.A.O. set these broad guidelines of control, and established committees from each locale to regulate more specific points so that each law could be adapted to the region.

The general guidelines of the I.N.A.O. are:

**Areas of Production:** Regulates soil types (compositions deemed fit for production) and establishes delimited areas (permitting only vineyards within these areas to use the region's names).

**Types of Grape Varieties Used:** Selects grape varieties that are best suited to the area. However, the same vine planted in different soils will produce grapes having totally different characteristics.

**Methods of Cultivation:** Closely regulates the types of pruning, fertilizing, and care given to the vine during its vineyard life for each area, to ensure quality and discourage over production.

**Methods of Vinification:** Strictly enforces winemaking procedures in each area, as they are largely responsible for the reputation of its wines and their distinctive characters.

## Categories of French Wines

French wines are divided into four categories:

1. **Vins de Table**

   Often sold under a brand name, these wines can be a blend of various wines produced in different regions and can vary in quality and character depending on the producer. The alcoholic content must not be less than 8.5% or more than 15%.

2. **Vins de Pays**

   These wines must be produced exclusively in regions whose name they bear. They must be made from approved grape varieties and their alcoholic content must not be less than 10% in Mediterranean areas and 9% or 9.5% in other areas. The characteristics and standards of these wines are analyzed through chemical and tasting tests.

3. **V.D.Q.S. (Vins Delimites de Qualite Superieur)**

   Strictly controlled and regulated by the I.N.A.O., V.D.Q.S. labels are granted only after successfully passing a taste test by an official commission. The conditions under which V.D.Q.S. wines can be produced are clearly defined and are as follows:

   - Areas of production
   - Grape varieties used
   - Minimum alcoholic content
   - Maximum yield per hectare
   - Methods of cultivation
   - Methods of vinification

4. **Appellation Controlee (A.O.C.) Wines**

   The laws governing the production of A.O.C. wines cover the same general conditions as those for the V.D.Q.S.

wines but are stricter, with production zones defined more narrowly. As with the V.D.Q.S. wines, labels are granted only after successfully passing a taste test by an official commission.

## The Pursuit of Excellence

The French wine laws were designed to protect the reputation of its famous wine areas, and also to protect the consumer with the assurance that wines bottled under V.D.Q.S. labels or Appellation Controlee standards are guaranteed by law to be what the labels profess them to be.

France has been the hub, the barometer of the wine business, for centuries. There are three reasons for the special esteem given French wines:

1. **Insistence on Quality:** The French rate and classify their villages and wineries. Quality comes first.
2. **Variety:** Certain areas are regarded as the pinnacle in the production of almost every type of wine:
   sparkling wines—Champagne
   light, dry whites—Loire, Alsace
   full, dry whites—Burgundy
   elegant, dry reds—Bordeaux, Burgundy, Rhone
   sweet whites—Sauternes
3. **The French Spirit:** The attitudes of the winemakers, shippers and government officials reflect very high standards. Sometimes overbearing or haughty to outsiders, the French wine industry nevertheless exudes excellence.

La Belle France has not rested on her laurels. She is in the mainstream of today's technology and her wine laws are the model for other countries. France is a world leader in wine expertise, and in the sale of wine shoots, yeasts, oak barrels, and other winery equipment. From Dom Perignon to Louis Pasteur to Emile Peynaud, France has not only kept up with trends but has also forged them. The very language of wine is French.

More often than not, the French have earned pre-eminence in the old-fashioned way—they have earned it.

# THE WINE REGIONS OF FRANCE

## BORDEAUX

The region of Bordeaux is located in the southwestern part of France near the Atlantic Coast and is one of the most celebrated wine regions on the earth. It produces wines of the very highest quality in greater varieties and greater quantities than any other vineyard area of France. Bordeaux's wines are constantly imitated but never equaled, and share a complexity and elegance that sets them apart from all other wines of the world.

This all-important region is centered around the port of Bordeaux and is the center of the Gironde Department, the largest of the French *departments,* which takes its name from the Gironde River. Of the two and a half million acres that make up the department or the viticulture district known as Bordeaux, a fifth of these are planted in vines that account for approximately one-tenth of the production of France. The Bordeaux appellation encompasses all of the regions on the Gironde that produce quality wines. There are at least fifty different appellations in the department of which the appellations Bordeaux and Bordeaux Superieur account for approximately half of the entire production.

Two important rivers of the region, the Dordogne and the Garonne, meet north of Bordeaux to form the Gironde River, which flows some fifty miles to the Atlantic Ocean. These rivers are natural boundaries and separate the region into four basic wine producing areas. On the left bank, the Haut-Medoc and Medoc produce red wines almost exclusively. To the south, the area of Graves produces both red and white wines, and the areas of Barsac and Sauternes produce a naturally sweet wine.

Between the Dordogne and Garonne is the area known as Entre-Deux-Mers, which means between the two seas. This area produces a large volume of white wines and Premiers Cotes de Bordeaux is responsible for the greatest percentage of wine labeled as Bordeaux Superieur in the region. On the right bank, the areas of Saint-Emilion and Pomerol with neighboring Fronsac produce quality red wines. To the north, facing the region of the Medoc, are the areas of Cotes de Bourg and Cotes de Blaye that produce both red and white wines of the appellation of Bordeaux.

Due to its size the Gironde has a diversity of soils and sub-soils, which have been deposited over the centuries from the east by the Dordogne and from the south by the Garonne. As a result the vintners of Bordeaux have carefully selected the species of vine that best suits each particular area.

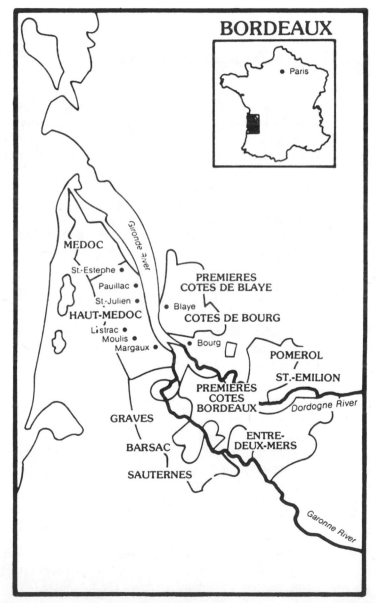

Wine from Burgundy is produced on small vineyard sites and from a single vine whose quality is dependent on a soil that has remained the same for centuries. In Burgundy all the finer reds are made from the Pinot Noir and the whites from the Chardonnay. Beaujolais has the Gamay and in Chablis, the Chardonnay again. But here in Bordeaux where you find vast vineyard estates, the wines are made from a blend of a variety of grape types, three or four for the whites and as many as five for the reds. This marriage of vines achieves a complexity and balance not possible from a single variety, as each has something special to impart to the desired blend. At harvest the vintners walk through the estate and pick only the grapes that have reached their peak, then put them in separate vats where the blending will be done at a later time, according to the decision of the cellar master. As the choice and percentage of grapes varies with each individual vineyard, the different varieties used in blending are responsible for the variations in the flavor, body, and bouquet of different vines.

---

## GRAPE VARIETIES OF BORDEAUX

**Red wine grapes:**

**Cabernet Sauvignon:** a classic grape that produces wines with great finesse and breed that require aging.

**Cabernet Franc:** known in Saint-Emilion and Pomerol as Bouchet, this grape is full-bodied with less color and stronger perfume than the Cabernet Sauvignon.

**Merlot:** velvety in style, highly perfumed, with less tannin than the Cabernet Sauvignon.

**Petit Verdot:** high in alcohol and acidity, rich in tannin.

**Malbec:** light and delicate grape that produces soft, well-colored wines.

**White wine grapes:**

**Semillon:** a fine, sturdy vine that gives smoothness and a certain texture to the wine.

**Sauvignon Blanc:** rich, with a strong flavor and bouquet, high in acidity.

**Muscadelle:** strongly perfumed with a high yield.

---

## The Regions of Bordeaux
## Medoc and Haut-Medoc

Medoc comes from the Latin phrase *in medio aquae* meaning in the middle of the water, and refers to a peninsula situated between the Gironde River and the Atlantic Ocean. Protected from harsh winds by dense forests, it has a unique micro-climate and a variety of soils making this area ideally suited for what are truly some of the world's greatest vineyards.

When you leave the city of Bordeaux, which is in the region of Graves, you cross over a small stream called La Jalle de Blanquefort, which acts as a natural boundary between the area of Graves and that portion of the Medoc called the Haut-Medoc. It is here, on the left bank of the Gironde, that most of the best red wines of Bordeaux are produced, accounting for nearly a quarter of the total production of the department; only 1% is white wine. It is in the Haut-Medoc that we find the all important communes (villages) of Saint-Estephe, Pauillac, Saint-Julien, Moulis, Listrac, and Margaux, each having their own appellation. Their *Chateaux* produce the most highly regarded wines in the world, those exceptional clarets of Bordeaux, wines that possess a great variety of styles. They are complex, with great breed, harmoniously balanced yet delicate, acquiring a rare bouquet over the years.

It was here in the Medoc that the custom of selling wines from individual estates, vinified separately, originated. And for many years after that there were attempts to grade the various *chateaux* with respect to their quality, long before the Appellation Controlee laws were developed. In 1855, in preparation for an international exhibition organized by Napoleon III, the Chamber of Commerce had the registered brokers establish a classification based on over a century's experience, analyzing the prices paid by the merchants of Bordeaux for the wines of various vineyards during that time. It was evident that the higher the price paid, the finer the quality. When you realize the quality of a wine is primarily dependent on the formation of a vineyard's soil and subsoil, it makes it easier to understand why the classification registered on the 19th of April, 1855, has stood the test of time so well. Credit must also be given to the skill and constant care given by the vintners to the cultivation and vinification of the vines.

As a result, 61 chateaux were designated *cru classes* in the Medoc-Grand Cru classification and were divided into five categories, reflecting the comparative prices paid for each, and were

# THE CLASSIFICATION OF 1855
## RED BORDEAUX

| WINE WITH CHATEAUX | COMMUNE | WINE WITH CHATEAUX | COMMUNE |
|---|---|---|---|

### FIRST GROWTHS (Premiers Crus)

| | |
|---|---|
| Château Lafite Rothschild | Pauillac |
| Château Latour | Pauillac |
| Château Mouton Rothschild* | Pauillac |
| Châteaux Margaux | Margaux |
| Château Haut-Brion | Pessac |

*Château Mouton Rothschild was elevated to first growth with the 1973 vintage.

### SECOND GROWTHS (Deuxièmes Crus)

| | |
|---|---|
| Rausan-Ségla | Margaux |
| Rauzan-Gassies | Margaux |
| Léoville-Las-Cases | St.-Julien |
| Léoville-Poyferré | St.-Julien |
| Léoville-Barton | St.-Julien |
| Durfort-Vivens | Margaux |
| Lascombes | Margaux |
| Gruaud-Larose | St.-Julien |
| Brane-Cantenac | Cantenac |
| Pichon-Longueville | Pauillac |
| Pichon-Longueville-Lalande | Pauillac |
| Ducru-Beaucaillou | St.-Julien |
| Cos-d'Estournel | St.-Estéphe |
| Montrose | St. Estéphe |

### THIRD GROWTHS (Troisiémes Crus)

| | |
|---|---|
| Kirwan | Cantenac |
| d'Issan | Cantenac |
| Lagrange | St.-Julien |
| Langoa | St.-Julien |
| Giscours | Labarde |
| Malescot-St-Exupéry | Margaux |
| Cantenac-Brown | Cantenac |
| Palmer | Cantenac |
| La Lagune | Ludon |
| Desmirail | Margaux |
| Calon-Ségur | St. Estéphe |

| | |
|---|---|
| Ferriére | Margaux |
| Marquis d'Alesme-Becker | Margaux |
| Boyd-Cantenac | Margaux |

### FOURTH GROWTHS (Quatriéemes Crus)

| | |
|---|---|
| St-Pierre-Sevaistre | St.-Julien |
| St-Pierre-Bontemps | St.-Julien |
| Branaire-Ducru | St.-Julien |
| Talbot | St.-Julien |
| Duhart-Milon | Pauillac |
| Pouget | Cantenac |
| La Tour-Carnet | St.-Laurent |
| Lafon-Rochet | St.-Estéphe |
| Beychevelle | St.-Julien |
| Le Prieuré-Lichine | Cantenac |
| Marquis-de-Terme | Margaux |

### FIFTH GROWTHS (Cinquiémes Crus)

| | |
|---|---|
| Pontet-Canet | Pauillac |
| Batailley | Pauillac |
| Haut Batailley | Pauillac |
| Grand-Puy-Lacoste | Pauillac |
| Grand-Puy-Ducasse | Pauillac |
| Lynch-Bages | Pauillac |
| Lynch-Moussas | Pauillac |
| Dauzac | Labarde |
| Mouton-Baronne-Philippe | Pauillac |
| Le Tertre | Arsac |
| Haut-Bages-Libéral | Pauillac |
| Pédesclaux | Pauillac |
| Belgrave | St.-Laurent |
| Camensac | St.-Laurent |
| Cos-Labory | St.-Estéphe |
| Clerc-Milon-Mondon | Pauillac |
| Croizet-Bages | Pauillac |
| Cantemerle | Macau |

*The only change in the Cru Classé of 1886 came in 1973 when Chateau Mouton-Rothschild was elevated from second to first growth. A Picasso label commemorated this historic event. The label says, "I am first; second I was; Mouton does not change!"*

referred to as growths. In Bordeaux, a growth or *cru*, refers to a chateau, vineyard, or wine estate. These Grand Crus represent 25% of the production of the Medoc.

Following the Grand Cru Classes, in order of quality, are a number of chateaux of the Haut-Medoc classified as Cru Exceptionnel followed by a number of estates of the Cru Bourgeois Supérieur category, with the finest labeled Cru Grand Bourgeois. These three categories are responsible for all the finer wines of the Medoc. All others fall into a bourgeois or ordinaire category.

Many of the classified growths have introduced some interesting wines under a second label, offering the opportunity to purchase a wine from one of these great chateaux at a more reasonable price than that of the primary label. Realizing that you have the same soil, same grape variety, and the same attentive care given by the same cellar master, the rewards can be great. For example, the extremely popular Grand Cru Classe Chateau from the commune of St.-Julien, Chateau Beychevelle, has recently released a second label, Amiral de Beychevelle, a fantastic wine that exhibits, quite naturally, all of the characteristics of this noted property. It is a selection of certain cuvees of the normal harvest by the cellar master (made from vines that have an average age of thirty years as opposed to a blend of younger vines), resulting in a typically complex, well-balanced wine showing luscious fruit and a great potential for cellaring.

Following is a list of a number of second labels of classified growths:

| WINE WITH CHATEAUX | COMMUNE |
| --- | --- |
| **FIRST GROWTHS** | |
| Haut-Brion — Bahans-Haut-Brion | Pessac |
| Lafite-Rothschild — Moulin des Carruades | Pauillac |
| Latour — Les Forts de Latour | Pauillac |
| Margaux — Pavillon Rouge | Margaux |
| **SECOND GROWTHS** | |
| Brane-Cantenac — Domaine de Fontarney and Notton | Margaux |
| Cos d'Estournel — de Marbuzet | St.-Estéphe |
| Ducru-Beaucaillou — La Croix | St.-Julien |
| Duforts-Vivens — Comaine de Curé Bourse | Margaux |
| Gruaud-Larose — Sarget de Gruaud-Larose | St.-Julien |
| Lascombes — La Gombaude | Margaux |
| Léoville-Las Cases — Clos du Marquis | St.-Julien |
| Léoville-Poyferré — Moulin Riche | St.-Julien |
| Pichon Lalande — Reserve de la Comtesse | Pauillac |
| Montrose — Demereaulemont | St.-Estéphe |
| **FOURTH GROWTHS** | |
| Duhart-Milon — Moulin de Duhart | Pauillac |
| Prieuré-Lichine — de Clairfont | Margaux |
| Talbot — Connétable Talbot | St.-Julien |
| La Tour-Carnet — Sire de Camin | St.-Laurent |
| Beychevelle — Amiral de Beychevelle | St.-Julien |
| **FIFTH GROWTHS** | |
| Grand-Puy-Lacoste — Lacoste-Borie | Pauillac |
| Haut-Batailley — La Tour L'Aspic | Pauillac |
| Lynch-Bages — Haut-Bages-Averous | Pauillac |
| Pontet-Canet — Les Haut Pantet | Pauillac |

There are three types of appellation wines that you will find in Bordeaux:

1. Proprietary or trademark wines, such as the Mouton-Cadet at the right, B & G Fonset-Lacour, La Cour Pavillon, or Beau Rivage. Mouton-Cadet has certainly been Bordeaux's most important proprietary wine.
2. Regional wines, such as those represented on page 123. We strongly recommend these wines, especially for beginners, because they manifest the style of specific villages and areas. They are consistent reflections of what their appellations stand for.
3. Chateau wines, such as the Château Fourcas Hosten shown at the right, are wines produced at any one of the 7,000 chateaux in the Bordeaux region.

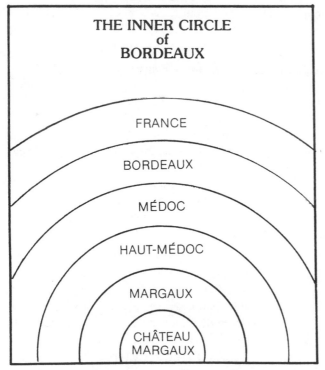

*Usually, the smaller the circle, the finer the wine.*

*Chateau Fourcas Hosten is located in Listrac, a commune near Margaux whose wines have consistently won gold medals—considered to be equal in quality to many of the fifth growths.*

BARON PHILIPPE DE ROTHSCHILD S.A.

Graves
Baron Philippe

une mise en bouteilles
de La Baronnie
par BARON PHILIPPE DE ROTHSCHILD S.A.
NÉGOCIANT A PAUILLAC GIRONDE
Appellation Graves Contrôlée

CONT 750 ml        Imported by        ALC BY VOL 12.5%
PALACE BRANDS COMPANY
WHITE BORDEAUX WINE     FARMINGTON, CT     PRODUCT OF FRANCE

BARON PHILIPPE DE ROTHSCHILD S.A.

St Emilion
Baron Philippe

une mise en bouteilles
de La Baronnie
par BARON PHILIPPE DE ROTHSCHILD S.A.
NÉGOCIANT A PAUILLAC, GIRONDE
Appellation St Emilion Contrôlée

CONT 750 ml        Imported by        ALC BY VOL 11.5%
PALACE BRANDS COMPANY
RED BORDEAUX WINE     FARMINGTON, CT     PRODUCT OF FRANCE

BARON PHILIPPE DE ROTHSCHILD S.A.

Pomerol
Baron Philippe

une mise en bouteilles
de La Baronnie
par BARON PHILIPPE DE ROTHSCHILD S.A.
NÉGOCIANT A PAUILLAC, GIRONDE
Appellation Pomerol Contrôlée

CONT 750 ml        Imported by        ALC BY VOL 11.5
PALACE BRANDS COMPANY
RED BORDEAUX WINE     FARMINGTON, CT     PRODUCT OF FRANCE

BARON PHILIPPE DE ROTHSCHILD S.A.

Pauillac
Baron Philippe

une mise en bouteilles
de La Baronnie
par BARON PHILIPPE DE ROTHSCHILD S.A.
NÉGOCIANT A PAUILLAC, GIRONDE
Appellation Pauillac Contrôlée

CONT 750 ml        Imported by        ALC BY VOL 11.5
PALACE BRANDS COMPANY
RED BORDEAUX WINE     FARMINGTON, CT     PRODUCT OF FRANCE

BARON PHILIPPE DE ROTHSCHILD S.A.

Sauternes
Baron Philippe

une mise en bouteilles
de La Baronnie
par BARON PHILIPPE DE ROTHSCHILD S.A.
NÉGOCIANT A PAUILLAC, GIRONDE
Appellation Sauternes Contrôlée

CONT 750 ml        Imported by        ALC BY VOL 13
PALACE BRANDS COMPANY
WHITE BORDEAUX WINE     FARMINGTON, CT     PRODUCT OF FRANCE

BARON PHILIPPE DE ROTHSCHILD S.A.

Médoc
Baron Philippe

une mise en bouteilles
de La Baronnie
par BARON PHILIPPE DE ROTHSCHILD S.A.
NÉGOCIANT A PAUILLAC, GIRONDE
Appellation Médoc Contrôlée

CONT 750 ml        Imported by        ALC BY VOL 11.5
PALACE BRANDS COMPANY
RED BORDEAUX WINE     FARMINGTON, CT     PRODUCT OF FRANCE

## COMMUNES OF THE HAUT-MEDOC REGION

### Margaux
*Appellation Contrôlée*

The commune of Margaux produces the most elegant wines of the Haut-Medoc. They are typically lighter and more delicate than their neighbors with a very distinctive, fragrant bouquet. With nearby Cantenac, there are no less than eight Cru Classe chateaux in their communes.

### St.-Julien
*Appellation Contrôlée*

An important commune in the center of the Haut-Medoc that has twelve Cru Classe properties producing clarets in a full luscious style, rich wines that are generous and complete. These wines tend to mature more quickly than the wines of Pauillac or St.-Estéphe.

### Pauillac
*Appellation Contrôlée*

The wines of Pauillac are classic clarets in every sense of the word, full-bodied wines with deep color that are long-lived and complex. At their best they are beyond praise. Sixteen Cru Classe chateaux make their home here.

### St.-Estéphe
*Appellation Contrôlée*

This is the northernmost of the wine-producing communes of the Haut-Medoc. St.-Estéphe has five Cru Classe chateaux whose wines are firm, full-bodied, and tannic, maturing more slowly than other wines of the Haut-Medoc. These attractive wines have less finesse than the wines of Margaux, St.-Julien, and Pauillac.

### Listrac and Moulis
*Appellation Contrôlée*

The communes of Listrac and Moulis produce some notable wines, but none with higher than a Cru Bourgeois classification.

*Les Forts de Latour is the second wine of Chateau Latour, a first growth of Pauillac. This world famous chateau is ranked as one of the five best in the Grand Cru Classe classification of Medoc.*

*Chateau Batailley is a classified growth (fifth) from the same commune (Pauillac) as Château Mouton, Lafite, and Latour. Some experts feel that Batailley, like Lynch-Bages, Palmer, and Talbot, should be reclassified higher. You should take note that to be listed among the best 61 out of 7,000 chateaux makes all classified Medocs first-rate.*

There are a number of estates that have been producing wines that are considered equal to those of the Grand Crus of the Fifth Growths, such as Chateau Fourcas Hosten of Listrac and Chateau Chasse-Spleen of Moulis. All of the other vineyard estates in the remaining communes are only entitled to the appellation Haut-Medoc.

## THE MEDOC REGION

North of the commune of St.-Estéphe to the tip of the Gironde estuary is the area having its own appellation classified simply as Medoc (formerly referred to as Bas-Medoc, or lower Medoc). The wines of this region generally lack the distinction of those wines of the Haut-Medoc. In recent years the vignerons have been working hard to improve their image, giving care and attention to their winemaking techniques and selectively replanting numerous vineyards that have achieved astonishing results. There are none that can compare to the classified growths in the Medoc, but there is an ever growing number of exceptional wines of the Cru Bourgeois. Eighty of these Cru Bourgeois properties represent about half of the total production of the region. Some of the more outstanding estates in this category are: Chateau La Tour de By, Chateau Livran, Chateau Patache D'Aux, Chateau Greysac, and Chateau Saint-Bonnet. Many of the remaining estates are small in size and belong to one of the five cooperatives that are responsible for most of the balance of the wines being produced. The region produces many sound, solid wines of exceptional value.

*Famous fourth growth Chateau Beychevelle places only its best lots under the Chateau Beychevelle label. Other lots, excellent but not quite good enough for the first label, are called Amiral de Beychevelle, the Chateau's second label.*

## GRAVES

To the south of the Medoc is the region of Graves, which begins within the city of Bordeaux and extends south around the appellations of Barsac and Sauternes. Bordeaux's finest white wines are produced in this region with Graves producing exceptional dry white wines that have a pronounced bouquet and velvet finish. Yet the vineyards of Graves produce a far greater amount of red wine than white, wines with a deep color that age very well and tend to be fuller in body than the wines of the Medoc.

The finest wines of the region are to be found closest to the city of Bordeaux within the communes of Pessac, Talence, Leognan, Martillac, Villenave d'Ornon, and Cadaujac. Unlike the Medoc, none of the communes are classified separately, but in 1953 the finest chateaux of the Graves were classified as Cru Classes by the Institut National des Appellations d'Origine Controlee. In 1959 it was revised to include 13 red wines and 9 whites, with the exception of Chateaux Haut-Brion which was included in the original classification of the Medoc in 1855.

*This is one of the most famous Grand Cru Graves. Semillon and Sauvignon yield dry, elegant whites. Proprietor Jean-Jacques de Bethmann is the winemaker of Chateau Olivier. A Grand Cru dry red is also produced at the Chateau.*

## CLASSIFIED GROWTHS OF THE GRAVES

### RED WINES (Classified in 1959)

| | |
|---|---|
| Château Haut-Brion | Pessac |
| Château La Mission-Haut-Brion | Pessac (Talence) |
| Château Pape-Clement | Pessac |
| Château Bouscaut | Cadaujac |
| Château Haut-Bailly | Leognan |
| Château Carbonnieux | Leognan |
| Domaine de Chevalier | Leognan |
| Château Fieuzal | Leognan |
| Château Olivier | Leognan |
| Château Malartic-Lagraviere | Leognan |
| Château La Tour-Martillac | Martillac |
| Château Smith-Haut-Lafitte | Martillac |
| Château Latour-Haut-Brion | Talence |

### WHITE WINES (Classified in 1959)

| | |
|---|---|
| Château Bouscaut | Cadaujac |
| Château Carbonnieux | Leognan |
| Domaine de Chevalier | Leognan |
| Château Olivier | Leognan |
| Château Malartic-Lagraviere | Leognan |
| Château La Tour-Martillac | Martillac |
| Chateau Laville-Haut-Brion | Pessac |
| Château Couhins | Villenave d'Ornon |
| Château Haut-Brion Blanc | Pessac |

## SAUTERNES AND BARSAC

Surrounded by the appellation of Graves is the southernmost region of Bordeaux known for producing the world's finest dessert wines—luscious wines, golden in color, rich in their sweetness and texture. Barsac is a little village in the area of Sauternes that produces wines that are a little lighter and somewhat drier than the wines of Sauternes. It has the choice of labeling its wines as either Barsac or Sauternes.

The wines of this region are produced by leaving the grapes on the vine long after the normal harvest. With the climate being more humid in this area than in any other of the Medoc, the grapes overripen and are affected by a mold or fungus, the *Botrytis cinerea* called *pourriture noble* or "noble rot." This fungus develops in the skin of the grape and dehydrates and shrivels it, leaving a high concentration of sugar. The result is a rich, golden nectar of white wine renowned the world over.

To ensure the very finest results, patience is required during the time of harvest. It is necessary to pick over the vines numerous times, selecting grapes berry by berry to ensure maximum maturity, as the noble rot does not develop on all of the grapes at the same time. The harvest starts in September and is repeated many times, taking a month, six weeks or even longer. It is a process that can only be afforded by select chateaux.

Chateau D'Yquem, the only chateau to be given Grand Premier Cru (first great growth) status in all of Bordeaux, uses only about 60% of the grapes harvested for their celebrated Sauternes. This degree of care is also reflected in their vinification and aging. Little wonder that D'Yquem is regarded as the world's finest dessert wine.

## ENTRE-DEUX-MERS

Entre-Deux-Mers, "between the two seas," is the largest of the wine-producing regions of the Gironde. It consists of all of the land that lies between the Garonne and Dordogne Rivers. Although it is best known for its white wines, it is the largest producer of red Bordeaux and Bordeaux Supérieur types. The white wines are entitled to the appellation Entre-Deux-Mers or Bordeaux when their alcohol strength reaches 10%, and to the appelation Bordeaux Supérieur when it exceeds 11.5%. For the red wines, the minimum alcoholic strength is 9.75% for Bordeaux and 10%, for Bordeaux Supérieur. Adjoining Entre-Deux-Mers are the appellations of Saint Foy, Saint Macaire, Graves de Vayres, and Premier Cotes de Bordeaux.

On the right bank of the Dordogne are the regions of St.-Emilion, Pomerol and Fronsac.

## SAINT-EMILION AND POMEROL

Approximately 20 miles east of the port of Bordeaux, on the right bank of the Dordogne, lies St.-Emilion and Pomerol, two exceptional wine producing areas. The wines are all red wines that have deep color, fairly full body with a soft, velvet texture, often referred to as the "Burgundies of Bordeaux." The principle

| THE CLASSIFICATION OF SAUTERNES IN 1855 | |
|---|---|
| **GRAND PREMIER CRU (First Great Growth)** | |
| Château D'Yquem | Sauternes |
| **PREMIER CRUS (First Growths)** | |
| Château La Tour-Blanche | Bommes |
| Clos Haut-Peyraguey | Bommes |
| Château Lafaurie-Peyraguey | Bommes |
| Château Rayne-Vigneau | Bommes |
| Château Suduiraut | Preignac |
| Château Coutet | Barsac |
| ChâteauClimens | Barsac |
| Château Guiraud | Sauternes |
| Château Rieussec | Fargues |
| Château Rabaud-Promis | Bommes |
| Château Sigalas-Rabaud | Bommes |
| **DEUXIEMES CRUS (Second Growths)** | |
| Château De Myrat | Barsac |
| Château Doisy-Daene | Barsac |
| Château Doisy-Vedrines | Barsac |
| Château d'Arche | Sauternes |
| Château Filhot | Sauternes |
| Château Broustet | Barsac |
| Château Nairac | Barsac |
| Château Caillou | Barsac |
| Château Suau | Barsac |
| Château de Malle | Preignac |
| Château Romer | Fargues |
| Château Lamothe | Sauternes |

grape of the region is the Merlot, with Cabernet Sauvignon and Bouchet (a local name for the Cabernet Franc). The vineyard areas of St.-Emilion and Pomerol are intensly cultivated by many small properties, unlike the great estates one finds in the Medoc.

The region of St.-Emilion is centered around a commune of the same name, which is one of the most charming, picturesque villages of France. It is situated on an escarpment overlooking the valley of the Dordogne. The region is divided into two distinct areas. One is the Graves, whose vineyards are located on a gravelly plateau bordering those of nearby Pomerol. Producers in this area tend to use a greater percentage of Cabernet Sauvignon in their blend, which adds additional tannin and backbone to these full-flavored generous wines. Two of the region's finest estates are located here, Chateau Figeac and Chateau Cheval Blanc, whose vineyards are only a path away from Chateau Petrus in neighboring Pomerol. The other vineyard area is known as the Cotes, which is situated on the escarpment around the village of St.-Emilion. Wines of the Cotes tend to have less fruit than those of the Graves, but at their best are the most intense, full-flavored, and generous wines of Bordeaux. Its most celebrated chateau is Chateau Ausone, believed to be named after the poet Ausonius. Some of the other top wines of the Cotes are Chateau Magdelaine, Chateau La Gaffeliere, and Chateau Pavie.

For whatever reason (oversight, or injustice, or the quality of wines may not have been of the high caliber that they are today), the wines of St.-Emilion were not included in the Classification of 1855. It was not until October 7, 1954 that the official classification of St.-Emilion was finally established through the efforts of the Syndicate Viticole of St.-Emilion. They requested that the Institut National des Appellation d'Origine ratify the long established practices of the wine trade by officially classifying the crus of St.-Emilion. Of more than 1,000 properties in the appellation of St.-Emilion, 84 were chosen for the classification. Of these, 72 were classified as Grand Cru Class, with 12 chateaux deemed the noblest expression of the wines of the region, as Premier Grands Crus Classe. In addition, Chateau Ausone of the Cotes and Chateau Cheval Blanc of the Graves were afforded special recognition as representing the finest example of the soil type of their respective areas. St.-Emilion achieved its reputation through these honored chateaux. Furthermore there were at least 100 or so chateaux that were classified simply as Grand Cru but only after an official tasting and analysis by a jury of peers. The classification of St.-Emilion is now subject to review every 10 years. In the recent revision of the classification on May 23, 1986, Chateau Beausejour-Becot, one of the original 12 chateaux in the Premier Grand Cru Classe category, was lowered to the lesser category of Grand Cru Classe. Also within the viticultural region of St.-Emilion are four communes to the south and east that bear the name of St.-Emilion which are also entitled to the appellation, producing noteworthy wines that have the same characteristics and wine making tradition of its larger neighbor. They are Montagne-St.-Emilion, Lussac-St.-Emilion, St.-Georges-St.-Emilion, and Puissequin-St. Emilion.

Pomerol is a vineyard area with no real village center, which includes and is part of the commune of Libourne, the port of Dordogne. It covers an area of less than 1,500 acres, is almost entirely covered with vines, and is one of the smallest wine growing regions of Bordeaux. Its unique subsoil, rich in iron oxides, imparts a special character and bouquet to its wines. The wines of Pomerol have a brilliant deep red color with rich concentrated flavors and a soft, elegant finish, lacking the acidity and tannin of the stronger wines of St.-Emilion. The countryside is dotted with modest houses that proudly bear the name of chateaux. The wines of Pomerol have not been officially classified because the region, unbelievable as it may seem, was not even seriously recognized until after World War II. But like all wines of Bordeaux, those of Pomerol are granted their right to the appellation by the Institut National des Appellations d'Origine after official taste samplings. Although not classified, a number of chateaux have been universally accepted as having outstanding wines. At the top of the list is

*Château Lagrange is an example of an estate-bottled Pomerol St.-Emilion. In this area the Merlot and Bouchet (Cabernet Franc) reign supreme. Chateaux are generally smaller in vineyard size here than in the Medoc.*

# CLASSIFICATION OF THE GRANDS CRUS OF SAINT-EMILION

*SAINT-EMILION, PREMIERS GRANDS CRUS CLASSÉS*

A Château Ausone
　Château Cheval-Blanc

B Château Beau-Se-jour
　　(Duffau-Lagarosse)
　Château Belair

　　Château Canon
　　Château Clos Fourtet
　　Château Figeac
　　Château La Gaffelière
　　Château Magdelaine
　　Château Pavie
　　Château Trottevieille

*SAINT-EMILION, GRANDS CRUS CLASSES*

Château Balestard La Tonnelle
Château Beau-Séjour (Bécot)
Château Bellevue
Château Bergat
Château Berliquet
Château Cadet-Piola
Château Canon-La Gaffelière
Château Cap de Mourlin
Château Chauvin
Château Clos des Jacobins
Château Clos La Madeleine
Château Clos de L'Oratoire
Château Clos Saint-Martin
Château Corbin
Château Corbin-Michotte
Château Couvent des Jacobins
Château Croque-Michotte
Château Curé Bon La Madeleine
Château Dassault
Château Faurie de Souchard
Château Fonplégade
Château Fonroque
Château Franc-Mayne

Château Grand-Barrail-
　Lamarzelle-Figeac
Château Grand Corbin
Château Grand Corbin-Despagne
Château Grand Mayne
Château Grand Pontet
Château Guadet Saint-Julien
Château Haut Corbin
Château Haut Sarpe
Château La Clotte
Château La Clusière
Château La Dominique
Château Lamarzelle
Château L'Angelus
Château Laniote
Château Larcis-Ducasse
Château Larmande
Château Laroze
Château L'Arrosée
Château La Serre
Château La Tour du Pin-Figeac
　(Giraud-Belivier)

Château La Tour du Pin-Figeac
　(Moueix)
Château La Tour-Figeac
Château Le Châtelet
Château Le Prieuré
Château Matras
Château Mauvezin
Château Moulin du Cadet
Château Pavie-Decesse
Château Pavie-Macquin
Château Pavillon-Cadet
Château Petit-Faurie-de-Soutard
Château Ripeau
Château Sansonnet
Château Saint-Georges Côte Pavie
Château Soutard
Château Tertre Daugay
Château Trimoulet
Château Troplong-Mondot
Château Villemaurine
Château Yon-Figeac

SAINT-ÉMILION

GRAND CRU CLASSE

# CHATEAU FONPLÉGADE

APPELLATION SAINT-EMILION GRAND CRU CLASSE CONTROLEE

1977

e
75cl

Armand MOUEIX
PROPRIETAIRE A SAINT-EMILION · GIRONDE
MIS EN BOUTEILLE AU CHATEAU

PRODUCE OF FRANCE

*The château-bottled St.-Emilion was granted Grand Cru status in 1955. St.-Emilion wine is softer and fuller than the wine of Medoc. Together with Pomerol, St.-Emilion is sometimes called the "Burgundy of Bordeaux."*

Chateau Petrus, perhaps today the most sought after chateau of the entire Bordeaux region, followed by Vieux-Chateau-Certan, La Conseilante, Petite-Village, L'Evangile, Trotanoy, Le Gay, Gazin, Nenin, Clos L'Eglise, Clos Rene, and others. Pomerol is a village whose producers have mutual respect for each other, whose standards are exceptionally high, and whose wines have a tremendous reputation for consistency.

## FRONSAC

Fronsac, named after its most important village, a little port on the Dordogne, is just two miles northwest of Libourne. The appellation includes five other parishes near the village: La Riviere, Saillans, St. Aignan, St. Germaine de la Riviene, and St. Michele de Fronsac. The landscape is similar to that of St.-Emilion with the soil closer in makeup to that of Pomerol. The vineyards fall

into two categories: the Canon-Fronsac, with its vineyards situated on a plateau or range of hills overlooking the river; and the adjacent vineyard slopes, referred to as the Cotes de Fronsac. These two areas are responsible for the finest crus of the region. Farther north where the plateau widens, a number of lesser wines are found. There is no order of classification, but the finest reds, many of which compare to fine St.-Emilions, all fall under the appellation of Cotes de Fronsac. The bulk of the region's wines are simply sold as Bordeaux or Bordeaux Supérieur.

## COTES de BOURG
## and COTES de BLAYE

Just north of Pomerol and Saint-Emilion on the right banks of the Dordogne and Gironde, facing the Medoc, is an area responsible for nearly a fifth of the entire production of Bordeaux. The countryside is charming with deep valleys and rolling hills that produce both red and white wines—not great wines, but sound, modest wines that are perfect for everyday drinking. It is here from the little ports of Bourg and Blaye that wines were exported long before the vineyards of the Medoc were planted.

Blaye is known primarily for its dry white wines and Bourg for red wine produced from the Cabernet. The better wines of the region are entitled to be labeled as Cotes de Bourg and Premier Cotes de Blaye,   provided the alcohol strength is not less than 10.5%. Lesser wines are labeled as Bordeaux and Bordeaux Supérieur.

## The A. O. C. of Bordeaux

The following is a list of the Appellations d'Origine Controlee (A.O.C.) in the region of Bordeaux, divided into six basic categories.

**RED WINES: MEDOC and GRAVES**
  **Appellations:**
    Medoc
    Haut-Medoc
    Graves

130

Saint-Estephe
Pauillac
Saint-Julien
Margaux
Listrac
Moulis

## RED WINES: SAINT-EMILION, POMEROL and FRONSAC
**Appellations:**
Saint-Emilion
Saint-Emilion Grand Cru
Saint-Georges-Saint-Emilion
Montagne-Saint-Emilion
Lussac-Saint-Emilion
Puissequin-Saint-Emilion
Pomerol
Lalande-de-Pomerol
Fronsac
Canon-Fronsac

## RED WINES: BORDEAUX
**Appellations:**
Bordeaux
Bordeaux Superieur
Bordeaux Rose
Bordeaux Clairet

## RED WINES: THE COTES
**Appellations:**
Premiers Cotes de Bordeaux
Cotes de Bourg
Premiers Cotes de Blaye
Cotes de Castillon
Cotes de Fronsac
Graves de Vayres

## WHITE WINES: SWEET
**Appellations:**
Sauternes
Barsac
Cerons

Loupiac
Sainte-Croix-du-Mont
Cadillac
Premiers Cotes de Bordeaux
Graves Superieures
Cotes de Bordeaux-Saint-Macaire
Sainte-Foy-Bordeaux
Bordeaux Superieur

## WHITE WINES: DRY
**Appellations:**
Graves
Entre-Deux-Mers and Entre-Deux-Mers Haut Benauge
Cotes de Blaye
Cotes de Bourg
Graves de Vayres
Bordeaux and Bordeaux Haut Benauge

1988

# CHATEAU LA GIROUETTE

PREMIÈRES CÔTES DE BLAYE

APPELLATION PREMIÈRES CÔTES DE BLAYE CONTRÔLÉE

OUDINOT S.A. PROPRIÉTAIRES A SAINT-GENÈS DE BLAYE (GIRONDE)

MISE EN BOUTEILLE AU CHATEAU

PRODUCT OF FRANCE

RED BORDEAUX WINE                                    CONTAINS SULFITES

IMPORTED BY :
FAVIN IMPORTERS, BAYONNE, NJ

ALC. 12,5% BY VOL.        PRODUCT OF FRANCE        CONT. 750 ML

# SELF-EVALUATION

BEFORE READING ON, see if you have mastered the data set forth in the last few pages. Check the answer section at the back of the book for the correct answers. If you have not answered at least 70% of the questions below correctly, please reread the previous section.

## BORDEAUX

| TRUE | FALSE | |
|------|-------|---|
| _____ | _____ | 1. Entre-Deux-Mers means "between two seas." |
| _____ | _____ | 2. The Bordeaux region produces more wine than any other region in France. |
| _____ | _____ | 3. The main difference between Bordeaux and Burgundy is the soil. |
| _____ | _____ | 4. There are three general categories in Bordeaux: Bordeaux, Bordeaux Superieur, and Bordeaux Mousseux. |
| _____ | _____ | 5. Medoc, Pomerol, and Haut-Medoc are the three primary subregions of Bordeaux. |
| _____ | _____ | 6. Wines of Margaux are generally lighter and more delicate than those of St.-Estèphe. |
| _____ | _____ | 7. Graves produces exceptional red wines, but more white wines than reds are produced in the area. |
| _____ | _____ | 8. The wines of Sauternes and Barsac are among the world's finest dessert wines. |
| _____ | _____ | 9. Blaye is known primarily for its dry red wines. |
| _____ | _____ | 10. In order for a white wine to have the appellation Entre-Deux-Mers, the alcoholic strength cannot be less than 10%. |

# NORTHERN BURGUNDY
## Chablis — Côte d'Or

The region of northern Burgundy is located within the limits of the Yonne and Côte d'Or departments and runs from Chablis southward through the great "Golden Slope" or Côte d'Or. The Côte d'Or contains a line of low lying hills that run some 30 miles, from Dijon in the north to Santenay in the south. It is an area responsible for some of the world's greatest table wines. The finest reds are made from the Pinot Noir grape, and the whites from the Chardonnay.

## Chablis

Chablis, often referred to as the "Golden Gate of the Côte d'Or" due to the golden color of its magnificent wines, is a delightful little village in the Department of Yonne, just a little over two hours' drive south of Paris. For many centuries this department accounted for two-thirds of all Burgundy wines produced, including red, white, and rose wines that came from vineyards in and around the villages of Tonnerre, Auxerre, and Chablis. Taking the name from the principle village, they became known as the "wines of Auxerre."

Phylloxera, that devastating scourge that nearly destroyed most of the vineyards of Europe, came to the area in 1893. By this time, the French vignerons from other regions had discovered that grafting French vines onto American root stocks was an effective way to combat the problem. Growers were forced to pull up their vineyards, and many, when replanting, opted for more productive varieties of vines that were generally inferior to the Chardonnay, a plant that shaped the future of the wines of Chablis. It was cultivated by the Cistercian monks many years before and underwent considerable testing of various combinations of vines and soils to bring about the most favorable results.

Today the vineyards of Chablis and those of a number of smaller communes nearby are the only significant ones to remain. As a result, even though Chablis is considered part of the region of northern Burgundy, it is separated from the Côte d'Or by some 75 miles.

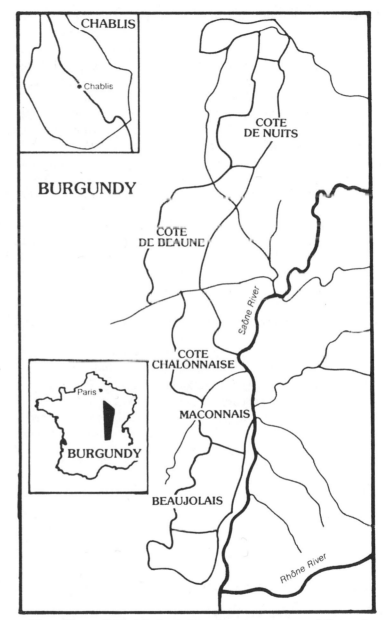

The village of Chablis has given its name to one of France's most prestigious white wines. The wines of Chablis are light golden in color, with just a hint of green in their youth. They are full-bodied wines, crisp and incredibly dry, having perfect balance between acidity and fruit. The finest categories of Chablis display a certain richness and may still show their attractiveness after 10 years of time, considerably longer than that of most other dry white wines. With an unrivalled worldwide reputation, the wines of Chablis are one of the premier white wines of France.

The Chardonnay is used exclusively for these wines and is referred to locally as the Beaunois. It is planted on chalky slopes whose soil is a mixture of limestone and clay with numerous amounts of oyster fossils, identical to that of Champagne some 20 miles away, making the grapes of Chablis ideal for sparkling wine. Some of the finest Crémant de Bourgogne, a sparkling wine made in the *Methode Champenoise* is produced in nearby Saint-Bris at the Caves Bailly.

The soil in this region is very delicate and traditionally has required periodic resting for as many as 20 years. Today, due to modern chemical treatments, that time has been greatly reduced. Still, only about one-third of the vineyards of Chablis are under cultivation at any one time.

Here, as is the case throughout Burgundy but even more so in Chablis, growers tend to have small holdings, many in several vineyards with neither the facilities to bottle or properly store their wine. For this reason, a *cave cooperative* was formed, La Chablisienne, that is now responsible for about one-third of the total production of the area. The remaining production is primarily in the hands of the *negociant* or shipper, whose role becomes an extremely important one. The negociants purchase various barrels from numerous growers and, in effect, create a blend or a house style under their own label. A few who also own their own parcels of land are called *negociant-eleveur*, shippers who do their own bottling. Some of the most respected of these are J. Moreau et Fils, whose holdings are quite extensive in both the Grand Cru and Premier Cru categories, as well as Domaine Laroche, Domaine Long-Depaquit, Albert Pic et Fils, and Simmonet-Fevre.

## CLASSIFICATION OF THE WINES OF CHABLIS

The wines of Chablis have been divided into four different categories of excellence: **Chablis Grand Cru, Chablis Premier Cru, Chablis,** and **Petit Chablis.**

First there are Chablis Grand Cru wines, the elite of Chablis—elegant wines, fuller-bodied than other Chablis. These wines may only come from seven small vineyards: Les Clos, Valmur, Blanchots, Vaudesir, Preuses, Bougros, and Grenouille. To illustrate the varying limits of yield per acre and alcoholic content, in the Grand Cru category, only 360 gallons per hectare may be made (150 cases of wine) and the alcoholic content may not fall below 11%. The wines must be made, as in each of the categories, exclusively from the Pinot Chardonnay grape, and each of the seven vineyards is specifically delimited. There are only some 5,000 cases of Chablis Grand Cru produced in a good year, an average of about 750 cases per vineyard.

Right under the Grand Crus are the Premier Crus, only very slightly "lesser" wines. There are 11 Premier Cru vineyards, such as Fourchaume, Vaillons, and Montmains. They may produce 420 gallons per hectare and may not fall below 10.5% alcohol by volume.

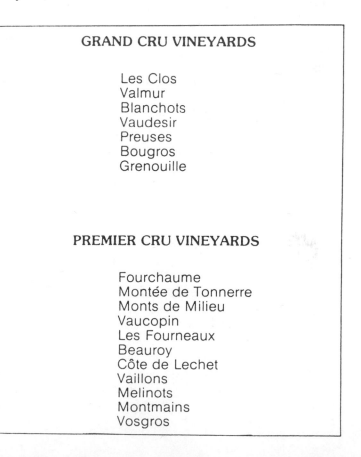

**GRAND CRU VINEYARDS**

Les Clos
Valmur
Blanchots
Vaudesir
Preuses
Bougros
Grenouille

**PREMIER CRU VINEYARDS**

Fourchaume
Montée de Tonnerre
Monts de Milieu
Vaucopin
Les Fourneaux
Beauroy
Côte de Lechet
Vaillons
Melinots
Montmains
Vosgros

*Les Clos ranks as a Grand Cru. A tiny parcel of vineyard area within Les Clos, called Clos des Hospices, is owned exclusively by J. Moreau. This may be the best example of authentic French Chablis. Flinty, steely Chablis is the "most naked of wines" because there is no room for disguises or imperfections. Chablis is either superb or unworthy of the name.*

A bottle simply labeled Chablis is the regional appellation which accounts for nearly half of Chablis' total production, and may come from any vineyard within the district of Chablis, and must contain at least 10% alcohol.

Finally, we come to Petit Chablis, a much lesser appellation, largely produced in the areas where the vineyards were not re-planted at the time of phylloxera. Although it is made solely from the Chardonnay, the subsoil differs from that of Chablis itself. Petit Chablis must contain at least 9.5% alcohol and is best when consumed young, even within the first year.

## Côte d'Or

The Côte d'Or is responsible for the greatest red and white wines of Burgundy. The reds are generous, velvety, full-bodied, with remarkable length and bouquet, and the whites are truly elegant, rich in flavor with exceptional depth. The Pinot Chardonnay is used exclusively for the whites. The Pinot Noir, responsible for the great reds of the Côte d'Or, gives its best here—a perfect match with the sun, soil, and climate. Many feel that no other area in the world attains such a high level for both its red and white wines.

This great area, approximately 30 miles long, is divided into two parts: the Côte de Nuits to the north and the Côte de Beaune to the south.

The Côte de Nuits, which produces red wines almost exclusively (small amounts of Musigny Blanc and Clos Vougeot Blanc are the exceptions), stretches for about 12 miles along the Côte d'Or and is comprised of the following villages or communes, (from north to south):

Fixin
Gevrey-Chambertin
Morey-St.-Denis
Chambolle-Musigny
Vougeot
Flagey-Echézeaux
Vosne-Romanée
Nuits-St.-Georges

To the south we have the Côte de Beaune, producing both red and white wines of superb quality, a little softer and less robust than those of Nuits. The communes are:

Ladoix
Aloxe-Corton
Pernand-Vergelesses
Savigny-Les-Beaune
Beaune
Pommard
Volnay
Monthélie
Auxey-Duresses
Meursault
St.-Aubin
Puligny-Montrachet
Chassagne-Montrachet
Santenay

*Faiveley is one of Burgundy's most esteemed negociants. Latricières-Chambertin is a Grand Cru. The red grape here, as throughout the Côte d'Or, is Pinot Noir.*

The finest burgundies, red and white, are all single-vineyard wines. At the top of the list, and designated through the Appellation d'Originé Contrôlée, are the Grand Crus identified only by their vineyard name without the name of the village. Examples are:

Chambertin
*Appellation Contrôlée*

Le Corton
*Appellation Corton Contrôlée*

Le Montrachet
*Appellation Contrôlée*

Following these are vineyards designated as Premier Cru — only slightly less distinguished than the Grand Crus that are labeled with the village name, followed by that of the individual vineyard:

Gevrey-Chambertin "Clos St. Jacques"
*Appellation Premier Cru Contrôlée*

Aloxe-Corton "Les Chaillots"
*Appellation Contrôlée*

Puligny-Montrachet "Les Pucelles"
*Appellation Puligny-Montrachet Premier Cru Contrôlée*

If the wine is a blend of two or more wines entitled to the classification of Premier Cru, the label will appear as:

Aloxe-Corton Premier Cru
*Appellation Contrôlée*

Puligny-Montrachet Premier Cru
*Appellation Puligny-Montrachet Premier Cru Contrôlée*

Meursault Premier Cru
*Appellation Contrôlée*

Finally we have the Commune wines named after the villages themselves:

Gevrey-Chambertin
*Appellation Contrôlée*

136

Beaune
*Appellation Contrôlée*

Meursault
*Appellation Contrôlée*

Years ago, many of the little known communes, experiencing the importance of their greatest vineyards, officially added them to their village name. For example:

Gevrey-Chambertin (Côte de Nuits)
   *(Village-Vineyard)*
Chambolle-Musigny (Côte de Nuits)
   *(Village-Vineyard)*
Aloxe-Corton (Côte de Beaune)
   *(Village-Vineyard)*
Puligny-Montrachet (Côte de Beaune)
   *(Village-Vineyard)*

Below these we have designations called Côte de Nuits-Villages and Hautes-Côtes de Nuits in the north, and Côte de Beaune, Côte de Beaune-Villages, and Hautes-Côtes de Beaune in the south. The breakdown, quite different in the two areas, is as follows:

Côte de Nuit-Villages: Wines in the northern and southernmost ends of the Côte de Nuits, consisting of the village Bronchon in the north between Fixin and Gevrey-Chambertin, and the villages Prissey, Comblancien, and Corgoloin to the south below Nuits St. George.

Hautes-Côtes de Nuits: A classification of lesser wines from an area to the west, behind the great slopes of the Côte that can be labeled Hautes-Cotes de Nuits along with the appellation Bourgogne Rouge, designating their true quality levels.

Côte de Beaune-Villages: A blend of various communes (primary included) of the Côte de Beaune, but excluding the wines of Aloxe-Corton, Pommard, and Volnay.

Hautes-Côtes de Beaune: A classification of lesser wines from an area to the west, behind the great slopes of the Côte that can be labeled Hautes-Côte de Beaune along with the appellation Bourgogne Rouge designating their true quality levels.

Following these we have the appellations Bourgogne Rouge, Bourgogne Blanc, and Bourgogne Clairete or Rose.

The complete breakdown of Burgundy wines in descending order of quality is as follows:

1. Grand Crus — single vineyard
2. Premier Crus — single vineyard
3. Commune Wines — Villages
4. a. Côte de Nuits-Villages
   b. Côte de Beaune-Villages
5. Bourgogne Rouge (red) — Pinot Noir
   Bourgogne Blanc (white) — Pinot Chardonnay
   Bourgogne Clairete or Rose (rose)
6. Bourgogne Grand Ordinaire and Bourgogne Ordinaire (lower in alcohol strength and do not travel as well)
7. Bourgogne Passe-Tout-Grains (red wine with 2/3 Gamay and 1/3 Pinot)
8. Bourgogne Aligoté (white wine using Aligoté grapes with some Chardonnay for balance)

Whenever you leave the single vineyard wines and are talking about commune wines, the shipper often becomes the most important factor affecting the quality of the wine.

Skill in vintning outweighs the luck of geography. At this level you may prefer a wine made by a scrupulous shipper from a lesser commune over a wine made by an inferior shipper from a commune of higher acceptance.

The single vineyard wines that are bottled at the property coinciding with chateau-bottling of Bordeaux are called Estate Bottled, Mis du Domaine or Mis a la Proprieté.

Burgundy is not France's largest wine region. In fact, all of the Côte d'Or, the heart of the region and the home of its most remarkable wines, produces about one-tenth that of Bordeaux. Yet, these wines include some of the finest in the world and make Burgundy one of the most important wine regions of France.

## PRINCIPAL VILLAGES (COMMUNES)
## of the CÔTE DE NUITS

### Marsannay
This little village just south of Dijon has gained a reputation

over the years for producing some remarkable dry rose wines (probably Burgundy's best) and some light red wines, all made from the Pinot Noir grape. Previously the wines were merely sold under the appellation Bourgogne-Marsanny or Bourgogne Rose-Marsanny, but in 1987 the village was given its own appellation, the first to be granted to a village since the 1930s. The appellation includes **Marsannay** for which it is named and two smaller villages, Couchey and Chenove. It is unique in that it is the only appellation that encompasses red, white, and rose wines in the Côte d'Or. There is an important cooperative here that has been producing roses since 1919. Other noteworthy wines can be found from Domaine Phillipe Charlopin-Parizot, Domaine Clare-Daü, Rene Bouvier, and Andre Bant.

### Fixin

The Côte de Nuits officially begins at this tiny little village just south of Dijon. Fixin produces red wines exclusively, modest wines that are robust, age well, and are good values, the best of which come from three Premiers Crus properties, Clos du Chapitre, Les Hervelets, and Clos de la Perriere. Lesser wines, coupled with those of nearby Brochon, are sold simply as Côte de Nuits-Villages.

### Gevrey-Chambertin

Known to wine lovers throughout the world, Gevrey-Chambertin is a commune blessed with some of the most magnificent red wines of Burgundy — if not the world. The first vines were planted in the commune in the seventh century, when the monks of the Abbey of Bèze were bequeathed a vineyard, which became known as the Clos de Bèze. Over the years great wines were consistently produced at the site.

In the twelfth century, a farmer by the name of Bertin, hoping to achieve the same results, decided to cultivate the same vines in an adjoining field. *Champ* is the French word for field. Obviously the *Champ of Bertin* was extremely successful, becoming the Grand Cru vineyard Chambertin as we know it today.

Chambertin and Chambertin Clos de Bèze are certainly the two finest wines of the commune, followed by seven other Crus that may also add the name of Chambertin to their own: Chapelle, Charmes, Griotte, Latriciere, Mazis, and Mazoyères and Ruchottes, i.e., Mazoyères-Chambertin. There are also a number of Premier Cru vineyards located throughout the commune, two of the best of which are Clos St. Jacques and Gazetieres. Wines from the Domaine Armand Rousseau (referred to as the father of Chambertin), Dujac, and growers like Henri Richard, are excellent representations.

### Morey St.-Denis

Upon leaving Gevrey-Chambertin, the next village one comes to dates back to the Gallo-Roman period and got its name by adding the name of its most prestigious vineyard, the property of the Abbey of St. Denis, to its original village name. There are four Grand Cru vineyards within the commune. St. Denis and Clos de la Roche to the north tend to have much the same characteristics as the wines of Gevrey. In the south, the Grand Cru vineyard of Clos de Tart is owned entirely by Didier Mommessin of Beaujolais and Macon fame, who along with the Gachet family that own Chateau Grillet in the Côte du Rhone, share the distinction of having the only two appellations in France under single ownership. Also in the south is Bonnes-Mares, the majority of which lies within the adjoining commune of Chambolle-Musigny, and exhibits much of the same soft character and graceful style found in the wines there.

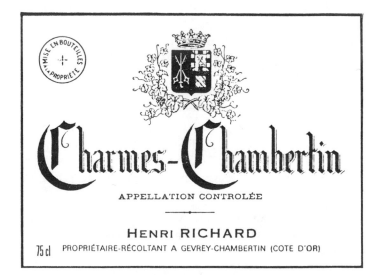

*Charmes-Chambertin is a famous Grand Cru red. Henri Richard is a proprietaire-recoltant, which means a grower-owner. His wines age in the bottle very well. Massive Chambertin wines were Napoleon's favorite.*

*Clos de Tart is an exceptional Grand Cru Estate from the commune of Morey St.-Denis in the Côte de Nuits. It is under single ownership by Didier Mommessin of Mâconnais, one of Burgundy's leading negotiants.*

## Chambolle-Musigny

The wines produced here are the softest wines to be found in the Côte de Nuits. At one time the site of a Roman camp, it was referred to as Campus Ebulliens (the boiling field), which in French became Champ Bouillant which was the origin of the village name, Chambolle. In the 1800s it added to its name the name of its most famous vineyard, Musigny, an ancient vineyard dating back to the twelfth century. The vineyard today is divided among at least 10 owners. One of the most wonderful wines of Musigny is produced by the Comte de Vogue, who also makes a small amount of Musigny Blanc, a rarity found here in the Côte de Nuits. Together with Bonnes-Mares that adjoins Morey St.-Denis in the north, you have the two greatest vineyards of the commune. There are a number of excellent Premier Cru vineyards to be found here, with Les Amoureuses, Charmes, Cras, and Les Combettes heading the list.

## Vougeot

Vougeot is a small, modest village, downhill from the vineyards of Musigny, which owes its name to a small stream, the Vougeot, that has its origin in the hillside above Chambolle-Musigny. By far, the most important property in the commune is the Clos Vougeot, a 125-acre estate that was established and culti-

vated by the monks of the Abbey of Citeaux who had the foresight to realize the importance of the Cote d'Or and became the real restorers of Burgundy's vineyards in the twelfth century. Surrounded by a wall (*clos*), it is the largest single estate of the Côte d'Or. Later in the sixteenth century, the Chateau of the Clos, which served as both a cuverie and cellars, was completed. Today the property is divided among well over 60 owners. To be sure, the quality overall is truly Grand Cru in stature, but as a result of its size alone, the property does lack in consistency. The very best wines seem to come from parcels located at the highest part of the slope, such as Musigny de Clos Vougeot, with many wines seeming to lose something as you proceed lower on the slope. Some excellent vineyards outside of the Clos include La Perriere, the Chateau de la Tour of Morin, and the Clos Blanc de Vougeot, which produces a tiny amount of white wine from La Vigne Blanche.

## Flagey-Echézeaux

There are two important Grands Crus in this commune, Les Echézeaux and Les Grand Echézeaux, that are now included among those of neighboring Vosne-Romanée, as well as the lesser wines of the commune that fall under the same appellation.

*As with many Premiers Crus (first growths), the vineyard name, Les Corvees Paget, is listed. Vienot, as negociant-eleveur of this wine, supervises the growing of the grapes as well as the production of the wine.*

## Vosne-Romanée

Perhaps the most celebrated vineyards of Burgundy are to be found here in this quaint little village. Seven Grands Crus are found here: the illustrious Romanée-Conti, followed by Richbourg, La Tache, Romanée St.-Vivant, La Romanée with Grands Echézeaux and Echézeaux (from adjoining Flagey-Echézeaux). They are easily the most highly prized of red burgundies. The vineyards are considerably smaller than most others in the Côte d'Or and are divided among relatively few owners, keeping the quality consistently high. One of the largest parcels is held by the Societé Civile du Domaine de la Romanée Conti, a joint venture between Messrs. de Villaine and Leroy, which includes all of Romanée-Conti and La Tache, with interests in Richbourg, Grands Echézeaux, Echézeaux, and Romanée St.-Vivant (and a small amount of Montrachet in the Côte de Beaune). After the Grands Crus there are a number of Premier Crus such as Grande-Rue, Gaudichots, Malconsorts, and Suchots.

## Nuits-St.-Georges

Regarded as the center of the wine trade for the Côte de Nuits, Nuits-St.-Georges is its largest commune. Many of the Côtes' most prominent shippers and wine merchants have made their headquarters here, including names like Charles Vienot, in whose ancient cellars lie examples of some of the Côtes' finest old wines. Faiveley, who has some of the most extensive holdings throughout the Côte d'Or, Morin, Bichot, and Jean Claude Boisset, whose innovations and contributions have certainly made their mark, are others found here. There are no Grand Cru vineyards in the commune, but a number of excellent Premiers Crus are to be found — Les St.-Georges, considered to be the best, was added to that of the village name. Boudots, Porets, and Les Vaucrains should be mentioned. In Premeaux, a little hamlet to the south whose vineyards are entitled to the same appellation, you have Clos de la Marechale, Aux Perdrix, and Les Corvees Paget, to list a few.

## Prissey, Comblanchien, and Corgoloin

The communes of Prissey, Comblanchien, and Corgoloin produce small amounts of red and white wine. They are lesser wines that are entitled to the appellation Côtes de Nuits-Villages.

*A regional wine from a reliable shipper combines the style of the Côte d'Or with affordability. This is a dry white from Chardonnay grapes.*

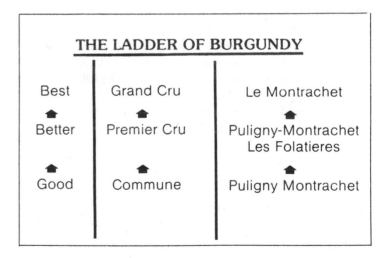

*The French have classified and reclassified their wines very well. This has inspired confidence in French wines internationally. France has also been a role model for the wine laws and classification systems of other nations.*

## PRINCIPAL VILLAGES (COMMUNES) OF THE CÔTE DE BEAUNE

### Ladoix-Serrigny

When leaving the Côte de Nuits, you come upon two tiny villages situated on either side of the Route de Grand Crus—Ladoix and Serrigny. The finest vineyards are located entirely within Ladoix, positioned on the eastern side of the hill of Corton, and have the right to be included among those of Aloxe-Corton in both Grand Cru and Premier Cru classifications. Lesser wines of the commune are usually sold as Côte de Beaune-Villages, rarely as wines of Ladoix.

### Aloxe-Corton

Just south of the Côte de Nuits, one comes upon the most impressive slope of the Côte d'Or, the isolated hill of Corton. Nestled within its vineyards is the picturesque village of Aloxe-Corton, the only commune of the Côte d'Or to have Grand Cru appellations for both red and white wine. Corton, the only red wine to be given Grand Cru status in the whole of the Côte de Beaune, is by far its greatest red.

The appellation of Corton is complicated somewhat in that it is not limited to the Corton vineyard alone, but also includes a number of adjoining parcels of equal stature. These parcels are entitled to include their name in the appellation, such as Corton-Renardes, Corton-Clos du Roi, Corton-Clos de la Vigne au Saint, Corton-Bressands, and Corton-Pougeots. The firm of Louis Latour, who many consider the dean of Burgundy shippers, has by far the most extensive holdings on this illustrious slope.

Apart from the village of Aloxe-Corton, nestled on one part of the slopes, is Chateau Grancey, Louis Latour's eighteenth century estate. An excellent proprietary wine, Corton-Grancey, is made from the wines of the Domaine that have the right to the appellation. Just behind the estate is the cuverie and cellars of the Domaine that are dug deep into the vineyard slope of Corton, certainly one of the most impressive in all of France.

Situated as it is, midway in the Côte d'Or, there are a number who feel that the red wines of Corton may well be the finest in all of Burgundy, having characteristics of both the Côte de Nuits and the Côte de Beaune.

With all the deserving praise focused on the red wines of Corton, we should not overlook the Grand Cru white wine vineyard of Corton Charlemagne. Interestingly, it was Louis Latour's great-grandfather who was instrumental in the creation of the appellation by pulling up the vines of Aligote and Pinot Noir that were planted on the southeast slope and replanting them with Chardonnay. Today, this magnificent Grand Cru is certainly on par with that of the great Montrachet of Puligny.

A number of Aloxe-Corton's excellent Premier Cru vineyards are Les Fournieres, Les Chaillots, Les Brunettes, and Les Meix. Producers such as Louis Latour, Reine Pedauque, and Bouchard Pere et Fils, and growers like Michele Voarick, make excellent wines. One of the musts when visiting Burgundy is to spend some time in this lovely commune at the Hotel Clarion. It is ideally located near the vines of Corton and Corton-Charlemagne. The proprietor, Christian Voarick, is the nephew of grower Michele Voarick.

*There is a tale that Charlemagne ruled Europe, but not his household. His wife would perpetually nag him if she found traces of red wine in his white beard. So he had white Chardonnay vines planted in his beloved Corton. We do not know how this affected his marriage, but we are certain that Corton-Charlemagne, together with Le Montrachet, is considered the finest dry white wine in the world. This rare gem from Reine Pedauque is estate-bottled.*

141

## Pernand-Vergelesses

Pernand-Vergelesses is a little town on a hill behind Corton. It produces both red and white wines, the best of which may be sold under the appellation of Corton and Corton-Charlemagne, parts of which lie within the commune. There are a number of Premiers Crus vineyards, the best of which are Le Vergelesses and Ile de Vergelesses.

## Savigny-lès-Beaune

Leaving Pernand, set well back from the main road is the quaint little village of Savigny-lès-Beaune, a commune known over the years as a forerunner in viticultural advances in the region. For example, it was the first village in Burgundy to plant its vines in rows and was the first to introduce the Guyot method of pruning. The wines produced here are somewhat lighter in style than those of Pernand or nearby Beaune. Its finest vineyard is considered to be Dominode. A number of others such as Marconnets, Aux Vergelesses, and Gravains produce excellent wines.

## Chorey-lès-Beaune

Facing Savigny-lès-Beaune on the other side of the Route National 74 (the Route de Grand Crus) are the vineyards of Chorey-les-Beaune. Sold usually as Côte de Beaune-Villages, they are rarely seen under their own appellation. Yet there are a number of excellent wines produced here. One of the finest is from the vineyard Les Beaumonts. A real treat when found is a previous bottling by Robert Voarick (father of Christian Voarick of the Hotel Clarion, and brother of Michele of Aloxe-Corton). He is also the proprietor of one of the truly fine restaurants of Burgundy, Le Bareuzai, located in Chorey on the Route de Grand Crus. Other fine wines are produced by Tollot-Beaut and the Chateau de Chorey.

## Beaune

Beaune is the largest commune in the Côte de Beaune and considered the capital of Burgundy wines. Many of the leading shippers of Burgundy wines are centered here — Bouchard Pere et Fils, Louis Latour, Patriarche Pere et Fils, Louis Jadot, and Joseph Drouhin, to name just a few. Beaune is most famous for the Hotel-Dieu or Hospices de Beaune, which for well over 500 years has devoted its service to the relief of the suffering of the poor. In 1443, Nicolas Rolin, chancellor to the Duke of Burgundy, and his wife Guigone de Salins, built the Hotel-Dieu as a charitable hospital and donated several parcels of vineyards in hope that the hospital would be able to support itself on the proceeds realized from the sale of their wines. Other vineyards were bequeathed over the years to the Hospices de Beaune, and as a result, the estates are spread over some of the finest Grand Cru and Premier Grand Cru vineyards in the Côte de Beaune. Recently a small amount of Mazis-Chambertin was donated, representing the only wine from the Côte de Nuit. Each year the annual auction at the Hospices de Beaune is held on the third Sunday in November. They are the first wines to be sold and seem to act as a guideline for the pricing of the current vintage. There are 29 Premiers Crus in Beaune. Some of the best are Clos du Roi, Clos des Mouches, Vignes Franches, and Beaune Grèves de L'Enfant Jésus. There is also a wine labeled simply as Côte de Beaune (not to be confused with Côte de Beaune-Villages) made up of wines found on the slopes around Beaune.

*This Premier Cru Beaune-Greves has a remarkable story. A monk tasting it centuries ago commented that it was so smooth that it tasted "like the baby Jesus in velvet trousers." It is produced today solely by the family of Bouchard Pere et Fils.*

## Pommard

Pommard is an attractive little village whose wines are easily the best-known of the Côte de Beaune and are probably the most widely consumed of all red wine from the region of Burgundy. With more than 850 acres that extend non-stop from Beaune in the north to Volnay in the south, it produces more wine than any other village in the Côte d'Or. The most imitated of wines, there is more Pommard consumed worldwide than the commune could ever hope to produce. There are no Grand Cru vineyards, but there are a number of very fine Premier Cru vineyards, examples of which are Les Epenots, Les Rugiens Bas, Les Rugiens Haut, Les Caillerets, and Clos Cammeraine from the Chateau de la Cammeraine, the property of Jaboulet-Vercherre.

## Volnay

Just south of Pommard lies the little hillside village of Volnay, where some very fine red wines are produced. They are softer, more elegant wines than are generally found in this area of the Côte. There is also some excellent white wine produced, but through an arrangement with nearby Meursault, they are sold under the appellation Meursault. In turn, the red wines of Meursault may be sold as Volnay. Some of the finer vineyards are Les Caillerets, Les Santenots, Les Mitants, and Clos des Chenes.

## Monthélie and Auxey-Duresses

These are two adjoining communes situated just behind the village of Meursault, which, prior to the Appellation d'Origine Controlée, sold their wines under the labels of Pommard and Volnay. Today some excellent wines can be found in both communes. They are extremely good values for red wines. In Auxey-Duresses there is some white wine produced that resembles those of Meursault.

## Meursault

The second largest commune in the Côte de Beaune, Meursault is the principle village in what is referred to as the Côtes de Blanc, an area just three miles in length that runs through the villages of Meursault, Puligny-Montrachet, and Chassagne-Montrachet. This is that special part of the Côte d'Or where, with the exception of Corton-Charlemagne in Aloxe-Corton, can be found what many feel to be the epitome of the world's dry white wines. The white wines of Meursault are charming wines, softer than those of Puligny and Chassagne. Its two finest wines are Charmes and Perrières from vineyards that border those of Puligny. Others include Genevrières, Goutte d'Or, and Porusot. Another excellent wine comes from the nearby little hamlet of Blagny—Louis Latour's Meursault Blagny "Chateau de Blagny" is a prime example. Ropiteau Freres, Prieur, and the Chateau de Meursault also have important holdings in this commune. A small amount of red wine is produced and is entitled to be labeled as Volnay.

## Puligny-Montrachet

Within this village and neighboring Chassagne can be found the most celebrated white wine vineyards in the world. There are a total of five Grands Crus, including Le Montrachet, a magnificent white wine that is perhaps the greatest dry white wine in the world. Scarcely the size of a football field, the vineyard produces an average of 1,200 cases per year. More than a dozen owners share the property, the most prominent of them being the Marquis de Laguiche, Louis Latour, Bouchard Pere et Fils, Roland

*Meursault is one of the Côte d'Or's most famous whites. Rich, complex, and dry, it is from the Chardonnay vine. The House of Ropiteau specializes in Meursault production. There is a red Meursault, but it is rarely seen.*

143

Thevenin, Baron Thenard, and the Domaine of Romanée-Conti. The remaining Grand Crus are Chevalier-Montrachet, Bienvenue-Bâtard-Montrachet and Criots-Bâtard-Montrachet, located exclusively within Chassagne. Both Le Montrachet and Bâtard-Montrachet are divided between the two communes.

Below the Grands Crus is an exceptional list of Premier Cru vineyards, some of the finer being Les Pucelles, Caillerets, Les Folatières, Clavoillons, Combettes, and Champ Canet. Some of the better known growers are Etienne Sauzet and the Domaine Leflaive, who consistently produce some exceptional wines.

### Chassagne-Montrachet

Producing excellent white wines, the vineyard of Criots-Bâtard-Montrachet is the only Grand Cru vineyard that lies entirely within the commune, sharing Le Montrachet and Bâtard-Montrachet with neighboring Puligny. Apart from the Grands Crus, a number of Premier Cru vineyards are worth mentioning— La Romanée, Les Chenevottes, Morgeot, and Cailleret. Known primarily for its white wines, the village produces some excellent red wines that actually represent the majority of its production, a fact which is easily overlooked. Vineyards like La Boudriotte and Clos St. Jean, along with the Abbaye de Morgeot, are prime examples. The Duc de Magenta and Chateau de la Maltroye are two of its most respected producers.

### Saint Aubin

Saint Aubin is a little village located behind the villages of Puligny and Chassagne that produces both red and white wines. The white wines are exceptional values, truly characteristic of its illustrious neighbors. Most of the red is labeled as Côte de Beaune-Villages. Raoul Clerget, a noted grower and shipper in Saint Aubin, is known for producing a full range of top quality wines. His St. Aubin Blanc "Le Charmois" is truly exceptional.

### Santenay

A number of pleasant red wines are produced here in the southernmost commune of the Côte d'Or. The wines seem to fall into two categories due to radical variations in the soil and subsoil throughout the vineyards. Some are full-bodied wines with deep color, having the potential to age, while others are light and delicate with more finesse. The two vineyards of note are Les Gravières and La Comme.

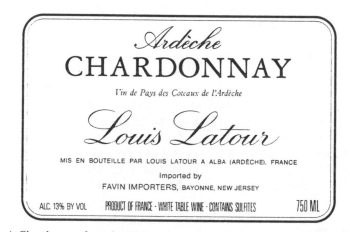

*A Chardonnay from Louis Latour, one of Burgundy's most respected shippers, it is a white wine to savor. As a Vin de Pays, it is affordable and possesses Latour's distinctive style.*

*Saint Aubin, a village nestled behind Puligny and Chassagne, has many of the same characteristics of its illustrious neighbors at half the price— it is an appellation destined for a great future.*

Smooth Pommard was Louis Pasteur's favorite. This is a first growth from the Rugiens vineyard. Louis Max is a high-quality negociant-eleveur.

A Grand Cru red from Louis Latour. Corton is one of Burgundy's most important names, since it produces Corton red and Corton-Charlemagne white. It is the median of the Côte d'Or, where the Côte-de-Nuit and the Côte-de-Beaune meet.

Although these two wine labels look alike, the wines are not the same. They are from different vintages. The 1984 is a Premier Cru from the Folatieres vineyard area. The 1985 is a commune wine. Both are from the prestigious shipper Olivier Leflaive. Puligny-Montrachet, made from the Chardonnay, is one of France's richest whites.

# OFFICIAL CLASSIFICATIONS OF THE CÔTE D'OR
## RED WINES OF THE CÔTE DE NUITS

| COMMUNE | GRANDS CRUS (Grand Vin de Borgogne or Grand Cru de Borgogne are often added.) | PRINCIPLE PREMIERS CRUS | COMMUNE WINES |
|---|---|---|---|
| FIXIN | | **Clos de la Perrière**<br>Clos du Chapitre<br>Les Hervelets | Appellation Fixin Contrôlée |
| GEVREY-CHAMBERTIN | Le Chambertin<br>Chambertin—Clos de Bèze<br>Latricières-Chambertin<br>Mazis-Chambertin<br>Mazoyères-Chambertin<br>Ruchottes-Chambertin<br>Chappelle-Chambertin<br>Charmes-Chambertin<br>Griotte-Chambertin | Clos des Ruchottes<br>Clos St.-Jacques<br>Variolles<br>Fouchère<br>Éstournelles<br> (or Étournelles)<br>Gazatiers<br>Les Combottes | Appellation Gevrey-Chambertin Contrôlée |
| MOREY-ST.-DENIS | Clos de Tart<br>Bonnes-Mares<br>Clos de la Roche<br>Clos St.-Denis<br>Clos-des-Lambrays | Calouère<br>Les Charnières | Appellation Morey-St.-Denis Contrôlée |
| CHAMBOLLE-MUSIGNY | Le Musigny<br>Bonnes-Mares | Les Amoureuses<br>Les Baudes<br>Les Charmes<br>Les Gras | Appellation Chambolle-Musigny Contrôlée |
| VOUGEOT | Clos de Vougeot | | Appellation Vougeot Contrôlée |
| FLAGEY-ÉCHÉZEAUX | Les Grands Échézeaux<br>Échézeaux | Champs-Traversin<br>Clos St. Denis<br>Les Cruots<br>Les Rouges-du-Bas<br>Les Poulaillières<br>Les Loachausses<br>Les Quartiers-de-Nuits<br>Les Treux<br>En Orveaux<br>Les Échézeaux-de-<br> Dessus | Appellation Vosne-Romanée Contrôlée |

| | | | |
|---|---|---|---|
| VOSNE-ROMANÉE | Romanée-Conti<br>La Romanée<br>La Tâche<br>Le Richebourg<br>Romanée St.-Vivant<br>La Grande Rue | Les Gaudichots<br>Les Malconsorts<br>Les Suchots<br>Aux Brûlées<br>Les Reignots<br>Clos de la Réas<br>Les Petits-Monts<br>Les Chaumes | Appellation Vosne-<br>Romanée Contrôlée |
| NUITS-ST.-GEORGES | | Les St.-Georges<br>Les Baudots<br>Les Cailles<br>Les Porrets<br>Les Pruliers<br>Les Vaucrains<br>Les Cras<br>Aux Murgers<br>Les Thorey | Appellation Nuits (or Nuits-<br>St.-Georges) Contrôlée |
| PRÉMEAUX | | Clos de la Maréchale<br>Les Didiers<br>Clos des Forêts<br>Les Corvées<br>Les Corvées-Paget<br>Le Clos St.-Marc<br>Clos des Argillières<br>Clos Arlot<br>Les Perdrix | Appellation Nuits (or Nuits-<br>St.-Georges) Contrôlée |

# WHITE WINES OF THE CÔTE DE NUITS

There is only one Grand Cru white wine from the Côtes de Nuits. It is Le Musigny Blanc. The white wine of the Clos de Vougeot called Clos Blanc de Vougeot is classified as a Premier Cru.

# RED WINES OF THE CÔTE DE BEAUNE

| COMMUNE | GRANDS CRUS<br>(Grand Vin de Borgogne or Grand Cru de Borgogne are often added.) | PRINCIPAL PREMIERS CRUS | COMMUNE WINES |
|---|---|---|---|
| PERNAND-VERGELESSES | | Ile-des-Vergelesses<br>Les Basses-Vergelesses | Appellation Pernand-Vergelesses Contrôlée |
| ALOXE-CORTON | Le Corton<br>Corton-Bressandes<br>Corton-Clos du Roi<br>Corton-Les Renardes<br>Corton-Chaumes<br>Corton-Corton-Languettes<br>Corton-Vigne-au-Saint<br>Corton-Les Perrières<br>Corton-Les Grèves<br>Corton-Pauland<br>Corton-Les Meix<br>Corton-Les Pougets<br>Corton-Vergennes | Les Maréchaudes<br>La Pauland | Appellation Aloxe-Corton Contrôlée |
| SAVIGNY-LES-BEAUNE | | Les Vergelesses<br>Les Marconnets<br>Les Jarrons | Appellation Savigny (or Savigny-les-Beaune) Contrôlée |
| BEAUNE | | Les Grèves<br>  (Grèves de l'Enfant Jésus)<br>Les Feves<br>Les Marconnets<br>Les Bressandes<br>Le Clos-des-Mouches<br>Le Clos<br>Le Clos-de-la-Mousse<br>Le Cras<br>Les Champs-Pimonts | Appellation Beaune Contrôlée |
| POMMARD | | Les Épenots<br>Les Rugiens-Bas<br>Le Clos Blanc | Appellation Pommard Contrôlée |
| VOLNAY | | Les Angles<br>Les Caillerets<br>Les Champans<br>Le Fremiet<br>Santenots<br>Les Petures | Appellation Volnay Contrôlée |

| COMMUNE | | PRINCIPAL PREMIERS CRUS | COMMUNE WINES |
|---|---|---|---|
| AUXEY-DURESSES | | Les Duresses<br>Le Bas-des-Duresses<br>Les Bretterins<br>Les Éccusseaux<br>Les Grands-Champs<br>Les Reugnes<br>Clos du Val | Appellation Auxey-Duresses Contrôlée |
| CHASSAGNE-MONTRACHET | | Le Clos St.-Jean-Morgeot<br>Clos de la Boudriotte<br>La Boudriotte | Appellation Chassagne-Montrachet Contrôlée |

# WHITE WINES OF THE CÔTE DE BEAUNE

| COMMUNE | GRANDS CRUS | PRINCIPAL PREMIERS CRUS | COMMUNE WINES |
|---|---|---|---|
| ALOXE-CORTON | Corton-Charlemagne<br>Corton Blanc | | Appellation Aloxe-Corton Contrôlée |
| BEAUNE | | Clos-des-Mouches-Blanc | Appellation Beaune Contrôlée |
| MEURSAULT | | Clos des Perrières<br>Les Perrières<br>Les Genevrières<br>La Goutte d'Or<br>Les Charmes<br>Les Santenots<br>Les Bouchères<br>La Pièce-sous-le-Bois<br>Sous-le-Dos-d'Ane<br>La Jennelotte | Appellation Meursault Contrôlée |
| PULIGNY-MONTRACHET | Le Montrachet<br>Bâtard-Montrachet<br>Chevalier-Montrachet<br>Bienvenues-Bâtard-<br>   Montrachet | Le Cailleret<br>Les Combettes<br>Hameau de Blagny Blanc<br>Le Champ-Canet<br>Les Pucelles<br>Les Chalumeaux | Appellation Puligny-Montrachet Contrôlée |
| CHASSAGNE-MONTRACHET | Le Montrachet<br>Bâtard-Montrachet<br>Criots-Bâtard-Montrachet | Les Ruchottes<br>Morgeot<br>La Maltroie | Appellation Chassagne-Montrachet Contrôlée |

# SELF-EVALUATION

BEFORE READING ON, see if you have mastered the data set forth in the last few pages. Check the answer section at the back of the book for the correct answers. If you have not answered at least 70% of the questions below correctly, please reread the previous section.

# NORTHERN BURGUNDY

| TRUE | FALSE | |
|------|-------|---|
| ———— | ———— | 1. The region of northern Burgundy extends from Chablis southward through the great "Golden Slope" or Côte D'Or. |
| ———— | ———— | 2. Primary grapes for red wines are Pinot Noir, and for white wine, Chardonnay. |
| ———— | ———— | 3. Appellation Contrôllée has decreed that Chablis must be sold under three different categories: Grand Cru, Premier Cru, and Chablis. |
| ———— | ———— | 4. Côte D'Or is approximately 30 miles long and divided into two parts: Côte de Nuits and Côte de Beaune. |
| ———— | ———— | 5. Côte de Nuits produces both red and white wines of superb quality, a little softer and less robust than those of Côte de Beaune. |
| ———— | ———— | 6. The finest Burgundies, red and white, are all single vineyard wines. |
| ———— | ———— | 7. Commune wines are named after the villages themselves. |
| ———— | ———— | 8. Gevrey-Chambertin is an example of a commune wine. |
| ———— | ———— | 9. Burgundy is France's largest wine-producing region. |
| ———— | ———— | 10. Burgundy is one of the most important wine regions in France. |

# SOUTHERN BURGUNDY
## Chalonnais — Mâconnais — Beaujolais

## Côte Chalonnais

The Côte Chalonnais is the smallest and northernmost region of southern Burgundy. The region begins just south of the village of Santenay in the Côte d'Or, where the "Golden Slopes" give way to an intermingling of vineyards with orchards, wheat fields, and assorted crops. The wines of the region have many of the same characteristics as those of the Côte de Beaune. The Pinot Noir for the reds and the Chardonnay for the whites are used exclusively, and the terrain and composition of the soil are nearly the same.

With the ever-increasing demand for the fine wines of the Côte d'Or and the accompanying rise in price, the wines of Chalonnais become real values.

There are four major communes, each having its own appellation, that are responsible for the fine wines of the Côte Chalonnais: Rully, Mercurey, Givry, and Montagny.

### Rully

Rully is an ancient village just 14 miles south of Beaune that produces both red and white wines. The whites are delicate with a pronounced bouquet and a certain finesse. A small amount of sparkling white wine is also produced here. The reds are fairly full wines that have some potential for aging.

### Mercurey

Named after the Roman god of the same name, this old Roman village is by far the most famous of the Côte Chalonnais. A limited amount of very pleasant white wine is produced here, and red wines that are deep in color, flavorful, and exceptionally soft like many lesser appellations of the Côte de Beaune, but with definite characteristics of their own.

### Givry

Both red and white wines are produced in this commune as well. They are similar to those of nearby Mercurey, but with less finesse. They are robust wines, displaying more depth.

### Montagny

This commune is the southernmost of the Côte Chalonnais and is known primarily for its white wine. They are truly excellent wines, some rivaling the better appellations of the Côte de Beaune. Much of the red wine produced here is used in the making of Sparkling Burgundy.

Negociants like Joseph Faiveley and Delorme represent some of the finest wines from this area, with Louis Latour of Beaune producing an exceptional Montagny.

## Mâconnais

Just an hour's drive south of Beaune, in the Côte d'Or, one enters the Region of Mâconnais, an area consisting of a line of gently rolling hills extending from north to south on the right bank of the river Saone. This viticultural area encompasses all of the vineyards that lie within three principle communes: Mâcon, the capital of the district for which the region derives its name; Tournus; and Cluny. Vineyards were found here in Roman times, but it was the Benedictine monks headquartered in Cluny that were responsible for cultivating the vines, making them flourish, and refining the winemaking techniques that have proven to play such an important role in the reputation of the wines of Mâconnais as we know them today. The region now produces more white

*A deep, flavorful, soft, dry red from Chalon. Mercurey and Rully can be as rich as wines from the neighboring Côte d'Or, but at a fraction of the price.*

151

*Montagny*
APPELLATION CONTROLÉE

*Louis Latour*

MIS EN BOUTEILLE PAR LOUIS LATOUR
NÉGOCIANT A BEAUNE (COTE-D'OR)

*A stunning Chardonnay-based white from the Chalon area of Burgundy. Montagny is a good alternative to the pricey Côte de Beaune wines.*

wine than that which is produced jointly in Chablis, the Côte d'Or, and the Côte Chalonnais.

There is an official classification to distinguish the several qualities produced. The first category is Mâcon and Mâcon Supérieur where the Mâcon Supérieur is bottled with a higher degree of alcohol. Following this there are 43 villages situated on more favorable slopes and soils that are entitled to the appellation Mâcon Villages or Mâcon followed by a village name. For example, there are Mâcon-Lugny, Mâcon-Viré, Mâcon-Chardonnay (a village that gives its name to the grape variety), and Mâcon-Clessé.

In the southernmost part of the region there are five neighboring villages that produce the finest wine of Mâconnais—Chaintré, Fuissé, Pouilly, Vergisson, and Solutré—whose vineyards make up the appellation for which the region has gained its reputation, Pouilly-Fuissé. Each village has something special to impart to the finished wine: Chaintré, has a flowery bouquet; Solutré has backbone and the ability to age; Vergisson adds acidity and freshness; Fuissé has fullness and body; and Pouilly gives elegance and fruit.

Nearby are two villages, Loché and Vinzelles, that have wines similar to those of Pouilly-Fuissé. They share a cooperative and tasting cellar for their production and are entitled to their own appellations, Pouilly-Loché and Pouilly-Vinzelles.

The youngest appellation of Mâconnais was created in 1971

and is called Saint Véran, a wine exhibiting all of the finesse and charm so characteristic of the area. It is made up of vineyards from six small villages: Prissé, Davayé, Leynes, Saint Vérand, Saint Amour, and Solutré. They surround the Pouilly wines and intertwine with the region of Beaujolais giving the producers a choice of two appellations, Beaujolais Blanc and Saint Véran. In these areas the granite type soil so suited to the Gamay and Beaujolais give way to chalky clay, which is ideal for Chardonnay.

Although the Chardonnay is used exclusively for the white wines, the region produces a small amount of red wines, the principle grape being Gamay, under the appellation of Mâcon or Mâcon Supérieur. With few exceptions, most tend to lack the fruit and smoothness of those of neighboring Beaujolais, yet are pleasant and light. There are a few wines that can be found from a select number of villages labeled as Mâcon Villages that seem to age well, showing more intesity and depth of flavor.

A small amount of Pinot Noir produced is labeled as Bourgogne, a wine with less body and lacking the finesse of the wines located in the Côte d'Or. There is also an interesting wine produced under the appellation Bourgogne-Passetoutgrains that uses a combination of Gamay with its characteristic fruitiness, and Pinot Noir adding fullness and body. This is a pleasant wine when consumed young.

PRODUCE OF FRANCE

POUILLY-FUISSÉ
APPELLATION POUILLY-FUISSÉ CONTROLÉE

Mis en bouteille en France par  MOMMESSIN  à La Grange St-Pierre - Mâcon

Alcohol by vol 13% · WHITE STILL BURGUNDY WINE · 750 ML
IMPORTED BY WILLIAM GRANT & SONS, INC. NEW YORK, N.Y.

*This wine is an excellent example of Pouilly-Fuissé from Didier Mommessin, a negotiant who has some of the finest and most extensive holdings in the regions of Beaujolais and Mâconnais.*

Chateau Fuissé is a famous tenth century estate in the village of Fuissé owned by the Vincent family. It has long been recognized at the "Tete de Cru" of all Pouilly-Fuissé.

This wine seems to be singled out by great restauranteurs the world over to grace their menus. The grandfather of Louis Latour was instrumental in introducing the first Pouilly-Fuissé to the U.S. market.

The most important wine from the Village of Viré, one of the very best viticultural areas in the Mâconnais. Château de Viré is a serious rival to Pouilly-Fuissé as Mâcon's finest white.

Mâcon-Villages is a suitable alternative to Pouilly-Fuissé. Prize-winning "Le Grand Cristal" is the trademark of one of Burgundy's most important shippers, Reine Pedauque. Enjoy it young, within a couple of years of its release.

153

The white wines of Mâconnais have certainly a far better reputation than the reds. Made from the noble Chardonnay, they can be exceptional wines. To understand this statement, one only has to experience the wine from the village of Fuissé, Chateau Fuissé, the only chateau in this renowned village that has been deemed the "Tete de Cru" of Pouilly-Fuissé. Owned by the Vincent family, this tenth century chateau is truly one of the very great white Burgundies of France. Pouilly-Fuissé has always been a favorite in the United States, and as a result, the demand far exceeds the supply and prices are continuously on the rise. Wines from nearby villages of Viré, Lugny, Chardonnay, and Clessé have nearly the same characteristics and represent excellent values for about half the price. A few examples are Mâcon-Lugny "Les Genièvres" from Louis Latour, Prosper Maufoux's "Chateau de Viré," "Le Grand Cristal" of Reine Pedauque, or "Les Chazelles" from the Caves Cooperative de Viré. Saint Véran is also an excellent choice when carefully chosen from a reputable shipper.

---

### APPELLATIONS OF MÂCONNAIS

MÂCON (Red and White)
MÂCON SUPÉRIEUR (Red and White)
MÂCON-VILLAGES (Red)
MÂCON-VILLAGES (White)
plus
MÂCON with the village name
MÂCON-LUGNY (White)
SAINT VERÁN (White)
POUILLY-LOCHÉ or POUILLY-VINZELLE (White)
POUILLY-FUISSÉ (White)

---

## Beaujolais

Nestled adjacent to the region of Mâconnais is the most southerly vineyard district in the wine region of Burgundy—Beaujolais. It is responsible for the most popular wine of France—a fresh, fruity, uncomplicated wine, brilliant in color, that has managed to capture the hearts of wine drinkers the world over.

The vineyard area begins near the village of Mâcon and extends south to the outskirts of Lyon. With its neighbor, Mâconnais, it produces more wine than all of the other vineyards of Burgundy

combined, with Beaujolais producing a much greater majority of red wine than white. The principle grape is Gamay, with the exception of a small amount of Chardonnay used to produce Beaujolais Blanc. The vineyards are planted on a series of rolling slopes and valleys in a picturesque countryside of small, charming villages that extend some forty miles from Villefranche to Mâcon.

Interestingly, Beaujolais is the only region that still uses the centuries-old system of *vigneronnage*, where vineyards are leased to vignerons who work the property in exchange for a percentage of the harvest and a place to make their home.

Much of the distinctive character of the wines that have made Beaujolais so famous the world over comes not only from the combination of the granite-type earth and the Gamay, but from the region's traditional and unique method of vinification, referred to as Carbonic Maceration or locally as the Beaujolais Method. At harvest the grapes are gathered in whole clusters and put intact into the fermentation vats (as opposed to the practice in other areas of running them through a "de-stemmer" or *egrappoir*, which removes the stems and gently breaks the skins, enabling the fermentation to start immediately). With carbonic mac-

*Thirty-nine of the best villages in northern Beaujolais produce the most charming expressions of the Gamay grape. They are entitled to be called Beaujolais-Villages. Here, as in all of the Burgundy, look for a quality shipper like Mommessin, Du Boeuf, Cruse, Prosper Maufoux, Louis Jadot, Joseph Drouhin, or Louis Latour.*

FONDÉE EN 1860

· GRAND CRU DU BEAUJOLAIS ·

# BROUILLY

APPELLATION BROUILLY CONTROLÉE

BURGUNDY TABLE WINE

*Prosper Maufoux*

MIS EN BOUTEILLES PAR MAISON PROSPER MAUFOUX
NÉGOCIANT A SANTENAY (COTE-D'OR) · FRANCE

IMPORTED BY THE HOUSE OF BURGUNDY, INC., NEW YORK N.Y.
PRODUCT OF FRANCE                    NET CONTENTS .750 ML.

*From the Grand Cru zone of Brouilly, this Beaujolais will hold up well in the bottle for a few years. Ordinarily Beaujolais should be drunk young. Some Grand Crus, like Morgon and Moulin-a-Vent, age very well.*

eration, the fermentation occurs very slowly within the grapes themselves, extracting a brilliant color and soft fruitiness so typical of fine Beaujolais.

The region of Beaujolais has been divided into two areas, the Bas-Beaujolais and the Haut-Beaujolais. The Bas-Beaujolais is located in the southern half of the region and consists of about 60 villages that produce the bulk of the wines of Beaujolais. The Bas-Beaujolais contains all of the vineyards entitled to the appellation Beaujolais and Beaujolais Supérieur. The soil, different from that in the Haut-Beaujolais, is a composition of clay and limestone, compared to the granite base found in the north. In addition, each area has its own method of pruning. The southern vineyards are pruned using the Guyot method (long pruning), and the northern vineyards train most vines in the Gobelet (short pruning) method.

The Haut-Beaujolais to the north has a geographical advantage of steeper slopes and granite-type soils and produces the finest wines of Beaujolais, classified as Beaujolais-Villages from some 39 villages, and ten Crus of Beaujolais that are sold under their individual village names.

As is the case in the other great wine areas, there is a classifica-

tion to distinguish between the several qualities produced. The first of the categories is a wine simply labeled "Beaujolais," produced by the 60-odd villages with the exception of a percentage of wine bottled with a higher degree of alcohol, labeled Beaujolais-Supérieur. In the northern part of the region, there are 39 villages with vineyards on somewhat steeper foothills that produce a wine of supérieur quality, both in strength and alcohol, which make up the second category of excellence, labeled as Beaujolais-Villages, or at times as Beaujolais followed by the name of the village of origin, such as, Beaujolais-St.-Etienne-la-Varenne and Beaujolais-Lancie.

The last category, with the classification of Cru Beaujolais, produces the finest wines of the region. These distinctive wines come from ten villages or communes whose vineyards are on the granite ridges to the north. These communes (which are detailed at the end of this discussion) produce elegant wines with more character and grace than the categories below and with the longest life of any of the wines of the district. The wines are labeled by the village or communal name alone.

There is a special wine in the region of Beaujolais that receives maceration for as short as three or four days, and is then bottled just weeks after the harvest and released in mid-November to celebrate each new vintage. It is labeled Beaujolais Nouveau or Beaujolais Primeur. Best consumed by the following April, it is a fresh, fruity, and delicate wine that brings out all of the charm of

IMPORTED BY DEINHARD AND PARTNERS, TENAFLY, NEW JERSEY

RED BEAUJOLAIS WINE

# CÔTE DE BROUILLY

APPELLATION CÔTE DE BROUILLY CONTRÔLÉE

*Château des Ravatys*

1986

REINE PEDAUQUE

*This Grand Cru Beaujolais is from Château des Ravatys. It is owned by the Louis Pasteur Institute. Côte de Brouilly is a small zone known for the production of elegant wine.*

155

Gamay; it may be produced from the two appellations, Beaujolais and Beaujolais-Villages.

A small amount of white wine is produced in Beaujolais exclusively from the Chardonnay grape, and called Beaujolais Blanc. It is produced in the northern part of the Haut-Beaujolais where it overlaps with the Mâconnais. In 1971 a new appellation was created for the white wines of this area, called Saint Véran. Due to the success of this new appeallation, Beaujolais Blanc has become a rarity and as a result commands an extremely high price. The wines resemble some of the better wines of the Mâconnais.

As in the case of the Côte d'Or, the most important factor in choosing the excellent wines of Beaujolais is the shipper or grower whose name appears on the label and not the name of the wine itself. People like Georges DuBoeuf, who has done such a magnificent job in this area, along with Marc Pasquier-DeVignes, Didier Mommessin (often referred to as the *Roi de Beaujolais* or King of Beaujolais), Louis Jadot, and Louis Latour are shippers you can rely on.

The varying skills and care in pruning, spraying and the many, many other tasks in the vineyard, along with the all important methods in cellaring and bottling, all have tremendous influences on the quality of the finished product.

## PRINCIPAL VILLAGES (COMMUNES) OF BEAUJOLAIS

### Regnie

A very deserving commune whose wines have consistently symbolized the finest of the Beaujolais-Villages over the years is the newest addition to the hierarchy of cru, with the vintage 1988. Bordered by Brouilly, Morgon, and Chiroubles, it produces elegant Beaujolais that truly epitomize the category.

### Chiroubles

One of the smaller crus of Beaujolais, Chiroubles produces a charming wine that is fairly light, fresh, full of fruit, and with a flowery bouquet. It lacks the firmness of Morgon, but exhibits more elegance than Fleurie. It is an excellent wine when consumed young.

### Brouilly

Brouilly is not an actual commune but a specific group of vineyards in a delimited zone on the lower slopes of Le Mont Brouilly. The wines are truly characteristic with a full, luscious flavor and some depth. Attractive when young, they lack the aging ability of Morgon or Moulin-a-Vent.

### Côte de Brouilly

Surrounded by the appellation Brouilly, the Côte de Brouilly occupies the vineyards on the upper slopes of Le Mont Brouilly. The wines are full bodied with a rich deep color and high alcohol, making them slower to develop than those of Brouilly.

### Saint Amour

Truly one of the finest and perhaps the most popular of all of the crus, Saint Amour seems to bring out the finest attributes of Beaujolais. Luscious fruit and flowery bouquet with a smooth graceful finish, this wine by comparison is softer than those of Julienas and shows less intensity than Moulin-a-Vent.

### Fleurie

Situated in the heart of the region, Fleurie produces one of the most typical and attractive wines of Beaujolais. It is often referred to as the "Queen of Beaujolais" bowing to its richness in flavor, deep brilliant color, and elegance of style.

### Chénas

Bounded by Julienas to the north and Fleurie to the south, Chénas is the smallest of the communes of Beaujolais with at least half of its vineyards entitled to the appellation Moulin-a-Vent. It is an extremely good wine, very dark in color, full-bodied, and has many of the same characteristics one finds in Moulin-a-Vent, yet tends to mature much earlier.

### Morgon

Morgon is the second largest commune of the region and produces the sturdiest and most robust wines of the area. Fine wines that have a deep garnet color and intense bouquet, they are the least typical of Beaujolais; after a number of years, these wines acquire qualities closer to those of Burgundy.

### Julienas

These vineyards are located northwest of Chénas and Saint Amour and produce some of the best wines of Beaujolais. They are full flavored wines, rich in color with deep aromas of wild fruit. These wines generally improve with age.

## Moulin-a-Vent

Regarded as the finest and most distinguished wine of the ten crus, Moulin-a-Vent, like Brouilly and Côte de Brouilly, is not a commune but a number of select vineyards in a delimited area situated on a series of slopes partly in Chénas and neighboring Romanèche-Thorins. It takes its name from an ancient windmill that stands majestically alone on one of the slopes. It is here that the soil imparts an intensity and richness of flavor and bouquet not found in any other part of Beaujolais. They are surely wines of great class.

---

### APPELLATIONS OF BEAUJOLAIS

#### GRAND CRU BEAUJOLAIS
(10 Villages)

| | |
|---|---|
| Brouilly | Julienas |
| Chénas | Morgon |
| Chiroubles | Moulin-a-Vent |
| Côte de Brouilly | St.-Amour |
| Fleurie | Regnie |

#### BEAUJOLAIS-VILLAGES
(39 Villages)

Arbuissonas, Beaujeu, Blance, Cercie, Chanes, Chapelle-de-Guinchay, Cherentay, Chénas, Chiroubles, Denise, Durette, Emeringes, Fleurie, Julienas, Jullie, Lancie, Lantigne, Leynes, Montmelas, Odenas, Perreon, Pruzilly, Quincie, Regnie, Rivolet, Romaneche, St-Amour-Bellevue, St-Etienne-des-Ouilleres, St-Etienne-la-Varenne, Ste-Julie, St-Lager, St-Symphorien-d'Ancelles, St.-Verand, Salles, Vaux, Ville-Morgon, Les Ardillats, Morchampt, Vauxremard

#### BEAUJOLAIS-SUPÉRIEUR
#### BEAUJOLAIS
#### BEAUJOLAIS BLANC

---

## THE APPELLATIONS CONTROLEES OF THE BURGUNDY REGION

### I – CÔTE D'OR

Aloxe-Corton
  Corton
  Corton-Charlemagne
Auxey-Duresses
Beaune
Blagny
Chambolle-Musigny
  Bonnes Mares
  Musigny
Chassagne-Montrachet
  Bâtard-Montrachet
  Chevalier-Montrachet
  Criots-Bâtard-Montrachet
  Montrachet
Chorey-les-Beaune
Côte de Beaune
Côte de Beaune-Villages
Côtes de Nuits-Villages
Dezize-les-Maranges
Fixin
Gevrey-Chambertin
  Chambertin
  Chambertin-Clos de Bèze
  Chapelle-Chambertin
  Griotte-Chambertin
  Latricières-Chambertin
  Mazis-Chambertin
  Mazoyères-Chambertin
  Ruchottes-Chambertin
Bourgogne Hautes-Côtes-de-Beaune
Bourgogne Hautes-Côtes-de-Nuits
Ladoix
Bourgogne Marsanny-la-Côte
Meursault
Monthélie
Morey-Saint-Denis
  Bonnes Mares
  Clos de la Roche
  Clos Saint-Denis
  Clos de Tart
Nuit-Saint-Georges
Pernand-Vergelesses

Pommard
Puligny-Montrachet
  Bâtard-Montrachet
  Bienvenue-Bâtard-Montrachet
  Montrachet
Saint-Aubin
Saint-Romain
Sampigny-les-Maranges
Santenay
Savigny-les-Beaune
Volnay
Vosne-Romanée
  Échézeaux
  La Tâche
  Richebourg
  Romanée-Saint-Vivant
  Romanée-Conti
  La Romanée
Vougeot
  Clos de Vougeot

### II – CHABLIS

Chablis Grand Cru
Chablis Premier Cru
Chablis
Petit Chablis

### III – MÂCONNAIS

Mâcon
Mâcon-Supérieur
Mâcon-Villages
Pouilly-Fuissé
Pouilly-Loché
Pouilly-Vinzelles
Saint Véran

### IV – CHALONNAIS

Givry
Mercurey
Montagny
Rully

# SELF-EVALUATION

BEFORE READING ON, see if you have mastered the data set forth in the last few pages. Check the answer section at the back of the book for the correct answers. If you have not answered at least 70% of the questions below correctly, please reread the previous section.

## SOUTHERN BURGUNDY

TRUE    FALSE

_____    _____    1. Pinot Noir is the basic grape for Beaujolais.

_____    _____    2. Chardonnay is used for fine whites in southern Burgundy.

_____    _____    3. The best wines in the Beaujolais area are called Beaujolais-Villages.

_____    _____    4. Grand Cru Beaujolais may be white or red.

_____    _____    5. Mâcon is better known for its whites than for its reds.

_____    _____    6. Mercurey and Rully produce red wines from Pinot Noir.

_____    _____    7. Pouilly-Fuissé is a Chardonnay-based white wine from the Mâconnais.

_____    _____    8. All Beaujolais taste the same.

_____    _____    9. The shipper is an important consideration in purchasing wine from southern Burgundy.

_____    _____    10. Pouilly-Fuissé is from the Côte d'Or.

# CÔTES-DU-RHÔNE

As the Rhône River sweeps south from Lyon to Marseille, it flows through virtually a valley of sun known viticulturally as the Côtes-du-Rhône, a lush agricultural area beginning just south of Lyon and extending some 130 miles down to the historical city of Avignon, the city of the Popes.

Some say the Phoenicians brought the first grapes to the valley as far back as 550 B.C. The Rhône vineyards may well be the oldest in France. Its wines are remarkable in both their greatness and diversity. The wines vary greatly due to the variations of both soil and climate that exist between the region to the north near Lyon and the southern half of the valley with its strong Mediterranean influence.

As the Rhône takes its course through the valley, it passes a great diversification of landscape. In the north there are numerous amounts of fruit and nut trees being cultivated along with the vine. The vineyards are situated on rugged, narrow, steep, almost inaccessible granite-based slopes topped off by a thin layer of limestone. Some of the longest-lived red wines of France find their home here. To the south, we find a land of gently rolling hills and flat sun-drenched fields, filled with a base of smooth, round, fist-sized stones and a rich soil that varies greatly with combinations of limestone, clay, and sand and gravel. This southern climate is also ideal and a primary source for the cultivation of olives.

With their long, intensely hot and sunny growing season, the wines of the Rhône are big, robust, and generally higher in alcohol than most French wines, with a whole variety of vine species rarely cultivated elsewhere, which produce some of France's most powerful red wines. Over 90% of all Rhône wines are red, with some interesting white wines and some of France's finest roses. Rhône wines are not as a rule made from one single grape variety as in other regions, but from a blend of anything from two to as many as 13.

The Appellation d'Origine Contrôlée classifies Rhône wines into three broad categories: Côtes-du-Rhône, Côtes-du-Rhône-Villages, and the best wines of the region, specific appellations classified as Grands Crus.

The Côtes-du-Rhône appellation is a category of red, white, or rose wines which have at least 10.5% alcohol and which are not

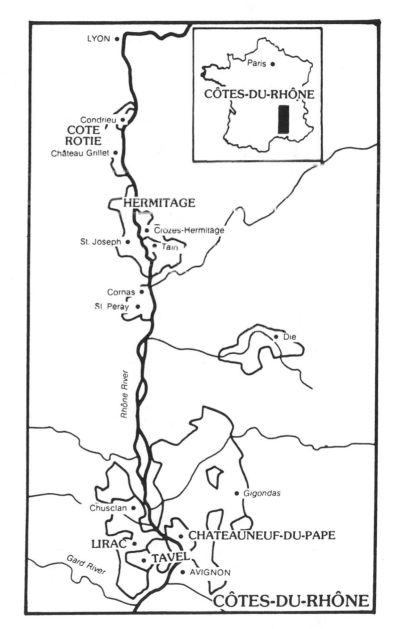

159

entitled to a more specific appellation. These wines may come from any of the 46 districts of the Rhône Valley, and may include grapes from any or all of the following varieties: Grenache, Syrah, Cinsault, Mourvedre, Roussane, Carignan, Bourboulenc, Coudoise, Muscadin, Picpoul, Terret Noire, Ugni Blanc and Viognier.

The Côtes-du-Rhône-Villages appellation is comprised of 17 villages whose producers must adhere to higher standards than those labeled simply as Côte-du-Rhône. When the wine comes from only one village it will be labeled Côtes-du-Rhône followed by the village name, as in Côtes-du-Rhône-Cairrane or Côtes-du-Rhône-Chusclan. When the wines of neighboring villages are used in the blend, the wine is required to be labeled as Côtes-du-Rhône-Villages.

The Grand Cru appellations are produced in two vineyard areas with eight Grands Crus in the northern Côte du Rhône:

1. Côte Rôtie (red)
2. Chateau Grillet (white)
3. Condrieu (white)
4. Hermitage (red and white)
5. Crozes-Hermitage (red and white)
6. Cornas (red)
7. Saint-Péray (white sparkling)
8. St.-Joseph (red and white)

In the southern Côte du Rhône there are four Grands Crus produced:

1. Châteauneuf-du-Pape (red and white)
2. Gigondas (red)
3. Lirac (red, white, and rose)
4. Tavel (rose)

## Northern Côtes-du-Rhône

Some of the finest red and white Rhône wines are found here in the northernmost part of the valley, wines that tend to be full-bodied, high in alcohol, and long-lived. All of these wines are made from the Syrah (red), Roussanne, Marsanne, and Viogner (white) grapes.

*Hermitage is one of the world's longest-lived wines. Côte Rotie and Hermitage, both based on the Syrah vine are the finest wines of the northern Rhône. You will find a small amount of White Hermitage.*

## GRANDS CRUS

### Côte Rôtie

The "Roasted Slope," northernmost of the Rhône vineyards, is made up of two parts, the Côte Blonde and the Côte Brune, named from their respective soils, one having more chalk than the other. Only a total of 150 acres make up this renowned appellation with less than 100 growers responsible for its cultivation. Côte Rôtie is a blend of two grape varieties, Syrah (red) and Viogner (white), which produce a rich robust, heady wine that improves greatly with age. Producers Guigal and Robert Jasmin seem to pave the way in this appellation.

### Condrieu

This is a picturesque little village that produces at its best a fairly full white wine that is crisp, dry, yet luscious with intense fragrance and exceptional length. To find a bottle from shippers like Delas Freres or George Vernay, who seem to bring out the best of the Viogner grape from which this wine is made exclusively, is a real treat.

### Chateau Grillet

This famous estate, just south of Condrieu, is one of the smallest of the French appellations. It is just seven and a half acres in size and has been in the hands of the Neyrat-Gachet family since 1820. The château produces a dry, soft, golden-colored white wine that is usually expensive and always extremely scarce.

### Hermitage

Considered the finest of Rhône wines, it derives its name from the legendary hermit, Henri Gaspard, the Chevalier de Sterimberg, who upon returning from the Crusades fell in love with this beautiful spot and built a chapel on top of what is now Hermitage Hill. He settled down to devote the rest of his life to the cultiva-

RHÔNE
WHITE WINE
PRODUCE
OF FRANCE

U.S. REPRESENTATIVES
FREDERICK
**WILDMAN**
AND SONS
NEW YORK CITY

CONTENTS
750 ML
ALCOHOL
13,5 % BY VOLUME

le Chevalier de Sterimberg
MARQUE DÉPOSÉE

# HERMITAGE
APPELLATION HERMITAGE CONTRÔLÉE

75cl **PAUL JABOULET AÎNÉ**
Mis en bouteilles par
PAUL JABOULET AÎNÉ, NÉGOCIANT ÉLEVEUR A TAIN L'HERMITAGE DRÔME FRANCE

*The firm of Paul Jaboulet Aîné has been a trend-setting grower and shipper in the Rhône Valley since 1834. Hermitage Blanc "le Chevalier de Sterimberg" is considered to be one of the great white wines of the world.*

tion of the vine. Since that time, magnificent full-bodied red and white wines have been produced here. They need many years to meet their full potential. The Syrah is used exclusively for the reds, and they seem to enjoy the longest life of any French wine. A blend of Rousanne and Marsanne is used for the whites.

Some of the finest examples of these magnificent wines are Chapoutier's "Chante Alouette" and Paul Jaboulet Ainé's "Le Chevalier de Sterimberg" for the white wines of Hermitage. For the red, "La Chappelle," produced at the famous vineyard site of the chapel, the sole property of the Jaboulet family, is acclaimed as one of the truly great wines produced in France.

### Crozes-Hermitage

Although excellent values for cellaring, the red and white wines of Crozes-Hermitage are less distinguished than those from the upper slopes of Hermitage.

### Saint-Joseph

Centered around the village of Tournon, opposite Hermitage, Saint-Joseph produces wines that are lighter, more delicate, and with less body than the wines of Hermitage. As in all of the northern Grands Crus, Syrah is used exclusively for the reds and Roussanne and Marsanne for the whites.

### Cornas

This dark ruby-colored red wine is produced entirely from the Syrah, which needs extensive aging to bring out its full potential. It is an intensely flavored wine that exhibits a rich, velvet finish.

### Saint-Péray

The vineyard of Saint-Péray produces both a still and a sparkling white wine using the vines of Roussanne and Marsanne. Many consider the sparkling one of the finest of France.

## Southern Côtes-du-Rhône

The southern vineyards are responsible for about 80% of the production of the Côtes-du-Rhône. The wines tend to mature earlier than their northern counterparts. They may be produced from more than a dozen grape varieties. By far, Chateauneuf-du-Pape is the most celebrated of all the Rhône wines—big, pungent, strong, and deep-colored.

*This multi-vintage blend is the leader in sales of Chateauneuf-du-Pape throughout the world.*

*One of the biggest, richest, most elegant of red Chateauneuf-du-Papes. Château-bottled, this wine is a blender's dream since 13 grape varieties are used. You may find some dry, rich, white Chateauneuf-du-Pape as well.*

## GRANDS CRUS

### Chateauneuf-du-Pape (Pope's New Castle)

This a village near Avignon that derives its name from a castle built as a summer palace for one of the Avignon popes in the fourteenth century (the only time the Papal palace was not in Rome). The original vineyards were planted in the park at this grand estate. Made from as many as 13 grape varieties, this full-bodied wine with a deep rich color is by far the most popular wine of the Rhône Valley. Estates like Chateau de Beaucastel, Domaine de Mont Redon, Chateau Rayas, Chateau La Nerthe, and Vieux Lazaret, along with shippers like Chapoutier, Pere Anselme, Paul Jaboulet Aîné, Delas, and Guigal are labels to look for. The village also produces an excellent white wine. Though very limited in production, it is exceptionally fine when consumed in its youth.

### Gigondas

A blend of Grenache, Syrah, Mourvedre, and Cinsault grapes, Gigondas is a well-balanced, fairly full-bodied red wine with a rich, spicy aroma that achieves its fullest after a number of years of cellaring. It received its own appellation in 1971.

### Tavel

Tavel is crisply clean with a clear pink color and a flowery, spicy bouquet. It is made from a blend of Grenache, Mourvedre, Clairette, Cinsault, Picpoul, Carignan, and Bourboulenc grapes. Chapoutier's "La Marcelle" seems to excel in this category.

### Lirac

The vineyards of Lirac, planted alongside Tavel, produced red, white, and rose wines. Mourvedre and Syrah are responsible for the red wine that reaches perfection only after two or three years of age. Vines such as Grenache, Cirsault, and Clairette are used to give the light, fresh, appealing style of the white and rose.

## Additional Appellations

A new appellation contrôlée status was given in 1974 to a lush vineyard area in the southern Rhône situated around the mountain of Ventoux from which the appellation derives its name—Côtes-du-Ventoux. Planted with Grenache, Syrah, Cinsault, and Carignan grapes, the result is a red wine that is fairly full with a remarkable smoothness and a hint of spice that seems to promise great things in the future. La Vieille Ferme is the most important expression of this wine.

For dessert wines, two villages in the southern Rhône seem to excel: Rasteau, home of one of the finest cooperatives in the Rhône Valley; and Beaumes-de-Venise. Rasteau, rarely seen in the U.S., is a naturally sweet, dark golden-colored wine produced primarily from the Grenache grape. On the other hand, the Beaumes-de-Venise is produced from the Muscat grape. It is a full-bodied, golden-hued nectar that is fortified to about 21% and can be served as both an aperitif or dessert wine. If you can find a bottle from Paul Jaboulet Aîné, you are in for a rare treat.

It seems the Rhône is finally getting the full attention it deserves for producing some of the finest and most interesting wines of France. We owe a lot to dedicated shippers such as Pere Anselme, Delas Freres, Chapoutier, Paul Jaboulet Aîné, and Guigal, just to name a few, for exhibiting the full potential of this area.

## APPELLATIONS OF CÔTES -DU-RHÔNE

### THE GRANDS CRUS
### Northern Côtes-du-Rhône (8)

Côte Rôtie (red)
Condrieu (white)
**Chateau Grillet (white)**
Saint-Joseph (red and white)
Hermitage (red and white)
Crozes-Hermitage (red and white)
Cornas (red)
Saint-Péray (sparkling white)

### THE GRANDS CRUS
### Southern Côtes-du-Rhône (4)

Châteauneuf-du-Pape (red and white)
Gigondas (red)
Tavel (rose)
Lirac (red, white, and rose)

### CÔTES-DU-RHÔNE-VILLAGES (17)

| | |
|---|---|
| Rasteau | Chusclan |
| Seguret | Laudau |
| Vacgueyras | Saint-Gervais |
| Sablet | Saint-Maurice-sur-Eygues |
| Beaumes-de-Venise | Rousette-les-Vignes |
| Visan | Rouchegude |
| Cairranne | Saint-Pantaleon-les-Vignes |
| Roaix | Vinsobres |
| Valreas | |

*La Vieille Ferme*
Côtes du Ventoux
APPELLATION COTES DU VENTOUX CONTROLÉE

*Récolte 1981*

*Mis en bouteille à la Vieille Ferme*

750 ml                                    Alc 12.5% by vol
LA VIEILLE FERME s a NÉGOCIANT A ORANGE (Vse) FRANCE

·TABLE WINE          IMPORTED BY **Vineyard Brands Inc.** CHESTER Vt          PRODUCE OF FRANCE
SHIPPED BY ROBERT HAAS SELECTIONS. FRANCE

*An up-and-coming area in the Rhône for excellent, affordable red wines. This brand has been the house wine of oenophiles for years. Recolte 1981 refers to the vintage of the wine.*

# SELF-EVALUATION

BEFORE READING ON, see if you have mastered the data set forth in the last few pages. Check the answer section at the back of the book for the correct answers. If you have not answered at least 70% of the questions below correctly, please reread the previous section.

# CÔTES-DU-RHÔNE

| TRUE | FALSE | |
|------|-------|---|
| ———— | ———— | 1. The vineyards of the Côtes-du-Rhône may be the oldest in France. |
| ———— | ———— | 2. Rhônes are bigger, more robust, and higher in alcohol than most other French wines. |
| ———— | ———— | 3. Rhône wines are generally a blend of two or more grape varieties. |
| ———— | ———— | 4. There are three broad categories of Rhône wine: Côtes-du-Rhône, Premieres Crus, and Grands Crus. |
| ———— | ———— | 5. The Côtes-du-Rhône appellation covers only 17 villages, which produce only red wines. |
| ———— | ———— | 6. The Grand Cru appellations are produced in two vineyard areas with four Grands Crus in northern Côtes-du-Rhône and four Grands Crus in the southern. |
| ———— | ———— | 7. Hermitage is a magnificent, full-bodied wine, which may be red or white. |
| ———— | ———— | 8. Northern Côtes-du-Rhône wines are made from red Syrah and white Roussane, Marsanne, and Viogner grapes. |
| ———— | ———— | 9. Wines from the souther Côtes-du-Rhône tend to mature earlier than their northern counterparts. |
| ———— | ———— | 10. Châteauneuf-du-Pape wines are made from 13 grape varieties and are by far the most popular wines of the Rhône Valley. |

# ALSACE

A generation ago, an old woman from Alsace was interviewed on television. She had been born French before the Franco-Prussian War. In 1871 the victorious Germans made her German, which she remained until World War I, when she again became French in 1918. She was German again for a few years during the second World War. At its completion she was French once more. She said that she viewed herself as Alsatian first and a citizen of the world second. She subsequently died a French citizen.

When we speak of Alsatian wines, we sometimes call them German wines made in the French manner. This region, Alsace, is one of France's most attractive. The Rhine is the eastern border, with the Vosges Mountains providing the western perimeter. Vineyards stretch along a narrow 80-mile line in the eastern foothills of the Vosges Range. These hills separate Alsace from the rest of France and provide a protective barrier against damp, cold weather. Strasbourg in the north and Mulhouse to the south are its major cities with Colmar almost directly in the middle.

The region is named for the River Ill, which flows south to north into the Rhine. The Romans had called it Elsus and the Germans Elsass; it finally became known as Alsace. The cuisine (*choucroute,* a mix of meats and sauerkraut, for example) and the language are clearly Germanic, even today. The wines are decidedly French.

Alsace is divided into two sections: the Bas-Rhin in the north and the Haut-Rhin, south of Colmar.

Alsace has given the world Bartholdi, who designed the Statue of Liberty, and the most renowned foie gras on earth. Picturesque, idyllic villages have given us wonderful, dry varietal wines of great value. Important villages include Barr, Riquewihr, and Guebwiller. We should point out that, unlike the rest of France, wines are not rated by villages or communes but rather by grape variety. Most of the wines are white. They are vinified to be completely dry. They are usually very fresh and lively, even spicy.

Lesser wines called Zwicker or Edelzwicker are ordinarily made from Chasselas, Müller-Thürgau, or Knipperle vines. The best wines come from the aristocratic Riesling and distinctive Gewürztraminer. Pinot Gris is called Tokay D'Alsace. One will also find very good Sylvaner, Pinot Blanc, and fragrant Muscat D'Alsace (the same grape that makes Asti Spumante). You may find a small amount of pink wine made from Pinot Noir. Red is

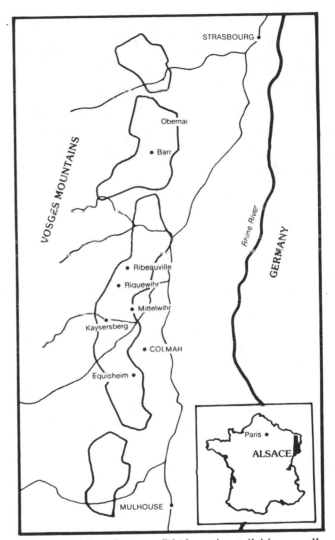

very rare. Sparkling Cremant D'Alsace is available as well.

A wine that reaches 11% alcohol is called a *grand vin*. Certain vineyard areas yield especially fine wines called Grands Crus. Alsatian wines are sold in green flute bottles similar to Mosels. Most of the Alsatian wine seen in the U.S. is from larger grower-shippers such as Hugel, Willm, Trimbach, Dopff and Irion, or Dopff au Moulin. Each of these export houses strives for a distinctive house style; for example, Schlumberger strives for big, earthy wines. Alsatian whites are generally dry. In great vintages, *vendange tardive* (late harvest) wines are made. These are lus-

165

VIN D'ALSACE
APPELLATION ALSACE CONTROLÉE

GEWURZTRAMINER

CLOS GAENSBROENNEL WILLM

13,3 % ALC./VOL. ALSACE WILLM – BARR – 67140 FRANCE    750 ml

Produit de France – Produce of France

*"Clos Gaensbroennel" is one of the few Gewurztraminers that is given the designation of Grand Cru. It is a single vineyard wine from the Domaine of Alsace Willm, founded in 1896 in the village of Barr located in the northern half of Alsace.*

and long-lived wines (a decade or more) and may have German terms such as *Auslese* or *Beerenauslese* to indicate the level of concentration.

Alsatian wines are excellent values. They are wonderful luncheon and picnic wines as well as ideal first course wines at formal dinners. This beautiful region is renowned not only for beer, but for *eaux-de-vie* (fruit brandies) called *alcools blancs* (white alcohols). They are rare and expensive. They have to be! It takes over 60 pounds of raspberries to make a single bottle of authentic framboise. They are not fruit-flavored cordials, but fruit distillates, just as cognac is a distillate of wine grapes.

**Alsatian Eaux-de-Vie**

| | |
|---|---|
| Kirsch | Cherries |
| Fraise | Strawberries |
| Framboise | Raspberries |
| Mirabelle | Yellow Plums |
| Quetsch | Blue Plums |
| Houx | Holly Berries |
| Mures | Blackberries |
| Reine Claude | Greengage Plums |
| Myrtilles | Bilberries |
| Enzian | Gentian Root |
| Alises | Sorb-Apples |

| | |
|---|---|
| Hugel | Reserve Exceptionnelle or Personnelle Riesling |
| Hugel | Reserve Exceptionnelle or Personnelle Gewürztraminer |
| Trimbach | Cuvee des Seigneurs de Ribeaupierre Gewürztraminer |
| Trimbach | Cuvee Frederic Emile Riesling |
| Beyer | Cuvee des Comtes d'Eguisheim Gewürztraminer |
| Dopff & Irion | Muscat Les Amandiers |
| Dopff & Irion | Domaine du Chateau de Riquewihr Gewürztraminer |
| Willm | Clos Gaensbroennel Gewürztraminer |
| Schlumberger | Cuvee Christine Schlumberger Gewürztraminer |

VIN D'ALSACE
APPELLATION ALSACE CONTRÔLÉE

Vin Blanc          White Wine

ALSACE WILLM®

GEWURZTRAMINER    700 ml

ALSACE WILLM, à 67140 / BARR – FRANCE

*Alsace is a French region where the grape variety and the shipper count far more than the geography. Willm is a premium shipper, and the Gewürztraminer (along with the Riesling) are the finest varietals.*

# THE LOIRE

The Loire is France's grandest river. It originates in the south-central mountains, flows northward to Nevers, then twists to the west where it eventually spills into the Atlantic Ocean some 650 miles from its source. It is the stream of Rabelais, of Joan of Arc, of majestic castles, and of charming wines fit for the newcomer or the most experienced oenophile. Legend tells us that at Tours in 345 A.D., in the heart of the Loire Valley, a donkey ate some young, tender springtime vine shoots as he waited for his master, the venerable St. Martin. Local monks were terrified to see their vines munched down to the very trunk. They were surprised in the fall to find more abundant and delicious grapes growing from those very vines which the donkey had nibbled. Thus did the custom of pruning begin.

Whites, dry and crisp reign here, but there are light reds, dessert whites, and off-dry roses as well. You will find superb sparkling wines. Except for a handful of the sweeter whites and one or two dry ones, the rule of thumb is to enjoy graceful Loire wines young and fresh.

In touring the major wine villages of the Loire, we should start in the east with the town Pouilly-Sur-Loire. A dry white wine named Pouilly-Sur-Loire is made here from Chasselas grapes. Pouilly-Fumé, also called Blanc Fumé de Pouilly, is a finer dry white fashioned from Sauvignon (Fumé) Blanc. Crisp and pungent, this wine may develop in the bottle for two or three years. Across the Loire on the west bank is the storybook town of Sancerre. A dry white, flinty and steely, called Sancerre, is made here, again from Sauvignon Blanc vines. Sancerre and Pouilly-Fumé are very close to each other in taste and quality, the primary difference coming from Sancerre's chalky soil. Both are superior to Pouilly-Sur-Loire. The nonpareil shipper of Pouilly-Fumé is de Ladoucette, whose special cuvee "Baron L" is probably the finest dry wine of the Loire. Other reliable producers are Bailly, Michel Redde, and Blanchet. Chateau de Sancerre is a fine example of Sancerre as are de Ladoucette's Comte La Fond, Laporte, and Vacheron. You will occasionally find a dry pink Sancerre, made from Pinot Noir or even more rarely, a red Sancerre, also derived from Pinot Noir. Both are distinguished. Nearby villages of Quincy and Reuilly produce dry whites based on Sauvignon

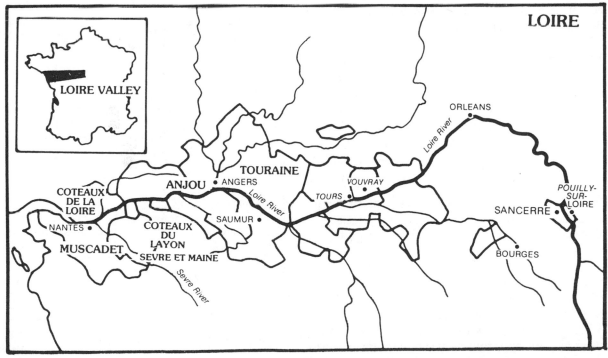

Blanc, the former on the earthy side, the latter high in acidity. Neither Quincy nor Reuilly are as fine as Pouilly-Fumé or Sancerre, but good nonetheless.

Sailing west 75 miles toward the sea, we come to Tours, "chateaux country," where stately Chenonceaux and Amboise grace the landscape. Tours means Vouvray, a versatile white based on Chenin Blanc. It can be made fully sparkling (*mousseux*), with a slight crackle (*petillants*), soft and dry, or sweet (*sec, moelleux, or demi-sec*). The sunnier the vintage, the greater the chance for the long-lived, sweet kind. The Vouvray firm with the highest reputation is Marc Bredif, which still has some bottles from the nineteenth century in its cellars. Chateau Moncontour is also highly regarded. The village of Montlouis, across the Loire from Vouvray, produces sound wine from Chenin Blanc.

The best reds of the area are the dry, young, fruity Chinon and Bourgueil. The grape for both is the Breton, a local name for Cabernet Franc. Rabelais called Chinon "taffeta wine." Usually these soft, smooth reds reach their peak in about five years and represent good value. Many tasters detect nuances of raspberries and strawberries.

West of the Touraine is the Côteaux de Saumur, acclaimed for sparkling wines made primarily from Chenin Blanc with a bit of Groslot and Cabernet. South of Angers along the Layon River is Côteaux du Layon, an area noted for hearty, sweet wines infected by the noble rot. The two most acclaimed Layon wines, full and long-lived, are Bonnezeaux and Quart de Chaume. Nearby, on the north bank of the Loire, is Savennières, a village that gives its name to sharp, lively, dry, long-lived whites based on Chenin Blanc. The best vineyard areas are La Coulée de Serrant and La Roche aux Moines. These are superb wines just waiting to be discovered.

Good, delicate, off-dry roses are made in the area. Superior Cabernet D'Anjou is based on Cabernet Sauvignon. Ordinary Rose D'Anjou is derived from Groslot, Gamay, Cot (Malbec), and Pineau D'Aunis. Rose D'Anjou is typically fragrant, light, pale in hue, pleasant, and slightly sweet.

Near the mouth of the Loire, close to the open Atlantic Ocean, we are in seafood territory and have France's most useful seafood wine. We are speaking of Muscadet, which is made around the town of Nantes. The vine used in Muscadet is the Melon de Bourgogne, which took on the new name Muscadet when it was first transplanted here in the early seventeenth century. It took

well to the temperate Atlantic climate, producing light, fresh, crisp white wine, perfect with oysters or, for that manner, linguini with clam sauce. There are three place names associated with Muscadet. In descending order, they are Muscadet de Sevre et Maine, Muscadet Coteaux de la Loire, and Muscadet.

The best is bottled *sur lie*, which means directly off its lees, so as to be fresh, fruity, and occasionally possessing a slight crackle (*petillants*). Called "the poor man's Chablis," Muscadet is best enjoyed young. There is even a Muscadet Nouveau. Aged Muscadet from a serious shipper such as Joseph Hallereau can be surprisingly appealing. Another vine, the Gros Plant, produces fresh whites in the area. These may be refreshing, but are sometimes high in acidity. Gros Plant du Pays Nantais is usually consumed locally.

Having reached the sea, we are tempted to reverse our steps. The Loire is so beautiful and charming, and so are the wines. The Loire is perfect for the initiate. Muscadet, Rose D'Anjou, Sancerre, Pouilly-Fumé, and Chinon are ideal instructors in what

de Ladoucette

STILL LOIRE WHITE WINE
Mis en bouteille par de LADOUCETTE
AU CHATEAU DU NOZET, POUILLY-S.-LOIRE (NIÉVRE)

CONTENTS 750 ml        ALCOHOL 12.5 % BY VOLUME        PRODUCE OF FRANCE

EXCLUSIVE IMPORTER
INTERNATIONAL VINTAGE WINE COMPANY
HARTFORD, CT 06101

*The aristrocrat of Pouilly-Fumé. Made from the Sauvignon (Fumé) Blanc. Dry, complex and distinctive, this wine will hold its own for a few years. Do not confuse it with the Burgundian Pouilly-Fuissé.*

wine should be. And like a Puccini aria, the Loire is a moving, touching place for even the most demanding oenophile to return on occasion. We should note that for the most part, Loire wines are the products of great shippers (negociants), who have contracts with growers. In this way, it is more like Alsace and Burgundy than Bordeaux.

*One of the best Muscadets, from the delimited "De Sevre et Maine" area. This estate-bottled wine is very fresh, as Sur Lie indicates. We like Muscadet with seafood, even linguini with clam sauce.*

## LOIRE REGION

Of the nine major Loire districts, Muscadet, Anjou, and Touraine are most important.

| DISTRICTS | SUB-DISTRICTS | PRIMARY GRAPES |
|---|---|---|
| Anjou | Savennieres<br>Coteaux du Layon<br>Saumur | Chenin Blanc<br>Cabernet Sauvignon<br>(for Cabernet D'Anjou) |
| Coteaux du Loir<br>(No "e" at the end; this is a tributary of the great Loire.) | | Chenin Blanc |
| Jasnières | | Chenin Blanc |
| Muscadet | | Melon de Bourgogne |
| Pouilly-Sur-Loire | Pouilly-Fume<br>Pouilly-Sur-Loire | Sauvignon Blanc<br>Chasselas |
| Quincy | | Sauvignon Blanc |
| Reuilly | | Sauvignon Blanc |
| Sancerre | | Sauvignon Blanc |
| Touraine | Bourgueil, Chinon<br>Vouvray, Mont Louis | Cabernet Franc<br>Chenin Blanc |

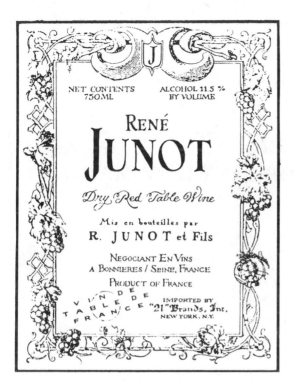

One very popular category of French wine that has emerged in the past few years is that of French table wines. These are light, fresh, quaffable, and affordable wines, very similar to what the French drink on a daily basis. Of the dozens available in the U.S., we have found the brands of Chantovent, Chantefleur, and René Junot to be among the best.

# OTHER WINE REGIONS OF FRANCE

## Provence

The distinctive, spicy cuisine of La Belle Provence has always made dry roses mandatory. Many experts consider Domaine Ott Château de Selle to be the world's very finest rose. Provencal rose is usually marketed in a festive bottle (similar to Italy's Verdicchio), and is often a blend of red and white wine. One can hardly resist the scenery, the people, the fresh herbs, fruits and vegetables, a bowl of Côtes D'Azur bouillabaisse (a seafood soup), and a chilled glass of Château de Selle or for that matter, Château Ste. Rosaline.

There is also dry white Bellet, and red Palette and Cassis. These are smaller appellations with not so small price tags. Full red Bandol, grown in unique, pebbly soil called pudding-stone, is a mouthful.

White vines in the area include Clairette and Ugni Blanc (the Italian Trebbiano, the basic grape in Cognac), with some Sauvignon, Doucillon, Marsanne, and Pascal. Red wines are made from Grenache, Cinsault, Carignan, Mourvedre, and Barbaroux. These grapes, for the most part unfamiliar to us Americans, can also be found in Spain and the Rhône Valley. Many areas that qualified only for V.D.Q.S. a decade ago, now produce wines protected by the Appellation Contrôlée.

## Corsica

From the wild, intriguing island of Napoleon and Prosper Merimee's "Matteo Falcone," come scented reds and whites that qualify for the single Appellation Vin de Corse. Unfortunately most of it is drunk locally or on the French Riviera. Important grape varieties are white Moscato, Vermentino, and Biancolella, and red Aleatico and Sciaccarello.

## Savoy

This Alpine area is most famous for white Seyssel, still or spar-

kling, but you may also find good white Crepy. White wines are made from Roussette, Altesse, and Jacquere. Rare reds are fashioned from Mondeuse and Gamay.

## Jura

We are in the land of "yellow" and "gray" wines. *Vin Jaune*, or yellow wine, is a pale, amber wine similar to Fino sherry. Château-Chalon, as the best is called, is based on the Savagnin grape. It is long-lived and must be listed among the ultimate aperitif wines of the world. The late Fernand Point, dean of French cuisine, said that there were five Grand Seigneurs among French whites, great wines that typify their regions:

Le Montrachet (Burgundy)
Château D'Yquem (Sauternes)
Coulée de Serrant (Loire)
Château-Grillet (Rhône)
Château-Chalon (Jura)

Good company, indeed!

*Gris* or gray wines are really pink. The Rosé D'Arbois is considered by many on par with Tavel and Provencal pinks.

*Vin de Paille*, or straw wine, is made in the area, after drying out grapes on straw mats or in special, well-ventilated rooms. These dessert wines are similar to the Italian passito wines. Vines in the Jura, the land of Louis Pasteur, include the red Gros Noiren (a local name for Pinot Noir), and white Savagnin, Pinot Blanc, and Melon D'Arbois (Chardonnay). This area has never recovered from the phylloxera. Alexix Lichine tells us in his wonderful *Encyclopedia of Wines and Spirits* that Jura boasted 46,000 acres of vines in 1836. Today fewer than 2,500 vineyard acres exist. Most of the wine is consumed locally. A bit goes to Alsace and Switzerland and eventually finds its way to the U.S.

## Midi

This southern area is France's San Joaquin and Central Valley, famous, or rather infamous, for producing large quantities of bulk wines, aimed at blending or being distilled into industrial alcohol.

As Serena Sutcliffe puts it in her excellent *Wine Handbook*, "A huge amount of awful wine is made here, from the wrong grape varieties, in the wrong way."

You will find some of the right stuff at fair prices among the reds. Corbières, Fitou, Faugeres, Minervois, and Côtes-de-Roussillon can be quite good and are protected by the Appellation Contrôlée or V.D.Q.S. Vines include Carignan, Grenache, and Cinsault. Most of the wine is made by co-ops. The Midi, also called the Languedoc-Roussillon, is most noted for its powerful, deeply colored, generous, dry reds.

## The Southwest

Over the last few years a lot of deserving attention has been given to the wines in the southwest of France, just east of Bordeaux. Rich in viticultural heritage, this area has produced some excellent wines using many of the same grape varieties as that of Bordeaux. Cabernet, Merlot, and Malbec are used for the reds, while Semillon, Sauvignon, and Muscadelle are used for the whites. The following are a few areas that are consistently producing sound, dependable wines.

### BERGERAC

A number of small vineyards fall under the appellations of Bergerac, Cotes de Bergerac and Monbazillac (whose Chateau Bazillac produces a luscious dessert wine of world class), and Pécharment, its finest red. The red wines tend to be fruity and full-bodied and the whites can be either dry or sweet. (We will resist the temptation to say Bergerac wines possess the finest "nose" of all French wines.)

### CAHORS

The region of Cahors produces red wines that are deep, powerful, full of tannin in their youth, and have great aging ability. The main grape varieties are Malbec, Merlot, and Tannat, a local variety. It was once remarked that the wines of Cahors are like "a strong hand in a velvet glove."

## COTES de BUZET
## and COTES de DURAS

These small vineyard areas produce wines similar to those of Bergerac and have their own appellations. The red wines are full in body, with deep color and intense bouquet, and are wines that will improve with some age. There is a little white wine produced in this region as well.

*Domaine Ott Château de Selle from Provence may be the very finest rose in the world. Grenache, Cabernet, and Cinsault grapes yield a coral-hued wine that evokes the fragrances of thyme, rosemary, blackberries, and vanilla.*

# FRANCE IN REVIEW

- Although many countries produce quality wines, France enjoys a paramount reputation in this regard.

- France is among the leaders in table and sparkling wine production and consumption.

- Each area of France is associated with its own particular grape varieties and types of wine:

| | |
|---|---|
| Champagne | — *Pinot Noir, Chardonnay* |
| | — Sparkling Wine |
| Bordeaux | — *Cabernet Sauvignon, Merlot* |
| | — Red Table |
| | — *Sauvignon Blanc* |
| | — White Table |
| Sauternes | — *Semillon* — Dessert |
| Burgundy | — *Pinot Noir* — Red Table |
| | — *Chardonnay* — White Table |
| Beaujolais | — *Gamay* — Red Table |
| Rhône | — *Syrah* — Red Table |
| Loire | — *Sauvignon Blanc, Chenin Blanc, Melon* — White Table |
| Alsace | — *Riesling, Gewürztraminer* |
| | — White Table |

- France's wine legislation, the Appellation Contrôlée, has been a model for other countries to follow.

- Chablis is France's most famous dry white wine.

- Bordeaux is the finest *large* wine producing-area in the world. Bordeaux wines are blends. Burgundy is made from only one grape.

- Côte d'Or produces the best in red and white burgundy.

- In Burgundy many people or companies own parcels of a single estate. The shipper is important in Burgundy.

---

**DO YOU KNOW YOUR POUILLYS (PWEES)?**

| Wine | Geographic Area | Grapes |
|---|---|---|
| Pouilly-Fumé | Loire | Sauvignon(Fumé)Blanc |
| Pouilly-Sur-Loire | Loire | Chasselas |
| Pouilly-Fuisse | | |
| Pouilly-Vinzelles } | Burgundy (Mâcon) | Chardonnay |
| Pouilly-Loche | | |

---

# SELF-EVALUATION

BEFORE READING ON, see if you have mastered the data set forth in the last few pages. Check the answer section at the back of the book for the correct answers. If you have not answered at least 70% of the questions below correctly, please reread the previous section.

## ALSACE - LOIRE - OTHER

TRUE     FALSE

———    ———   1. The expression "German wine made in the French manner" typifies the wines of Alsace.

———    ———   2. The Appellation Contrôlée of Alsace divides the region into three sections.

———    ———   3. Wines of Alsace are usually very fresh and lively, even spicy.

———    ———   4. Alsatian wines are named after grape varieties.

———    ———   5. The Loire is better known for red wines than for whites.

———    ———   6. Wines from Loire generally are to be consumed young.

———    ———   7. Melon de Bourgogne is the basic grape in Sancerre wines.

———    ———   8. Muscadet, Anjou, and Touraine are districts within the Loire.

———    ———   9. Provence produces only dry roses.

———    ———   10. "Straw wine" is another term for dessert wine.

———    ———   11. The Midi is France's "bulk wine" area.

# GLOSSARY OF FRENCH TERMS

**Chai** — An above ground storage facility for wine casks, as opposed to a cellar. Especially in Bordeaux.

**Chaptalisation** — The addition of sugar at the time of the crush to assure a higher alcohol content. Not a sweetening process. Especially in Bordeaux.

**Château** — A wine-producing estate attached to a specific vineyard. May be a cottage or a splendid castle. Especially in Bordeaux.

**Climat** — A vineyard, a Cru in Burgundy, such as Le Montrachet. Equivalent to a growth in Bordeaux.

**Clos** — A vineyard enclosed by a wall. Especially in Burgundy.

**Commune** — A parish or township.

**Cooperative** — A group of growers or winemakers that join together to grow grapes or make and cellar wines.

**Côte** — A vineyard slope.

**Cru** — A growth, a vineyard of high quality.

**Domaine** — A wine estate. Especially in Burgundy.

**Gout** — The taste of a product. In Champagne, dry versions are called Gout Anglais (British style); sweeter ones are Gout Americain (American style). A wine with an earthy taste has the Gout de Terroir.

**Hectare** — 2.47 acres.

**Hectoliter** — 100 liters or about 26.5 gallons.

**Mis en Bouteilles au Chateau** — "Chateau-bottled." Especially in Bordeaux. This just tells us where the wine was bottled and is not automatically a sign of quality. But you should recall that the less a wine is handled, the better.

**Moelleux** — Soft, smooth, not completely dry.

**Mousseux** — Sparkling.

**Negociant** — A shipper; one who buys grapes or wine, then produces, blends, bottles, and sells the wine.

**Negociant-Eleveur** — A shipper who does not own but supervises the growing of grapes that will eventually be transformed into wine.

**Oeil de Perdrix** — "Eye of the Partridge," a pale-hued rosé wine.

**Pelure D'Oignon** — "Onion Skin," a tawny rosé wine.

**Petillant** — Crackling, slightly effervescent.

**Pourriture Noble** — "Noble Rot," a special mold (*Botrytis cinerea*) that forms on white grapes. Essential to the production of Sauternes.

**Proprietaire** — The proprietor or owner of a vineyard, winery or château.

**Recoltant** — A grower of grapes.

**Tonneau** — A measure equal to four barriques or 900 liters (237 gallons). A Tonneau yields 1,152 bottles or 96 cases of wine. Used as a measurement in Bordeaux.

**Ullage** — Space inside the bottle caused by the evaporation of wine.

**Vendange** — The vintage, the harvest, the year in which the grapes were picked.

**Vin Doux Naturel** — Unfortified, sweet dessert wine with alcohol of at least 14%, such as Muscat de Beaumes-de-Venise.

**Vigneron** — A vine grower. Sometimes broadly used to mean a wine maker.

# NOTES

# THE WINES OF ITALY

## INTRODUCTION

Truly Italy is an enigma: No country can rival her in the variety or volume of wine production, and she boasts some of the world's oldest estates and most prestigious wines. Yet other countries generally view her as a source of wines of average quality at reasonable prices. Familiar standbys such as Soave, Chianti, Asti Spumante, and Lambrusco dominate sales figures, and formidable brands such as Bolla, Ruffino, Martini and Rossi, and Riunite must be viewed as leaders within these popular categories.

In the U.S., Italian wines outsell all other imports combined. With regard to fine wines, we have experienced only the tip of the Italian iceberg. Surely in the next few years, Italy will provide the U.S. with a steady stream of esoteric discovery which will vie the well-known estates of France and California.

The wines of Italy are steeped in the history of its peninsula. As a country Italy is only a bit more than one century old, but her rich heritage dates back almost 4,000 years. Slavs, Germans, the French, Spanish, and Arabs have left indelible marks on Italian culture. Before them, Greeks, Romans, Etruscans, Jews, and Phoenicians influenced Italian thought. Add the native genius of the Italians themselves and it is not difficult to imagine how such a broad rainbow of colors, flavors, and styles are found among Italian wines.

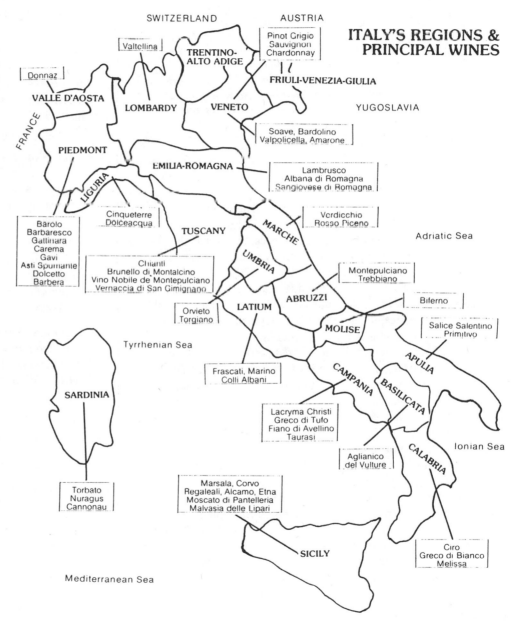

ITALY'S REGIONS & PRINCIPAL WINES

SWITZERLAND

AUSTRIA

Valtellina

TRENTINO-ALTO ADIGE

Pinot Grigio
Sauvignon
Chardonnay

Donnaz

FRIULI-VENEZIA-GIULIA

VALLE D'AOSTA

LOMBARDY

VENETO

YUGOSLAVIA

FRANCE

PIEDMONT

Soave, Bardolino
Valpolicella, Amarone

EMILIA-ROMAGNA

Lambrusco
Albana di Romagna
Sangiovese di Romagna

LIGURIA

Cinqueterre
Dolceacqua

Verdicchio
Rosso Piceno

Adriatic Sea

Barolo
Barbaresco
Gattinara
Carema
Gavi
Asti Spumante
Dolcetto
Barbera

TUSCANY

MARCHE

UMBRIA

Chianti
Brunello di Montalcino
Vino Nobile de Montepulciano
Vernaccia di San Gimignano

Montepulciano
Trebbiano

ABRUZZI

Biferno

Orvieto
Torgiano

LATIUM

MOLISE

Salice Salentino
Primitivo

Tyrrhenian Sea

Frascati, Marino
Colli Albani

APULIA

CAMPANIA

BASILICATA

SARDINIA

Lacryma Christi
Greco di Tufo
Fiano di Avellino
Taurasi

Ionian Sea

CALABRIA

Aglianico
del Vulture

Torbato
Nuragus
Cannonau

Marsala, Corvo
Regaleali, Alcamo, Etna
Moscato di Pantelleria
Malvasia delle Lipari

Ciro
Greco di Bianco
Melissa

SICILY

Mediterranean Sea

177

Italy is about the same size as California but with over twice its population. Most of the country is hilly or mountainous with a great diversification of soil. The Alps help protect the peninsula from the harsh winters of Northern Europe. There are micro-climates in Southern Italy that are as cool as Burgundy and Bordeaux due to altitude and lake or sea breezes. All in all, the climate is ideal for wine production. There is significant variation, however, from vintage to vintage. Well over 1,200 grape varieties are planted. These yield over 3,000 different kinds of wines.

Each year over seven billion liters of wine are produced. More than 22 gallons per capita are consumed (about 10 times as much as in the U.S.). Red wine is generally preferred to white. Italy is a world leader in table wines, in aromatized (vermouth), and, sparkling wines. Marsala, Italy's famous fortified wine, lags far behind sherry in popularity. Italian production and consumption figures must be viewed as conservative, since even today many families produce their own wine for personal use.

Italy is divided into 20 regions which are similar to our states. Regions are then broken down into provinces, like our counties. Each region possesses its own government, its own dialect, cuisine, pasta shapes, grape varieties, and wines. Very few wines sell outside of their respective regions. Most grape varieties, although they are first rate vinifera, have not been planted throughout the rest of Europe or the U.S. Exceptions include Barbera (California), Moscato (many countries including France), and Trebbiano (the basic grape of cognac). Within Italy, most varietals are planted only in two or three adjacent regions. Italian wines are invariably linked to food.

## How Italian Wines Are Named

*You will understand this better after reading the section on the Italian wine laws.*

1. **Geographical Names** — Usually the name of the town from which the wine comes, such as Barbaresco, Chianti, Gavi, Soave, Barolo, or Orvieto. Many geographical areas are D.O.C. zones. All of these listed are D.O.C. or D.O.C.G. Sometimes the wine is named for a vineyard plot within an approved zone, for example: "Zonchera" Barolo, "Asij" Barbaresco.

2. **Grape Names** —
   a. In combination **with non-D.O.C.** geographical names (such wines are not D.O.C.): Barbera (del Piemonte), Pinot Grigio (del Veneto), Trebbiano (di Sicilia).

   b. In combination **with D.O.C.** geographical names (these wines are D.O.C.): Barbera (D'Asti), Pinot names (these wines are D.O.C.): Barbarera (D'Asti), Pinot Grigio (dell'Alto Adige), Trebbiano (D'Abruzzo).

3. **Legendary Names** — That is, wine whose names are based upon folklore or tradition: Est! Est!! Est!!! (di Montefiascone) D.O.C., Lacryma Christi (del Vesuvio) D.O.C., Vino Nobile (di Montepulciano) D.O.C.G. When combined with an approved area, the wine will qualify for D.O.C. or D.O.C.G.

4. **Proprietary Names** — That is, trademark names ordinarily fantasy names, vineyard names or estate names:

| PROPRIETARY NAMES | WINERY WHICH OWNS THE TRADEMARK |
|---|---|
| Ca del Pazzo | Caparzo Estate |
| Corvo | Duca di Salaparuta |
| Regaleali | Count Tasca |
| Tignanello | Antinori Winery |
| Terre Alte | Livio Felluga Winery |

**"LE RAGOSE"**
1981

AZIENDA AGRICOLA DI M. MARTA GALLI NEGRAR VERONA

SHIPPED BY ENOTECA INTERNAZIONALE DE RHAM M.

| NET CONTENS 750 ML | RECIOTO DELLA VALPOLICELLA | Alcohol 13.50% By Vol. |
|---|---|---|
| | DENOMINAZIONE DI ORIGINE CONTROLLATA V.Q.P.R.D. | |
| | **AMARONE** | |
| | RED DRY WINE · **ESTATE BOTTLED** · PRODUCT OF ITALY | |
| | BY AZ. AGR. «LE RAGOSE» DI M.M. GALLI · NEGRAR · ITALIA | |

*Riserva 1983*

*Chianti* ✠ *Rufina*
*denominazione di origine controllata*

FATTORIA
**SELVAPIANA**
*imbottigliato da*
*Francesco Giuntini A.*
*proprietario viticoltore*

NELLE CANTINE DI RUFINA - ITALIA
R.I. 296/FI

0,750 ℓ. ℮                                    12,5% vol.

*1987*

**DECUGNANO DEI BARBI** ®
*Orvieto Classico*
*denominazione di origine controllata*

IMBOTTIGLIATO ALL'ORIGINE DA
*Azienda Agricola Decugnano dei Barbi*
ORVIETO - ITALIA

*There are several famous, high quality firms, such as Neil Empson and Marc de Grazia, who search Italy for rare, small precious estates. These wineries have been organized by Baron Armando De Rham of Enoteca Internazionale De Rham. It is safe to say that without his company, these fine holdings would be too small to attract international success.*

IMPORTED BY **FREDERICK WILDMAN AND SONS, LTD.** NEW YORK, N.Y.

U.S. REPRESENTATIVES

DRY WHITE WINE

PRODUCT          OF ITALY

LEONE

# SOAVE

DENOMINAZIONE DI ORIGINE CONTROLLATA

BOTTLED BY FOLONARI s.c.a r.l. CALMASINO
AT ITS OWN CELLARS OF PASTRENGO - ITALIA

**FOLONARI**®

NET CONTENTS          ALCOHOL 11%
750 ml          BY VOLUME

## The Italian Wine Laws

Laws governing the wines of Italy are as ancient as the classical Romans. Limitations as to where Chianti and Carmignano may come from date back to an edict from the early eighteenth century. The great leap forward, however, came in 1963 with a presidential decree, more commonly known as the D.O.C. Wine Laws.

D.O.C. stands for *Denominazione di Origine Controllata,* which indicates a wine comes from a protected or controlled place of origin. These regulations run parallel to the French A.O.C. The standards imposed under the D.O.C. are administered by the Italian government's Ministry of Agriculture and Forestry and the National Committee. This committee consists of growers, wine

dealers, winery officials, members of professional wine associations, certain members of the wine press, and the National Union of Consumers. Together with local associations called Consortia, inspectors make certain that the prescribed standards of production are maintained.

Once a wine is granted a D.O.C., the consumer can be assured of the following and more:

1. Vintage dating is entirely accurate.
2. The wine is from the area designated on the label.
3. The wine has not been overproduced, that is, the yield per acre has been kept low.
4. Only prescribed grape varieties have been used.
5. The wine has been vinified and aged properly.

In other words, the wine must be typical and exemplary. The finished product must meet high standards of taste, color, fragrance, and flavor as well as chemical composition, alcohol, and acidity. Sales ledgers of wineries are inspected to confirm compliance. Strict penalties are exacted upon violators. These regulations are considered to be among the most stringent of their type.

IMPORTED

PRODUCED AND BOTTLED IN ITALY
ALCOHOL 12% BY VOLUME

NET CONT. 750 ML

ITALIAN DRY          WHITE WINE

# BERTANI (R)

## SOAVE

DENOMINAZIONE DI ORIGINE CONTROLLATA
CLASSICO SUPERIORE

PRODOTTO ALL'ORIGINE ED IMBOTTIGLIATO
A GREZZANA DALLA CASA VINICOLA

*Cav. Gio. Batt. Bertani*
VERONA - ITALIA
SOLE U.S.A. DISTRIBUTOR CARILLON IMPORTERS, LTD. TEANECK, NEW JERSEY

*Soave, Italy's favorite white D.O.C. wine, may be vinified to be a reasonably priced rival to American Chablis, as is the Folonari brand. Bertani, whose grapes come from a few select villages, is a "Classico." Because it is richer and higher in alcohol, it is "Superiore." Of course, it will be more expensive. Both are excellent within their genre.*

Although some wines are permitted to incorporate dried grapes, concentrates, and wines from other regions into their blends, the use of sugar (chaptalization) is strictly forbidden. Sulphur and other additives are kept to a minimum. It may be said that Italian wines are the most heavily scrutinized in the world. Today over 220 zones or about 800 types of wine fall under the D.O.C. This accounts for about 12% of Italy's production.

---

### HOW ITALY CLASSIFIES ITS WINES

**Denominazione di Origine Controllata** *(day-noh-mee-nah-tzee-OH-nay dee oh-REE-jee-nay kohn-troh-LAH-tah)* **D.O.C.** — Approximately 220 zones of production fall within this category, or about 12% of Italy's wine production. In addition to strict control in the field and at the winery, the finished wine must conform to high standards of fragrance, color, alcohol content, acid level, chemical composition, and flavor, or they face declassification.

**Denominazione di Origine Controllata e Garantita** *(day-noh-mee-nah-tzee-OH-nay dee oh-REE-jee-nay kohn-troh-LAH-tah ay gah-rahn-TEE-tah)* **D.O.C.G.** — In addition to meeting the above-mentioned standards for a D.O.C. wine, this category of wines has undergone a very rigorous tasting analysis by the Italian Ministry of Agriculture. Successful wines are awarded a special government seal. Unsuccessful wines are declassified and must be sold as table wines. Only six Italian wines are designated D.O.C.G. at this time:

1. Barbaresco
2. Barolo
3. Brunello di Montalcino
4. Chianti
5. Vino Nobile di Montepulciano
6. Albana di Romagna

(Soon Gattinara, Carmignano, and Torgiano Rosso Riserva will become D.O.C.G.)

**Vino da Tavola** *(VEE-noh dah TAH-voh-lah)* — Table wine. These wines represent a broad category. We will see a deeper classification of table wines in the years to come, just as we saw the D.O.C.G. emerge in the late 1970s. You must note that these table wines simply do not fit any D.O.C. statute at this time. They vary in quality from the adequate to the sublime.

---

Note that the Italian wine laws are in a constant state of flux. Wines are continually requesting D.O.C. status. In fact, when these rules were enacted in the mid-1960s, there was an entire classification for which no single wine could qualify. This was the D.O.C.G. category (G is for guaranteed). It was not until the early 1980s that a cluster of excellent Italian D.O.C.G. wines made their way into the general market. D.O.C.G. wines have a special government seal affixed to the capsule at the top of the bottle. This neckband indicates that the wine has not only met all the difficult D.O.C. requirements but has also undergone a severe tasting analysis by a special panel selected by the national committee.

To date there are five reds that qualify for the D.O.C.G. They are Barolo and Barbaresco from Piedmont, and Chianti, Vino Nobile di Montepulciano, and Brunello di Montalcino from Tuscany. Recently a white wine, Albana di Romagna from Emilia-Romagna, was granted D.O.C.G. If a wine fails to meet the requirements of the D.O.C.G., it must be declassified, then labeled and sold as simple table wine.

In a land of over 3,000 wines, it is impossible for each and every wine to fall under legal, governmental guidelines. Nor can the government be the final arbiter of quality. There is a broad spectrum of wines that do not fit under any D.O.C. or D.O.C.G. umbrella. They are called *Vino da Tavola* or table wine ( or *Vini da Tavola*, table *wines*). They range from the adequate to the sub-

---

### The D.O.C.G. Capsule Band

| MINISTERO DELL'AGRICOLTURA E DELLE FORESTE |
| --- |
| CAMERA DI COMMERCIO I.A.A. - SIENA |
| VINO A D.O.C.G. VINO NOBILE DI MONTEPULCIANO |

serie **AB**    lt. 0,750    N° 009054

*A special committee of the Ministry of Agriculture awards a band to D.O.C.G. wines. These wines have not only met strict requirements but have been tasted and approved by a panel of experts. These bands are severely counted and controlled and are usually placed across the top of the bottle or around the capsule. Please note that some producers, independent of D.O.C.G. requirements, affix their own quality control bands over the capsule.*

## QUALITY:
## What No Label Can Tell Us

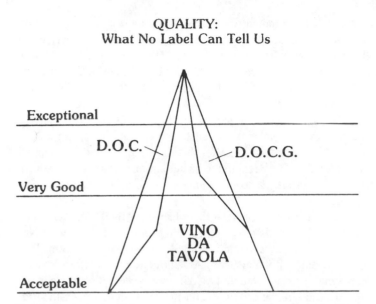

*No label can, by itself, be a guarantee of quality. There are significant quality variations within each D.O.C. or D.O.C.G. By that we mean that there is acceptable Soave, very good Soave, and exceptional Soave, all depending on the standards of the individual producer, not on government regulations. Do not think that D.O.C.G. wines are automatically better than D.O.C. wines or that D.O.C. wines are, in themselves, superior to Vini da Tavola. Some of the most exquisite and expensive Italian wines are Vini da Tavola that do not fit into any official classification. As in all other countries, the quality wines of Italy are always the conscious result of quality producers, not government mandates.*

lime. Some of Italy's elite wines are Vino da Tavola. Perhaps they use grapes that are not approved; perhaps their geographic area is not sanctioned. But for one reason or another, they do not fit into any of the 800 D.O.C. or D.O.C.G. boxes.

A look at the quality winery of the Antinori family may help explain this situation. Antinori produces a Chianti Classico Riserva, which satisfies the requirements of the D.O.C.G. He also produces a rare single-vineyard dry red wine called Tignanello, which is a blend of Sangiovese, Cabernet Sauvignon, and Cabernet Franc grapes. Since this blend does not conform to any existing D.O.C. or D.O.C.G. regulation, Tignanello is a Vino da Tavola. Antinori's Chianti is wonderful, but experts would place

his Tignanello upon a much higher rung of the ladder. The Vino da Tavola is more prestigious and expensive in this case than the D.O.C.G. wine.

This is not an isolated example. Sassicaia, Solaia, Rosso del Conte, San Giorgio, Vigorello, Grifi, Ca del Pazzo, and Sammarco are only a few of these highly priced and prized Vini da Tavola. The worth of a wine in Italy, as elsewhere, is based on the quality of the producer, not on a government mandate. Please note that this category makes Italian wines different from their French and German counterparts, where almost universally, quality wines conform to Appellation or Qualitäts mit Prädikat standards.

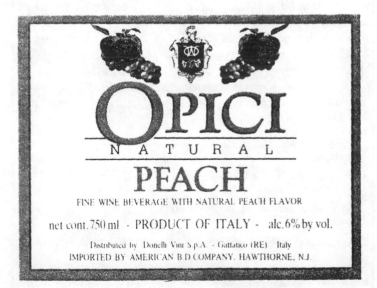

*Technically this is not a wine because of its very low (6%) alcohol. "Wine" statistics for Italy and Spain (Sangria) do not include products like this. This category of wine beverages led by Riunite, Giacobazzi, Cella, Bosca, and Opici has been extremely popular, especially in the summer. Now sales are dropping off, but these wines are still great alternative to wine coolers.*

Five reds now qualify for the D.O.C.G. Three are from Tuscany and are based on the Sangiovese grape: Chianti, Brunello di Montalcino, and Vino Nobile di Montepulciano. Two are from Piedmont and are based on the Nebbiolo: Barolo and Barbaresco. The first and only white is Albana di Romagna from Emilia-Romagna and is based on the Albana vine.

*Estate-bottled, this Brunello di Montalcino is from the most successful importer of Italian wines, Banfi.*

*Martinenga, owned by Marchese di Gresy, is considered to be the finest vineyard area in Barbaresco. 1982 was an outstanding vintage for Barolo and Barbaresco. As with Barolo, the wine is 100% Nebbiolo.*

*This estate-bottled Vino Nobile is from an Azienda Agricola (Az Agr.), a farm which does not buy grapes but grows its own. The estate, Sanguineto (bloody) is so named because it is an ancient battleground.*

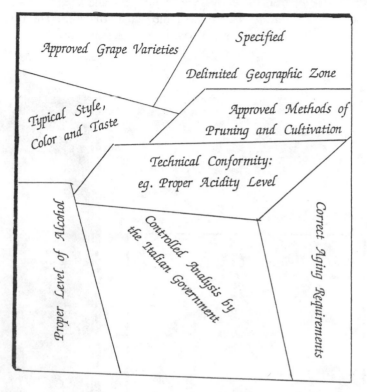

Approved Grape Varieties

Specified Delimited Geographic Zone

Typical Style, Color and Taste

Approved Methods of Pruning and Cultivation

Technical Conformity: eg. Proper Acidity Level

Proper Level of Alcohol

Controlled Analysis by the Italian Government

Correct Aging Requirements

*Without any one of the pieces the puzzle is incomplete and, therefore, the wine cannot be D.O.C. or D.O.C.G.*

**Barolo**

*Product of Italy*

CANTINE VILLADORIA

*Denominazione di origine controllata e garantita*

*Riserva*

*Dry Red Wine*

*bottled by C.E.D.I.V.I.-Serralunga d'Alba*

Imported by: AMERICAN B.D. COMPANY
Hawthorne New Jersey - N. J.

**VILLADORIA**

Alcohol 13% by vol.   Reg.imb.2236/2 CN   Net contents 750 ml

*Riserva Speciale means that the wine was aged for at least five years. Under the new D.O.C.G. laws the category of Riserva Speciale will disappear. There will only be Barolo and Barolo Riserva, like the above label.*

PRODUZIONE LIMITATA

# Colle del Re

## ALBANA DI ROMAGNA
DENOMINAZIONE DI ORIGINE CONTROLLATA E GARANTITA
**1987**
SECCO

*Umberto Cesari*

750 ML   PRODUCT OF ITALY   ALC.
IMBOTTIGLIATO DA CESARI - CASTEL S. PIETRO - ITALIA   11.5% BY VOL.

*This dry white is produced from 100% Albana grapes. Fewer than 6000 cases are made annually from the Colle del Re vineyard site.*

---

### Three Types of Wineries

1. **Azienda Agricola** — "A grape-wine estate." Similar to a French château. They produce their own grapes and do not purchase any.

2. **Casa Vinicola** — "A wine house." Like the French negociants and negociant-eleveurs, they buy grapes and make wine.

3. **Cantina Sociale** — "A cooperative winery." Some are excellent, such as Barbaresco and Barolo.

The House of Bolla, popularizers of premium Soave, Bardolino, and Valpolicella in the U.S., have recently launched their Franco Bolla signature selections. In Italy there is a trend toward upscale wines and super-premium varieties. Bolla is a brand in the vanguard. Even with the untimely death of Franco Bolla, his family continues his work.

- *Fruity, fresh Pinot Grigio from the Dolomite Alto Adige region goes well with fish or poultry.*

- *Flinty, dry Gavi, based on the Cortese grape, is perfect for seafood.*

- *Full, rich Amarone, the Bolla family favorite, is ideal for cheeses, game, beef, or lamb.*

185

# SELF-EVALUATION

BEFORE READING ON, see if you have mastered the data set forth in the last few pages. Check the answer section at the back of the book for the correct answers. If you have not answered at least 70% of the questions below correctly, please reread the previous section.

## THE WINES OF ITALY
### INTRODUCTION

TRUE     FALSE

_____ _____ 1. It has been said many times that Italy is known for her red wines more than for her whites.

_____ _____ 2. Italy has become the largest supplier of wines to the United States.

_____ _____ 3. The addition of sugar to the fermenting grape (chaptalization) is legal in Italy using the Denomination Laws recently passed by the Italian government.

_____ _____ 4. Italy produces over three billion gallons (12 billion liters) of wine each year.

_____ _____ 5. Italy is divided into over 26 regions.

_____ _____ 6. In Italy, vintage is not a large contributing factor to the quality of a wine.

_____ _____ 7. The average Italian consumes about three times as much wine as the average American.

_____ _____ 8. Italian grape varieties are widely planted throughout the world.

_____ _____ 9. Wine is produced in every region of Italy.

_____ _____ 10. All of the D.O.C.G. wines are red.

_____ _____ 11. Barolo may be red or white.

_____ _____ 12. All of the best wines of Italy are D.O.C. or D.O.C.G.

_____ _____ 13. Italian wines are best served by themselves, that is, without food.

# THE WINE REGIONS OF ITALY

## NORTHERN ITALY

Northern Italy is one of the most affluent and chic areas in the world. The landscape is dominated by lofty mountains, great lakes, and the fertile Po River Basin. Major business centers can be found in Milan, Turin, and Genoa in the west. Venice and Verona attract tourists in the east, as does Trieste. Although each region will boast that its cuisine is the best, one city in Emilia-Romagna, Bologna, has been nicknamed "La Grassa," the Fat One, and has been called the Lyons of Italy. Museums, architecture, universities, and hospitable people make northern Italy a must for tourists. It is a great place to enjoy a wine tour, since many of Italy's best and most famous wines originate here, including Barolo, Barbaresco, Asti Spumante, Soave, Valpolicella, Bardolino, Amarone, Pinot Grigio, and Lambrusco.

*Fratelli Oddero is located in La Morra in the Piedmont section of northwest Italy. Of their approximately 55 acres of vineyards, half produces Barolo. Fratelli Oddero's reputation in Italy and in the United States is excellent, and their wines continually support that reputation.*

### Val D'Aosta

Mt. Blanc, lofty Alpine terraces and minuscule quantities of wine from Europe's highest vineyards are the trademarks of this "Valley of Augustus," nestled in the northwest corner of Italy. French is spoken as well as Italian, as can be seen on wine labels. This is the smallest and least populated region of Italy. It is also last in wine production. Most of the wine is consumed locally. These distinctive wines are regarded as curiosities. French (Gamay, Pinot Noir), Italian (Nebbiolo, Moscato) and German (Müller-Thürgau) varieties are planted, as well as local Petit Rouge and Malvoisie. Of the 15 wines that qualify for D.O.C., the reds, Donnaz and Enfer D'Arvier, and white Blanc de Morgex are the most interesting and most likely to be found in the U.S.

### Piedmont
#### Italy's Cote D'Or

Piedmont means "foot of the mountains," the mountains being the Alps and Apennines which hem it in. It is famous for Fiat and for white truffles, for Vermouth and Asti Spumante, and for the king and queen of Italian wines. The king is Barolo, a generous mouth-filling red from the Langhe Hills in southern Piedmont outside of the town of Alba. The queen is Gattinara, an elegant red wine from the Novara Hills far to the north, close to Switzerland and Lake Maggiore. Both are based on the Nebbiolo vine.

Piedmont is most famous for its reds but actually produces a great quantity of whites. Fruity Moscato D'Asti and Asti Spumante from a zone just south of the Tanaro River lead the way. Gavi, a dry flinty white based on the Cortese grape, has been called the most French of Italian whites. Crisp and light, Gavi is compared to French Chablis and matches up well to the seafood of the Italian Riviera just to the south.

Barbera is the most popular red wine vine. Dolcetto produces deep purple, fragrant, soft, dry wines. Often compared to Beaujolais, Dolcetto has a style all its own.

The most impressive grape is the Nebbiolo, which means foggy. The name comes from the fog, which lingers on the hillsides during autumn mornings. Nebbiolo D'Alba, Barolo, and Barbaresco are made exclusively from the Nebbiolo vine. Barolo

Certain outstanding wineries produce superb wines that fit into each Italian classification. The wines below are fashioned at the Colombini estate, Fattoria dei Barbi (a Fattoria is a farm, not a factory). All are limited, estate-bottled, dry reds.

*Vino da Tavola-Brusco dei Barbi – This rustic, hearty wine is about 80% Sangiovese and 20% Canaiolo. It shows its best with hard, aged cheeses. Will hold for six to eight years.*

*D.O.C.-Rosso di Montalcino – Since 1983 a D.O.C. wine. This wine spends up to 18 months in the cask before release. Try it with poultry, game birds, or chops.*

*D.O.C.G.-Brunello di Montalcino – Aristocratic Brunello must be aged for four years, three and a half of which are in cask. A "Riserva" is held for one additional year at the winery. Barbi uses different color labels (red for Riserva; blue for regular) plus a neck label to distinguish theirs.*

and Barbaresco are named for towns just outside of Alba in the Langhe Hills. If Barolo is the king, Barbaresco is the crown prince. Both wines are powerful in structure, rich in tannin and extract, and capable of long cellaring. Traditionalists keep these wines in wooden casks for five or ten years in certain vintages. Some producers choose to age Barolo (three years) and Barbaresco (two years) only as briefly as required by D.O.C.G. mandates. This results in a wine that is more moderate in size and more approachable in its youth. Whether you are a traditionalist or lover of innovation, seek out the quality producers of each school. There are many but would include Gaja, Ceretto, Giacosa, Aldo Conterno, Giacomo Conterno, Ratti, and Di Gresy.

In the Novara Hills to the north, the Nebbiolo is called *Spanna*.

In the hands of a master like Antonio Vallana, non-D.O.C. Spanna del Piemonte can be a glorious wine. You will also find interesting dry reds such as Ghemme, Fara, Sizzano, and Boca based on Nebbiolo with a bit of Bonarda and Vespolina added. Carema, especially that of the house of Ferrando, is one of the most fragrant and delicious wines made from the Nebbiolo vine. Here the Gattinara reigns as queen. Napoleon is said to have preferred it to his beloved Chambertin. Quality producers include Monsecco, Dessilani, Antoniolo, and Travaglini.

Piedmont leads Italy by having the greatest number of registered D.O.C. vineyards (over 31,000) as well as the most D.O.C./D.O.C.G. zones (37). Many towns have their own wine museum. The climate of the area can be quite severe, especially the winters. In some years entire productions of Barolo and Barbaresco must be declassified. Lighter reds are made from Grignolino and Freisa grapes. New dry whites include Erbaluce di Caluso and Arneis, which may rival Gavi in a few years. The key in these wines is the excellence of the producer. For example, the prolific Barbera, which usually yields a dry red wine of average quality, is responsible for Giacomo Bologna's brilliant Bricco Dell'Uccellone, which must be regarded as one of Italy's most respected wines.

Piedmont is a center for sparkling wines. Sweetish, fragrant Asti Spumante is so successful that we Americans tend to think that *all* Italian *spumanti* are sweet. Nothing could be farther from the truth. Piedmont is a leading producer of brut spumante, much of it based on Pinot Noir and Chardonnay grapes, which come from Lombardy and Trentino Alto-Adige.

There has also been a renewed interest in table wines made from Cabernet Sauvignon and Chardonnay which have been growing in Piedmont since the early 1800s. Gaja's versions have achieved critical success at high prices. Still the big, rich, dry, generous reds, Barolo, Barbaresco, and Gattinara are what come to mind when the oenophile thinks of Piedmont.

*Gavi or Cortese di Gavi may come from several communities in eastern Piedmont. Gavi di Gavi comes exclusively from the town of Gavi itself.*

*This Barolo from the exceptional 1978 vintage has been aged in large oak barrels for at least five years, as we see from the words "Riserva Speciale." Cerequio is a preeminent vineyard area, adjacent to the illustrious Brunate vineyard.*

ANTICHI VIGNETI DI CANTALUPO
GHEMME — ITALIA

COLLIS BRECLEMAE
# GHEMME
DENOMINAZIONE DI ORIGINE CONTROLLATA
VINTAGE
1983

DRY RED WINE                    NUMBERED BOTTLE

NET CONTENTS 750 ML - PRODUCT OF ITALY - ALCOHOL 13.5% BY VOL. ESTATE BOTTLED BY ANTICHI VIGNETI DI CANTALUPO OF ALBERTO & MAURIZIO ARLUNNO & C. - GHEMME - ITALY - 10.953 NUMBERED BOTTLES HAVE BEEN SELECTED FORM THE 1983 HARVEST

IMPORTED BY: AMERICAN B.D. - COMPANY
HAWTHORNE, N.J.

*This austere dry red based on the Nebbiolo vine is not well-known yet in the U.S. In Italy it is quite renowned, however, having been enjoyed by heads of state and even the papacy.*

This estate has been in the Broglia family for many years. Piero Broglia, the present director, is its sole proprietor. In a few short years he has imposed his name on the market with his production of Cortese Di Gavi. This single vineyard limited production of "Gavi in Barrique" is a fine example.

"Il Favot" Vino Rosso da Tavola is a special blending of Nebbiolo, produced by Aldo Conterno, who is without question one of the great producers of Barolo wines in the region.

The La Chiara Estate is situated in a lovely valley about two kilometers from the town of Gavi, which itself is located on the border between the Liguria and Piedmont regions. The proprietor of the estate is Nando Bergaglio, a traditional and talented wine maker who had dedicated his life to seeking perfection in the production of the Cortese di Gavi wine.

The Estate of Giacomo Conterno is located in the picturesque village of Monforte D'Alba in the heart of Piemonte's finest wine producing area. Traditionally produced, Conterno wines use only the most carefully selected grapes from the best vintages to achieve the full-bodied, ample, long-lived, old-style Barolo at its very best.

*The House of Contratto, Italy's most renowned name in sparkling wines, was one of the first to market a delicate Gavi in the U.S. Enjoy Contratto Gavi young with seafood. Based on the Cortese vine.*

*Uniting modern wine making with traditional methods, Castello di Neive produces only wine of the highest quality. The grapes for these outstanding wines come exclusively from Castello di Neive's estates, which include the famous vineyards of Santo Stefano. Estate bottled, this wine received a coveted four stars in the Wasserman book,* Italy's Noble Red Wines. *This Barbaresco, which should age for many years, is ruby red, big, rich, and velvety.*

*The wines of Produttori del Barbaresco — one of the world's truly exceptional co-operatives — includes nearly one quarter of the vineyards in the Barbaresco zone. Many feel these superbly made wines are the epitome of excellence for this prestigious region.*

## Liguria

Liguria, the Italian Riviera, is most noted for the flowers of San Remo and the Port of Genoa, Christopher Columbus's birthplace. This narrow strip of hilly coastline abounds in fish and in a green paste made from basil, oil, cheese, and pine-nuts, called *pesto*. Wines are made in small quantities, sometimes under almost impossible circumstances due to the difficult terrain. Only Val D'Aosta produces less wine.

Dry whites based on local vines called Pigato and Vermentino are quite exquisite. A soft, attractive red, Rossese di Dolceacqua, comes from the western corner of Liguria, close to Monaco and France's Cote D'Azur. The most prized wine of the region is Cinqueterre, or Five Lands. This is an ancient, delicate white wine made from grapes grown around five villages between coastal cliffs and the sea. Harvesting and transporting these grapes requires boats, since some vineyard sites are not otherwise accessible. Cinqueterre is usually dry; there is a very rare, highly prized sweet Cinqueterre, called Sciacchetra, made from sun-dried raisin-like grapes.

The only problem with these wonderful and interesting wines of Liguria is that we seldom can find them in the U.S. Perhaps we will see more of them in the near future, especially Pigato and Vermentino.

*Banfi chose to name their Gavi after the Princess Gavia, who once ruled this idyllic area in eastern Piedmont. Principessa Gavi, when very fresh, will contain a slight, attractive petillance, a natural result of the cold fermentation process.*

## Lombardy

Lombardy is one of the most diverse of the Italian regions. With Milan, the hub of Italy's commerce, Lombardy is the most affluent and populous region. The rich culture includes the famous violin makers of Cremona: Stradevari and Guarneri. The peninsula's most famous river, the Po, flows through it and all three lakes, Como, Magggiore, and Garda, grace it. The climate, tempered by the Alps to the north, is fine for viticulture. Yet the reds of its westerly neighbor, Piedmont, and whites from the east, Veneto, outshine Lombardy's wines, as do the frothy Lambruscos of Emilia-Romagna to its south.

Still we would refer to Lombardy as an up-and-coming region, with a few shining stars already. Much good wine comes from the area south of the Po River, called Oltrepo (beyond the Po). Grapes from the Pinot family plus Barbera, Bonarda, Riesling, and Moscato thrive there. Farther east on the slopes overlooking Lake Garda, many fine D.O.C. wines are made including Lugana, a crisp white which stands up to the very best Soaves.

Outstanding estates in the area include Frecciarossa (Red Ar-

row). At one time Frecciarossa wines were world-renowned, perhaps due to the French label designations used by then-proprietor, Dr. Giorgio Odero. A red called Grand Cru and a rosé, St. George, were based on Barbera, Croatina, and Uva Rara grapes. A dry white was called La Vigne Blanche and a sweet white bore the name Sillery. Today the wines meet the Oltrepo Pavese D.O.C. and no longer carry the French terms. Close by, Angelo Ballabio produces superb, distinctive wines, including an oakaged white called Clastidum and a lordly red Narbusto, aged for at least eight years in wood. Both are very limited.

On the hillsides near Lake Iseo not too far east of Milano is Franciacorta. This superlative wine zone is home to Bella Vista, Ca Del Bosco, Berlucchi, and Barone Pizzini, some of the finest houses and grower-producers of premium dry sparkling wines. Excellent table wines are made there as well. Franciacorta Red is based on noble Cabernet Franc, Nebbiolo, Barbera, and Merlot.

*The estate-bottled Gavi of Piero Broglia is from La Meirana Estate. Flinty, delicately scented, Gavi has been called the most French of Italian whites because of its similarity to French Chablis.*

Franciacorta White is made from the aristocratic Chardonnay and Pinot Bianco. Quality is consistently high and should make Franciacorta one of Italy's premier wine areas.

In the mountains of the far north, around the town of Sondrio, is the Valtellina district. Here the Nebbiolo is called Chiavenasca, and yields the finest reds of the region. The steep vineyards require handpicking of grapes as well as placing them in baskets on cables for transport to the wineries. Wines from four subdistricts, Interno, Grumello, Sassella, and Valgella, are the most widely known. These wines are lighter in color and in body than a Gattinara or Barolo, but more fragrant and straightforward.

There is an Amarone-like red called Sforsato or Sfursat, which is made from dried raisinized grapes. Sfursat and other Valtellina reds mentioned here age quite well, sometimes for a decade or more. The only problem with these wonderful, discovery wines is that they are traditionally bought and consumed by their Swiss neighbors. Recent attempts by the Swiss government to promote and sell their own wines may be a blessing in disguise for those of us in the U.S. who would like to see (and to drink) more of the fine reds of Valtellina. Quality producers include Nino Negri, Tona and Rainoldi.

*Franciacorta white is based on the aristocratic Chardonnay vine. This brand is estate grown and estate bottled.*

## Emilia-Romagna
### Land of the "Fat"

This is the land of prosciutto, Parma ham, Parmigiano-Reggiano cheese, Mortadella (bologna), Lambrusco, and Luciano Pavarotti. Although the great tenor has voiced the praises of his region's wines and brought attention to the rich cuisine of Bologna, Modena, and Parma, there is much more to sing about.

From the northwestern province of Piacenza, not far from composer Verdi's idyllic estate in Bussetto, comes a rich, dry red called Gutturnio. Based on Barbera and Bonarda grapes, it is named for the classical Roman wine, Gutturnium. Produced by Castello di Luzzano, it is stunning and shows the potential for moderate aging. In the U.S., it is all but completely unknown and yet to be discovered.

Bologna "La Grassa," the "Fat One," is in the middle of the region and is revered as the culinary center of Italy. It has been referred to as the "Lyons of Italy." Lyons would be honored to be called the "Bologna of France." It is clearly the fresh, handmade pasta capital of Italy, as the tagliatelle, tortellini, gnocchi, cappelletti, and other shapes would confirm. Not only are the recipes and dishes divine, but with the balsamic vinegar of Pavarotti's home, Modena, Grana grating cheeses, and the aforementioned prosciutto ham, Bologna provides ingredients for the great recipes and dishes throughout Italy.

The wine that cuts most deliciously into this wealthy cuisine is Lambrusco. There are four D.O.C. zones for this red varietal, but most of what is imported into the U.S.A. is not D.O.C. Lambrusco is a frothy wine which has won popularity in the U.S. due to its crackle, residual sweetness, low alcohol and fresh, clean taste. It has outlasted Sangria and other "pop" wines, and although sales are slipping, we can safely say that more Lambrusco is shipped to the U.S. than all the wines of Germany combined.

Traveling east of Bologna toward Ravenna, famous for its mosaics, and the sea resort of Rimini, the land of Federico Fellini, the wine philosophy changes. Whereas in western Emilia there is a preference toward round, bubbly wine, in Romagna in the east they lean toward the dry, still types. Vines change as well, with Barbera and Lambrusco yielding to Sangiovese, Trebbiano, and Albana. Albana di Romagna is quite a versatile white wine. It can be dry, off-dry, still, crackling, or fully sparkling. A small estate, owned by Umberto Cesari, produces a single-vineyard dry Albana di Romagna called Colle del Re (hill of the king). It appears to be the king of the hill with regard to Albana and is one of Italy's finest white wines. In the hands of a quality producer such as Fattoria Paradiso, Albana di Romagna can be quite divine and can age for up to four or five years. It is the region's first D.O.C.G. wine and Italy's first white to gain the D.O.C.G. As with Gutturnio, we have yet to see a significant campaign to launch this wine onto our shores.

This is true also of the delicate, graceful Pagadebit wine, a stunning white which is made to be either dry or slightly sweet and is based on the legendary Pagadebit Gentile grape. One of the best producers of the entire region is Vallania, whose Terre Rosse estate in the hills southwest of Bologna produces topflight Sauvignon Blanc, Cabernet Sauvignon, and Chardonnay. The summit of Emilia-Romagna's wine peak is clearly the Castellucio estate of Gian Matteo Baldi. In the Romagna hills the Sangiovese Grosso grape grows to perfection. Baldi ages this red in small barrels of new French oak to produce three elegant, complex, long-lived wines, named after single-vineyard sites. His barrel fermented Sauvignon Blanc, called Ronco del Re, is one of the most sought after and costly dry white wines of the world. As you might expect, the supply is extremely limited.

Emilia-Romagna is a section that typifies the current Italian wine scene. There is a good supply of dependable D.O.C. Sangiovese and Trebbiano di Romagna, plus the ancient Gutturnio, and the modern esoteric wines of Gian Matteo Baldi. We see a new D.O.C.G. white, Albana di Romagna, as well. There is much more than just Lambrusco. Add the great and varied cuisine, and newly revived wine houses and *enotecas,* and Emilia-Romagna surely merits a side trip from the more popular Florence, Venice, or Milano.

*Zonchera is a small vineyard area where the Nebbiolo grapes for this wine are grown. This lordly Barolo is made by Bruno and Marcello Ceretto, who have been called "The Barolo Brothers." The Ceretto house style is elegant and well balanced.*

# SELF-EVALUATION

BEFORE READING ON, see if you have mastered the data set forth in the last few pages. Check the answer section at the back of the book for the correct answers. If you have not answered at least 70% of the questions below correctly, please reread the previous section.

## NORTHERN ITALY

TRUE      FALSE

_____    _____    1. In Piedmont, every vintage is outstanding.

_____    _____    2. Barolo is considered "the king of wines and the wine of kings."

_____    _____    3. Barbera is widely planted in Piedmont.

_____    _____    4. Valpolicella, when very young, has been compared to a French Beaujolais.

_____    _____    5. Bardolino is made from almost the same grapes as Valpolicella.

_____    _____    6. Northern Italy includes the area of Piedmont.

_____    _____    7. Piedmont is known for its red wines and among them are some of Italy's best.

_____    _____    8. Asti Spumante is a white sparkling wine that comes from anywhere in Piedmont.

_____    _____    9. Lugana wines are dry white wines from the area of Lombardy.

_____    _____    10. Soave, produced in the Veneto, takes its name from the ancient town of Soave.

_____    _____    11. The wines of Liguria and Val D'Aosta are very popular in the U.S.A.

_____    _____    12. Lugana is a crisp, light dry white wine which is similar to Soave in style and taste.

# NORTHEASTERN ITALY
## "The Three Venices"

We can safely refer to the northeastern corner of Italy as the "School of Italian Wines." This area is called the "three Venices" or "Tre Venezie" and consists of the regions of the Veneto, Friuli-Venezia Giulia, and Trentino-Alto Adige. Not only are there two outstanding viticultural schools in Conegliano and Trentino, but we witness a more sophisticated level of technology here than elsewhere, especially in the production of white wines. These three regions share a climate blessed by the Alps, which ward off the cold, harsh winters of Northern Europe. Burton Anderson calls this area the "sunny side" of the Alps.

Although culturally linked to the historic Venetian Republic, each region is unique. Trentino is pronouncedly Germanic, and Friuli points toward the Slavic countries to the east. The result of this diversity is a cosmopolitan mix of both native and foreign grape varieties. This interesting area is a consistent leader of high quality D.O.C. wines. No other section of Italy can claim to grow a greater variety of fine varietals.

## The Veneto
### "Wines of Today's Italy"

As to the specific region of the Veneto, we should point out that Italy's leading wine fair, Vinitaly, is held here in Verona. Usually among the top four regions in total production, the Veneto constantly ranks first in D.O.C. production.

This is the land of the famous white Soave, the D.O.C. wine most heavily imported into the U.S. Soave, a dry wine based on the Garganega and Trebbiano vines, is sometimes called "Italy's Chablis." This wine can be of the good value, dependable, jug style, of the consistent, high quality type, or of the costly, subtle, esoteric ilk. Leaders in the low price category include Folonari, followed by Barbella. Bolla leads the pack in sales among premium brands, outdistancing Bertani and Santa Sofia, which are also of excellent quality and reflect solid value. Super-premium producers include Pieropan, Masi, and Anselmi. You may also find a sparkling version of Soave, or a sweetish dessert type, called Recioto di Soave. Both of these are quite rare. Gambellara and Bianco di Custoza are crisp and light and will remind many of Soave.

Light, fruity reds from and around the idyllic villages of Bardolino and Valpolicella are often compared to France's Beaujolais because of their freshness. Both wines are made from the same grapes, Corvina, Molinara, and Rondinella. Bardolino is sometimes vinified to be a light, dry rose called Chiaretto. Valpolicella can be quite complex and robust, especially in the hands of a producer like Bertani, Masi's Serego Alighieri, Allegrini, or Tedeschi.

Soave, Bardolino, and Valpolicella have special *classico* zones, which consist of those villages that produce the very best grapes. If these wines are aged for a certain period of time and achieve a higher level of alcohol, they can be called *superiore*.

The richest wine of the region is a variety of Valpolicella called Amarone. This long-lived, dry red is made from partially dried grapes and must be viewed as one of the world's fullest wines. Quality producers include Bolla, Bertani, Masi, Le Ragose, Tommasi, Allegrini, Santa Sofia, as well as Cesari and La Colombaia (owned by the Montresor family).

Very popular dry sparkling wines, made from the ancient Prosecco grape, hail from the Veneto. Good by itself, Prosecco has also become the leading sparkler used in the Bellini cocktail. Great names in table wines include Maculan from Breganze, whose dessert wine, Torcolato, is of world-class stature. Count Loredon's Venegazzu estate wines from the Montello-Colli Asolani area include a Cabernet-Merlot blend which ranks with Italy's finest. The trend in the area has been toward varietal wines, such as the native Tocai and French imports such as Cabernet, Merlot, Chardonnay, and Pinot Blanc. Surely the hottest, most "camp" wine of the region is Pinot Grigio.

## Trentino-Alto Adige
### "The Tyrol"

One of Italy's most distinctive regions is that of Trentino-Alto Adige. The southern section is centered around the town of

Trento. The northern part, Alto Adige, named for the Adige River which winds south through Verona and into the Adriatic, is centered around Bolzano or Bolzen. If Bolzen sounds Germanic to you, you are right. This area, which touches Switzerland and Austria, is called the Sudtirol or South Tyrol. It was part of Austria until the end of the first World War. Much of the land is mountainous and impossible to cultivate. The emphasis is on quality. Over half of the region's production is D.O.C.; over one-third of the wine is exported. Much of the red and the dry, crisp Alpine white goes to Austria and to Germany. Some cases find their way to the United States.

German and Italian names exist side by side. Magdalenerwein is Santa Maddalena, Kalterersee is Lago di Caldaro, and Eisacktaler is Valle Isarco. Producers have names like Kettmeier, Conti Wallenburg, Lageder, and Tieffenbrunner. Native red grape varieties include Lagrein (called Dunkel or Scuro, meaning dark), Teroldego, Marzemino, and Schiava (a.k.a. Vernatsch). The renowned aromatic white grape from the town of Tramin, Gewürztraminer, has been transplanted in Alsace and other parts of Europe, the Americas, and Australia.

Fragrant whites based on Riesling, Sylvaner, Müller-Thürgau, and Moscato are in good supply. There are a few D.O.C. zones for Chardonnay. Sauvignon Blanc and Pinot Blanc do well, but the most popular white in the U.S. is clearly Pinot Grigio. Floral, fresh, light, and clean, Pinot Grigio displays the Italian style very clearly, as does the Chardonnay. This style tends toward leanness and crispness with good fruitiness and mouth-cleansing acidity. You will not usually find oaky, buttery, long-lived whites, but varietal character is not sacrificed.

Sparkling wines from the area, some made by the methode Champenoise, reflect this philosophy as well. Quality producers of dry spumanti include Ferrari, Equipe 5, and Vivaldi. Seldom are these wines as yeasty as their French counterparts. Crisp, light roses are made here, including the Lagrein Kretzer.

As to the reds of the region, Santa Maddalena has survived, being Mussolini's favorite. The wine is good, but very few would place it among Italy's top five. Lago di Caldaro is one of Italy's leading D.O.C. reds. Both are based on the Schiava vine. Surely we will see a good supply of fresh Cabernet Franc and Sauvignon, Pinot Nero (Pinot Noir), and Merlot as well as a smaller quantity of Lagrein Scuro, Marzemino, and Teroldego Rotaliano.

Outstanding small-production wines include Hoffstatter dry

*When the people of Friuli ask for "Vino Bianco" (white wine), they mean Tocai! Perfect with light cuisine, Tocai has not yet been "discovered" by Americans.*

white DeVite, based on the Kerner vine, and Count Bossi-Fedrigotti's red Cabernet-Merlot blend, called Foianeghe. Luna dei Feldi, a dry white from the Santa Margherita firm, is an exquisite white based partially on the Traminer grape.

## Friuli-Venezia Giulia
### "The Next Hot Region"

Friuli-Venezia Giulia borders Yugoslavia and Austria. Even within the region, sectionalism is rampant. Is Udine, Trieste, or Aquileia the cultural center of the region? It depends on whom you ask. Friuli might well become the next "discovery" area for the U.S., since it is responsible for avant-garde, dry whites, which we Americans love so much. Friuli is quite small and does not appear among the leaders in production. This region is, how-

Marco Felluga makes two Pinot Grigios. Both are from the same zone, Collio, and qualify for the same D.O.C., but one is made with grapes grown exclusively on the Russiz estate. Russiz Superiore is estate-bottled, one of Italy's very finest wines. The lion on the label is the emblem of Venice. The Latin reads, "Peace to you, Mark, my Evangelist."

Bertani Valpolicella is from the Valpantena area. You will note 13% alcohol. This is no light wine. It is full-bodied, ages well, and is similar to the fine reds of Piedmont.

199

No country has more tiny gems than Italy. The Maso Poli estate in Atesino in the hills of the northeast produces one of the finest Pinot Grigios and Chardonnay in all of Italy.

Bertani Amarone is unique insofar as it is aged at least eight years before release. Bertani Amarone that is 20–30 years old drinks beautifully. Full, round, rich, and elegant, this limited bottling is costly but well worth the price.

ever, constantly at the very top in percentage of high quality wines.

The cuisine, based upon fresh Adriatic fish, demands fruity, fresh, delicate whites. Most popular is the Tocai, but we see Sauvignon Blanc, Pinot Bianco, and Chardonnay as well. In addition, there are dry Verduzzo and Malvasia among the whites. Perhaps the most exquisite dry wine of the area is the Pinot Grigio, which is sometimes left in contact with the reddish skins of the grapes in the traditional, costly manner. This results in an intense, copper-colored wine, referred to locally as *ramato*. Friulian whites go very well with salty dishes.

There are light reds based on Cabernet and Merlot, which complement dishes based on game caught in the mountains in the north. These dry fruity reds are delightful when young. It is unfair to categorize them as white wines with red color. We are seeing a trend toward the use of *barriques* (small oak barrels of about 55 gallons; used for aging) among the reds, as is evidenced in Fantinel's exquisite "Rosso della Ponca."

Although there are seven D.O.C. zones, the most renowned are the hills of Collio (Goriziano) and Colli Orientali, close to Yugoslavia. There are many quality producers in the region. We could list Walter Filiputti of Ronco del Gnemiz, Schioppetto, Marco Felluga, Jermann of Vintage Tunina fame, Volpe Pasini, and the Abbazia di Rosazzo. Patriarch and perhaps foremost among the quality producers is Livio Felluga. With Livio Felluga and others we see a trend toward single-vineyard wines. Esoteric, proprietary wines, such as Vintage Tunina, Terre Alte, and Ronco delle Acacie, represent the pinnacle of production for the premium wineries.

For good wine at fair prices, it is difficult to beat the Cantina Casarsa in Grave del Friuli. There is a revival of local grape varieties such as the red Refosco and Schioppettino and the white Ribolla Gialla. The luscious, shy-bearing Picolit, the legendary "Dowager Empress" of dessert wines, is enjoying a revival, especially in Colli Orientali, which is the only D.O.C. zone for Picolit. The Verduzzo grape also provides exquisite dessert wine. Lire for lire, Verduzzo di Ramandolo may be the best dessert wine in Friuli, even in Italy on the whole.

It is surprising that in this bastion of fine white wines, more red is produced than white.

*Only those grape clusters that get the most sun are used in Amarone. This full, rich red is from the La Colombaia estate. It is a limited production with individually numbered bottles.*

*The Picolit vine is a shy-bearer due to a disease called floral abortion. From 7.5 acres you can get only 4,000 bottles in a good year. The vigneron normally gets 16,000 bottles from such acreage. Picolit is one of only two Italian wines used on the Orient Express. The other? Biondi-Santi Brunello di Montalcino.*

TORRE
DI LUNA

THIS WINE IS BOTTLED WITH THE NEW
MOON FOLLOWING IN OLD TRADITION
THAT GIVES IT A TASTE OF TIMES PAST

PINOT GRIGIO ATESINO

*"Torre di Luna" (tower of the moon) Merlot (red) and Pinot Grigio (white) are two wines of extremely good value that are produced from vineyards along the Adige River in the region of Trentino-Alto Adige. Following in the old tradition, the wines are only bottled with the new moon.*

TORRE
DI LUNA

THIS WINE IS BOTTLED WITH THE NEW
MOON FOLLOWING IN OLD TRADITION
THAT GIVES IT A TASTE OF TIMES PAST

TRENTINO MERLOT

№ 21008                          1985

BARONE
FINI
VALDADIGE

D.O.C.
PINOT GRIGIO
QUALITY DRY WHITE WINE

PRODUCED IN ITALY AND BOTTLED AT ORIGIN BY
CASCOM, MEZZOCORONA, TRENTO ITALY 486 TN

NET CONTENTS 750 ML.          ALCOHOL 12 % BY VOLUME

IMPORTED BY THE HOUSE OF BURGUNDY, INC., NEW YORK, N.Y.

*A floral, crisp Pinot Grigio is made by Barone Fini in the Adige Valley. This mountainous area around the town of Trento is responsible for some of Italy's most fragrant whites. Fini Pinot Grigio represents solid dollar value.*

## SerègoAlighieri

PRODUCE OF ITALY

Valpolicella Classico Superiore
Denominazione di origine controllata
Possessioni in Gargagnago di Valpolicella

### MASI·

Imbottigliatore: Masi Agricola Spa in S. Ambrogio di Valpolicella - Italia
Viticoltore e vinificatore: Conte di Serego Alighieri - Gargagnago Verona

750ml e ALC. 12% VOL.          Bott. n.

Valpolicella is usually light-bodied. This Classico Superiore is an exception. The Serego Alighieri Estate was
owned by the family of Dante Alighieri. Masi supervises
the production of this fine red like a French negociant-
eleveur.

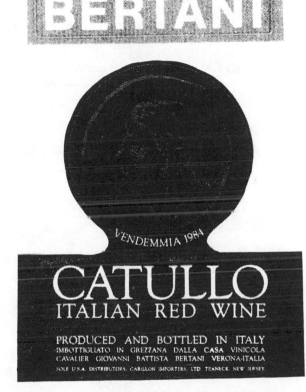

Catullo is the name of the classical Roman lyric and elegaic poet from
the Lake Garda area where this wine hails from. It is an exquisite Valpo-
licella-type wine vinified together with Amarone, so you get the body of
an Amarone at a Valpolicella price. Catullo is a trademark for the Bertani winery.

# SELF-EVALUATION

BEFORE READING ON, see if you have mastered the data set forth in the last few pages. Check the answer section at the back of the book for the correct answers. If you have not answered at least 70% of the questions below correctly, please reread the previous section.

# NORTHEASTERN ITALY

| TRUE | FALSE | |
|------|-------|---|
| _____ | _____ | 1. "Tre Venezie" consists of three regions: Veneto, Friuli-Venezia Giulia, and Trentino-Alto Adige. |
| _____ | _____ | 2. By D.O.C. law, all Soave must come from the Veneto. |
| _____ | _____ | 3. Wines from Bardolino and Valpolicella are often compared to French burgundies because of their mouth-filling, full-bodied style. |
| _____ | _____ | 4. Friuli is renowned for dry white wines. |
| _____ | _____ | 5. Friuli consistently produces small quantities of quality wines. |
| _____ | _____ | 6. There are seven D.O.C. zones and one D.O.C.G. zone in Friuli. |
| _____ | _____ | 7. The two basic red grapes in Friuli are Merlot and Sangiovese. |
| _____ | _____ | 8. The richest, fullest red wine of the Veneto is a variety of Valpolicella called Amarone. |
| _____ | _____ | 9. Pinot Grigio is a famous white grape in the Trentino-Alto-Adige region. |

# CENTRAL ITALY

There is a saying in the wine business that as you go south in Italy, you sacrifice technology but gain climate. Certainly the latter is true as testified by the fact that the vine has thrived in central Italy from the days of the ancient Greeks and Romans. One should note that there are hilly areas in Italy's midsection and south that are as cool as the north. In addition, premier wineries such as Antinori, Lungarotti, and most notably, Villa Banfi, have kept up with technological progress and possess state-of-the-art facilities.

Altogether, six regions comprise central Italy: Tuscany, Umbria, Marches, Abruzzi, Molise, and Latium. They not only produce over 25% of Italy's wine and provide 35% of the D.O.C./D.O.C.G. output, but they are also responsible for some of Italy's most popular types: Chianti, Orvieto, Verdicchio, and Frascati.

On the western side of the Apennines toward the Tyrrhenian Sea, the red Sangiovese grape reigns supreme. It is the basis for Chianti, Brunello di Montalcino, Vino Nobile de Montepulciano, and Torgiano Rosso. Whites are based on Malvasia and Trebbiano (the ancient Procanico grape). Orvieto, Frascati, and Est! Est!! Est!!! are all derived from these vines. You will also find French varietals, especially Cabernet Sauvignon, brought back from France centuries ago by the De Medici family.

The Adriatic coast on the eastern side of the mountains produces whites from the Trebbiano and Verdicchio, and reds from the Sangiovese and the underrated Montepulciano vine.

## Tuscany
### The Etruscans, the Renaissance, and Wine

Tuscany is an ancient area of civilization, renowned today as the epicenter of Italian art. It has always been a region closely tied to agriculture, and to the kitchen as well. We know that the Etruscans used wine in their religious services in Tuscany as far back as the ninth century B.C. There are fossilized vines from Tuscany dating to the dawn of history—even before the entrance of mankind

*A Sangiovese and Cabernet blend that started a revolution when the 1971 vintage was released. This wine usually takes 7–10 years to develop. It is made by Giacomo Tachis for the Antinori's, a family that has been in the wine business for over 600 years.*

*The finest wine of the Marches Region is Le Moie. It is one of a handful of Italian whites that prosper from a few years of bottle aging. It is made by Fazi-Battaglia, who produce the famous Verdicchio.*

Much of Tuscany consists of beautiful hillside landscapes, ideal for grape growing (about 1500 feet above sea level). Usually about seventh in production among all the regions of Italy, Tuscany is the source of three D.O.C.G. wines (Brunello di Montalcino, Chianti, and Vino Nobile di Montepulciano), all of which are based on the Sangiovese Grosso vine.

Well-known and esteemed for the Renaissance cities of Florence, Siena, and Pisa, Tuscany possesses wine properties that predate the Renaissance. Often called the "Bordeaux of Italy," Tuscany's renowned estates have been producing elegant, long-lived, dry red wines for centuries. This is not only the land of Michelangelo and DaVinci but also of Catherine of Medici, who helped to elevate French cuisine to new heights.

Today's Tuscan table epitomizes the triumph of nature with diversified yet simple recipes, reflecting freshly picked ingredients. Soups and bean dishes are very important. The Chianti zone is world famous for its olive oil. The seaport of Livorno has given us the seafood soup called caciucco and Florence is well-known for its steak, bistecca alla Fiorentina.

There is good wine to grace this varied cuisine, with dry whites such as the light Galestro, Montecarlo, and Vernaccia di San Gimignano. There is no longer any white Chianti. Most noteworthy are the rich dry reds, such as the ageless Brunello di Montalcino, elegant Carmignano, Chianti, and Vino Nobile di Montepulciano, all derived from the noble Sangiovese grape. Almost every high-quality producer is making a non-D.O.C. super-premium wine, usually referred to as a "discovery" or "fantasy" wine. New "fantasy" wines based on Cabernet and Sangiovese are fast becoming Italy's most fashionable and sought after wines. They include Sassicaia, Solaia, Grifi, and Sammarco as well as Ca del Pazzo, Tignanello and Vigorello. There is a trend toward small French oak barrique which are replacing the larger, more traditional Slavonian (Yugoslavian) oak casks. Finally, there is "Vin Santo," the "holy" amber nectar so rare and so perfect as an aperitif or dessert wine.

*A new wave, chic dry white from the Castelvecchio Estate. Called Libaio after a slope area ideal for white grapes, this single-vineyard wine consists of 85% Chardonnay and 15% Sauvignon Blanc. Cold-fermentation and controlled stainless steel aging keep the fruit and flavor very fresh.*

*Ruffino and other key Tuscan producers have developed a system called "Predicato" for classifying new-style Tuscan wines. Such Predicato wines must pass a taste analysis, similar to the D.O.C.G. This elite Cabreo white is a wood-aged Chardonnay from the lofty La Pietra Vineyard site. There is also a classy Cabreo red based on Cabernet and Sangiovese.*

## PREDICATO – A QUALITY VARIATION
## FOR SOME OF TUSCANY'S LEADING WINERIES

The decade of the 1980s saw dramatic, exciting changes for Tuscan wines. Standards were raised to new heights. The D.O.C.G. was granted to Brunello, to Vino Nobile, and to Chianti. "Fantasy" red wines, such as Grifi, Sammarco, Tignanello, Sassicaia, Vigorella, and Ornellaia began garnering prizes in international competitions, as well as securing top marks from wine journalists.

In addition, several leading estates and wineries, among them Ruffino, Melini, Villa Cilnia, Frescobaldi, and San Felice introduced a new, light, dry, vivacious white wine called Galestro. Named for the special soil of Tuscany laced with Galestro limestone, this fresh, crisp clean Galestro was recently rewarded by the Italian government as the "Wine of the Decade."

These same estates and wineries introduced a series of new upscale wines, which allow for the innovative genius of the "Fantasy" wines, while clinging to disciplines as strict as those of the D.O.C.G. These are the *Predicato* wines. There are four types, all of which should prove interesting to wine lovers:

1. **Predicato di Biturica:** Red wines consisting of blends of Cabernet Sauvignon (at least 30%) and Sangiovese.
2. **Predicato del Muschio:** Dry whites based on Chardonnay or Pinot Bianco with up to 20% Riesling permitted.
3. **Predicato del Selvante:** White wines based on Sauvignon Blanc.
4. **Predicato di Cardisco:** Red wines based on Sangiovese with up to 10% other red grapes. Cabernet or Merlot may *not* be part of the blend.

*Vigorello, whose first vintage was in 1968, is the original Tuscan fantasy wine. It is a blend of 85% Sangiovese and 15% Cabernet Sauvignon.*

*Situated between Florence and Siena, in the hamlet of Gaiole in Chianti, impressivly stands Badia a Coltibuono. Historically, it is believed to be the birthplace of Chianti. Factually, it is source of world class Italian wines. A fruity, charming white Tuscan wine made from the Trebbiano and Chardonnay grapes, it has a light straw color with greenish tinges. The wine is fruity, delicate, and fresh.*

Several of the best Chianti producers are making small quantities of "fantasy" wines. The one above is from the prestigious Castello Dei Rampolla and is called Sammarco. It is a blend of Sangiovese and Cabernet Sauvignon aged in barriques (small oak barrels of about 55 gallons) for up to two years. Often referred to as the "Mouton Rothschild" of Italy.

Avignonesi, the preeminent producer of D.O.C.G. Vino Nobile di Montepulciano, produces a Vino da Tavola of extraordinary quality. It is a "fantasy" blend consisting of Prugnolo Gentile (Sangiovese Grosso) and Cabernet Franc aged in French barriques for about one year.

## Some Changes in Chianti Classico

| D.O.C. | vs. | D.O.C.G. |
|--------|-----|----------|
| Up to 20% white grapes | | As little as 2% white grapes |
| May be sold March 1 after the harvest | | Must wait until June 1 |
| *Vecchio* category (2 years of age) | | *Vecchio* eliminated – only regular and Riserva (3 years) exist |
| 861 gallons per acre allowed | | 561 gallons per acre allowed |
| Vine age unregulated | | Vine age – at least 5 years old |
| No standard, official taste test | | Wines must pass "blind tasting" by experts. |

### Chianti and Bordeaux Similarities

Chianti is not one wine, but 8,000.

BOTH – are best known for medium-bodied, elegant dry reds.

– produce two styles of red: one light and young, the other austere and capable of great age.

– are marketed in the Bordeaux bottle.

– are blends with one dominant grape (Sangiovese in Chianti, Cabernet Sauvignon in Bordeaux).

– are large production areas.

– are blessed with grandiose Chateaux (You know Bordeaux already. Chianti has Badia a Coltibuono, Monsanto, Villa Cafaggio, Villa Capezzana, Castello di Nipozzano, etc.)

– have communes within them that produce distinctive styles of wine.

### The Seven Chianti Zones

Chianti Classico
Chianti Colli Aretini (Hills of Arizzo)
Chianti Colli Fiorentini (Hills of Florence)
Chianti Colli Senesi (Hills of Siena)
Chianti Colline Pisane (Hills of Pisa)
Chianti Montalbano
Chianti Rufina

1987

GIANNINA

Vernaccia
di San Gimignano
Denominazione di Origine Controllata
**SANGIMINO**

Bottled by: Teruzzi · San Gimignano · Italy
White wine · Product of Italy
Contains sulfites

750 ml · Alc. 11,5% by vol. · R.I. 1402/SI

Imported by:
AMERICAN B.D. Co. · Hawthorne · N.J.

CONTAINS SULFITES

*Vernaccia is the grape variety and San Gimignano the town from which the wine comes. Giannina is the brand name. Vernaccia di San Gimignano was Michelangelo's favorite wine. It was made differently then, almost copper-colored with a taste like sherry. Today it is dry and crisp.*

1989

GIANNINA

Vernaccia di San Gimignano
Denominazione di Origine Controllata

PRODUCED AND BOTTLED BY GIANNINA · SAN GIMIGNANO
WHITE WINE · PRODUCT OF ITALY · CONTAINS SULFITES
CONTENTS 750 ML · ALCOHOL 11,5% BY VOLUME

*Italy's Grand Cru. This Cabernet Sauvignon is aged two years in barriques and has been the trendsetter for the new Italian "fantasy" wines. Only 4,000 to 5,000 cases are produced annually. Sassicaia stands up to the best of Bordeaux or California.*

SASSICAIA
**1982**
TENUTA SAN GUIDO
BOLGHERI

Imbottigliato all'origine dal produttore
C I T A I S p A - Bolgheri (107 LI)
Distribuito dai M s L e P Antinori Fi

VINO DA TAVOLA DI SASSICAIA

RED TABLE WINE · PRODUCT OF ITALY

750 ml ℮    ITALIA    Alcohol 12,5% vol

210

*Chianti Riserva is aged for three years before being sold. Riserva wine lots are always better wines to start with. A lesser wine will not stand the test of time.*

IL MARZOCCO

*There is no longer a white Chianti. Many Chianti producers still make a dry Bianco Toscano (Tuscan white), based principally on Trebbiano grapes. Antinori's is one of the best.*

*As one of Tuscany's finest producers of Vino Nobile di Montepulciano, Avignonesi produced a limited amount of exceptional barrel fermented white wines, such as Sauvignon Blanc and "Il Marzocco" the remarkable Chardonnay pictured here.*

RUFFINO

RISERVA DUCALE®

Chianti Classico

DENOMINAZIONE DI ORIGINE CONTROLLATA

VENDEMMIA 1982

Bottiglia

750 ml e

ALCOHOL 12.5% BY VOL

BOTTLED BY

I. L. RUFFINO

PONTASSIEVE ITALIA 26(471)

With all the changes in Chianti laws and blends, one might think that there was something missing from traditional Chianti. Nothing could be farther from reality. People have been savoring Ruffino Riserva Ducale and Ducale Gold for over a century, ever since the Duke of Alba first requested it. It was Giuseppe Verdi's favorite.

*Marsilio Ficino*

CHIANTI

COLLI FIORENTINI

1985

0.75 l e  12% vol.

Chianti from the Florentine Hills is lighter and matures more quickly than Classico. You can enjoy this wine within a few years of the vintage.

s. quirico

Vernaccia di S. Gimignano

DENOMINAZIONE DI ORIGINE CONTROLLATA

Proprietà Vecchione

PRODUCE OF ITALY

PRODOTTO E IMBOTTIGLIATO ALL'ORIGINE DA
AZIENDA AGRICOLA S. QUIRICO S. GIMIGNANO (SIENA) · ITALIA

750 ml.    13% vol.

VENDEMMIA 1985

This fine estate-bottled wine is one of Tuscany's best whites. San Quirico is a brand that can be enjoyed young or be held for a few years.

212

Many fine Chianti estates, quite like the Chateau of Bordeaux, are famous for their architecture and art. This is true of the fourteenth century Luiano Villa. In addition to producing fine wine, Luiano is known for its olive oil.

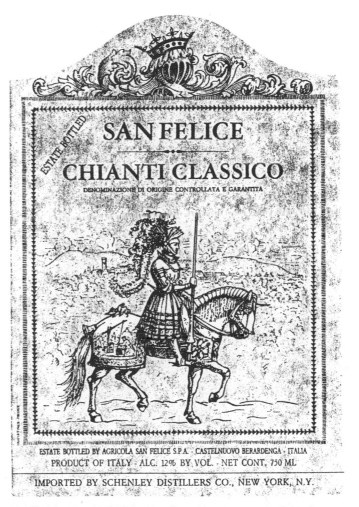

This Chianti Classico is from the San Felice Estate, not far from picturesque Siena. Estate grown and estate bottled, each bottle bears the Gallo Nero (black rooster) Consonzio seal. Recently the black rooster group was enjoined not to use the word "gallo" to promote their wine due to a trademark infringement with the E & J Gallo winery of California.

*Riccardo Falchini is located in the ancient Tuscan town of San Gimignano in the heart of Tuscany. Coupling the ancient tradition of the region with modern wine-making methods is the hallmark of this outstanding producer. When you consider his commitment, drive, and expertise, it is no wonder Falchini's wines are among the best in Tuscany.*

## Umbria
### Orvieto Plus

Umbria is Italy's heartland. Still relatively unexplored by tourists and surprisingly so, since it is on the road between Rome and Florence, and boasts of the Spoleto Festival, the Assisi of St. Francis, and Perugina candies. It can boast, too, of black and white truffles, sublime pork dishes, a cuisine based on rosemary, fennel, "liquid gold" (that is, Umbrian olive oil, perhaps Italy's finest), and Orvieto wine.

Some of us are old enough to recall "red" Orvieto. The D.O.C. laws did away with that. Today Orvieto must be white. Orvieto used to be marketed in short, squat, wicker *fiaschi,* and traditionally was a golden off-dry or *abboccato.* Current production is almost exclusively pale and dry (secco), and shipped in glass bottles. Known as the "Wine of Popes," Orvieto is named for a hillside cathedral town in southern Umbria. The D.O.C. zone stretches from Umbria across the regional border into Latium (Lazio).

Based largely on Trebbiano vines, commercial versions are crisp and pleasant but almost neutral. Some brands with style are Bigi, Antinori, Barberani, and Vaselli. Often, dependable Orvieto is made by Chianti or Roman wineries, such as Ruffino, Fontana Candida, or Fassati. Perhaps the very best Orvietos, Decugnano dei Barbi and Bigi's "Vigna Toricella."

There has been a trend in Umbria to grow French grape varieties. The master of these, as well as native wines, is Dr. Giorgio Lungarotti. His family winery (daughter Maria Teresa is his winemaker) dominates the region, producing both a Cabernet Sauvignon and Chardonnay of worth and interest. Lungarotti's most important wines are D.O.C.s, Torgiano Rosso and Torgiano Bianco. The red, from Sangiovese with a touch of Canaiolo and Ciliegiolo grapes, is called Rubesco. A limited, single-vineyard, rich Rubesco Riserva ranks as the region's best and one of Italy's most renowned wines. The floral, dry white, based on Trebbiano and Grechetto, is trademarked as Torre di Giano. It is available in both a fast-maturing regular version and a wood-aged, single-vineyard Riserva. A fairly new red, non-D.O.C. San Giorgio, from Cabernet Sauvignon and Sangiovese vines, is long-lived, full of body and class, and very distinguished. Lungarotti also produces a fine Vin Santo. Soon, Torgiano Rosso Riserva will become D.O.C.G.

*Because Antinori now uses the noble Chardonnay in his blend, he can no longer call Castello della Sala "Orvieto." This is an example of the enigma of the Italian wine law. This superb wine is not D.O.C., but simply white table wine of Umbria. Raccolto means vintage.*

*Count Vaselli's Orvieto is not only Classico and Secco but also estate-bottled.*

*Umbria's best wine. This single-vineyard (Monticchio) wine qualifies for the D.O.C. Torgiano Riserva. Dr. Giorgio Lungarotti, proprietor of the finest winery in the area, calls his Torgiano "Rubesco." Pit this deep red against a classified Bordeaux growth. You may be surprised.*

215

Many Orvietos are produced by Chianti or Frascati firms. This fine Secco (dry) Orvieto is bottled by Fontana Candida in Orvieto itself.

This Orvieto, a U.S. favorite, is a Classico, which means that the vines for it are from the original and best section for grapes, destined to be called Orvieto. The cathedral on the label is that of the picturesque hillside town of Orvieto.

Rome's eternal white wine. Fontana Candida, number one in the United States, should be enjoyed young to savor the fresh, crisp style. This is a "Superiore," that is, a Frascati that has a bit more alcohol than a regular Frascati. This comes from better, riper grapes.

216

## The Marches
### The Land of Verdicchio

Picturesque hills within sight of the Adriatic Sea capture the wine-producing areas of the Marches region. It is the Adriatic water that stabilizes the temperature of the region and which provides a bounty of fresh fish as well. The local fish soup (it is more of a stew, similar to bouillabaisse), called brodetto Anconese, after the city of Ancona, is reputed to be Italy's best. Of course, fresh fish requires a fresh white wine.

The wine is Verdicchio, often called "Italy's Muscadet" because of its crispness. Verdicchio wine is made from the Verdicchio grape, so called due to its deep green colored skin (*verde* in Italian means green). This is an ancient varietal. We are told that Alaric and the Goths in 410 A.D. quaffed Verdicchio before their final assault on Rome. The traditional amphora bottle dates back to the Classical Greeks, who stored wines in similarly shaped jars. Verdicchio is a versatile grape which makes attractive sparkling and crackling (*frizzante*) wine as well as table wines. It grows to perfection in the Castelli di Jesi (D.O.C.) zone, where we witness a dry white wine that will develop character after two years or so in the bottle.

The Verdicchio of the higher Matelica (D.O.C.) zone are of greater body and strength, although of lesser delicacy. It is difficult to find a white wine more suited to grace fine seafood than Verdicchio. Fazi-Battaglia is the area's best-known producer. Fa-

*Antonio Pulcini, as delightful as the wine he makes, has emerged as the leader in fine Frascati production. For the past three years in "Decanter's" tasting, Colli Di Catone's Frascatis have won the first, second, and third place. Pale straw colored, fresh, dry, good fruit, and balanced acidity mark this as a classic Frascati. The wine is round, mellow, and full flavored.*

zi's single-vineyard "Le Moie" may very well be the best wine of the region. Bucci is another producer of high quality. It is a shame that Verdicchio sales have slipped of late in the U.S. It is good wine that has never been better. One would have to search to find a Soave, Pinot Grigio, Orvieto, or Frascati as good as a typical young Verdicchio.

Red wines of the region are usually based on Sangiovese and Montepulciano grapes. These dry red wines are vibrant in their youth and in some vintages show the stuff to age a decade or more. There is good Rosso Conero (Montepulciano primarily), but foremost is the hearty Rosso Piceno, made from Sangiovese grapes. These dry reds are usually quite limited in production and since they have not yet been "discovered," they represent excellent dollar value.

Red or white, still or sparkling, the finest tribute to local wine making is that the Marchegiani, the people who live in the Marches region, consume much more wine per capita than in any other region in Italy. The average is over 31 gallons or about fifteen times as much as here in the United States.

### The Neck Label

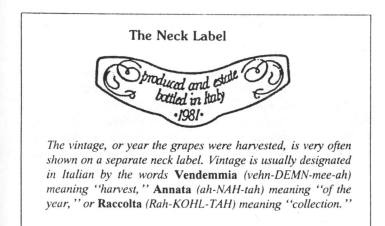

*The vintage, or year the grapes were harvested, is very often shown on a separate neck label. Vintage is usually designated in Italian by the words* **Vendemmia** *(vehn-DEMN-mee-ah) meaning "harvest,"* **Annata** *(ah-NAH-tah) meaning "of the year," or* **Raccolta** *(Rah-KOHL-TAH) meaning "collection."*

217

## Abruzzo
### Wines from the Land of "Abbondanza"

Each region in Italy has a little phrase that is supposed to capture the spirit and essence of its inhabitants. For the Abruzzesi it is *forte e gentile* or strong and gentle. How well this captures the wines of the region as well! They are generous, honest wines, usually with a price tag that is surprising an more than fair.

This is the land of *abbondanza!* — the land of plenty. Clearly this is Italy's dried pasta capital. A bevy of Adriatic fish, meat, and game from the Apennines make for hearty meals. There is also the Gargantuan *la panarda,* a magnificent 30-course banquet that makes the smorgasbord look like a snack. True, in diet-conscious twentieth-century Italy, one does not see such festive dining too often, but we could make a strong case for Abruzzo as the torch bearer of Italian cuisine. In fact, one town, Villa Santa Maria, is almost exclusively dedicated to culinary arts. This may partially explain the great number of Abruzzesi restaurateurs in the United States. Truly, food is important in Abruzzo.

Wine is indispensable as well. Red wine is based on Montepulciano grapes. Sometimes a dry rose called Cerasuolo is made from these same grapes. The white is usually from Trebbiano Toscano grapes. Hence we have only two D.O.C. wines to speak of, complex wines but uncomplicated: red or rose Montepulciano D'Abruzzo and white Trebbiano D'Abruzzo.

Important quality producers include Emidio Pepe and Edoardo Valentini. Pepe still crushes by foot, ages his red in glass, and does many other things that seem unusual. What results is a long-lived, glorious, incomparable wine. Valentini has cultivated the true Trebbiano D'Abruzzo grape, also called Bombino Bianco. His unfiltered dry white wine has a texture and aroma that experts have likened to fine burgundies. Unfortunately, these controversial and colorful personalities do not produce large quantities of wine.

The most important winery of the region is Casal Thaulero. Located in the foothills of the northern sector where yield per acre is low and quality is high, Casal Thaulero makes full, round, rich reds that are eminently drinkable. The white wines are crisp, consistent, and complex. Under the leadership of Piero Ciglia, Casal Thaulero has become a pioneer in developing the export market, bringing these wonderful wines to the shores of the U.S. Other leading shippers include Cantina Tollo, Barone Cornacchia, and the outstanding Duchi di Castelluccio and Illuminati. Newcomer Santangelo is already earning praise, especially for its single vineyard red, Colli del Moro.

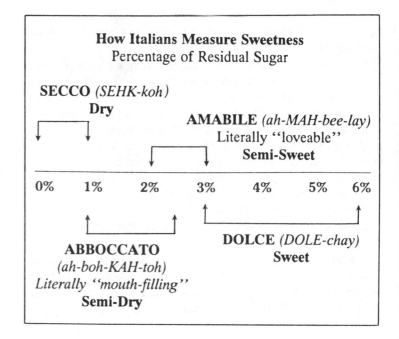

**How Italians Measure Sweetness**
Percentage of Residual Sugar

SECCO (*SEHK-koh*)
**Dry**

AMABILE (*ah-MAH-bee-lay*)
Literally "loveable"
**Semi-Sweet**

| 0% | 1% | 2% | 3% | 4% | 5% | 6% |

ABBOCCATO
(*ah-boh-KAH-toh*)
*Literally "mouth-filling"*
**Semi-Dry**

DOLCE (*DOLE-chay*)
**Sweet**

## Molise

This tiny region just south of Abruzzo has been viewed as a footnote to its northern neighbor. Wines are largely from the red Montepulciano and white Trebbiano. There are only two D.O.C. zones, Bieferno and Pentro D'Isernia, which produce red, white, and pink wines. It is a rustic, mountainous region with a little strip of coastline along the Adriatic. The area is new for sophisticated viticulture, but the potential is very good. Until 1963, Molise was part of Abruzzo.

## Latium (Lazio)
**"When in Rome do as the Romans do; that is, drink Frascati with everything!"**

In a country where each region considers its cuisine without peer, even the most loyal outsider would have to list Latium as one of the top three. Pungent, colorful, piquant sauces include *matriciana* (tomatoes, red pepper, bacon, salt pork or *pancetta*) and *arrabbiato* (tomatoes, onions, and red pepper). Then there are the creamy Fettucine al Burro (butter), Alfredo, or Carbonara. Don't forget the salty, flavorful grated Pecorino Romano cheese, please! How about Saltimbocca (veal with prosciutto), so delicious that it "jumps into your mouth" *(salta in bocca)*. Extravagant spring baby lamb called *abbacchio* is sometimes made "hunter's" style, with anchovies, garlic, vinegar, and rosemary. (And you thought these were all "northern" Italian.)

What is common to these varied dishes is that no wine seems to go with them. This is where the wines of the Castelli Romani, the hillside towns just south of Rome, come in. There *must* be wine with every meal! The symbol of the area is a three-breasted woman (two for milk, one for wine). In these Alban Hills, the Colli Albani, white wine proliferates. Malvasia and Trebbiano vines yield wines from towns like Cori, Zagarolo, or more famously, Marino and Frascati. Frascati was historically sweetish. You will still find some called Cannellino or the off-dry Abboccato. There was once a red Frascati.

What we almost exclusively find in the U.S. is the dry, delicate, fragile version, usually a Superiore (12% alcohol), which aids in the shipping. Fontana Candida dominates sales. Other dependable brands include Pallavicini, Gotto D'Oro, and Colli di Catone. Rare and esteemed are Mennuni and Zandotti. Marino is a wine very close to the crisp, clean Frascati in style. It is usually a bit bolder, deeper, softer, and with a pleasantly bitter almond finish.

There are three superb red gems based on Merlot or Cabernet, sometimes with a bit of the native Cesanese blended in. They are Fiorano (which also makes white wines), Colle Picchione, and Torre Ercolana. A D.O.C. zone around Aprilia is farmed by Italians who emigrated from North Africa after World War II. Wines include Merlot, Sangiovese, and Trebbiano di Aprilia.

The most colorful story (if not wine) of Latium is that of Est! Est!! Est!!!, from the northern town of Montefiascone near Lake Bolsena. The legend is that a certain bishop, named Fugger, sent an emissary south from Germany to highlight the outstanding hostels along the road to Rome. Fugger was going to visit the Pope, you see. If the food and wine were good, this servant would inscribe "Est!" ("This is it!" in Latin) outside the inn. It seems this was a precursor to the *Guide Michelin*. When the bishop's emissary reached Montefiascone, he flipped out over the cuisine and wine, as the name implies. We are told that Fugger never did see the Pope, preferring to remain in Montefiascone and enjoy its legendary wine. Over his grave there is an annual libation poured to Fugger's memory — even today, centuries later. The story ranks with those of Bernkasteler Doktor, Lacryma Cristi del Vesuvio, and Dom Perignon in the annals of wine folklore.

# SELF-EVALUATION

BEFORE READING ON, see if you have mastered the data set forth in the last few pages. Check the answer section at the back of the book for the correct answers. If you have not answered at least 70% of the questions below correctly, please reread the previous section.

## CENTRAL ITALY

| TRUE | FALSE | |
|------|-------|---|
| _____ | _____ | 1. Tuscany is the source of three of Italy's six D.O.C.G. wines. |
| _____ | _____ | 2. The Brunello di Montalcino, Chianti, and Vino Nobile di Montepulciano are based on Nebbiolo grapes. |
| _____ | _____ | 3. There are six regions that comprise central Italy. |
| _____ | _____ | 4. Verdicchio is from the Marches region. |
| _____ | _____ | 5. Abruzzo is called the "Land of Plenty." |
| _____ | _____ | 6. Trebbiano D'Abruzzo and Montepulciano D'Abruzzo are two primary wines of the Abruzzo region. |
| _____ | _____ | 7. Umbria's Orvieto is always made to be bone dry. |
| _____ | _____ | 8. Molise has no famous wines at this point in time. |
| _____ | _____ | 9. Lazio is known for dry red wines such as Frascati. |

# SOUTHERN ITALY
## The Original "Enotria" or "Land of Wine"

The ancient Greeks called southern Italy *Enotria,* the land of wine. When they colonized this area, as early as 750 B.C., they brought with them certain grape varieties that still abound today. They include the Aglianico, Greco, Moscato, and Malvasia. This area later felt the influence of the Romans. The poet Horace praised the charms of its Falernian and Caecubian wines. Cato, Pliny the Elder, and Columella wrote treatises on farming and viticulture, as did the poet Virgil. Later, Arabs, Spaniards, Normans, French, and Germans made their influences felt.

Today southern Italy is known for producing tremendous quantities of high-alcohol bulk wine, which it ships to vermouth houses and to other EEC countries for blending or "cutting" purposes. True, Sicily and Apulia alone produce more wine than Hungary, Germany, Australia, and Chile. However, the quality of this bulk wine is on a par with or superior to those of the French Midi and California's San Joaquin region. Also remarkable is the fact that despite having a climate viewed by experts for almost 3,000 years as perfect for viticulture, we are just now learning about some excellent underrated and underpriced wines.

The mountainous sections of the Mezzogiorno (that is, the noonday sun, another name for southern Italy), do not bake. The Irpinia Valley in Campania, the central highlands of Sicily, Mount Vulture in Basilicata, and the Apulian Plateau are all high enough and cool enough to produce world-class wines. Names like Mastroberardino, D'Angleo, DeCastris, Taurino, Villa Matilde, Count Tasca, and Simonini will provide oenophiles with great discovery wines in the next few years.

## Campania
### Campania Felix of the Romans

The Romans called this region *Felix,* – Happy, Lucky, Blessed, or all three. It was their breadbasket. The Happy Fields yielded classic Falernum and Caecubum wine, in addition to grains, fruits and vegetables. Today, Campanian San Marzano is the tomato capital of the world. The tomato or *pommarola* (golden apple) as it is known locally, is the hub of the local cuisine. Pizza, eggplant parmigiana, and *spaghetti alla vongole* (spaghetti with clam sauce) are dishes that are enjoyed so much worldwide that they have become cursed with popularity. The cuisine, based upon freshly picked vegetables and fruits and the day's catch from the sea, operates on a very high level. Visitors to Capri and Ischia, the Amalfi coast, Sorrento, Pompeii, and the Naples area will attest to that. And have we forgotten sun-dried tomatoes, basil, and *mozzarella bufala*, a soft, mild cheese made from the milk of water buffaloes?

Less than half of 1% of Campania's wines are D.O.C. Non-D.O.C. Ravello is worth searching out, as is the rare Torre Gaia You may find a little D.O.C. Capri, Ischia, or Solopaca in the U.S.A. Campania is Mastroberardino territory. The family of Antonio and Walter Mastroberardino dominates the area. They are the principal producers of D.O.C. Lacryma Cristi del Vesuvio wines, the red based on ancient Piedirosso (pigeon's foot) vines, the white on the classic Coda di Volpe (fox-tail) grape. Both varietals were named by Pliny in the first century A.D. "Mastro," as Antonio is known, produces a salmon-colored dry rose called Lacrimarosa D'Irpinia. He is renowned for the distinctive dry whites, Greco di Tufo and Fiano di Avellino. The former is derived from the ancient Greco vine, the latter from the Latino or Fiano vine. Rare single-vineyard versions of both are available. They age well, especially the Fiano whose delicate, complex scent of pears takes on nuances of hazelnuts when held for a decade or more.

A full, dry, D.O.C. red called Taurasi is the region's finest red wine. One of Italy's best and longest-lived wines, Taurasi is based on the classic Aglianico (Hellenic or Greek) vine. This grape, planted in the hills of Irpinia, is left on the vine sometimes until November. The resulting wine is rich and supple but without a hot, alcoholic nature. Some experts feel that the expensive and rare 1968 Taurasi Riserva of Mastroberardino is one of the very finest examples of Italian winemaking. Another quality producer of Taurasi, Greco di Tufo, and Fiano di Avellino is Giovanni Struzziero.

An estate (Villa Matilde) in northern Campania has resurrected small quantities of lofty ancient Roman wines. The enthusiasm and passion of the Avallone family toward the Roman Falernum and Cecubum wine types has led to the D.O.C. Falerno del Mas-

*Legend has it that when Satan left Heaven, he took part of it with him, dropping it into the Bay of Naples. Awed at the beauty of this bay, God wept on the hills of Mt. Vesuvius. His tears (the Lacryma Christi) caused the first vines to shoot forth. Today, D.O.C. white Lacryma Christi del Vesuvio is made by Antonio Mastroberardino from the ancient Coda di Volpe (fox-tail) grapes. A D.O.C. red is fashioned from Piedirosso (red pigeon-foot) vines.*

*Basilicata's best wine from its best producer. The Aglianico (Hellenic) vine was brought by the Greeks to southern Italy around 650 B.C. Vulture is an inactive volcano. The wine is rich, harmonious, and capable of moderate aging. Aglianico is also the grape in Campania's best red, Taurasi.*

sico red and white and the red Cecubo. These wines are worth searching out.

## Basilicata

This small region, called Lucania by the Romans, has one D.O.C. wine of worth, produced in the north around Rionero. The volcanic slopes of Mt. Vulture yield this wonderful, dry red called Aglianico del Vulture. Quality producers include Martino, Sàsso, and Paternoster. They are rare in the United States. We are fortunate, however, to have the very best, namely that of D'Angelo. His is a robust, complex wine that ages well beyond a decade, if from a good vintage. D'Angelo also produces a note-

worthy dry white based on Chardonnay and Malvasia, called Lucanello.

## Calabria

The most famous wine from the "toe" of Italy is Ciro. It is the heir to Cremissa wine, drunk by the famous athletes in ancient days from the Greek towns of Sybaris and Kroton. This makes it the oldest wine in the world. Red Ciro is based on the classical Greek Gaglioppo vine; the dry white Ciro is basically Greco. Notable producers of Ciro include Ippolito, Caparra and Siciliani, Scala, and Librandi.

Although Ciro is the region's most famous wine, the very best is Umberto Ceratti's Greco di Bianco. This luscious dessert wine, unfortunately so limited, ranks with the great Sauternes of France and German TBAs as the most delectable after a meal.

## Apulia
### Kicking Up Its Heel

Noted originally as a bulk contributor to Italy's "Wine Lake," Apulia does have some 23 D.O.C.s and a handful of other classy wines. It must be viewed as up-and-coming. Apulia produces some of Italy's most esteemed dry roses, including the Five Rose of DeCastris, Rosa del Golfo, and Rivera's Castel del Monte Rosato. A clean, crisp, white Locorotondo is perfect with seafood.

In northern Apulia around the town of Foggia, Attilio Simonini makes superb wines based upon Pinot Blanc, Chardonnay, and Cabernet Franc. These distinctive wines are called Favonio, after the refreshing sea breeze of the same name. Cool winds and altitude are factors in Apulian viticulture. Still north of the Taranto-Brindisi line, we find D.O.C. Castel del Monte wines. A non-D.O.C. red made by Rivera and called Il Falcone, is excellent. It is derived from Montepulciano, Uva di Troia, and Bombino Nero vines.

The southern tip of the heel provides us with a luxuriant red, Salice Salentino. As made by DeCastris and Taurino, Salice ages nicely. Taurino's version is one of Italy's best price-quality values. The Negroamaro grape is used in Salice Salentino. A rose is made from the same vine. Like the red, it can age a bit.

Of more than passing interest is the fact that the all-American mystery vine, the Zinfandel, most probably is the Apulian Primitivo vine. This versatile grape, in Italy as in California, yields blush type wines, dry table wines, and long-lived dessert wines. The spicy, berry-like character comes through in all versions.

Apulia has much to see: Greek ruins in Gallipoli, the octagonal Castel del Monte fortress, the city of Bari, the port of Taranto. Apulia has much to eat as well: good pasta and bread, game, lamb and cheeses, fresh vegetables, fruits, pungent herbs, and hearty olive oil, and not least of all, outstanding mussels and oysters. One thing is certain: you will not run out of interesting wine to drink.

*This dry, generous estate-bottled red exemplifies what we have come to expect of Italian wines—superb quality, exceptional value.*

### The Italian Back Label

*Quite often an Italian wine bottle will have a helpful and informative back label. Since Italian grapes are so diverse and not usually found outside of Italy, these labels provide descriptions of the grape variety or the wine, as well as food match-ups and serving instructions. Data on a particular vineyard site, a bottle number of limited bottlings, or awards won by a wine are sometimes also mentioned. Such information is important since more often than not Italian wines are made from vines unfamiliar to Americans.*

## Sardinia
### A Footprint in the Mediterranean

The ancient Greeks called Sardinia *Ichnusa* (footprint) because of its shape. It is an island that has been owned by Carthage, Rome, Spain, and now Italy. But no one has really ever taken possession of it. Sardinians have adapted foreign influences to their own use. These fiercely independent people have retained a distinctive, unspoiled character throughout history, especially in the kitchen and in their wines.

One must journey to the Costa Smeralda to sample *malloreddus,* a special tiny gnocchi, or *culingiones,* a type of ravioli, or *carasau* (sheet music), the paper-thin Sardinian bread. And though the grapes for their wines may have originated in the Middle East, North Africa, or other parts of Europe, the style is uniquely Sardinian. These vines are not planted elsewhere. They have names like Canonau, Monica, Nuraghus and Torbato.

The two main zones for wine production center around Cagliari in the south and Olbia in the north. Co-ops abound, but the most famous producer is Sella and Mosca, a private firm in the commune of Alghero in the northwestern sector of the island.

Sardinia is also Italy's cork center. It vies Portugal in the closure business.

Sardinia produces good dry white Vermentino, an amber, sherry-like Vernaccia di Oristano, and sound Malvasias and Moscatos. Perhaps the best white is new D.O.C. Torbato di Alghero, crisp, pale, refreshing, and well-balanced. The most prolific D.O.C. white is Nuraghus di Cagliari.

Hearty dry reds of interest are made from the Cannonau grape. A rich, heady dessert version, made from dried grapes, is called Anghelu Ruju (Red Angel). It is reminiscent of porto, ages extremely well, and is Sardinia's finest wine. As with other things Sardinian, it is a discovery experience for us in the United States.

*Sicily's grandest red. Rosso del Conte (The Count's Red Wine) is a late-harvest, single-vineyard wine aged in chestnut barrels. It will age for 20 years or more. One wine critic, surprised by the wine's extract, called it "high fiber" wine.*

*You may see a neck label on a bottle with a* **VIDE** *seal.* **VIDE** *is the logo of a voluntary association which promotes wineries that produce their own grapes. Current membership is about 30 wineries. Throughout all of Italy these estate bottled wines aim for high quality and standards.*

## Sicily
### The Cradle of Italy

Goethe once said, "The key to everything (in Italy) is in Sicily. It happened there first." Always in the vanguard of history, the Mediterranean's largest island has experienced much. This enchanted island, the land of sun and toil, has given birth to the Greek genius Archimedes, composers Bellini and Mascagni, and countless authors, among them Nobel Laureate Luigi Pirandello. It has borne ice cream and sherbet, the meatball — even pasta itself. It has been the home to various wine gods and goddesses, including Roman Bacchus, Greek Dionysus, and Phoenician Tanit. And yet what we know and say of this cosmopolitan crossroads seems to boil down to two things: foreign conquest (by Normans, Arabs, Spaniards, etc.), and the Mafia. How unfortunate! And inaccurate!

As to wine production, Sicily has almost doubled its annual production since 1964 to a staggering one trillion liters. It is Italy's leader, together with Apulia. Sicily's most famous wine is the fortified Marsala, which can be sweet or dry, even contain flavors. Marsala is indispensable in the kitchen for *veal scallopini alla Marsala* or the egg-yolk and sugar dessert, *zabaglione*. A dry type, Marsala *vergine*, stands alongside white porto, fino sherry and French Chateau-Chalon as one of the world's very best aperitifs.

One dessert wine of worth is Moscato di Pantelleria. Pantelleria is an island closer to Tunisia than to Sicily itself. The wine is made from the large Moscato or Zibibbo vine, from dried grapes in the passito fashion. Quality brands include Tanit and Bukkuram. Much of the production is fortified. There is a lighter, sparkling version called Solimano. Dessert wines abound in Sicily, as do desserts themselves. We have Sicilians to thank not only for ice cream and sherbet but also for cannoli and cassata. Surely the most exquisite dessert wine is from the volcanic chain of Aeolian islands north of Sicily. Called Malvasia delle Lipari, this amber nectar evokes praise for its subtle fragrances of apricots, eucalyptus, and oranges. The premium producer is Carlo Hauner.

Sicily drinks far less table wine per capita than other regions do, but certain wines are widely respected, especially in foreign markets. Etna and Faro are leaders among D.O.C. wines, which account for less than 3% of Sicily's total production. One brand of D.O.C. Alcamo that is worth searching for is Rapitala, with its

*Many new brands are causing a stir in Italy. One successful one, Ligorio, is now available in the U.S. Both red and white are crisp, chic, and very modern Italian.*

nutty yet crisp character.

The island's two most respected brands are Corvo and Regaleali, and with completely contrasting philosophies! Corvo buys grapes from different parts of the island and masterfully blends them into a line that has developed a loyal following worldwide. The green label dry white is the brand leader. Made from Inzolia, Catarratto, and Trebbiano vines, this dry white is consistently balanced and flavorful. The Colomba Platino version is finer and more delicate. A very good red from Nerello Mascalese, Perricone, and Nero D'Avola grapes is sold after being aged in oak and in the bottle. A new, limited world-class red wine called Duca Enrico was recently introduced. Full, rich, and dry, it is one of

Italy's finest. Corvo markets a Brut Spumante made by Charmat, and a fortified Stravecchio di Sicilia. They also produce a uniquely elegant aperitif called Ala.

Regaleali is an estate owned by the Count Tasca family for over 150 years. Seven generations of Tascas have seen to it that not one grape from outside the estate is used. Cool ocean breezes and lofty altitude (about 1500–2000 feet) provide an almost ideal micro-climate. Sauvignon Blanc has been present at the estate for over 40 years. There are new plantings of Cabernet Sauvignon, Pinot Noir, Pinot Grigio, and Chardonnay. A crisp white is the flagship item. There is a dry rose, and a red aged in chestnut and oak casks. Limited single-vineyard wines, red Rosso del Conte and white Nozze D'Oro, are regarded as the island's finest table wines. A new Barrique-aged chardonnay and a method champenoise Cremant round out this interesting estate's line of wines.

*Nozze D'Oro means golden wedding. This Sauvignon Blanc-based wine was created by Count Tasca to honor his wife on their 50th anniversary. The Regaleali Estate, which he owns, has been in his family for over 150 years.*

*The "Cherub"*
*The symbol of the Chianti Putto Consorzio*

### Consorzio
*(kohn-SORE-tzee-oh)*

*A Consorzio (consortium) is an association of growers and wine producers who supervise and control production in specific geographic areas. Such groups are involved in promoting the wines of their associate members. These groups award colorful neck labels which signify membership. Noteable Consorzi include Asti Spumante, Frascati, Brunello di Montalcino, and Chianti Classico with its famous black rooster. Be aware that there are neck bands that are not Consorzio labels. Look for the Consorzio quality control number and the word "Consorzio." But remember: Membership in a Consorzio is not an absolute guarantee of quality.*

# SELF-EVALUATION

BEFORE READING ON, see if you have mastered the data set forth in the last few pages. Check the answer section at the back of the book for the correct answers. If you have not answered at least 70% of the questions below correctly, please reread the previous section.

## SOUTHERN ITALY

| TRUE | FALSE | |
|------|-------|---|
| _____ | _____ | 1. Sicily and Apulia together produce more wine than Hungary, Germany, Australia, and Chile combined. |
| _____ | _____ | 2. Taurasi is Campania's most famous white wine. |
| _____ | _____ | 3. Apulia is most famous for its white wines. |
| _____ | _____ | 4. Sardinia produces not only wine but corks as well. |
| _____ | _____ | 5. VIDE is a voluntary association for quality producers of Italian wines. |
| _____ | _____ | 6. Marsala is from Sicily. |
| _____ | _____ | 7. Sicily consumes more table wine than any other Italian region. |
| _____ | _____ | 8. A *Consorzio* is an association of growers and producers of Italian sparkling wines. |
| _____ | _____ | 9. A *Tenuta* is an estate, a vineyard, and a winery combined. |
| _____ | _____ | 10. VQPRD is a European Economic Community (Common Market) abbreviation. |

# VINI DA TAVOLA OF QUALITY OR INTEREST

Below is a partial listing of table wines of considerable merit which are not under the control of the Italian government's D.O.C. or D.O.C.G. laws.

| REGION | PRODUCER/WINE TYPE | STYLE |
|---|---|---|
| ABRUZZI | Coroso, Citra | Dry Red |
| APULIA | Simonini, Favonio Pinot Bianco | Dry White |
| | Simonini, Favonio Chardonnay | Dry White |
| | Simonini, Favonio Cabernet Franc | Dry Red |
| | Cirillo-Farrusi, Torre Quarto | Dry Red |
| BASILICATA | D'Angelo, Lucanello | Dry White |
| CALABRIA | We have not found any exceptional non-D.O.C. wines from this region. | |
| CAMPANIA | Tenuta Ocone, Greco del Sannio | Dry White |
| | Torre di Gaia, Il Gaio | Dry White |
| | Mastroberardino, Lacrymarosa D'Irpinia | Dry Rose |
| | Episcopio, Ravello Rosso | Dry Red |
| | Gran Caruso, Ravello Bianco | Dry White |
| | Tenuta Ocone, Aglianico del Sannio | Dry Red |
| EMILIA-ROMAGNA | Paradiso, Barbarossa di Bertinoro | Dry Red |
| | Terre Rosse, Chardonnay | Dry White |
| | Umberto Cesari, Malise | Dry White |
| | Paradiso, Pagadebit | Dry White |
| | Castelluccio, Ronco del Re | Dry White |
| | Umberto Cesari, Liano | Dry Red |
| | Castelluccio, Ronco Casone | Dry Red |
| | Castelluccio, Ronco dei Ciliegi | Dry Red |
| | Castelluccio, Ronco delle Ginestre | Dry Red |
| FRIULI-VENEZIA GIULIA | Fantinel, Rosso della Ponca | Dry Red |
| | Borgo Conventi, White Table Wine | Dry White |
| | Associated Picolits (from outside Colli Orientali D.O.C. zone) | Sweet White |
| | Ronco del Gnemiz, Müller-Thürgau | Dry White |
| | Abbazia di Rosazzo, Ronco Acacie | Dry White |
| | Abbazia di Rosazzo, Ronco dei Roseti | Dry Red |
| | Ronchi di Cialla, Schioppettino | Dry Red |
| | Livio Felluga, Terre Alte | Dry White |
| | Jermann, Vintage Tunina | Dry White |
| | Fantinel, Bianco della Ponca | Dry White |
| LATIUM | DiMauro, Colle Picchioni | Dry Red |
| | Ludovisi, Fiorano Rosso | Dry Red |
| | Ludovisi, Fiorano Bianco | Dry White |
| | Colacicchi, Torre Ercolana | Dry Red |
| LIGURIA | We have not found any exceptional non-D.O.C. wines from this region. | |

| REGION | PRODUCER/WINE TYPE | STYLE |
|---|---|---|
| LOMBARDY | Berlucchi, Bianco Periale | Dry White |
| | Nino Negri, Castel Chiuro | Dry Red or White |
| | Ballabio, Clastidium | Dry Red |
| | Ballabio, Narbusto | Dry Red |
| MARCHES | Fazi-Battaglia, Le Moie | Dry White |
| MOLISE | We have not found any exceptional non-D.O.C. wines from this region. | |
| PIEDMONT | Various Arneis | Dry White |
| | Cascina Drago, Bricco del Drago | Dry Red |
| | Valentino, Bricco Manzoni | Dry Red |
| | Dessilani, Caramino | Dry Red |
| | Scarpa, Rouchet | Dry Red |
| | Various Spannas | Dry Red |
| SARDINIA | Sella and Mosca, Anghelu Ruju | Dessert Red |
| | Sella and Mosca, Torbato di Alghero | Dry White |
| SICILY | Duca di Salaparuta, Duca Enrico | Dry Red |
| | Duca di Salaparuta, Corvo | Dry Red & White |
| | Duca di Salaparuta, Corvo Colomba Platino | Dry White |
| | De Bartoli, Vecchio Samperi | Aperitif |
| | Count Tasca, Regaleali Estate Wines | Dry Red, Wht, Rose |
| | Count Tasca, Regaleali Nozze D'Oro | Dry White |
| | Count Tasca, Regaleali Rosso del Conte | Dry Red |
| TRENTINO-ALTO ADIGE | Santa Margherita, Luna dei Feldi | Dry White |
| | Hofstätter, de Vite | Dry White |
| | Count Bossi-Fretriotti, Foianeghe Rosso | Dry Red |
| TUSCANY | Antinori, Santa Christina | Dry Red |
| | Antinori, Solaia | Dry Red |
| | Antinori, Tignanello | Dry Red |
| | Barbi, Brusco dei Barbi | Dry Red |
| | Caparzo, Ca del Pazzo | Dry Red |
| | Capezzana, Ghiaie della Furba | Dry Red |
| | Avignonesi, Grifi | Dry Red |
| | Banfi, Fontanelle Chardonnay | Dry White |
| | Castello di Volpaia, Coltassala | Dry Red |
| | Castellare, I Sodi di San Niccoló | Dry Red |
| | Monte Vertine, Le Pergole Torte | Dry Red |
| | Altesino, Palazzo Altesi | Dry Red |
| | Castello dei Rampolla, Sammarco | Dry Red |
| | Incisa della Rocchetta, Sassicaia | Dry Red |
| | M. Castelli, Vinattieri Rosso | Dry Red |
| | Villa Cilnia, Vignacce | Dry Red |
| | San Felice, Vigorello | Dry Red |
| | Villa Cafaggio, San Martino | Dry Red |
| | Villa Cafaggio, Solatio Basilica | Dry Red |
| | Gabbiano, Ania | Dry Red |
| | Fontodi, Faccianella delle Pieve | Dry Red |

| REGION | PRODUCER/WINE TYPE | STYLE |
|---|---|---|
| TUSCANY (con'd) | Villa Cilnia, Vocato | Dry Red |
| | Villa Cilnia, Poggio Garbato | Dry White |
| | Villa Cilnia, Campo del Sasso | Dry White |
| | Villa Cilnia, Sassolato | Sweet White |
| UMBRIA | Antinori, Castello della Sala | Dry White |
| | Decugnano dei Barbi, Rosso | Dry Red |
| | Lungarotti, San Giorgio | Dry Red |
| VAL D'AOSTA | Voyat, Chambave Rouge | Dry Red |
| VENETO | Masi, Campo Fiorin | Dry Red |
| | Maculan, Torcolato | Sweet White |
| | Gasparini, Venegazzú | Dry Red |
| | Bertani, Catullo | Dry Red |
| | Quintarelli, Ca del Merlo | Dry Red |

RISERVA

*Vigneti*

*La Selvanella*

LOCALITÀ SELVANELLA

PRODUCT OF ITALY

*Chianti classico*

DENOMINAZIONE DI ORIGINE CONTROLLATA
E GARANTITA

Questa bottiglia porta il numero D  00553

BOTTLED IN GAGGIANO BY

*Melini s.c.a.r.l.*

NET CONTENTS    POGGIBONSI    ALCOHOL 12.5%
750 ML ℮     ITALIA      BY VOLUME

IMPORTED BY
FREDERICK WILDMAN AND SONS, LTD.,
NEW YORK, N.Y.

## ITALY IN REVIEW

- No country can rival Italy in sheer volume and variety of wines.

- All 20 regions of Italy produce wines. Each of these regions has its own specialties.

- Italy dominates in exporting wines to the United States. One of two bottles of imported wine consumed in the U.S. is Italian.

- In spite of recent price increases, Italian wines still represent superlative quality for value.

- The trend in Italian wines is toward esoteric "discovery" wines.

- Italian wines have become popular in the United States through the Italian-American restaurants.

- Italy is better respected for its reds than for its whites, especially big reds like Barolo, Gattinara, Brunello di Montalcino, and Amarone.

- Although each region produces significant wines, Piedmont and Tuscany may be singled out for their important wines.

- Italy's wine laws and export control standards are very strict (the D.O.C. and D.O.C.G.).

# GLOSSARY OF ITALIAN TERMS

**Azienda Agricola** *(ah-dzee-ENN-day ah-GREE-koh-lah)* — A firm whose whole business is agriculture. These firms grow their own grapes. Their wines are, therefore, estate bottled.

**Bianco** *(bee-AHN-koh)* — A white wine.

**Brut** *(BROUT)* — Very dry sparkling wine.

**Cantina** *(kahn-TEE-nah)* — Literally a wine cellar, where wine is served. Usually and more broadly for a winery itself.

**Cantina Sociale** *(kahn-TEE-nah soh-chee-AH-lah)* or **C.S.** — A cooperative group which makes wine.

**Casa Vinicola** *(KAH-zuh vee-NEE-koh-lah)* — A wine house, a winery. They buy grapes and/or wines. Similar to a *negociant* or *negociant-eleveur* in France.

**Classico** *(KLAH see-koh)* — A geographic term, under D.O.C. laws. A smaller portion of a larger area where a wine is produced. Considered the original, or best subzone within the area.

**Fattoria** *(fah-toh-REE-ah)* — Not a factory, rather a farm.

**Imbottigliato** *(eem-boh-tee-LYAH-toh)* — Means "bottled." Usually followed by "at the zone of production," "at the origin," or "at the estate."

**Liquoroso** *(lee-Kwoh-ROH-zoh)* — A wine high in alcohol, usually fortified and sweet.

**Passito** *(pah-SEE-toh)* — A wine made from partially dried, raisin-like grapes.

**Riserva** *(ree-ZAYR-vah)* — Under D.O.C. and D.O.C.G. rules, an aging term. The wine is aged at the winery for a longer period than regular wine. For example, Barolo must be aged for three years. If held at the winery for four years, it is a Riserva.

**Rosato** *(roh-ZAH-toh)* — A rose or light red wine.

**Rosso** *(ROHS-soh)* — A red wine.

**Spumante** *(spou-MAHN-tay)* — Frothy, sparkling wine. May be dry or sweet.

**Superiore** *(sou-peh-ree-OH-ray)* — This does not mean that the wine is superior. It means that under D.O.C. regulations the wine has been aged longer and is higher in alcohol than regular wine (such as Soave 10.5%, Soave Superiore 11%).

**Tenuta** *(teh-NOU-tah)* — An estate. A vineyard and winery combined.

**Vigneto** *(veen-YAY-toh)* — A vineyard site, or plot of land. The equivalent of the French term *cru*.

**VQPRD** — A European Economic Community (EEC) or a common market abbreviation, signifying a wine of quality produced in a regulated region.

# NOTES

# THE WINES OF GERMANY

## INTRODUCTION

It is a tribute to the determination of the German people that there *is* a German wine industry today. Much of the country is above 50° latitude (similar to the Saint Lawrence River in Canada) where grape growing is extremely difficult. Almost 70% of the terrain is very hilly, virtually impossible to work. During storms, soil is often swept down to the bottom. There is not a comfortable amount of growing days, light units, and warm autumns to ensure ease of harvest. It is always a struggle.

Each year the people combat the elements. They place ropes on steep hillside vineyards to assist them in working the fields without slipping downhill. They gather eroded soil from the lower slopes, pack it into pails, and carry it back to the hilltop sites. They have reconstructed almost half of their vineyard area in the past 30 years in order to gain a more efficient, economical harvest. They have developed grape varieties that can withstand nature's fickle way.

What is most amazing is that German wines not only exist, but they excel! No country can claim to produce more appealing white wine, fresh, fruity, sufficient to grace almost every dish or to be enjoyed alone without food. Of Germany's total production, 85% is white. Most of these whites are low in alcohol, light, and with abundant fruitiness. This luscious fruit is balanced by mouth-cleansing acidity which leaves the drinker with a pleasant, clean finish and not a cloying aftertaste. It is interesting to note that the Germans drink the national beverage, beer, with their meals, and wine by itself.

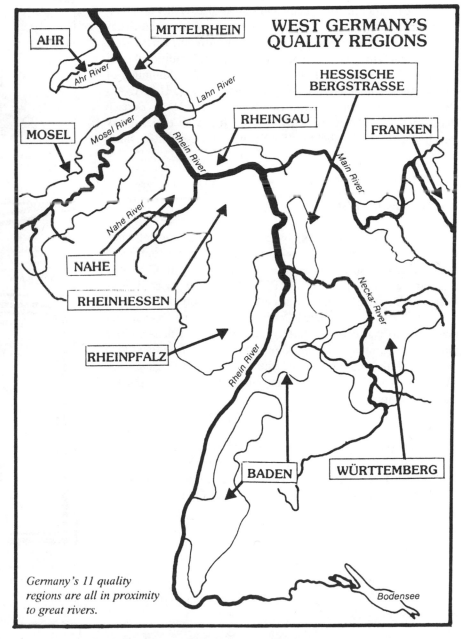

WEST GERMANY'S QUALITY REGIONS

*Germany's 11 quality regions are all in proximity to great rivers.*

233

## The Wine Laws of 1971

Wine legislation in 1971 helped to standardize quality and minimize label confusion. In truth, consumers in the United States still find the estate and village names a bit difficult. There are a group of wines that have bypassed and conquered traditional label wording. The prime example is Blue Nun, a Liebfraumilch of good quality, which has enjoyed great success in the U.S.A. Another is the prestigious firm Deinhard's example of Bereich Bernkastel, which they call Green Label. It is a lot easier to ask for a bottle of Green Label than for Bereich Bernkasteler Riesling!

## Categories of Wines

These 1971 wine laws established two main headings of wine: simple table wine and quality wine. Table wines must conform to strict standards and be made of grapes grown only in Germany. They are marked by the letters DTW (*Deutscher Tafel Wein* — German table wine). These wines are rarely exported to the U.S.

For a wine to be designated *Qualitäts,* it must pass an examination at an official control center. There are nine of these centers throughout Germany. Samples are tasted and analyzed and then given a control number called the *Amtliche Prüfungsnummer* (A.P.Nr.), which will appear on the label. Samples are retained at least two years for reference.

Quality wines are divided into two categories:

1. **QbA** (Qualitätswein eines bestimmten Anbaugebietes): A quality wine from a specific German region.
2. **QmP** (Qualitätswein mit Prädikat): Quality wine with special attributes. High quality QmP wines are subcategorized into:

   • Kabinett
   • Spätlese (late picked)
   • Auslese (select picked)
   • Beerenauslese or BA (select berry picked)
   • Trockenbeerenauslese, or TBA (select, dry berry picked).
   • Eiswein (ice wine)

*This is a Grosslage (several individual vineyards combined together) wine from the Mosel's Central Cellars. As a QmP Kabinett wine, it would be a fine alternative to Black Cat wine. An estate-bottled Kabinett.*

*This is an estate-bottled, light wine from one of Germany's finest shippers, Deinhard. The label tells us the town (Wehlen), the single-vineyard (Sonnenuhr "Sundial"), the grape (Riesling), the vintage (1985), and the quality level (Kabinett, QmP).*

Although sugar is permitted to be added to table wines and regular quality wines (a process called chaptalization), it may not be added to QmP wines. Please note, however, that a special unfermented grape juice called *Süss-Reserve* (sweet reserve) may be used for even QmP. Sugar is added at the time of fermentation to assist the conversion of sugar and yeast to alcohol and carbon dioxide. Süss-Reserve is added *after* fermentation to sweeten the wine and lower the alcohol content.

The quality of QmP is determined not by when the grapes are picked, as the names imply, but by how much sugar is in the unfermented grape must. This is measured by the Oechsle Scale (*see chart*).

**Kabinett.** The term "cabinet-wine" is derived from a centuries-old custom of keeping the finest wines in a special chamber or cabinet. We could call Kabinett the best wine from the main harvest. These wines should always be smooth, well-balanced, with an elegant finish. They usually represent excellent dollar value.

**Spätlese.** There is a tale that in 1775 at the famous Schloss Johannisberg monastery, abbots sent a courier to the town of Fulda to get permission to harvest the grapes. The courier fell ill and by the time he returned, the grapes looked quite rotten. The fearful monks harvested anyway and what resulted from the "late-picking" was a much finer nectar. Spätlese was born. Today a statue of the courier stands at Schloss Johannisberg.

This elegant Rheingau hillside vineyard was named for Queen Victoria. Since the English could not pronounce the village name, Hochheim, they began calling this wine, then virtually every other Rhein wine, "hock."

| Oechsle "Ripeness" Measurement | | |
|---|---|---|
| QmP Rating | Oechsle Scale | When to Drink |
| Kabinett | 70- 76 | 4- 6 Years |
| Spätlese | 76- 90 | 4- 7 Years |
| Auslese | 90-110 | 6-10 Years |
| Beerenauslese (BA) | 110-125 | 8-15 Years |
| Trockenbeerenauslese (TBA) | 150+ | Up to 50 Years |
| Eiswein | 106 (Frozen Grapes) | 5-15 Years |

These wines are picked usually two to four weeks after the main harvest. They have a special luscious character, which is best appreciated when drunk without food.

**Auslese.** These "select-pickings" are essentially the ripest clusters of the Spätlese harvest. They are sweeter, smoother and more costly. They match up well to fruit and dessert cakes. As with Spätlese, they are best when tasted alone.

**Beerenauslese (BA).** These astonishing and rare wines are produced from individually picked berries that have been attacked by a special fungus which the Germans call *Edelfaule*. This is the same "noble rot" *(Botrytis cinerea)* that is present in the famous French Sauternes and Barsac. This attack must be followed by a spell of dry weather, so that the fungus can settle into the grape's skin to promote water evaporation. As you can imagine, this phenomenon is extremely rare. It occurs usually only about three years each decade. Very few cases are produced. Wine lovers feel that no food is good enough for BA wines. They are served and savored as after-dinner liqueurs.

**Trockenbeerenauslese (TBA).** This is the ultimate in Russian roulette. Berries attacked by noble rot are left on the vine to shrivel and lose up to 85% of their liquid volume. The resulting raisinized grapes are individually picked and made into a fabulous nectar, which may develop in the bottle for half a century or more. Realize that we are into December now and that adverse weather conditions can destroy the berries completely. Of course, TBAs are phenomenally expensive.

**Eiswein.** "Ice-wine" must be exposed to temperatures below 18° F and picked frozen. When crushed, the ice is separated from the must, causing the juice to be very luscious and concentrated in sweetness. It is very rare, expensive, and usually somewhere between Auslese and Beerenauslese in taste. You will usually find an additional Prädikat designation on the label, such as *Nikolauswein*, December 5–6; *Christwein*, December 24–25; or *Drei Königenwein* (Three Kings Wine), January 6. These are among the most esoteric treasures in all of winedom!

Remember that these five designations (Kabinett to Eiswein) are only designations. The quality of the wine will vary according to the grapes used, the vintage, the soil and climate, and most of all, the excellence of the winemaker.

*We applaud the labeling on this dry QbA Riesling from the Rheinhessen from one of Germany's preeminent shippers. We applaud the wine, too.*

*This Bereich wine is a QmP, Spätlese. Expect it to be luscious and concentrated but with a balanced, crisp finish. From Leonard Kreusch, the U.S.'s number one importer of German wines.*

Each QbA and QmP has a control number on its label, for example:

**A.P.NR. 2 576 510 14 82**

2 — The German government's testing control center where the wine was tasted and approved. There are nine altogether.

576 — This grouping designates the source, the grower.

510 — These digits identify the specific bottling plant.

14 — This number represents the specific batch application number of the bottler. In other words, this is the fourteenth batch of wine for which bottler 510 has sought approval.

82 — The year the wine was tasted by the board.

## The Grapes

Over 85% of all German wines are white. The majority come from three grapes: Müller-Thürgau (31%); Riesling (20%); and Sylvaner (10%). Riesling is considered the finest. It is Germany's finest vinifera and grows to its zenith in the Mosel-Saar-Ruwer district and the Rheingau. Müller-Thürgau, originally thought to be a cross between Sylvaner and Riesling, now appears to be a cross of two clones of Riesling. It was developed by a Dr. Müller from Thürgau in Switzerland. Müller-Thürgau vines like early ripening and usually provide a large, agreeable, dependable source of good, not great wine. Silvaner (Sylvaner) is gradually losing ground. It is a vinifera which is considered to be quite neutral; that is, it allows the character of the soil or other grapes to dominate its taste. It thrives in the Rheinhessen and in Franken.

Other white grapes include the Scheurebe, Morio-Muskat, Gutedel (known as Chasselas in France and Switzerland), and Kerner. White wine is derived from the red-skinned Ruländer (Pinot Gris or Pinot Grigio) and Traminer (Gewürztraminer). There is also some Weiss-burgunder (Pinot-Blanc).

Red or "blue" vines include the Spätburgunder (Pinot Noir), which yields wines more reminiscent of a Beaujolais than of a burgundy from the Cote d'Or. Much of the Spätburgunder is planted in Baden. The Trollinger vine produces sound red wine in Württemberg. One red varietal, the Blauer Portugieser, is responsible in the Rheinpfalz for a fresh, lovely rose called Weissherbst (white autumn). You may find Weissherbst from other districts and other grape varieties.

## The Climate

It is precisely the difficult climate of Germany that provides its wines with vitality and vigor. Unstressed vines from hot plains usually produce wines that are alcoholic, flabby, and rich. German wines are light, aromatic, refreshing, and have good acidity to balance the ample fruit and touch of residual sweetness. However, without the stabilizing factor of great rivers—the Mother Rhein, the Mosel, Saar, Ruwer, Nahe, Main, Ahr, and Neckar—viticulture would probably cease in Germany. These rivers also provide moisture necessary for the noble rot to create BA and TBA wines.

Slopes facing the south provide the most favorable micro-climates, the most famous of which are the Rheingau and the Moselle near Bernkastel. These steep slopes require a great human effort, since mechanization is impossible. The Germans say, "Where the plow can go, vines should not grow."

## The Soil

Germany has a fine variety of soils. Much of it is light in color, which reflects sunlight and releases heat very slowly. It is very good for light-colored and light-bodied wines. Some soils are rich in minerals. Soils of loam, humus, loess, and clay retain moisture to feed the vines' root stock. This can cause rot. Germany's best wines come from thin, light soils, such as slate, basalt, volcanic rock, and weathered red sandstone. Into such soil, with a good southern exposure, surely the wise German vintner will plant the lordly Riesling, one of the world's finest white varietals.

This is a "quality wine" from a broad area (Bereich) around the Bernkastel Village. The house of Deinhard, founded in 1650, makes it easy for us. We just have to remember to ask for "Green Label."

A luscious Spätlese from the village of Flonheim in the Rheinhessen. Do you find the English script clearer and easier on your eyes than the Germanic?

# SELF-EVALUATION

BEFORE READING ON, see if you have mastered the data set forth in the last few pages. Check the answer section at the back of the book for the correct answers. If you have not answered at least 70% of the questions below correctly, please reread the previous section.

## THE WINES OF GERMANY
### INTRODUCTION

| TRUE | FALSE | |
|------|-------|---|
| _____ | _____ | 1. German wine production is equally divided between red and white. |
| _____ | _____ | 2. QbA and QmP are two designated categories within quality wines (Qualitätswein). |
| _____ | _____ | 3. Deutscher Tafelwein (DTF), that is, simple German table wine, is seen very frequently in the United States. |
| _____ | _____ | 4. Süss-Reserve is added before fermentation to raise the alcohol content of the wine. |
| _____ | _____ | 5. Kabinett wines are the best wines from the main harvest, which are well-balanced and smooth. |
| _____ | _____ | 6. Spätlese wines result from late picking, usually two months after the main harvest. |
| _____ | _____ | 7. Auslese wines are essentially the ripest clusters of the Spätlese harvest. |
| _____ | _____ | 8. The luscious nature of Beerenauslese (BA) wines is the result of the grapes being attacked by a special fungus, called Edelfaule. |
| _____ | _____ | 9. Trockenbeerenauslese (TBA) wines are picked very late, usually in December, and are extremely expensive. |
| _____ | _____ | 10. For Eiswein or "ice wine," the grapes are picked frozen. |
| _____ | _____ | 11. The three leading German grape varieties are Müller-Thürgau, Riesling, and Trollinger. |
| _____ | _____ | 12. Germany's moderate climate ensures a steady crop of healthy grapes year in and year out. |

# THE WINE REGIONS OF GERMANY

## The Regions for Tafelwein

The 1971 wine law divided Germany into wine-growing regions. For German table wine (DTW) there are five large Weinbaugebiete, or regions:

1. Mosel
2. Rhein
3. Main
4. Neckar
5. Oberrhein

Since we see so little DTW in the United States, we will turn our attention to the divisions for Qualitätswein.

## Anbaugebiete (Regions) for QbA and QmP Wines

There are 11 *Anbaugebiete* or wine regions alongside the great network of rivers in western Germany. Each *Anbaugebiet* (region) has its own personality and character. Unfortunately, in the U.S. we usually see wines from only six or seven of these regions. The 11 regions are:

1. Ahr
2. Mittelrhein
3. Mosel-Saar-Ruwer*
4. Nahe*
5. Rheingau*
6. Rheinhessen*
7. Rheinpfalz*
8. Franken*
9. Hessische Bergstrasse
10. Württemberg
11. Baden*

*Generally available in the United States.

## REGION BY REGION
### The Ahr

We in the U.S. see almost no wine from this small, romantic region. Many restaurants and inns dot the rocky countryside where Beethoven was wont to spend his summers. Surprisingly, more red than white is produced here.

### The Mittelrhein

This is the land of the Grimm Brothers' tale *Snow White and the Seven Dwarfs*. Breathtaking landscapes have inspired both Lord Byron and Dostoevsky, as well as Heine's *Die Lorelei*.

Riesling dominates here, showing a hearty, spicy style. Mittelrhein is a major region for Sekt. Ninety-nine percent of the production is white.

### Mosel-Saar-Ruwer

Slopes along these three rivers are almost impossible to work. The saying, "Where the plow can go, vines should not grow" originated here. But it is worth it! As the Romans used to say, "There is no palm of victory without a swallowing of the dust of the arena." For over 140 miles along the Mosel, slatey peaks climb to 800 feet at a steepness of up to 60 degrees.

The rivers reflect the sun's rays by day, and create fog banks to protect against frost and promote noble rot. Some of Germany's most famous wine villages are here, especially in the Middle Mosel section. They include Bernkastel, Piesport, Wehlen, and Graach. Riesling accounts for about 65% of the wine. Ninety-nine percent of the region's production is white. Mosel-Saar-Ruwer wines are sold in green flute bottles.

Saar wines are slatey, delicate, crisp and fragrant. Ruwer wines are less slatey, but more robust and spicy. Mosel-Saar-Ruwer wines generally are refreshing, clean, racy, and very low in alcohol. They surely beat a coffee break at 10:00 a.m.

### The Nahe

This is the melting pot of German viticulture. The Nahe is not as well known as its famous neighbors, and therefore provides wines of good value. At their best, Nahe wines combine the charm of a Mosel, the elegance of a Rheingau, and the fruitiness of a Rheinhessen.

Soil composition varies from red sandstone to slate, quartz, and volcanic porphyrite. White wines dominate to the tune of 99% with an equal balance of Silvaner, Riesling and Müller-Thürgau. This region of small estate producers is undervalued and, as yet, untapped by the U.S. market.

## The Rheingau

The Rheingau, Germany's most prestigious wine region, is pre-eminent because of a turn in the Mother Rhein River. From Hochheim to Lorch, a distance of about 25 miles, the northern slope of the river has a southern exposure, enabling the grapes to soak up the extra sun rays. Morning mists create conditions for noble rot. The Taunus Mountains ward off cold north winds. The soil of red clay and slate stores moisture and reflects heat. All in all, it is a perfect microclimate for the lordly Riesling, which accounts for almost 80% of the wine produced here. Ninety-eight percent of Rheingau wine is white. Even if Rheingau wines are costly, they are fairly priced, because they are very elegant and require time to show their best colors.

This is a region with many small growers (about 2,250), but large, famous estates dominate. High on the list are Steinberger, Schloss Vollrads, and Schloss Johannisberger. Wine folklore includes Charlemagne, Cistercian monks, and Roman legionnaires. The Wine Museum and Academy in Geisenheim are world-renowned. The "Wine Alley" in Rudesheim is colorful and festive, a source of good wine, *gemütlichkeit* (conviviality), and a song or two. Hochheim is famous because the English could not pronounce it. German wines are still called "hocks" today. Rheingau wines, as well as neighboring Rheinhessen and Rheinpfalz, are sold in brown flute bottles. One of Germany's best reds, Assmannshausen, is from the Rheingau.

## Franken

Franken wine, sometimes called Steinwein, differs from other German wines. It is marketed in the squat, flagon-shaped bocksbeutel. It is often very dry with a strong, earthy character, reminiscent of a Chardonnay from France. The grape is usually Silvaner or Müller-Thürgau, with white wines accounting for about 99% of total production. We do not see much Frankenwein in the U.S. When we do, it can be pricey. The center of the region is the famous beer city, Würzburg.

## Rheinhessen

The Rheinhessen is Germany's largest wine-producing region. Wines range from cabbages to kings. Silvaner and Müller-Thürgau account for over 75% of the wines. Many cross-vines, including Scheurebe, are used here. Only 5% of the total production is red, with some of the country's best coming from the village of Ingelheim. The soil here is as varied as its wines; loess, quartzite, slate, and volcanic rock are found.

Except for Bingen, many of the best and most famous wines come from towns between Mainz and Worms on the Rhein's west bank. Mainz was the home of Gutenberg, who modified a wine press to invent the printing press. Worms is the home of the original Liebfraumilch vineyard site behind its Church of the Blessed Mother. Some of Germany's best estates are in the noteworthy wine villages of Nierstein and Oppenheim.

## Hessische Bergstrasse

Until 1971, the wines of this small region, famous for its almond and cherry trees, were considered as part of Baden. Ninety-eight percent of the production is white with Riesling accounting for over half. Many of the small "weekend vineyardists" sell their grapes to cooperatives. The wines are often compared, quite flatteringly, to those of the Rheingau. However, to get a taste, you will have to visit the region. The wines of Hessische Bergstrasse are very rarely exported.

## Rheinpfalz (Palatinate)

A close second to the Rheinhessen in volume, the Rheinpfalz is divided into three sectors:

1. Unterhaardt (north)
2. Mittlehaardt (between Kallstadt and Ruppertsberg)
3. Oberhaart (southern Wineroad)

CROWN of CROWNS

750 ml e **Liebfraumilch** A. P.Nr. 4333145/37/84
ALCOHOL 9.5% BY VOLUME **Qualitätswein** RHEINHESSEN
Produce of Germany

*Liebfraumilch, which means "milk of the blessed Mother," derives its name from the original vineyards around the Liebfrauenkirch, a church in Worms. "Crown of Crowns" is an excellent proprietary label bottled by the firm of Langenbach.*

The northern and southern sections yield soft, mild, pedestrian wines which go into Liebfraumilch blends. Silvaner and Müller-Thürgau dominate here. The Rheinpfalz produces about 13% red wine.

In the Mittelhaardt, the Riesling emerges in all its glory in the famous wine villages of Forst, Deidesheim, Wachenheim, and Ruppertsberg. Some of Germany's finest wine producers are here, including the three "B's" — Bürklin-Wolf, von Bassermann-Jordan, and von Bühl. Germany's most significant wine festival, the Würstmarkt, is held in nearby Bad Dürkheim.

Rheinpfalz wines at their best are complex, earthy, rich, deep in color, lush, almost meaty, and long-lived.

## Württemberg

This is a small region dominated by co-ops. Fifty percent of the grapes are red, but white wines account for 70% of the wine production (we hope you can figure that one out). Württemberg has the highest per capita consumption in Germany. Perhaps that is why very little is exported. A pink wine, Schillerwein, is a specialty in this region.

## Baden

They say you can taste the sun in Baden wines. We are not sure, but this is Germany's most southerly region and officially placed in Zone B (or Region II). The rest of Germany is Zone A (Region I). Many different vines thrive in the varied soil of this large geographic zone that stretches from the Swiss frontier north to the Neckar River.

About 21% of Baden's wines are red, mostly from the Spätburgunder (Pinot Noir). Some pink Weissherbst is made as well. Müller-Thürgau, Ruländer (Pinot Gris) and Gutedel (Chasselas) lead the way among white wines.

Most of the wine is handled by Baden Central Cellar Cooperative Winery. Although styles vary from Bereich to Bereich, the trend is toward lighter, crisper wines, sometimes slightly *spritzig* or crackling.

## Bereiche (Districts)

Within the 11 regions there are about 30 districts or *Bereiche*. A Bereich or district is a broad combination of vineyard sites. A wine with Bereich on the label must come from within the boundaries of the district, which may encompass several towns. A Bereich wine is always fresh, pleasant, consistent, everyday fare that will not hurt your pocketbook. One example would be Deinhard's Bereich Bernkastel. Bereich wines are QbA (Quality wines).

## Grosslagen (Collective Vineyard Sites)

*Grosslagen,* or great sites, are collections of individual vineyard sites. They are smaller than Bereiche. Before the 1971 wine laws, there were over 25,000 individual sites in West Germany. Today there are some 2,600 *Einzellagen* (individual sites) and 150 or so Grosslagen. There is no limit in size for Grosslagen. The Saumagen Grosslage in Kallstadt is only 100 acres. Hofstück in Deidesheim covers 3,000 acres.

The Grosslage Badstube around the town of Bernkastel encompasses the five Einzellagen of Lay, Graben, Doktor, Matheisbildchen, and Bratenhöfchen. A Grosslage is a marketing unit that allows a shipper to produce a larger quantity of similarly styled wine. Grosslage wines are ordinarily better than Bereich wines. Quite often the best wine of a grower will be offered under the name of an Einzellage. Grosslage wines may be QbA or QmP (Quality or Predicate wines).

Most Grosslagen are associated with famous wine towns. There are approximately 1,400 of these villages, called *Gemeinden.* Well-known Grosslagen include Zeller Schwarze Katz, Piesporter Michelsberg, Niersteiner Gutes Domtal, Kröver Nacktarsch, and Johannisberger Erntebringer.

## Einzellagen (Individual Vineyard Sites)

The *Einzellage* is an individual vineyard site and is the smallest unit recognized by German law. The 2,600 registered Einzellagen vary in size from one acre to over 600 acres. They represent the flower of German viticulture. It is due to a glaring label weakness that one is not able to tell a Grosslage from an Einzellage except through memorization. For example:

| GROSSLAGE | EINZELLAGE |
|---|---|
| Bernkasteler Kurfurstlay | Bernkasteler Doktor |
| Graacher Münzlay | Graacher Himmelreich |
| Niersteiner Rehbach | Niersteiner Hipping |
| Forster Mariengarten | Forster Jesuitengarten |
| Piesporter Michelsberg | Piesporter Goldtröpchen |

As in French Burgundy, there may be several owners and producers of a single Einzellage. Einzellage wines may be QbA, but they are generally QmP, that is Kabinett or higher. Below is a list of some of Germany's most famous individual vineyard sites with their associated villages. Some vineyards are so famous that they are marketed without their village name. For example:

- Steinberger — owned by the German State (Rheingau)
- Schloss Vollrads — from Winkel (Rheingau)
- Schloss Johannisberg — owned by the von Metternichs (Rheingau)
- Schloss Eltz — from Eltville (Rheingau)
- Scharzhofberger — from Wiltingen on the Saar; the most famous owner is Egon von Müller (Mosel-Saar-Ruwer)

Several vineyard sites, including all of the renowned Steinberg plus parts of Rudesheimer Berg Roseneck, Berg Rottland, Berg Schlossberg, Erbacher Marcobrunn, and Hochheimer Domdechaney among others are owned by the German government. Excellent, elegant wines are produced under the direction of Dr. Hans Ambrosi, one of the country's most respected professors, scholars, and experts on German viticulture. The labels are simple and classy with a distinctive gold and black eagle on the top. In a way, one of Germany's finest producers of wines is Germany itself.

## Cooperative Cellars

Many growers (almost 70%) do not make wine. Rather they sell their grapes to any of the more than 300 cooperative cellars. Some of these co-ops have existed for over 100 years and produce very sound wine. There are six large *Zentralkellerei* (central cellars), one each in Baden, the Rheinhessen, the Mosel-Saar-Ruwer, the Nahe, Württemberg, and Franken. They are impressive large-scale winemaking facilities with almost 40,000 grower-members.

# POPULAR GERMAN WINES

**Liebfraumilch:** Originally from a vineyard behind the Church of the Blessed Mother in Worms (Rheinhessen), Liebfraumilch (blessed mother's milk) now is merely a generic term for a pleasant quality (QbA) wine from the Rhein or Nahe Regions. They do not bear vineyard names, cannot be QmP (predicate), and must have the taste of Riesling, Silvaner, or Müller-Thürgau grapes. Many of those which appear in the U.S. have memorable names such as Sichel Blue Nun, Valkenberg's Madonna, and Deinhard's Hanns Christoff.

**Moselblümchen:** The "Little Flower of the Mosel," Beethoven's favorite, may be Tafelwein or Quality Wine. It is a light and crisp blend of secondary vineyard sites. It should be enjoyed young.

**Zeller Schwarze Katz:** This Grosslage is usually a QbA, rarely a QmP. "Black Cat" wine is fragrant and fresh. It can be enjoyed at 10 a.m. or 10 p.m. The story goes that a black cat helped wine merchants in the village of Zell pick the best wine by jumping onto its barrel. It is almost always 100% Riesling from the Mosel.

**Kröver Nacktarsch:** This is another Mosel Grosslage, a popular QbA, with a smiling man slapping the "bare bottom" of a young boy. It seems the lad had gone into the cellar and helped himself to wine — now he must pay the price! Fresh and clean, it has perhaps the most memorable label in the world.

**May Wine:** A Rhein wine flavored with Waldmeister (Woodruff) herbs, it is simple, festive, and delicately scented.

**Affenthaler:** This pricey German red from Baden has a distinctive gold monkey embossed on the bottle. Made from the Spätburgunder (Pinot Noir) grape, the wine is dry and fruity, reminiscent of a Beaujolais. The name is interesting. *Thal* means valley. This valley was named at one time for the Blessed Virgin, *Ave Maria Thal*. As years progressed, it became *Ave Thal* and finally *Affenthal*. Since *Affe* means *ape* in German, Affenthal wine came to be known as "Monkey Wine."

With these popular, familiar types of wines, always look for a quality shipper. Some recommended shippers are Leonard Kreusch, Deinhard, St. Ursula, Sichel, Langenbach, Anheuser, and Hallgarten.

*In Worms one of the Gothic churches, the Liebfrauenkirch, is surrounded by 26 acres of vineyards called Liebfrauenstift, which literally means the churches endowment. It was this vineyard that gave its name to Liebfraumilch, and its wine.*

## The German Label

### WHAT IT TELLS US

The German wine label provides us with a lot of information. It tells us the specific region (Anbaugebiet), the village name (with "-er" on the end), the district (Bereich) or vineyard site (Grosslage or Einzellage), and the vintage. If a wine bears a vintage date, at least 85% of the grapes must have been grown during that year and the wine must be characteristic of the vintage. The label usually states the grape variety or varieties. We can easily determine the quality level (Tafelwein, QbA or QmP) as well as the Prädikat designations (Kabinett, Spätlese, Auslese, BA, TBA, or Eiswein). Words like *Halbtrocken* (half dry — between 33 and 50 grams per liter of sugar) and *Trocken* (dry — between 4 and 9 grams of sugar per liter) let us know the level of dryness. The official control number (A.P.Nr.) as well as the name and address of the bottler are shown. Estate bottling is designated by the term *Erzeugerabfüllung*.

## WHAT IT DOES NOT TELL US

It is impossible to determine a Grosslage from an Einzellage except by memorization. Shippers and producers are not rated. Here is where an informed wine merchant can be of great help. German wine labels are surely the most colorful and striking in the world. What is most difficult for the initiate is the German language, the German script, and the repetition of names. For example, there are 72 different vineyard sites called Schlossberg, 11 Steinbergs but only 1 Steinberger, 34 Herrenbergs plus Herrengarten, Herrenbuckel, Herrenstuck, Herrentisch, *und so weider!* There are many producers and shippers of varying quality named Schmitt or Müller or Schneider. We could go on!

We sincerely feel that the wines of Germany, especially the finest ones, should be even more popular than they are in the U.S.A. Americans say they like their wines dry, but not too dry. Witness the success of Lambrusco, Canei, and other off-dry wines of light alcohol. Is the consumer intimidated by the thought of ordering a bottle of Deidesheimer Höfstuck Riesling Spätlese? We think so. We also think that without further label simplification and reform, Americans will not be motivated to move beyond the German wines that they can pronounce. These wonderful, distinctive, fragrant, delicious, light, low-alcohol wines that go with any meal or no meal deserve a better fate.

## Buying Tips

One approach to buying German wines that has worked well for us is:

1. Determine what level of concentration, sweetness, or style you would like to try (Trocken, Kabinett, Spätlese, etc.).
2. Zero in on a district which may interest you (if you like Liebfraumilch, you might look to Rheingau, Nahe, Rheinpfalz or Rheinhessen; if you prefer the "Black Cat," seek out a Mosel).
3. Pick a recent vintage of good quality.
4. Select a well-known wine village.
5. Ask your wine merchant to show you a Grosslage and Einzellage from that village.

## THE GERMAN "WINE SEAL" AND AWARDS BANDS

*No other country shows us more clearly which of its wines have won national contests and prizes. The Wine Seal and Award Bands are coveted indicators of high quality.*

6. Ask your merchant's advice on the stature of the producer, bottler and shipper.
7. Look at the price tag.

We have found that quite often one can find a superb wine of Kabinett or Spätlese quality at about the same price as a Lieb or Zeller Schwarze Katz.

The following is a list of some of Germany's most famous individual vineyard sites with their associated villages:

| Region | Village | Vineyard Site |
|---|---|---|
| Mosel-Saar Ruwer | Graach | Himmelreich |
| | Brauneberg | Juffer |
| | Bernkastel | Doktor |
| | Ürzig | Würzgarten |
| | Bernkastel | Graben |
| | Trittenheim | Altärchen |
| | Piesport | Goldtröpchen |
| | Zelting | Sonnenuhr |
| | Wehlen | Sonnenuhr |
| Rheingau | Rudesheim | Bischofsberg |
| | Oestrich | Lenchen |
| | Eltville | Sonnenberg |
| | Hochheim | Domdechaney |
| | Erbach | Markobrunn |
| | Hattenheim | Nussbrunnen |
| | Rudesheim | Berg Rottland |
| Rheinhessen | Nierstein | Hipping |
| | Nierstein | Hölle |
| | Oppenheim | Kreuz |
| | Oppenheim | Sackträger |
| | Bingen | Scharlachberg |
| Rheinpfalz | Forst | Jesuitengarten |
| | Deidesheim | Nonnenstuck |

# GERMANY IN REVIEW

- Germany is recognized as the premium producer of light, white wines.

- The Riesling vine is the nation's most aristocratic.

- Wines are produced in 11 quality zones. Most of what we see in the U.S. originates in: Mosel-Saar-Ruwer, Rheingau, Rheinhessen, Rheinpfalz or Nahe.

- Germany has very stringent wine laws.

- These laws divide wines into three categories: German Table Wines (DTW), Quality Wines (QbA) and Quality Wines with Attributes (QmP).

- Quality Wines with Attributes (QmP) are subdivided by law into six levels of sweetness and concentration:

  Kabinett
  Spälese
  Auslese
  Beerenauslese (BA)
  Trockenbeerenauslese (TBA)
  Eiswein

- It is a tribute to Germany that she produces such fine wines in spite of the tremendous difficulties presented by her climate.

# SELF-EVALUATION

BEFORE READING ON, see if you have mastered the data set forth in the last few pages. Check the answer section at the back of the book for the correct answers. If you have not answered at least 70% of the questions below correctly, please reread the previous section.

## GERMAN REGIONS

TRUE     FALSE

_____   _____   1. A wine with *Bereich* on the label must come from within the boundaries of the district.

_____   _____   2. *Grosslagen* or "great sites" may come from several different towns and villages.

_____   _____   3. An *Einzellage* is a unit larger than a *Grosslage*.

_____   _____   4. Rheinhessen is Germany's largest wine-producing region.

_____   _____   5. Most wines of Baden tend to be very light and crisp.

_____   _____   6. Bernkasteler Doktor is an example of a wine from an Einzellage.

_____   _____   7. Rheingau and Rheinhessen are two of the most famous regions of West Germany.

_____   _____   8. The Ahr region is the smallest of the wine regions of Germany.

_____   _____   9. The words earthy, rich, deep in color, and lush describe the wines of the Franken region.

_____   _____   10. In Germany several people may own different parts of one *Einzellage* or vineyard site.

# GLOSSARY OF GERMAN TERMS

**Amtliche Prüfung** (certification) — One of the most important factors introduced in the new German wine laws of 1971. A sample of each quality wine is tasted by professionals in the government to determine whether it is worthy of certification. If so, the label is marked with a certification number.

**Anbaugebiete** (regions) — Broad geographic designations. There are 11 for quality wines and 5 for table wines.

**Auslese** (selected harvest) — Wines produced from fully ripe grape clusters, sometimes affected with *Botrytis cinerea* (noble rot). The Oechsle Scale will determine if a wine is rich enough to be called Auslese. Auslese is a QmP designation.

**Badische Weinstrasse** (Baden Wine Road) — The route extending from Weil near Basel to Laudenbach, north of Weinheim.

**Beerenauslese** (selected grapes) — Rare wines produced from overripe grapes, usually having noble rot. Sweet and spicy with an unmistakable *Botrytis* aroma. These long-lived dessert wines score high on the Oechsle Scale.

**Bereich** (district) — A subregion which is an amalgamation of several large vineyard areas located in communities of close proximity and yielding wines with similar taste characteristics.

**Bocksbeutel** — A flagon used for Franconian wines. The name of the bottle is said to be derived from its similarity to an unmentionable part of a male goat's anatomy. Also used by the famous Portuguese rose, Mateus.

**Deutsches Weinsiegel** (German wine seal) — This quality seal is given to wines that have gained an extremely high number of points in a voluntary sensory examination. This rare seal is given in addition to the official certification number.

**Diabetiker Wein** (diabetic wine) — The 1971 wine law provides that completely fermented dry wines, usually more robust than the typical German wine, may bear a designation on bottles *Für Diabetiker Geeignet,* meaning suitable for diabetics.

**Edelfaule** — The rare noble rot that affects the more luscious dessert types of wine.

**Einzellage** (individual vineyard) — This is the smallest vineyard area recognized by the 1971 German wine laws.

**Eiswein** (ice wine) — Fully ripened grapes, harvested frozen. Only the concentrated, sugary nectar is pressed. The frozen water from the grapes is separated away. A rarity among German wines, Eiswein is a tribute to their determination and appreciation of esoterica.

**Erzeugerabfüllung** — Estate-bottled.

**Grosslagen** (collective sites) — Each individual vineyard is part of a legally defined, larger collective site. These Grosslagen are usually not as good as Einzellagen (individual sites).

**Hock** — This British term is applied to any white wine from the Rhine. From the town of Hochheim in the Rheinhessen.

**Jahrgang** — This word simply means vintage.

**Kabinettwein** — These are elegant, mature wines of better quality, the driest of the Prädikat category. The term "cabinet" was first used as a quality description on the label of an 1811 Steinberger by the Duke of Nassau.

**Prüfungsnummer** (national certification number) — These numbers on a label indicate that the QbA or QmP wines have passed an official government quality-control tasting.

**Rotwein** — Red wine.

**Sekt** — Sparkling wine, usually produced by the Charmat or transfer processes.

**Spätlese** (late harvest) — Fully ripened grapes picked later than the normal harvest. Between Kabinett and Auslese on the QmP Oechsle Scale.

**Süss-Reserve** — Sweet unfermented grape juice added to some wines before bottling to enhance and balance the blend.

**Tafelwein** (table wine) — Light, fresh wines. Must be produced from grapes harvested in Germany. A lower category than Qualitätswein. Usually not exported.

**Trockenbeerenauslese** — The word means selected dried grapes. This type of wine is made exclusively from shrivelled grapes, overripe and afflicted with noble rot. Extremely rare and long-lived. The highest on the Oechsle Scale.

**Weingut** — This is a winery and vineyard that has its own equipment for cultivating, pressing, and making wine.

**Weissherbst** — A fresh, fruity rose made from red wine grapes.

# THE WINES OF IBERIA
## *Spain and Portugal*

Aside from geographic proximity, Spain and Portugal do not have much in common. And yet they are always grouped together, especially at wine tastings, as "Iberian." True, their languages are similar and they are both religiously Catholic countries, but they remind us a lot of Italy, where each region has its own dialect, dishes, wines, and way of life. One thing that they share (and this is Italy's problem, too) is that we do not know enough about them. And what we do know may be the wrong thing.

For example, we do know Portuguese rose—sweetish, inexpensive blends of red and white wines, sometimes carbonated and marketed in gimmicky bottles. And how about Spanish Sangria—that ubiquitous wine and citrus punch, inexpensive and made to stay that way! Truly there is much, much more to viticulture in the Iberian Peninsula. One thing Spain and Portugal do have in common is that they offer us a bevy of wines, traditionally well made in an assortment of styles. In addition, a technological explosion exists, which bodes a sunny future. Our ignorance of their excellence has kept their price tags low. To the oenophile, they have emerged as suitable alternatives to much more costly Bordeaux and burgundies. Very often they are superior wines, price notwithstanding.

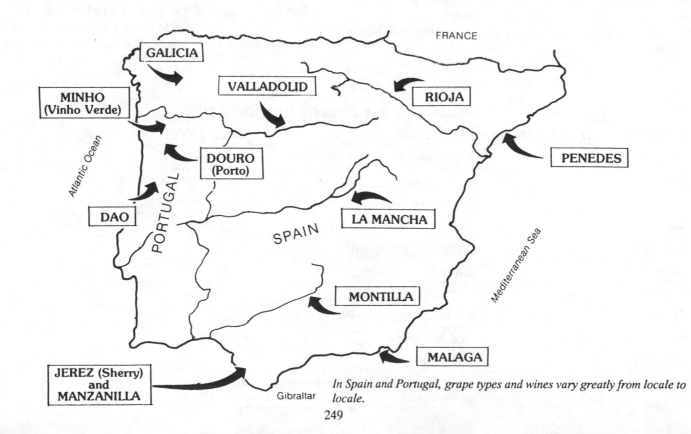

*In Spain and Portugal, grape types and wines vary greatly from locale to locale.*

249

# WINES OF PORTUGAL

The vine flourished in Portugal (or Lusitania) during the Classical Age. Phoenicians, Greeks, and Romans introduced their own grape varieties. Later Arab invaders slowed the wine industry, but with Portugal's formation as a nation in the twelfth century, wine-making soared once again. Today Portugal ranks seventh in the world in production and is always among the top three (with Italy and France) with a per capita consumption of over 20 gallons. Portugal has had a demarcation system in effect since 1908 (similar to Italy's D.O.C. and France's A.O.C.). The country's porto trade has been regulated since 1756. Today there are 10 *Regiaoes Demarcades*.

The *Regiao Demarcada* controls grape varieties, yield per acre and aging requirements. It also imposes analytical standards for degree of alcohol and the like. Successful wines receive carefully counted back label seals or strip seals that go over the cork. This seal is called the *Selo de Origem*. By the way, Portugal is the cork center of the world. Its cork oak trees are considered to be the very finest.

**Rose:** The best are made in the *Bica Aberta* system, that is, with the juice left in contact with the skins and pits for a brief time to pick up color. The sweetness comes from adding a sweet, partially fermented or concentrated must. Sometimes carbon dioxide is added to provide crispness. With Mateus and Lancers leading the way, Portuguese roses account for two-thirds of the nation's exported table wines.

**Vinho Verde:** "Green wine" accounts for 25% of Portugal's total production. It is available in white and red and comes from the Minho in the far north. The countryside here is a lush green from ample rainfall, but the wine is called green because it is fresh, light, young, and exuberant with acidity, like a green apple. Azal Branco, Loureiro, Trajadura, and the famous Alvarinho grapes make up the white version. Although 80% of the production is an astringent red, most of it is consumed locally. We rarely see it in the U.S.

Vines here are trained to grow high, sometimes over trees and hedges or on pergolas. The result is a lack of reflected sunlight from the soil, which results in lower grape sugar. It is this factor that makes Vinho Verde low in alcohol, crisp and fresh, and with

## PORTUGAL'S REGIONS OF DEMARCATION

| DEMARCATED REGION | LOCATION | SOIL TYPE |
|---|---|---|
| Vinho Verde | Northwestern | Granite |
| Douro | Northeastern | Slate, Granite, Schist |
| Donro | Northeastern | Slate, Granite, Schist |
| Dao | Northern, below Douro | Granite, Schist |
| Bairrada | Northern, on Atlantic | Clay |
| Colares | Central, on Atlantic | Sand |
| Carcavelos | Central, near Lisbon | Limestone |
| Bucelas | Central, near Lisbon | Loam |
| Moscatel de Setubal | South Central | Sand, Chalk |
| Algarve | Far South | Sand, Clay |
| Madeira | An island 500 miles southwest of Portugal | Volcanic |

a slight *petillance* or crackle (captured $CO_2$ from the fermentation). Although some companies add sweeteners or extra carbon dioxide to their export lots, we have found the following brands to be authentic, reliable, and wonderful: Aveleda (they also make Casal Garcia), Gatao, and Casalinho. If you journey to "Little Lisbon," Ferry Street in Newark, New Jersey, you might find 20 different brands of Vinho Verde on wineshop shelves. It is hard to think of a more refreshing summer wine or a better match to fresh seafood. Drink young!

**Dao:** Red Dao must spend 18 months in the cask according to law. Most spend three to five years, resulting in a full-bodied, dry wine with a smooth taste due to high glycerine. White Dao, if made in the lighter style, can be steely and flinty like a French Chablis. Red Dao comes from Tourigo, Tinta Pinheira, and Alvarelhao, the white from Arinto and Dona Branca—as you can see, all local vines. Important brands are Grao Vasco, J.M. Da-Fonseca's Terras Altas (look for his Periquita also), Caves Velhas and Carvalho, Ribeiro, and Ferreira. Dao, especially the red, is an exceptional value.

**Bairrada:** We've sampled some delicious reds from this zone. They are from the local Baga grape and spend two years in cask and bottle before being sold. The name comes from the Barro or clay soil that dominates the region. Look for the Caves Alianca brand. Whites, sparklers, and roses are also produced here.

**Colares:** The Ramisco vine grows down through the sandy soil to a depth of 30 feet. Special windbreakers are put up to prevent the salt of the Atlantic from striking the grapes. Viticulture in the area is so difficult that even the ravenous phylloxera, the dreaded vine louse of the nineteenth century, never established itself here. And so we have rare pre-phylloxera vines for Colares wines. Dry red Colares is rich in tannin. It ages extremely well, sometimes for a generation or more.

We doubt if you'll find either of the following wine types in the United States, since they are consumed locally in Lisbon or Estoril:

**Bucelas:** A light, dry white made from the Arinto vine.

**Carcavelos:** A topaz-colored, fortified wine from the Galego, Dourado and Arinto vines.

**Setubal:** You may find what some consider to be the world's greatest Muscat. About 40,000 cases of Moscatel de Setubal are produced annually. Fonseca markets two styles here, and orange-colored, honey-like five-year-old and a darker, richer, more elegant 25-year-old. Muscat vines here develop the same *Botrytis*

*This dry, full red has been compared to Barolo, Rhône, and Côte d'Or wines. Made from Castelao Frances grapes, Periquita has a style and flair all its own. Periquita is an outstanding value. One taste will illustrate why this is Robert Parker's favorite Portuguese wine. It is named for the vineyard area, Quinta da Periquita, where the wine was originally produced.*

*"Green wine" is fresh, light, crisp, almost tart, like a green apple. One of the best wines with seafood. The Portuguese call these easy-drinking wines "Wines of Passion."*

251

*cinerea* (noble rot) that attacks French Sauternes and German BAs and TBAs. After fermentation, fortification with brandy takes place, and a new sweet must is introduced to enhance the fruitiness. The wine fuses for a year, after which it is placed into casks for maturation. The resulting wines are unique and exquisite.

Perhaps one wine typifies Portuguese table wines. It is the dry red and white Serradayres brand of Carvalho, Ribeiro, and Ferreira. These are subtle, complex, generous, well-made wines with an unbelievably low price tag. Portuguese wines are an excursion from which the oenophile will return with many souvenirs.

*An elegant dry red with some Cabernet Sauvignon in it. The prestigious Torres family winery uses their trademark Coronas (crowns) to signify a trio of superb reds: Coronas, Gran Coronas, and Gran Coronas Black Label. Good, better, best!*

# WINES OF SPAIN

Spain has more land under vine than any other country in the world (over 4 million acres). Whether it is the dry climate, difficult terrain, or outdated husbandry, Spain is not first in production. She is usually third, behind Italy and France. Spaniards consume about 16 gallons per capita or roughly seven times as much as Americans do. It is an understatement to propose that the future of Spanish viticulture is bright.

The vine has thrived in Spain for 3,000 years. It is interesting to point out that Columbus brought wine with him to the New World in 1492, as did Captain John Smith of Virginia in the early 1600s. We can surmise that Spanish wine was the very first drunk in the New World. Spanish missionaries spread viticulture throughout California, Chile, and Argentina.

In the 19th century, the vine plague, *Phylloxera vastatrix*, caused vignerons from France to emigrate to Spain, especially to the Rioja sector. The pesty wine louse unfortunately followed them. Regardless, many of these Frenchmen remained in Spain, spreading their wine and grape growing expertise. The first demarcated zone of production was Rioja (1926). Jerez (1933) and Malaga (1937) followed soon after. Today about 26 official *Denominaciones de Origen* (D.O.) exist, all controlled by the government's Ministries of Agriculture and Commerce. There are subzones as well.

## SPAIN'S DEMARCATED AREAS

| REGION | D.O. ZONES and SUB-ZONES | MAJOR GRAPE VARIETIES |
|---|---|---|
| Aragon | Cariñena<br>Campo de Borja<br>Somontano | White: Garnacha Blanca<br>Red: Bobal, Cariñena, Garnacha Tinta |
| Catalonia | Ampurdan-Costa Brava<br>Alella<br>Penedes<br>Conca de Barbera<br>Tarragona<br>Priorato<br>Terra Alta | White: Macabeo, Xarel-Lo, Malvasia Garnacha Blanca, Parellada, Pedro Ximenez (P.X.), Chardonnay.<br>Red: Ull de Llebre, Monastrell, Carinena, Garnacha Tinta, Cabernet Sauvignon. |

| REGION | D.O. ZONES and SUB-ZONES | MAJOR GRAPE VARIETIES |
|---|---|---|
| Extremadura (and Southwest) | Condado de Huelva<br>Tierra de Barros | White: Zalema, Airen, P.X., Palomino.<br>Red: Morisca, Garnacha Tinta. |
| Galicia | Ribeiro<br>Monterrey<br>Valdeorras<br>Val de Salnes<br>Condado de Tea<br>El Rosal | White: Albarino, Dona Blanca.<br>Red: Alicante, Garnacha Tinta,<br>Tinta Fina. |
| Malaga | Malaga | White: Moscatel, P.X. |
| Montilla-Moriles | Montilla-Moriles | White: P.X., Airen, Moscatel |
| Navarra | Navarra | Red: Garnacha Tinta.<br>White: Viura, Malvasia. |
| New Castille-La Mancha | Mentrida<br>La Mancha<br>Valdepenas<br>Manchuela<br>Almansa | White: Airen.<br>Red: Cencibel. |
| Old Castille - Leon | Rueda<br>Ribera del Duero | White: Verdejo.<br>Red: Tinto Fino. |
| Rioja | 3 Sub-Zones:<br>Rioja Alta<br>Rioja Alvesa<br>Rioja Baja | White: Viura, Malvasia, Garnacha Blanca.<br>Red: Tempranillo, Graciano, Mazuelo, Garnacha Tinta. |
| Sherry (Jerez) | D.O. Villages or Districts:<br>Anina<br>Balbaina<br>Los Tercios<br>Macharnudo | White: Palomino, Pedro Ximenez, Moscatel. |
| Valencia | Utiel-Requena<br>Valencia<br>Yecla<br>Jumila<br>Alicante | Red: Monastrell, Bobal.<br>White: Moscatel, Verdil. |

## RIOJA SUBREGIONS

| SUBREGION | RATING | SOIL & CLIMATE | GRAPES USED | NOTEABLE PRODUCERS |
|---|---|---|---|---|
| Rioja Alta | Best | Climate is similar to Bordeaux; Clay, Silt, Limestone. | Tempranillo and a high proportion of Mazeulo, Graciano & Garnacha | 30 altogether, including the Bodegas Berberana, Bilbainas, Paternina, Lan, Olarra, Marques de Caceres, Marques de Murrieta, R. Lopez de Heredia, C.U.N.E. |
| Rioja Alavesa | Very close to Alta | Temperate climate; mostly limestone & clay. | Mostly Tempranillo with a little Viura and Garnacha | 12 altogether, including Bodegas Alavesas, Marques de Riscal, Cantabria, Palacio. |
| Rioja Baja | Lowest of the three | Semi-arid, Mediterranean; Alluvial silt, clay | Mostly Garnacha Tinta | |

In addition to these D.O.s there is one *Denominacion Especifica* (D.E.) called *CAVA* (which means cellar). This D.E. regulates sparkling wines. The regulation reads: "Natural sparkling wine whose production process and fermentation, from the start to the removal of residues, takes place in the same bottle into which the wine was originally filled." In other words, CAVA is your guarantee of the methode Champenoise process.

## Rioja

Rioja is Spain's most famous and most important table wine region. Named for the River Oja, this northcentral district is divided into 3 subregions (see chart).

Rioja wines are blends, the various grapes providing color, power, flavor, or longevity. The most important single varietal for the reds is Tempranillo. Generally speaking, *tinta* refers to a fuller-bodied red and *clarete* to a lighter, more delicate one.

These reds are sometimes made the way Bordeaux used to be, that is, with four to five years in the barrel, sometimes more. To be called Reserva, a red Rioja must be aged for three years, one of which must be in oak. Gran Reserva reds spend two years in oak, plus three in the bottle for a total of five years. Historically Rioja

has been criticized for overwooding wines and for using old barrels. This is an unfair generalization, which random tasting will prove. Rioja Reservas and Gran Reservas are among the world's very finest wines, with an aging potential to rival Bordeaux and Brunello di Montalcino. Great vintages *(cosechas)* include 1982, 1978, 1970, 1964, 1955, 1948, and 1947.

White Rioja is made from Viura, Malvasia, and Garnacha Blanca. Cold fermentation and aging in stainless steel has led to a new wave of clean, crisp whites. Old style whites can still be found. Reserva whites are aged for two years, six months of which must be in oak. Gran Reserva spends at least six months in oak and a minimum of four years of total aging.

## Penedes

This area, just outside of Barcelona, is the center for CAVA sparkling wines. It is also a section that has pioneered planting foreign vinifera vines, such as Cabernet Sauvignon and Pinot Noir, Chardonnay, Sauvignon Blanc, Gewürztraminer and Riesling. Native vines of worth include Ull de Llebre, Monastrell, Carinena, and Garnacha. World-class wines are made in specific microclimates, at elevations of up to 2,000 feet with favorable exposures.

The firm of Jean Leon caused heads to turn a decade ago when his Cabernet Sauvignon defeated first growth Bordeaux at an international tasting. Masia Bach also produces top-class wines. The firm of Miguel Torres in Vilafranca has done more to elevate the status of Spanish wine, cuisine, and culture than any other winery. Their entire line of wines merits tasting. Outstanding are the reds, Coronas and Sangre de Toro, and the whites, Vina Sol and Esmeralda (based on Gewürztraminer). In a class by itself is the Black Label Gran Coronas, one of the world's most aristocratic and elegant red wines.

## Valdepenas

The flat plains of La Mancha, southeast of Madrid, yield an interesting light red wine. Called Valdepenas, this dry red is made from 90% white Airen grapes, its pale, brilliant ruby red color coming from the 10% black Cencibel and Garnacha. When drunk fresh, it is fragrant, well-balanced, amply flavored, and of superlative value. This is the jug wine of Madrid.

## Esoterica Hispanica

Which wine won renown as Winston Churchill's favorite claret? Not a claret at all, it is Vega-Sicilia, a lordly red from northcentral Spain, from Old Castille-Leon just east of Valladolid. This is a D.O. Ribera del Duero, made from a blend of Cabernet Sauvignon, Merlot, Malbec, Tinto Aragenes, Garnacha, and a little white Albillo. The must is lightly pressed and later aged in oak for 10 years or more. The finished wine is usually 13.5% alcohol or more, full and rich, with great depth of color, complex and fragrant, with a lingering finish unrivalled in the world of wine. It is priced up with the classified growths of Bordeaux, as it should be. A similar, substantial wine called Valbuena is made from the same grapes but is aged less, usually three to five years.

Another brilliant red from this area has burst onto the American scene of late, Tinto Pesquera, also a D.O. Ribera del Duero. It tastes of Cabernet Sauvignon and Tempranillo. A costly Reserva from an older vintage is absolutely sensational. It indicates that even though this wine may be hot and trendy, there is a fine tradi-

*Proprietor Henri Fournier also owns Bordeaux's Chateau Trintaudon-La Rose. These red Riojas are both from Rioja Alta, the best zone. Do not think the only difference between them is the aging factor. A Reserva wine is better to start with. It shows a potential to age well.*

tion as well, at least for the Alejandro Fernandez Winery.

Surely we will hear more from this region. In fact, wine writers speak of the "Spanish Crescent." This is an arc on the northern side of the Sierra Morena to Sierra de Guadarrama and finally the Iberian Mountain chain, sweeping from the south to the north and then east to the sea. The southern slopes are hot and better suited to bulk style wines. Microclimates along this arc include the Ribera del Duero, Rioja Alta, Rioja Alavesa, and Pencdes. The wines of Spain and Portugal, like those of Italy, should provide the U.S. market with excellent alternatives to the costly growths of France. In almost every category and price range, carefully selected Iberian wines are first rate. The variety and the potential of this great peninsula's wines are promising. The U.S. is also discovering the charms and glories of Paella Valenciana from Spain and Portuguese Mariscada, and a bounty of other distinctive dishes from Iberia's fields, hills, rivers, and seas. Could there be a better opportunity to try a bottle of Spanish or Portuguese quality table wine? And with sherry and porto, no one can deny Iberia's preeminence in the area of fortified wines.

*The wine is a rare Rioja produced only in the very best years. The minimum aging requirements are 24 months or longer in oak; then for the balance of 60 months it is aged in glass. A Gran Reserva cannot leave the bodega until the sixth year after vintage. The bouquet is outstanding and memorable, the wine full, rich, soft and silky, balanced as only carefully made and aged wine can be.*

*The finest Tempranillo and Grenache grapes are vinified at least 12 months in oak, then spend the remainder of their 36 month aging in bottles. The reserva cannot leave the bodega until the fourth year after vintage. The wine has a lovely fruity nose, is round and supple, and delicious.*

ALCOHOL 12.5%
BY VOLUME

**RIOJA**
DENOMINACION DE ORIGEN

NET CONTENTS
750 ML.

RED WINE

# AÑARES

BOTTLED BY

**Bodegas Olarra,** s.a.

LOGROÑO - RIOJA - ESPAÑA
PRODUCT OF SPAIN

## RESERVA 1983

*Made from the Tempranillo and Grenache grape varieties, this is a soft, silky rich red full of fruit flavor. To achieve world class status, a wine must be meticulously vinified from superior grapes under the guiding genius of a master wine maker whose commitment to excellence increases each vintage. Fortunately, Bodegas Olarra has just such a man in Ezequiel Garcia, the recognized dean of Rioja wine making.*

# IBERIA IN REVIEW

- The wines of Spain and Portugal provide us with superb "discovery" wines, which are fine alternatives to the growths of France, Italy, and California.

- The Spanish and Portuguese are important producers and consumers of wine.

- There is much more to Iberian wine than Spanish Sangria and Portuguese Rose.

- Each local area of Iberia has its own particular wines and grape varieties.

- The Iberian Peninsula is a most renowned source for fortified wines: sherry, porto, Madeira, Malaga, Montilla, Setúbal.

- Portugal's most important table wines are Vinho Verde and Dao.

- Spain's most important table wines are Rioja, and the wines of the Penedes and Ribera del Duero.

- Spain is the primary source for reasonably-priced sparkling wine made by the champagne method.

- Many quality producers make wines that rank with the world's best (such as Rioja Reserva).

# SELF-EVALUATION

BEFORE READING ON, see if you have mastered the data set forth in the last few pages. Check the answer section at the back of the book for the correct answers. If you have not answered at least 70% of the questions below correctly, please reread the previous section.

# SPAIN AND PORTUGAL

TRUE     FALSE

_____    _____ 1. There are 10 demarcated regions in Portugal.

_____    _____ 2. Vinho Verde means "green wine."

_____    _____ 3. According to law, all red Dao must spend time in casks.

_____    _____ 4. Colares grapes produce full-bodied sweet wines.

_____    _____ 5. Both Bairrada and Carcavelos wines are often seen in fine U.S. wineshops.

_____    _____ 6. Spain leads the world in acreage under vine.

_____    _____ 7. Rioja is Spain's most famous and important table wine region.

_____    _____ 8. Rioja whites are more famous than Rioja reds.

_____    _____ 9. Rioja is subdivided into three areas: Alta, Alavesa, and Baja.

_____    _____ 10. Rioja Reserva wines are aged for three years, one of which must be in oak.

# THE WINES
# OF OTHER COUNTRIES

The shelves of U.S. wineshops are blessed with an assortment of wines, the spectrum of which no other nation can rival. These wines, since they are so-called "export" quality, are not only curiosities to the oenophile, but also usually represent excellent dollar value. We call this chapter "Other Countries" for want of a more creative name. We question our use of "other" in two ways: (1) How can we group elite wines such as Hungary's Tokaji Essencia, Chile's Cousino Macul Antiguas Reservas, or Australia's Penfolds Grange Hermitage under the same ignominious heading of "other;" and (2) How can we refer to nations like Argentina, which is fifth in the world in production or Greece whose colorful wine history is 3,000 years old, as "other" countries?

Perhaps we should title this chapter, "High Quality and Interesting Wines from Significant Countries that for Some Reason or Other Do Not Get the Attention They Deserve." Truly, the adventurous shopper will find gems from these areas which are less familiar than France, Italy, Spain, Portugal, Germany, or the U.S.A.

We divide this chapter into three sections:

1. Other European Countries
2. North Africa and Asia
3. Wines of the Southern Hemisphere

# OTHER EUROPEAN COUNTRIES

## Switzerland

From the lofty land of fondue, cuckoo clocks, and cheeses comes fresh, clean, fragrant, sky-born wines with a distinctive, vibrant character. Grapes are grown in virtually every canton (over 300 areas), but there are four well-known winemaking areas:

1. Valais (Valley of the Rhone) — southwest
2. Lake Geneva (Vaud) — far west
3. See Land (Lake Neuchatel) — northwest
4. Ticino (Italianate Section) — southeast

The most renowned wines include the following:

1. **Neuchatel:** A crisp, dry, sprightly white wine based on the Chasselas grape, commonly bottled Sur Lie.
2. **Oeil de Perdrix** (Eye of the Partridge): A pale, dry rose of Pinot Noir from the Seeland area.
3. **Fendant:** A soft, fruity, fragrant white from the Chasselas vine grown in the Valais.
4. **Dole de Sion:** Also from the Valais, a noble, deep, generous, dry red that may possess a crackle. Based on Pinot Noir and Gamay, this is Switzerland's best red.

Although one does not need a Swiss bank account to finance the purchase of a bottle or two, Swiss wines are never inexpensive. They are always a bit more costly than the popular wines of their French, Italian, and German neighbors.

## Austria

Austrian viticulture dates back to Roman times, but reached its peak in the sixteenth century, when their neighbor and rival, Hungary, was forbidden to produce wine by her Turkish conquerors. Today Austria is noted for a variety of crisp, light, fast-maturing whites, often made from the Grüner Veltliner grape. The four principal wine regions are:

1. **Lower Austria:** You will find good whites from the town of Krems, based on Grüner Veltliner or Rheinriesling. Also rich, flavorful Gumpoldkirchner from these lowlands along the Danube near the border of Czechoslovakia.

2. **Burgenland:** A part of Hungary until 1919, this southeastern area borders a lake called the Neusiedlersee. *Botrytis cinerea*, "noble rot," is common here, so we see Spätlese and Auslese wines made from Rieslings or Muscat-Ottonel.
3. **Styria:** The wines of this eastern area are consumed locally, much of it in Graz, its capital city.
4. **Vienna:** Here you can waltz to zithers, violins, and guitars and sip on *Heurige* (today's wine). Fresh, new, crisp whites with high acidity and a little carbon dioxide recaptured from the fermentation process is an apt description. It is a gay, happy wine, more often than not made from Grüner Veltliner.

# EASTERN EUROPE

## Yugoslavia

All six republics from this crossroads of east and west produce wine. It is a land of 1,000 grape varieties. Vines of Asiatic or European origin thrive here, including the red Prokupac, Pinot Noir, Kadarka, and Cabernet, and the white Riesling, Kevedinka, and lately, Chardonnay. Yugoslavians consume about 25 liters per capita or about 80% of their homeland's production.

Yugoslavia is usually in the top 10 worldwide in total wine production. Most of the wine is produced by larger cooperatives which are closely watched over by the government. Varietal wines, such as Cabernet Sauvignon and Riesling of the Avia brand, a subsidiary of Coca-Cola, represent excellent dollar value. Alexandria Cabernet Sauvignon is flavorful and quite elegant for a wine of its price.

Today there are 10 wine zones and 23 subzones throughout the six republics. Annual production from these states usually is of the following proportions:

1. Serbia: 45%
2. Croatia: 35%
3. Slovenia: 9%
4. Macedonia: 9%
5. Bosnia-Herzegovina: less than 2%
6. Montenegro: less than 1%

*Yugoslavia has a perfect climate for viticulture and a winemaking history of two millenia old. We found this Cabernet Sauvignon to be of exceptional value. You can still find excellent Yugoslavian wines for under $3.00 a bottle.*

## Hungary

No one would dispute Hungary's claim to preeminence in viticulture in Central Europe. Today winemaking is controlled by a government agency named Hungarovin. Hungarian wines are marketed abroad by trading companies, such as Monimpex, and to a lesser extent, Generalimpex and Konsumex. The biggest customers are in Eastern Europe, but we get a share of Hungary's most typical and best in the United States.

The Hungarians have fortunately tried to spare us the difficulty of their language. For example, from Northern Transdanubia (the ancient Roman Pannonia), the excellent Pinot Grigio, Badacsonyi Szurkebarat, is labeled "Grey Friar."

260

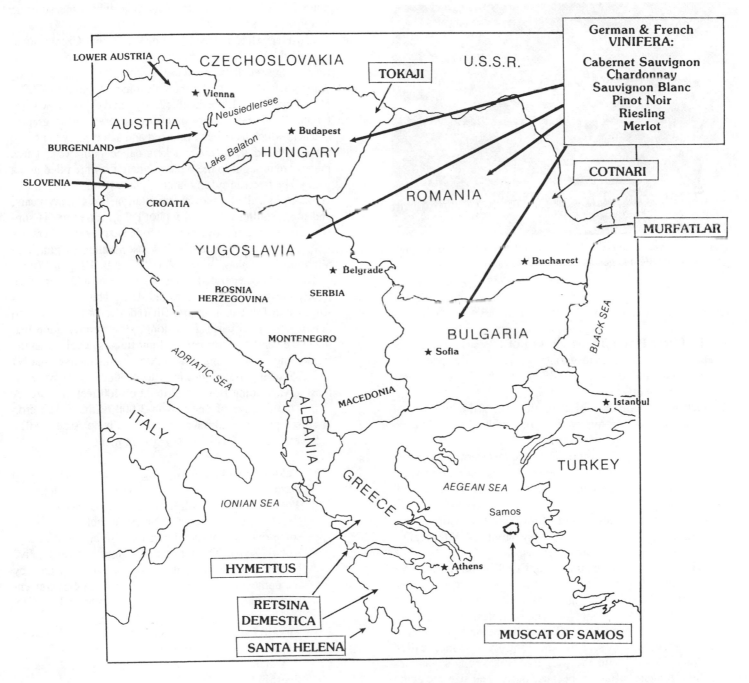

LOWER AUSTRIA

CZECHOSLOVAKIA

U.S.S.R.

TOKAJI

German & French
VINIFERA:

Cabernet Sauvignon
Chardonnay
Sauvignon Blanc
Pinot Noir
Riesling
Merlot

★ Vienna

Neusiedlersee

AUSTRIA

BURGENLAND

Lake Balaton

★ Budapest

HUNGARY

ROMANIA

COTNARI

SLOVENIA

CROATIA

MURFATLAR

YUGOSLAVIA

★ Belgrade

★ Bucharest

BOSNIA
HERZEGOVINA

SERBIA

BLACK SEA

MONTENEGRO

BULGARIA

ADRIATIC SEA

★ Sofia

ALBANIA

MACEDONIA

★ Istanbul

ITALY

TURKEY

GREECE

AEGEAN SEA

IONIAN SEA

Samos

HYMETTUS

★ Athens

RETSINA
DEMESTICA

MUSCAT OF SAMOS

SANTA HELENA

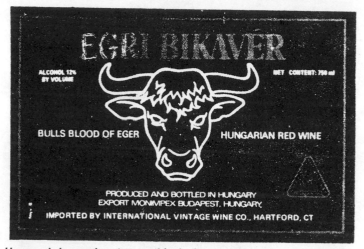

*Hungary's best red, quite possibly the best red wine of Eastern Europe. It ages very well. Big and generous, like a Barolo.*

There are five zones of production in Hungary:

1. **The Great Plain:** The sandy soil of this eastern area enables pre-phylloxera vines to grow. Seventy-five percent of the production is white. Half of Hungary's wines come from this plain.
2. **Northern Transdanubia:** In the west, the villages of Somlo and Badacsonyi produce fine whites. Lake Balaton helps to stabilize the climate here.
3. **Southern Transdanubia:** This southwestern area which borders Yugoslavia is best known for reds based on Cabernet and the Kekrankos vines in the communes of Szekszardi and Villanyi.
4. **Northern Hungary:** Look for excellent whites from Olaszrizling, Leanyka, and Harslevelu vines. Of these, Debroi Harslevelu is the most famous.

   Hungary's most acclaimed red, Egri Bikaver, is from this area. According to legend, in the sixteenth century, the women of the village of Eger gave their men a rich red wine based on Kadarka, Pinot Noir, and Merlot, to instill in them the courage to face a strong Turkish invading force. Apparently this generous, smooth, long-lived wine, called "Bull's Blood," did the job. Egri Bikaver is sometimes called Hungary's Barolo, because of its great size and aging

potential. It has a character of its own, which measures up to spicy paprika dishes.

5. **Tokaj-Hegyalja:** This small zone, bordering Czechoslovakia and the U.S.S.R. in the north, produces Hungary's finest and most acclaimed wines. Around the village of Tokaj white vines are planted in the volcanic soil: Furmint (70%); *Hars-Levelu* or Lime-Leaf (20%); and Yellow Muscat (about 10%). Harvesters carefully separate these grapes. Clusters which have been infected and affected by the noble rot are placed in special buckets called *puttonyos*. These grapes are brought to the winery where they are piled into a press. The free-run syrupy juice is placed into small fermentation casks called *gonci*. Fermentation takes many years, and the resulting nectar, the rare Tokaji Essencia, is supposed to have restorative and aphrodisiac powers. There is a Latin expression, "Vinum Tokayense, Vinum Regum, Rex Vinorum" or Tokay Wine, Wine of Kings, King of Wines.

The grapes, separated from the free-run juice, are then lightly pressed into a paste called *Aszu*. This Aszu paste is stirred into fresh wine must, filtered after a few days and drawn into gonci casks for a long, slow fermentation that may take years to complete. A light fungus develops on the fermenting must, giving Tokaji Aszu its distinctive bouquet and character. Grapes destined to produce Aszu wine almost always come from an altitude of 400 feet or more. A minuscule average of one part in 3,000 of the Tokaji crop has Aszu potential; in many years there is no Aszu at all.

Several types of Tokaji (Tokay) are made:

- **Tokaji Furmint:** A dry, light, fruity wine with no Aszu.
- **Tokaji Szamorodni:** *Szamorodni* is Slavonic for "such as it was grown." No Aszu, but there may be some ripe, nobly rotted berries. Can be sweet or dry.
- **Tokaji Aszu:** Three puttonyos, four puttonyos, five puttonyos—the amount of Aszu paste, indicated by the number of puttonyos, provides a scale of concentration which deepens the color, and adds to longevity and luscious sweetness.
- **Tokaji Essencia:** This is the magical, amber wine whose price and glory place it together with Chateau D'Yquem, German TBA, and Italian Picolit as the finest in the world.

*A dry white flavored with chalky resin. This distinctive wine, so popular in Greece, takes some getting used to. Achaia Clauss is one of Greece's most important wine companies.*

## Greece

What wine feast of today can compare with those of the ancient Greeks? Prisoners were released, the state treasury was displayed, and dramas were performed, all to celebrate the miracle of the rebirth of vine shoots in the spring. If we trust the Roman poet Vergil, the Greeks boasted of a variety of vines as numerous as the grains of sand in the desert. Islamic influence curtailed interest in viticulture, but Greece can claim today that she produces wine in almost every province and island.

Some of the main types include:

- **Retsina:** A distinctive wine, white or red, flavored with pine resin. Drink cold and young. White from the Savatiano grape is preferred. Most of the production is from Central Greece.
- **Muscat of Samos:** One of Greece's best-made dessert wines, luscious with a complex bouquet of citrus and apricots.
- **Mavrodaphne:** The best come from Patras, a port on the Corinthian Gulf in the southern area called the Peloponnesus. Sometimes called the "poor man's porto." Based on the red Mavron grape, it is heady, sweet, and best enjoyed unchilled.
- **Kokkineli:** A good rose. The best comes from Central Greece.
- **Hymethus:** Dry white from Central Greece.
- **Santa Helena:** Dry, clean white from the Peloponnesus.
- **Demestica:** Dependable dry red or white.

Major wineries include Achaia-Clauss, Cambas, Metaxa, and Boutari, whose Grand Reserve Naoussa Red is the best we have tasted. Some of these also produce brandy and Ouzo, an aperitif based on anis.

## Cyprus

Winemaking on this island of the love goddess, Aphrodite, dates back to before 1,000 B.C. The Greek poet, Hesiod, around 750 B.C., describes a Cypriot dessert wine called Nama, made from sun-dried grapes. During one of the Crusades, Nama was renamed Commandaria by the Knights Templar. This luscious wine is still made, mostly from the white Xynisteri, but with some red Mavron grapes blended in. A system similar to the sherry *solera* insures a consistent, uniform taste with a guarantee of some older wine in the mix.

Also available are a dry white, Aphrodite; a sweet white, St. Pantalemon; and a rich, full, dry red called Othello. This wine is similar to the Italian Amarone and marries well to strong cheeses and spicy cuisine. Keo and Sodap are the brands that you will find in the United States.

## Romania

Romania produces more wine than Germany and just a bit less than Portugal. The two most acclaimed wines are Murfatlar, a dessert wine based on Muscat grown in the shadow of the Black

*This vintage-dated Sauvignon Blanc from Romania's Tarnave Region is supple and soft. Premiat wines are bargains when compared to Sauvignons from France, Italy, the U.S.A., and Australia.*

tion that dates back to the Greeks. Turkish Moslem influence and World War II disturbed Bulgarian viticulture, but in 1948 Vinprom was created to guide the fortunes of some 500,000 peasant farmers who grow grapes. The results have been very successful.

Much of Bulgaria's wines are exported, to Russia especially, but to West Germany as well. Recently a red Mavrud won a Gault-Millau competition, which turned some heads. Superb, good value wines based on popular varietals such as Cabernet Sauvignon and Chardonnay are sold in the United States under the Trakia label, once again a marketing coup for Monsieur Henri. Collectively the 17 wine zones of Romania and the 13 of Bulgaria have been meticulously plotted by U.S. researchers, an effort of cooperation between PepsiCo and the communist governments. Prospects for the future are very high. This project proves the old saying, "Waters separate countries; wine unites them."

Sea, and Cotnari, a natural dessert wine from Moldavia in the northeast close to Russia. This historic wine is based on the Grasa vine and has been made since at least the mid-1600s. Very little of either wine is seen in the West.

What we do see in the U.S. are excellent French varietals. Cabernet Sauvignon, Pinot Noir, Riesling, and Chardonnay are sold under the Premiat label. Marketed wisely and handsomely by Monsieur Henri, these are among the finest values for those of us who enjoy a glass of wine on a nightly basis and not just on special occasions.

## Bulgaria

Surprisingly, Bulgaria can lay claim to having the most modern and progressive wineries in the world, as well as an ancient tradi-

*Bulgaria has a long, checkered history of viticulture. It came into prominence with a major government campaign after World War II. The affiliation with PepsiCo has proven to be wonderful. This Merlot from Haskovo is one of the best values among dry red wines today.*

## Czechoslovakia

Although some wine is produced in all three regions—Bohemia, Moravia, and Slovakia—the Czechs must import wine to satisfy their needs. They consume about four gallons per capita. They grow western varietals and produce a wine similar to the Hungarian Tokay. For the time being, we in the West will have to be content enjoying Czech Pilsner Urquell beer, by reputation the world's finest light brew.

## Luxembourg

The wines of this small grand duchy have been described as Mosels with Alsatian style. Very little wine is exported. Luxembourg has a system called *Appellation Complete*, similar to the A.O.C. of France. Good wines carry the vintage, the grape varieties, and the name and address of the producer. The best wines bear the Marque Nationale, a seal indicating that the wine has passed stringent government standards. You are more likely to see sparkling wine from Luxembourg in the United States. Table wines are almost entirely white, based on Riesling, Müller-Thürgau, Pinot Blanc, and Pinot Grigio.

## Great Britain

Small quantities of boutique English wines are finding their way to the United States. Usually German vinifera or French hybrids are utilized in their production. Viticulture is difficult here due to the climate. When the last Russian czar commented that the best British wine was Irish, he meant whiskey, not wine. (Maybe that is why he was overthrown!)

## U.S.S.R.

Russia is usually third or fourth in total production worldwide, but we see almost no Soviet wine in the West. Much wine originates in the areas north of the Black and Caspian Seas, where emphasis is on sweet and on sparkling wines. The Crimea, Moldavia, Ukraine, and Georgia continue a winemaking tradition that dates back at least to 700 B.C. Table grapes, wine, and brandy are basic to Armenia and Azerbaijan.

The Soviets must deal with extremely cold winters. Many varietals from Aligote, Cabernet, and Riesling to Matrassa, Napureouli, and Mzvane are planted. We see "Russian champagne," Armenian brandy (Ararat), and the national beverage, vodka, in the U.S.A.

## Denmark

Berry wines and liqueurs are produced here. Most popular are black currant, cherry, and blackberry. Grapes cannot thrive because of the cold climate.

# NORTH AFRICA

## Morocco, Tunisia and Algeria

Although wine is produced in North Africa, emphasis has been on heady bulk wines. For generations, Algeria, Tunisia, and Morocco shipped wine to France to be blended into lighter French fare. Tunisia and Morocco make commendable reds based on Carignan, Grenache, Cinsault, and Alicante. Algeria produces a ripe, rich Cabernet Sauvignon called Le Sable, which represents one of the best values in the U.S. today. The best vineyard sites are in mountain regions or in areas cooled by coastal zephyrs. The finest wines qualify for an *Appellation D'Origine Garantie*, similar to the French.

# THE MIDDLE EAST

## Egypt

The ancient Roman poet, Horace, wrote about Maereotic wine from Egypt. He claimed that it made Cleopatra and Mark Anthony drunk and foolish enough to challenge the might of Rome. No current Egyptian wine is so famous, but some good wines are produced, mostly west of the Nile Delta.

Any Egyptian success is a reflection of the genius and dedication of Nestor Gianaclis, who in the early twentieth century analyzed soils, planted dozens of grape varieties, and sought to revive the wines of his ancient pharoahs. Today one can find—in lands as diverse as the U.S.S.R. and England—Egyptian wines based on Chasselas, Pinot Blanc, Pinot Noir, and Gamay. These wines have not yet made their way to the shores of the United States.

## Turkey

Turkish wines were traditionally made by Greeks, Armenians, and other non-Islamic people who resided in Turkey. War, politics, and early-twentieth century migrations virtually halted wine production by the 1920s. Formation of state wine monopolies and the 1928 decree eliminating the Moslem faith as the nation's official religion have caused a turnaround. Wines are produced in Thrace, Marmara, the Aegean Isles, and throughout Anatolia. Today the Turk prefers eating table grapes to drinking wines, but there has been an effort by the Turkish government to increase wine production and exports. We see more of Club Raki, an aperitif based on anis, in the United States than we do of Turkish wines. We should recall that the very first wines may have been made here by the Sumerians in the third millenium B.C., when the region was broadly called Mesopotamia. This area may also have been the birthplace of the great wine grape family, *Vitis vinifera*.

## Lebanon

From the Bekaa Valley, the scene of so much bloodshed and turmoil today, comes a line of wines of stature from Serge Hochar, called Chateau Musar. The best are full-bodied, dry reds that age well. They are based on Cabernet Sauvignon and other vinifera. They are well worth searching for.

## Iran

The ancient Persians were hearty drinkers. There is even a tale that one of the Great King's lovers attempted suicide by imbibing on forbidden, fermented grape juice which, until then, had been considered the most potent of poisons. She soon realized that this interesting beverage had a euphoric, not fatal, effect. Thus, wine drinking was born.

The Syrah vine, of Rhone wine renown, is named for the Iranian town of Shiraz. It may well have been carried back to France by a Crusader. Current warfare and a strict Islamic revival have all but eliminated the heady red wines of Shiraz. Such folly cannot diminish the words of the Iranian poet, Omar Khayyam, who sang wine's romantic praises in his *Rubaiyat:*

> *I wonder often what the vintners buy*
> *One-half so precious as the stuff they sell.*

and

> *Here with a little bread beneath the bough,*
> *A flask of wine, a book of verse—and thou*
> *Beside me singing in the wilderness—*
> *Ah, Wilderness were paradise enow!*

## Israel

Jewish viticulture is as old as Noah. The custom of using wine with religious services is ancient, as are the rules for making clean, Kosher wines. But a discussion of modern Israel's wine industry begins with the donation of vines by Baron Edmond de Rothschild, of banking and Bordeaux fame. Cooperative wineries, with French vines and French know-how, developed. Even today 75% of Israel's wines are produced by co-ops. Since the foundation of the Jewish state (1948), the wine industry has flourished. Production has gradually shifted from heavier, traditional, ceremonial wines to lighter table wines. Israel produces almost every type of wine: dry red or white, sparkling, sacramental, fortified, vermouth, as well as brandies and liqueurs. Exports are

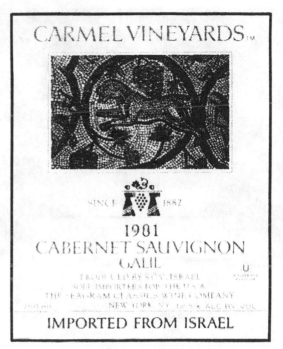

*This Cabernet Sauvignon hails from Galilee (Galil). The first vines for Israel's Carmel Cooperative were donated by the Rothschilds. This is a fine dry Kosher wine. Notice the circle with the "U" in it on the lower right portion of the label. It is the seal of the Union of Rabbis. The logo of Carmel, the two men carrying grapes, is from the Old Testament.*

directed almost exclusively by the Carmel Wine Company. All exports are prepared under strict Rabbinical religious supervision.

Winegrowing areas include Galil, Sharon, Samson, and Shomron. Vines include red Carbernet Sauvignon, Carignan, and Petit Sirah, as well as white Sauvignon Blanc, Chenin Blanc, and Semillon. Good wines are Carmel Hock, Sauvignon Blanc, and Carbernet Sauvignon. Of superior quality are President's Sparkling Wine and a limited bottling, Special Reserve Cabernet Sauvignon, both under the Carmel label. The fine wines of Yarden, Richon, and Gamla can be found in U.S. wineshops. Generally speaking, Israeli wines represent excellent dollar value.

## ASIA

### India

India has had a checkered history when it comes to viticulture. The Greek god of wine had a tiger as his symbol. Folklore tells us that Dionysus journeyed to India to learn winemaking from wise men and brought the tiger back with him as his emblem. Today very few wines are made, most of them by western missionaries.

## Japan

Viticulture is difficult in Japan, largely due to a humid climate and acid soil. However, Asian varietals (the Konshu, for example), as well as American Labrusca (Delaware), hybrids (Seyval), and European vinifera (Cabernet Sauvignon) do grow throughout the Honshu island.

The Japanese are great importers of expensive European and, lately, U.S. wines. They are also avid beer drinkers. Sake, a double fermented rice brew, and sweetish plum wine are not only popular in Japan, but are also exported to the West. Grape wine production is controlled by large companies, including Suntory, which is better known for fine whiskey and a melon cordial. Formidable brands of sake and plum wine are Gekkeikan, Genji, and Kiku.

## China

With a tradition dating back to 2500 B.C., Chinese viticulture reached its apex in the eleventh century A.D. Since then, winemaking has had more downs than ups, but sherry-type wine is as necessary to the Chinese kitchen as soy sauce. Traditional rice "wine" has been made since the 4th century B.C.

Very recently the People's Government hired several European winemakers, including Antonio Mastroberardino, as wine consultants. Remy Martin, the number one cognac in China, built a winery which has produced a decent light Muscat called Dynasty.

*Japanese Sake is actually a double-fermented rice brew, not a wine. When served warm, like the heart of the host who offers it, it is very memorable. Gekkeikan also offers deliciously sweet plum wine.*

# SELF-EVALUATION

BEFORE READING ON, see if you have mastered the data set forth in the last few pages. Check the answer section at the back of the book for the correct answers. If you have not answered at least 70% of the questions below correctly, please reread the previous section.

## OTHER COUNTRIES
### Europe, North Africa, The Middle East, and Asia

| TRUE | FALSE | |
|------|-------|---|
| _____ | _____ | 1. Neuchatel is the name of Switzerland's most renowned red wine. |
| _____ | _____ | 2. Austria is noted for its crisp, light white wines. |
| _____ | _____ | 3. Special buckets to hold clusters of grapes with noble rot and called *puttonyos* in Hungary. |
| _____ | _____ | 4. *Gonci* in Hungarian means "small cluster of grapes." |
| _____ | _____ | 5. Retsina is a distinctive wine flavored with pine resin. |
| _____ | _____ | 6. Wines from Romania are usually very high in alcohol. |
| _____ | _____ | 7. Bulgaria can claim to have one of the most modern and progressive winery networks in the world. |
| _____ | _____ | 8. Most wines from North Africa are heady, bulk-type wines. |
| _____ | _____ | 9. Anis is the basic grape for all Turkish wines. |
| _____ | _____ | 10. Baron Edmond de Rothschild of Bordeaux donated vines to Israeli wineries. |

# SOUTH AMERICA

## Brazil

Southern Brazil, especially the cooler, hilly area west of Porto Alegre in Rio Grande do Sul, is a section that shows promise. A century ago, Italian settlers brought red Barbera, Bonarda, and white Trebbiano and Moscato with them to this region, which borders Uruguay. Much of Brazil's production is from French-American hybrids, which are better suited to the damp climate. White Isabella is Brazil's most widely planted vine. We have tasted some superior dessert Malvasia under the Granja Uniao label. European and U.S. vermouth and sparkling wine firms and distillers have established operations throughout South America, especially in Brazil. They include Cinzano, Martini and Rossi, Moët-Hennessy, National Distillers, and Heublein.

## Uruguay

Uruguay is a small wine producer, specializing in French-American hybrids and, more recently, in vinifera such as Cabernet Sauvignon. The red Harriague vine from the Pyrenees is most widely planted. One can find Barbera and Nebbiolo as well in the low hills of Salto, Canelones, and Colonia. For the time being, one must visit Montevideo in order to savor Uruguayan wine. As in Brazil, thirsty Uruguay consumes all that it can produce.

## Peru

Although viticulture dates back to 1566, Peru is not renowned for winemaking today. Recent University of California at Davis studies indicate that there are several microclimates in the lower mountains that show great promise. Peruvian Pisco brandy, a distillate of Moscato similar to Grappa, is the country's most renowned spirit. The black figurine bottles in which Pisco is marketed have become collector's items in recent years.

## Argentina

In the land of beef and gauchos, the natives demand large quantities of sound wine. Argentina is South America's production leader, fifth worldwide, and is among the pacemakers in consumption with well over 20 gallons per capita. The wine for Buenos Aires, at times called "Italy's second largest city," comes from the western and northern stretches of Argentina, some 600 miles away. Over 45,000 small growers sell their grapes to large wineries, called here, as in Spain, *bodegas*. Wine is made in Mendoza, San Juan, Rio Negro, and farther north where it is hotter, in La Rioja, Catamarca, and Salta.

Vines were planted as early as 1556 by a Jesuit priest, Father Cedron. The story really begins in 1870 when a wave of Italian immigrants settled in Mendoza and set up an elaborate irrigation system that made large-scale viticulture a possibility. The melted snow from the caps of the Andes are funneled into reservoirs. These lead to a network of canals that feed the dry, sometimes parched soil in a zone that receives very little rainfall. In this flat, semi-arid area, the red Malbec vine dominates. We also find Cabernet Sauvignon, Barbera, Tempranillo, and Merlot, among others. White grapes include Riesling, Chardonnay, and Chenin Blanc. The historic grape of Argentina is the pink Criolla.

Argentine reds have been labelled as too massive, too high in alcohol, and reminiscent of "hot climate" wines. Whites are said to be overlooked. Recent tastings indicate that these criticisms are outdated. Early picking of white grapes, especially from cooler zones of Rio Negro, and cold fermentation result in crisp, clean wines with no hint of flabbiness or oxidation. Reds are richly balanced, perfect matches to the ubiquitous Argentine steak. Almost 75% of Argentina's wine comes from Mendoza, where we find the second largest winery in the world, Penaflor. Owned by the Pulenta family, a Trapiche, this winery's "oak cask" label Cabernet Sauvignon, Malbec, and Chardonnay are receiving world acclaim. Modern, massive wineries dominate here, over 200 in all, with diverse European names like Lopez, Toso, Bianchi, Gargantini, Weinert, Suter, and Norton.

The reputation for making decent table wines is well founded. Argentine wines are good values. The entire Andean line—Trapiche's "oak cask" Cabernet, Malbec, and Chardonnay, Toso's Cabernet, and Gargantini's Emenencia—are all high quality products. The Argentine is also a passionate consumer of vermouth. Cinzano has had a plant here for some time.

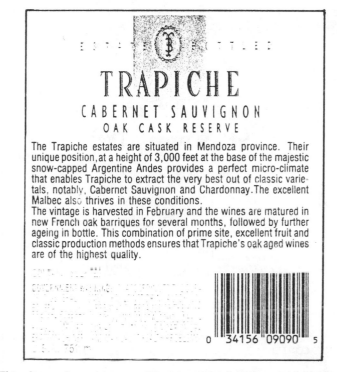

*This elegant dry red is a candidate for Argentina's best wine. Made at Penaflor, the largest winery in South America, second only to Gallo in the world.*

*A soft, generous wine from the Mendoza Valley in Argentina. A perfect, reasonable match-up for Argentine beef (or Texas steak, for that matter).*

## Chile

Although missionaries planted vines as early as 1535, it was not until 1851 that Chile started on the path that would lead to its preeminent position today. A Basque immigrant, Silvestre Ochagavia, the "Father of Chilean Viticulture," saw great potential for the Central Valley, the area nestled between the Maipo and Aconcagua Rivers inland from Valparaiso near Santiago. He brought in French agronomists, winemakers, and technicians, who pulled up some historic Pais vines and replaced them with Cabernet Sauvignon, Riesling, and Sauvignon Blanc.

The dreaded phylloxera wine louse which devastated Europe and Argentina has never made its way here across the Atacama Desert or over the Andes Mountains barriers. Chile's climate

## SANTA ANA

**QUALITAS**

## CEPAS PRIVADAS

### MENDOZA

*Cabernet Sauvignon '87*

RED ARGENTINE WINE

NET CONTENTS 750 ML      ALCOHOL 12.5% BY VOLUME

PRODUCED AND BOTTLED BY BODEGAS Y VIÑEDOS SANTA ANA S.A. EST. N° A-71071 - MENDOZA
IMPORTED BY: S.M.R. WINES & SPIRITS MIAMI, FLORIDA

PRODUCT OF ARGENTINA            ENVASADO EN ORIGEN

## SANTA ANA

**QUALITAS**

## CEPAS PRIVADAS

### MENDOZA

*Chardonnay '88*

WHITE ARGENTINE WINE

NET CONTENTS 750 ML      ALCOHOL 11.5% BY VOLUME

PRODUCED AND BOTTLED BY BODEGAS Y VIÑEDOS SANTA ANA S.A. EST. N° A-71071 - MENDOZA
IMPORTED BY: S.M.R. WINES & SPIRITS MIAMI, FLORIDA

PRODUCT OF ARGENTINA            ENVASADO EN ORIGEN

*Santa Ana S.A., one of Argentina's oldest and most respected wine producers, offers an exceptional value to the American consumer in its top quality 100% varietal, Cabernet Sauvignon and Chardonnay, described by many as a best buy!*

makes it free from *oidium* and virtually all other rots, pests, and diseases. Today Chile is tenth in total production, has a per capita consumption of 15 gallons, and clearly makes the best wines of South America. Wine is made in a northern and a southern zone, but most of Chile's best originates in the central and south central area.

Chile's government regulates the wine industry with an iron fist in an attempt to control alcoholism. Export wines must meet aging requirements, color and taste standards, and minimum alcohol levels, all mandated by the National Council for External Commerce. This prevents low-quality wine from being dumped into foreign markets. A Vino Courant is less than two years old; Special on a label indicates two years of aging; Reserva, four years; Gran Vino, six years.

Outstanding Chilean wines are made from red Cabernet Sauvignon and white Sauvignon Blanc, Riesling, Semillion, and Chardonnay. The country's most significant exporter is Concha y Toro. Landowners (over 1,000 acres) as well as winemakers, Concha y Toro has an extensive line of excellent, consistent wines of super value. Their Casaleiro del Diablo wines, especially the red, are complex wonders. In the last 18 years, this winery has garnered 45 medals.

272

Chile's first growth is Vina Cousino Macul, a 650-acre estate founded in 1882. Their Antiguas Reservas Cabernet Sauvignon, with three years in cask and up to two more in the bottle, stands up to the Bordeaux growths. The Canepa winery is best known in the United States for their whites, especially Sauvignon Blanc. Undurraga is a quality winery, which was the first to export Chilean wines to the U.S. Santa Rita's Cabernet won kudos at recent international tastings, and Santa Carolina's varietals are easy on the palate and pocketbook.

# MEXICO

Mexico is thirty-second in total wine production worldwide and is not listed among 30 nations in consumption. There is some promise for Baja, California, but the biggest news is that international giants, including Cinzano, Domecq, Gonzalez Byass, Hennessy, Martini and Rossi, Martell, Osborne, Seagrams, and Suntory have set up operations south of the border, mostly for brandy and vermouth production and distribution.

For the time being we will have to enjoy excellent Mexican beer (Corona, Dos Equis, Superior, Carta Blanca, etc.) or a Tequila Margarita with hot and spicy fajitas, burritos, and enchilladas.

# CANADA

Wine is made in seven of Canada's provinces, with Ontario leading the way, followed by British Columbia and Quebec. The most important vineyard area is in the Niagara Peninsula or southern Ontario, where French-American hybrids grow as well as a little vinifera. This area is known as "Canada's Vineland." In British Columbia, by and large, grapes are brought in from the west coast of the United States, then made and bottled. Much of the wine is made from French-American hybrids and vinifera such as Pinot Noir and Chardonnay, which can be made to endure difficult winters.

In a recent survey we found only Chateau Gai Canadian Sparkling Wine in a few U.S. wineshops. Traveling to Canada you may want to look for wines from Andres Wines Ltd., Bright and Company's DuBarry Wines, or London Winery Ltd. Canada is about twenty-five in the world in total wine production. Per capita consumption is about two and a half gallons, or slightly more than that of the U.S. There are some serious wineries in Canada today, and some light-hearted ones as well. Witness wines named Entre Deux Poissons, Caberneaux, and similar titles for Italianesque and Germanic-Canadian wines. Low alcohol, sweetish sparklers such as Baby Duck, Golden Goose, Cold Turkey, and Lonesome Charlie are quite popular. Often wines are transported from Europe, then blended and bottled in Canada.

In every nation there are serious, outstanding wineries. We have found two in Canada: L'Orpailleur Vineyards and Domaine des Cotes D'Ardoise. Both are in Quebec and specialize in hybrids and early ripening vinifera.

# SELF-EVALUATION

BEFORE READING ON, see if you have mastered the data set forth in the last few pages. Check the answer section at the back of the book for the correct answers. If you have not answered at least 70% of the questions below correctly, please reread the previous section.

## OTHER COUNTRIES
### South America, Mexico, and Canada

| TRUE | FALSE | |
|------|-------|---|
| —— | —— | 1. Barbera and Trebbiano are two grape varieties that grow in Brazil. |
| —— | —— | 2. Most of Brazil's production is from the French-American hybrids. |
| —— | —— | 3. Argentina is South America's largest producer of wine. |
| —— | —— | 4. Penaflor in Argentina is the world's largest winery. |
| —— | —— | 5. Chile's climate and terrain make it free from oidium and other rots, pests, and diseases, even the phylloxera. |
| —— | —— | 6. Chile produces the best wines of South America. |
| —— | —— | 7. Concha y Toro is one of Brazil's most famous export wineries. |
| —— | —— | 8. Although Peru is not noted for winemaking, Pisco Brandy is its most renowned spirit. |
| —— | —— | 9. Uruguay consumes just about all of its wine production. |
| —— | —— | 10. *Vino Courant* is a Chilian designation for a reserve-quality wine aged more than two years. |
| —— | —— | 11. Widely used grapes in Canadian wines are French-American hybrids and certain vinifera such as Pinot Noir and Chardonnay. |
| —— | —— | 12. Mexico is not a factor in the production of brandy. |

# AUSTRALIA

Perhaps it was the America's Cup yacht race or the movie *Crocodile Dundee*, but our fascination with the "Land Down Under" has hit a new peak. This colorful country, as large as the continental U.S.A., with a population only slightly more than the metropolitan New York City area, has tickled our imaginations with its tennis players, kangaroos, platypusses, koalas, and boomerangs for some time now—but more recently, with its beers and wines.

Aussies are avid beer drinkers (about 35 gallons per capita annually); even their Foster's Lager can is bigger than life. They consume about twice the quantity of wine per capita than we do in the U.S.A. (about five gallons). They will pass Germany in this decade. The trend is up. We produce five times as much in the United States; Italy and France each make 20 times as much. But only seven percent of Australia's land is currently sown. What is most newsworthy is that in the past 20 years Australia has emerged as a recognized producer of quality table wines which have stood up to be counted among the best that Europe and California can offer.

Recent trends in Australian viticulture closely parallel those of California. For example, in the 1950s, fortified wines outsold table wines two to one; today the scale is tilted in favor of table wines six to one. The best table wines are named for grape varieties. The style and taste of Australian wines are varied, but many do have a "New World" character, Californian rather than European. We have not seen a great push toward standardization and appellation legislation in Australia. Emphasis is rather on experimentation and a quest for producing more enjoyable wines.

## History

Australia, like California, was settled in the second half of the 18th century. Wine was made out of necessity, not for the religious zeal of Californian's Padre Junipero Serra and Fr. Juan Ugarte, but as a rum substitute. Rum and fortified wines were not only consumed in abundance but served as a form of currency for early colonists in Australia.

The first commercial winery dates back to 1827. The "Father of Australian Viticulture," James Busby, brought vines from various European countries a few years after 1827 and donated them to the government. Trade was so good in the nineteenth century that Australia became known as "John Bull's Vineyard." As viticulture spread, Australia's climate ensured consistent crops without the peaks and valleys which Western Europe must endure. Recent decades have seen the development of the "bag-in-the-box" business. In fact, the inexpensive wines in these boxes are so good that the wine-loving Aussie does not have to invest in costlier bottles of varietals to drink well. Although we have spoken of the Australian wine industry as a recent phenomenon, we should point out that several estates date back to the middle of the nineteenth century. Fortunately they have made wine uninterruptedly, not having experienced Prohibition.

**BLACK OPAL**

1987

CHARDONNAY

HUNTER RIVER VALLEY

PRODUCED AND BOTTLED BY:
MARK CASHMORE WINES PTY LTD.
HERMITAGE RD. POKOLBIN N.S.W.

ALCOHOL 11.8% BY VOLUME.

PRODUCT OF AUSTRALIA. 750 ml.

*A delicious Chardonnay named for the gem most associated with southern Australia. This wine was judged high for quality and value by wine critics. Australian varietals are similar to California's and often a bit lower in price; this makes them easy to swallow for Americans.*

We can understand why European giants, like Cinzano and Remy Martin, have invested in Australian viticulture. We look for more, especially from the Hunter and Barossa Valleys. The best, most respected, and costliest wine of Australia is Penfold's Grange Hermitage, a dry, rich red that can stand beside the world's finest. We have found the best producers of Australian fortified Muscats and port-style wines to be Campbells, Morris, Rosewood, and Yalumba. One of Australia's most dynamic wine figures is Wolfgang Blass, who produces extraordinary wine under the Wolf Blass and Tollana banners.

By their own admission, Australia is in the kindergarten stage of its wine development. We think they are being too modest. What is most exciting and refreshing about the Australian approach to wines is their positive ability to enjoy fine wine without being too technical. As far as we're concerned, the wines and the wine people from "down under" are "tops."

*Flamboyant Wolfgang Blass puts some of his best wines under the "Yellow Label." Product information is given on the left. Recent awards are shown on the right. Try this wine with Napa Valley Cabernets or fine Bordeaux. Wolfgang Blass "Black Label" wines represent some of Australia's finest.*

*Vinifera like Chardonnay and Sauvignon thrive in South Australia. They still require an excellent winemaker to display their potential. Bilyara Cellars wines exhibit great balance and style. The U.S. market is finding them to be wonderful alternatives to French and Californian wines. Colorful winemaker Wolf Blass is one of Australia's "New Guard."*

# THE TERRITORIES OF AUSTRALIA

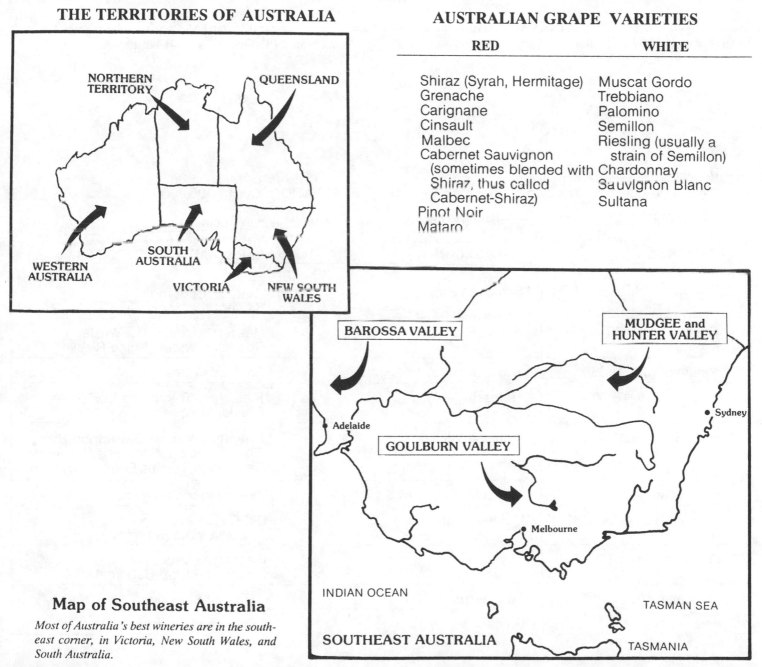

NORTHERN TERRITORY

QUEENSLAND

WESTERN AUSTRALIA

SOUTH AUSTRALIA

VICTORIA

NEW SOUTH WALES

# AUSTRALIAN GRAPE VARIETIES

| RED | WHITE |
|-----|-------|
| Shiraz (Syrah, Hermitage) | Muscat Gordo |
| Grenache | Trebbiano |
| Carignane | Palomino |
| Cinsault | Semillon |
| Malbec | Riesling (usually a |
| Cabernet Sauvignon | strain of Semillon) |
| (sometimes blended with | Chardonnay |
| Shiraz, thus called | Sauvignon Blanc |
| Cabernet-Shiraz) | Sultana |
| Pinot Noir | |
| Mataro | |

BAROSSA VALLEY

MUDGEE and HUNTER VALLEY

GOULBURN VALLEY

Adelaide

Sydney

Melbourne

INDIAN OCEAN

TASMAN SEA

TASMANIA

SOUTHEAST AUSTRALIA

## Map of Southeast Australia

*Most of Australia's best wineries are in the southeast corner, in Victoria, New South Wales, and South Australia.*

# WINE REGIONS

Wine is produced in every state and on several islands, including Tasmania. Many wineries have land holdings and winemaking facilities in all four major states. The four states are (1) South Australia, (2) New South Wales, (3) Victoria, and (4) Western Australia.

## SOUTH AUSTRALIA

PRODUCTION: 60% of Australia's production  
CAPITAL CITY: Adelaide, founded 1836

SIZE: 13% of Australia  
POPULATION: Over 1,000,000

This state has never suffered the ravages of the phylloxera, as did other states in Australia.

| WINERY | SUBREGION | RECOMMENDED WINES |
|--------|-----------|-------------------|
| Penfolds (Est. 1844) | Barossa Valley | Bin 707 Cabernet, Kaiser Stuhl Riesling |
| Seppelt (Est. 1851) | Adelaide | Dessert Wines, Great Western Sparkling Wines, Rhine Riesling |
| Yalumba (Est. 1863) | Barossa Valley | Fortified Wines |
| Orlando (Est. 1847) | Barossa Valley | Rieslings, "Bag-in-the-Box", Sparkling Wines |
| Wolf Blass (Est. 1973) | Barossa Valley | Oak-aged Whites, Sauvignon Blanc, Chardonnay, Yellow Label Cabernet Sauvignon, Tollana Eden Valley Shiraz |
| Marc Swann | Adelaide | "Roo's Leap" Fume and Chardonnay |
| Thomas Hardy (Est. 1857) | McLaren Vale | Old Castle Riesling Reynella Vintage Ports |
| Petaluma (Est. 1976) | Adelaide | Riesling, Chardonnay, Cabernet-Shiraz, Cabernet |
| Lindemans (Est. 1908) | Coonawarra | Cabernet Sauvignon, Chardonnay |
| Peter Lehmann | Barossa Valley | Cabernet Sauvignon |

# NEW SOUTH WALES

PRODUCTION: 24% of Australia's total
CAPITAL CITY: Sydney

SIZE: 10.4% of Australia
POPULATION: Over 5,000,000

| WINERY | SUBREGION | RECOMMENDED WINES |
| --- | --- | --- |
| Wyndham Estate (Est. 1928) | Hunter Valley | Cabernet, Chardonnay, Hunter Riesling |
| Tyrrells (Est. 1858) | Hunter Valley | Excellent whites, especially Semillon, Chardonnay; Red Shiraz |
| Rosemount (Est. 1969) | Hunter Valley | Chardonnay, Pinot Noir |
| Rothbury | Hunter Valley | Shiraz, Pinot Noir, Cabernet, Semillon, Chardonnay |
| Montrose | Mudgee | Chardonnay, Shiraz |
| Richmond Grove | Hunter Valley | Black Opal Chardonnay |

# VICTORIA

PRODUCTION: 13% of Australia's total
CAPITAL CITY: Melbourne, founded 1834

SIZE: 3% of Australia
POPULATION: About 4,000,000

| WINERY | SUBREGION | RECOMMENDED WINES |
| --- | --- | --- |
| Chateau Tahbilk (Est. 1860) | Goulburn Valley | Shiraz, Cabernet, Long-lived reds |
| Brown Bros. (Est. 1889) | Milawa | Muscats, Shiraz |
| Taltarni (Est. 1972) | Great Western | Cabernet, Merlot, Shiraz |

# WESTERN AUSTRALIA

PRODUCTION: 1.5% of Australia's total
CAPITAL CITY: Perth

SIZE: 33% of Australia
POPULATION: Over 1,000,000

| WINERY | SUBREGION | RECOMMENDED WINES |
| --- | --- | --- |
| Leeuwin (Est. 1974) | Margaret River | Chardonnay, Riesling, Pinot Noir, Cabernet |
| Houghton (Est. 1835) | Swan Valley | Cabernet Rose, Verdelho |

**Penfolds**

*Grange Hermitage*

BIN 95

VINTAGE 1977    BOTTLED 1978

Grange Hermitage is generally recognised as Australia's finest red wine and has received international acclaim. This great wine developed by Max Schubert, commencing with the 1952 vintage, is made from premium Hermitage grapes grown at selected vineyards in South Australia and matured in small oak casks prior to bottling.

During an extensive tour of the Bordeaux region of France in 1950, Max Schubert studied numerous wine-making practices that have now become an integral part of Penfolds wine-making technique. He also observed the practice of maturing wine in new oak casks, a method previously untried in Australia. The development of Grange Hermitage represented the beginning of a new era in Australia's red wine making tradition.

This knowledge combined with Max Schubert's foresight, skill and dedication has resulted in Grange Hermitage, the definitive Australian dry red table wine, acknowledged to be amongst the world's classic wine styles.

It is recommended that Grange Hermitage should always be decanted before serving.

**Bottled by PENFOLDS WINES PTY. LTD.**

PENFOLDS WINES PTY. LTD. SYDNEY N.S.W. AUSTRALIA 2044 · ALC 13.8% VOL

750 ml · WINE MADE IN AUSTRALIA

*Since the mid-1950s, Penfold's Grange Hermitage has been considered Australia's classic red. Max Schubert's stunning masterpiece is aged in new oak. The process is costly; so is the wine. It may run between $35 and $40. Penfold's is one of Australia's "Old Guard" wineries.*

# NEW ZEALAND

Samuel Marsden planted New Zealand's first vines in 1819, but as late as 1960 fewer than 1,000 acres of vineyards had been planted. Since then, acreage has increased almost twenty-fold. The future seems bright due to promising microclimates in Hawkes Bay, Poverty Bay, and Marlborough, and also to the fact that New Zealand abounds with the latest in technology and the enthusiasm of a newcomer. The cool climate favors white grapes. Reds so far have been generally lighter in body. Over two-thirds of the production is in table wines; the balance is split between fortified wines and brandies.

The best wines are named for grape varietals; white Müller-Thürgau is the most popular; producing wines are labeled "Riesling." Red varietals include Cabernet Sauvignon, Pinot Noir, Pinotage, and Shiraz. Other whites range from Chardonnay and Traminer to Palomino. Some good New Zealand wines under the Corbans, Cooks, Glenvale, and Seagram-owned Montana labels have made their way to the United States lately.

The New Zealander consumes a bit over two gallons per capita, about the same as we Americans do. Like their Australian neighbors, they are more enthusiastic toward beer, drinking over 30 gallons per head.

# SOUTH AFRICA

It is ironic that South Africa, the object of criticism in the United States for its political injustice, has initiated a system of regulating wine production that is the very model and envy of the civilized world. We are told also that the wine industry is very progressive when it comes to anti-apartheid reforms, with blacks in many important decision-making positions on the winery level. South African wines are widely available in the U.S. They are super values, but most go unnoticed, or rather are the objects of boycotts and censure. The biggest export market for South African wines is England.

South Africa was settled in 1655 by the Dutch. They brought cuttings of German vinestocks with them. They soon discovered a climate that is paradise to viticulture. In addition to the Dutch, French Huguenots contributed to South Africa's history.

The modern era has seen the creation of the Cooperative Wine Growers Association of South Africa Ltd. (the K.W.V.) in 1918. The Wine and Spirit Control Act came in 1924 and was amended in 1940. We can safely say that the government, with their W.O. and W.O.S. (Wines of Superior Origin), initiated in 1972, completely guarantees and endorses its wines. The K.W.V. now supervises export distribution, quality, and pricing worldwide for its 6,000 members. Nonmembers must adhere to these same high standards, according to the Wine and Spirit Control Act.

## Wine Regions

The best viticultural areas are the Coastal Belt and Little Karoo, south and east of Cape Town. Cool ocean breezes and coastal mountains provide ideal conditions to grow vinifera. The soil, which consists of sand and granite, provides for good drainage. The best subregions in the Coastal Belt, Stellenbosch, Paarl, Malmesbury, Worcester, and Constantia, are blessed with sparse rainfall. Little Karoo is known for fortified wines and brandy.

## SOUTH AFRICAN VARIETALS

| Reds | Whites |
| --- | --- |
| Pinotage | Steen |
| *(Pinot Noir & Cinsault)* | *(Chenin Blanc)* |
| Shiraz | Muscats |
| Cabernet Sauvignon | Sultana |
| Tinta Barocca | Semillon |
| Malbec | Riesling |
| Merlot | Clairette Blanche |
| Gamay | |

## WINES

South African ports, sherries, and fortified Muscatels are quite good. The trend is toward varietal-named table wines. The South African reportedly consumes about two gallons per capita, or about the same as we do in the United States.

## WINERIES

**Oude Meester:** Producer of dependable Fleur du Cap Cabernet Sauvignon and Grunberger Steen.

**Nederberg:** South Africa's most renowned cellar. They produce the botrytis-affected Chenin Blanc Edelkeur and Baronne, considered the continent's finest Cabernet Sauvignon.

**K.W.V.:** A complete line of brandies, ports, sherries. Dry, red table wine, Roodeberg, is a combination of Pinotage, Shiraz, Tinta Barocca, and Cabernet Sauvignon. K.W.V. stands for Ko-operative Wijnbouwers Vereniging or Cooperative Wine Growers Association.

# OTHER COUNTRIES IN REVIEW

- Some countries, not ordinarily viewed by U.S. consumers as significant wine nations, produce exceptional wines, such as:

  > Switzerland — Red Dole de Sion; White Fendant
  > Austria — White Kremser or Gumpoldkirchner
  > Hungary — Red Egri Bikaver and White Tokaji
  > Yugoslavia, Romania, Bulgaria — Cabernet, Chardonnay, etc.

- In South America, Chile has the reputation of producing the best wine.

- Argentina's finest wines come from the Mendoza Valley.

- Argentina is best known for its rich red wines.

- Chile and Argentina are world leaders in both the production and consumption of wine.

- Australia has an uninterrupted wine history dating back to 1827.

- Australian varietals are popular today in the U.S., perhaps due to similarities to Californian wines.

- Outstanding wines from other countries are very often comparable to more familiar wines but at great savings to the consumer.

# SELF-EVALUATION

BEFORE READING ON, see if you have mastered the data set forth in the last few pages. Check the answer section at the back of the book for the correct answers. If you have not answered at least 70% of the questions below correctly, please reread the previous section.

## OTHER COUNTRIES
### Australia, New Zealand, and South Africa

TRUE    FALSE

_____    _____   1. Recent trends in Australian viticulture parallel those of California.

_____    _____   2. Australia helped develop and popularize the "bag-in-box."

_____    _____   3. Wine is produced in every state in Australia.

_____    _____   4. South Australia is the only state not to have suffered from phylloxera.

_____    _____   5. New South Wales is Australia's largest wine-producing state.

_____    _____   6. Penfold's Grange Hermitage is Australia's most respected and expensive red wine.

_____    _____   7. Müller-Thürgau is New Zealand's most popular white wine.

_____    _____   8. Oude Meester, Nederberg, and K.W.V. are South Africa's most famous wineries.

_____    _____   9. W.O.S. stands for Wines of Superior Origin.

_____    _____   10. Most of South Africa's wines are fortified.

# ALCOHOLIC BEVERAGES REFERENCE GUIDE
## PART ONE: DISTILLED SPIRITS

**DISTILLED SPIRITS:** Alcoholic beverages produced by distillation. These are the whiskies, gins, vodkas, brandies, rums, and cordials. (The secret of alcoholic distillation from grains and fruits was stumbled upon more than 4,000 years ago, and through these centuries this discovery has been cherished and elaborated upon, to produce the liquors we know today.)

Grain is the basic ingredient of Whiskey. Grain, distilled to a tasteless neutral spirit, is the base from which the Gins, Vodkas and many Cordials are derived, the latter flavored with fruits, roots, herbs and barks drawn from across the face of the earth. From grapes come Brandy, and from the different fruits—apples, plums, cherries and apricots, among others—the family of Fruit Brandies. Grape Brandy shares with the grain spirits the role of base for the Cordials. Sugar cane produces the Rums in all their varieties.

# A

**ABISANTE:** A distinctive liqueur produced by subtle blending of aniseed and aromatic herbs. Clear green in color, becomes milky in water. Enjoyed especially in the Absinthe Drip and Suisee Cocktails.

**ABRICOTINE:** See **Apricot Liqueur.**

**ABSINTHE:** Light yellow-green high-proof liqueur with a pronounced aromatic aroma in which licorice dominates. The primary aromatic is Artemisia, or wormwood. Absinthe, with wormwood, has been prohibited in the U.S. and a number of other countries; Absinthe substitutes are marketed. These are without wormwood, are sweeter, and are not as strong.

**ADVOKAAT:** Creamy, thick egg liqueur, similar in taste to prepared eggnog but still delightfully different. Made by the addition of fresh yolks of eggs to basic liqueur. **Uses:** Straight for all occasions (serve chilled in liqueur glass); combined with whiskey to suit personal taste; tall drink (1 jigger in 8 oz. glass, 2 cubes ice, fill with ginger ale or milk).

**AGAVE:** A fermented beverage made throughout Mexico and South America. Also known as Maquey and **Pulque** (see).

**AGUARDIENTE:** A generic term for spirits in Portugal, Spain, and South America. It may refer to grape brandy or, more generally, to any distillate.

**ALCHERMES:** A spicy Italian liqueur utilizing cinnamon, sweetflag, cloves, roses, nutmeg, iris root, sugar, and alcohol.

**ALDABO:** A Cuban rum liqueur with a touch of orange flavoring.

**ALIZE:** From France, a blend of passion fruit and cognac. A proprietary brand.

**ALLASCH KUEMMEL:** Traditional **Kuemmel** (see **Kummel**). Not as dry as **Berliner Kuemmel** (see) or **Doeppel Kuemmel** (see).

**AMARETTO:** A sweet, almond tasting Italian liqueur, derived from the kernels of apricot stones. The most popular brand is Amaretto di Saronno.

NOTE: Alcoholic Beverages Reference Guide—From the Mohawk *Complete Encyclopedia of Alcoholic Beverages*. Published with the permission of Mohawk Liqueur Corporation.

*Basilica Amaretto—A romantic, popular liqueur, based not on almonds but on the stones of apricots. Enjoy it neat, on the rocks, in mixed drinks or in Cappucino.*

**ANESONE:** White liqueur with licorice-like flavor, higher in proof and drier than **Anisette** (see). Produced by distillation of anise seed. **Uses:** Straight, sometimes added to coffee, popular as highball and frapped. See also **Cordial.**

**ANGOSTURA:** A strong, flavorful tonic bitters from the Caribbean. It is used by the drop as a cocktail ingredient to add flavor or color.

**ANIS DEL MONO:** The trade name for a high quality Spanish Anisette, produced by Vicente Bosh.

**ANISETTE:** Sweet, mild, delicate aromatic liqueur with pleasant flavor reminiscent of licorice; sweeter and lower in proof than **Anesone** (see); white and red. Produced as a flavor-blend of aniseeds and aromatic herbs. **Uses:** After-dinner liqueur, frappe, with soda, in coffee, ingredient in many cocktails and cooking recipes, over ice cream. See also **Cordial.** See **Mastic, Ouzo.**

**APPLE BRANDY:** Brandy distilled from apples. See **Applejack, Brandy.**

**APPLEJACK:** (Apple Brandy) Brandy distilled from apples; mild, pleasant apple flavor. **Uses:** All-occasion liquor, excellent

"on the rocks," in highball, in many drinks to which it gives distinctive character, an ingredient in many cooking recipes. See **Fruit Brandy, Brandy.**

**APRICOT FLAVORED BRANDY:** Pure grape brandy, with the true flavor and aroma of fresh, ripe apricot; generally drier, lighter bodied and more potent than **Apricot Liqueur** (see); classified as cordial. Amber. **Uses:** Straight, as after-dinner liqueur, frapped, with soda, as ingredient in many cocktails and tall drinks, in fruit punches, over ice cream, in fresh fruit sherbets and compotes, for "flaming" desserts, over sliced pound cake, in many food recipes. See also **Cordials.**

**APRICOT LIQUEUR:** Sweet, rich liqueur, with the flavor and aroma of fresh, ripe apricots, sweeter, fuller-bodied and lighter proof than **Apricot Flavored Brandy** (see). Amber. **Uses:** Straight, as after-dinner liqueur, in tall drinks, with soda, "over the rocks," in fruit punches, over ice cream, in fresh fruit sherbets and compotes, over sliced pound cake, in candying vegetables and basting meats and fowl. See also **Cordial.**

*The original "Berentzen Appel" Liqueur is produced in Germany using only 100% pure, natural apple juices—a real, refreshing favorite in the market today.*

**APRY:** See **Apricot Liqueur.**

**AQUA D'ORO:** A sweet Italian liqueur containing gold leaf, similar to **Goldwasser** (see).

**AQUAVIT (Akvavit):** Smooth, light, dry, white liquor with the flavor of caraway; like **Kummel** (see), but much drier. National beverage of the Scandinavian countries. Produced as highly refined spirit flavored with caraway seeds and other aromatics. **Uses:** Neat (chilled) as appetizer, with smorgasbord, canapes, hors d'oeuvres, buffet suppers or anytime; ingredient in a number of cocktails. See also **Cordial.**

**ARAKI:** A date brandy produced in Egypt.

**ARMAGNAC:** A grape brandy of France, probably second only to cognac. Armagnac is produced in a legally delimited region in the Gers Department in southwest France. It is dry, less delicate and less ethereal than cognac, but compensates with a fuller body.

**Uses:** Straight, as an after-dinner drink; with soda; in coffee; an ingredient in cocktails; with various cooking recipes; flavoring for desserts. See **Brandy.**

**ARRACK:** A type of brandy from rice, millet, and other items. It possesses a taste suggestive of rum. From the Dutch East Indies.

**ARRAKI:** A variety of sloe gin produced in Tatary, Asia.

**AURUM:** A sweet, golden, orange-flavored liqueur from Italy.

# B

**B & B:** A mixture of brandy and a sweet French herb-based cordial called Benedictine D.O.M. The brandy preserves the flavor of the Benedictine but cuts its sweetness.

**BALSAM:** The West Indian banana liqueur popular with the natives of Haiti.

*Bas-Armagnac – Considered a superior area to Haut-Armagnac and Tenarèze. These two are unblended vintage-dated distillates which have been aged in 400 liter casks for much more than 7 years. The term "aged in wood for 7 years" satisfied a BATF requirement. Armagnac hails from Gascony, the land of the Three Musketeers. The Gascons are reputed to have gargantuan appetites and sometimes Armagnac is sipped in the middle of the meal to make "a hole in the stomach" so that more food may fit.*

**BANANA LIQUEUR:** Sweet, yellow liqueur with the full flavor of fresh, ripe bananas. **Uses:** Straight, as after-dinner liqueur, over ice cream, fruits, parfaits, grapefruit; in fruit punches, in a number of cocktails. Also used in cooking as a flavoring; delicious in cakes and especially banana cream pie. See also **Cordial.**

**BARBADOS RUM:** Medium-bodied rum, dry, heavier and more pungent than **Puerto Rican Rum,** but lighter and not as pungent as **Jamaica Rum.** Produced in pot stills; amber in color. **Uses:** Straight in highball with soda (add slice fresh lemon or lime), in many rum cocktails, as flavoring in pudding and mince pie, in making Cumberland Rum Butter, as topping over ice cream and cake. See **Rum.**

**BARENFANG LIQUEUR:** Honey-flavored German liqueur; yellow. **Use:** after-dinner liqueur. See also **Cordial.**

**BATAVIA ARRAC:** Dry, highly aromatic, colorless, brandy-like rum of great pungency and rumminess; distilled in Indonesia in the East Indies. **Uses:** straight, as Hot Toddy, as Hot Punch, excellent for flavoring fruit salads, cakes and pastries. See **Rum.**

**BEAGA:** A Russian spirit made from oatmeal and hops.

**BENAI:** Herb-flavored cordial, produced as a flavor in old brandy. Amber color. **Uses:** After-dinner liqueur. See also **Cordial.**

**BERGAMOTTE LIQUEUR:** Pear-flavored German liqueur; also called **Kaiserbirn Liqueur** (see). **Uses:** See **Cordial.**

**BERLINER KUEMMEL:** Traditional **Kuemmel** (see **Kummel**). Drier than **Allasch Kuemmel** (see).

**BITTERS:** An infusion of roots, barks, herbs and other botanicals, produced by private formulas. There are three primary varieties — aromatic, flavoring and laxative. One should never be stubstituted for the other. *Aromatic Bitters* are aromatic and pungent, with distinctive aroma and bouquet. They whet the appetite and stimulate the digestive processes, and are frequently used in cocktails that are primarily appetizers. *Flavoring Bitters,* like Orange Bitters, are important as flavorings in a number of drinks, particularly when a fragrant aroma is sought.

**BLACKBERRY FLAVORED BRANDY:** Pure grape brandy with the true flavor and aroma of fresh, ripe blackberries; generally drier, lighter bodied and more potent than **Blackberry Li-**

queur (see); classified as a cordial. Blue-black. **Uses:** Straight, as after-dinner drink, frapped, with soda, ingredient in many cocktails and tall drinks, "On the Rocks;" in fruit punches, over ice cream, in fresh fruit sherbets and compotes; for "flaming" desserts, over sliced pound cake topped with fresh or preserved fruit. See also **Cordial.**

**BLACKBERRY LIQUEUR:** Sweet, rich liqueur, with the flavor and aroma of fresh, ripe blackberries; sweeter, fuller bodied and lighter proof than **Blackberry Flavored Brandy** (see). Blue-black. **Uses:** Straight, as after-dinner liqueur, with or in coffee, in tall drinks, "On the Rocks," with soda, in fruit punches, over ice cream, in fruit sherbets and compotes, over sliced pound cake. See also **Cordial.**

**BLEND OF STRAIGHT WHISKEYS:** Two or more Straight Whiskeys combined to create a distinctive Straight Whiskey character. The Straight Whiskeys used (all 2 years or over) may be different kinds — Straight Bourbon, Straight Rye, Straight Corn, etc. Or all the Straight Whiskeys may be of one kind, as Straight

*Mohawk Blackberry Flavored Brandy—A cordial with a brandy base and the flavor of natural blackberries. Mohawk is a brand leader in the production of liqueurs and flavored brandies.*

Bourbon. Each will be a whiskey distilled to highlight different characteristics of body, flavor and aroma. Each is selected for the special contribution it makes, in balance, to the final product. The blend of Straight Whiskeys is full-bodied, with well-defined aroma and flavor. It may also be labelled Blended Straight Whiskeys. When the Straight Whiskeys in this blend are all of one type, the distiller may carry the grain tag over to the label as Blend of Straight Bourbon Whiskeys or Blend of Straight Rye Whiskeys. **Uses:** See **Whiskey.**

**BLEND OF STRAIGHT BOURBON WHISKEYS:** Two or more Straight Bourbon Whiskeys blended to create a distinctive Straight Bourbon Whiskey character. This blend always consists of 100% Straight Bourbon Whiskeys. However, if less than 100% of the bottle, but more than 51%, consists of Straight Bourbon Whiskey, the distiller may still use the Bourbon grain tag, provided a back label is added showing the percentage of various type whiskeys used. This whiskey may also be labelled Blended Straight Bourbon Whiskeys. See also **Blend of Straight Whiskeys. Uses:** See **Whiskeys.**

**BLEND OF STRAIGHT CORN WHISKEYS:** Two or more Straight Malt Whiskeys, blended together. Also labelled Straight Corn Whiskeys.

**BLEND OF STRAIGHT MALT WHISKEYS:** Two or more Straight Malt Whiskeys, blended together. Also labelled Blended Straight Malt Whiskeys.

**BLEND OF STRAIGHT RYE WHISKEYS:** Two or more Straight Rye Whiskeys blended to create a distinctive Straight Rye Whiskey character. This blend always consists of 100% Straight Rye Whiskeys. However, if less than 100% but more than 51% consists of Straight Rye Whiskey, the distiller may still use the Rye grain tag, provided a back label is added showing the percentage of the various types of whiskeys used. This whiskey may also be labeled Blended Straight Rye Whiskeys. See also **Blend of Straight Whiskeys. Uses:** See **Whiskey.**

**BLEND OF STRAIGHT RYE MALT WHISKEYS:** Two or more Straight Rye Malt Whiskeys blended together. Also labeled **Blended Straight Rye Malt Whiskeys.**

**BLEND OF STRAIGHT WHEAT WHISKEYS:** Two or more

*Fleischmann's Preferred Blended Whiskey — One of America's most popular Blended Whiskeys. Fleischmann's has retained a higher proof (90°), even though other producers have dropped to 80°. This means that less Fleischmann's needs to be used in a cocktail for a full flavor.*

Straight Wheat Whiskeys blended together. Also labeled **Blended Straight Wheat Whiskeys.**

**BLENDED BOURBON WHISKEY:** Blended Whiskey produced as a mixture or blend of Neutral Spirits and Straight Whiskey but differing this way: Contains minimum of 51% Straight Whiskeys, instead of a minimum of 20% Straight Whiskeys as in the Blended Whiskey. Light in body, like the Blended Whiskey, but with a more clearly defined bourbon character. Also labeled **Bourbon Whiskey — a Blend. Uses:** See **Whiskey.**

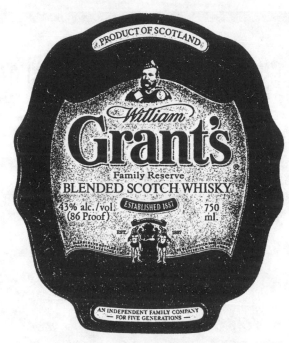

*William Grants "Family Reserve" Scotch Whisky is a special blend from one of the worlds most prestigious Scotch distilleries.*

**BLENDED CANADIAN WHISKY:** Distinctive whisky of Canada. See **Canadian Whisky.**

**BLENDED CORN WHISKEY:** Blended Whiskey containing a minimum of 51% Straight Corn Whiskey and Neutral Spirits. Also labeled **Corn Whiskey — A Blend.**

**BLENDED IRISH WHISKEY:** Distinctive whiskey of Ireland. See **Irish Whiskey.**

**BLENDED MALT WHISKEY:** Blended Whiskey containing a minimum of 51% Straight Malt Whiskey and Neutral Spirits. Also labeled **Malt Whiskey — A Blend.**

**BLENDED RYE MALT WHISKEY:** Blended Whiskey containing a minimum of 51% Straight Malt Whiskey and Neutral Spirits. Also labeled **Malt Whiskey — A Blend.**

**BLENDED RYE WHISKEY:** Blended Whiskey containing a minimum of 51% Straight Rye Whiskey and Neutral Spirits.

Light in body, like the Blended Whiskey, but with more clearly defined Straight Rye Whiskey character. Also labeled **Rye Whiskey — A Blend. Uses:** See **Whiskey.**

**BLENDED SCOTCH WHISKY:** Distinctive whisky of Scotland. See **Scotch Whisky.**

**BLENDED STRAIGHT BOURBON WHISKEYS:** Two or more Straight Bourbon Whiskeys combined. Also labeled **Blend of Straight Bourbon Whiskeys** (see).

**BLENDED STRAIGHT CORN WHISKEYS:** Two or more Straight Corn Whiskeys blended together. Also labeled **Blend of Straight Corn Whiskeys** (see).

**BLENDED STRAIGHT MALT WHISKEYS:** Two or more Straight Malt Whiskeys blended together. Also labeled **Blend of Straight Malt Whiskeys.**

**BLENDED STRAIGHT RYE MALT WHISKEYS:** Two or more Straight Rye Malt Whiskeys blended together. Also labeled **Blend of Straight Rye Malt Whiskeys.**

**BLENDED STRAIGHT RYE WHISKEYS:** Two or more Straight Rye Whiskeys combined. Also labeled **Blend of Straight Rye Whiskeys** (see).

**BLENDED STRAIGHT WHEAT WHISKEYS:** Two or more Straight Wheat Whiskeys blended together. Also labeled **Blend of Straight Wheat Whiskeys.**

**BLENDED STRAIGHT WHISKEYS:** Two or more Straight Whiskeys combined. Also labeled **Blend of Straight Whiskeys** (see).

**BLENDED WHEAT WHISKEY:** Blended Whiskey containing a minimum of 51% Straight Wheat Whiskey and Neutral Spirits. Also labeled **Wheat Whiskey — A Blend.**

**BLENDED WHISKEY:** Light bodied, soft whiskey, mild in flavor and aroma, made as a mixture, or blend, or Neutral Spirits and Straight Whiskey. By law, this whiskey contains a minimum of 20% Straight Whiskey by volume at 100° proof. In most brands, different Straight Whiskeys are blended with Neutral Spirits. Each is selected for its individual character and contribution to the flavor, aroma, color and body of the Blend as a whole. The Neutral Spirits — highly refined, without important taste, flavor or body — round out the base whiskeys The Blend, one of

America's two great whiskey types, is the "Rye" of popular consumer preference in the East. Also labeled **Whiskey—A Blend.** When 51% or more Straight Whiskey of one type is used in this blend, a "grain tag" may be added to the label, as **Blended Bourbon Whiskey** or **Blended Rye Whiskey** (see). **Uses:** See **Whiskey.**

**BOGGS:** A cordial from the U.S.A. based on cranberries.

**BOTTLED-IN-BOND WHISKEY:** A Straight Whiskey, blood brother of the Straight Bourbons and Straight Ryes, but a higher caste, with full-bodied flavor and aroma complementing its 100° Strength Bottled-in-Bond Whiskey, is **always** bottled at 100° (Straights may be bottled at any legal proof); Bottled-in-Bond Whiskey is **always** 4 years old and may be older (Straights may be 2 years or older). The Bottled-in-Bond Whiskey in the bottle is always produced in a single distillery by the same distiller and must be the product of a single season or year. Bottled-in-Bond Whiskey earns a grain tag like the Straights—Bonded Straight Bourbon or Bonded Straight Rye—when the mash of grain from which it is made contains at least 51% corn or rye grain, respectively. Bottled-in-Bond Whiskey is identified by its distinctive green strip stamp. **Uses:** See **Whiskey.**

*Royal Stock—The best lots of Distillerie Stock's vast brandy reserve goes into Royal Stock X.O. One of Italy's very best. World class.*

**BOURBON:** Type name for one of the two great American whiskies. Named for Bourbon County, Kentucky, where Bourbon was first produced soon after the Revolutionary War. See **Bourbon Whiskey, Straight Bourbon Whiskey.**

**BOURBON WHISKEY:** Like Straight Bourbon Whiskey, except for age. When the label says only, "Bourbon Whiskey," without the word "Straight," the whiskey may have **any age up to 2 years. Straight Bourbon Whiskey** (see) must be a minimum of 2 years old.

**BOURBON WHISKEY—A BLEND:** A mixture, or blend, of Neutral Spirits and a minimum of 51% **Straight Bourbon Whiskey** (see); also labeled **Blended Bourbon Whiskey** (see).

**BRANDY:** A family of liquors distilled from the wines of grapes or other fruits. Brandy is a soft, smooth, velvety liquor, amber in color, distinguished by its great bouquet and the subtle fragrance of grapes. Brandy, unless otherwise identified on the label, is always a distillation of the wines of pure grapes. When brandy is

*Asbach Uralt—Produced from the wines of Charlemagne's vineyards on the Rhine, Asbach-Uralt is Germany's world-famous brandy. Aged in oak casks, this mellow, distinctive brandy should be enjoyed as you would a fine cognac.*

distilled from other fruits, the fruit must be stated, as **Apple Brandy**, or **Apricot Brandy**. Brandy is famed as an after-dinner drink, straight or with many cordials, and as the Brandy & Soda. It is a basic ingredient in favorite cocktails; makes a perfect blend in drinks that call for fruit juices and wines. Over fruit salad and compote, brandy brings out the natural flavors of the fruit. See **Apple Brandy, Applejack, Apricot Brandy, Armagnac, Calvados, Cognac, Eau de Vie de Marc, Framboise, Fruit Brandy, Fruit Flavored Brandy, German Brandy, Grappa, Greek Brandy, Kirschwasser, Marc, Mirabelle, Quetsch, Slivovitz, Spanish Brandy.**

# C

**CACAO MIT NUSS LIQUEUR:** Cocoa and hazel nut flavored German liqueur; white. Characteristic bouquet and taste derived from blend of cocoa powder and extract from hazel nuts. **Use:** Straight. See also **Cordial.**

**CALISAY:** The national aperitif of Spain, containing cinchona and flavored with Peruvian bark. Basically a sherry with a quinine flavor.

**CALVADOS:** Apple Brandy produced in a legally delimited region of Normandy, France. Uses: See **Applejack, Brandy.**

**CANADIAN WHISKY:** Distinctive whisky of Canada, characteristically light, mild and delicate. Most Canadian Whiskies are blended whiskies, combining heavy and light-bodied whiskies. They are distilled from mashes of corn, rye and malted barley, much like those used by American distillers, and are aged in new white oak barrels or in reused barrels. Most are blended during the aging process, although a final blending usually precedes the bottling of the brand: Canadian regulations require that all whiskies be aged a minimum of 2 years. Most brands sold in the U.S. are aged a much greater period. **Uses:** See **Whiskey.**

**CANADIAN WHISKY—A BLEND:** Label designation also authorized by U.S. regulations for Canadian Whisky produced as a mixture of distilled spirits.

**CASCARILLA:** A popular South American liqueur flavored with spices and various barks.

**CHAMBORD LIQUEUR ROYALE DE FRANCE:** Rich

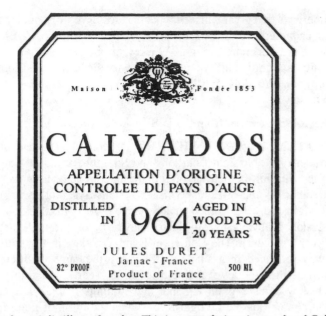

*Calvados—A distillate of apples. This is a superlative vintage-dated Calvados aged in barrels for twenty years. Enjoy it as you would a fine Cognac. The U.S.-made apple distillate is called Apple Jack.*

aroma and taste of framboises (small black raspberries) and other fruits and herbs combined with honey. A proprietary liqueur in a distinctive spherical bottle.

**CHARTREUSE:** A trio of liqueurs from France, based on 130 different herbs. Green is stronger, costlier and more renowned than yellow, which is nonetheless powerful, stylish stuff. A special aged V.E.P. is rare and expensive. The green is the basis for the mixed drink, the Swampwater.

**CHERRY HEERING (also called Kirsebaer):** A cherry liqueur made by Peter F. Heering (see also **Peter Heering**).

**CHERRY KARISE:** A trade name for distilled spirits from cherry liqueur with other natural flavors added. Ripe cherries from Northern Europe and other natural flavors are used in strict compliance with a centuries-old Danish formula.

**CHERRY LIQUEUR:** Sweet, rich liqueur, with the flavor and aroma of fresh, ripe cherries; sweeter, fuller-bodied and lighter proof than **Cherry Flavored Brandy** (see). Cherry red. **Uses:**

Straight as after-dinner liqueur, in tall drinks, with soda, in fruit punches, "Over Rocks," over ice cream, in fresh fruit sherbets; wonderful over hot compote of black cherries and other compotes; over sliced pound cake, in candying vegetables and basting meats and fowl. See also **Cordial.**

**CLARISTINE:** Golden amber herb liqueur of the monastery type; rich, sweet, honey-like flavor. **Uses:** After-dinner liqueur, straight or half-and-half with brandy; delightful also in mixture of two parts Scotch and one part Claristine.

**COCORIBE LIQUEUR:** Refreshing coconut and rum liqueur from the Virgin Islands. A proprietary brand. Used in Coladas.

**COGNAC:** Superb brandy of France; probably one of the most delicate and ethereal of all alcoholic beverages, with great aroma and the bouquet of grapes. Cognac is produced in a legally delimited 150,000 acre area surrounding the ancient city of Cognac in the departments of Charente and Charente-Maritime in the southwest of France. For the classification of Cognacs, the district is subdivided into seven sections, which, in order of quality, are: Grande Champagne, Petite Champagne, Borderies, Fins Bois, Bons Bois, Bois Ordinaires, Bos Communs. This division is based primarily on the composition of the soil, which by nature, is limy. The more lime, the finer the wines produced for the Cognac. The Grande Champagne has the most lime — the other sec-

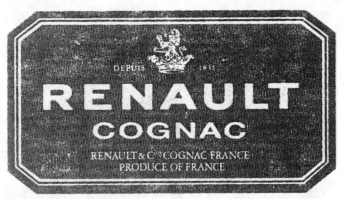

Renault Cognac — A refined Cognac of good bouquet and flavor. Cognac must come from a delimited zone just north of Bordeaux in France. It is a distillate of wine; that is, a grape brandy.

tions, a successively lower lime content. Under French law, only brandy distilled from wine made from grapes grown within this district may be called Cognac. Various qualities of Cognac are sometimes indicated by stars, in ascending quality, and by letters: "E" meaning Especial; "F," Fine; "V," Very; "O," Old; "S," Superior; "P," Pale; "X," Extra; "C," Cognac. Thus, "V.S.O.P." on a Cognac label means "Very Superior Old Pale." **Uses:** Straight, as an after-dinner drink; in highball with soda; in coffee; as an ingredient in many cocktails; in cooking recipes and flavoring for desserts. See **Brandy.**

**COFFEE LIQUEUR:** Delicious piquant liqueur with distinctive coffee flavor. **Uses:** After-dinner liqueur; "On the Rocks;" ingredient in numerous cocktails; over ice cream or other desserts; as food flavoring.

**COINTREAU:** The best-known **Triple Sec** (see)or **Curacao** (see), that is, a dry, clear, orange-flavored liqueur.

**CORDIAL:** Sweetened, flavored family of liquors; also termed **Liqueur.** (Both describe the same product.) The cordial is produced in great varieties of flavors drawn from fruits and plants from across the face of the earth. These are combined with a previously prepared spirit base — generally brandy or neutral spirits. By law, the cordial must be sweetened — sugar, or dextrose, or both, must be added in an amount equal to at least 2.5% by weight of the finished product. These tasteful spirits have outstanding palatability — are renowned for their pleasures as after-dinner top-

"Mocaríbe" is a distinctive, quality-tasting product, produced in the same tradition of other premium quality coffee liqueurs.

*A. de Fussigny – Most significant producers take exceptional lots of cognac and lay them aside for special aging and blending. These rare cuvees are among the best examples of the ancient art of distillation.*

*Monnet V.S.O.P. – The salamander is the logo of the firm of Monnet, which has been making Cognac for 150 years. Paul Masson once said that Cognac is "Something good to drink, made from something good to drink!"*

*Delamain Cognac – Made from grapes grown in the tiny Grand Champagne vineyard area. This section, in the heart of Cognac country, accounts for less than 15% of the entire grape growing Cognac zone.*

**Cognac Prunier**

Reserve of the Prunier family

Grande Fine Champagne

REGISTRE 1ᵉʳ        Cté de la Rochelle

Nᵒ 336

PAR ORDONNANCE RENDUE

le 9ᵉ du mois de Decembre de l'an 1701 par
Mʳ les Commissaires Généraux du Conseil
députés sur le fait des Armoiries.
Celles de chez PRUNIER, Notable de la Rochelle.

Telles qu'elles sont ici peintes & figurées, après avoir été
reçues, ont été enregistrées à l'Armorial Général dans le Registre cotté La Rochelle en conséquence du payment des droits
reglés par la Tarif & Arrest du Conseil, du 20ᵉ de Novembre
de l'an 1696 et n'y a pû être délivré qu'à été obtenu
à Paris par Nous CHARLES D'HOZIER, Conseiller
du ROI & Garde de l'Armorial Général de France 1701

Monsieur Jean Prunier the
founder of Maison Prunier S.A
and a recognized tasting
expert had elaborated his
personal blend for private
use.
His descendants give you
now the opportunity to
appreciate rare vintage
cognac brandies blended
according to family tradition.

750 ml        PRODUCE OF FRANCE        80 Proof

Maison PRUNIER S.A.
16100 COGNAC FRANCE

*Cognac Prunier – From the distinguished Prunier firm. This is the family blend. Prunier is illustrious for vintage Cognac. "Grande Fine Champagne" refers to the very best source for Cognac grapes.*

**REMY MARTIN**

PRINTED IN FRANCE        80 PROOF
500 ml

Maison fondée en 1724

Rémy Martin

V.S.O.P.        COGNAC        PRODUCE
FRANCE        OF FRANCE

DISTILLED AND BOTTLED BY REMY MARTIN A COGNAC - FRANCE

FINE CHAMPAGNE COGNAC

*Remy Martin V.S.O.P. – The most successful V.S.O.P. in the U.S. V.S.O.P. stands for "Very Special Old Pale." It is a notch above V.S. ("Very Special").*

*Remy Martin X.O. – Prestigious Cognac firms produce several blends. Remy Martin X.O. (Extra Old) fits between the popular V.S.O.P. and Louis XIII in age, quality, and price.*

*Jules Duret Cognac – Fewer than 300 cases of Lot 024/98 were made by Jules Duret. These grapes were from the Grande Champagne area, the best in the Cognac zone. Other areas in descending order are: Petite Champagne, Borderies, Fins Bois, Bons Bois and Bois Ordinaires.*

pers. Many have wide appeal for persons who prefer a sweeter and milder drink and are outstanding suggestions for service at entertainments and parties. They are used in numberless cocktails as well as for flavorings in cooking and over desserts.

**CORDIAL MÉDOC:** A fine liqueur from Bordeaux based on brandy, fruits and herbs.

**CORN WHISKEY:** Like Straight Corn Whiskey, except for age. When the label says only "Corn Whiskey" without the word "Straight," the whiskey may have any age up to 2 years. **Straight Corn Whiskey** (see) will be a minimum of 2 years old.

**CREAMS:** A category of thick, luscious cream-flavored cordials with brandy or whiskey. The cream may be either dairy or non-dairy. Most popular is Bailey's Irish Cream, based on Irish Whiskey and chocolate cream.

**CREME DE ALMOND:** Rich, nutty cordial, brilliant clear red; made by a distillation of the almonds of apricot kernels. **Uses:** Popular in cocktails. See also **Cordial.**

**CREME DE BANANA:** See **Banana Liqueur.**

**CREME DE CACAO: (Creme de Cocoa):** Rich, creamy cordial blending cocoa-cholcolate and vanilla flavors; brown (regular) and white. Made from selected cacao and vanilla beans. **Uses:** Straight, as an after-dinner liqueur; ingredient in many cocktails, (notably, Alexander and Angel's Tip), on desserts in place of chocolate sauce or as syrup over vanilla or chocolate ice cream. White (colorless) is the base of the Grasshopper and Pink Squirrel, among other cocktails. See also **Cordial.**

**CREME DE CASSIS:** Sweet, reddish-brown cordial, fairly heavy with the flavor of currants. Made by macerating black currants in spirit. **Uses:** Popular, particularly for the Vermouth Cassis, straight as an after-dinner liqueur, in highballs, over vanilla ice cream, ingredient in a number of cocktails. See also **Cordial.**

**CREME DE COFFEE:** Coffee-flavored cordial made by the percolation of coffee and vanilla beans. **Uses:** Straight, as an after-dinner liqueur; in coffee; over ice cream. See also **Cordial.**

**CREME DE MANDARINE:** Tangy, tempting liqueur with the bouquet of tangerine oranges; slightly more delicate taste than

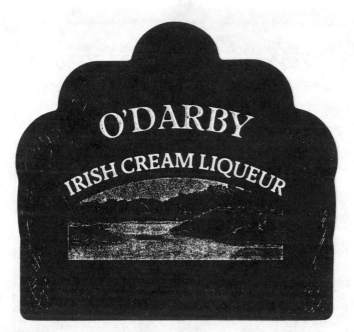

*From the fertile dairy lands in the south coast of Ireland comes some of the finest cream in the world. O'Darby's takes this cream and blends it with Irish Spirits and a hint of chocolate to make O'Darby's Irish Cream.*

**Curacao** (see). Made by infusing natural fruit flavors or orange peels in spirit. **Uses:** As an after-dinner liqueur. See **Cordial.**

**CREME DE MENTHE:** Refreshing, tangy, natural mint-flavored cordial, cool, clean and very pleasant to the taste; green and white. Made as a spirit, flavored with slips of fresh peppermint plant. **Uses:** Straight, as after-dinner liqueur, frapped. Green is used in many cocktails, is popular "over rocks" and with soda; decorates (splash) Collins, Fizz or Highball, in gourmet recipes; White is the mint for the Stinger and other cocktails; both wonderful over ice cream or in a parfait, and on grapefruit. See also **Cordial.** See **Gold-O-Mint. Peppermint Schnapps.**

**CREME DE MENTHE (Gold):** Same mint flavor as other Creme de Menthes (above), but with a gold color. Uses: After-dinner liqueur, frappe and in various cocktails, particularly the Stinger. See also **Cordial.**

**CREME DE NOYA (Creme de Noyaux):** Exquisite, rich liqueur, with delicious nutty flavor; flavoring derived primarily from oil of bitter almonds or the oil of apricot kernels. **Uses:** After-dinner liqueur, in highball, ingredient in number of cocktails, especially the Pink Squirrel. See also **Cordial.**

**CREME DE PRUNELLE:** Cordial made from plums. **Uses:** See **Cordial.**

**CREME DE ROSES:** Cordial, flavor obtained from the essential oils of rose petals and vanilla. **Uses:** as an after-dinner liqueur, over ice cream and other desserts.

**CREME DE VANILLE (Vanilla):** Velvety-brown liqueur with the pleasant flavor of vanilla. **Uses:** After-dinner liqueur; tasty on chocolate ice cream and parfaits; flavoring in cooking. See **Cordial.**

**CREME DE VIOLET:** Cordial, flavor obtained from the essential oils of violets and vanilla. **Uses:** After-dinner liqueur, over ice cream and other desserts.

**CREME DE YVETTE:** Cordial with violet color and flavor drawn from the petals of fresh violets. Uses: Ingredient in a number of cocktails. See also **Cordial, Ivette (creme d').**

**CUARENTA-Y-TRES ("43"):** A marvelous, sweet Spanish cordial based on herbs with a dominant vanilla taste. So called, allegedly, because it was the firm's forty-third attempt at producing a successful liqueur.

**CUBAN RUM:** Dry, light rum, brandy-like to the taste, with slight molasses flavor. Produced in two labels—White Label, more delicate in flavor and aroma and Gold Label, a little sweeter and with more pronounced rum flavor (Cuban Gold Label tends to be slightly bolder than Puerto Rican Gold). Distilled at high proof in column stills. **Uses:** Straight, "on the rocks" (with twist of lemon peel), in highball with favorite mixer, in many mixed drinks, in gourmet dishes, as flavoring for puddings, cakes and other desserts, as topping over ice cream. See **Rum.**

**CURACAO:** Light, delicate, orange-flavored cordial, produced as a flavor blending of the peels of tangy Curacao and sweet oranges. Amber. Curacao has a subtle orange character, contains slightly less total flavor than **Triple Sec** (see), has more sweet orange peel taste, contains more sugar and is lower in proof. **Uses:** Straight as an after-dinner liqueur; ingredient in many cocktails and punches, over ice cream, with or in black coffee. Because it is more subtle in flavor than Triple Sec, it is not used frequently in cooking. See also **Cordial.**

**CURACAO (BLUE): CURACAO (GREEN):** Same flavor as Curacao, different colors. Distinctive after-dinner liqueur (because of the color); ingredient in preparation of colorful cocktails. Teaspoon of Green in Tom Collins adds to its icy look.

**CYNAR:** A bitter-sweet, high quality aperitif or digestivo from Italy, based on the artichoke.

# D

**DAMSON GIN:** A gin specially flavored with the juice of Damson plums.

**DELECTA LIQUEUR:** Light herb-flavored cordial produced as a flavor blending of spices and many varieties of honey. Amber. **Use:** After-dinner liqueur. See also **Cordial.**

**DEMERARA RUM:** Full-bodied dark rum made from molasses of sugar cane grown along the Demerara River in British Guyana; distilled in pot stills. **Uses:** Ingredient in Planter's Punch and many other rum cocktails; in cooking; in making puddings; as flavoring on cakes, ice cream and in frostings. See **Rum.**

**DOEPPEL KUEMMEL:** Traditional **Kuemmel** (see **Kummel**). Drier than **Allasch Kuemmel.**

**DRY GIN:** The version of gin (also called **London Dry Gin**) which dominates the American market. Dry Gin—the gin product of the U.S. and England—is crisp, clean, delicate, a white liquor, aromatic of juniper, with the flavor toned down but with enough of the bouquet to give it independent character. There is no grain taste. Like Dry Gin, the Dutch gin types—**Hollands** and **Geneva Gins**—draw their primary flavor from juniper, but otherwise differ completely from the American and English gins. Dry Gin may be enjoyed straight (chilled), but is geared most to combine with other flavors—vermouth, fruit juices, peels, quinine water, cordials and other liquors. Taste-tempting mixed drinks have earned Dry Gin its following. Dry Gin is produced by distillation, or redistillation of Neutral Spirits in the presence of juniper and such other roots, herbs and berries as angelica root, coriander, cardamon and cassia. See **Gin.** See also **Hollands Gin, Geneva Gin, London Dry Gin.**

**DRAMBUIE:** A sweet, strong, mead-like cordial, based on Scotch Whiskey, herbs and honey. With Scotch it becomes the "Rusty Nail."

**DUTCH GIN:** Gin pungent of juniper and with pronounced grain flavor. See **Geneva Gin, Hollands Gin;** also **Dry Gin, Gin.**

# E

**EAU-DE-VIE ("Water of Life"):** Literally, any distillate, but usually applied to colorless distillations of fruits. The French call these "white alcohols" or alcools blancs. Popular types include cherries (**Kirsch**), apples (**Calvados**), raspberries (**Framboise**), pears (Poire Williams or **Pear William**), golden plums (**Mirabelle**), purple plums (**Quetsch**) and strawberries (Fraise or **Fraisette**).

**EAU DE VIE DE MARC:** A French brandy. See **Marc, Brandy.**

**EDELKIRSCH LIQUEUR:** German cherry liqueur; cherry red. Derives characteristic cherry taste and bouquet from flavor-blend of fresh cherry juice and Kirschwasser (cherry brandy). **Uses:** See **Cordial.**

**EXQUISIT LIQUEUR:** Orange-flavored golden-yellow German liqueur, differs distinguishably from **Triple Sec** and **Cuarcao** (see). Produced as a flavor-blend of orange peels and brandy. **Uses:** See **Cordial.**

# F

**FALERNUM:** A trademark for a liqueur of low alcoholic content with an almond taste. A flavoring ingredient in exotic mixed drinks.

**FLAVORED GIN:** Traditional Dry Gin, with fruit or other flavors added, together with sweetening. Flavored Gin is classified as a Cordial by U.S. Government regulations. Sugar or dextrose or both must be added in an amount not less than 2.5% by weight of the finished product. See **Gin.**

**FERNET BRANCA:** Italian aromatic bitters. A digestive tonic of great reputation. A mint version is available.

**FIOR DI ALPE (also called Flora Alpina):** A spicy Italian li-

*Frangelico Liqueur—A premium cordial based on the hazelnut, and other natural ingredients like berries and flowers. This Italian product is very popular in the U.S. in mixed drinks, on the rocks, even as an ice cream topping.*

queur with a sprig inside of the bottle, made with an excess of sugar which crystallizes on the sprig.

**FLENSBURGER FEUER:** Blend of blackberry liqueur and bitters. Tart after-taste. Like a bitter. **Uses:** Enjoy straight.

**FLEUR DE MOCHA: Coffee liqueur** (see).

**FRUIT BRANDY:** (See also Fruit-flavored Brandy below). Fruit Brandy is a distillation of the fermented juice of fruit. It is colorless (white), except it may draw color from the barrel during aging; it has the subtle fragrance of the fruit from which it is distilled. See **Brandy.**

**FRANGELICO:** A hazelnut-flavored Italian liqueur in a stately, distinctive bottle. When combined with Bailey's Irish Cream, it makes the "Nutty Irishman."

**FRAISETTE:** The trade name for a strawberry liqueur made by Distillerie de la Fraisette, La Plaine St. Denis, France.

**FRAMBOISE:** May be a dry, colorless **Eau-de-Vie** from raspberries or a purple, sweet liqueur derived from raspberries.

**FRUIT-FLAVORED BRANDY:** (See also Fruit Brandy above). Fruit-flavored Brandy is a fruit **flavoring** of a previously prepared brandy spirit base—unlike Fruit Brandy which is made by **distilling** the fruit. Generally, the Fruit-flavored Brandy is produced by soaking the fruit in the spirit until the spirit takes on the color and pronounced flavor of the fruit. Fruit-flavored Brandy is classified as a cordial. Sweetening—sugar or dextrose, or both—must be added in an amount not less than 2.5% by weight of the finished product. See **Brandy.**

# G

**GALLIANO:** A sweet Italian herb liqueur in a long bottle. It is named after the Italian major who defended the fort pictured on the label during the Abyssian campaign. It is the spirit used in the "Harvey Wallbanger." The firm which makes this Liquore also markets a **Sambuca** and an **Amaretto.**

**GEBIRGS-ENZIAN LIQUEUR:** Yellow German liqueur with flavor drawn from the blue flowered species of the Gentian plant which grows in the Bavarian Alps. **Use:** Straight. See also **Cordial.**

**GENEVA GIN:** (also Genever Gin; Hollands Gin). A Dutch Gin, the national drink of Holland. Unlike mildly flavored Dry Gin, Geneva Gin is heavy in body and pungent of juniper, with pronounced grain character. Geneva Gin is distilled at low proof from a fermented mash of barley malt, rye and corn. After this distillation, juniper berries, which give the Gin its typical flavor, are added to the malt-wine, and it is then redistilled. Geneva Gin should always be served ice cold—never at room temperature. It is served straight, and except for the possible addition of a dash of bitters is never used in mixed drinks. See also **Dry Gin, Gin.**

**GERMAN BRANDY:** A blend of specially selected distillates of European wines, matured in oak wood; characteristic mellow brandy taste. **Uses:** German Brandy is enjoyed straight, both before dinner and after dinner with coffee; a refreshing drink with soda. See also **Brandy.**

**GIN:** A family of liquors flavored with juniper and other aromatics. Two distinctive types of gin are produced—the **Dry Gin** or **London Dry Gin** type that dominates the American market and the Dutch **Geneva** or **Hollands Gin.** See **Dry Gin, Dutch Gin, Flavored Gin, Geneva Gin, Hollands Gin, Lemon Flavored**

Fleischmann's Gin—A distillate of juniper berries and other botanicals, Fleischmann's is "today's" style of Gin—clean, clear, smooth.

Gin, London Dry Gin, Mint Flavored Gin, Old Tom Gin, Orange Flavored Gin, Steinhager.

**GINGER FLAVORED BRANDY:** Pure grape brandy with the true flavor and aroma of ginger roots and other aromatics. Light brown. **Uses:** Straight, as an after-dinner liqueur; in highball; ingredient in a number of mixed drinks. Especially invigorating with a pleasant, warming effect on cold days. See also **Cordial.**

**GOLD LIQUEUR: Goldwasser** (see).

**GOLD-O-MINT:** Golden-colored **Creme de Menthe** (see).

**GOLDWASSER:** (also called **Liqueur d'Or;** Gold Liqueur; Gold Water.) Sweet white cordial with a citrus fruit peel and spice flavor. Contains tiny flakes of gold leaf so slight they cannot be felt on the tongue. **Use:** Straight, as an after-dinner liqueur. See also **Cordial.**

**GRAND MARNIER:** An aristocratic French liqueur of oranges and Cognac. Used in cooking. Spectacular 100 and 150-year commemorative cuvees can be found at high, but fair, prices.

*Der Lachs Goldwasser—A liqueur based on anise and caraway seeds, with flakes of gold added into the bottle. The port of Danzig, now Gdansk, is renowed for Silberwasser (silver flaked liqueur) as well as gold. Der Lachs has been producing brandies and cordials for almost 400 years.*

**GRAPPA:** Brandy distilled from the pulpy residue—the grape pomace—of the wine press. In France, this brandy is called **Marc** (Eau de Vie de Marc). **Uses:** See **Brandy.**

**GREEK BRANDY:** Soft, mellow liquor, comparatively sweet, as Cognac used to be. Distilled from grapes, with the gum of native Greek pine added to impart much of its unique flavor. **Uses:** After-dinner drink, straight, before dinner, in many cocktails, especially the Old Fashioned and Manhattan, with soda as a brandy highball. See also **Brandy.**

**GRENADINE:** Bright red flavoring syrup blending the tastes of pomegranate, strawberry and raspberry fruits.

**GUIGNOLET:** A special liqueur distilled in France from Guignes, a type of sweet cherries.

# H

**HIMBEER LIQUEUR:** German raspberry liqueur; red. Derives characteristic bouquet and taste from fresh raspberry juice. **Uses:** After-dinner liqueur, in mixed drinks. See also **Cordial.**

**HIMBEERGEIST:** German raspberry brandy.

**HOLLANDS GIN:** A Dutch gin type, also called **Geneva Gin** (see). See also **Gin.**

# I

**INGWER:** German ginger liqueur.

**IRISH WHISKEY:** Distinctive whiskey of Ireland. This whiskey is produced in two types: (1) the traditional Irish, a blend of straight pot still whiskeys, hearty and full-bodied; and (2) the new style, light, soft and mellow in taste, a blending of the heavy pot still and lighter column still grain whiskeys. Irish whiskey is made from barley principally, both malted and unmalted, together with oats, wheat and sometimes a small proportion of rye. Unlike Scotch, Irish Whiskey does not have a "smokey" taste—the malted barley is dried in kilns constructed so that the smoke from the fuel does not come in contact with the malt. **Uses: See Malt.**

**IRISH MIST:** From Ireland, a secret blend of four whiskeys, honeys, heather, clover, and essence of a dozen herbs. A proprietary brand.

**IRISH WHISKEY—A BLEND:** Label designation also authorized U.S. regulation for Irish Whiskey produced as a mixture of distilled spirits.

**IVETTE (Creme d'):** The trade name for a purple liqueur with the taste of violets. Similar to **Parfait Amour** (see).

**IZARRA:** Green and yellow cordials, similar to Chartreuse, from the Basque region of the Pyrenees on the French-Spanish frontier.

# J

**JÄGERMEISTER:** From Germany, a popular blend of 56 roots, herbs, and fruits. Used as an aperitif or as a digestive.

**JAMAICA RUM:** Full-bodied rum, heavy of rum flavor and pungent of bouquet and body; rich golden hue and dark color; distilled in pot stills. **Uses:** Popular in Planters' Punch and many

*"Black Bush" is an enormously satisfying and rich whiskey, best saved for drinking as one would the fine cognac or armagnac.*

other rum cocktails; in cooking; as flavoring on cakes, ice cream and in frostings. See **Rum.**

**JACOJBINER:** Rich, German monastery-type liqueur prepared by an ancient formula of selected fruits, herbs and flowers, aged in grape brandy.

## K

**KAHLUA:** Mexican coffee-flavored liqueur. The ingredient in the "Black Russian" and "White Russian" as well as "Mexican Coffee." Very popular.

**KAISERBIRN LIQUEUR:** (Also called **Bergamotte Liqueur**). Yellow, pear-flavored German cordial, deriving characteristic

bouquet and taste from juice of a variety of pears native to southern Europe. **Use:** After-dinner liqueur. See also **Cordial.**

**KIRSCHWASSER (Kirsch):** Fruit brandy distilled from cherries. Smooth, mellow, with the subtle fragrance of cherries. Colorless. **Uses:** Straight, in highballs; in cooking; in flaming desserts, notably Cherries Jubilee. See also **Brandy.**

**KONRADINER LIQUEUR:** Yellow German liqueur with an herb-like flavor; produced as a flavor blend of selected fruits, plants and flowers. **Uses:** After-dinner liqueur, in mixed drinks. See also **Cordial.**

**KROATZBEER LIQUEUR:** Dark red German cordial with a blackberry-like flavor derived from the juice of fresh Kroatzbeer (a berry native to Germany and similar in taste and color to the blackberry). **Use:** After-dinner liqueur. See also **Cordial.**

**KUMMEL: (Kuemmel):** White liqueur with the pleasing, piquant flavor of the caraway seed. Neither too sweet nor too dry, and thus appealing to both masculine and feminine tastes. Also comes in very dry type. Produced as a flavor-blend of caraway and other seeds, herbs and spices. **Uses:** Straight, in a number of cocktails, in cooking recipes, as an after-dinner liqueur, in coffee, ingredient in Coffee Royal, with Kummel a long-time favorite. See also **Cordial.**

## L

**LE GRANDE PASSION:** French blend of armagnac with passion fruit. A proprietary brand.

**LEMON FLAVORED GIN:** See **Flavored Gin.**

**LIQUEUR:** Sweetened, flavored family of liquors; also termed **Cordial** (see).

**LIQUEUR ST. MONICA:** Smooth, rich amber liqueur deriving characteristic bouquet and flavor from many different roots, leaves and peels, predominantly Angelica, Hyssop and Melissa, along with spices. **Uses:** Straight: as an after-dinner liqueur, frappe, in numerous cocktails. See also **Cordial.**

**LIQUEUR D'OR:** Also called **Goldwasser** (see).

**LIQUEUR MONASTIQUE:** Herb-like liqueur of monastic tradition produced from ancient formula using over 30 herbs, seeds, roots and flowers. **Uses:** As an after-dinner liqueur; sometimes preferred half and half with brandy. See also **Cordial.**

**LOCHAN ORA:** Trade name for a delightful Scotch Whiskey liqueur with so-called Monastery overtones. Produced by Chivas Regal.

**LONDON DRY GIN:** Crisp, clean, white liquor, aromatic of juniper to the taste. See **Dry Gin.**

# M

**MALIBU:** From Canada, flavor blend of white rum and coconut. A proprietary brand.

**MALT WHISKEY:** Like **Straight Malt Whiskey,** except for age. When the label says only, ''Malt Whiskey,'' without the word ''Straight,'' the whiskey may have **any age up to 2 years. Straight Wheat Whiskey** will be a minimum of 2 years old.

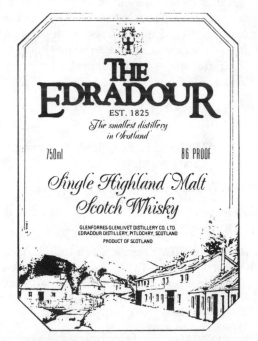

*The Edradour Single Malt Scotch Whisky—A delicious single malt from the highlands of Scotland. The Edradour is the tiniest distillery in Scotland. Extremely high quality. Lofty, like a great cognac.*

**MALT WHISKEY—A BLEND:** Blended Whiskey containing a minimum of 51% Straight Malt Whiskey and Neutral Spirits. Also labeled **Blended Malt Whiskey.**

**MANDARINE NAPOLEON:** Belgian liqueur based on tangerines and Cognac.

**MARASCHINO:** White Aromatic liqueur with the clean, rich taste of marasca cherries. **Uses:** After-dinner liqueur; excellent in Daiquiris, punches, wines cups, over chilled melon balls, peaches, berries, fruit salads. See **Cordial.**

**MARC (Eau de Vie de Marc):** In France, brandy distilled from the pulpy residue—the grape pomace—of the wine press. Elsewhere, this brandy is called **Grappa. Uses:** See **Brandy.**

**MARTINIQUE RUM:** Rum distilled in Martinique and shipped to Bordeaux, France, where it is blended and reshipped to world markets. Pronounced rum flavor. Amber. **Uses:** In Planters' Punch and other rum drinks; in black coffee; in cooking; as flavoring in baking and desserts. See **Rum.**

**MASTIC:** Sweet, white Greek liqueur, licorice-like in flavor. Slightly drier than **Ouzo;** much drier and more potent than **Anisette** (see). Flavor derived from aniseed and sap of tree of Cashew family. **Uses:** All-occasion liqueur, enjoyed both before and after meals.

**MASTICHA:** White Greek-type liqueur with anise and mastic taste. Made by distillation of aniseeds and gum mastic.

**METAXA:** A world-renowned Greek brandy. The Metaxa firm bottles several starred versions, as well as a resinated Mastic and a Grande Fine liqueur.

**MIDORI:** Light refreshing taste of fresh honeydew in this green liqueur from Japan. A proprietary brand.

**MINT FLAVORED GIN:** See **Flavored Gin.**

**MIRABELLE:** Fruit brandy distilled from plums. Generally, Mirabelle designates plum brandy originating in Alsace, France, where it is also called **Quetsch.** More popularly, plum brandy is known as **Slivovitz** (see). **Uses:** See **Brandy.**

**MOCCA:** Coffee liqueur type; aromatic coffee flavor drawn from mocca and vanilla beans. **Uses:** After-dinner liqueur, straight.

Metaxa—Greece's most renowned brandy. Metaxa produces several ages and grades of brandy, giving star designations to distinguish between them. This is the superlative 7-star. Enjoy it as you would a fine Cognac.

Midori Melon Liqueur—A delicious cordial with the fragrance and flavor of a honeydew melon. It is the main ingredient in the Melon Ball cocktail. It can be used neat, over ice, as a topping on ice cream or in baking.

# N

**NEUTRAL SPIRITS:** An alcoholic spirit purified in the still to a minimum of 95% absolute alcoholic purity. At that degree of proof—190°—the spirit is considered to have no important taste, and little body or flavor. By U.S. law, Neutral Spirits may be distilled from "any material." Almost always, they are distilled from grain. Neutral Spirits are used to make **Blended Whiskey.** In original distillation, or redistillation, over juniper berries and other aromatics, Neutral Spirits become **Dry Gin.** Filtered through charcoal, Neutral Spirits become **Vodka.** Neutral Spirits are also the base for many **Cordials** and **Liqueurs.**

**NEW ENGLAND RUM:** Full-bodied rum produced in U.S. from molasses shipped from the West Indies; distilled at less than 160° proof and always a **straight** rum. **Uses:** Popular in the Planters' Punch and many other rum cocktails; used in cooking and as flavoring on cakes, ice cream and in frostings. See **Rum.**

# O

**OCHA:** Japanese cordial. Green. Produced with flavor drawn from green tea. Rich sweet tea taste. **Uses:** After-dinner liqueur; 1 jigger Ocha in glass of hot water with twist of lemon makes delightful hot tea; 1 jigger Ocha in glass of cold water with twist of lemon makes cold tea refreshment.

*Metaxa Ouzo—A popular aperitif in Greece, based on anis. Similar to France's Ricard or Pernod or Italy's Anisette. Ouzo is clear, but turns milky and cloudy when chilled or poured over ice.*

**OLD TOM GIN:** Traditional Dry Gin, sweetened by the addition of sugar syrup. See **Dry Gin, Gin.**

**ORANGE CURACAO:** See **Curacao.**

**ORANGE FLAVORED GIN:** See **Flavored Gin, Gin.**

**ORGEAT (Sirop d'):** A syrup flavored with almonds and oranged flower water and emulsified with tragacanth gum.

**OUZO:** Sweet, white Greek liqueur, licorice-like in flavor. Slightly sweeter than **Mastic;** much drier and more potent than **Anisette** (see). Flavor derived from aniseed. **Uses:** All-occasion liqueur, enjoyed both before and after meals either straight, on the rocks or with water.

# P

**PARFAIT AMOUR:** Exotic liqueur, with flavors produced from flowers. Color ranges from ruby to pale lilac. **Uses:** After-dinner liqueur or frappe.

**PASTIS:** A colorful anis-based spirit. It becomes cloudy if poured over ice or mixed with water. Popular brands are Pernod and **Ricard.**

**PEACH FLAVORED BRANDY:** Pure grape brandy with the true flavor and aroma of fresh, ripe peaches; generally drier, lighter-bodied and more potent than **Apricot Liqueur** (see). Classified as a cordial. Amber. **Uses:** Straight, as an after-dinner liqueur, frapped, with soda, as an ingredient in many cocktails and tall drinks, in fruit punches, over ice cream, in fresh fruit sherbets and compotes, for "flaming" desserts, over sliced pound cake, in many food recipes. See also **Cordial.**

**PEACH LIQUEUR:** Sweet, rich liqueur with the flavor and aroma of fresh, ripe peaches; sweeter, fuller-bodied and lighter proof than **Peach Flavored Brandy** (see). Amber. **Uses:** Straight, as after-dinner liqueur, in tall drinks, with soda, in fruit punches, over ice cream, in fresh fruit sherbets and compotes, over sliced pound cake, in candying vegetables and basting meats and fowl. See also **Cordial.**

**PEAR WILLIAM:** Delicate liqueur or eau de vie from fresh Anjou pears from France's Loire Valley. Some Pear William comes from Switzerland as well.

**PECHER MIGNON:** French liqueur made from white peaches. A proprietary brand.

**PEPPERMINT GET:** A trade name for a **Creme de Menthe.** High quality.

**PEPPERMINT SCHNAPPS:** Dry, white peppermint-flavored liqueur; lighter-bodied and not as sweet as **Creme de Menthe** (see). Has pleasant aftertaste in which the odor of alcohol is not discernable. **Uses:** After-dinner liqueur; enjoyed by many as all-occasion drink; frequently used in place of White Creme de Menthe when lighter-bodied, less sweet peppermint cordial is required. See also **Cordial.**

**PERONETTE:** Light green cordial with anise taste. **Uses:** See **Cordial.**

**PERSICO (or Persicot):** This ancient liqueur is made from bitter almonds, parsley, cloves, cinnamon, sugar, and alcohol.

*Mohawk Peach Flavored Vodka—Vodka with flavors added has been popular in Russia for centuries. Mohawk Peach Flavored Vodka is well-balanced. Not syrupy like a cordial; not strong like a Vodka. Clean and fresh.*

**PETER HEERING:** Danish **Cherry Liqueur.** Flavor and aroma from the juices of fresh, ripe Danish cherries. Proprietary brand. See also **Cherry Heering.**

**PETITE LIQUEUR:** From France, cognac and sparkling wine with a hint of coffee. A proprietary brand from Moët and Chandon.

**PFLUMLIWASSER:** German plum brandy.

**PIMM'S CUP #!:** A concentrate from Great Britain of gin, aromatics and sweetners. It is recommended that you add some ice, lemon soda and a rind of cucumber. Substitution of Champagne makes it a Pimm's Royal.

**PINEAU DES CHARENTES:** A sweet aperitif consisting of Cognac and grape juice.

**PISCO:** A **Marc** or **Grappa** from a Latin American country. Most acclaimed is Inca Pisco from Peru.

**PRALINE LIQUEUR:** Rich mellow vanilla and pecan-based flavor of the original New Orleans Praline confection. Proprietary brand. Popular in baking.

**PRUNELLE (Liqueur de):** This is made from the meat of the plum pit, figs, vanilla beans, sugar, and alcohol. Popular as a digestive in Italy.

**PUERTO RICAN RUM:** Dry, light rum, brandy-like to the taste, with slight molasses flavor. *White Label* is more delicate in aroma and flavor; *Gold Label* is a little sweeter, with a more pronounced rum flavor. Distilled at high proof in column stills, aged one to three years and blended by traditional methods. **Uses:** Straight, on the rocks (with a twist of lemon peel), in highball with favorite mixer, in many mixed drinks, in gourmet dishes, as flavoring for puddings, cakes and other desserts, as topping over ice cream. See **Rum.**

**PULQUE:** A Mexican beverage made of the fermented juice of the agave plant, which is the plant used to create **Tequila.**

# Q

**QUETSCH:** Fruit brandy distilled from plums. See **Mirabelle.**

# R

**RASPBERRY LIQUEUR:** Sweet, rich liqueur with the flavor and aroma of fresh raspberries. Deep red color. **Uses:** Straight, as an after-dinner liqueur with soda, as topping over vanilla ice cream, in fruit punches. See also **Cordial.**

**RAKI:** A Near Eastern distillate, usually based on anis.

**RATAFIA:** A name formerly used in France to designate a liqueur obtained by the maceration of fruits in alcohol or brandy with distillation. A festive drink created originally to celebrate "ratifications" of treaties.

**RICARD:** Anise and herb liqueur from France. A proprietary brand, extremely successful in France. See **Pastis.**

**ROCK & RYE:** Sweet, hearty rye whiskey-flavored cordial.

Amber made as a blending of rye whiskey with rock candy and fruits — lemon, oranges and cherries. **Uses:** Straight, in toddies, gives a new taste character to the Old Fashioned, an ingredient in many other drinks.

**ROCK & RYE CRYSTALLIZED:** Like Rock & Rye, but sweeter. Made as a blending of rye whiskey with rock sugar which crystallizes out when cooled. **Uses:** Straight, as Hot Toddy, in highball.

**ROSOLIO (also called Rossolis or Rosoglio):** A liqueur consumed mostly in Italy and Turkey, made from petals of red roses, orange blossom water, cinnamon, clove, jasmine, alcohol, and varying amounts of sugar. Very popular in Italy.

**RUM:** A family of liquors distilled from the fermented juice of sugar cane or molasses. Rum is produced in virtually all of the various sugar countries in New England (from West Indies molasses). There are many differences in these rums — that is why rum's geography is important. The differences result from the methods of distilling, aging and blending, and the water, climate and soil in which the sugar cane grows. Rum is attractive straight, but earns its major following in America as a mixed drink. Rum blends perfectly with fruits and other liquors, makes an ideal base for a great many cocktails pleasing to most people. See **Barbados Rum, Batavia Arrac, Cuban Rum, Demerara Rum, Jamaica Rum, Martinique Rum, New England Rum, Puerto Rican Rum, Virgin Island Rum.**

**RYE:** Popular Eastern name for Blended Whiskey. "Rye" is widely applied to this whiskey type, although by Federal definition it is a misnomer. Actually, the typical Blended Whiskey brand is likely to contain both Straight Rye and Straight Bourbon, and possibly other grain flavors, balanced with Neutral Spirits.

**RYE WHISKEY:** Like **Straight Rye Whiskey,** except for age. When the label says only "Rye Whiskey" without the word "Straight" this whiskey may have **any age up to 2 years.** Straight Rye Whiskey will be a minimum of 2 years old.

**RYE WHISKEY — A BLEND:** A mixture, or blend of Neutral Spirits and a minimum of 51% Straight Rye Whiskey; also labeled **Blended Rye Whiskey.**

**RYE MALT WHISKEY:** Like **Straight Rye Malt Whiskey,** except for age. When the label says only "Rye Malt Whiskey"

*Lemon Hart Demerara Rum — This rum from Guyana is named for the Demerara River where sugar cane grows. The firm of Lemon Hart and Sons makes several rums including this "overproof" of 151 proof rum. This type of rum is used not only cocktails but in cooking, especially in the preparation of flaming desserts.*

without the word "Straight" the whiskey may have any age up to 2 years. Straight Rye Malt Whiskey will be a minimum of 2 years old.

# S

**SABRA:** Flavors of Jaffa orange and fine chocolate are combined in this Mediterranean liqueur. A proprietary brand from Israel.

**SAMBUCA:** A colorless Italian cordial with a sweet anise-like taste. On the rocks or with water, it becomes opalescent. Often used as a sweetener for espresso. Based on the Black Elder plant.

**SAURER MIT PERSIKO LIQUEUR:** Red fruity-flavored German liqueur with a bouquet and taste derived from a flavor-blend of the juice of ripe cherries, peaches and peach pits. **Use:** After-dinner liqueur. See also **Cordial.**

*Sambuca Romana—America's favorite Sambuca, a cordial derived from the elder shrub. Enjoy it neat or as a "sweetener" for demitasse or espresso coffee.*

*Basilica Sambuca—A delicious Sambuca that offers quality at a reasonable price. At its best in Italian coffee.*

*Sambuca Molinari—A high quality Sambuca that enjoys great success in Italy. The luscious, complex texture and taste are increasing its popularity in the U.S.*

**SCHNAPPS:** Light, refreshing, and easy to enjoy, these untraditional liqueurs are made primarily for after-dinner sipping, because they are too sweet and syrupy for straight drinking. Enjoyed with many mixers, especially peach with orange juice. Some proprietary schnapps brands: Apple Barrel, Aspen Glacial (peppermint), Cool Mint, Cristal (anise), DeKuyper Harvest Pear (Bartlett pears), DeKuyper Peachtree (peaches), Dr. McGillicuddy (menthomint), Hot Shot (peach), Minttu Pepp (peppermint), Rumple Minz (peppermint), Steel (peppermint), Super Schnapps (peppermint).

**SCOTCH WHISKY:** Distinctive whisky of Scotland. Scotch is renowned as a blending of hearty barley malt whiskies produced in traditional pot stills and the light grain whiskies made in column stills. Scotch is soft, light-bodied, mellow to the taste, with the subtle, gentle aroma of peat (heather, evergreen and fern compressed by nature over the ages)—the "smoky" flavor for which Scotch is famed. Scotch draws its special character from two primary factors: (1) The drying of the malted barley over peat fires—the smoke impregnates the barley and gives Scotch its smoky taste; and (2), the use, in the original mash, of the native soft waters which flow down from the Highlands.

**SINGLE MALT SCOTCH:** Unblended Scotch Whisky.

**SLIVOVITZ:** Fruit brandy distilled from plums; soft, pleasant, with mellow plum fragrance. Comes gold and white (colorless). **Uses:** See **Brandy.**

**SLOE GIN:** Rich, red cordial with delicate bouquet and tangy fruity flavor resembling wild cherries. Made generally as a blend of sloe berries, from which it derives its primary flavor, and other fruits in a pure spirit. **Uses:** Main ingredient in Sloe Gin Fizz, in highball with soda or ginger ale, ingredient in icy fruit punches and other mixed drinks. See **Cordial.**

**SOUTHERN COMFORT:** Sweet, rich American liqueur based on peaches, whiskey, oranges and herbs. Used in the "Old Fashioned" and in many other cocktails.

**SOUR MASH:** Term often used in connection with Straight Whiskey, identifies a production process, distinguished from the "Sweet Mash" technique of distillation. The name has nothing to do with the taste of the whiskey — Sour Mash Whiskeys are rich and mellow. It is inherited from the early distillers and refers to the natural fermentation of the yeast and the grain. In the Sour Mash process, strained de-alcoholized "beer" from the previous fermentation is mixed with the mash of grain. This is done because certain properties in the spent "beer" are said to aid in developing the individuality of the whiskey.

**SPANISH BRANDY:** Brandy distilled from sherry wine, soft, mellow, not quite as dry as traditional brandy. **Uses:** Straight as an after-dinner drink; with soda or tonic in a highball; in coffee; as an ingredient in many cocktails; in cooking recipes, as flavoring for desserts. See also **Brandy.**

**SPIRIT WHISKEY:** A whiskey type, in today's market, containing less than 20% Whiskey or Straight Whiskey in combination with Neutral Spirits. By legal definition, it may consist of Neutral Spirits and not less than 5% by volume of Whiskey or Neutral Spirits and less than 20% by volume of Straight Whiskey, but not less than 5% by volume of Straight Whiskey, or Straight Whiskey and Whiskey.

**ST. DOMINIC:** Spicy, straw-colored liqueur made by a distillation of roots and herbs in brandy; proprietary brand. **Use:** After-dinner liqueur, straight or half-and-half. See also **Cordial.**

**ST. PAULI LIQUEUR:** Dark red German liqueur with the aromatic taste of cherries and rum. Derives characteristic bouquet and taste from flavors of **Kirschwasser (cherry brandy)** and **rum. Use:** After-dinner liqueur. See also **Cordial.**

*This 12 year old whisky by Glen Moray is one of the finest examples of a single malt (unblended) Scotch from the region of the Highlands. It is pale gold in color, elegant, smooth yet firm, with exquisite dryness and length of finish.*

*Glenfiddich — "Glenfiddich" means "the valley of the deer" in Gaelic. This is a single malt, or an unblended Scotch. Very fine. Enjoy it neat.*

**STEINHAGER:** German Westphalian Gin, white and dry like the **London Dry** types. Steinhager has the faint taste of herbs, like all **Dry Gins,** but with slightly more pronounced juniper character. **Uses:** Almost always enjoyed neat on the Continent; featured in U.S. for use in the Martini (4 to 1 with Dry Vermouth). "Over Rocks," Steinhager itself has the taste of a Dry Martini. See also **Dry Gin.**

**STONSDORFER KRAUTER LIQUEUR:** Brown German liqueur with herb-like flavor. **Use:** After-dinner liqueur. See also **Cordial.**

**STRAIGHT WHISKEY:** An alcoholic distillate of a fermented mash of grain, indentified by characteristic taste, body and aroma, and bottled exactly as it comes from the barrel in which it has matured, except for the addition of pure water to reduce the proof to bottle proof. By law, Straight Whiskey is aged a minimum of 2 years in new charred oak barrels. Distillation may not exceed 160°, it must be withdrawn from the cistern room (for barreling) at not more than 110° or less than 80° proof; it must be bottled at not less than 80° proof. The distiller may call this product Straight Whiskey without a grain tag whether or not one grain predominates in the mash from which it is made. The distiller may use the grain tag (as **Straight Bourbon Whiskey** or **Straight Rye Whiskey**) when 51% or more of the grain from which the whiskey is fermented consists of that grain. **Straight Corn Whiskey,** an exception, is made from a mash containing at least 80% corn. Two or more Straight Whiskeys may also be combined as **Blends of Straight Whiskeys** or **Blends of Straight Bourbon (or Rye) Whiskeys. Bottled-in-Bond Whiskeys** are blood brothers of the Straight Whiskeys. Among the Straight Whiskeys identified by a grain tag, Straight Bourbon primarily and Straight Rye are the only whiskeys important in the market. Federal law also identifies **Straight Corn Whiskey, Straight Wheat Whiskey, Straight Malt Whiskey** and **Straight Rye Malt Whiskey.** Each is distilled from a mash in which the grain specified constitutes 51% of the formula. **Uses:** See **Whiskey.**

**STRAIGHT BOURBON WHISKEY:** Mellow, full-bodied whiskey with characteristic Bourbon flavor and taste; light and yet well-defined in aroma and bouquet. This distinctive whiskey type is produced form fermented mash of corn, rye and barley malt and is aged a minimum of 2 years in new charred oak barrels. The

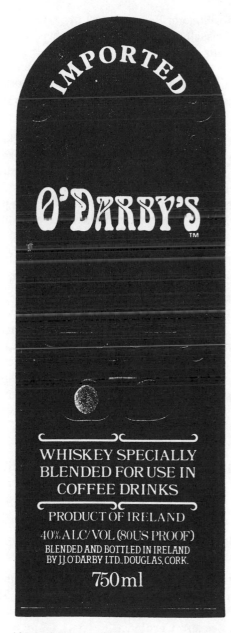

IMPORTED

O'DARBY'S
™

WHISKEY SPECIALLY
BLENDED FOR USE IN
COFFEE DRINKS

PRODUCT OF IRELAND
40% ALC/VOL (80 US PROOF)
BLENDED AND BOTTLED IN IRELAND
BY J.J. O'DARBY LTD., DOUGLAS, CORK.
750ml

*O'Darby's, a blend of 80% Canadian Whisky and 20% Scotch Whisky, is specially blended to form a perfect marriage with the distinctive flavor of good American coffee.*

grain formula for Straight Bourbon must by law contain not less than 51% corn; usually the proportion is higher—about 65% to 75%. (A larger proportion of corn tends to produce a lighter-bodied whiskey; more of the rye and barley grains produce heavier-bodied Bourbon.) Straight Bourbon is the most important of the Straight Whiskey types identified by a grain tag. **Uses:** See **Whiskey.**

**STRAIGHT CORN WHISKEY:** A white or colorless whiskey produced from a grain mash of which not less than 80% must be corn and aged in uncharred oak containers or reused charred oak containers a minimum of 2 years. Somewhat lighter in body than Bourbon. Corn Whiskey, like Bourbon and Rye, is a product of early America. Today, its primary market is in the South.

**STRAIGHT MALT WHISKEY:** Whiskey distilled from a mash of grain of which not less than 51% consists of malted barley, and aged a minimum of 2 years in new charred oak barrels.

**STRAIGHT RYE WHISKEY:** A hearty, rich whiskey, heavier-bodied than Straight Bourbon and with more pronounced aroma and bouquet; characteristic Rye flavor. This distincitive type whiskey is produced from fermented mash of rye, corn and malted barley and aged a minimum of 2 years in new charred oak barrels. By law, the grain formula for Straight Rye Whiskey must contain not less than 51% rye. Typically, a higher proportion of rye grain is used to bring out the characteristic taste, body and aroma of this whiskey—usually about two-thirds of the mash. **Uses:** See **Whiskey.**

**STRAIGHT RYE MALT WHISKEY:** Whiskey distilled form a mash of grain of which not less than 51% consists of malted rye, and aged a minimum of 2 years in new charred oak barrels.

**STRAIGHT WHEAT WHISKEY:** Whiskey distilled from a mash of grain of which not less than 51% consists of wheat grain, and aged a minimum of 2 years in new charred oak barrels.

**STRAWBERRY LIQUEUR:** Sweet, rich liqueur with the flavor and aroma of fresh ripe strawberries. Light red. **Uses:** Straight, as an after-dinner cordial, in cocktails, with soda in a highball, in fruit punches. See also **Cordial.**

**STREGA:** A green-gold, herb-flavored sweet liqueur from Benevento in Southern Italy.

*Suntory Whiskey—A blended whisky from the Far East's most important distiller. This noteworthy product has a taste described as "slightly east of Scotch."*

**SWEDISH PUNSCH:** A sweet liqueur made from a base of **Batavia Arrac** (see) and flavored. The national liqueur of Scandinavia. **Use:** Straight as after-dinner drink.

# T

**TAFEL AQUAVIT:** See **Aquavit.**

**TEQUILA:** Mexican spirits distilled from the fermented jucie of the Mescal plant. Distinctive dry character; white and gold. The Mescal plant takes years to grow; when picked resembles a huge pineapple. Plant is baked in ovens, crushed and the juice extracted. Juice is fermented and distilled in pot stills. Spirit comes from still. White. Tequila Gold is the result of aging in oak barrels. **Uses:** Principally, in the U.S., in mixed drinks—the Margarita; in virtually all gin and vodka drinks.

**TIA MARIA:** "Aunt Mary." Jamaican coffee and rum cordial.

**TRIPLE SEC:** White orange-flavored liqueur. Made from the same ingredients as **Curacao.** A flavor-blend of the peels of tangy Curacao and sweet oranges, but differs from Curacao as follows: Triple Sec has more tangy orange character, more total flavor, higher in proof, drier and is water clear. **Uses:** After-dinner cordial; ingredient in numerous cocktails; in food recipes such as crepe suzettes; over fruit cup, ice cream and fruit compote. See also **Cordial.**

**TUACA:** Golden liqueur with hint of herbs and fruit peels in a brandy base. A proprietary brand from Italy.

# V

**VANDERMINT:** Dutch chocolate with touch of mint. A proprietary brand. Imported from Holland.

**VIRGIN ISLAND RUM:** Light and dry rum; also produced as more intermediate type. *White Label* is pale and light and *Gold Label* has more pronounced rum flavor. **Uses:** Straight; on the rocks (with twist of lemon peel); in highball with favorite mixer; in many mixed drinks; as flavoring for puddings, cakes and other desserts; as topping over ice cream. See **Rum.**

**VODKA:** Light, crisp, dry distilled spirit—colorless and flavorless; leaves little, if any, aromatic odor on the breath. Vodka is made by passing highly refined Neutral Spirits through charcoal, by redistillation or other government approved process. **Uses:** Straight as an appetizer (always chilled); over rocks (with twist of lemon peel or few drops of aromatic or orange bitters); in tall drinks with virtually every kind of juice and flavor of cider, ginger beer, orange, tomato, pineapple, apple, grapefruit juice; in many cocktails, notably the Vodka Martini. See **Zubrovka.**

# W

**WACHOLDER:** A German distillate with juniper and other botanicals. In other words, "German Gin."

**WESTPHALIAN GIN:** See **Steinhager.**

**WHEAT WHISKEY:** Like **Straight Wheat Whiskey,** except for age. When the label says only "Wheat Whiskey," without the word "Straight," the whiskey may have **any age up to 2 years.** Straight Wheat Whiskey will be a minimum of 2 years old.

*Elduris is a quality, premium-priced, imported vodka from Iceland. Pronounced "El-dur-ees," the name comes from* Eldur, *which means "fire," and* Is, *which means "ice." That unusual combination gives Iceland one of the most beautiful and pure environments on earth, and a vodka unlike any in the world.*

*Suntory Vodka – Vodka can be produced anywhere. It does require an excellent distiller to capture the clean style associated with Vodka. Suntory, Japan's biggest and best distiller, is one of the world's most important producers of spirits.*

*The world's best Vodka is Russian. The U.S.A. has Vodkas from Sweden, Finland and many other lands. From the U.S.S.R. we have the exceptional Stolichnaya.*

*Fleishmann's Vodka, a popular, clean, crisp, dry distilled spirit, is made by passing refined neutral spirits through charcoal.*

310

**WHEAT WHISKEY—A BLEND:** Blended Whiskey containing a minimum of 51% **Straight Wheat Whiskey** and Neutral Spirits. Also labeled **Blended Wheat Whiskey.**

**WHISKEY:** America's national alcoholic beverage. Whiskey is distilled from a fermented mash of grain, identified by characteristic taste, body and aroma, and distilled in conformity with the laws of the Federal Government. Federal Standards of Identity list more than 30 different types of whiskey. In this family of whiskeys are Straight Whiskeys (whiskeys as they come from the barrel, aged 2 or more years, and including also the Blends of Straight Whiskeys); Blended Whiskeys (whiskeys containing Straight Whiskeys and Neutral Spirits); Whiskeys (whiskeys without age or with brief age); and the imported whiskeys (Scotch, Canadian, Irish). **Uses:** Whiskey is an all-purpose liquor for every serving occasion; enjoyed straight, in highball with favorite mixer (water, soda, ginger ale, Seven-Up or cola); on the rocks (plain or with twist of lemon peel); in numerous mixed drinks, blending with the widest variety of fruit juices and other flavors.

*Cutty Sark Blended Scots Whisky—One of the leading brands of Scotch in the world. Cutty Sark is light in style and smooth tasting. This aristocratic blend is distilled, aged and bottled in Scotland.*

*Clan MacGregor Blended Scotch Whisky—A light-bodied, smooth Scotch blend. Great value. Note that the Scotches and Canadians are Whiskies (Whisky); Americans and Irish are Whiskeys (Whiskey).*

**WHISKEY—A BLEND:** A mixture or blend of Neutral Spirits and Straight Whiskey; also labeled **Blended Whiskey.**

**WHISKEY—NO EARNED AGE:** Straight Whiskey identifies aged whiskey—whiskey which is aged a minimum of 2 years. The label "Whiskey" without the word "Straight," identifies a type of whiskey not required to earn age. Usually, it is artificially colored. By Government Standards, it must be distilled from a mash of grain at under 190° proof, compared with Straight Whiskey's maximum 160° proof. (Occasionally, a distiller may choose to label a brand only "Whiskey," followed by a statement "4 years old" or "5 years old." Actually, this whiskey is "Straight Whiskey.")

**WILD TURKEY LIQUEUR:** Bourbon base, herbs, spices, and other natural flavorings. Proprietary brand. Amber color. From Kentucky.

**WISHNIAK:** A Polish liqueur made from cherries and spices.

**WISNIOWKA:** Red cherry liqueur made by the percolation and distillation of wild cherries. **Uses:** After-dinner liqueur; may be enjoyed straight at any time. See also **Cordial.**

# Y

**YUKON JACK:** A Canadian liqueur reminiscent of **Southern Comfort.**

# Z

**ZITRONEN EIS LIQUEUR:** Yellow lemon-flavored German liqueur with characteristic bouquet and taste derived from flavor-blend of fresh lemon juice, sugar and distillate of fresh lemon peel. **Uses:** Refreshing drink, especially in warm weather, over ice cubes; half-and-half with Dry Gin over ice. See also **Cordial.**

**ZUBROVKA:** Vodka-flavored by Zubrovka grass. The grass steeped in Vodka six months to a year gives it green or yellow color and distinctive flavor. **Uses:** Straight or on the rocks; in Martini, with tonic water, in Collins—in any recipe that calls for Vodka. See **Vodka.**

*Suntory Draft Beer—Modern technology makes it possible to ship fragile draft beer in consumer packages. Draft beer is unpasteurized and has an unforgettable taste when enjoyed young.*

# PART TWO: MALT BEVERAGES

*Eins, Zwei, Drei, Vier,*
Lift your stein and drink your beer!

*The Student Prince*

Beer, an ancient beverage, is produced today in many countries. Whether made at a large brewery or a microbrewery, beer is the result of good natural ingredients, scientific technology, and the artistry of the brew master. Increased use of refrigeration has accelerated beer's popularity. Increased also is interest in beer memorabilia, such as trays and posters, some of which are both beautiful and priceless.

## The History of Beer

Beer, or fermented cereal brew, predates written history. A document, dating back to 6000 B.C. in Babylonia, speaks of beer preparation to be used at a religious service. Cereal brews were commonly used in ancient Egypt and China. The Greek goddess Demeter and her Roman counterpart, Ceres, both had barley malt brews. A minor diety, Gambrinus, appeared in the Roman Pantheon. He was the God of Beer, and friend to Ceres and to Bacchus, God of Wine. Gambrinus was later made a King in Holland and Belgium, where he became the Parton Saint of Beer.

Hops, a bittering agent, has been used since antiquity. We know that Pepin had a hop garden in the eighth century A.D. Germany became the hub of beer made in the Middle Ages. In the fourteenth century there were over 1,000 brew masters in Hamburg alone. The town of Einbeck was exporting beer as far as the Holy Land.

## GERMANY'S PURITY LAW (Reinheitsgebot)

Enacted in 1560 A.D. by the Duke William IV of Bavaria, only the following ingredients could be used to make beer:

1. Barley Malt
2. Hops
3. Yeast
4. Water

This simple rule, started in 1516 A.D., is still followed in Germany.

In Great Britain, heirs to the Celtic brewing traditions developed new types of brews, such as porter. Pubs became quite common throughout England. In the American colonies, the first brewery was built in New Amsterdam in 1612. William Penn himself constructed a brewhouse in 1685. George Washington maintained a brewhouse at Mt. Vernon.

The nineteenth century saw an influx of German immigrants into America and the beer industry blossomed. Old country recipes, coupled with new technology and an effervescent spirit, led to a clear favorite type of American beer, the light lager.

## Principal Types of Beer

**Lager:** These are pale gold in color, light in taste, medium in hops and high in carbonation. They are usually 3.5–4.0% alcohol by volume. Light lagers are sometimes called pilseners, after the town of Pilzen, Czechoslovakia, where this style of brew was perfected. Vienna type lagers are amber hued and mildly hoppy. Munich lagers are dark, sweet, and rich in body. The color comes from roasted barley. Oktoberfest beer is an amber variation of a Munich type. Originally created for seasonal use, you can usually enjoy Oktoberfest year round today. Bock beer is a heavy, dark brew made in winter for spring use. Bock beer and other hearty dark beers can reach 10% alcohol, but most are around 5%. In lager beers the yeasts settle in the bottom of the brew, that is, they are bottom fermented.

**Ale:** These brews are more aromatic, hoppier, tarter, and possessing greater alcohol strength (4–5%). Ale is top fermented, ferments at a hotter temperature than lager, and is aged in the bottle longer. Britain is the champion of ale. You will find both bitter and mild ales in British pubs.

**Stout:** This is a rich, almost ebony-colored malty brew, with a pronounced bitter hop taste. Alcohol is usually 5–6%, and stout is served at a cool room temperature.

**Porter:** Dark brown, full bodied, sometimes sweet with overtones of licorice, porter is smoother and lighter than stout. About 5% in alcohol, it has less hop dominance than ale.

**Malt Liquor:** This beer has more than 5% alcohol and is usually a lager type.

Coors—Two trends in the American beer business have been: (1) National marketing of local breweries (Coors is associated with Colorado and that pure Rocky Mountain water); and (2) The emergence of "Light" or low-calorie beer (Coors Light is called "The Silver Bullet").

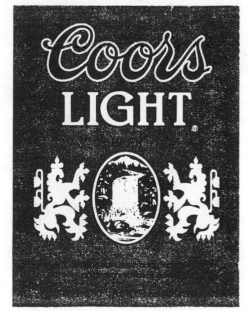

**Weiss Beer:** A wheat brew made in Berlin and Munich today, this beer was developed in England and Hamburg. Yeasty and cloudy, it is served with raspberry syrup or lemon and known for its rich, foamy head.

**Sake:** Although reminiscent of rice wine, sake is actually a rice brew.

## Trends Today

Modern technology has enabled the brew master to produce beers that have little or no alcohol. Americans seem to be looking for lighter beers, especially those that finish clean and dry. "Dry," "Light," and "Low Alcohol" all seem to be chic today.

The number of brewers in the U.S.A. has been declining each year. Mergers and buyouts have caused most of the beers in the U.S. to be manufactured and sold by fewer companies. Dominant giants include Anheuser-Busch, Miller, and Coors. In addition to these larger breweries, there are many microbreweries, which make great beers in smaller quantities. Big or small, the general rule of thumb is to buy your beer fresh and drink young.

## How Beer Is Made — A Quick Look

Making beer involves the conversion of sugar in grain to alcohol with the assistance of yeast. Barley is the best and oldest grain to make beer, but corn, wheat, or rice may be used in substitution for or in conjunction with barley. To prepare grain for fermentation, the brewmaster soaks the grain in water to cause sprouting or germination. This process is called malting. The grain is then dried.

At the proper time, heated water is added to the grain. This is called mashing and in the mashing kettle maltose and dextrins, fermentable sugars, appear. This fermentable liquid is called wort. The wort is transferred to a brew kettle where hops are added. Every aspect, from the temperature of the water to the strain of hops, is handled by the skillful brewmaster.

After the hops are removed, yeasts are added to assist fermentation in special fermentation tanks. This process, which usually takes one week, is done under strict temperature control.

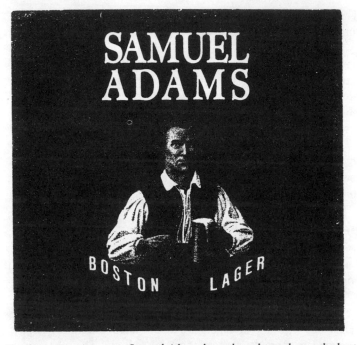

For three years in a row, Samuel Adams beers have been chosen the best in the United States. Our extraordinary dedication to purity has made Samuel Adams the only U.S. beer to pass the German Beer Purity Law and be sold in Germany.

After fermentation, the green or young beer is aged in a storage cellar, where a slow secondary fermentation takes place. Filtration takes place when the flavor is just right and the beer is ready for processing and bottling.

Although $CO_2$ can be added and carmel and other substitutes may be used to improve the color or the sparkle of a brew, it must be noted that a brewmaster needs only four things to make a fine beer:

1. Pure water
2. Special yeast strains
3. Hops
4. Barley

*Coors Extra Gold – brewed from the finest barley, selected grains, and choicest hops – is a full bodied beer with extra flavor and a deep golden color.*

*George Killians Irish Red is the result of an agreement with George Killian Lett, an independent brewer in Ireland, and Coors. This unique Irish lager is carefully blended to result in a lager with robust character, distinctive flavor, smoothness, and deep amber color.*

## Some Recommended American Brews: National, Regional, and Microbreweries

| BRAND AND TYPE | LOCATION OF BREWERY |
| --- | --- |
| Augsburger Lager | Monroe, WI |
| Prior Double Dark | Philadelphia, PA |
| Genesee Bock | Rochester, NY |
| Genesee Cream Ale | Rochester, NY |
| Olympia Gold | Olympia, WA |
| Mickey Malt Liquor | LaCrosse, WI |
| McSorley's Cream Ale | Philadelphia, PA |
| Ballantine, IPA | Cranston, RI |
| Andeker Lager | Milwaukee, WI |
| Lowenbrau | Fulton, NY et al. |
| National Premium | Baltimore, MD |
| Coors | Golden, CO |
| Samuel Adams | Boston, MA |
| Rolling Rock | Latrobe, PA |
| Stroh's Bohemian | Detroit, MI |
| Yuengling Chesterfield Ale | Pottsville, PA |
| Yuengling Porter | Pottsville, PA |
| Anchor Steam | San Francisco, CA |
| Anchor Porter | San Francisco, CA |
| Michelob | Newark, NJ et al. |
| Old Chicago Dark | Chicago, IL |
| Rainier Ale | Seattle, WA |
| Matt's Premium | Utica, NY |
| Maximus Super | Utica, NY |
| Sierra Nevada | Chico, CA |

## Some Recommended International Brews

| | |
| --- | --- |
| Cooper Best Extra Stout | Australia |
| Foster's Lager | Australia |
| Swan Lager | Australia |
| Gosser Bier | Australia |
| Orval Abey Ale | Belgium |
| Biere des Trappistes | Belgium |
| Stella Artois | Belgium |
| Corsendonk | Belgium |

| | | | |
|---|---|---|---|
| Frambois | Belgium | Dos Equis Amber | Mexico |
| Duval | Belgium | Superior Light | Mexico |
| Molson Golden | Canada | Tecante Cervesa | Mexico |
| Labatt's 50 Ale | Canada | Hansa Fjond Lager | Norway |
| Moosehead Pale Ale | Canada | Ringnes Export | Norway |
| Tsing-Tao | China | San Miguel Dark | Philippines |
| Pilsner Urquell | Czechoslovakia | Okocim Light | Poland |
| Albani Porter | Denmark | Krakus | Poland |
| Carlsberg Elephant Malt | Denmark | Zywiec | Poland |
| Bass Ale | England | Red Stripe | Jamaica |
| Guiness Stout | Ireland | Feldschlossen Special | Switzerland |
| Harp Lager | Ireland | Niksicko Pivo | Yugolslavia |
| MacEwan's Tartan Ale | Scotland | | |
| Theakston Old Peculier | England | | |
| Whitbread Tankard | England | | |
| Mackeson Stout | England | | |
| Samuel Smith | England | | |
| Royal Oak | England | | |
| Kronenbourg 1664 | France | | |
| Fischer Gold | France | | |
| Augustinerbrau | Germany (Munich) | | |
| Beck's Light and Dark | Germany (Bremen) | | |
| Dinkelacker Privat | Germany (Stuttgart) | | |
| Dortmunder Actien (DAB) | Germany (Dortmund) | | |
| Dortmunder Union | Germany (Dortmund) | | |
| Dortmunder Ritter Brau | Germany (Dortmund) | | |
| Hacker-Pschoor | Germany (Munich) | | |
| Hofbrau Bavarian Dark | Germany (Munich) | | |
| Spaten | Germany (Munich) | | |
| St. Pauli Girl Light and Dark | Germany (Hamburg) | | |
| Wurzburger Bock Beer | Germany (Munich) | | |
| Fix Beer | Greece | | |
| Heineken | Holland (Amsterdam) | | |
| Amstel Light | Holland (Amsterdam) | | |
| Grolsch Natural | Holland (Enschede) | | |
| Birra Moretti | Italy | | |
| Peroni Mastro Azzurro | Italy | | |
| Asahi Lager | Japan | | |
| Kirin | Japan | | |
| Suntory | Japan | | |
| Carta Blanca | Mexico | | |
| Corona Light | Mexico | | |

*Since 1786 Molson has been providing us with some of the most out-standing ales produced in Canada—Molson Export, Extra Dry, Light, and Molson Golden—and has certainly captured the heart of America.*

316

# Glossary of Brew Terms

**ALE:** Derived from the Norse *oel*, this is a top fermented brew, usually fuller-bodied, tarter, and containing more alcohol than a lager beer.

**BARLEY:** a cereal grass very well suited for making malt beverages.

**BARREL:** A standard measurement for malt drinks; 31.5 gallons in the U.S.A., 36 imperial gallons in Great Britain.

**BEER:** A bottom-fermented brew. In some cases, beer is used to describe *all* malt beverages.

**BOCK:** A strong, light or dark, seasonal German beer.

**CARBON DIOXIDE:** $CO_2$, the ingredient that gives bubbles to beer.

**CASK:** Brewers' casks come in seven sizes:
Butt (108 gallons)
Puncheon (72 gallons)
Hogshead (54 gallons)
Barrel (31.5 to 36 gallons)
Kilderkin (18 gallons)
Firkin (9 gallons)
Pin (4.5 gallons)

*Coors "Winterfest" is a traditional full-bodied lager, brewed once a year in celebration of the season in limited quantity from the choicest all natural ingredients, characterized by a rich, full-flavored, robust taste.*

**CERVESA:** Spanish term for beer, from the latin *Cevesvis* (strength of grain).

**DRAUGHT (DRAFT):** Beer drawn from a cask. Fresh, unpasteurized.

**GRAIN:** Corn, rice, wheat, and other grains are sometimes used in addition to or in place of barley to make beer.

**HOPS:** Dried cones used to make brews attractively bitter. Also a preserving agent.

**I.P.A.:** A strong ale. "India Pale Ale" was hearty enough to survive the long passage from England to India by the nineteenth century ship route.

**KRAUSENING:** Cross brewing; that is, blending young beer into aged beer to effect a better, more natural infusion of carbon dioxide.

**LAGER:** From the German, *lagern*, "to lay aside, to store," the term used to apply to bottom-fermented, aged beer.

**MALT:** Grain steeped in water to produce sprouting. Later, malt is dried.

**MALT LIQUOR:** A brew containing 5% or more alcohol.

**MASH:** Crushed or ground malt which is then soaked in water.

**NEAR BEER:** A very low alcohol brew.

**OKTOBERFEST:** A harvest festival in Germany for which a dark, luscious lager is prepared.

**PASTEURIZATION:** Named for Louis Pasteur, a process for stopping fermentation and destroying bad bacteria by raising the temperature to 140 – 150 degrees for a short period of time.

**PILSENER:** A pale lager, named in honor of Pilzen, Czechoslovakia, where this type was perfected.

**PORTER:** A very dark brew, created in England.

**SHANDY:** A blend of beer and lemonade or lemon soda.

**STOUT:** A hearty dark beer, very popular in Great Britain.

**WEISS:** From the German word meaning "white." Popular in Munich and Berlin today. A pale, yeasty, cloudy beer made from wheat. It has a large head and is traditionally served with raspberry syrup or fresh lemon juice.

**WORT:** Malt extract in water.

# NOTES

# EPILOGUE

We are constantly amazed and humbled by how much there is to know and by how little we really do know about wine. Like Socrates, our wine wisdom lies in the realization that we are only amateurs — people who love wine very much. And so we apologize for all we have left out. We do hope that we have passed along the great affection and respect that we feel for wine.

This book is a collection of our lectures, of techniques which we have used to train professionals in the wine trade for the past 18 years. We have seen these methods work effectively and are confident that you have learned something from our efforts. We feel that they will better prepare you to read and enjoy the newsletters and books of more specialized and detailed wine authors. We have no hesitation recommending the fine wines, spirits, and beers mentioned throughout the text. Many of those products have elevated the sciences of vinification, distillation, and brewing to an art form.

Truly the most attractive wine is the one not yet tasted. The best vintage is next year's. So it is with the S.E.C.'s *Vintage Wine Book.* Periodic updating will take place. Next year's book will be better than this year's.

We could recommend that to further your knowledge you take some formal instruction, join wine societies, read books, subscribe to newsletters and magazines. Our best advice is to listen to the words of the late Frank Packard: "There are three important things to remember in trying to learn about wine: (1) Taste, (2) Taste, and (3) Taste some more."

# PRODUCTION AND CONSUMPTION INFORMATION

## THE TOP TEN WINE PRODUCING COUNTRIES
1985 (Approximated in millions of gallons)

1. France ............................ 1,850
2. Italy ............................. 1,650
3. U.S.S.R. ............................ 930
4. Spain ............................... 870
5. Argentina .:., ...................... 540
6. UNITED STATES OF AMERICA ....... 460
7. Portugal ........................... 230
8. Romania ............................ 230
9. South Africa ....................... 200
10. West Germany ...................... 140
   All others ......................... 1,030

TOTAL                                  8,130

## ESTIMATED PER CAPITA CONSUMPTION
1985 (In Gallons)

1. Portugal ............................. 23
2. Italy ................................ 22
3. France ............................... 21
4. Argentina ............................ 21
5. Luxembourg ........................... 16
6. Spain ................................ 13
7. Switzerland .......................... 13
8. Chile ................................ 11
9. Greece ............................... 10
10. Austria ............................... 9

26. UNITED STATES OF AMERICA ....... 2.42

## WHAT AMERICANS ARE DRINKING

| Drink Type | 1960 Gallons per Capita | 1980 Gallons per Capita | Predicted Trend |
|---|---|---|---|
| Soft Drinks | 12.3 | 36.0 | ⬆ Greatly |
| Milk | 37.9 | 25.0 | ⬇ Greatly |
| Coffee | 35.7 | 24.0 | ⬇ Greatly |
| Beer | 15.1 | 23.0 | ⬆ Moderately |
| Tea | 5.6 | 12.0 | ⬇ Moderately |
| Juice | 2.7 | 4.0 | ⬆ Moderately |
| Spirits | 1.3 | 2.0 | ⬇ Moderately |
| Wine | 0.9 | 2.0 | ⬆ Almost Even |
| TOTAL | 111.5 Gallons | 128.0 Gallons | ⬆ Greatly |
| Bottled Water, not included, is ⬆ greatly. | | | |

# SELF-EVALUATION ANSWERS

**INTRODUCTION, PART I – page 12**
1.F  2.T  3.T  5.T  6.T  7.T  8.F  9.F  10.T

**INTRODUCTION, PART II – page 34**
1.F  2.T  3.F  4.T  5.T  6.F  7.T  8.F  9.T  10.T

**SHERRY – page 41**
1.T  2.T  3.F  5.T  6.T  7.T  8.T  9.T  10.T

**PORTO, MARSALA, MADEIRA, AND OTHER FORTIFIED WINES – page 49**
1.T  2.F  3.F  4.T  5.F  6.T  7.F  8.F  9.T  10.T

**AROMATIZED WINES – page 57**
1.T  2.F  3.T  4.T  5.T  6.T  7.F  8.F  9.F  10.F

**CHAMPAGNE – page 72**
1.T  2.T  3.T  4.T  5.F  6.T  7.F  8.F

**VARIATIONS IN THE CHAMPAGNE METHOD – page 75**
1.F  2.T  3.T  4.T  5.T  6.F  7.F  8.F  9.T  10.F

**OTHER SPARKLING WINES – page 85**
1.T  2.F  3.T  4.F  5.T  6.T  7.T  8.T  9.F  10.T

**WINES OF THE UNITED STATES – page 113**
1.T  2.F  3.T  4.T  5.F  6.F  7.T  8.F  9.F  10.T

**BORDEAUX – page 132**
1.T  2.T  3.F  4.F  5.F  6.T  7.F  8.T  9.F  10.T

**NORTHERN BURGUNDY – page 150**
1.T  2.T  3.F  4.T  5.F  6.T  7.T  8.T  9.F  10.T

**SOUTHERN BURGUNDY – page 158**
1.F  2.T  3.F  4.F  5.F  6.T  7.T  8.F  9.T  10.F

**CÔTES-DU-RHÔNE – page 164**
1.T  2.T  3.T  4.F  5.F  6.F  7.T  8.T  9.T  10.T

**ALSACE-LOIRE-OTHER – page 174**
1.T  2.F  3.T  4.T  5.F  6.T  7.F  8.T  9.F  10.F  11.T

**THE WINES OF ITALY - INTRODUCTION – page 186**
1.T  2.T  3.F  4.F  5.F  6.F  7.F  8.F  9.T  10.F  11.F  12.F
13.F

**NORTHERN ITALY – page 196**
1.F  2.F  3.T  4.T  5.T  6.T  7.T  8.F  9.T  10.T  11.F  12.T

**NORTHEASTERN ITALY – page 205**
1.T  2.T  3.F  4.T  5.T  6.T  7.F  8.F  9.T  10.T

**CENTRAL ITALY – page 221**
1.T  2.F  3.T  4.T  5.T  6.T  7.F  8.T  9.F

**SOUTHERN ITALY – page 228**
1.T  2.F  3.F  4.T  5.T  6.T  7.F  8.F  9.T  10.T

**THE WINES OF GERMANY – INTRODUCTION – page 239**
1.F  2.T  3.F  4.F  5.F  6.F  7.T  8.T  9.T  10.T  11.F  12.T

**GERMANY REGIONS – page 247**
1.T  2.T  3.F  4.T  5.F  6.T  7.T  8.F  9.F  10.T

**SPAIN AND PORTUGAL – page 258**
1.T  2.T  3.T  4.F  5.F  6.T  7.T  8.F  9.T  10.T

**OTHER COUNTRIES – page 269**
1.F  2.T  3.T  4.F  5.T  6.F  7.T  8.T  9.F  10.T

**OTHER COUNTRIES – page 274**
1.T  2.T  3.T  4.F  5.T  6.T  7.F  8.T  9.T  10.F  11.T  12.F

**OTHER COUNTRIES – page 282**
1.T  2.T  3.T  4.T  5.F  6.T  7.T  8.T  9.T  10.F

# Indexes

**NOTES:**

Letter-symbols and terms are used to denote the following:

— *l:* label illustration
— *n:* notation, legend, or caption
— *t:* table or summarized information
— *also:* additional, related information (for **Name Index, Producers,** *also* pages indicate other categories of wines by the producer and/or other countries in which the company is located)
— *mentioned:* references occur to some extent on each of the inclusive pages
— **boldface type:** indicates cross-references between the **Subject Index** and the **Name Index,** or to the **Alcoholic Beverages Reference Guide.**

The content and international scope of this book may create the necessity to refer to multiple index(es) entries to achieve comprehensiveness for particular subjects. Users are encouraged to seek all topics related to subjects of interest.

Many wines are named for geographic origin; significant regions and towns may be listed only as subentries to countries.

The **Alcoholic Beverages Reference Guide, Parts One and Two** is an alphabetized supplement to the book and is therefore only selectively indexed, primarily to cross-reference subjects, beverages, and producers which are discussed in the main text of the book.

# Subject Index

Abboccato, defined 214, 218*tn*
  Frascati type 219
A.C. or A.O.C. and wines of
  France. *See* Appellation
  Controlee; Appellation
  d'Origine Controlee system
*Academie du Vin Complete Wine*
  *Course* (Spurrier and Dovaz)
  24
Acidity
  of grapes, effect of climate, and
    ripeness 5*n*, 8,62-63
  of wine
    as longevity factor 14
    types of acids in, defined 10,29
Additives to wine, in ancient history
  1,51,52
Additives to wine, types of
  alcohol 2,40,46,54
  botanicals 51,52,54,244
  brandy
    to fortified wines 35,38,40,42,
      47,48,252
    to vermouth 54
  carbon dioxide 74,250,251
  clarifiers 40,54
  flavorings 51,52,54
    and regulation of for Marsala
      45
  grape juice, unfermented 54,235,
    248
  sweeteners 38,40,235,248,250,
    251,252
    addition of to imperfect wines
      10
  sugar 65,67,68,74,175,181,235

sulphur dioxide (sulfites) 2,10,
  14-15,181
wines. *See* Blending
yeast 7,65,67
Affenthaler wine 244
Africa. *See* North Africa; South
  Africa
After-dinner drinks. *See* Aperitifs;
  Cordials; Dessert wines;
  Digestivos; Liqueurs
Aging and maturing in production of
  wine. *See also* Vessels
  decisions regarding 8
  oxygen exposure during and effect
    on wine 10
  production processes for
    Madeira 46
    Marsala 45
    porto 42,43,44*ln*
    sherry 36,38-39,40
    sparkling wines 73-74
      CAVA wines 79,79*t*,254
      Champagne, true French 67,
        68,69,70,73
      Sekt and other German 77-78
  of table wines, label designations
    indicating aging as
    classification factor
    in Chile 272
    in Italy. *See* Riserva; Riserva
      Speciale; Superiore;
      Stravecchio; Vecchio
    in Spain. *See* Reserva
Aging potential of wines, factors
  affecting, and examples of
  wines 14. *See also* Fresh vs.
  aged wine; Storage of wine;

*specific factors; additional*
  *wines*
Aglianico grape and wines 2,6
  of Italy 221,222,228*t*, *map* 177
    a.k.a., Hellenic or Greek grape
      221,222*l*
Agriculture. *See also* Viticulture
  European investment in U.S. 83.
    *See also* Joint ventures
  wine as product of 14
  other types, of wine-producing
    regions. *See* Food items of
    origin or specialty; *specific*
    *regions*
Agronomists, winemakers as, and
  training for 8
Airen grape and wines 6,253*t*,255
Akvavit (Aquavit) aperitif 56*t*,295
Albana grape 6
  and Albana di Romagna wine 16,
    181,181*t*,183,184*l*,194-195,
    *map* 177
Albarino grape 253*t*
Albillo grape and wine 255
Alcamo wine 225, *map* 177
Alcohol
  as additive to wine 2,40,46,54
  as component of wine, defined 9
  conversion of sugar and grape
    sugar to 2,64,67-68
Alcohol content of wines
  and grape ripeness and sugar
    content, effect of 62-63,69,
    250-251
  brix indication of 29
  of dried grapes 47
  of late harvest grapes 29,47

high level, fortified wines, levels specified 11t,35,47,95. *See also other fortified wines*
Beaumes-de-Venise wine 163
Madeira 46
Marsala 45
porto 42,43
sherry 38,40
label identification of, examples illustrated 29-33
as longevity factor 14,43
low levels, wines with 51,78t,80, 194,240,245,250,273. *See also* Wine beverages
of sparkling wines 11t,78t,80,273
of table wines 11t
additives to, in production, to control level of 175,235
government regulation of
in Chile 272
in France, for categories 117
in France, for appellation and classification entitlements 127,130,134-135,159,165
in Italy 181t. *See also* Superiore
in Portugal 250
Alcohol by volume, defined 29
Alcohol, industrial, sources of 64, 171. *See also* Bulk wines
Alcohols, white 166
Alcoholism, control of by Chilean government 272
*Alcools blancs* 166
Aleatico grape 6,171
Alexander grape 89
Algeria 265
Alicante grape and wines 6,100,107, 253t,265
Aligote grape and wines 6,137,141, 265
Alkalinity of wine 29. *See also* Acidity
Alsatian. *See* France, Alsace
Altar wine. *See* Religious aspects

Altese grape and wines 171
Altitude, significance of in viticulture 5n,8,178,205,221, 223,226,237,240
Alvarelhao grape and wine 251
Alvarinho grape and wines 6,250
Amabile, defined 218tn
Amarone wines. *See under* Valpolicella
Amber (ambra) wines 11t,45
AmerPicon aperitif 55t
*Ampelidaceae*, defined 2
America's Cup yacht race 275
Amontillado sherry, as type of oloroso 36,37n,40. *See also* Oloroso sherry; Sherry
Ampelography, defined 6n
Amphora bottle 217
Amtliche Prüfungsnummer (A.P.Nr.), defined 234,248
example, illustrated 237
*Anada* wine, defined 39
Analysis, of wine. *See* Components; Tasting
of grapes, to determine harvest time 62-63
Anbaugebiet(e), defined 240,248
Anghelu Ruju wine 224,229t
Anis(e) aperitifs, and types of 56t, 266,284. *See also specific types*
Anjou wines 17,168,169t
Annata, defined 217
Ansonica grape and wines 45
a.k.a., Inzolia 6,32ln,45,225
A.O.C. and wines of France. *See* Appellation Controlee; Appellation d'Origine Controlee system
Aperitifs. *See also specific beverages, comparisons, and producers*
aromatized wines, spirits, and types 51,52-56

complementary foods for, examples 20
fortified wines 35,47,48
and types of 40,42,46,47t,55t, 226
and comparisons to 225
serving order for, examples 16
Aphrodisiac, supposed 262
Aphrodite wine 263
A.P.Nr. *See* Amtliche Prüfungsnummer
Appearance of wine, as factor in tasting 24,26. *See also* Cloudy wine; Colors; Crystals; Sediment; Viscosity
*Appellation Complete* of Luxembourg 265
Appellation Controlee designations of France, for classification of wine quality, summarized. *See also specific subregions and communes (villages)*
of Bordeaux 130t-131t
of Burgundy 157t
Beaujolais 157t
Chablis 134-135
of Chalonnais 157t
Cote d' Or 146t-149t
Maconnais (Macon) 154t
of Corsica 171
of Cotes-du-Rhone 163t
of Midi 172
of Provence 171
single-ownership appellations 138
for Calvados brandy 290l
for sparkling wines and laws regarding 61,74,76,77
*Appellation d' Origine Controlee* (A.O.C.) system of France, function of, defined 116-117
comparisons to 28,182,250,265
*Appellation D' Origine Garantie* of Algeria 265
Appellation-type ruling for U.S. 96, *also* 98

Appetizer wines and spirits. *See* Aperitifis

Arabs, roles and influences of 35*n*, 221,225,250

Ararat brandy 265

Arbois wine 76*t*,171

Argentina 270-271
  influences of Spain in 252
  production and consumption, and rankings 259,270,320*t*
  for vermouth 52,271
  sparkling wines of 84

Arinto grape and wines 6,251

Arkansas 97

*Armazens,* defined 42

Armenia, and persons from 265,266

Arneis grape and wines 6,189,229*t*

Aroma of wine, defined 24

Aromatized wines 11*t*,51-56. *See also* Aperitifs; Cordials; Dessert wines; Vermouth; *specific wines, comparisons, and producers*

*Arrope* wine, defined 40

Assmannshausen wine 241

Asti, town of, and wines named for. *See* Asti Spumante; Moscato D' Asti

Asti Spumante. *See also* Spumante
  as Consorzio (Consortia) member 226*n, also* 180
  grape variety used for 80,165
  popularity of in U.S. 80,189
  producers of 53*ln*,80
  production area 80,187,189
  production methods 73,80
  sales of 177
  serving order for 17

*Aszu,* defined and use of 262

Atmospheres (atmospheric pressure) in sparkling wines. *See also* Cremant wines; Pettilance; Pettilant

for Champagne, true French 65, 73,76
for other sparkling wines 73,76, 78*t*

Auction of wines, at Hospices de Beaune 142. *See also* Pricing

Aurora grape and wines 7,83,90

Auslese wines
  of Germany, defined 234,236,248
    aging potential of 14,235,235*t*
    serving order for 17
  of Austria 260
  of France 166

Australia *v*,1,14,47,84,275-280

Austria 79,198,259-260,281,320*t*

Autoclave Process Method for sparkling wines. *See* Charmat Method

Averna aperitif 56*t*

Awards to wines
  of Australia 276*ln*
  of Bulgaria 264
  of Chile 272,273
  of France 122*l*,153*l*
  of Germany 245
  of Italy 191*ln*,207,217*ln*
  of Spain 255
  of U.S. 89
    California 82,91,106*ln*
    Idaho 98
    New York State 82
    Texas 97

Azal Branco (Branco) grape and wines 6,250,251*l*

Azienda Agricola (Az. Agr.), defined 183*ln*,184*t*,231


BA wines. *See* Beerenauslese

Bacchus grape 7. *See also* **Name Index, Persons**

Baco Noir grape and wines 2,7,90, 97

"Bag in a box." *See* Box wines

Baga grape and wines 251

Bairrada wine and region 250*t*,251

Balling (brix), defined 29

Banyuls wine 47*t*,55*t, map* 35

Barbaresco wines 178,184*t*,187-188, *map* 177
  D.O.C.G. status of 181,181*t*,183, 188,189
  examples of 183*l*,191*l*,192*l*
  serving order for 17

Barbaroux grape and wines 171

Barbera grape and wines 6,100
  of Argentina 271
  of Brazil 270
  of Italy 178,187,189,193,194, *map* 177
  of Uruguay 270
  of U.S. 90,95,96,106,111*l*

Barberone (Big Barbera) wines. *See* Barbera grape, U.S.

Bardolino wine 17,187,197, *map* 177

Barolo wines 178, 184*t*,187-188, *map* 177
  aging potential of 14,188
  comparisons to 194,251*ln*,262*ln*
  decanting of 21
  D.O.C.G. status of 181,181*t*,183, 184*ln*,188,189,231
  examples of 55*t*,184*l*,187*l*,189*l*, 190*ln*,191*l*,195*l*
  serving order for 17

Barrel fermentation, defined 29. *See also under* Vessels

Barrels. *See* Vessels

Barriques, use of 175,201,206,208*ln*

Barsac wines. *See under* France, Bordeaux

Baskets, use of
  for harvesting grapes 42,63
  for wine service, and illustrated 27

Bastardo grape and wines 42,46

BATF. *See* United States Bureau of Alcohol, Tobacco, and Firearms

Beaujolais wines. *See under* France,
    Burgundy
Beaumes-de-Venise. *See under*
    France, Cotes-du-Rhone
Beaunois grape and wine 134. *See*
    *also* Chardonnay
Beer, consumption and/or production
    of 312-317
    in Australia 275
    in Czechoslovakia 265
    in France 166
    in Germany 233,241
    in Japan 268
    in Mexico 273
    in New Zealand 280
    in U.S. 320*t*
Beerenauslese (BA) wines
    of Germany, and defined 234,
        236,237,248
      aging potential of 14,235*t*
      crystals and acids in (i.e., late
        picked wines) 10,28
      serving order for 17
    of France 166
Bereich(e), defined and wines of
    234,236*ln*,242,248
    compared to Grosslage(n) wines
      243
Berries
    distillates of 166,296. *See also*
      Brandy, fruit
    grape variety having fruit
      resembling 97
    wines from 1,98,265
Bianco, translated 231
Bianco di Custoza wine 197
Bianco Sarti aperitif 56*t*
Biancolella grape 171
Bica Aberta system 250
Bieferno (Biferno) wine 218, *map*
    177
Bitters, defined 286
    types of, examples 53*ln*,55*t*,56*t*
Black Cat wine. *See* Zeller Schwarze
    Katz

Blanc de blancs, defined 61
    sparkling wine, types of 79*t*, 80*l*,
      83
    Champagne 61,66*l*,69,70
    table wine, example of 170*l*
Blanc Fume de Pouilly. *See*
    Pouilly-Fume
Blanc de Morgex wine 187
Blanc de Noir, defined 95. *See also*
    Blush wines; Rose wines;
      Zinfandel: California; white
    examples of 83,83*ln*,95,99
    serving order for 16
Blanquette de Limoux wine 76*t*,77
Blauer Portuguieser grape and wine
    237
    as Portuguieser grape 6
Blending of wines. *See also specific*
    *and other wines; grape*
    *varieties and wines of*
    for champagne and sparkling 61,
      64-65,68-70,73
    for fortified wines 37,38-40,42,
      43,45
    reserve stocks of wine for. *See*
      Cuvees
    vs. single-vineyard, in France
      119,134,136,137,159. *See*
      *also other countries, regions,*
      *and specific wines of*
    for vermouth 54,221
    wines produced for (bulk) 221,
      223,265,273
Blue Nun wine. *See* Liebfraumilch
Blush wines 11*t*. *See also* Blanc de
    Noir; Rose wines
    of Italy 223
    of U.S. 95,97*l*,112*l*
Boal (Bual) grape and Madeira 46
Bobal grape 6, 252*t*,253*t*
Boca wine 188
Bocksbeutal 13,241,248
Bodegas, uses and functions of 38,
    39,40,256*ln*,270
Bodies of water, proximity of

    vineyards to, and effect 8,
      217,237,240,241,262
Body, tasting of wine to define 24
Bombino Bianco grape and wine
    218. *See also* Trebbiano;
      Trebbiano Toscano
Bombino Nero grape and wine 223
Bonarda grape and wines 6,193,194,
    270
Bonnezeaux wine 168
Books. *See* Publications
Boonekamp aperitif 56*t*
Bordeaux wines. *See* France,
    Bordeaux
Botanical additives to wine
    to aperitifs 51,52
    to German Rhine wines 52,244
    to vermouth 54
*Botrytis cinerea* (*Edelfaule*; noble
    rot; *pourriture noble*),
      defined 126-127,175,236,248
    climate and geographic
      requirements for 126,236,
      237,240,241
    wines from *Botrytis*-affected
      grapes
      glycerine and tartar as
        components of 9-10,28
      of Austria 260
      of France 126-127,168
      of Germany 235,236,248
      of Hungary 262
      of Portugal 251-252
Bottle fermentation of sparkling
    wines. *See* Charmat Method;
      Classic Method; Methode
      Champenoise; Transfer
      Method; Vessels
Bottles, sizes of, and shapes
    illustrated 13-14
    alternatives to (i.e., box wines)
      13,110*ln*,275,278*t*
    of ancient cultures 1,217
    for Champagne, true French, vs.
      other sparkling wines 61

collectors' item, example of 270
first uses of 116
for French wines 13,70,116,165,
171
for German wines 13,240,241,248
for Italian wines 13,171,214,217
opened, storage of 14,71
opening, techniques for 19,21,22.
*See also* Decanting; Serving
and corkscrews, use of and
illustrated 27
for Portuguese wines 13,248,249
Bottling, production process of
Bottling, production process of
for Champagne and sparkling
wines 65,67,73,74
decisions regarding 8
by shippers 134
by *sur lie* 168,169*ln*,259
terms on labels indicating source
of bottling production
for French 137,175
for German 244,248
for Italian 183*ln*,184*t*,231
for U.S. 29,96,102*ln*,107*ln*
Bouchet (Bouschet) grape and wines
107,119,127,128*l*. *See also*
Breton; Cabernet Franc
Bountiful grape 7
Bouquet of wine, defined 24
Bourboulenc grape and wines 160,
162
Bourgogne wines. *See also* France,
Burgundy. *See also under*
Muscadet
classification of 137,138,157*t*
types of 76*t*,134,140*l*,152
Bourgueil wine 17,168,168*t*
Boutique shippers of sherry 40
Boutique wines and wineries
of England 265
of U.S. 83,91,92*t*-93*t*,98
Bouzy champagne, serving of 70
Box wines ("bag in a box"
dispensers; cardboard casks;

winecasks) 13,110*ln*,275,
278*t*
Brands, label identification of,
examples illustrated 29-33.
*See also* Naming wines;
*specific wines*; **Name Index,
Producers**
Brandy, fruit, as distilled spirits,
defined 166,283,289-290
eaux-de-vie of Alsace and types of
166. *See also specific and
other types in* **Alcoholic
Beverages Reference Guide,
Part One**
Brandy, grape
as additive
to fortified wines 35,38,40,42,
47,48,252
to vermouth 54
alternatives to, for after-dinner 40
as distilled spirits, defined 283,
289-290
grappa 3,270,298
marc 3,300
production of, and including types
source of grape juice used for
3,37
in Greece 263
in Israel, and exports of
266-267
in Mexico, and distribution by
international corporations 273
in New Zealand 280
in Peru 270
in South Africa 281
in U.S.S.R., regions for 265
Brandy producers (companies) 83,
102*ln*,273. *See also*
**Alcoholic Beverages
Reference Guide, Part One;**
*specific companies under*
**Name Index, Corporations**
Brazil 270
and Uruguay, wine consumption
in 270

"Breaking Away," movie 53*ln*
"Breathing" of wine, defined 21
"Breeding" vs. blending of wine 43
Breton grape and wines 168. *See
also* Bouchet; Cabernet Franc
Brix, defined 29, *also* 94
Bronze grape varieties 7. *See also*
Scuppernong; Vitis
muscadine
Brown wines 10,11*t*,36
Brunello di Montalcino wines
aging potential of 14
and comparisons to 254
aging requirements for 188*ln*
as Consorzio (Consortia) member
226, *also* 180
D.O.C.G. status of 181,181*t*,183,
207
examples of 183*l*,188*l*,201*ln*
grape based on 183,206
map 177
serving order for 17
Brut, defined 68,231
Bruto, style of 79
Bual (Boal) grape and Madeira 46
Bucelas wine and region 250*t*,251
Bulgaria 264, *map* 261
Bulk wines, production areas for and
users of 221,223,265,273.
*See also* Alcohol, industrial
Bulk Process Method for sparkling
wines. *See* Charmat Method
Bureau of Alcohol, Tobacco, and
Firearms. *See* United States
Burger grape 6
Burgundy wine. *See also* France,
Burgundy
of U.S., and labeling of 36,89,94
Buying wines, selection advice for
8-9,28,33. *See also* Labels;
Naming wines; Quality
factors; *specific wines,
producers, and regions*
and freshness
of sparkling wines 68*ln*,82,84

of winecask boxes 110*ln*

mentioned in book, and labels appearing for *x*, 319

selecting by producer, importance of 152,182,188,189. *See also* Shippers, role of

sparkling wines, vs. true French Champagne 73

vs. table wines 84

French wines, consumer assurances for 117

Bordeaux wines, recommended for beginners 122

German wines 182,236,245

Italian wines, consumer assurances for 180-181,182, *illus*. 178

BV (Beaulieu Vineyards). *See under* **Name Index, Producers, Table Wines, U.S.**

Byrrh aperitif 55*t*


Ca del Pazzo wine 178,182,206,229*t*

Cabernet, Ruby, grape 7,100

Cabernet Franc grape and wines 6

of France 76*t*,169*t*

and a.k.a., Bouchet 119,127

and a.k.a., Breton 168

of Italy 193,198,223,228*t*

of U.S., as Bouschet (Bouchet) 107

Cabernet Sauvignon grape and wines 2,6,90,100

of Algeria 265

of Argentina 271

of Australia 277,278,279

of Bulgaria 264, *map* 261

of Chile 271,272,273

of France 76*t*,119,127,168,169*t*

of Hungary 262, *map* 261

of Israel 267

of Italy, *map* 177

central 205,206,214,219

northeastern 197,201

northern 195

of Sicily 266

of Japan 268

of Lebanon 266

of New Zealand 280

of Romania 264, *map* 261

of South Africa 281

of Spain 252*t*,254

of Uruguay 270

of U.S. 90

California 17,32*l*,92,93,95,101, 103*l*,108*l*-111*l*

New York State 90

Texas 96

Washington State 99

of U.S.S.R. 265

of Yugoslavia 260, *map* 261

Caecubian (Caecubum, Cecubum) wine, ancient, and influence on modern 221,222

Calabrese grape and wine 45

California

role and influence of in U.S. wine industry 1,89,90-91,94,95-96

University of, at Davis 7,8,25,89, 96,98,270

vines and viticulture 4,10, *map* 88

areas 5*t*,91,96, *mentioned* 100-112, *map* 101

influence on, by immigrants and missionaries 1,89,96, 111*ln*,252

wines and wineries 32*l*,90-91, 101-112

boutique wineries 83,91,92*t*-93*t*

bulk wine production areas 171,221

comparisons to California wines 210*ln*,257,275,276*ln*,281

consumption of California wines in U.S. *x*

sparkling wines and production methods 74,77,82-83

"California wine language" 28-29

Calisay aperitif 56*t*,290

Campari aperitif, and comparisons to 52,56*t*

Canada 4,46,273

Canaiolo grape and wines 6,188*ln*, 214

Canei wine, popularity of in U.S. 245

Canonau (Cannonau) grape and wine 6,224, *map* 177

Cannellino, as Frascati type 219. *See also* Frascati

Cantina, translated 231

Cantina Sociale (C.S.), defined 184*t*,231

Capri wine 221

Carbonated wines, Portuguese 249

Carbonation Method of sparkling wine production 74,79

Carbon dioxide

as additive to wines 74,250,251

as result of fermentation 1-2,59, 67,74

Carbonic maceration, defined 29. *See also* Maceration

Beaujolais method of 154-155

Carcavelos wine and region 250*t*, 251

Cardboard cask. *See* Box wines

Carema wine 188, *map* 177

Carignan (Carignane) grape and wines 6,7

of Australia 277

of France 160,169,171,172

of Israel 267

of North Africa 265

Carinena grape 252*t*,254

Carlos grape 7

Carmignano wine 180,181*t*,206

Carnelian grape and wine 7,97

*Cartizze* wines 81

Casa Vinicola, defined 184*t*,231

Cascade grape 7

Cask numbers on labels 29

Casks. *See* Vessels, wood

Castel del Monte wines 223

Castelao Frances grape and wines
251
Castillo de Perelada wine 79
and Perellada grape 79,252t
Catarratto grape and wines 6,32l,45,
225
Catawba grape and wines 2,7,82,83,
89,90
CAVA sparkling wines of Spain 59,
79,79t,80l,254
*Cave cooperative*, function of and
examples of 76t,134
Cayuga grape 7
Cecubum wine. *See* Caecubian
Cencibel grape and wine 253t, 255
Cerasuolo wine 218
Cellar master, role of
in Bordeaux 119,121
in Champagne region 64,65
"Cellared by," defined 29
Cellaring wine for personal use. *See*
Storage
Cellars
advantages of 14
of French producers, notable 62,
140,141,175
Ceremonial wine. *See* Religious
aspects
Cesanese grape and wines 219
Chablis wines. *See also under*
France, Burgundy
serving order for 16
of U.S.
comparison to 180ln
examples of 32ln,95
labeling of 36,89,94
Chai, defined 175
Chalybon wine 1
Chambertin wine. *See*
Gevrey-Chambertin *under*
France, Burgundy, Cote d'
Or, Cote de Nuits
Chambourcin grape 7
*Chambrer*, defined 21-23
Champagne. *See* Sparkling wines

Champagne, true French and region
of. *See* France, Champagne;
Sparkling wines
Champagne Method of sparkling
wine production (a.k.a.,
Classic Method, Methode
Champenoise). *See* Methode
Champenoise
Champagne Method Institute, Italian
82
Champagne stopper 14, *illus.* 71
Chancellor Noir grape 2,7
Chaptalisation(-zation), defined 175,
181,235. *See also* Additives,
sugar
Charbono grape and wine 6,107
Chardonnay grape and wines 2,6,
100. *see also* Pinot
Chardonnay
of Argentina 271,277,278,279
of Australia *mentioned* 275-279
of Bulgaria 264, *map* 261
of Canada 273
of Chile 272
of France, comparison to French
Chardonnay 241
Alsace 76t, 77
Burgundy region 119
Burgundy, northern 133,137,
140l,141,143l,144l
a.k.a., Beaunois 134
Burgundy, southern 151,154,
173t
and origin of name (village)
152,154
Champagne 61,62,66ln,69,71l
sparkling wines of other
regions 76t,77
Cotes-du-Rhone 76t
Jura 76t,77
a.k.a., Melon D' Arbois 171
Limoux 76t,77
of Hungary *map* 261
of Italy 228t,229t
central 206ln,211ln,215ln

northeastern 197,198,200l,201,
*map* 177
northern 194,195
southern 223,226
sparkling wines, 82,189
of New Zealand 280
of Romania 264, *map* 261
of Spain 252t,254
of U.S. 90
California 16,92,93,101-104,
107l,109l
Michigan 97
New York State 97
Oregon 98,99ln
southeast 97
Washington State 99
sparkling wines 83
of Yugoslavia 260, *map* 261
Charmat Method (Autoclave
Process; Bulk Process; Cuve
Close Method) of sparkling
wine production, and wines
73-74
of Germany 77,78,248
of Israel 84
of Italy 73,80,226
of Spain 79
of U.S. 73,82,83
Chasselas grape and wines 6
of Egypt 266
of France
Alsace 165
Loire 167,169t,173t
Savoy (Savoie) 76t
of Germany, a.k.a., Gutedel
grape 6,237,242
of Switzerland 259
Chateau, defined 175
"Chateau-bottled" and French term
for, defined 175. *See also*
Estate wines, French
Chateau (cru class) wines of
Bordeaux
of Graves, summarized 126t
red wines, summarized 120t

second labels of, examples 121*t*
of Saint-Emilion, summarized
129*t*
of Sauternes, summarized 127*t*
*See also* Cru (growth)
classes; France, Bordeaux
*and regions*; **Name Index,
Producers, Table wines,
France**
Chateau-Chalon wines 47*t*,171
and comparisons to 45,171,225
Chateauneuf-du-Pape, and wines of
5*t*,17,21,160,161-62,163
Chateau D'Yquem and wines 127,
127*t*,171,262
Chateau Grillet and wines 138,160,
161,171
Chelois grape and wine 7,90,97
Chemicals as components of wine.
*See* Components
Chenin Blanc grape and wines 2,6,
16
of Argentina 271
of France 168,169*t*,173
a.k.a., Pineau de la Loire 6,
76*t*. *See also* Pineau D'Aunis
of Israel 267
of South Africa, a.k.a., Steen 6,
281
of U.S. 90,92,93,97,110*l*
Chianti wine
of Italy. *See* Italy, Chianti zone
of U.S., example of 107
labeling of 36,89,94
serving order for Chianti 17
Chiaretto wine 17,197
Chiavenasca grape and wine 194.
*See also* Nebbiolo
Chief grape 7
Chile, and wines of 84,259,271-273,
*map* 270
influence of Spain in 252
production and consumption
rankings 272,320*t*
Chilling. *See* Serving; Temperatures

China 268
Chinon wine 17,168,169*t*
Christianity. *See* Religious aspects
*Christwein* 236
Ciliegiolo grape and wines 214
Cinqueterre wine 192, *map* 177
Cinsault grape and wines 160,162,
171,265,277
as Cinsault (Hermitage) 6,7,281.
*See also* Hermitage grape;
Pinotage grape
Ciro wine 221,222, *map* 177
Clairete. *See* Claret wine, France
Clairette grape and wines 76*t*,162,
171,281
Claret bottle 110*ln,illus.* 13
Claret wines
decanting of 21
of France (clairete) 119,124,137
of Spain (clarete) 254,255
of U.S., labeling of 94
Clarification, production process of.
*See also* Decanting
cold stabilization, defined 29
for sherry, fining of 40
for sparkling wines 73-74
for Champagne, true French 64,
65,67
for vermouth 54
Classic Method for sparkling wines
(a.k.a., Champagne Method,
Methode Champenoise). *See*
Methode Champenoise
Classico, designation of, for Italian
wines, defined 231
for Bardolino 197
for Chianti, and zone of 180*ln*,
197,213
for Orvieto 216*ln*
for Soave 180*ln*,197
for Valpolicella 197
Classification of wines for quality.
*See specific countries,
regions, and types of wines*

Classification of wine (categorizing),
FA.S.T. method for 11*t*
*Climat*, defined 176
Climate, as factor of wine
production and quality,
general 2,4,5,8,9. *See also*
Altitude; Bodies of water;
*Botrytis cinerea*; Irrigation;
Late harvest; *specific
countries and regions*
cool or cold regions, and
suitability of grape varieties
or viticulture 98,265,273,
280,281
degree days, defined 100
and diseases, deterrence of 272
for fortified wine production 38,
46,47
in France 115
Champagne region 60,61-62
in Germany, and weather
obstacles in 233,237
in Italy, effect on classification of
wines 188-189
of world viticultural areas 100,
*map* 5
Clinton grape 7
Clos, defined 139,175
Cloudy wine
drinkability of 28
effect on senses, regarding tasting
51
in sparkling wine, cause of 74
Club Raki (Raki) aperitif 56*t*,266,
303
C.M. (Cooperative-Manipulant) 70
Cocktails
alternatives to 40,47. *See also*
Aperitifs
made with sparkling wines 70,81
use of vermouth in 54
Coda di Volpe grape and wines 221,
222*ln*
Cognac, defined 166,291
aperitif based on 55*t*

of China, most popular 268
custom for use of 47
grape used for, basic 171,178
types and brands. *See* **Alcoholic Beverages Reference Guide, Part One**
Colares wine and region 250*t*,251
Cold fermentation and wines made by 193*ln*,206*ln*,254,271
Cold stabilization, defined 29. *See also* Clarification
Colheita, defined 43
Colle Picchione(i) wine 219,228*t*
Colombard, French, grape 100
Color wines (wines for coloring), source of, types, and uses for 39*n*,40
Color of wine 11*t*. *See also* Ramato; *specific colors and wines*
as analysis characteristic 24,26
avoiding, in Champagne production 64
derivation of 6*n*
label identification of, examples illustrated 29-33
as longevity factor 14
regulation of 28. *See also specific countries and regulations*
and sediment 28
Commandaria wine 263. *See also* Commanderie of St. John
Commanderie of St. John wine 47*t*, map 35. *See also* Commandaria
Common Market. *See* European Economic Community
Commune, defined 175
Commune (villages) wines. *See under regions of* France
Communist governments
comparison of U.S. Prohibition to 89
and U.S. cooperation with 264
Comparisons or similarities to wines. *See specific wines*

*Complete Encyclopedia of Alcoholic Beverages* (Mohawk Liqueur Corporation) 283*n*
Components of wine. *See also* Additives; Methanol levels; *specific components*
analysis and appreciation of 108. *See also* Tasting
definitions of 9-10
with nutritional value 14,15
Concord grape and wines, 2,7,89, 90,96,98
Consortia. *See* Consorzio
Consorzio (Consortia) of Italy, functions of 180
and memberships in, types of wines 213*ln*,226
Constitution, U.S., 18th Amendment of 89
Consumption of wines and other beverages, trends and behavior
aperitifs and aromatized wines 35, 52
champagne and sparkling wines 52
cocktails 52
fortified wines 35,36,42,47
moderation of consumption *x*,15, 26,47,54,94
non-alcoholic beverages 52,320*t*
white table wine 52
Consumption of wines by countries
country consuming its entire production 270
in Italy, of types and types produced 178,217
in U.S.
of blush wines 95
during colonial era, favorite wine 46
of domestic vs. imported wines *x*
of German wines, and limiting factors of popularity of 245

of Iberian wines 249
of Italian wines vs. other imports 177
of Italian sparkling wines 80
per capita, for wine and other beverages, summarized 320*t*
per capita comparisons of U.S. to other countries
Australia 275
Canada 273
Italy 178,217
New Zealand 280
South Africa 281
Spain 252
of "pop" wines and low-alcohol wines 51,52,80, 95,194,245
of sherry, popularity of types of 36
of sparkling wines 59,73,80
and suppression of consumption by Prohibition, with cultural comparisons 89. *See also* Social pressures
of varietal wines 95
per capita, for countries
top three 250
top ten and U.S., summarized 320*t*
Argentina 270
Australia 275
Canada 273
Chile 272
Czechoslovakia 265
Germany 77,242
New Zealand 280
South Africa 281
Spain 252
Yugoslavia 260
Cooking of wine during production 37,40,54
Cooking with wine
leftover, including champagne 14, 71
Madeira 46

Marsala 44*ln*,45,225
sherry 268
vermouth 54
Cooperative-Manipulant (C.M.) 70
Cooperatives of growers and/or
    producers, including terms
    for, translated
of France 70*t*,175
    Bordeaux 125
    Burgundy 134,138,140,152
    Cotes-du-Rhone 76*t*,163
    Midi 172
of Germany 241,242,243
of Israel 266
of Italy 184*n*,192*ln*,224,231
of South Africa 280,281
of Yugoslavia 260
Cordials. *See also* Aperitifs; Dessert
    wines; Liqueurs; *specific*
    *beverages, comparisons, and*
    *producers*
    alternatives to 40,47
    as distilled spirits, defined 283,
    291
Cordon pruning, defined 4
Corks
    as agricultural product, areas for
    224,250
    in champagne production, uses of
    types of, and illustrated 67,
    68
    crystallization on 10. *See also*
    Crystals
    defective seal, indication of 9,10,
    14
    extraction from bottles 21,22,27,
    70
    history of, pre-invention and first
    uses 1,116
    presentation by waiter 19
    storage of bottles with 14
        of opened bottles, alternatives
        to corks to reseal 14,17
Corkscrews, types of, illustrated 27
    uses of 21,22

Corporations, international, with
    alcoholic beverage- and
    wine-industry interests. *See*
    *also specific companies*
    *under* **Name Index,**
    **Corporations**
    in Argentina 271
    in Australia 276
    in Brazil 270
    in Bulgaria 264,264*ln*
    in China 268
    in Japan 268
    in Mexico 273
    in New Zealand 280
    in U.S. 83,91,104*ln*. *See also*
        Joint ventures
    in Yugoslavia 260
Corsica. *See under* France
Cortese grape and wines 6,185*ln*,
            187,189*ln*,190*ln*,
    191*ln*
Corton-Charlemagne wine 16,141*l*,
    143
Corvina grape and wine 6,197
Corvo wine 81,178,225-226,229*t*,
    *map* 177
    serving order for types of 16,17
Cot grape and wine 168. *See also*
    Malbec
Cote (Cotes), defined 175. *See also*
    *named regions and*
    *subregions under* France
Cosechas, defined 254
Cotnari wine 264, *map* 261
Cotto, defined and use of 45
Coudoise grape and wine 160
Coulee de Serrant, La, and wines
    168,171
Cowart grape 7
Crackle in wine. *See* Petillance;
    Petillant(s); Spritzig
Cream sherry, as type of oloroso 36,
    37*n*. *See also* Oloroso sherry;
    Sherry
    comparison to 45

example of 40*l*
    of U.S. 47,97
Cremant wines, defined according to
    atmospheres 76
    of France 76*t*,77,134,165
    of Sicily 226
Cremissa wine, ancient and modern
    222
Crepy wine 171
Criadera, defined and function of
    38,39
Criolla grape 6,271
*Crocodile Dundee*, movie 275
Croatina grape and wine 193
Cru, defined 175
    equivalent of in Italy 231
Cru (growth) classes of France
    Alsace 165,166*ln*
    Bordeaux (chateau) 119-121,
        124-130
    Burgundy
        Beaujolais 155-157,
            *summarized* 157*t*
        Chablis 134-135, *summarized*
            157*t*
        Cote d'Or 135-144,
            *summarized 146t*-149*t*
        Cotes-du-Rhone 159-162,
            *summarized* 163*t*
Crusades, the 1,263,266
Crushing and pressing grapes for
    wine
    alternatives to. *See* Maceration
    for Champagne, true French 68,70
    and regulation of 62,63,64
    decisions regarding 8
    by foot 37,38,42,218
    mechanical methods 37,38, *illus.*
    3
Crystals in wine 10,28
    German wines with. *See*
        Beerenauslese; Eiswein;
        Spätlese;
        Trockenbeerenauslese

C.S. (Cantina Sociale), defined
    184t,231
Cultivation. See Vines; Viticulture
Customs regarding wine use 15. See
    also Religious aspects
  of aperitifs 51,52
  of champagne 70
  of cognac and port 47
  of Europeans, including
    Mediterranean and Italian 1,
    14,96,178,218,219
  and toasting with wine x
"Cutting," wine produced for, of
    Italy 221. See also Alcohol,
    industrial; Bulk wines
Cuve Close Method for sparkling
    wines. See Charmat Method
Cuvees of wine, defined 68
  use of in Champagne 64,65,68-70
  use of for fortified wine
    production 39,43
Cynar aperitif 56t,295
Cynthiana grape 7
Cyprus 47t,263, map 35
Czechoslovakia 265

D'Anjou wines 17,168,169t
Damaschino grape and wine 45
Dao wines and region 17,250t,251
Dates on labels. See also Vintage
    dates and dating
  of bottling, example 44l. See also
    specific wines regarding
    production aging
  of disgorgement, on champagnes
    68ln,82, also 67
  for quality control tasting of
    German wines 237t, also 234
D.E. and wines of Spain. See
    Denominacion Especifica
Dearing grape 7
"Decanter" 217ln
Decanting of wine 21, illus. 22
  of porto 42,43ln
    See also Sediment

DeChaunac grape 7
Degree day, defined 100
Delaware grape 7,83,268
Delimited areas for wine production.
    See Demarcation; all
    cognates of Appellation;
    Denominacion(e);
    Denominazione;
    Qualitätswein; specific
    wine-producing countries and
    regions
Demarcation areas (delimited zones)
  in Portugal 42,46,250,250t
  in Spain 36,252-256
Demestica wine 263, map 261
Demi-sec, translated 68
Denmark 265
  aperitif of 56t,295
Denominacion Especifica (D.E.) for
    CAVA wines of Spain 28,
    254. See also CAVA wines
Denominacione de Origen (D.O.)
    for table wines of Spain 28,
    252,254-256, summarized
    252t-253t
Denominazione di Origine
    Controllata (D.O.C.) wine
    laws of Italy 28
  aging requirements of and
    terminology for. See Riserva;
    Riserva Speciale; Superiore
  comparisons to 28,250
  defined 180-182,184. See also
    D.O.C.G. category
  for Marsala 45
  non-D.O.C. wines. See Vino da
    Tavola
  for sparkling wines 81
  zones for D.O.C. wines. See
    Italy, regions and wines
Denominazione di Origine
    Controllata e Garantita
    (D.O.C.G.) category of
    wines of Italy 28

defined 181-182,184. See also
    D.O.C. wine laws
  requirement failures and
    declassification of wines 181,
    188-189
  Riserva Speciale designation for,
    and change in law regarding
    184ln,189l
  wines qualified as D.O.C.G. See
    Albana di Romagna;
    Barbaresco; Barolo; Brunello
    di Montalcino; Chianti; Vino
    Nobile di Montepulciano
  wines with impending D.O.C.G.
    qualification. See
    Carmignano; Gattinara;
    Torgiano Rosso Riserva
Dessert wines. See also Aperitifs;
    Cordials; Digestivos;
    Liqueurs; specific wines,
    comparisons, and producers
  examples of, and serving order for
    17
  and foods to serve with, examples
    20
  fortified, types of 35,36,40,42,43,
    45,46,47
  pH level of 29
  vin doux naturel, defined 175
  of Australia 278t
  of Austria 260
  of Brazil 270
  of France 126-127,163,167,171,
    172
  of Germany 235-236
  of Greece 263
  of Hungary 262
  of Italy 201,206,223,224,225
  of Romania 263-264
Deutscher Tafel Wein (Tafelwein)
    (DTW) 28
  defined and standards for 234,
    244,248
Deutsches Weinsiegel, defined 248,
    illus. 245

Diabetiker Wein, defined 248
Diamond grape 7
*Die Lorelei* (Heine) 240
Digestivos, defined 53*ln*
  types of 52*l*,53*l*,56*tn*
"Discovery" wines. *See also*
    Esoteric wines; Fantasy
    wines, Super-premium wines;
    *specific wines and producers*
  of France 168, *also* 171
  of Germany, untapped by U.S.
    markets 241,245
  of Italy 198,198*ln*,206,221,224
    defined 206
    and regarded as upcoming 217,
      223
  of Portugal and Spain 257
Diseases, insects, rots, and maladies
    encountered in viticulture 4,
    8*t*,201*ln*,237. *See also*
    Phylloxera vastatrix
  climate as deterrant of 272
Disgorgement, in champagne
    production, defined 67
  date of on labels 68*l*,82
Distilled spirits (distillates). *See*
    Brandy *and types*; Cordials;
    Eaux-de-vie; Rum; Vodka;
    Whiskey; **Alcoholic
    Beverages Reference Guide,
    Part One**
Dixie grape 7
D.O. and wines of Spain. *See*
    Denominacione de Origen
D.O.C. and wines of Italy. *See*
    Denominazione di Origine
    Controllata
D.O.C.G. and wines of Italy. *See*
    Demoninazione di Origine
    Controllata e Garantita
Dolce, defined 45, 218*tn*
Dolceacqua wine 192, *map* 177. *See
    also* Rossese
Dolcetto grape and wines 6,17, *map*
    177

and comparison to 187
Dole de Sion wine 17,259
Domaine, defined 175
  Mis (mise) du Domaine,
    translated 137
Dom Perignon, production director
    for, and U.S. winery
    affiliation of 83*ln*
Dona Branca grape and wine 251,
    253*t*
Donnaz wine 187, *map* 177
Dosage de l'expedition 68. *See also*
    Liqueur d'expedition
Dosage de tirage 65,67. *See also*
    Liqueur de tirage
Dosage Zero, dryness designation
    of, example 82
Doucillon grape 171
Dourado grape and wines 251
Doux, translated 68
  vin doux naturel, defined 175
*Drei Königenwein* 236
Drug dealers, equating of wine
    industry with 90
Drunk driving *x*, 15. *See also* Health
    issues; Social pressures
Dry berry-picked wines. *See* Botrytis
    cinerea
Dry coalition in U.S. 90. *See also*
    Prohibition
Dry sack. *See under* Sherry
Dryness and sweetness of wines,
    levels of and designations
    for. *See also* Sugar, residual;
    *specific wines*
  and brix 29
  control of during production 2,38,
    40,42,68
  serving of, and examples 15,
    16-17,20
  terms used for, on labels. *See also
    specific and additional terms*
  for Champagne, and
    imprecision of 68

Common Market designations
    81*t*
  French 68,168
  German 81*t*,244
  Italian 218*t*
  Spanish 79
Dubonnet wine aperitif 52,55*t*
Dunkel, defined 198
Duriff, French, grape and wines
    105. *See also* Petite Sirah
Dutch, role of, in South African
    viticulture 280
Dutchess grape 7

Eaux-de-vie, defined 296
  quality control of, by French
    government agency 116-117
  and types of Alsatian 166
*Edelfaule*, defined 236,248. *See also*
    Botrytis cinerea
Edelzwicker wines 165
"Education" of wine, in sherry
    production 38,39
Egrappoir, defined and use of 154
Egri Bikaver wine 17,262
Egypt 1,265-266
Einzellage(n), defined and wines of
    243,248
Eisacktaler wine 198
Eiswein, category of and defined
    234,235,248. *See also* Ice
    wine
  aging potential of 14,235*t*
  crystals and acids in (i.e., late
    picked wines) 10,28
  serving order for 17
Elvira grape 89
Emerald Riesling grape 7,100,107.
    *See also* Muscadelle; Riesling
*Encyclopedia of Wines and Spirits*
    (Lichine) 171
Enfer D'Arvier wine 187
England, wines and viticulture in
    265

consumption and serving of
fortified wines 36,40,45
imports to 40,42,46,266,280
En masse production 67,73. *See also*
Tirage
En tirage. *See* Tirage
Enotecas 195
example of 179*ln*
Enotria 221
Entre-Deux-Meers. *See under*
France, Bordeaux
Epluchage, defined and use of 63,73
Epernay. *See under* France,
Champagne
Erbaluce di Caluso wine and
comparison to 189
Erosion, and vineyard reconstruction
in Germany 233
Erzeugerabfüllung, defined 244,248
Escarchardo aperitif 56*t*
Esoteric, wines regarded as. *See also*
Discovery wines; Fantasy
wines; Super-premium wines;
*specific references*
of France 171
of Germany 236
of Italy 195,197,201,219
comparisons to 177
of Spain 255-256
Espalier (Trellis Method) pruning,
defined 4
and use of pergolas in Portugal
250
similarity to. *See* Guyot
Esparto, defined 37
Espumoso, defined 79. *See also*
CAVA wines
Est! Est!! Est!!! wine 178,205,219
Estate wines, production and
bottling of, and terms for
French 137,175
German 244,248
Italian 183*ln*,184*t*,231
U.S. 2,96,102*ln*,107*ln*

Estufagem system, defined and use
of 46. *See also* Maderization
Etna wine 225, *map* 177
Etruscans 177,205
European Economic Community
(EEC, Common Market),
agreements and labeling
terms. *See also specific terms*
for dryness/sweetness levels 81*t*
for Italian wines, V.Q.P.R.D.
quality designation 231
and translation of, examples on
labels 199*l*
for sherry 36
for sparkling wines 61
"Eurowines." *See* Joint ventures
"Export quality" wines 259
and control of
by Chile 272
by Israel 267

Faber grape 7
Fairs. *See* Festivals
Falernian wine. *See* Falernum
Falernum wine 221-222,296
and ancient Falernian 52,221
"Fantasy wines" of Italy 178*t*,206,
207,207*l*,208*ln*. *See also*
Discovery wines; Esoteric
wines; Super-premium wines;
*specific wines*
Fara wine 188
Faro wine 225
F.A.S.T. wine classification
memory-method 11*t*
Fattoria, translated 188*ln*,231
Favonio wines 223,228*t*
Fendant wine 259
Fermentation, defined 1-2
additives introduced to assist
process of
alcohol 2,40
brandy 40,42
sugar 10,65-67,74,175,235

sulphur dioxide (sulfites) 2,10,
14-15
yeast 7,65,67
alternative to crushing grapes to
cause 29,154-155
and brix 29
cold fermentation, use of and
wines made by 193*ln*,206*ln*,
254,271
components resulting from 9,10
and crackle in wine, production of
251. *See also* Petillance
duration of, decisions regarding 8
oxygen exposure during, and
effect on wine 10. *See also*
Oxidation
of porto, and fortification stage 42
of sherry 38
of sparkling wines 59,73-74
of true French Champagne 61,
64,67
label terms regarding 74
spontaneous fermentation, defined
74
unfermented sugar. *See* Sugar,
residual
vessels used for, illustrated 3
barrels 3,64
barrel fermented, defined 29
bottles 61,67,73,74,96
tanks 3,29,64,73,80
vats 3,65,74
Fernet Branca aperitif 53*l*,296
and comparisons to 56*t*
Festivals and fairs for wine and
viticulture *v*,197,214,242,
263
Fiacre bottle, use of 1
Fiano grape and wines 6,16, *map*
177
a.k.a., Latino grape 221
Fiaschi bottle, use of 214
Filtration. *See* Clarification
Fino sherry. *See also* Sherry

production process for 38, *illus.*
37
serving order and occasions for
16,40
types of 33*l*,36,55*t*
and comparisons to 45,55*t*,171,
225
of U.S., example 47
Fiorano wines 219,228*t*
"Financed" vs. blended, for porto
production 43
Fining, process of. *See also*
Clarification
sequence of process in
winemaking 3
in sherry production 40
Finish, the, of wine, regarding
tasting 24
Flavored wines, categorizing 11*t*.
*See also* Additives,
flavorings; Wine beverages
Flavorings. *See under* Additives
Flor, development of in sherry
production 33*ln*,36, *illus.* 37
defined 38
similarity to, in Tokaji production
262
Flora grape 7
Floral abortion 201*ln*
Foch grape 2,7
Folklore. *See* Gods; Legends;
Literature; Naming wines,
proprietary
Folle Blanche grape 6
Food and wine, general
with champagne, types and
occasions 70
classic combinations of 19
enemies of wine 19
European customs regarding 1,14,
178,218,219
Italian label advice regarding 223*n*
serving of food at wine tastings 10
with table wines 87

U.S. cuisine and wines,
international status of 94
wine as food item, and nutritional
value of 14,15,94
wines served without food,
German types 236
Food items with suggested
complementary wines
cheeses 19,20,45,47,185*ln*,188*ln*
desserts 20,70,80,236
finger foods 20,40
fish and seafood 19,20,70,168,
169*ln*,185*ln*,187,191,217,
223,251,251*ln*
fruit 19,236
light cuisine 20,198*ln*
meats, including game 19,20,70,
185*ln*,188*ln*,271,271*ln*
nuts 47
poultry, including game 20,70,
185*ln*,188*ln*
salty dishes 46
soup 19,20,46
styles of wines for foods 20
and serving order for styles,
examples 16-17
Food items of origin or specialty of
wine-producing regions
almonds 241
balsamic vinegar 194
bean dishes 206
candies, Perugina 214
cannoli, origin of 225
carasau bread 224
cassata 225
cheeses 194,219,221,223,259
cherries 241
eggplant parmigiana 221
fish and seafood, including soups
of 171,201,206,217,223
foie gras 165
fondue 259
herbs and types of 214,223
ice cream and sherbet, origins of
225

*la panarda* banquet 218
mariscada 256
meatball, origin of 225
meats 194,201,206,214,219,223,
270,271
Mexican, types of 273
olives and oil 159,206,213*ln*,214,
223
paella valenciana 256
paprika (spicy) dishes 262
pasta, types of and dishes 194,
218,219,221,223,224
and origin of 225
pizza 221
sauces, including pesto 192,219
sauerkraut *choucroute* 165
soy sauce 268
tomatoes and sauces of 219,221
truffles 187,214
Foods with wine as ingredient. *See*
Cooking with wine
*Ford's Illustrated Guide to Wines*
(Ford) 90
Formulas, for flavoring aromatized
wines 52,54
Fortified wines. *See also* **Name**
**Index, Producers**
defined 11*t*, 35
liquoroso, defined 231
popularity of during Prohibition
89
types of. *See also types named*
ancient 1
aperitifs 35,47,48
and types of 40,42,46,47*t*,
55*t*,226
and comparisons to 225
dessert wines, types of 35,36,
40,42,43,45,46,47
major types 11*t*,35
and production of 35-48
"pocket wines" 95
miscellaneous: additional
production areas 280,281

"Fox tail" grape. *See* Coda di
   Volpe
"Foxy," described, as characteristic
   of Native American grapes
   10
Fragrance of wine, as factor of
   tasting 24
France, general
   aperitifs produced in 53*l*,55*t*,56*t*
   bulk wines, production of 221
      imports of 265
   categories of wines, legal qualities
      of, defined 28, 117. *See also*
      *specific categories for*
      *regulations regarding quality*
      *and production*
     *also,* legal regulation for
      cognac 291
   characteristics of wines by region
      117. *See also regions*
   fortified wines produced in 47*t*.
      *See also wines named*
   glossary of terms 175. *See also*
      *specific and additional terms*
   grape varieties
      and climate, compared with
         U.S. regions 100
      of French origin grown in
         California 101,104-106
      of major regions, and wines,
         summary 173
      vinifera origin in France 1
   history of viticulture and
      winemaking, overview
      115-116
   imports to 42,265
   influence of France in other
      countries 117,180,221,252,
      265,266,271. *See also under*
      Immigrants
   joint ventures with U.S. 61,83,91
   maps
      fortified wines, partial 35
      wine regions, general 115
         Alsace 165

Bordeaux 118
Burgundy 133
Champagne 60
Cotes-du-Rhone 159
Loire 167
   production and consumption
      statistics and rankings 77,
      252,275,320*t*
   sparkling wine production
      methods 73,74,76,77. *See*
      *also* Methode Champenoise,
      France
   sparkling wines by region
      Alsace 76*t*,77,165
      Burgundy 76*t*,77
         Chablis 134
         Montagny and Rully 151
      Champagne. *See* France,
         Champagne
      Cotes-du-Rhone
         Die 74,76*t*
         St. Peray 161
      Gaillac 74
      Jura, Arbois 76*t*,171
      Limoux 74,76*t*,77
      Loire 76*t*,77,167
         Saumur 76*t*,168
         Touraine 76*t*
         Vouvray 76*t*,77,168
      Savoy (Savoie) 74
      Seyssel 76*t*,77,171
   summary review 173
   table wines. *See regions*
   vermouth production in 52,54
France, Alsace 76*t*,77,117,165-166
   comparison to 265
France, Ardeche 144*l*
France, Bergerac 172
France, Bordeaux, general
   aging potential of wines of 14
   Appellation Controlee, wine types
      122
      by type and region, summarized
         130*t*-131*t*

   comparisons to Bordeaux region
      119,209*t*
      to wines of, general 119,210*ln*,
      209*t*,249,254,256,273,276*ln*
   cru (growth) classes of chateaux,
      defined and levels of
      119-121,124-129
   map 118
   serving order of dry red wine,
      type of 17
   University of 8
France, Bordeaux, subregions of,
   and wines
   Barsac 14,17,118,126-127,131*t*,
      236
   Cotes de Blaye 118,130,131*t*
   Cotes de Bourg 118,130,127,131*t*
   Entre-Deux-Mers 16,118,127,131*t*
   Fronsac 118,130,131*t*
   Graves 5*t*,16,118,123*l*,126,130*t*,
      131*t*
   Graves, communes (villages) of
      Cadaujac 126
      Leognan 126
      Martillac 126
      Pessac 120,121,126
      Talence 126
      Villenave d'Ornon 126
   Graves de Vayres 127,131*t*
   Haut-Medoc 118,119,121,130*t*
   Haut-Medoc, communes of
      Cantenac 120,124
      Listrac 119,122*l*,124-125,131*t*
      Margaux 119,120,121,124,131*t*
      Moulis 119,124-125,131*t*
      Pauillac 119,120,121,123*l*,124,
         131*t*
      St.-Estephe 119,120,124,131*t*
      St.-Julien 119,120,121,124,
         125*l*,131*t*
   Medoc 118,119,121,122*l*,123*l*,
      125,130*t*
   Pomerol 30*l*,118,119*t*,123*l*,
      127-128,130,131*t*

Premiers Cotes de Bordeaux 118,
127,131*t*
Saint-Emilion 118,119*t*,123*l*,
127-128,129*t*,130,131*t*
Saint Foy 127,131*t*
Saint Macaire 127,131*t*
Sauternes 14,17,117,118,123*l*,
126-127,131*t*,171
comparisons to 222-223,236
France, Burgundy, general. *See also*
Burgundy wine
Appellation Controlees regions
and villages, summarized
157*t*
comparison of, to Bordeaux 119,
137,175
grape varieties, major 119,173
map 133
sparkling wines of 76*t*,77,151
wines of, general 117
comparisons to 218,249
decanting of 21
France, Burgundy, subregions of
Beaujolais 17,31*l*,119,152,
154-157,173
comparisons to wines 187,197,
237,244
Chablis 16,119,133-135. *See also*
Chablis wines
comparisons to wines 197,251
Cote Chalonnais and communes
151,157*t*
Cote d'Or 133,135-137
aging potential of wines 14
Appellation Controlees and
classifications (crus) of,
summarized 146*t*-149*t*,157*t*
comparisons to 137,151,187,
251*ln*
Cote d'Or subregions and villages
(communes)
Cote de Beaune 17,142,
148*t*-149*t*,151
Aloxe-Corton 16,136,137,
141,142,145*ln*

Auxey-Duresses 136,143
Beaune 136,137,142
Chassagne-Montrachet 136,
141*ln*,143,144
Chorey-les-Beaune 136,142
Cotes de Blanc 143
Ladoix-Serrigny 136,141
Meursault 16,136,137,143
Monthelie 136,143
Pernand-Vergelesses 136,142
Pommard 17,136,137,143,
145*l*
Puligny-Montrachet 16,136,
137,140,140*t*,
141,143-144,145*l*,171
St.-Aubin 136,144
Santenay 136,144
Savigny-les-Beaune 136,142
Volnay 17,136,137,143
Cote de Nuits 135,137,
146*t*-147*t*
Bonnes-Mares 138,139
Brochon (Bronchon) 137,138
Chambolle-Musigny 137,
138,139
Comblanchien 137,140
Corgoloin 137,140
Fixin 137,138
Flagey-Echezeaux 139,140
Gevrey-Chambertin 17,136,
137,138, *also* 188
Marsannay 137-138
Morey-St.-Denis 138,139*l*
Nuits-St.-Georges 137,139*l*,
140
Premeaux 140,147
Prissey 137,140
Vosne-Romanee 139,140
Vougeot 135,139
Mâconnais (Mâcon) 16,151-152,
153*l*,156
Appellation Controlees of,
summarized 157*t*
Pouilly, village of, and related
apellations 152-154. *See also*

*specific* Pouilly wines. *See
also under* France, Loire
Saint Veran 152,156
France, Cahors 172
France, Champagne, general
Appellation Controlee and
designations 31*ln*,75
Champagne sparkling wine, true
French, defined 60-61
comparisons to 61,73,80,82,83,
83*ln*. *See also* Methode
Champenoise
Grande Marque producers and
styles of 61,64,69,70*t*
examples 31*l*,63*l*-66*l*,68*l*,71*l*
map 60
production, and methods, of
region 60-70,117
viticultural aspects of region 5*t*,
61-62
similarity to 134
France, Champagne, vineyard areas
of
Cotes des Blancs 61,62
Epernay 31*l*,61,62,65*l*,68*l*,71*l*
comparison to 80
Marne, Valley of the 61,62
Ay 61,65*l*
Rheims (Reims), Mountain of 61,
62,63*l*,64*l*,66*l*
comparisons to 80
France, Corsica, island of 171
France, Cotes de Buzet 172
France, Cotes de Duras 172
France, Cotes-du-Rhone, general.
*See also Rhone valley of
Switzerland*
Appellation Controlee categories
159,160
appellations summarized 163*t*
map 159
wines of region, style of and
similarities to 117
comparison to 171

serving order for, examples 16, 17
sparkling wines of 74,76t,161
France, Cotes du-Rhone, subregions and villages of and wines of
Beaumes-de-Venise 55t,163,175
Chateau Grillet 138,160,161,163, 171
Chateauneuf-du-Pape 5t,17,160, 161,162,163
Condrieu 160-161,163
Cornas 160,161,163
Cotes-du-Ventoux 162-163
Cotie Rotie 17,160,163
Crozes-Hermitage 160,161,163
Die 74,76t
Gigondas 160,162,163
Hermitage 160,160l,161,163
Lirac 160,162,163
Rasteau 163
St.-Joseph 160,161,163
St.-Peray 160,161,163
Tavel 17,95,160,162,163,171
villages summarized 163t
France, Gaillac, sparkling wines of 74
France, Jura, wines of 47t,171
comparisons to 45,171,225
sparkling wines of 76t
France, Languedoc-Roussillon. See France, Midi
France, Limoux, sparkling wines of 74,76t,77
France, Loire
map 167
sparkling wines of 76t,77,167,168
style of wines, general, and similarity to 117
villages (districts), and wines
Anjou (D'Anjou) 17,168,169t
Bourgueil 17,168,169t
Chinon 17,168,169t
Coteaux du Layon 168,169t
Coteaux du Loir 169t
Coteaux de la Loire 168

Coteaux de Saumur 76t,168, 169t
Jasnieres 169t
Mont Louis (Montlouis) 168, 169t
Muscadet 168,169t
comparison to 217
Pouilly-Sur-Loire 167,168, 169t,173t
Quincy 167-168,169t
Sancerre 167,168,169t
Savennieres 168,169t
La Coulee de Serrant vineyard of, wine and comparisons to 168,171
Touraine 76t,77,169t
Vouvray 16,76t,77,168,169t
France, Midi (Languedoc-Roussillon) 47t,171-172
bulk wine production of, uses for and comparisons to 54,171, 221
France, Provence 17,95,171,172l
comparison to wines of, with Jura and Tavel 95,171
France, Savoy (Savoie) 171
Chambery wine of, and vermouth production using 54
sparkling wines of 74,76t,77,171
Franciacorta and wine of 82,193-194
Franconian wine. See Frankenwein
Frankenwein 240,241
bottle used for 13,248
Frascati wine 81,205,216l,217l,219
comparisons to 217,219
as Consorzio (Consortia) member 226n, also 180
serving order for 16
Freisa grape and wines 6, 189
French-American hybrid grapes. See Hybrids
French Colombard grape 100
French Duriff grape and wines 105. See also Petite Sirah
French Huguenots 88,250

Fresh vs. aged wines 14, also 110ln
sparkling wines 84
and disgorgement dating 68ln, 82, also 67
Frizzante, defined 217
Fruit distillates. See Brandy, fruit
Fruit brandy. See Brandy, fruit
Fruit wines 268. See also Berries
categorizing 11t
Fruit-flavored wines. See Wine beverages
Fruitiness, of dry wines 10
Fume Blanc grape and wines. See Sauvignon (Fume) Blanc
Fungus (mold)
beneficial, to winemaking. See Botrytis cinerea; Flor
destructive, to viticulture. See Diseases
Furmint grape 6, 262

Gaglioppo grape and wines 6,222
Galego grape and wine 251
Galestro wine 206,207
Galleries of Champagne region 62. See also Cellars
Gamay grape and wines 6
of Egypt 266
of France 137,168,171,173. See also Gamay Beaujolais; Gamay Noir
of Italy 187
of South Africa 281
of Switzerland 259
of U.S. 94,95
Gamay Beaujolais grape and wines 6,31l,119,152,154
Gamay Noir grape and wines 76t
Gambellara wine 197
Garganega grape 6,197
Garibaldi Dolce (GD) Marsala 45
Garnacha. See Grenache
Gasificado, indication of, for Spanish sparkling wines 79

Gattinara wine 17,181*t*,187,188, 189, *map* 177
  comparisons to 194
Gauls, role of, in early French viticulture 115-116
Gavi wines 16,178,185*l*,190*l*,191*l*, 193*l*, *map* 177
  and comparisons to 187,189,193*ln*
Gelatin, as additive 54
Gemeinden, defined 242
Geographic location as quality factor for wine production 2,8. *See also* Climate; Soil; *specific countries and regions*
  altitude, significance of 5*n*,8,221, 226,237,240
  proximity to bodies of water 8, 118,119,217,237,240,241, 262
German wine names in Italy 198
German wines made in French manner 165,166
Germany, West, general
  aperitifs of 52*l*,56*t*
    and vermouth, origin of 52
  climate as production factor 8, 237,240
    and Regions (Zones) of 100*t*, 242
  comparison of U.S. area to Rhine 97
  glossary of terms 248. *See also specific and additional terms*
  grapes 100,105,106,237. *See also specific varieties*
  imports to 198,264
  influence of Germany and Germans in other countries 90,96,165,166,198,221,280
  introduction of viticulture to 1
  labels of wines, interpreting 234, 234*ln*,236*l*,237*t*,238*l*,243, 244-245,248
  legal standards for quality of wines, and categories of 28,

234-236. *See also specific subcategories*
  comparisons to 182
  map, quality regions 233
  production ranking of 77,252,320*t*
  soil 5*t*,233,237,241
  sparkling wines 59,73-74,77-78, 78*t*,81*t*
  table wines. *See also specific wines, and regions for additional types*
    popular types of 244
    review of chapter on 246
  University of Geisenheim 8,241
  vineyards of 243
    and most famous, by region and village 246*t*. *See also specific regions*
Germany, West, regions of
  for Deutscher Tafelwein (DTW) 240
  for Qualitäts wine (QbA and QmP)
    Ahr 237,240
    Baden 242, *mentioned* 240-244, 248
    Franken 240,241,243
      and Franconian wine bottle 13,241,248
    Hessische Bergstrasse 240,241
    Mittelrhein 77,240
    Mosel-Saar-Ruwer 5*t*,8,234, 237,240,242,243,246*t*
      comparison to wines of 265
      examples of wines of 31*l*, 234*l*,236*l*,238*l*,244
      serving order for wines 16
    Nahe 240-241,243,244
    Rheingau 8,77,235,240,241, 243,246*t*
    Rheinhessen 240,241,243,246*t*
      examples of wines of 236*l*, 238*l*,242*l*,244,244*l*
    Rheinpfalz (Rheinland-Pfalz;

Rhineland-Palatinate) 240, 241-242,243,245,246*t*
    Württemberg 240,243
Generic names of wines. *See also* Naming wines
  for port (porto) 36,47
  for sherry 36
  for sparkling wines and champagne 61,79,83,83*ln*
  for U.S. wines, various types 36, 47,83,83*ln*,89
  and defined for U.S. wines 94
Gevrey-Chambertin. *See under* France, Burgundy, Cote d'Or
Gewürztraminer grape and wines 6, 7
  of France 165,166,173
  of Spain 254,255
  of U.S. 90,98,99,106
  origin of name 106,198
  a.k.a., Traminer grape
    in Germany 237
    in New Zealand 280
Ghemme wine 188,189*l*
Girasol, use of 79. *See also* Riddling
Glassware for serving wines, types of, illustrated 18,71
  and copita, use of 40
Glossaries of terms. *See also specific and additional terms*
  French 175
  German 248
  Italian 231
Glycerine, and viscosity of wine 9-10,24,251
Gobelet pruning, defined and illustrated 4
  use of 155
Gods and goddesses of mythology
  Greek *v*,225,263,267,312
  Phoenician 48*ln*,225
  Roman *v*, 8,151,225,312
Gold (oro) color wines 11*t*,45
Gonci, defined and use of 262
Goths, wine consumed by 217

Gout, defined 175
Government regulation of wine
    industries and quality,
    general 28
  designations for on lablels,
    examples illustrated 29-33
  and abbreviations for,
    commonly seen 28
  *See also terms and*
    *regulations for* Aging;
    Alcohol content; Bottling;
    Delimited areas; *additional*
    *quality factors; specific*
    *countries, regions, and wines*
Graciano grape 253t,254t
Grafting of vines, of *Vitis labrusca*,
  to control phylloxera
  devastation 2,2n,116,133
Grand Seigneurs of French white
  wines 171. *See also specific*
  *wines*
*Grand vin* of Alsace 165
Grande Marque producers of
  Champagne. *See under*
  France, Champagne
Gran-vas, indication of, for Spanish
  sparkling wines 79
Grappa 3,270,298. *See also* Brandy,
  grape
Grape brandy. *See* Brandy, grape
Grape juice
  inferior, uses for 37
  unfermented, a.k.a., *must* or
    *mosto*, and uses of
    in Champagne 63
    in fortified wines 37,40,45,252
    in table wines, German 235,248
    in vermouth 54
Grape products (non-wine or -spirits)
  10,96,266
Grapes. *See also* Climate; Vines;
  Viticulture; *specific wines,*
  *countries, and regions*
  components of 6n,9-10. *See also*

  *specific and related*
  *components and terms*
  ripeness and sugar content of, and
    effect on wine 29,62-63,69,
    235,235t,236. *See also* Late
    harvest; Select harvest
  species of. *See* Hybrid grapes;
    *Vitis labrusca; Vitis*
    *muscadine; Vitis vinifera*
  varieties of species, partial
    summary 6t-7t. *See also*
    *specific and additional*
    *varieties*
  study of 6n
Grapes, dried (raisinized; raisin-like)
  and wines. *See also* Botrytis
  cinerea; Late harvest
  effect of on alcohol content 47
  of Cyprus 263
  of Greeks, ancient 52
  of Italy 181,192,194,197,224
    a.k.a., *passito* grapes and wines
    48l,225,231
    similarity to *passito* 171
  use of in sherry production 40
Grasa grape 264
Graves. *See under* France, Bordeaux
Great Britain 265. *See also* England
Grechetto grape and wines 214
Greco grape and wines 6,16,81,221,
  222-223,228t, map 177
Greece and wines of 1,47t,263,320t,
  maps 35,261
Greek (Hellenic) grape. *See*
  Aglianico
Greeks, ancient v,263. *See also*
  Gods; Literature
  roles and influences of 1,4n,177,
    205,221,222ln,250,264,266
  ruins of, in Italy 223
  wines and uses of 1,52,217,222
Green Hungarian grape 6. *See also*
  Harslevelu
Green wine 11t,250-251,251l

Grenache grape and wines 6,7
  of Australia 277
  of France 47t,160,162,163,171
  of North Africa 265
  of Spain, a.k.a., Garnacha grape
    254,255,256ln,257ln
    Garnacha Blanca 252t,253t,254
    Garnacha Tinta 252t,253t,254t
  of U.S. 95,99
Grey wines 11t,171
Grifi wines 182,206,207,208l,229t
Grignolino grape and wines 6,95,
  107,189
Grillo grape and wine 6,32l,45
Gris (grey) wines 11t,171
Gros Noiren grape. *See* Pinot Noir,
  France
Groslot grape and wines 76t,168
Gros Plant grape and wine 168
Grosslage(n), defined and wines of
  234ln,243,248
Growers. *See also* Cooperatives
  French terms for 70t,175
  responsibilities of 8
  in Champagne region 62-63
Growths (crus), and classes of. *See*
  Chateau wines; Cru classes
Grumello wine 194
Grüner Veltliner grape and wines 6,
  79,259,260
Gumpoldkirchner 259,281
Gutedel grape. *See* Chasselas,
  Germany
Gutturnio (Gutturnium) wine 194,
  195
Guyot pruning, defined and
  illustrated 4
  and uses of 142,155
  similarity to. *See* Espalier
Gyropalettes, use of 73


Halbtrocken, defined 244
  and Common Market equivalent
  of 81t
Harriague grape 6,270

Harslevelu (Hars-Levelu; Lime-leaf)
grape and wines 262. *See
also* Green Hungarian
Harvest of grapes and methods of
decisions regarding 8
hand-picking method, use of 37,
42,119
late harvest grapes and wines. *See
also* Botrytis cinerea
defined 29
glycerine and tartar as
components of 9-10,28
of France, term for 165
of Germany 235,236,248. *See
also specific wines*
of Italy, example 224*l*
mechanical method, use of 42
select harvest grapes and wines
of Germany 234,235,236,248.
*See also specific wines*
for sherry 37
work at time of harvest 8*t*
Health issues *x*,14-15. *See also*
Medicinal uses
allergies to sulfites 10,15
diabetics, German wine suitable
for use by 248
labeling response to 15,94
Heat Summation Chart 100*t*
Hectare, defined 175
Hectoliter, defined 175
Hellenic grape. *See* Aglianico
*Herb*, translation equivalent 81*t*. *See
also* Brut
Hermitage grape and wines. *See
under* Rhone Syrah
Hermitage, appellation of. *See under*
France, Cotes-du-Rhone
Higgins grape 7
Hippocras 52
Hock wine, of Germany, and origin
of name 235*l*,241,248
of Israel 267
Huguenots, French 88,280

Human factor in vinification process
8. *See also* Growers;
Producers; Shippers
Hungary and wines of 84,260,262,
*map* 261
Hybrid grapes, French-American.
*See also* Vitis labrusca,
hybrid of
dominant geographic areas for 4,
10
process of creating 2
types of 2,7. *See also specific
varieties*
in Brazil 270
in Canada 4,273
in Great Britain 265
in Japan 268
in Uruguay 270
in U.S.
Early American wines 89
popularization of 90
viticultural areas for 4,10,83,
96,97, *map* 88
Hymethus (Hymettus) wine 263,
*map* 261

Ice
to chill wine 23
wine served over 40
"Ice wine," U.S. produced,
example 99. *See also*
Eiswein
Idaho 83,98
Illinois 97
Immbottigliato, translated 231
Immigants, influence of, on
viticulture and wine
industries. *See also*
Missionaries
in Australia *v*,2
in South Africa 1,280
European, in U.S. *v*,2,89,90,96
French
in Chile 271

in U.S. 90,96
in Spain 252
German, in U.S. 90,96
Italian
in Argentina 270-271
in U.S. 96,110*ln*
Italo-Swiss, in U.S. 96
Import quotas, U.S., and social
pressures regarding 90. *See
also* Social pressures
Importers, label identification of,
examples illustrated 29-33
India 267
Industrial Revolution, impact on
winemaking technology 52.
*See also* Technology
Infusion, production method of,
defined 54. *See also*
Botanicals
Inlandischen Schaumwein 78*t*, *also*
77
Interno wine 194
Inzolia grape and wines 6,32*l*,45,
225
a.k.a., Ansonica 45
Iran 266
and ancient Persians, wine used
by 1
Irrigation systems 2*n*,99,270-271
Isabella grape 7,89,270
Ischia wine 221
Islamic (Muslim; Turkish Moslem)
governments, comparison of U.S.
Prohibition to 89
influence, on viticulture and/or
winemaking
in Austria 259
in Bulgaria 264
in Greece 263
in Lebanon 266
in Turkey 266
Israel and wines of 84,266-267
ancient (Palestine) 1
Italia Particolare (IP) Marsala 45

Italian Champagne Method Institute
82
Italy, general
  aperitifs of 52,53*l*,55*t*,56
    and vermouth production 52
  comparisons to
    California, grapes and climate
      100,105,106
    characteristics of country 249
    wines of 257
  culture of, and historical foreign
    influences 1,177,178
  fortified wines 47*t*,35 *and map.*
    *See also specific wines*
  glossary of terms 231. *See also*
    *specific and additional terms*
  legal standards and designations
    for quality 28,178,180-182,
    184. *See also specific*
    *classifications*
  maps
    fortified wines 35
    regions and principal wines 177
  production and consumption,
    including rankings 77,178,
    252,275,320*t*
  sparkling wines 59,61,73,80-82
    comparisons to 80,82
  table wines 177-230. *See also*
    *specific regions and wines*
    chapter review 230
  universities, with viticultural
    programs 8, 197
Italy, regions of and wines
  Abruzzo(i) 205,218,228*t*, *map*
    177
  Apulia 95,221,223,228*t*, *map* 177
  Basilicata (Lucania) 221,222,
    228*t*, *map* 177
  Calabria 222,228*t*, *map* 177
  Campania 95,221-222,222*ln*,228*t*,
    *map* 177
  Chianti zone. *See also* Chianti
    wine
    comparisons to

Bordeaux 209*t*,210*ln*
California 210*ln*
Consorzio (Consortia)
  memberships of producers,
    examples 213*ln*,225, *also*
    180
  examples of wines 30*l*,179*l*,
    182,208*l*,211*l*,212*l*,213*l*
  grape based on 206
  laws regarding 180,212*ln*
    and D.O.C.G. classification
    30*ln*,181,181*t*,183,207,209*t*
  map 177
  origin of, historical 207*ln*
  origin of name 178*t*
  regarding sales of 177
  white Chianti 206,211*ln*
  zones of, summarized 209*t*
Emilia-Romagna 181,183,187,
  193,194-195,228*t*, *map* 177
Friuli-Venezia Giulia 5*t*,197,198,
  201,228*t*, *map* 177
Latium (Lazio) 205,219,228*t*,
  *map* 177
Liguria 192,228*t*, *map* 177
Lombardy 82,189,193-194,229*t*,
  *map* 177
Marches 205,205*l*,217,229*t*, *map*
  177
Molise 205,218,229*t*, *map* 177
Piedmont 80,181,183,187-189,
  193,229*t*, *map* 177
  Serralunga region of 5*t*,82
Sardinia 224,229*t*, *map* 177
Sicily 95,221,224*l*,225-226,229*t*,
  *map* 177
  fortified wines of 47*t*,226
    Marsala and types of 32*l*,35,
    44*l*,45,55*t*,178,225
Trentino-Alto Adige (Tyrol) 29*l*,
  82,185*l*,189,197-198,229*t*
Tuscany 30*l*,181,183,188*l*,
  205-207,229*t*-230*t*, *map* 177
Umbria 181,205,214,230*t*, *map*
  177

Val D'Aosta 187,230*t*, *map* 177
Veneto 193,197,230*t*, *map* 177
*Italy's Noble Red Wines* (Wasserman
  and Wasserman) 191*ln*


Jacquere grape and wines 171
Jägermeister aperitif 52*l*,56*t*,298
Jahrgang, translated 248
Japan 268
Jerez. *See under* Spain
Jerez-Quina aperitif 55*t*
Jewish customs and wine. *See*
  Religious aspects
Johannisberg. *See* Johannisberger;
  Schloss Johannisberg(er)
Johannisberg Riesling grape and
  wines 6,93,99,105,106*l*,260.
  *See also* Riesling
  a.k.a., White Riesling 6,98
Johannisberger Erntebringe,
  vineyard of 243
Joint ventures. *See also*
  Corporations, international
  of California, with French and
    Europeans 61,83
  of U.S. with Bulgaria 264


Kabinett wines, category of, and
  defined 234,235,243,248
  aging potential of 235*t*
  comparison to 245
  example os 234*l*
Kadarka grape and wines 6,260,262
Kalterersee wine 198
Kekrankos grape and wine 262
Kerner grape and wine 7,198,237
Kevedinka grape 260
Knights Templar 263. *See also*
  Crusades
Knipperle grape and wines 165
Kokkineli wine 262
Konshu grape 268
Kosher wines. *See under* Religious
  aspects

Kremser wine 281
Kröver Nacktarsch vineyard and
    wines 243,244


Labels (on bottles). *See also* Aging
    terms; Bottling terms; Buying
    wine; Dates; Dryness levels;
    Estate wines; Government
    regulation; Health issues;
    Naming wines; Numbers;
    Winemaking methods
appearing in book, regarding
    authors' recommendations *x*,
    *also* 312
back labels, including
    wraparound, and information
    on
    Californian 94,108*l*
    Italian 223*n*
champagne vs. sparkling wine,
    authenticity terms for 61,74
French, with German terms 166
German, confusion of and
    interpreting 234,234*ln*,236*l*,
    238*l*,243,244-245
interpreting information on,
    examples illustrated 29-33
Italian
    with German terms 198
    misconceptions of government
        designations on 181-182,
        *illus.* 182
    Italian Champagne Method
        Institute emblem 82. *See also*
        Riddling
Kosher wines, symbol identifying
    267*ln*
seals and bands, neck
    German, defined 248, *illus.* 245
    Italian 181,181*t*,213*ln*,217,
        226*n*
    illustrated 178,181,217,224,
        226
    of Luxembourg 265
    Portugese 250

"serve very cold," quality
    implication of 10
terms found on, defined 28-29.
    *See also specific, related,
    and additional terms*
Labels (quality classifications),
    granting of to French wines
    117. *See also* Appellation
    Controlee; Appellation d'
    Origine Controlee system;
    Cru classes of France;
    *regulatory systems of other
    countries*
Labrusca (Native American) grapes.
    *See* Vitis labrusca
Lacryma Cristi del Vesuvio wines
    178,221,222*l*, *map* 177
Lacrymarosa D'Irpinia wine 221,
    228*t*
Lagars (lagares), defined and use of
    37,42
Lago di Caldaro wine 198
Lagrein grape and wines 6,198
Lairen grape and wine 47*t*
Lambrusco grape and wines 6
    of Italy 177,193,194,*map* 177
    in U.S., consumption and
        popularity of imports of 194,
        245
Landot grape 7
Late Bottled Vintage (LBV) porto,
    43,44*ln*
Late harvest grapes and wines. *See
    also* Botrytis cinerea
defined 29
glycerine and tartar as components
    of 9-10,28
of France, term for 165
of Germany 235,236,248. *See
    also specific wines*
of Italy, example 224*ln*
Latino vine. *See* Fiano
Laws and legal regulation of wine
    industries and quality. *See*
    Government regulation

Leanyka grape and wines 262
Lebanon 266
Lees, and defined 64,73
    and *sur lie*, defined, and wines
        bottled as 168,169*ln*,259
Legal regulation and laws for wine
    industries and quality. *See*
    Government regulation
Legends
    drinking of wine, origin of 266
    of Madeira's burnt taste 46
    of naming wines
        Est! Est!! Est!!! 219
        Lacryma Cristi del Vesuvio
            222*ln*
        Punt e Mes vermouth 53*ln*
        Zeller Schwarze Katz 244
    of pruning, origin of 167
    of Spätlese wine, origin of 235
"Legs" of wine 24
Le Moie wine 205*ln*,217
Le Monrachet wine 136,143. *See
    also under* France,
    Burgundy, Cote d'Or
    comparisons to 140,141,171
Lenoir grape and wines 97
Le Sable wine 265
Liebfraumilch wines 241,242*l*,244,
    244*l*
    as Blue Nun 77,234,244. *See also*
    **Name Index, Persons,**
    Sichel, Peter
    comparison to 245
"Light" wines 95. *See also* Alcohol
    content, low; Wine beverages
Lillet aperitif 55*t*
"Lime-leaf" (Harslevelu) grape and
    wines 262. *See also* Green
    Hungarian
Liqueur de tirage 74. *See also*
    Dosage de tirage; Tirage
Liqueur d'expedition 74. *See also*
    Dosage de l'expedition
Liqueurs. *See also* Aperitifs;
    Cordials; Dessert wines;

Digestivos; Eaux-de-vie;
*specific beverages,*
*comparisons, and producers*
defined 299
of Denmark 265
of Israel 266-267
sparkling, type of 53*ln*,303
Liquoroso, defined 231
Literature, historical, with references
to viticulture and winemaking
Biblical *xi*,1,266
Greek (poets, writers,
philosophers) *v,xi*,1,33,52,
263
Roman (poets, writers) 52,128,
203,221,263,265 266
London Particular (LP) Marsala 45
Longevity of wine. *See* Aging
potential
Loureiro grape and wines 250
Lucanello wine 222,228*t*
Lugana wine 81,193
Luxembourg and wines of 84,265,
320*t*

Macabeo grape and wines 6,79,252*t*
Marceration, defined 29,54
carbonic (Beaujolais method) 29,
154-155
Mâcon (Mâconnais). *See under*
France, Burgundy
"Made and bottled by," defined 29.
*See also* Bottling terms
Maderia, island of 35,45-46,250*t*
aperitifs of 55*t*
fortified wine (Madeira) of 35
aging potential of 45
comparisons to 45,55*t*
production method for 10,46
types of 46,55*t*
serving order for types 16,17
Maderization, defined 10
as controlled process
for Madeira wines (estufagem)
46

for vermouth 54
Maereotic wine 265-266
Mafia, the 225
Magdalenerwein 198
Magnolia grape 7
Mahogany-color wine 11*t*
Malaga wines and region 47*t*,252,
253*t*,*maps* 35,249
Malbec grape and wines 6
of Argentina 271
of Australia 277
of France 119,172
a.k.a., Cot grape 168
of South Africa 281
of Spain 255
Malmsey (Malvasia) Madeira 46
comparison to 45
Malt beverages. *See* Beer; **Alcoholic**
**Beverages Reference Guide,**
**Part Two**
Malvasia grape and wines 6
of Brazil 270
of Italy
central 205,219
northeast 201
south 221,222
Sardinia 224
Sicily 47*t*,225, *maps* 35,177
of Mediterranean basin 47
of Portugual 42,46
of Spain 252*t*,253*t*
of U.S. 47
Malvoisie grape 187
Manzanilla sherry, as type of fino
36,37. *See also* Fino sherry;
Sherry
serving of 16,40
Maps
Australia 277
Europe
Eastern, vinifera and wines 261
Mediterranean basin, fortified
wines 35
France, wine regions 115
fortified wines, examples 35

Alsace 165
Bordeaux 118
Burgundy 133
Champagne 60
Cotes-du-Rhone 159
Loire 167
Germany, West, quality regions
233
Italy, regions and principal wines
35,177
Portugal, regions and wines 35,
249
South America, southern tip 270
Spain, regions and wines 35,249
U.S., grape species, regional 88
California, wine-producing
counties 101
world isothermic 5
Marc (brandy) 3,300. *See also*
Brandy, grape
Marc (weight), defined 64
Marino wine 81,219, *map* 177
Marque d'Acheteur (M.A.), defined
70*t*
Marsala wine 35, *map* 177
for cooking, uses of 44*ln*,225
popularity of in Italy compared
with sherry 178
production of 10,45
serving order for types 16,17
types
Fine 32*l*,44*l*,45
Rubino Fine 45
Superiore and types of 45
Vergine, and comparisons to
45,55*t*,225
Mash, source and use of 37
Mass, the 116. *See also* Religious
aspects
Massachusetts 96
Matrassa grape 265
Marsanne grape and wines 160,161,
171
Marzemino grape and wines 198
Mataro grape 277

Maturation of wine. *See* Aging
Maury wine 47*t*,55*t*
Mauzac grape and wine 76*t*
Mavrodaphne wine 47*t*,263, *map* 35
Mavron (Mavrud) grape and wines 6,47*t*,263,264
May wine 244. *See also* Infusion process
Mazuelo grape 253*t*,254*t*
Medicinal uses of wine. *See also* Health issues
  by Arabs, historical 35*n*
  as digestive aids, and types of 52*ln*,53*ln*,56*tn*
  by Greeks, ancient 52
  during Prohibition, U.S. 89
  restorative powers, supposed, wine with 262
Melissa wine *map* 177
Melon D' Arbois grape and wine 171,173. *See also* Chardonnay
Melon de Bourgogne. *See* Muscadet
Mennuni wine 219
Merchant, asking advice of 28,245
Merlot grape and wines 2,6
  of Argentina 271
  of Australia 279
  of Bulgaria 264*ln*, *map* 261
  of France 30*l*,119,127,128*ln*,172, 173
  of Hungary 262, *map* 261
  of Italy 193,197,201,202*ln*,219
  of Romania *map* 261
  of South Africa 281
  of Spain 255
  of U.S. 92,93,106
  Yugoslavia *map* 261
Mesopotamia 266
Methanol levels, assurance of safety of, in Italian wines 178
Methode Champenoise, sparkling wine production method (a.k.a., Champagne Method; Classic Method) and wines

label indication of
  in Spain 79,254
  in U.S. 74
uses of
  in Argentina 84
  in France 73,74,74*ln*,134
    Champagne region, and true French Champagne 60-70, 71*l*,73
  in Germany 77-78
  in Hungary 84
  in Italy 73,80,82,198,226
  in Portugal (Metodo Champanhes) 84
  in Spain 59,73,79,79*t*,80*l*,254
  in U.S. 73,74,82,83,83*l*,99
variations of. *See* Carbonation Method; Charmat Method; Rural Method; Transfer Method; *Methode Champenoise production in areas of France outside of Champagne region and in other countries*
Methyl anthranilate, defined 10
Meursault. *See under* France, Burgundy
Mexico 273
Michigan 97
Microclimates for viticulture
  France 60,119
  German 237,241
  Italy 178,226
  New Zealand 280
  Peru 270
  Spain 254,256
  U.S. 96,98
*Mild*, translation equivalent 81*t*. *See also* Doux
Millot grape 7
Mineral content of wine. *See* Components, nutritional
Mis (Mise) du Domaine, Mis a la Proprieté, translation equivalents 137

Mis en Bouteille(s) au Chateau, translated and defined 175
Mission grape and wines 6,82
Missionaries. *See under* Religious aspects
Missouri 77,82,97
Mistelas wine, use of 40
Mistelle, defined and use of 54
Moderation. *See under* Consumption
Moelleux, translated and defined 168,175
Mold. *See* Fungus
Molette grape and wine 76*t*
Molinara grape 197
Monastrell grape and wines 6,79, 252*t*,253*t*
Mondeuse grape and wines 171
Monica grape 224
"Monkey Wine" 244
Monks and monastic influences. *See under* Religious aspects
Montalcino wines. *See* Brunello; Rosso
Montecarlo wine 206
Montenegro aperitif 56*t*
Montepulciano D'Abruzzo grape and wines 6,217,218,223, *map* 177
Montrachet wine. *See* Le Montrachet
Montilla wines and region 36,47*t*, 55*t*,253*t*, maps 35,249
Morio-Muskat grape 7,237
Morisca. *See* Mourisca
Morocco 265
Moscatel grape 253*t*. *See also* Muscat
Moscatel de Setubal wine 46*l*,47*t*, 250*t*,251-252, *map* 35
Moscatellone grape 48*ln*. *See also* Muscat
Moscato grape. *See* Muscat
Moscato D'Asti wine 80-81,187
  serving order for 17
  use of in vermouth production 54

Moscato (Passito) di Pantelleria wine
47*t*,48*l*,225, *maps* 35,177
Mosel (Moselle) river, region, and
wines. *See* Germany,
Mosel-Saar-Ruwer
Moselblümchen wine 244
Moslem. *See* Islamic
Mosto. *See* Grape juice,
unfermented
Mourisca (Morisca) grape and wine
42,253*t*
Mourvedre grape and wines 160,
162,171
Mousseux, or vin mousseux, and
defined 76,77,168,175
Mouton-Cadet wine 122,122*l*
Mouton-Rothschild, Chateau and
wines 111*l*,120*t*,121*l*,122,
122*l*,123*l*. *See also* **Name
Index: Persons,** Rothschild,
Baron Philippe de; *under*
**Producers, Table wines,
France**
comparisons to 124*ln*,208*ln*
Müller-Thurgau grape and wines 7
of France 165
of Germany 241,242,244
deviation of species and name
7,237
of Italy 187,198,228*t*
of Luxembourg 265
of New Zealand 280
Mulsum, defined 52. *See also*
Falernum
Murfatlar wine 263, *map* 261
Muscadelle grape and wines 7,
119*t*,172
Muscadet grape and wines
a.k.a., Melon de Bourgogne 168,
169
comparison to 217
serving order for 16
Muscadin grape and wine 160
Muscadine grapes. *See* Vitis
muscadine

Muscat (Moscatel; Moscatellone;
Moscato) grape and wines 2,
6,47,100
of Brazil 270
of China 268
of France
Alsace 165,166*t*
Corsica 171
Cotes-du-Rhone 47*t*,55*t*,76*t*,
100*t*,163
Midi 47*t*
of Greece, Samos 47*t*,263, *map*
261
of Italy 81,178,221
Lombardy 193
Piedmont 80-81,187
Sardinia 224
Sicily, Pantelleria island 47*t*,
48*l*,225
Trentino-Alto Adige 198
Tuscany 100*t*
Val D' Aosta 187
of Peru 270
of Portugal 46*l*,47*t*,250*t*,251-252
of Romania 263, *also map* 261
of South Africa 281
of Spain 253*t*
of U.S. 47,100,107
and sales of Italian based-types
in 81
Muscat, Yellow, grape and wines
262
Muscat D' Alsace gape 163
Muscat de Beaumes-de-Venise wine
47*t*,55*t*,163
as vin doux naturel, defined 175
Muscat de Frontignan wine 47*t*,55*t*,
*map* 35
Muscat Gordo grape 277
Muscat-Ottonel grape and wine 260
Muscat of Samos wine 47*t*,263, *map*
261
Muscatel wines 281. *See also*
Muscat grape and wines
Museums, wine 188,241

Muslim. *See* Islamic
Must. *See* Grape juice, unfermented
Mythology. *See* Gods; Legends;
Literature
Mzvane grape 265


Nama wine 263
Naming of wines, general methods
and examples
generic names 83,83*ln*,89,94
and conflicts regarding 36,47
geographic names (towns, etc.)
135-137,155,160,167,178
for grape varieties 46,90,94,137,
178,275,280,281. *See also*
*specific grapes*
proprietary (trademark, fantasy,
folklore, legendary) names
95,122,178
for vineyards or estates 134,
136-137,178,243,246. *See
also* Estate wines
Napa Gamay grape and wines 6,17
Napureouli grape 265
Native American (Labrusca) grapes.
*See* Vitis labrusca
Nebbiolo grape and wines 2,6,100
of Italy
Lombardy 193
a.k.a., Chiavenesca 194
Piedmont 183,187,189,189*l*,
190*l*,195*ln*
a.k.a., Spanna 188,229*t*
Nebbiolo D' Alba wine 17,
187
Val D' Aosta 187
of Uruguay 270
Negociant, defined 175
role of in Chablis 134
comparison to, in Italy 184*n*,231
Negociant-eleveur, defined 134,
139*ln*,175
comparison to, in Italy 184*n*,231

Negociant-Manipulant (N.M.), defined, and role of in Champagne 68-70
Negra Mole grape and wine 46
Negroamaro grape and wine 6,223
Nerello Mascalese grape and wines 6,45,225
Nero D' Avola grape and wines 6, 225
Neuchatel wine 259
New Jersey 15,97,251
New York State 8,15,89,90,96-97
  sparkling wines 74,82,83,90
Niagara grapes 7,90
*Nickolauswein* 236
Nitrogen, inert, use of in sparkling wines 74
Noble grape 7
"Noble rot." *See* Botrytis cinerea
Non-vintage (N/V, n.v.). *See* Vintage dates
Norton grape 7
New Zealand 280
Normans, conquests and influences of 221,225
North Africa 265
  introduction of viticulture to 1
  similarity to California, climate and grapes 100
Numbers on labels. *See also* Dates
  alcohol content, identifying, examples illustrated 29-33
  bottle sizes, names for and equivalent measurements 13
  identifying, examples illustrated 29-33
  cask numbers 29
  German control numbers (A.P.Nr.) 234, *illus*. 237*t*
  harvest dates on champagne 69
  on Italian D.O.C.G. capsule bands, illustrated 181
  on Italian Consorzio labels, illustrated 226
  lot numbers 29, *example* 201*l*

Nuraghus (Nuragus) grape and wine 6,224, *map* 177
Nutritional value of wine 14,15

Oidium. *See* Diseases
Oechsle Scale 235,235*t*
Oeil de Perdrix wine 175,259
  and partridge-eye color of 11*t*
Ohio 82, 97
Okanagan Riesling grape 7
Olaszrizling grape and wine 262
Oloroso sherry 17,36,37*n*,38,39*l*,40.
  *See also* Cream sherry; Sherry
  comparison to 45
Onion-skin color and wine 11*t*,175
"Opening up" vs. oxidation 24. *See also* Oxidation
Orange-color wines 11*t*,251. *See also* France, Cotes-du-Rhone, Tavel
Oregon 98,99*l*,104
Orient Express, wines served on 201*ln*
Origins of wines, label identification of, examples illustrated 29-33. *See also specific countries and regions*
Ornellaia wine 207
Oro (gold) color wines 11*t*,45
Orvieto wine 16,178,179*l*,205,214, 216*l*,*map* 177
  and comparison to 217
  law regarding labeling of 215*ln*
Othello wine 263
Ouzo aperitif 56*t*,263,302,302*l*
Oxidation (exposure to oxygen) of wine, beneficial and detrimental 10,14,21,24,29, 51,54,74

Pagadebit Gentile grape and wine 195,228*t*
Pais grape 6,271

Palestine. *See* Israel
Palomino grape and wines 6,33*ln*, 37,40,253*t*,277,280
Partridge-eye color and wine 11*t*, 175,259
Pascal grape 171
Passito-style grapes and wines 48*ln*, 225,231. *See also* Grapes, dried
  similarity to 171
Pasteurization, in vermouth production 54
Pastis aperitif 56*t*,302
  types of and comparisons to 302*ln*
  Pernod 56*t*
  Ricard 56*t*,303
Pedemonte. *See* Italy, Piedmont
Pedro Ximenez(s) (P.X.) grape and wines 6,37,40,47*t*,252*t*,253*t*
Pelure d'Oignon wine 175
  and onion-skin color of 11*t*
Pennsylvania, and site of first U.S. winery 89
Periquita wine 251*l*
Perlant wines, defined 76
Perlwein, characteristics of 78*t*
Pernod. *See* Pastis
Perellada (Perelada) grape and wines 79,252*t*
Perricone grape and wines 6,45,225
Persians, ancient 1,266
Peru 270
Petillance, defined 250. *See also* Spritzig
  and wines with 193*l*,251
Petillant(s), defined 168,175
  and as level of sparkling wine 76
Petite chateau 91. *See also* Boutique wineries
Petite Liqueur 53*l*,303
Petite Rouge grape 187
Petite Sirah grape and wines 6,90, 92,93,105,108*ln*,267
  as French Duriff variety 105
Petite Verdot grape 6,119

pH, defined 29. *See also* Acidity
information on labels regarding 94
Phoenicians, roles and influences of
1,46,48*ln*,159,177,250
*Phylloxera vastatrix*, illustrated 2
areas and devastation by 2,2*n*,89,
116,133,135,171,252,278*n*
areas unaffected by 2*n*,65*ln*,251,
262,271,278*n*
Picolit grape and wines 6,201,201*l*,
228*t*
comparisons to 262
Picpoul grape and wines 160,162
Piedirosso (red pigeon-foot) grape
and wine 6,221,222*ln*
Piemonte. *See* Italy, Piedmont
Pigato grape and wine 192
"Pigeon's foot" grape. *See*
Piedirosso
Pineau D'Aunis grape and wine of
Loire 168. *See also* Pineau
de la Loire
Pineau de la Loire (a.k.a., Chenin
Blanc) grape and wines 6,
76*t*. *See also* Chenin Blanc;
Pineau D'Aunis
Pineau des Charentes aperitif 55*t*,
303
Pink wines. *See* Rose
Pinkish-gray wines. *See* D'Anjou
wines; Gray wines
Pinotage grape and wines 7,280,281
Pinot Beurot grape and wine 76*t*
Pinot Bianco grape and wines 194,
201,228*t*. *See also* Pinot
Blanc
Pinot Blanc grape and wines 6. *See
also* Pinot Bianco
of Egypt 266
of France 76*t*,165,171
of Germany, a.k.a.,
Weissburgunder 6,237
of Italy 82,197,223
of Luxembourg 265
of U.S. 83,107

Pinot Chardonnay grape and wine
134,135,137. *See also*
Chardonnay
Pinot Grigio grape. *See under* Pinot
Gris
Pinot Gris grape and wines 6
of France 76*t*
a.k.a., Tokay D'Alsace 6,165
of U.S. 98
a.k.a., Pinot Grigio 6,16
in Hungary 260
in Italy 82,187
comparison to 217
Friuli-Venezia Giulia 199*l*,
201
Sicily 226
Trentino-Alto Adige 29*l*,198,
200*l*,202*l*
Veneto 197
in Luxembourg 265
a.k.a., Rülander 6
in Germany 237,242
Pinot Meunier grape and wines 6,61,
62,82
Pinot Nero grape. *See* Pinot Noir,
Italy
Pinot Noir grape and wines, 2,6,7,
100
of Australia 277,279
of Bulgaria *map* 261
of Canada 273
of Egypt 266
of France
Alsace 76*t*,165
Burgundy 76*t*,119,137
Cote Chalonnais 151,152
Cote d'Or 135,136*ln*,138
Champagne 61,62
Jura 76*t*
a.k.a., Gros Noiren 171
Loire 167
of Germany, a.k.a.,
Spätburgunder 237,242,244
of Hungary 262, *map* 261
of Italy 82,187,189,226

a.k.a., Pinot Nero 198
of New Zealand 280
of Romania 264, *map* 261
of Spain 254
of Switzerland 259
of U.S. 90,95
California 83,92,93,104-105
serving order for wines of 17
Oregon 98,99*ln*,104
Washington State 98
of Yugoslavia 260, *map* 261
Pinot St. George grape 6
*Pipes*, defined and use of 42
Pisco, grape brandy distillate 270,
303
Poison, wine regarded as 266
Pommard. *See under* France,
Burgundy
"Pop" wines. *See* Wine beverages
Popes
French papal palace 159,162
wines enjoyed by 189*ln*,214
Port wines. *See also* Porto
comparison to 55*t*
grapes for, growing regions for
100
labeling of 36,47,94
of Australia 47,276,278*t*
of U.S. 47,93*t*
Porto wines. *See also* Port wines
comparisons to 224,263
decanting of types 21,42,43*ln*
examples of 43*l*,44*l*,55*t*
grape varieties for 42
world growing regions for 100
as major fortified wine type 35
production methods 42-43
regulation of production 42,250
serving of types 16,17,42,43
vintage porto 42,43*l*,44
aging potential of 14,42,44*ln*
comparison to late bottled
(LBV) 43,44*ln*
white (blanco) porto 16,42,43
comparisons to 225

wood portos, types and examples
43,43*l*,44*l*
Portugal
aperitifs of 55*t*,56*t*
fortified wines and producing
regions
Carcavelos 250*t*,251
Douro 250*t*. *See also* Porto
wines
Madeira. *See* Madeira, island
and wine
Setubal 46*l*,47*t*,250*t*,251
maps, wines and regions 35,249
production and consumption
rankings 250,320*t*
sparkling wines 84
table wines and producing regions
chapter summary 257
comparisons to 249
Bairrada 250*t*,251
Bucelas 250*t*,251
Colares 250*t*,251
Dao 17,250*t*,251
Minho (Vinho Verde wine)
250,250*t*,251*l*
Portuguieser grape 6
as Blauer Portuguieser grape and
wine 237
Pouilly-Fuisse wines 16,152,153*l*,
153*ln*,154,157*t*,168*ln*,173*t*
Pouilly-Fume (Blanc Fume de
Pouilly) wines 16,106*ln*,167,
168*l*,169,173*t*. *See also*
Sauvignon (Fume) Blanc
Pouilly-Loche wines 152,154*t*,157*t*,
173*t*
Pouilly-Sur-Loire wines 167,169,
173*t*
Pouilly-Vinzelles wines 152,154*t*,
157*t*,173*t*
Pouring wines. *See* Serving
*Pourriture noble*, defined 126-127,
175. *See also* Botrytis
cinerea

Prädikat wines. *See* Qualitäts mit
Prädikat
"Praises of Wine, The" (Firestone)
106*ln*
Predicate wines
of Germany. *See* Qualitäts mit
Prädikat
of Italy. *See* Predicato
Predicato wines of Tuscany (Italy),
and types of, defined 206*ln*,
207. *See also specific wines*
Pregnant women, and wine and
alcoholic beverage
consumption by *x*,15,94
Prehistoric evidence
of vines 115,205
of wine use 1
Premium wineries and wines. *See
also* Discovery wines;
Esoteric wines; Fantasy
wines; Super-premium wines
of California 91,99
of Italy 185*ln*,201
of Washington State 99
Preprandial drinks, sherry as 40. *See
also* Aperitifs; Cocktails
Pressing. *See* Crushing
Pressure in sparkling wines. *See*
Atmospheres; Charmat
Method; Corks; Methode
Champenoise; Transfer
Method
Pricing
as factor in establishing
Classification of 1855 of
Bordeaux 119
and Hospices de Beaune auction
as factor for certain
Burgundy wines 142
of wines, expense/affordability of.
*See specific wines*
Primitivo di Gioia grape and wines
107,223, *map* 177. *See also*
Zinfandel

Procanico grape 205. *See also*
Trebbiano
"Produced and bottled by," defined
29. *See also* Bottling terms
Producers. *See also* **Name Index,
Producers,** *by category and
country*
importance of, in selecting wines
156,182,188,189. *See also*
Shippers
largest. *See under* Rankings
Production methods. *See*
Winemaking
Production rankings. *See* Rankings
Prohibition, period of
in Canada 89
in U.S. 89-90,97
Prokupac grape 6,260
Proprietaire, defined 175
Prosecco grape and wines 6,81,197
Provencal (Provence). *See* France,
Provence
Prüfungsnummer, defined 248
Amtliche Prüfungsnummer
(A.P.Nr.) 234,248, *illus.* 237
Prugnolo grape. *See under*
Sangiovese Grosso
Pruning and training of vines, and
methods of 4,8*t*,142,155,250
decisions regarding 8
origin of, legendary 167
regulation of 28,62,63
Publications referenced
*Academie du Vin Complete Wine
Course* (Spurrier and Dovaz)
24
*Complete Encyclopedia of
Alcoholic Beverages*
(Mohawk Liqueur
Corporation) 283*n*
"Decanter" 217*ln*
*Die Lorelei* (Heine) 240
*Encyclopedia of Wines and Spirits*
(Lichine) 171

*Ford's Illustrated Guide to Wines*
(Ford) 90
*Italy's Noble Red Wines*
(Wasserman and Wasserman)
191*ln*
*Matteo Falcone (Maltese Falcon)*
(Merimee) 171
"The Praises of Wine"
(Firestone) 106*ln*
*Rubaiyat* (Khayyam) 266
"Spirits and Beer A to Z
Supplement" (Mohawk
Liqueur Corporation) *x*
*Snow White and the Seven Dwarfs*
(Grimm) 240
*Wine Handbook* (Sutcliffe)
171-172
*Wines of America* (Adams) 97
Puligny-Montrachet. *See under*
France, Burgundy
Punt e Mes vermouth 53*l*,55*t*
Pupitre(s) 67,82. *See also* Riddling
Purple wine 11*t*
Puttonyos, defined 262
P.X. wine, use of in sherry
production 40. *See also*
Pedro Ximenez grape

QbA wines of Germany. *See*
Qualitätswein eines
bestimmten Anbaugebietes
QmP wines of Germany. *See*
Qualitätswein mit Prädikat
Qualitätsschaumwein 78*t*
Qualitätswein, or Qualitätswein
eines bestimmten
Anbaugebietes (QbA) of
Germany 28,237*t*,244
category of, defined 234
for Sekt, defined 78*t*
regions and vineyards for QbA
wines 240-242,243
wines designated as QbA,
examples 31*l*,235*l*,236*l*,238*l*,
242*l*,244

Qualitätswein mit Präikat (QmP) of
Germany 28,237*t*,244
category, subcategories, and
standards for, defined
234-237,243
comparison to France and Italy
182
regions and vineyards for QmP
wines 240-242,243
wines designated as QmP,
examples 234*l*,236*l*,238*l*,
244,244*l*
Quality of wines, basic factors for
achieving, defined 2-9. *See
also specific factors*
Quality, classification for. *See*
Government regulation
Quarte de Chaume wine 168
Quintas, defined 42
Quotas, import, U.S., and social
pressures regarding 90. *See
also* Social pressures

Rabelo, defined 42
Rabigato grape and wine 42
Raccolta, translated 217
Raccolto, translated 215*ln*
Racking, defined 64
decisions regarding 8
sequence of tasks of during
production 3
Rainwater wine 46
Raisin palate, wine described as
having 40*ln*
Raisin wine, ancient Greek 52
Raisins (raisinized, raisin-like). *See*
Grapes, dried
Raki (Club Raki) aperitif 56*t*,266,
303
Ramato, defined 201
Ramisco grape and wine 6,251
Rankings, consumption per capita,
top ten countries and U.S.
320*t*. *See also specific and
additional countries*

Rankings, production
by company
for champagne and sparkling
wines, largest and former
largest, worldwide 77,96
for wine production, general,
worldwide
first place 108*ln*
second place 271
by country, for wine production
top ten 320*t*
first 77,252
second 77,252
third 252
third or fourth 265
fifth 259,270
sixth 88
seventh 250
tenth 273
twenty-fifth 273
thirty-second 273
of Australia, compared with
U.S., Italy, and France 275
within U.S.
for grape production, by state,
first through third 99
for wine production, state
ranked third 97
for vermouth, largest producing
country 52
for viticulture, country with
largest area under vines 250
Ratafia aperitif 55*t*
Ravat grape and wines 7,83
Ravello wine 221,228*t*
Rayas, defined and use of 39
R.D. (Recently Disgorged). *See*
Disgorgement
Recommendations by authors of
book. *See also* Buying wine
to further knowledge 319
regarding labels shown and wines
mentioned *x*, 319. *See also
specific wines and regions*
Recoltant, defined 175

Recoltant-Manipulant (R.M.),
defined 70
Recolte, translated 163
Red grape varieties, examples 6,7.
*See also specific and
additional varieties*
Red wines. *See also specific wines*
production process for, illustrated
3
shades of 11*t*. *See also specific
shades*
styles of, and serving of,
examples, 15,16,17,20
Refosco grape 6,201
Refrigeration
to chill wine 23
in vermouth production 54
Regaleali wine 178,224*l*,225,226,
226*l*,229*t, map* 177. *See also*
**Name Index: Persons,**
Tasca; **Producers,** Count
Tasca
*Regiao Demarcada* for Portugal,
defined 250
regions designated as, and wines
of 250*t*,250-251
Regulations and laws for
classification of wines. *See*
Government regulation
Religious aspects of viticulture,
winemaking, and use of wine
Biblical and religious literature,
references to *xi*,1,266
Christianity, use and customs *v*,1,
14,116
Etruscans, wine use by 205
French Huguenots, influences of
88,280
Islamic (Muslim; Turkish
Moslem) influences
comparison of U.S. Prohibition
to governments under 89
in Austria 259
in Bulgaria 264

in Greece 263
in Lebanon 266
in Turkey 266
Jewish customs, wine use, and
influences *v*,1,14,177,266
Kosher wines
of Israel 266-267,267*l*
symbol on label identifying
as 267*ln*
of U.S. 10,90,96,97
for the Mass 116
missionaries, roles and influences
of in viticulture
in California 1,89,252,275
in India 267
in South America 1
Argentina 252,270
Chile 252,271
monks and monastic roles and
influences 1
in flavoring wines, art of 52
in France
Abbey of Beze 138
Abbey of Citeaux 139
Abbey of St. Denis 139
Benedictines 116,151
Cistercians 133
Saint-Hilaire, and wines of
76*t*,77
at Tours, and St. Martin and
pruning origin legend 167
for Vigne de l'Enfant Jesus
wine, naming of 142*ln*
in Germany 235,241
in Ohio River region, during
Prohibition 97
in U.S., influence on wine
industry 90
during Prohibiton, religious
wine production 89,97
Remuage, defined 67. *See also*
Riddling
invention of 63*ln*

Reserva, designation of for wines.
*See also* Riserva
of Chile 272,273
of Spain 80*ln*,254,255*ln*,256*ln*
Reserve stocks of wine for blending.
*See* Blended wines; Cuvees
Restaurants
a preferred wine of, named 153*l*
and restauranteurs, named 94,142
and Italian influence on, in
U.S. 218
wine service in 19,21,27,28
Resting, production phase of, for
Champagne 68
Retsina wine 1,262, *map* 261
Rheims (Reims). *See under* France,
Champagne
Rhine (Rhein) wines
serving order for 16
German. *See also under* Germany:
Mittelrhein; Rheingau;
Rheinhessen; Rheinpfalz
English name for 235*ln*. *See
also* Hock wines
with botanical additives 52,244
of U.S., labeling for 89,94
Rheinriesling grape and wines 259.
*See also* Riesling
Rhode Island 96
Rhone wines. *See* France,
Cotes-du-Rhone; Switzerland
(Rhone valley of)
Rhone Syrah grape and wines
origin of grape and name 266
of France
Cotes-du-Rhone 160
Cotie Rotie 160,160*l*
Giogondas 162
Hermitage appellation 160*l*,
161
a.k.a., Shiraz grape
in Australia 277,278*t*,279*t*
a.k.a., Hermitage grape (in
Australia) 259,276-277,280*l*.

*See also* Cinsault (Hermitage) *under* Hermitage grape
in Lebanon, and origin of name 266
in New Zealand 280
in South Africa 281
Ribolla Gialla grape 201
Ricard. *See* Pastis
Riddling, process of
hand method 73,79,79*t*
as *remuage*, and defined 63*ln*, 67
mechanical method 73,79
rack used for 67
and Italian labels depicting 82
Riesling grape and wines 2,6,7,100. *See also* Emerald Riesling; Johannisberg Riesling; Müller-Thurgau; Okanagan Riesling; Olaszrizling; Rheinriesling; Welschriesling; White Riesling
of Argentina 271
of Australia 277,278,279
of Austria 260
of Bulgaria *map* 261
of Chile 271,272
of France 16,76*t*,165,166,173
of Germany, 237
Mittelrhein 77,78*l*
Mosel-Saar-Ruwer 31*l*,234, 234*l*,237,238*l*,240,241
Nahe 244
Rheingau 235*l*,237,241
Rheinhessen 236*l*,244,244*l*
Rheinpfalz 242
of Hungary *map* 261
of Italy 193,198
of Luxembourg 265
of New Zealand 280
of Romania 264, *map* 261
of South Africa 281
of Spain 254
of U.S. 90,92,97,98,99,105

of U.S.S.R. 265
of Yugoslavia *map* 261
Rioja. *See under* Spain
Ripeness. *See under* Grapes
Riserva, designation of for Italian wines, defined 231. *See also* Reserva
for Barolo 184*ln*,231
for Brunello di Montalcino 188*ln*
for Chianti 30*ln*,209*t*,211*ln*
for Marsala 45
wine lots for Riserva 211*ln*
Riserva Speciale, designation of for Italian wines, and change in law regarding 184*ln*,189*ln*
Riviera, French (Cotes D'Azur), wines consumed on 171
Rkatsiteli grape 6
Romania 1,263-254,320*t*, *map* 261
Romans, ancient, roles and influence of in viticulture and/or winemaking *v*, 1,115-116, 205,221,241,250. *See also* Gods; Literature
province of, in Hungary 260,262
quotation from, applied to German viticulture 240
wines of, and used by 1,52,266
Ronco (della) Acacie wine 201,228*t*
Rondinella grape 197
Rosato wine, defined 231
Rose (Rosé) wines. *See also* Blanc de Noir; Blush wines
dry, serving order for, examples 17. *See also specific wines*
and complementary foods for 20
shades of 11*t*. *See also specific shades*
of Australia 279*t*
of France
Alsace 165
Burgundy 137,138
Champagne 66*l*
Cotes-du-Rhone 159

Lirac 160,162,163*t*
Tavel 17,95,160,162,163*t*
Jura 171
Loire 167,168, *also* 17
Provence 17,95,171,172*l*
as *vin mousseux* 77
of Germany 237,242,248
of Greece 263
of Italy, terms used to denote 231
Abruzzo 218
Apulia 95,223
Campania 95,221,228*t*
Lombardy 193
Molise 218
Sicily 95,226,229*t*
Trentino-Alto Adige 198
Veneto 197, *also* 17
of Portugal 249,250. *See also* Bocksbeutal
of Spain 251
of Switzerland 259, *also* 175
of U.S., and popularization of 95
California 17,95
Washington State 95,99
Rosette grape 7. *See also* Seibel
Rossese grape 6
Rossese di Dolceacqua wine 192, *map* 177
Rosso wine, defined 231
Rosso Antico wine 55*t*
Rosso del Conte wine 182,224*l*,229*t*
Rosso Conero wine 217
Rosso di Montalcino wine 188*l*
Rosso Piceno wine 217, *map* 177
Rosso della Ponca wine 201,228*t*, *also* 5*t*
Rotwein, translated 248
Reoussane grape and wines 160,161
Roussette grape and wines 76*t*,171
*Rubaiyat* (Khayyam), excerpted 266
Rubesco wine 214,215*l*. *See also* Torgiano
Ruby Cabernet grape 7,100
Ruby wines 11*t*,43,45

Rülander grape. *See under* Pinot Gris

Rum
  as distilled spirit 283
  defined, and types of 304
  use of as currency 275
Rustic (Rural) Method of sparkling wine production 74

Sack sherry 36,37
  dry, example 39*l*
  Shakespearian references to 36,77
Sacramental wine. *See* Religious aspects
St. Pantalemon wine 263
St. Rafael aperitif 55*t*
Sake (Saki) 268,268*l*,314
Salice wine 222,222*l*, *map* 177
Sammarco wine 182,206,207,208*l*, 229*t*
Samos. *See* Greece
Sancerre wine 106*ln*,167
  comparison to 168
Sancorcho wine, defined 40
San Giorgio wine 182,214,230*t*
Sangiovese (Sangiovese Grosso) grape and wines 2,6
  a.k.a., Prugnolo Gentile grape 208*ln*
  of Italy, wines of. *See also* Brunello di Montalcino; Ca del Pazzo; Grifi; Rosso Piceno; Sammarco; San Giorgio; Sassicaia; Solaia; Tignanello; Torgiano Rosso; Vigorello; Vino Nobile di Montepulciano
    Chianti wine. *See* Italy, Chianti zone
    Emilia-Romagna 194,195
    Latium 219
    Marches 217
  of U.S. 107
Sangria wine 95,194,249
Santa Helena wine 263, *map* 261

Santa Maddalena wine 198
Sardinia. *See under* Italy
Sassella wine 194
Sassicaia wine 182,206,207, 210*l*,229*t*
Saumur wine (Coteaux de Saumur) 76*t*,168,169*t*
Sauterne wine, U.S. labeling of 89, 94
Sauternes wine. *See under* France, Burgundy
Sauvignon (Fume) Blanc grape and wines 2,6
  growing regions for 100
  of Australia 277,278*t*
    comparisons to 264*ln*
  of Bulgaria *map* 261
  of Chile 271,272,273
  of France
    comparisons to 264*ln*
    Bordeaux 105,106*ln*,119
    Loire 105,106*ln*,167,169,169*t*, 173*t*
    Provence 171
    southwest 172
  of Hungary *map* 261
  of Israel 267
  of Italy
    comparisons to 264*ln*
    map 177
    Emilia-Romagna 195
    Friuli-Venezia Giulia 201
    Sicily 226,226*ln*
    Trentino-Alto Adige 198
    Tuscany 206*ln*,207,207*ln*,211*ln*
  of Romania 264*ln*, *map* 261
  of Spain 254
  of U.S.
    comparisons to 264*ln*
    California 92*t*,93*t*,105,105*ln*, 107*ln*
      and popularization of 105, 106*ln*
    serving order for 16
  Oregon 98

Washington State 99
  of Yugoslavia *map* 261
Sauvignon Vert grape 6
Savagnin grape and wines 6,47*t*,76*t*, 171
Savatiano grape and wines 263
Savoring (sipping) a wine 24,26
Scandinavia
  Denmark 265
    aperitif of 56*t*,295
  Finland, winemaker and U.S. immigrant from 96
Scharzhofberger, vineyard of 243
Schaumwein 77,78*t*
Scheurebe grape and wines 7,237, 241
Schiava grape 6
  a.k.a., Vernatsch, and wines 6, 198
Schillerwein 242
Schioppettino grape and wines 201, 228*t*
Schloss Eltz, vineyard of 243. *See also* Germany, Rheingau
Schloss Johannisberg(er), vineyard and wines of 77,241,243
  and legend of Spätlese wine origin 235
Schloss Vollrads, vineyard and wines of 241,243
Schools with viticultural programs
  France, Bordeaux 8
  Germany, Geisenheim 8,241
  Italy
    Conegliano 8,197
    Trentino 197
  U.S.
    Christian Brothers 96
    University of California at Davis 7,8,25,89,96,98,270
Sciaccarello grape 171
Sciacchetra wine 192
Scoring wines to record impressions from tasting 23

Scuppernong grape and wines 7,89,
    90,97
Scuro, defined 198
Sealing. *See* Corks
Seasonal phases of work for
    viticulture and winemaking
    8*t*. *See also related subjects*
    for Champagne production 62,67
Sec, defined 68
Secco, style of 79
Secco, translated and defined 45,
    216*ln*,218*tn*
Sediment in wine, defined and types
    of 28. *See also* Cloudy wine;
    Crystals
    in champagne and sparkling wines
        during production 64,67,74
    in porto, types of 21,42,43
    in sherry 40
    separating from wine
        by decanting and straining 21,
            22
        by use of wine basket 27*n*
"Seeing" wine. *See* Appearance
Sehr Trocken, translated 81*t*
Seibel grape 2,7
Sekt sparkling wines
    of Germany 59,61,77-78,240,248,
        *also* 73-74
    of Austria 61,79
Select harvest grapes and wines. *See
    also* Harvest: hand-picking
    method; late harvest
    for German wines 234,235,236,
        248. *See also specific wines*
    for sherry 37
Selecting wines. *See* Buying
Semillon grape and wines 6,7,100
    of Australia 277,279
    of Chile 272
    of France 119,172,173
    of Israel 267
    of South Africa 281
    of U.S. 98,99
Sercial grape and Madeira 46,55*t*

Sereksia grape 6
Serradayres wines 252
Serving wine 15-23,27,28. *See also*
    Food; *specific wines*
Setubal wines and region 46*l*,47*t*,
    250*t*,251, *map* 35
Seyssel wine 76*t*,77,171
Seyval Blanc grape and wines 2,7,
    83,90,97,268
Sforsato (Sfursat) wine 194
Sherry
    in cooking, use of 268
    comparisons to 36,224
    defined, as major fortified wine
        35,36
    grape varieties used for 40
        and world growing regions for
            100
    labeling of 36
        and in U.S. 94
    popularity of
        in Italy, compared with Marsala
            178
        in U.S., type of 36
    production of, and methods for
        10,37-40
        comparison to, for type of porto
            42
        in South Africa 36,281
        in Spain, Jerez region 36,252,
            253*t*,256
        in U.S., and examples 47,96,97
    serving of types of 16,17,40
    types
        amontillado, as type of oloroso
            36,37*n*
        cream sherry, as type of oloroso
            36,37*n*,40*l*
            comparison to 45
            of U.S., examples 47,97
        fino, and types of 33*l*,36,55*t*
            comparisons to 45,55*t*,171,
                225
            of U.S., example 47

oloroso, and types of 36,37*n*,
    39*l*
    comparison to 45
manzanilla, as type of fino 36,
    37
    as sack 36,37,77
    dry sack, example 39*l*
Shippers, roles and importance of.
    *See also* Producers
    in France
        in Beaujolais 156
        in Burgundy region, commune
            wines 137
        in Chablis (Cote d'Or) 134,156
        for Champagne houses 68-70
        in Loire, and comparison with
            other regions of France 169
        terms used to denote French
            shippers 68,70*t*,134,139*ln*,
                169,175
    for German wines, and shipper
        rating 244,245
    in Italy 179*ln*
        terms used to denote Italian
            shippers 184*t*,231
    for porto production, and cuvees
        of 43
    for sherry production 38,39,40
Shiraz grape and wines. *See under*
    Rhone Syrah
Sicily. *See under* Italy
Sifone, defined and use of 45
Silvaner grape. *See* Sylvaner
Similarities or comparisons of
    wines. *See specific wines*
Single-vineyard wines. *See also
    specific and additional wines*
    of Burgundy, and classification of
        134,137
    custom of, and origin in France
        119
    in Italy, trend toward 201
Sipping, wines for

Marsala, types of 45
    *See also* Aperitifs: Cordials;
        Dessert wines; Liqueurs
Sipping (savoring) a wine, defined
    24,26
Sirah. *See* Petite Sirah
Sizzano wine 188
Smelling (sniffing) a wine, defined
    24,26
*Snow White and the Seven Dwarfs*
    (Grimm) 240
Soave wines and types of 81,177,
    178*t*,180*l*,187,197, *map* 177
    comparisons to 180*ln*,193,197,
    217
    serving order for 16
Social pressures and negative
    attitudes regarding wine
    consumption and industry *x*,
    94,90
"Soda pop" method of sparkling
    wine production. *See*
    Carbonation Method
"Soda pop" wines. *See* Wine
    beverages
Soil, as quality factor for wine
    production 2,4. *See also*
    *wine-producing regions and*
    *countries*
    chemical treatment and resting of
    134
    as contributing factor to taste of
    Madeira 46
    effect of different types on
    identical grape varieties 115
    erosion of, in Germany 233
    types of, notable 5*t*
    with moisture retention and
    effect on vines 237
Solaia wine 182,206,229*t*
Solera system of production
    for Marsala 45
    for sherry, of Spain 38-39
    for U.S. types 47,96
    process similar to 263

Solera-dated Madeira 46
Solimano wine 225
Solopaca wine 221
Sousao (Souzao) grape and wines 6,
    42,47
South Africa 1,280-281,320*t*
Southside wine 46
South America 1,270-273. *See also*
    *specific countries*
Spain 1,221,225,257
    aperitifs of 55*t*,56*t*
    CAVA and sparkling wines of 59,
    73,79,80*l*,254
    grape varieties of 37,40,79
    major, by region 252*t*-254*t*
    of Jerez, and climate, with
    comparisons 100
    legal standards and designations
    for wine quality 28,252,254
    maps 35,249
    production and consumption
    rankings 77,252,320*t*
    regions, and wines of
    Jerez 36,100,252,253t. *See also*
    Sherry
    Malaga 47*t*,252,253*t*
    Montilla 36,47*t*,55*t*,253*t*
    Old Castille-Leon 253*t*,255
    Penedes 79,80*l*,252*t*,254-255,
    256,257
    Ribera del Duero 253*t*,255,256,
    257
    Rioja 17, *mentioned* 252-257
    Valdepenas 253*t*,255
    other regions 252*t*-253*t*
"Spanish Crescent" 256
"Spanish earth," use of in sherry
    production 40
Spanna grape and wines 17,188,
    229*t*. *See also* Nebbiolo
Sparkling wines 11*t*,59,81*t*,84. *See*
    *also* **Name Index,**
    **Producers**
    production methods. *See*
    Carbonation; Charmat;

    Methode Champenoise;
    Rustic; Transfer; *specific*
    *processes of and related*
    *terms*
    serving of 16,17,18,20,21,23,27,
    70-71
    opened bottle, storage of 14,71
    of Argentina 84
    of Australia 84,278*t*
    of Austria 61,79
    of Brazil 84,270
    of Canada 84,273
    of Chile 84
    of France 73,74,76-77,134,151,
    161,165,167,168,175
    Champagne, true French 59-70
    comparisons to 61,73,80,82,
    83,83*ln*
    of Germany 59,61,73-74,77-78,
    240,248
    of Hungary 84
    of Israel 84,266,267
    of Italy 59,61,73,80-82,191*ln*,
    197,225,231. *See also* Asti
    Spumante
    of Luxembourg 84,265
    of New Zealand 84
    of Portugal 84,249,251
    of South Africa 84
    of Spain 59,61,73,79,80*l*,254,257
    of U.S. 59,73,80,82-83
    California 61,74,82-83
    New York State 74,82-83,96
    labeling of 83*ln*,89,94
    of U.S.S.R. 84,265
Spätburgunder grape. *See* Pinot
    Noir, Germany
Spätlese wines, category of and
    defined 234,235-236,248
    aging potential of 235*t*
    comparisons to 245
    crystals and acids in (i.e.,
    late-picked wines) 10,28
    examples of 236*l*,238*l*
    of Austria 260

Special, designation of, for wines of Chile 272. *See also* Riserva Speciale
"Spirits and Beer A to Z Supplement" (Mohawk Liqueur Corporation) *x*
Spitting vs. swallowing a wine, defined 15,26
Spoletto Festival 214
Spritzig, defined 242. *See also* Petillance
Spumante (spumanti) 59,61. *See also* Asti Spumante; Sparkling wines, Italy
defined 80,231
types of 80,189
brut (dry) types 189,198
comparison to 226
Steen grape and wines 6,281. *See also* Chenin Blanc
Steinberg(er), vineyards and wines of 241,243,248
Steinwein 241
Steuben grape 7
Still wine, defined 36
in Champagne production
blending of 68-69
conversion of to sparkling 64, 65,67
Storage of wine 14. *See also specific wines regarding aging potential*
bottles recommended for 13-14
in cellars 14,23
of French producers 62,141,175
of opened bottles 14,71
of porto 43
Straining wine. *See* Decanting
Stravecchio, designation of, for wines of Italy 45,226
Straw-color wine 11*t*,171,217*ln*
Sugar. *See also* Additives, sweeteners
as additive

to assist fermentation 10,65-67, 74,175,235
as chaptalization, and defined 175,181,235
to champagne, various production phases and effects 65,67,68
regulation of 181,235
content, in grapes
conversion of during fermentation 1-2,10,38,74
and ripeness, effect of 5,8,9, 29,62 63,69,235,235*t*,236
of late harvest grapes 29
of *Botrytis*-affected grapes 10
residual (unfermented) in finished wines 14,29,42,80,81*t*,95, 194,218*t*
Sulfites (sulphur; sulphur dioxide), as additive to wine production 2,10,14-15,181
and labeling of wines containing 15,90,94
Sultana grape and wines 6,277,281
Sumerians, ancient 266
Superior Old Marsala (SOM) 45
Superiore, designation of for Italian wines, defined 231
for Bardolino 197
for Frascati 219, *also* 216*ln*,217*ln*
for Marsala 45
for Soave 231, *also* 180*ln*,197
for Valpolicella 197,200*l*,203*l*
Super-premium wines and wineries. *See also* Discovery wines; Esoteric wines; Fantasy wines; Premium wines
of Italy 197,206
of U.S. 91
*Sur lie*, defined, and wines bottled as 168,169*ln*,259
and lees 64,73
*Sur pointe*, defined 67
Süss, translation equivalent 81*t*. *See also* Doux

Süss-Reserve, defined 235,248
Swallowing a wine vs. spitting, defined 15,24,26
Sweetness of wine. *See* Dryness
Sweetening of wine, production process of. *See* Additives: sugar, sweeteners
Switzerland 1,171,194,259,320*t*. *See also* France, Cotes-du-Rhone
Sylvaner (Wilvaner) grape and wines 7
of France 165
of Germany 77,237,241,242,244
of Italy 198
Syrah. *See* Rhone Syrah
Syrians, ancient, wine of 1

Table wines 87-281. *See also* **Name Index, Producers;** *specific wines, countries, and regions*
defined 11*t*,87
Tafel Wein (Tafelwein), Deutscher (DTW), defined and standards for 234,244,248
Tanks. *See* Vessels
Tannat grape 172
Tannin, defined and source of 9,28, 37
as longevity factor 14
tannic wines, examples of 172, 188,251
Tasting of wine, for analysis and appreciation 319
approach to popularized by California producers 108
art of, defined 24,26*t*
components of wine influencing 9-10
score card to record impressions, illustrated 23
and senses, combined reactions of 51
sensory analysis chart 25
by waiter 21

Tasting of wine, official, for
     classification and regulation
     of quality
  in Chile 272
  in France 117,128
  in Germany 234
  in Italy 181*n*,181*t*
  for sherry 38
Tastings (events for sampling wines)
  "blind" competitive, advocate of
     90
  competitive, for awards. *See*
     Awards
  guidelines for attending 15,24
  Iberian wines, presence at 249
  legal regulation of 15
  types of 10
Taurasi wine 17,221,222*ln*, map 177
Tawny-color wines 11*t*,43
Taxation related to wine industry,
     U.S.
  exemptions to promote viticulture
     89
  loss of during Prohibition 90
  social pressures regarding *x*,90
  of sparkling wines, rates of 74
Tavel. *See under* France,
     Cotes-du-Rhone
TBA wines. *See*
     Trockenbeerenauslese
Technology, influence and role of
  of Industrial Revolution for
     flavoring wines 52
  in Italy 197,205
  in New Zealand 280
  in Portugal 249
  for vermouth production 54
  and terms on labels related to 94
Temperatures
  control of during production 8
     of sparkling wines 62,64,67,73,
     74
  for serving wine 10,21,23
  for storing wine 10,14,21,23

viticultural requirements 5,8. *See
     also* Altitude; Bodies of
     water; Climate
Tempranillo grape and wines 6
  of Argentina 271
  of Spain *mentioned* 253-257,271
Tent wine 46
Tenuta (tenute), translated 231
Teroldego grape and wine 198
Terrantez grape and wine 46
Terre Alte wine 178,201,228*t*
Terret Noire grape and wine 160
Tête de cuvee 70. *See also* Cuvees
Texas 97-98
Thompson Seedless grape 6
Tignanello wine 178,182,205*ln*,206,
     207,229*t*
Tinta Barocca grape and wines 281
Tinta Cao grape and wine 42
Tinta Fina (Tinto Fino) grape 253*t*
Tinta Francisca grape and wine 42
Tinta Madeira grape 6
Tinta Pinheira grape and wines 251
Tinta wine 46,254
Tinto Aragenes grape and wine 255
Tinto Fino (Tinta Fina) grape 253*t*
Tinto Pesquera wine 255-256
Tirage (stacking procedure) 67,80
Tirage (sweetening procedures)
  dosage de tirage 65-67
  liqueur de tirage 74
Toasting *x*
Tocai Friulano grape and wines 6,
     197,198*l*,201
Tokaji wines and types of 259,262,
     map 261
  aging potential of 14
  comparisons to 265
  serving order for 17
Tokay D'Alsace grape. *See under*
     Pinot Gris
Tonneau, defined 175
Torcolato wine 197,230*t*
Torbato grape and wines 224,228*t*,
     map 177

Torgiano wines, *map* 177
  Bianco 214
  Rosso 205,214,215*l*
  Rosso Riserva 181*t*,214,215*l*
Torre Ercolana wine 219,228*t*
Torre di Gaia wine 221,228*t*
Touraine wine 76*t*
Tourigo grape and wines 6,42,251
Tours (sightseeing) for wine,
     recommended area of Italy
     187
Trajadura grape and wines 250
Traminer grape. *See*
     Gewürtztraminer
Transfer Method of sparkling wine
     production, and uses of
     73-74
  in Germany 77,248
  in U.S. 74,82,83,96
Trebbiano grape and wines 2,6
  of Australia 277
  of Brazil 270
  of France, a.k.a., Ugni Blanc
     grape 6,160,171
  of Italy 47*t*,178, *map* 177
     ancient varietal of 205
     a.k.a., Trebbiano Toscano
        in Tuscany 211*ln*
     in Abruzzo, as Trebbiano
        D'Abruzzo, a.k.a., Bombino
        Bianco 218
     in Emilia-Romagna 194,195
     in Latium 219
     in Sicily 225
     in Umbria 214
Trellis pruning, defined 4
  and use of pergolas in Portugal
     250
Trocken, translated and defined
     78*ln*,81*t*,244
Trockenbeerenauslese (TBA) wines,
     category of and defined 234,
     236,248
  aging potential of 14,235*t*,236
  comparisons to 222-223,262

360

crystals and acids in (i.e., late-picked wines) 10,28
growing conditions required to produce 237
serving order for 17
Trollinger grape and wine 7,237
Tunisia 265
Turkey 266. *See also* Islamic aperitif of. *See* Raki
Types of wines, label identification of, examples illustrated 29-33 *See also specific types; grape varieties*

Ugni Blanc grape and wines. *See* Trebbiano grape, France
Ull de Llebre grape 252t,254
Ullage, defined 175
Underberg aperitif 56t
Unicum apritif 56t
Universities. *See* Schools
United States. *See also specific states*
  aperitifs of 55t
  California, role of in U.S. wine industry 1,89,90-91,94,95-96
  exports *x*
  fortified wines of 36,47,96
  history of viticulture and wine industry, overview *v*,2, 88-91,94
  imports of wine. *See also* Discovery wines; *additional countries and wines*
    from France 61,69,77,171
    from Germany 77,234,240
    from Italy 177,183*ln*,194,198, 218,221,222
    of Madeira 46
    of sparkling wines 59,80-82
    from Spain 40,254-256
    from various other countries *mentioned* 259-281
  joint ventures with Europeans and countries 61,83,264

maps
  isothermic zone of U.S. 5
  major grape varieties, regional 88
production and consumption, and rankings *x*,52,77,88,96-97, 108*ln*,320t
regulation of wine industry 15
  and appellation-type ruling for, and approved zones, examples 96,98
  taxation related to *x*,74,89,90
  sparkling wines of 59,61,73,74, 80,82-83,96
  comparisons to 82,96
  serving customs for champagne 70
  viticultural areas 96-112. *See also specific states*
United States Bureau of Alcohol, Tobacco, and Firearms (BATF) and regulation of wine industry by 15,96,98
Uruguay 270
U.S.S.R. 265,320t
  Armenians in Turkey 266
  imports to 264,266
Uva di Troia grape and wine 223
Uva Rara grape and wines 193

Valbuena wine 255
Valdepenas wine 255
Valgella wine 194
Valle Isarco wine 198
Valpolicella wine 17,185*l*,187,197, 199*l*,203*l*, *map* 177
  Amarone, type of Valpolicella 17, 179*l*,185*l*,187,197,200*l*,201*l*
  comparisons to 194,263
  wine based on 203*ln*
Valtellina wines 194, *map* 177
Varietal wines. *See* Naming wines, for grapes
Vats. *See* Vessels

V.D.Q.S. wines of France. *See* Vins Delimites de Qualite Superieure
Vecchio, designation of for Italian wines 45,209t
Vecchio Samperi aperitif 45,229t
Vega-Sicilia wine 255
Veltliner grape. *See* Grüner Veltliner
Vendange, translated 175
  vendange tardive, translated 165
Vendemmia, translated 217*n*
Verdeca grape 6
Verdejo grape 253t
Verdelho grape and wines 42,279
  and Madeira 46,55t
Verdicchio grape and wines 6,16,81, 205,206*ln*, *map* 177
  comparisons to 171,217
Verdil grape 253t
Verduzzo grape and wine 6,201
Vermentino grape and wines 171, 192,224
Vermouth, and production of 51, 52-54
  methods for 54
  source of wines for 221
  in Central America 54
  in France 52,54
  in Israel 266-267
  in Italy 52,53*l*,54,187
  in Mexico 273
  in South America 54,270
    Argentina 52,271
    Brazil 270
  in U.S. 52
  types of 52-54,55t
  serving order for 16
Vernaccia grape and wines 6,16, 206,210*l*,212*l*,214*l*,224, *map* 177
Vernatsch grape 6
  a.k.a. Schiava, and wines 6, 198
Vespolina grape 6
Vessels used in winemaking, illustrated 3

for fermentation
    bottles, for sparkling wines 61,
      64,67,73,74,96
    tanks, advantages of 29,80
    tanks, for sparkling wines 64,
      73,80
    wood (barrels, casks) 64,262
    wood, disadvantages of 29
    vats, for sparkling wines 65,74
for maturation (aging in
      production). *See also specific*
      *wines for aging requirements*
    bottles, for porto 42
    tanks vs. wood, effect on wines
      103*ln*,254
    tanks, for sparkling wines 77,
      78*ln*
    wood, for fortified types 36,43,
      44*l*
    wood, barriques, uses of 206,
      208*ln*,210*ln*,226
    for mixing 65
    for purifying 64
Vidal grape and wine 7,83,97
Vigneron, defined 175
Vigneronnage, defined 154
Vigneto, translated 231
Vignoles grape 7. *See also* Ravat
Vigorello wine 182,206,207,207*l*,
    229*t*
Villages (commune) wines. *See*
    *under various regions of*
    France
Villiard grape and wine 7,97
Vin. *See also* Vinho; Vino; Vins
Vin jaune wines 171
Vin de paille wines 171. *See also*
    Straw-color
Vin de taille, defined 64
Vin doux naturel, defined 175
Vin mousseux, or mousseux, and
    defined 76,77,168,175
Vin ordinaire 28. *See also* Vins de
    table
Vin Santo 47*t*,206,214, *map* 35

Vinegar, source of 37
"Vineland", U.S. 2,88
    Canada 273, *map* 88
Vines. *See also* Climate; Diseases;
    Grafting; Grapes; *Phylloxera*
    *vastatrix*; Pruning; Soil;
    Yields
    life span of 61
    prehistoric evidence of 115,205,
      *also* 1
    and quality of wine, factors
      affecting 2,4,5,8-10
    regulation of 28. *See also specific*
      *countries*
Vineyards, terms used to denote
    French 119-122,175
    Italian 231
    German 248
Vinho Verde wines 250,251*ln*
Vinifera grapes. *See* Vitis vinifera
Vinification. *See* Winemaking
Vinitaly wine fair 197
Vino (Vini) da Tavola of Italy,
      category of, defined 181*t*
    and types of 181-182,228*t*-230*t*.
      *See also specific wines and*
      *producers*
Vino di Qualita Prodotto in (una)
      Regione Determinata
      (V.Q.P.R.D.), defined 231
    examples of on labels 199*l*
Vino Nobile di Montepulciano
      D.O.C.G. classification of 178,
      181,181*t*,183,207
    and capsule band for, illustrated
      181
    examples of 183*l*,208*l*,211*ln*
    grape based on 183,206,208*ln*
    map 177
    serving order for 17
Vins Delimites de Qualite Superieur
      (V.D.Q.S.) wines of France,
      and defined 28,117,172
Vins de Pays wines, category of,
      and defined 28,117

Vins de table wines, category of,
      and defined 28,117
Vintage (process of vinting). *See*
      Winemaking
Vintage dates and dating. *See also*
      Dates on labels
    vs. bottling dates, example, for
      porto 44*ln*. *See also specific*
      *wines regarding production*
      *aging*
    consumers' reliance on and
      quality expectations of 8,9,
      14,33,73,80
    exceptional or notable, and years
      for
      Barbaresco 183*ln*
      Barolo 183*ln*,189*ln*
      California wines, 109*ln*,110*ln*
      Madeira 46
      porto, Vintage Porto 42
      Rioja Reserva 254*ln*
      Taurasi Riserva 221
    identifying on labels, examples
      illustrated 29-33
    and terms denoting vintage
      French 165,175
      German 234*ln*,244,248
      Italian 215*ln*,217*n*
    for Italian wines, and accuracy of
      180
    on Luxembourg wines 265
    significant factors related to,
      regarding law/classification
      changes
      for Chateau Mouton-Rothschild
      120*t*,121*l*
      for Italian wines 180,181
      Barolo 184*ln*,189*ln*
      Chianti 181,209*t*
      impending changes 181*t*
      for Predicato wines 206*ln*,
      207
    for sparkling wines, vintage and
      non-vintage dated
      Champagne, true French,

determining factors for 65, 69-70

comparison of with other sparkling wines 73

examples 31*l*,63*l*-66*l*,68*l*,71*l*

German QbA Sekt, specifications for 78*t*

Italian sparkling wines 80

Vintage Chart, and excerpt from 9

Vintage Tunina wine 201,228*t*

"Vinted by," defined 29

Viognier (Viogner) grape and wines 160,161

Viscosity, as analysis characteristic 24

and glycerine, as contributing component 9-10,251

Vitamin content of wine. *See* Components, nutritional

Viticulture, general factors of 2,4-5, 8. *See also* Vigneronnage; Vines

origin of 1,266

*Vitis labrusca* (Labrusca; Native American) grapes and wines

characteristics of 10

hybrid of 89

for kosher wines 90,96

other products and uses of 10,96

predominant geographic areas for 2,4,10

root stock and use of for *phylloxera*-control 2,2*n*,116, 133

varieties of 2,7*t*. *See also specific varieties*

in Japan 268

in U.S. 2,4,10,83,88,89,90,96,97

*Vitis muscadine* (Muscadine) grapes and wines 7*t*,88,89,90,97

*Vitis vinifera* (Vinifera) grapes, defined 2

birthplace of, probable 266

European origins of 1

predominant geographic areas for 4,10, *map* 88

in Canada 273

in Japan 268

varieties of 2,6*t*. *See also specific and additional varieties*

"crosses" of 7*t*

Viura grape and wines 6,253*t*,254

Vodka, as distilled spirit and defined 283,309

of U.S.S.R. 265

Voeslauer grape and wines 79

Volnay. *See under* France, Burgundy, Cote d'Or

Volstead Act 89

Vouvray wine. *See under* France, Loire

V.Q.P.R.D. (Vino di Qualita Prodotto in (una) Regione Determinata), defined 231

examples of on labels 199*l*


Wars, and effect of on viticulture and wine industries

in Bulgaria 264,264*ln*

in France, Alsace 165

in Lebanon 266

in Spain, Napoleanic era 46

in Turkey 266

Washington State 83,98-99

Water, as component of wine 1,5,9. *See also* Bodies of water

Weather. *See* Climate

Weinbaugebiete, defined 240

Weingut, defined 248

Weissburgunder grape 6,7,237. *See also* Pinot Blanc

Weissherbst wine 11*t*,237,242,248

Welschriesling grape and wines 79. *See also* Riesling

West Germany. *See* Germany

Whiskey (Whisky), as distilled spirits. *See* **Alcoholic Beverages Reference Guide, Part One,** *and specific types*

as "Irish wine" 265

White alcohols 166

White grape varieties, examples 6,7. *See also specific and additional varieties*

White Riesling. *See* Johannisberg Riesling

White wines. *See also specific wines*

production process for, illustrated 3

shades of 11*t*. *See also specific shades*

styles of, and serving of, and examples 15,16,17,20

Wine, defined 1,38

Wine beverages

flavored wines 77,182*l*

of Italy 81,182*ln*,245

"pop" (soda pop) wines 11*t*,194

Sangria 95,194,249

wine coolers *x*,11*t*,95,182*ln*

Wine brick, defined 89

Winecask. *See* Box wines

Wine coolers. *See under* Wine beverages

Wine merchant, asking advice of 28, 245

Wine fairs. *See* Festivals

*Wine Handbook* (Sutcliffe) 171-172

Winemaking, methods of. *See also* Aging; Additives; Aromatized wines; Bica Aberta system; Clarification; Fermentation; Infusion; Maceration; Vessels; *specific wines; additional and related terms*

basic 1-2, *illus.* 3

for fortified wines. *See* Madeira; Marsala; Porto; Sherry

for sparkling wines. *See* Carbonation; Charmat; Methode Champenoise; Rustic; Transfer

for Champagne, true French.
*See* Methode Champenoise,
France, Champagne region
Wineries. *See terms for under*:
Producers; Shippers. *See*
**Name Index, Producers,** *by
category and country*
Winery, seasonal phases of work at
8*t*
*Wines of America* (Adams) 97
Wines of Superior Origin (W.O.S.)
designation of South Africa
280
"Wine thieves" 39
Wood, fermentation and aging in.
*See* Vessels
Würstmarkt wine festival 242

Xarel-Lo grape and wines 6,79,252*t*
Xynisteri grape and wine 6,47*t*,263

Yeast
as additive to wine production 7,
65,67
in grapes, and fermentation 1-2
in Champagne and sparkling wine
production 64,67,73
as lees 64,73
and *sur lie* 168,169*ln*,259
Yellow Muscat grape and wines 262
Yellow wines 11*t*,171
Yield of vines, factors affecting,
general 4,5. *See also specific
factors*
regulation of 4,28,117,134,180,
250
Yugoslavia 260, *map* 261
Yugoslavian oak casks, use of 206

Zagarolo wine 219
Zalema grape 253*t*
Zandotti wine 219
Zapatos, defined and use of 37
Zeller Schwarze Katz wine 31*l*,243,
244
comparisons to 234*ln*,245
Zibbibo grape and wines. *See*
Muscat, Italy, Sicily
Zinfandel grape and wines 2,6,100
origin of, probable 107,223
in U.S. 90
California 93,95,107,108*ln*
fortified type 47
white 95,112*l*. *See also* Rose
wines
Oregon 98
Zwicker wines 165

# Name Index

(includes: **PERSONS; BUSINESSES, CORPORATIONS, AND ORGANIZATIONS;**
and **PRODUCERS** by wine category and country)

## PERSONS

Adams, León, *Wines of America* 97
Alaric I 217
Alba, Fernando Alvarez de Toledo,
   Duke of (Alba) 212*ln*
Alighieri, Dante, family of 203*ln*
   and Masi 197, 230*t*
Ambrosi, Hans 243
Amerine and Winkler, professors
   100
Anderson, Burton 197
Antinori family 205*ln*
   and winery of 82,178,182,205,
     211*l*,214,215*l*,229*t*,230*t*
Antoinette, Marie 18*n*
Aphrodite, Greek goddess and wine
   named for 263
Archimedes 225
Arrowood, Richard 109*ln*
   and winery of 92,101,104
Ausonius, Decimus Maximus,
   Roman (Latin) poet 128
Avallone family 221-222

Bacchus (Bacchae), Roman god *v*,8,
   225. *See also* Bacchus grape
Baltimore, Lord (Sir George
   Calvert) 89
Bartholdi, Frederic Auguste 165
Bass, Gordon *x*
Beethoven, Ludwig von, favorite
   wine of 244
Bellini, Vincenzo 225

Benzinger, Bruno 103*ln*
   and Glen Ellen winery 95,101,
     104,108*l*
Bergaglio, Nando 190*ln*
Beringer brothers 96
   and winery 47,89,91,95,99,101,
     102*l*,104,105
Berlin, and origin of Chambertin
   vineyard 138
Bethmann, Jean-Jacques de 126*ln*
Blass, Wolfgang (Wolf), and winery
   276,276*ln*,278
Bolla, Franco, and family 185*ln*
   and winery 81,177,197
Bonaparte, Charles Louis Napoleon
   (Napoleon III) 119
Bonaparte, Napoleon (Napoleon I)
   46,138*ln*,171,188
Bonarrigo, Paul 97
Bonetti, Bill 102*ln*
   and winery 93,104
Broglia, Piero 190*ln*,193*ln*
Burgess, Tom 91
Busby, James 275
Byron, Lord George Gordon 240

Call, Gloria *x*
Callaway, Ely 91
   and winery 92,95,103*l*,104,106
Calvert, Sir George (Lord
   Baltimore) 89
Capon, Robert, quoted *xi*
Capus, role in French A.O.C. laws
   116

Carpano, Antonio Benedetto 52,53*ln*
Catherine de Médicis (Catherine of
   Medici) 206
Cato, Marcus Porcius, Roman writer
   221
Catullo (Gaius Valerius Catullus),
   Roman poet and wine named
   for 203*l*,230*t*
Cedron, Father 270
Ceres, Roman goddess 312
Ceretto, Bruno and Marcello,
   brothers 80,188,195*ln*
Charlemagne 141*ln*,241,289*ln*
Charmat, Eugene and Maumene 73
Chrysostom, St. John, quoted *xi*
Churchill, Winston 255
Ciglia, Piero 218
Cleopatra 265-266
Columbus, Christopher 192,252
Columella, Lucius Junius
   Moderatus, Roman writer
   221
Contratto family 80
   and winery 82,191
Coury, Charles 98
Czar, last Russian (Nicholas II),
   comments of 265

daVinci, Leonardo 206
de Grazia, Marc, firm of 179*ln*
Delaware, Lord (Baron Thomas
   West De La Warr) 89
De Medici. *See* Medici
Demeter, Greek goddess *v*,312

De Rham, Baron Armando, and firm
  of 179*ln*
de Villaine and Leroy, Messrs. 140
Devrient, Ludwig 77
Dionysus, Greek god *v*,225,267
Dostoevsky, Fyodor Mikhailovich
  240
Dovaz, Michel and Steven Spurrier,
  *Academie du Vin Complete
  Wine Course* 24
Du Boeuf, Geoerge 91,154*ln*,156
du Bois, Andre 82
  and winery affiliated with 193

Empson, Neil, firm of 179*ln*
Erath, Richard, and winery 98
Ericson, Leif 2,88
Euripides, Greek poet, quoted *v*

Fellini, Federico 194
Filiputti, Walter 201
Firestone, Brooks 91
  and winery 92,104,105,106
Forbes, Patrick, paraphrased 60
Ford, Gene, *Ford's Illustrated
  Guide to Wines* 90
Ford, Gerald 97
Ford-Coppola, Francis 91
Forgione, Larry 94
Fournier, Charles 83,90
  and winery 96
Fournier, Henri 255*ln*
Francis of Assisi, St. 214
Frank, Konstantin 90,96, *quoted* 77
Frank, Willibald 90,97
Fugger, bishop, and legend
  regarding 219

Gachet family (Neyrat-Gachet) 139,
  161
  and Chateau Grillet 160,171
Galileo, quoted *xi*

Gallo (Ernest and Julio) family 90,
  108*l*
  and winery 47,77,82,95,101,105*l*,
  106
Gambrinus, Roman diety 312
Gancia, Carlo, and family and
  winery 74,80,82
Garcia, Ezequiel 257*ln*
Garrett, Paul 90
Gaspard, Henri (Chevalier de
  Sterimberg) 161
Gavia, Princess, wine name for 193*l*
Gianaclis, Nestor 266
Gianinni, Amadeo Peter, and Bank
  of America 96
Goethe, Johann Wolfgang von,
  quoted 225
Gourdin, Robert *x*
Grimm Brothers (Jacob Ludwig Carl
  and Wilhelm Carl) 240
Guarneri, Giuseppe Antonio 193
Gutenberg, Johannes 241

Haraszthy, Agoston, 89,97,103*ln*
Heck, Adolf 77
Heine, Henrich, *Die Lorelei* 240
Heitz, Joe 91
  and winery 94,95,101,107
Helen of Troy 18*n*
Henry the Navigator 45
Heracleitus, Greek philosopher,
  paraphrased 33
Hesiod, Greek poet 263
Homer, Greek poet, and literature of
  1,52
Horace, Roman poet and literature
  of 52,221,265-266

Jaboulet-Aine, Paul and family 161
  and winery 160*l*,162,163
Jefferson, Thomas 77,89, *quoted xi*
Joan of Arc, St. 162
Jordan, Tom 91
  and winery 93,101

Khayyam, Omar, *Rubaiyat*
  excerpted 266
Kogan, Smitty *x*

Latour, George(s) de 96
  and winery 91,94,101,105,106*l*
Latour, Louis 141,142,144,156
  and grandfather of 153*ln*
  and great-grandfather of 141
  and winery 143,144*l*,145*l*,151,
  152*l*,153*l*,154,156
LeFranc, Charles 96
Leroy and de Villaine, Messrs. 140
Lichine, Alexix, *Encyclopedia of
  Wines and Spirits*,
  paraphrased 171
Long, Zelma 96
  and winery affiliated with 91,101,
  104,106,107
Longworth, Nicholas 82
Loredon, Count 197
  and winery 81, *also* 230*t*
Lunelli family 82
Lungarotti, Giorgio 214,215*ln*
  and Maria Teresa 214
  and winery 205,230*t*

Mark Anthony (Antony) 265-266
Martin, Remy 91
  and corporate affiliations 83,268,
  276,293*l*
Martin, St., Bishop of Tours 167
Mascagni, Pietro 225
Masson, Paul 96, *quoted* 292*ln*
  and winery 47,83,89,107
Mastroberardino family
  Antonio 221,222*ln*,268
  Michele 222*l*
  Walter 221
Maudiere, Edmond, and wineries
  affiliated with 83*ln*
Medici (De Medici) family 205
Médicis, Catherine de 206

Mercurey, Roman god and village named for 151
Merimee, Prosper, *Maltese Falcon (Matteo Falcone)* 171
Metternich, von, family, vineyard and wines 77,235,243
Michelangelo 206,210*ln*, *quoted xi*
Mirassou, Pierre 96
  and winery 82,83,91,106
Mommessin, Didier 138,139*l*,154, 156
Mondavi family 111*ln*
  Peter 96
    and Charles Krug wines 91,96, 105,106
    and C. K. Mondavi wines 91, 95,96
  Robert, and winery 95,96,99,101, 104,105,106*l*,107
    and role of in California wine industry 108
    and Opus One project 83,91, 95,96,111*ln*. *See also* Rothschild, Baron Philippe de
Montressor family 197
  and winery 29*l*,201*l*
Moueix, of Chateau Petrus 91, *also* 128-130
Müller, Egon von 243
Müller, doctor of Thurgau 237
Mussolini, Benito 198

Napoleon I (Napoleon Bonaparte) 46,138*ln*,171,188
Napoleon III (Charles Louis Napoleon Bonaparte) 119
Nassau, Duke of 248
Neyrat-Gachet (Gachet) family 138, 161
  and Chateau Grillet 160,171
Nicholas II (last Czar of Russia), comments of 265
Niebaum, Gustafe 96

Noah 266, *quoted* 1
Noilly, Louis 52

Ochagavia, Silvestre 271
Odero, Giorgio 193
Opici family 111*ln*
  and wineries 32*l*,96,182,182*l*

Packard, Frank *x*, *quoted* 319
Parker, Robert 251*ln*
Pasteur, Louis 145,171, *quoted* 14
  Institute 155*ln*
Paul, St. (the Apostle), quoted *xi*
Paulsen, Pat, and winery 91,109*l*
Pavarotti, Luciano 194
Penn, William 89,313
Pepin III 312
Phelps, Joseph 91
  and winery 93,95,101,104,105, 106
Pirandello, Luigi 225
Plato, quoted *xi*
Pliny the Elder 221
Point, Fernand, paraphrased 171
Puck, Wolfgang 94
Pulcini, Antonio, and winery 217*ln*, 219

Qualia family and winery 97

Rabelais, François 167,168
Rolin, Nicolas 142
Rothschild, Baron Edmond de 266, 267*ln*
Rothschild, Baron Philippe de, quoted 91
  and French wine industry affiliation 111*l*,120*t*,121*l*, 122,122*l*,123*l*. *See also* **Subject Index,**

Mouton-Rothschild
  and Opus One project, U.S. 83, 91,95,96,111*ln*. *See also* Mondavi, Robert

Salins, Guigone de 142
Sansevain Brothers 82
Schoonmaker, Frank *x*, 90
Schubert, Max 280*ln*
  and winery 259,276
Selfridge, Tomy 110*ln*
  and winery affiliated with 91,94, 96,101,105
Serra, Padre Junipero 89,275
Shakespeare, William 36,39*ln*, 77
Sichel, Peter *x*
  and winery (Blue Nun) 77,234, 244
Smith, John (Captain) 88,252
Smothers Brothers, Dick and Tom 91
Sommer, Richard 98
Spurrier, Steven and Michel Dovaz, *Academie du Vin Complete Wine Course* 24
Starr, Leo 90
Sterimberg, Chevalier de (Henri Gaspard) 161
Stradivari, Antonio 193
Strong, Rodney
  and Chalk Hill Vineyard 102*ln*, 104
  and Sonoma Vineyards 101,104
Sutcliffe, Serena, *Wine Handbook* quoted 171-172

Tachis, Giacomo 205*ln*. *See also* Antinori family
Tanit, Phoenician goddess and wine named for 48*ln*,225
Tasca D'Almerita, Giuseppe (Count Tasca), family of 226,226*ln*
  and wines 178,221,224*l*,225,229*t*
Taylor, Walter S. 97

Torres, Miguel and family 91,252*ln*, 255
Tower, Jeremiah 94
Trefethen, Eugen and winery 91,93
Truffini, Guido *x*

Ugarte, Father Juan 275

Verdi, Giuseppe 194,213*ln*
Vignes, Jean Louis and winery 89
Virgil (Vergil), Roman poet 221,263
Voarick, Christian and Michele 141, 142
Voarick, Robert 142

Wagner, Philip 90
Washington, George 313
Wasserman, Sheldon and Pauline, *Italy's Noble Red Wines* 191*ln*
Welch, Charles Edgar (Dr.) 96
Wile, J., family 104*ln*
    and winery 32*l*,95,107*l*
Wilson, Benjamin 82
Winkler and Amerine, professors 100
Winthrop, John 89
Woodhouse, John 45

Zanella, Maurizio 82
Zarco, captain in Madeira legend 46

## CORPORATIONS, BUSINESSES, AND ORGANIZATIONS

Bank of America. *See* PERSONS, Giannini

Cinzano 53*ln*,54,80,82,270,271, 273,276
Coca-Cola, wine subsidiary of 260
Comite Interprofessional du Vin de Champagne (C.I.V.C.) 62,63
Comite National des Appellations d' Origine des Vins et Eaux-de-Vie 116
Consorzio (Consortia) of Italian wines 180,209*ln*,226
Domecq 273
Enological Society of Pacific Northwest 98
Enoteca Internazionale De Rham 179*ln*
Gault-Millau competition 264
Generalimpex 260
Gonzales Byass 273
Grand Met of England 91
Hennessy 273
    and Moët-Hennessy 91,104*ln*
Hospices de Beaune (Hotel Dieu) 142
Hotel Clarion 141,142
Hotel Dieu (Hospices de Beaune) 142
Hungarovin 260
Institute National des Appellations d'Origine des Vins et Eaux-de-Vie (I.N.A.O) 116-117,126,128
International Standardization Organization 18
Konsumex 260
Le Bareuzai (restaurant) 142
Louis Pasteur Institute 155*ln. See also under* PERSONS
Martell 273
Martini and Rossi 54,80,82,177, 270,273
Ministries of Agriculture and Commerce (Spain) 252
Ministry of Agriculture and Forestry (Ministero Dell'Agricoltura e

Delle Foreste) (Italy) 180, 181*n*
Moët-Hennessy 91,104*ln*
    and Hennessy 270
Mohawk Liqueur Corporation *x*, 283*n*,303*l*
Monimpex 260,262*l*
National Committee (Italy) 189
National Committee for External Commerce (Chile) 272
Nestlé Co. 91
Osborne 40,273
PepsiCo 264,264*ln*
Racke USA 91
Remy Martin 91,268,276,293*l*
    and RMS (Remy Martin-Schramsberg) 83, *also* 82
Seagrams 91,273,280
Service de la Repression des Fraudes 116
Societé Civile du Domaine de la Romanee Conti 140
Sommelier Executive Council *x*,23, 319
Suntory 91,268,273,300,301*l*,308*l*, 310*l*,312*l*
Syndicate Viticole of Saint-Emilion 128
Tattinger 91
United States Bureau of Alcohol, Tobacco, and Firearms (BATF) 15,96,98
Vinprom 264

## PRODUCERS*

**Aromatized Wines and Spirits**

---

*See also* CORPORATIONS; **Alcoholic Beverages Reference Guide, Parts One and Two**

*Argentina*
Cinzano 271; *also* 53*ln*,54,80,82, 270,273,276

*Australia*
Cinzano 276; *also* 53*ln*,54,80,82, 270,271,273

*Brazil* 270. *See also* Table wines, U.S., Inglenook; *specific other companies under* CORPORATIONS

*France*
Dubonnet 52,55*t*
Moët and Chandon 53*ln*,303; *also* 61,65*l*,69,70*t*,80,83,83*ln*,96

*Germany*
Jägermeister 52*l*,298

*Greece*
Metaxa 263,300,301*l*,302*l*

*Israel*
Carmel Wine Company (exports of) 266-267

*Italy*
Cinzano 53*ln*,54,270,271; *also* 80,82,270,273,276
Carpano 52,52*l*
Corvo. *See* Duca di Salaparuta
DeBartoli 45,229*t*; *also* 45
Duca di Salaparuta (Corvo) 225-226; *also* 16,17,81, *map* 177,178,229*t*
Fratelli Branca (Fernet Branca) 53*l*,296
Martini and Rossi 54; *also* 80,82, 177,270,273

*Mexico* 273. *See also specific companies under* CORPORATIONS

*U.S.*
Dubonnet 55*t*; *also* 52
Tribuno 52

**Brandy, Cognac, and Distilled Spirits.** *See specific entries under* **Subject Index;** *specific entries and labels in* **Alcoholic Beverages Reference Guide, Part One**

**Fortified Wines**

*Australia*
Baily and Chambers 47
Campbells 276
Thomas Hardy 278*t*; *also* 84
Morris 47,276
Rosewood 276
Yalumba 276,278*t*

*Israel*
Carmel Wine Company (exports of) 266-267

*Italy*
Bukkuram 225
Corvo. *See* Duca di Salaparuta
DeBartoli 45; *also* 229*t*
Duca di Salaparuta (Corvo) 225-226; *also* 16,17,81, *map* 177,178,229*t*
Fici 45
Florio 32*l*,44*l*,45
Carlo Hauner 225
Mineo 45
Mirabella 45
Pellegrino 45
Rallo 45
Tanit 48*l*,225
Woodhouse 45

*Portugal*
Barros, Almeida, & C.44*l*
Blandy 46
Cockburn Smithes 42,43
Cossart Gordon 46
Dow 43
Fonseca 46*ln*,251; *also* 251*l*
Henriques and Henriques 46
Leacock 46
Quinta do Noval 43*l*

Sandeman 43
Warre & C. 43*l*,44*l*

*Spain*
Duff Gordon 40
Garvey 40*l*
Harveys 40
Lustau 40
Macenista 40
Osborne 40; *also* 273
Williams and Humbert 33*l*,39*l*

*South Africa*
K.W.V. 280,281

*U.S.*
Almaden 47; *also* 82,83,91,106, 110*l*
Beringer 47; *also* 89,91,95,96,99, 101,102*l*,104,105
Christian Brothers 47; *also* 91, 101,102*l*,104,106,110*l*
Ficklin 47; *also* 91
Gallo 47; *also* 77,82,90,95,101, 105*l*,106,108*l*
Paul Masson 47; *also* 83,89,96, 107,292*ln*
Meiers Wine Cellars 97
Messina Hof Vineyards 97
J.W. Morris 47, 93*t*
Novitiate 47
Papagni 47; *also* 82,91,96,107
Quady 47,93*t*
Taylor 47; *also* 83,95,96
Widmer 47; 96
Woodbury 47,93

**Sparkling Wines**

*Argentina*
*additional producers* 271
Cinzano 271; *also* 53*ln*,54,80,82, 270,273,276
Toso 84; *also* 271

*Australia*
   Cinzano 276; *also* 53*ln*,54,80,82,
      270,271,273
   Thomas Hardy 84; *also* 278*t*
   Mildara 84
   Seppelt 84,278*t*
   Taltarni 84; *also* 279*t*

*Brazil. See same as* Aromatized
   wines

*Canada. See also under* Table wines
   Chateau Gai 273

*Chile*
   Concha y Toro 84,272
   Santa Carolina 84; *also* 273
   Undurraga 84; *also* 273

*France*
   *additional producers* 76*t*
   Alsace Willm 76*t*; *also* 165,166,
      166*l*
   Ayala 69,70*t*
   Caves de Bailly 74*l*,76*t*,134
   Bollinger 65*l*,69,70*t*
   Bouchard Aine 76*t*
   Bouchard Pere et Fils 76*t*; *also*
      141,142,142*l*,144
   Marc Bredif 76*t*,77: *also* 168
   Champs D'Ore 77
   Chauvenet 77
   Veuve (Widow) Clicquot
      Ponsardin 63*l*,69,70*t*,83
   Delorme 76*t*; *also* 151
   Deutz 70*t*,77; *also* 83
   Dopff and Irion 76*t*; *also* 165,166
   Dopff au Moulin 76*t*; *also* 165
   Duval 77
   Gosset 69,70*t*
   Grandin 77
   Charles Heidsieck 69,70*t*
   Heidsieck Monopole 70*t*
   Jacquesson 70*t*
   Kriter 77
   Krug 66*l*,69,70*t*,77
   Lanson 69,70*t*

Laurent-Perrier 69,70*t*,83
Moët and (et) Chandon 53*ln*,61,
   65*l*,69,70*t*,80,83,83*ln*,96,
   303
Mumm 69,70*t*,83
Perrier-Jouet 69,70*t*
Piper-Heidsieck 61,63*l*,64*l*,69,70*t*
Pol Roger & Co. 31*l*,69,70*t*,71*l*
Pommerly-Greno 69,70*t*
Remy-Pannier 77
Roederer 69,70*t*,77,83
Ruinart 69,70*t*
Schlumberger 79; *also* 165,166
Taittinger 69,70*t*,77
Willm. *See* Alsace Willm

*Germany*
   Deinhard 77,78*l*; *also* 234,234*l*,
      236*l*,238*l*,242,244
   Henkell 77,78*l*,96
   Kroneck 77
   Langenbach 77; *also* 242*l*
   Furst von Metternich (Schloss
      Johannisberg) 77; *also* 235,
      243
   Sohnlein 77

*Israel*
   Carmel Wine Company 84,267;
      *also* 266-267,267*l*

*Italy*
   Banfi (Villa Banfi) 80,82,90; *also*
      183*l*,205,229*t*
   Antinori 82; *also* 182,205,205*l*,
      211*l*,214,215*l*,229*t*,230*t*
   Berlucchi 82; *also* 193,229*t*
   Domenico de Bertiol 81
   Bolla 81; *also* 177,185*l*,197
   Giacomo Bologna 80; *also* 189
   Ca del Bosco 80; *also* 193
   Carpene-Malvolti 81,82
   Cella 80; *also* 182
   Ceretto 80; *also* 188,195*l*
   Cinzano 53*ln*,80,82; *also* 54,270,
      271,273,276
   Contratto 80,82; *also* 191

Corvo. *See* Duca di Salaparuta
DeFaveri 81
Duca di Salaparuta (Corvo) 81,
   225-226; *also* 16,17, *map*
   177,178,229*t*
Equipe Five (5) 82,198
Ferrari 82,198
Fontanafredda 82
Nino Franco 81
Carlo Gancia 74,80,82
Martini and Rossi 80,82; *also* 54,
   177,270,273
Nando 80
Barone Pizzini 82; *also* 193,194*l*
Riccadonna 82
Santa Margherita 81; *also* 198,
   229*t*
Torresella 81
Tosti 80
Valdo 81
Venegazzu 81,197; *also* 230*t*
Zardetto 81
Zonin 80

*Luxembourg*
   Bernard-Massard 84

*Mexico*
   Cinzano 273; *also* 53*ln*,54,80,82,
      270,271,276

*Portugal*
   Caves Alianca 84; *also* 251
   Caves do Barrocao 84
   Caves Sao Joao 84

*Spain*
   Castellblanch 79*t*
   Paul Cheneau 79*t*,80*l*
   Codorniu 79,79*t*; *also* 83
   Covides 80*l*
   Freixenet 79,79*t*; *also* 83
   Segura Viudas 79*t*

*U.S.*
   Almaden 82,83; *also* 47,91,106,
      110*l*
   Batavia Wine Cellars 83

Jacques Bonet 82
Canandaigua 82
Chateau St. Jean 83; *also* 91,92,
    101,104,105,109*ln*
Chateau Ste. Michelle 83; *also*
    95,99,99*l*
Codorniu 83; *also* 79,79*t*
Cooks 77,82
Domaine Chandon 82,83,83*l*,91.
    *See also under* France: Moët
    and Chandon
Freixenet Sonoma 83; *also* 79,79*t*
Gallo 77,82,90; *also* 47,90,95,
    101,105*l*,106,108*l*
Geldermann 77,83
Gold Seal 83,90,96
Great Western (formerly Pleasant
    Valley Wine Co.) 82,83,96;
    *also* 89
Robert Hunter 83
Iron Horse 83
Korbel 77,82,83
Hanns Kornell 77,83
Maison Deutz 83
Paul Masson 83; *also* 47,89,96,
    107,292*ln*
Mirassou 82,83; *also* 91,96,106
Moët-Hennessy 91; *also* 104*ln*,
    273. *See also* Domaine
    Chandon; *under* France:
    Moët and Chandon; Table
    wines, U.S.: Simi
Papagni 82; *also* 47,91,96,107
Piper-Sonoma 82,83
Pleasant Valley Wine Company.
    *See* Great Western
Ste. Chapelle 83; *also* 98
Scharffenberger 83
Schramsberg 83; *also* 82
Sebastiani 83; *also* 91,95,96,106,
    107
Shadow Creek 83
Sterling Vineyards 83; *also* 91,
    101,104,106
Taylor 83, 96; *also* 47,95

Tijsseling 83
Van der Kamp 83,95
Vietti 80

**Table Wines**

*Argentina*
    *additional producers* 271
    Penaflor (Trapiche) 271,271*l*
    Santa Ana 272*l*

*Australia*
    *additional producers* 278*t*-279*t*
    Wolf Blass (Bilyara Cellars;
        Tollana) 276,278
    Mark Cashmore 275*l*
    Thomas Hardy 278; *also* 84
    Penfolds 259,276,280*l*
    Taltarni 279; *also* 84

*Brazil*
    Granja Uniao 270
    Heublein 270; *also* 91. *See also*
        *under* U.S.: Inglenook

*Bulgaria*
    Monsieur Henri 264; *also*
        *Romania* 264,264*l*
*Canada*
    Andres Wines Ltd. 273
    Bright & Co. (DuBarry) 273
    Domaine des Cotes D'Ardoise
        273
    London Winery Ltd. 273
    L'Orpailleur Vineyards 273

*Chile*
    Canepa 273
    Concha y Toro 272; *also* 84
    Cousino Macul (Vina,) 259,273
    Santa Carolina 273; *also* 84
    Santa Rita 273
    Undurraga 273; *also* 84

*Cyprus*
    Keo 263
    Sodap 263

*France*
    Alsace Willm 165,166,166*l*; *also*
        76*t*
    Pere Anselme 162,162*l*,163
    Bailly 167
    Andre Bant 138
    Beyer 166
    Blanchet 167
    Jean Claude Boisset 140
    Bouchard Pere et Fils 141,
        142,142*l*,144; *also* 76*t*
    Rene Bouvier 138
    Marc Bredif 77,168; *also* 76*t*
    Caves Chantefleur a Beaucaire
        170*l*
    Chantovent 170*l*
    Chapoutier 161,162,163
    Chateaux (cru/growth classes) of
        Bordeaux region, summaries
        120*t*,121*t*,126*t*,127*t*,129*t*.
        *See also specific*
        *corresponding Chateau*
        *names, as applicable:*
    Ausone 128,129*t*
    Batailley 120*t*,124*l*
    Beausejour-Becot (Beau-Sejour
        (Becot), Beau-Se-jour) 128,
        129*t*
    Beychevelle 121,121*t*,125*l*
    Chasse-Spleen 125
    Cheval Blanc 128,129*t*
    D'Yquem 127,127*t*,171,262
    Figeac 128,129*t*
    Fonplegade 129*t*,130*l*
    Fourcas Hosten 122*l*,125
    Greysac 125
    Grillet 138,160,161,171
    Haut-Brion 120*t*,121*t*,126,126*t*
    Lafite Rothschild 120*t*,124*ln*
    La Gaffeliere 128,129*t*
    La Tour de By 125
    Latour 120*t*,121*t*,124*l*,124*ln*
    Livran 125
    Lynch-Bages 120*t*,121*t*,124*ln*
    Magdelaine 128,129*t*

Margaux 120*t*,121*t*
Mouton-Rothschild 111*l*,120*t*,
121*l*,121*t*,124*ln*,208*ln*. *See*
*also* PERSONS: Rothschild,
Baron Philippe de
Olivier 126*l*,126*t*
Palmer 120*t*,124*ln*
Patache D'Aux 125
Pavie 128,129*t*
Saint-Bonnet 125
Talbot 120*t*,124*ln*
Chateau Bazillac 172
Chateau de Beaucastel 162,162*l*
Chateau de Chorey 142
Chateau de la Cammeraine 143
Chateau de Meursault 143
Chateau de Sancerre 167; *also*
106*ln*,168
Chateau de Selle (Domaine Ott)
171,172*l*
Chateau Fuissé (M. Vincent et
Fils) 153*l*,154
Chateau Lagrange 128*l*
Chateau La Nerthe 162
Chateau de la Maltroye 144
Chateau Petrus 128-130; *also* 91
Chateau Moncontour 168
Chateau Rayas 162
Chateau Ste. Rosaline 171
Chateau Taillefer 30*l*
Chateau Trintaudon-LaRose 255*ln*
Raoul Clerget 144
Clos de la Perriere 138
Clos de Tart (Mommessin) 138,
139*l*,154,156
Clos du Chapitre 138
Clos L'Eglise 130
Clos Rene 130
Comte de Vogue 139
Coulee de Serrant, La 168,171
Cruse 31*l*,154*ln*
de Ladoucette 167,168*l*
Delas Freres 161,162,163
Delorme 151; *also* 76*t*

Domaine Phillipe
Charlopin-Parizot 138
Domaine Laroche 134
Domaine Clare-Dau 138
Domaine Leflaive (Olivier
Leflaive Freres) 144,144*l*,
145*l*
Domaine Long-Depaquit 134
Domaine du Mont Redon 162
Domaine Ott (Chateau de Selle)
171,172*l*
Domaine of Romanee-Conti 144
Domaine Armand Rousseau 138
Dopff and Irion 165;166; *also* 76*t*
Dopff au Moulin 165; *also* 76*t*
Joseph Drouhin 142
Dujac 138
DuBoeuf 154*ln*,156; *also* 91
Duc de Magenta 144
Faiveley 140,140*l*,151,151*l*
Gazin 130
Guigal 160,162,163
Joseph Hallereau 168,169*l*
Hugel 165,166
Paul Jaboulet-Aine 160*l*,161,161*l*,
162,163
Jaboulet-Vercherre 143
Louis Jadot 142,154*ln*,156
Robert Jasmin 160
Rene Junot et Fils 170*l*
La Chablisienne 134
La Conseilante 130
La Coulee de Serrant 168,171
Ladoucette, de 167,168*l*
Louis Latour *mentioned* 141-145
*and* 151-154,156
La Vielle Ferme 163,163*l*
Olivier Leflaive Freres (Domaine
Leflaive) 144,144*l*,145*l*
Le Gay 130
Les Gay 130
Les Forts de Latour. *See* Chateaux
of Bordeaux, Latour
L'Evangile 130
Marquis de Laguiche 143-144

Prosper Maufoux 153*l*,154,154*ln*
Louis Max 145*l*
Mommessin (Clos de Tart) 138,
139*l*,154,156
J. Moreau et Fils 134
Morin 140
Nenin 130
Marc Pasquier-DeVignes 156
Patriarche Pere et Fils 142
Reine Pedauque 141,141*l*,153*l*,
154
Petite-Village 130
Albert Pic et Fils 134
Prieur 143
Michel Redde 167
Henri Richard 138,138*l*
Ropiteau Freres 143,143*l*
Baron Philippe de Rothschild. *See*
*under* PERSONS
Etienne Sauzet 144
Schlumberger 165,166; *also* 79
Simmonet-Fevre 134
Tallot-Beaut 142
Baron Thenard 144
Roland Thevenin 144
Trimbach 165,166
Trotonoy 130
George Vernay 161
Charles Vienot 138*l*,140
Vieux-Chateau-Certan 130
Vieux Lazaret 162
M. Vincent et Fils (Chateau
Fuissé) 153*l*,154
Robert Voarick 142. *See also*
*under* PERSONS
Willm. *See* Alsace Willm

*Germany*
Anheuser 244
von Bassermann-Jordan 242
von Bühl 242
Bürklin-Wolf 242
Deinhard 234,234*l*,236*l*,238*l*,242,
244; *also* 77,78*l*
German government-owned
vineyards 243

Hallgarten 244
Leonard Kreusch 31*l*,236*l*,238*l*, 244,244*l*
Langenbach 242; *also* 77
von Metternich (Furst von Metternich; Schloss Johannisberg) 235,243; *also* 77
G. M. Pabstmann 235
St. Ursula 244
Sichel (Blue Nun) *x*,234,244; *also* 77
Valkenberg 244
Zentrallkellerei (Central Cellar Cooperative Wineries)
    of Baden 242,243
    of Franken, Nahe, Rheinhessen, Württemberg 243
    of Mosel-Saar-Ruwer 234*l*,243

*Greece*
Achia-Clauss 263,263*l*
Boutari 263
Cambas 263

*Hungary*
Debroi 262
*exporters* 260

*Israel*
Carmel Wine Company 267,267*l*; *also* 84,266-267

*Italy*
*additional producers for Vini da Tavola* 228*t*-230*t*
Abbazia di Rosazzo 201,228*t*
Allegrini 197
Anselmi 197
Antinori 178,182,205,205*l*,211*l*, 214,215*l*,229*t*,230*t*; *also* 82
Antoniolo 188
Alberto and Maurizio Arlunno 189*l*
Avigonesi (Grifi) 182,206,207, 208*l*,211*l*,229*t*

Badia a Coltibuono 30*l*,207*l*,209
Gian Matteo Baldi (Castellucio) 195,228*t*. *See also* Duchi di Castelluccio
Angelo Ballabio 193,229*t*
Banfi (Villa Banfi) 183*l*,205,229*t*; *also* 80,82,90
Barbaresco, Produttori del 192*l*
Barbella 197
Barberani 214
Decugnano dei Barbi 179*l*,214, 230*t*
Fattoria dei Barbi (Colombini) 188*l*,229*t*
Bella Vista 193
Berlucchi 193,229*t*; *also* 82
Bertani 180*l*,197,199*l*,200*l*,203*l*, 230*t*
Bichot 140
Bigi 214
Biondi-Santi 201*ln*
Bolla 177,185*l*,197; *also* 81
Giacomo Bologna 189; *also* 80
Bosca 81,182*ln*
Count Bossi-Fedrigotti (Fredriotti) 198,229*t*
Piero Broglia 190*l*,193*l*
Bucci 217
Ca del Bosco 193; *also* 80
Villa Caffagio (Coffagio) 209,229*t*
Canelli (Canei) 245
Cantinas. *See* Casarsa; Tollo
Caparra & Siciliani 222
Villa Capezzana 209
Carparzo Estate (Ca del Pazzo) 178,182,206,229*t*
Casal Thaulero 218
Cantina Casarsa 201
Castellos. *See* Neive; Nipozzano; Rampolla
Castellucio (Gian Matteo Baldi) 195,228*t*. *See also* Duchi di Castelluccio
Castelvecchio Estate 206*l*
Cella 182; *also* 80

Cerequio 189*l*
Ceretto 188,195*l*; *also* 80
Umberto Ceratti 222
Umberto Cesari 184*l*,195,197, 228*t*
Villa Cilnia 207,229*t*,230*t*
Colli Di Catone 217*l*,219
Villa Coffagio (Caffagio) 209,229*t*
Colombini (Fattoria dei Barbi) 188*l*,229*t*
Aldo Contero 188,190*l*
Giacomo Contero 188,191*l*
Conti Wallenburg 198
Giuseppe Contratto 191; *also* 80, 82
Barone Cornacchia 218
Corvo. *See* Duca di Salaparuta
Count Tasca. *See* Tasca
D'Angelo 221,222,222*l*,228*t*
DeCastris 221,223
Dessilani 188,229*t*
Di Gresy 183*l*,188
Duca di Salaparuta (Corvo) 16,17, *map* 177,178,225-226,229*t*; *also* 81
Duchi di Castelluccio 218. *See also* Castellucio
Riccardo Falchini 214*l*
Fantinel 201,201*l*,228*t*
Fassati 214
Fattorias. *See* Barbi; Luiano; Paradiso
Fazi-Battaglia 205*l*,217,229*t*
Livio Felluga 178,201,228*t*
Marco Felluga 198,199*l*,201
Ferrando 188
Marsilio Ficino 213*l*
Barone Fini 202*l*
Folonari 180*ln*,197
Fontana Candida 214,216*l*,219
Fratelli Oddero 187
Frecciarossa 193
Fresscobaldi 207
Gaja 188,189
Il Gaia 221,228*t*

Giacobazzi 182*ln*
Giacosa 188
Giannina (Teruzzi) 210*l*
Francesco Giuntini 179*l*
Gotto D'Oro 219
Hofstatter 198,229*t*
Il Gaia 221,228*t*
Illuminati 218
Ippolito 222
Jermann 201,228*t*
Kettmeier 198
La Chiara 190*l*
La Colombaia 29*l*,197,201*l*
Lageder 198
Le Ragose 179*l*,197
Librandi 222
Ligorio 225*l*
Fattoria di Luiano 209*l*
Lungarotti 205,214,215*l*,230*t*
Maculan 197,230*t*
Martino 222
Masi 197,203*l*,230*t*
Maso Poli 200*l*
Mastroberardino 221,222*l*,228t,
 268
Villa Matilde 221-222
Melini 207
Monsecco 188
Monsanto 209
Nino Negri 194,229*t*
Castello di Neive 191*l*
Castello di Nipozzano 209
Fratelli Oddero 187
Opici 182,182*l*; also 32*l*,96,111*l*
Pallavicini 219
Fattoria Paradiso 195,228*t*
Paternoster 222
Emidio Pepe 218
Pieropan 197
Barpone Pizzini 193,194*l*; also 82
Produttori del Barbaresco 192*l*
Rainoldi 194
Castello dei Rampolla 182,206,
 207,208*l*,229t
Rapitala 225

Ratti 188
Regaleali Estate. *See* Count Tasca
Riunite 81,177,182*ln*
Rivera 223
Incisa della Rochetta (Sassicaia
 182,206,207,210*l*,229*t*
Ronco del Gnemiz 201,228*t*
Ruffino 177,206*l*,207,212*l*,214,
 216*l*
Russiz Superiore 199*l*
San Felice (Chianti; Vigorello)
 182,206,207,207*l*,209*l*,229*t*
S. (San) Quirico 212*l*
Sanguineto 183*l*
Santa Margherita 198,229*t*, *also*
 81
Santangelo 218
Santo Sofia 197
Sasso 222
Scala 222
Schioppetto 201
Sella and Mosca 224,229*t*
Simonini 221,223,228*t*
Giovanni Struzziero 221
Count Tasca (Regaleali Estate)
 178,221,224*l*,225,226,226*l*,
 229*t*
Taurino 221,223,223*l*
Tedeschi 197
Terre Rosse (Vallania) 195,228*t*
Teruzzi (Giannina) 210*l*
Tieffenbrunner 198
Cantina Tollo 218
Tommasi 197
Tona 194
Torre di Luna 202*l*
Travaglini 188
Edoardo Valentini 218
Antonio Vallana 188
Vallania (Terre Rosse) 195,228*t*
Vaselli 214,215*l*
Venegazzu 230*t*; *also* 81,197
Villas. *See* Banfi; Capezzana;
 Cilnia; Coffagio; Mathilde
Villacosta 189*l*

Villadoria 184*l*
*Vini da Travola, additional*
 *producers* 228t-230t
Vivaldi 198
Volpe Pasini 201
Conti Wallenburg 198

*Japan*
Gekkeikan; Genji; Kiku 268

*Lebanon*
Serge Hochar 266

*New Zealand*
Cooks; Corbans; Glenvale;
 Montana 280

*Portugal*
Caves Alianca 251; *also* 84
Avelada 251,251*l*
Caves Carvalho 251,252
Casalinho 251
Ferreira 251,252
Fonseca 251,251*l*; *also* 46*l*
Gatao 251
Grao Vasco 251
Lancers 250
Mateus 250; *also* 13,248
Ribeiro 251,252
Caves Velhas 251

*Romania*
Monsieur Henri 264,264*l*; *also*
 *Bulgaria* 264

*South Africa*
K.W.V. 280,281
Nederberg 281
Oude Meester 281

*Spain*
*additional producers, Rioja region*
 254t
Masia Bach 255
Bodegas Olarra 256*l*,257*l*
Alejandro Fernandez 256
Jean Leon 255
Marques de Caceres 255*l*
Miguel Torres 252*l*,255; *also* 91

U.S.
  *additional producers; California boutique wineries* 92t-93t
Acacia 92,104,105
Adelsheim 98,99*l*
Alba 97,97*l*
Almaden (formerly National Distillers. *See under* CORPORATIONS) 106, 110*l*; *also* 47,82,83,91
Amador Foothills (Sutter Home) 95,10*l*
Arrowood 92,101,104,109*l See also under* PERSONS
Associated Vintners 98
Barengo 96
Beaulieu Vineyard (BV) 91,94, 96,101,105,110*l*
Ben-Marl 95,96
Beringer 89,91,95,96,99,101, 102*l*,104,105; *also* 47
Blossom Hill 107*l*
Bonny Doon 92,107
Brotherhood Winery 89
David Bruce 91,104,105
Buena Vista 91,101,103*l*,104, 106. *See also* PERSONS: Haraszthy, Agoston
Bully Hill 97
Burgess 92,101,104,106,107
Cakebread 92,101,104,105
Calera 92,105
Callaway 91,92,95,103*l*,104,106
Carneros Creek 92,105,107
Cattani 96
Caymus 92,101
Chalk Hill Vineyard 102*l*,104. *See also* PERSONS: Strong, Rodney
Chalone 92,104,105,107
Chappellet 92,101,105,106
Chateau Montelena 92,101,104
Chateau St. Jean 91,92,101,104, 105,109*ln*; *also* 83
Chateau St. John 106

Chateau Ste. Michelle 95,99,99*l*; *also* 83
Chateau Souverain 91,106
Chicama Vineyards 96
Christian Brothers 91,101,102*l*, 104,106,110*l*; *also* 47
Clos du Bois 92,105,106
Clos Pegase 92,101,104
Clos du Val 92,101,106,107
Colony 90,95
Columbia Crest 98*l*
Concannon 91,92,105
Charles Coury Vineyards 98
Cribari 90,96
Cuvaison 107
Delinger 107
Domaine Caraleros 91
Domaine St. George 95
Dominus 95
Dry Creek 92,105,106,107
DuBoeuf 91; *also* 154*ln*,156
Duckhorn 92,106
Edelwein. *See* Freemark Abbey
Elk Cover Vineyards 98
Eyrie Vineyard 98
Fall Creek 97
Far Niente 92,104
Felton-Empire 105
Fetzer 95,105,106,107
Firestone 91,92,104,105,106,106*l*
Flora Springs 101,104
Foppiano 96
Franzia 90,96
Freemark Abbey (Edelwein) 92, 95,101,104,105
Gallo 90,95,101,105*l*,106,108*l*; *also* 47,77,82
Gaver Estate 104
Giumarra 91,96
Glen Ellen 95,101,103,104,108*l*
Glenora Wine Cellars 97
Grand Cru 106
Grgich Hills 92,104,105
Great Western (formerly Pleasant

Valley Wine Company) 89; *also* 82,83,96
Gross 97
Groth 101
Guasti 89
Guild 90
Gundlach-Bundshu 89,92
Hacienda 106
Hanzell 91,104,105
Hargrave Vineyard 96
Heitz 91,94,95,101,107
Heron Hill 97
Heublein 91; *also* 270. *See also* Inglenook
Hillcrest Vineyard 98
Hinzerling Vineyards 98
Honeywood Winery 98
Inglenook (formerly Heublein) 91, 94,96,101,102,106,107,109*l*; *also* 270
Italian Swiss Colony 89
Jekel 105
Johnson Turnbull 93,101
Jordan 91,93,101
Kalin Cellars 93,101,104,105
Robert Keenan 93,104,106
Kendall-Jackson 101
Kenwood Vineyards 93,106,107
Kings Road 97
Knudsen-Erath 98
Charles Krug 91,96,105,106. *See also* C. K. Mondavi; Peter Mondavi
La Crema 93,105
Lambert Bridge 104
Les Pierres Vineyards. *See* Sonoma-Cutrer
Llano Estacado Winery 98
Long Vineyards 104
Lytton Springs 107
McDowell 105
Manischewitz (Monarch Wine Company) 90
Louis Martini 91,96,101,106

Paul Masson 89,96,107; *also* 47, 83,89,292*ln*
Mayacamas 91,101,104
Meredyth 97
Meridian 91,93,104
Messina Hof Vineyards 97
Mirassou 106; *also* 82,83,91,96
Moët-Hennessey 91,104*ln*; also 270,273. *See also* Simi; Sparkling wines: Domaine Chandon; France: Moët and Chandon
Mogen David 97
Monarch Wine Company (Manischewitz) 90
C. K. Mondavi 91,95,96. *See also* Charles Krug; Peter Mondavi
Peter Mondavi 96. *See also* Charles Krug; C. K. Mondavi
Robert Mondavi 95,96,99,101, 104,105,106*l*,107,108,111*l*. *See also* Opus One
Monterey Peninsula 107
Monterey Vineyard 105
Montevina 107
Mount Eden 101
Mt. Eden Vineyards 105
Villa Mt. Eden 101
Nalle 107
Napa Ridge 91
National Distillers. *See* Almaden
Newton 93,101,104,105,106
Nichelini 96
Oak Ridge Vineyards 112*l*
Opici 32*l*,96,111*l*; also 182,182*l*
Opus One 83,91,95,96,111*l*. *See also* PERSONS; Mondavi,

Robert; Rothschild, Baron Philippe de
Papagni 91,96,107; *also* 47,82
Parducci 91,96,105,106
Pat Paulsen Vineyards 91,109*l*
Pedrizetti 91,96,105
Pedroncelli 91,96
Pennsylvania Vine Company 89
Robert Pepi 93,105,107
Perelli-Minetti 96
Petri 90
Phelps 91,93,95,101,104,105,106
Pleasant Valley Wine Company. *See* Great Western
Preston Wine Cellars 98,105
Martin Ray 91,104
Raymond 101,104
Renault 97
Ridge 93,105,107,108*l*
Carlo Rossi 95
Rutherford Estate 95,103*l*
Rutherford Hill 105
St. Clement 93,104
Ste. Chapelle 98; *also* 83
Sakonnet Winery 96
Santa Cruz Mountain Vineyard 105
Santino 107
Sausal 107
Scotto (Villa Armando) 96
Sebastiani 91,95,96,106,107; *also* 83
Seghesio 107
Silver Oaks 93,101
Simi 91,96,101,104,104*l*,106,107
Sokol Blosser Vineyards 98
Sonoma (Vineyards) 101,102*ln*, 104. *See also* PERSONS: Strong, Rodney

Sonoma-Cutrer Vineyards (Les Pierres Vineyards) 93,102*l*, 104
Stag's Leap Vineyards 93,105
Stag's Leap Wine Cellars 93,101
Robert Stemmler 93,105
Sterling Vineyards 91,101,104, 106; *also* 83
Stony Hill 104,105
Storybook 107
Rodney Strong. *See under* PERSONS
Sutter Home (Amador) 95,107
Tabor Hill Vienyard 97
Tamuzza 97
Walter S. Taylor (Bully Hill) 97
Taylor 95; *also* 47,83,96
Tewksbury 97
Three Sisters 97
Miguel Torres 91; *also* 252*l*,255
Trefethen 91,93
Tualatin 98
Val Verde Winery 97
Veedercrest 105,106
Villa Armando (Scotto) 96
Villa Mount Eden 101. *See also* Mount/Mt. Eden
Villa Zapu 104
Vinifera (Vineyards) Winery 90, 97
Vose 95
Wente Bros. 91,105
Widmer. *See under* Fortified Wines
Wiederkehr Wine Cellars 97
J. Wile & Sons 32*l*,95,104*l*,107*l*
Winery Lake 106

*Yugoslavia*
Alexandria 260,260*l*
Avia 260

# LEARNING MORE

## THE S.E.C. CORRESPONDENCE COURSE

As an owner of the **Vintago Wine Book**, you can test your knowledge and earn the diploma granted by The Sommelier Executive Council to those who pass a series of exams. These tests reflect data contained in this text. It is an excellent way for you to review at your own pace and check your level of proficiency. A self-explanatory test packet will be mailed to you. As soon as we receive your completed exam, we will grade it, and upon passing the exam you will receive an attractive certificate of merit, suitable for framing. A one-time charge of $14.95 includes all mailing fees, exam gradings, and the S.E.C. diploma. Simply fill out the form below and return it to the S.E.C. at:

Sommelier Executive Council Publishing
222 Main Street
New Milford, NJ 07646

----------------------------------------------------------------------------------------

☐  Yes I would like to participate in the S.E.C. Correspondence Course at the cost of $14.95.

Name _____

Address _____

City/State/Zip _____

☐ Check enclosed ☐ Money order enclosed ☐ Credit Card: VISA - AMEX - MasterCard

Card _____ Card # _____ Expir. Date _____

Comments on the Text: _____

_____